Skills, outlooks and passions

A psychoanalytic contribution to
the study of politics

A. F. DAVIES

Professor of Political Science, University of Melbourne

CAMBRIDGE UNIVERSITY PRESS
Cambridge
London   New York   New Rochelle
Melbourne   Sydney

Published by the Press Syndicate of the University of Cambridge
The Pitt Building, Trumpington Street, Cambridge CB2 1RP
32 East 57th Street, New York, N.Y. 10022, U.S.A.
296 Beaconsfield Parade, Middle Park, Melbourne 3206, Australia

First published 1980

320.01
D255s

Printed in Malta
by Interprint Limited

Library of Congress Cataloguing in Publication Data

Davies, Alan Fraser.
Skills, outlooks and passions.

Includes bibliographical references and index.
1. Political psychology. I. Title.
JA74.5.D378   320'.01'9   78-54575
ISBN 0 521 22081 5 hard covers
ISBN 0 521 29349 9 paperback

Contents

Illustrations and tables

To my parents

Preface

The purpose of this book is to put students of politics in touch with a body of unobtrusive yet tenacious and steadily growing work, which has addressed itself, over the last generation and a half, to certain deeper problems in the individual's relation to social life. Freud's general explanation of why psychoanalysis is ignored, if not reviled — that it offends against man's narcissism and his wish to feel thoroughly in control[1] —no doubt applies with undiminished force today, and not least in politics. But there are excuses for this indifference, too: analytic writing is often hard to read and harder to swallow (one's sense of incredulity must be stretched and calibrated by introspective work into a personal resource). It is not always clear, for that matter, who *are* the Freudians,* what they are agreed on, and where their ideas may be consulted.† Nor has it been very obvious over these years that psychoanalysis *has* had things of major political importance to report. Indeed, intelligent and cultivated people have long held a suspicion (recently strengthened, maybe, by new work on Freud's life, demonstrating that his keenest adolescent ambition was a political career and that he relinquished this goal only with painful reluctance)[3] that psychoanalysis was at bottom a kind of anti-politics or species of reproof to it — a project which, perhaps in resignation, perhaps in defiance, turned its back on collective solutions, and opted for the individual cure.

I have found, however, that once the student of politics knows reasonably clearly what he wants to find out, psychoanalysis rarely fails to offer something relevant, and the bulk of this book is some measure of how much it has to give. It is bulky, however, because analysis, as a 'psychology

---

* It is the psychoanalysis of the journals, not of the paperbacks, that this essay attends to and celebrates — the work of the private practitioners and 'unknown' analysts. Writers such as Reich, Fromm, Marcuse, Norman O. Brown and R. D. Laing have remarkably little to the point to contribute (as does, to my surprise, Erik Erikson).

† A quick spot-test for acquaintance with psychoanalysis: Do you know if your library possesses, and have you ever consulted, Grinstein's *Index of Psychoanalytic Writings*? This work (fourteen volumes to 1975) makes it possible to trace any reference to any topic in writings by analysts.[2]

of whole lives', is given to presenting its discoveries in biographical contexts of some amplitude — indeed, the reader may be advised to read somewhat against the conventions, to hurry over the broad summaries and exposition, and concentrate on the fine detail of the 'little stories', which may offer from time to time items of personal resonance.

I would like to stress the discrete particularity of analysts' contributions — for example, there is not much under 'Politics' in Grinstein — and the dependably indirect, even serendipitous, character of their work. It is evidently because they maintain an even, circumambient eye, alert to the most minute detail or discrepancy, that political novelties — or any others — can be made to emerge. For example, it is through pondering the mythic quality of the fantasies of orphans in public institutions in Paris that Maryse Choisy finds something significant to tell us about pathological (and perhaps especially *political*) ambition (see below, p. 436, n. 22). Ernest Jones perceived the nature and sensed the power of Hitler's 'secret weapon' in London in 1940 from two dreams of finding Hitler 'friendly', which were reported by homosexual patients (see below, pp. 243–5). And the 'motiveless' enmity of certain colleagues in the American Psychoanalytic Association put Heinz Kohut on the track of 'narcissistic rage' (see below, pp. 337–8), a notion no political journalist should be without.

Of course, such items would remain mere curiosities, albeit important and amiable curiosities, if there were not some structure in social science organised to receive and set them to advantage, to give them cumulative force, and, by linking them with the more familiar surfaces of didactic politics, to maximise their explanatory power. And these are the aims, indeed, of 'political psychology', which, like many of the newer academic specialisms, is young enough to have held its first national meetings within the decade, and to be taught so far in no more than a score of universities.

Harold Lasswell, the founder of political psychology, wrote his *Psychopathology and Politics*[4] in 1930, after a double training in social science and analysis; he *pre-thought* the discipline in a remarkable way, discovering every lode in its mine, yet allowing ample freedom of choice to later workers in their method of attack. This single, brilliant essay thought through all the ways in which analytic perspective and the kind of knowledge of people that it alone affords might some day enrich our understanding of politics, and indeed our power to do more for good through politics.[5] Lasswell brooded particularly on the new techniques of investigation and new types of investigator needed to carry through the programme. So soundly did he plan that part I of this book simply re-employs his master-scheme of types of political actor — agitator, administrator, and theorist — and gently presses back into its mould much later work whose authors may have fancied they had outgrown such simplicities. Lasswell called for a systematic dissection of political roles and role-performances, and for a progressive elaboration of sub-types, always against the double frame of contemporary work-style and formative developmental history. To ferret out the necessary information, he called for persons somewhere between analysts and political scientists, and for occasions somewhere between the analysis over several years and the single sharply focused interview. The later work that I summarise below has, I believe, substantially fulfilled these demands.

There were grandiose elements in Lasswell's scheme: he seemed at times to wish to recruit not only all political scientists to the new method of work, but to enlist, as part-time helpers, all analysts as well. Political scientists at first proved massively resistant to his ideas, and analysts' contributions to his scheme remained obstinately oblique. But in the next decades, social scientists who had reached out for psychoanalytic understanding (though the full double training remained almost unknown) carried out important work in central areas of the new study. When Nevitt Sanford, for example, reports on the authoritarian personality,[6] or David Riesman on political culture,[7] or Brewster Smith or Robert Lane on political ideology,[8] we see not merely gifted feats of individual pioneering scholarship but a vindication of the strategy of the double training and the tactic of the depth-interview, case-study method. And the *craft*, which was to underpin the development of political psychology, was carried further forward in the same years with the refinement of the analytically-informed biography.[9] Now, after four and a half decades of lively frontiersmanship and with new contributions and new recruits doubling each year, it seems a good time to take stock,* to point to gaps and weaknesses, to cordon off cul-de-sacs, to recommend avenues of promise, and above all, to study why the best work succeeds and how it can be more widely promoted.

Despite its apparent size, this book is actually three slim volumes bound as one — one on each term of the title. And they are slim because it is still early in the day, and much remains to be done.† As reviewer, I have faced a somewhat different predicament in each part.

In *Skills* I begin with some stunningly good contemporary sketches dissecting the work-styles of living administrators,[12] and I trace the history

---

* Two other recent surveys of the political psychology 'literature' are Fred I. Greenstein's exemplary *Personality and Politics* (and the Reader which goes with it)[10] and Jeanne Knutson (ed.,), *Handbook of Political Psychology*,[11] which, though copious and useful, sadly underlines the solipsism of pioneers who seem able only to discuss past work *of their own*. Though much the same studies are reviewed in each book — and here — they are discussed in three very different ways.

† The sense of work done in isolation — as if each writer were the first person in the world to consider the point he is making — is extraordinarily strong in the studies under review. Putting people with strikingly similar interests 'in touch' has been a large pleasure in my work.

of such commentary. To this end I resurrect Lasswell's largely forgotten scheme of political types, and illustrate these types afresh from recent biographical materials, including Freud's own maliciously witty (and absurdly apologised for) assessment of Woodrow Wilson. My worry in this part is that readers may not already have read the main works I discuss, which are simply beyond my capacity and present space to summarise. I must warn the reader, then, that unless these works are directly sampled before, or while reading, part ɪ, it will seem more drab and pointless than I believe it is.

For the ground plan of *Outlooks* I raid the closet of small-group psychology and bear away an astonishingly ambitious scheme, much too significant to remain a 'laboratory system' — Robert F. Bales's classification on Theophrastian lines of 26 types of character *and matching world view*.[13] On this provocative frame I string a liberal sampling of the 'personal outlooks' analysed in the political psychology files, including the whole set of Henry Murray's brilliant Harvard student cases.[14] (This 'exposition-through-cases' tactic owes much to Fred Greenstein's chance reference in conversation to 'Hilary Sullivan' (see below, pp. 183–8) as if he were a real person well known to us both. 'How ridiculous!' I first thought — and then, 'How right!') Some amends for the comparative ruthlessness of this exercise are made in chapter 6, glancing at the testimony on outlooks as outlook-holders themselves see them.

In *Passions*, I revive a quest that psychologists tacitly dropped around 1908, because of its difficulty; it has no psychoanalytic heroes, but it establishes beyond doubt the solid virtues of the profession. It has been a pleasure, here, to redeem from neglect the valuable work, and harness the system-building instincts, of three forgotten non-analytic writers: Alexander Shand, Max Scheler and Kurt Riezler. (Lasswell, least with us in this part, still contrives to have some of the best things to say.)

In concentrating this review on studies which are relevant to one or more of my three topics, I pass over much work that arguably applies psychoanalysis quite as centrally to politics and yet suffers greater undeserved neglect than work I do discuss. I think particularly of Nathan Leites's fine writing on exotic political cultures (especially France)[15] and national character studies generally; of Abram Kardiner's grand scheme of the dynamics of social change pivoted upon the family as 'primary institution';[16] of the substantive findings of the small-group movement itself (especially the work of Bales, Slater and Mills);[17] and the many achievements of those who have worked to develop social philosophy from Freudian writings, particularly Christian Bay and Erik Erikson.[18]

Finally, I must own to a certain sense of engulfment by the new tide of historical psycho-biography centred on the *Journal of Interdisciplinary History* and the *History of Childhood Quarterly*.[19] Though I have dipped into this, I have not reviewed it systematically. However, it is future psycho-biographers of political actors — along with commentators on contemporary politics — for whom I hope parts I and II in particular will be useful. With the prospect of an impending revolution in information-sorting and storing methods, may I commend, in Lasswell's spirit, the project of a general biographical code in whose design the chief objects of political psychologists' curiosity will be given a central place? For, as Elias Canetti has written:

> Man considers himself the measure of all things, but he is still almost unknown. His progress in self-knowledge is minimal; every new theory obscures more of him than it illuminates. Only unimpeded concrete inquiry into particular human beings makes gradual advance possible.[20]

Acknowledgements

I should like to thank Christian Bay, Fred Greenstein, Robert Lane, David Barber and Arnold Rogow for the privilege and sustainment of membership of their 'invisible college'; my teachers in analysis, Hedwig Hoffer and Roger Money-Kyrle; Tom Pocklington for the happy term at the University of Alberta where much of part III was written; Robyn Moodie and Neil Whitlock who each produced a handsome monograph from earlier drafts; Alan McBriar who nobly read the proofs; and, above all, my family and friends, for their patience, support and forbearance over a long haul.

Right at the end when I thought the task done, Fred Greenstein showed me a much sounder arrangement of the three parts, and the typescript received wonderfully sympathetic and searching 'readings' from W. H. Morris Jones, and Susan Allen-Mills of the Cambridge University Press, which enabled me to cut out much slack and adipose tissue, especially in part II. Thanks finally to Paul Chipchase: no book can owe more to its subeditor than this one.

University of Melbourne

PART ONE

Skills

Political mountebanks continue, and will continue, to puff nostrums and practise legerdemain under the eyes of the multitude: following a course as tortuous as that of a river, but in a reverse process; beginning by being dark and deep, and ending by being transparent.

Thomas Love Peacock
(Introduction to *Headlong Hall*, 1837)

1 *Introduction*

For most of those engaged in it, politics is work. 'Professionals', whose concern is steady or even life-long, produce the bulk of it — and almost all that is effective. Even 'temporaries', those in it for one campaign or turn of duty, soon come to feel its characteristic weight.

The band of political workers — a fraction, indeed, of the total population[1] — has bold enough markings, especially in broad clusters. Administrators, politicians, association heads, journalists and critics clearly comprise the 'unhappy few' who produce society's politics. Complexity ensures, as democracy enjoins, that power at the centre, as well as the boundaries of inclusion, be kept a little ambiguous and fluid. Leaders shade off into the led; aides, cronies and subordinates trail away into inconsequence; opinion leaders in work-place or district press up towards notice. Leaders in special fields feel themselves sadly led elsewhere.[2]

To see politics as work strains no perceptual habits — and sheds no sudden light. But questions that might have seemed obvious — how work is learnt, how personal skills become political resources, how personality affects both learning and performance — have for some reason failed entirely to rouse scholarly curiosity. Let us extend these questions a little, rehearsing what it is in general terms we may wish to know.

Selection and recruitment. What draws people to political work? Where does its inner appeal lie, and what sorts of people does it most strongly attract? What childhood experiences confirm political actors not only in the aspiration, but also in the talents, needed for tasks at the core of politics? How and when in their lives does political work become a goal? What are the 'fixation points', as it were, for political learning? How do actors learn what they must have or be to enter politics, and how do they set about shaping themselves, or showing others they are equipped?

Work learning. How is political work learnt? Is there much coaching or apprenticeship, or must recruits remain largely self-taught? How much is learnt in groups? in cool or passionate ways? in a hurry?[3] Which skills, learnt elsewhere, can be carried over to politics?

3

What shapes careers in politics? Is there a ladder of promotion, and how far is it standardised? How ceremonial or necessary are the steps? Is it dangerous to skip any? Are there at each level tests of maturity or competence (especially of the capacity to *continue* learning)? Who makes such tests, and with what degree of assurance?

Work performance in relation to personality. How clear to the opposing players, to the public, to the actor, himself, are the tasks and task priorities in the main political jobs? What scope does each offer for individual redefinition? What are the acceptable limits to eccentricity and autism? What are the principal moral and psychic strains produced by the work? How is poor performance detected and punished?

How far by mid-career has the chosen occupation, taken seriously, subtly re-worked the personality to fit its requirements? What is learnt, perhaps uniquely, 'on the job' – in the course of each kind of political work? What does a life-time spent in one or other of the main political occupations do to a man's character?[4] Does politics help to encourage certain emphases or biases in character types in society? Does it in any way ennoble?

Although they seem artless enough, these questions run deeply against the grain of conventional political studies. The one-country conspectus especially, whether on institutional or functional lines, seems to wish to exclude people entirely, or, if it is unable to do this, to make use only of superficial traits and labels. Nor are biographers much help, limited as they are by the rudimentary character of their subjects' self-awareness, though few 'lives' lack telling items. Yet it must always have been something in the work-style of their subjects which provoked these studies, with the aim of pinning down and accounting for this. Our questions will seem most familiar to political journalists, whose daily résumés of reputation and accomplishment trip lightly over this large territory; in one sense we seek simply to refine and elaborate their harried curiosity. For faster progress, political actors must be coaxed into new habits of attention and confidentiality. Yet both quest and strategy have been plainly before us for almost fifty years. Lasswell propounded both in *Psychopathology and Politics* (1930), and this essay merely follows and bodies out his original conceptual scheme.

The context is set by three introductory questions. First, as Lasswell himself asked, suppose one could discover a general motive for taking up politics – would not this, under the vast confusion of their surface activities, enormously clarify what people involved in politics were up to? Secondly, if politics *is* work,[5] what general characteristics does this stamp it with? Does a new understanding of the meaning of work in men's lives sharpen our eye for the special qualities in diligent application to politics? Thirdly, in what sense can we, or in what sense are we required to, talk of individual styles of work in politics?

The appetite for political work

Lasswell sought to identify[6] a political *type*, who is concentrated in government, but active in institutions of every kind, and whose mark is the desire for power — although it may sometimes be difficult to relate the strength of the desire to the degree of its attainment, or the appearance of power to the private sense of satisfaction.[7] Self-aggrandisement, the imposition of his will on others, is this type's preferred 'mode of dealing with the world', and he is unusually adept in the use of *political* means — rhetoric, wheedling, diplomacy, negotiation, intimidation, violence. It should not be too hard to make out his ruling traits. To start with, he must have a certain capacity for self-deception and imposture, since he must cloak his ambitions under a pretence of group loyalties and collective ideals in order to win support. He is, *par excellence*, the rationaliser — his 'reasons' will ideally be plausible enough to hide the private motives behind his commitments (even from himself) and make them 'irrelevant'. He is restless, and also radical, in the sense of 'strongly moved to reject or modify the patterns offered in the secondary environment'. He liberally displaces his private affects ('nurtured and organized in relation to the family constellation and the early self') on to politics; indeed, he moulds his life in order to do this more fully.[8] Analysis must help us find the developmental paths leading to these unique propensities, but Lasswell turns at once to the 'sub-types' — agitators, administrators, theorists — as more immediately manageable.

Returning almost twenty years later to his question,[9] Lasswell wished to add a new 'ruling need', the urge to exact deference, and he somewhat muted the central notion of power-seeking. His 'political type' is not the classical *homo politicus*, or wolf-man, single-mindedly set on ruthless self-aggrandisement. His cravings are *relative*, and to be taken in full cultural context: he is the man steering by power chances — recognisable by the unerring way that, in each situation in which he finds himself, he responds to and selects the power possibilities, and by his 'intense and ungratified craving for deference'.[10]

In this second study he identified the infantile spur: 'Our key hypothesis about the power seeker is that he pursues power as a means of compensation against deprivation. Power is expected to overcome low estimates of the self.' Cravings for power, respect and deference are encouraged by the type of family discipline which holds the child to high standards of achievement but treats him now harshly, now indulgently, leaving a sense of problematical self-worth and the lesson that affection and respect are contingent on demonstrating skill and achievement. It is the child 'exposed to a relatively elaborate set of requirements, which are rewarded or punished with special intensity' who grows into the political man.

The sense of an 'under-rated self' merges with a sense of deprivation in one's environment, and Lasswell's rather casual list[11] of early settings likely to provoke a preoccupation with power rather emphasises this sociological side: political parents, especially those serving the cause of a rising or exploited group; those brought up in middle-class 'hothouses of ambition' — particularly by mothers who married beneath them; small-town boys; those lacking standard qualifications, or with blighted first careers, with real or fancied physical handicaps, or with long, immobilising illnesses. He is surely right to insist that early identifications with primary political groups are part of the ego — slights to the group inflict personal wounds; but the psychological texture of a strong son proudly groomed by his elders for minority-group leadership is hardly that of the family 'weakling' out to prove his parents wrong.

Few hypotheses of note can have suffered such general neglect. So far some half-dozen biographers have testified that, indeed, something very like this drove on their subjects (Lincoln, Woodrow Wilson, Forrestal, Schumacher, Churchill, Nixon)[12] and two writers surveying sample groups of politicians have added their qualified agreement. Wilson's biographer points out, reasonably enough, that even where the power demand is very strong, other major needs, say, for affection or achievement (themselves also perhaps largely compensatory), may well reinforce or cut across it; that even compulsive striving for power will tend to be concentrated in certain areas of choice or decision, only, and often not run 'across the board'; and that Wilson's special inability to find satisfaction even in considerable achievement paved the way for a series of ruinous provocations of opponents who openly questioned his worth.[13]

Making resourceful use of TAT cards,[14] a 1960 study of some eighty political and business leaders in an urban and two small rural communities in the U.S. showed that the politicians in the livelier offices were, indeed, ahead in levels of 'power need'; but also that politicians in bulk lots combined preoccupations with achievement, friendship and power in highly various ways (many sought affability above all), and that in places where political jobs were realistically seen as largely ineffectual, 'hard-driving, active types' turned to business instead.[15]

An interview study of 100-odd recruits to the Connecticut legislature in 1959 found the 'compensatory urge to exact deference' not uncommon, but strongest in the least powerful and least productive members; sheer zest for problem-solving outweighed in the most productive any latent drive for personal power.[16] Even sensitive readings of current levels of self-esteem, however, cannot tell directly against Lasswell's hypothesis, unless (as seems unlikely) none of those now 'self-assured' suffered as children from low self-estimates.[17]

Eric Hoffer came independently on a formulation that supports Lasswell's, in his spirited attack on the problem of fanaticism (*The True Believer*, 1951).[18] Fanatics, he suggested, were basically in flight from a 'spoilt' or 'damaged self', seen as worthless, guilty, helpless, cowardly or incomplete, and sought, above all, to lose themselves in followership, in the higher, 'historic' identity conferred by membership of a great cause. Half a dozen recent biographies amply confirm this attachment to ideological extremes, and capacity for tireless service.[19] Hoffer's 'spoilt self' is Lasswell's 'insecure self' one shade darker: the fanatic's affects are correspondingly a shade more lurid, and their politicisation total, with the onset of fanaticism resembling a conversion experience. Such crises should demonstrate uniquely Lasswell's 'displacement' mechanism, as oppressive self-dislike is deflected into political channels, often with startling relief.

In a final return to the question in 1960,[20] Lasswell changed his focus to 'power-centred' personalities, 'individuals who come to rely upon power practices . . . as the preferred means' of gaining their ends. The childhood wounds become 'deprivations' dealt out by otherwise 'indulgent' parents, occasioning 'life-long rage'. Then, however, Lasswell suddenly began to have doubts about the enterprise. Politics, he mused, in huge, industrial nations with traditions of popular government will use no single personality type but a great variety; people drop into it at all ages and stages from all sorts of other work; it changes and even matures them as they labour. It may even be becoming positively *difficult* for classic power-types to go far, as 'gate-keepers' get better at recognising their compulsive rigidity, and reject them or determinedly relegate them to the very fringes of the system.

It seems too early to retract Lasswell's hypothesis: there has simply not been enough close work so far to tease out the really strong threads in it.* We lack, above all, informed biographies, but we also need more, light on the origins of 'low self-estimates', and on the disposition to externalise psychic anxieties and affects generally (note the peculiar aptness of politics to paranoids),[25] and the link between early feelings of impotence and the resolve to reverse the situation, to take control.[26] There are many branching questions — yet Lasswell's legacy includes one splendid practical hint: whatever politics is doing for a man, it should show when, at some 'dead end or blind drop', it ceases to do anything: veterans and victims are as much our quarry as recruits.

---

* Three later essays done in ignorance of Lasswell's work, in my view, rather powerfully support and supplement it: Henry Murray's case study of inordinate ambition in a Harvard undergraduate, which he traces back to a revengeful rejection of the mother and urethral-erotic fixation;[21] Lucille Iremonger's application of Maryse Choisy's 'Phaeton complex' to British prime ministers, and especially the cases of the fatherless Macdonald and the mother-rejected Rosebery,[22] and David Winter's reflective essay on the Don Juan myth, linking the drive for power with defence against female incorporation, and with mothers who bind their sons in a life-long ambivalence of feeling.[23] Abraham Zaleznik explicitly resuscitates Lasswell's thesis for a brief discussion in his 1975 study of power in business and government.[24]

Psycho-dynamics of work

If, as we have naively noted, politics is work for most of those involved in it, what general characteristics does this stamp it with? What do we know about the broad nature of work that reflects back on men's involvement with it, that calls them to it with a special force, or that changes them afterwards? In what distinctive ways do political actors choose to work, and how far is their choice modified by the exigencies of politics?

In the social sciences one has often only to propose a slightly new-sounding question to find that there is not much useful thinking on the subject. Even so, the neglect of the psycho-dynamics of work is extraordinary. What has been done is curiously limited — psychologists, for example, will obligingly find out for headmasters how to point school-leavers towards jobs, or advise business managers on what will make routine workers work harder or more cheerfully, or what will render junior executives more loyal or adaptable. But the actual work of headmasters, managers, and psychologists themselves has been little studied.

Certainly this has all the marks of a tough research field — one cannot at the same time work and watch how one does it! Also, work seems rather sacred: one hesitates to tackle so central a bastion of rationality. And it also borders on creativity, an awesome thing, which we tend to wish to keep dark. Yet psychiatrists have for several generations drawn a large part of their living from patients whose complaint has been an inability to work, or to find enjoyment in working. (Karl Menninger once estimated them as three-quarters of the whole.) Even if psychiatry is only a moderately successful craft, it is still odd that it should have offered so little to clarify the nature of straightforward, successful work.

One or two very general points certainly emerge from the psychological and psychiatric literature.[28] First, work *hurts* — because it involves 'renunciation of the instincts'. But it is not all pain; planning and finishing are often pleasurable and there is pleasure, too, in re-experiencing a familiar sense of mastery. One works in cycles of tension, of build-up and release.

Secondly, work is serious. It has to involve an element of self-preservation and sturdy independence, of pressure from the super-ego. Children may depend on others for their needs, but the adult *by definition* needs to earn his keep and win his own bread — and if he ceases to, because of illness, for example, or retirement, he finds the reversion to the dependent state deeply unsettling. Ferenczi discovered the 'Sunday neurosis' in many patients, a lost feeling particularly intense in the middle of the afternoon, as people who managed to cope with their difficulties during the week found their symptoms flooding out on their workless day.[29] Elliott Jaques, too, draws our attention to times when the super-ego turns harshly on work, one comes to feel persecuted by the rules governing the task, and even one's job knowledge seems harassing.[30] We all have a tendency to rest on the knowledge we have, and to resent the need to add to it, or revise it. When work is resented, we may retreat into a restrictive perfectionism — doing the thing exactly as it should be done, but without any enjoyment — or into carelessness and negligence.

Thirdly, work does not entirely over-ride sexual and aggressive instincts: they are smuggled into it ('sublimated') in socially acceptable forms. Work very often, for example, involves aggressive or compulsive activity directed towards solving problems; and we may, indeed, one day classify work-styles by the particular affect, or mixture of affects, a man characteristically demands of and exacts from his work.[31]

Fourthly, the main body of energy available for work is energy that is neutralised and freed from internal conflict. There are ego gratifications in work — of the intelligence and its competent use — that are their own reward. In our society it is increasingly work that confirms a man's essential identity. Jaques sees a perpetual tension between the weight of responsibilities accepted and the anxiety that one will not have the personal resources to meet them.[32] Very long projects produce uncertainty, confusion and anxiety that undermine the conditions for unconscious creativity. The side-tracking of so much mental energy into coping with the anxiety and confusion that are building up further undermines the ability to work. Jaques also explains the so-called 'neurotic flight to work':

> Such flight generally contains as a dominant feature the treating of one's work as the whole of one's life, something rigidly separated from the rest of life, with the result that the work tends to be soulless and lacking in humanity. The internal reflection of this work is a rigid compartmentalization of parts of the mind, so that mental processes which might enrich the work process are not available and creativity is inhibited. One of the paradoxical results of making a 'success' of such work is that an impoverishment of the personality occurs.
>
> Processes of narrowing and compartmentalizing our mental activities are always going on to some extent in the unconscious, and they are reinforced by the failure and anxiety they induce. These processes require constantly to be reversed, and the creativity in daily work is one of the means by which this reversal occurs. Working — and especially working for a living — can therefore be a fundamental activity in a person's retention and strengthening of his mental health.[33]

Work, then, as Abraham Maslow has pointed out, can be therapeutic — and self-therapeutic — at the point where the self-actualising job is

> assimilated into the identity or into the self by introjection . . . This is because the work or the task out there which has become part of the self can be worked on, attacked, struggled with, improved, corrected in a way that the person cannot do directly with his own inner self. That is to say, his inner problems can be projected out into the world as outer problems where he can then work with them far more easily

and with less anxiety, less repression than he could by direct introspection. As a matter of fact this may be one main unconscious reason
for projecting an inner problem into the outer world i.e. just so that
it can be worked on with less anxiety. I think probably the best
examples here and the most easily acceptable ones are, first, the artist
(certainly everybody will agree that he does exactly this with his inner
problems, putting them on his canvases), and second, many intellectual workers who do about the same thing when they select some
problems to work with which are really projections of their own inner problems, even though they don't recognise them as such.

We recall, too, the words of Marlow in Conrad's *Heart of Darkness*:
> I don't like work — no man does — but I like what is in the work —
> the chance to find yourself. Your own reality — for yourself — not for
> others — what no other man can ever know.[35]

The central question we wish to put to psychologists is simple enough:
What is the state of mind of a man deeply engrossed in a piece of serious
work? A general answer will be adequate, but one which is sufficiently
detailed to tell us what parts of the self are drawn into the task in what
strengths and in what order, and which features in the work-face or work
situation provoke and respond to these efforts?

The best account of what is going on in the mind of a person working
is that given by Elliott Jaques in *Glacier Project Papers*. The processes in
work, he explains, span six main stages: first, an objective is set or adopted,
and a relationship set up with it — it may be the achievement of a definite
task, or the experience of a problem and the intention of solving it; next,
an appropriate amount of mental capacity is allocated to the task; then
an integrative net ('reticulum') must be constructed and elaborated, more
or less unconsciously, within which the work is organised and out of
which a mental model may grow; concentration on the task now teases
out the contents of those areas of the mind concerned with it, and scans
them, searching for elements that will help in solving the problem; then
follows a gathering, linking and synthesis of the elements that fit, and the
building of a conscious mental model of the solution or result; finally,
decisions are taken and significant resources committed. The central
feature of the process is the interplay between the conscious and unconscious areas of the mind, with the focus of emphasis switching repeatedly —
each one now figure, now ground; neither wholly inactive.

A glance at each stage brings out the anxieties and uncertainties involved.

Relationship with objective. Work satisfies when it appeals to unconscious,
intuitive or symbolic aims as well as to conscious purpose. It is because of
these unconscious elements that we often cannot altogether explain why
certain types or stages of work interest us, and others do not. In favourable
conditions one 'throws oneself into' the work, 'loses oneself' in it; where

there is unconscious resistance or ambivalence, one feels confused and 'lost' in it, which stirs up fears of failure, making it still harder to work.

Mustering of energy involves a genuine act of mental investment: a segregation of the invested area from interference by other mental activities, and an allocation of attention and time – the more time given, the greater the area of the mental apparatus brought into play. In neurosis, so much mental capacity is absorbed in internal conflict that little is left over – or can be freed – for work.[36]

Integrative net: 'the more or less unconscious network of connections joining all the areas of the mind intuitively experienced as likely to be of help in solving the problem, and organized in such a manner that the gaps in the mental resources available for its solution are established'.[37] Consciously, it is a combination of any or all relevant factual knowledge, concepts, theories, hypotheses, working notions or hunches; unconsciously, it is a mixture of ideas-in-feeling, memories-in-feeling, fantasies and intuitions brought together and holding firm enough to direct behaviour (even if not firm enough to become conscious). The conscious mental effort, the concentrating on the task, calls out a proportionate mobilising of the unconscious effort and activity, and directs it along the required paths. (Problem-solving dreams illustrate how this unconscious effort is mustered, and show that, once they are set going, problem-solving activities may operate on their own.) Conversely, the strength of the mental activity mobilised for the task, the capacity to concentrate on the problem or objective, and the coherence and synthesising power of the 'net' depend largely on the coherence in the organisation of the unconscious mental processes and effort.

Teasing out and scanning relevant items is largely making the unconscious conscious. Items organised within distant sets of ideas are loosened, abstracted and made available for this task. At the same time the 'net' itself is loosened, prepared for the linking of new items, and perhaps modified and built up in the process.

Mental model building. As the gathering and linking proceed – maybe with trial-and-error testing – those items that fit together and that fit also into the scheme begin to form a unity. When ideas are consciously seen to fit, one experiences 'clicks' of insight; when the fit is unconsciously sensed, there is more a notion of 'right feel'. Increasing coherence and synthesis spur on the transformation of intuitions into conscious mental models.

At the moment of decision and trial anxieties about the task rise to their highest pitch. If one's work or capacity are intuitively felt to be insufficient, not only is anxiety consciously felt, but catastrophe is unconsciously anticipated. One may try to evade the strain by obsessional indecisiveness, paralysis of action, or by a careless or 'grandiose' decisiveness, based on omnipotent fantasies and an off-hand disregard of the result. After this strain, to learn that the work has been successful augments one's capacity to tolerate similar anxieties in the future without disintegration; each overcoming of unconscious anxiety and inhibition being a forward step in maturity and in the capacity for creativeness.

Jaques's account gives, I think, a nice sense at least of the challenge ahead of us. Knowing now roughly what it would be like to have the *autobiography of a project*, we may ask ourselves where in political writing we have come across a description of a piece of constructive work done — not just with this detail — but with this type of care and attention to internal processes?[38] Jaques's model immediately suggests questions we would like to add to the normal, commonsense (journalistic) effort to get the 'story behind' some political accomplishment or accommodation. We begin also to calculate the self-awareness necessary for good testimony.

Most political work, of course, is not done in privacy or isolation; and where men are deeply implicated with colleagues and/or superiors and subordinates, additional questions arise about their '*role-task* work'. This term is Abraham Zaleznik's, who uses it to cover the individual's sustained, conscious effort to synthesise his own needs, interests and aspirations with the organisational requirements of his position and to implant his particular value preferences into the organisation's working shape.[39] This work-face where individual and organisation meet is consciously problematical to the person himself, and he not only can, but often wants to, talk about it. The testimony of those he works with can also be gathered to substantiate or correct his view of how organisational events impinge on him and he on them. Our time-scale expands to an interest in how the individual represents to himself his career in an organisation, and how differently this presents itself to his colleagues.

Political work seems, finally, to call in particular on the 'sculpted' type of creativity (Jaques)[40] characteristic of the work performance of those in the second half of their lives. The spontaneous, naive and fluid character of youthful creativity draws on simpler fantasies, and seeks more private, narcissistic channels. Politics is carved out, co-operatively, in the face of death.

Individual styles of work

Lasswell launched the concept *style of work* in 1930, putting the question in its most general form: How may we characterise and account for the significantly different ways people carry out relatively standard political tasks?[41] Alternatively, how may we assess the impact of individuals on affairs, and separate the parts which are 'inevitable', 'obvious' or 'automatic' from those which are done that way solely because this man, A., is doing them?

We may define style *in* work as that part of the way a job is done which is not standard, which does not go without saying. And we may define style *of* work as a person's characteristic way of handling given tasks. (We encounter a fringe of it subjectively from time to time, in a realisation, usually rather unpleasant, of being unable to change what seems to be the one way we can do certain parts of our work.)

Lasswell's questions may be summarised as follows:

> How does the individual react as a subordinate when confronted by superiors of various kinds (strong and brutal; masterful but objective; or simply weak)? How does he act as a superior confronted by sub-ordinates of various kinds (strong, hostile, dangerous rivals; -strong and objective; weak)? What is his style of expression? What is his characteristic mode of thought and style of decision? Is he inventive or uninventive; quick or slow to suggest policies and tactics; influenced by facts and arguments, appeals to sentiment, personal inducements, sense of public interest, or coercion? Does he behave in a traditional manner or self-consciously? Does victory or defeat elate or depress him?

The questions are critical ones to be asked of administrators or executive politicians. Different questions suggest themselves for judges (as they did to Lasswell himself in *Power and Personality*, 1948)[42] or for journalists or ideologists. But the strategy is to break a performance into its standard, routine and institutionalised part (the basic role requirements) and a supererogatory part which gives play to individual temperament and ability.

The concept 'style of work' cuts in two directions: towards tracing out a personal pattern of going at things, and relationships, behind a whole range of instances, and fixing its emotional logic; and towards clarifying the requirements, strains and satisfactions inherent in, and peculiar to, particular roles in the political system.

Role is, of course, a splendidly elastic notion. Lasswell himself, as we shall see, kept to the grand level: agitator-administrator-theorist (with mixed types) — role-*families*, we might rather think them. One can imagine research teasing out twenty main political roles, or fifty, or a hundred. Some role prescriptions will be very much tighter than others: that of the auditor-general or ombudsman, for example, compared to that of the founder of a new party, or a new journal, who can be totally self-expressive. And some temperaments will seek far firmer prescriptions from stock roles than others. David Shapiro has noted in obsessional personalities the peculiar 'self-awareness of a person who is working under pressure with a stopwatch in hand' — an awareness which shows itself in characteristic role-playing:

> It is important for the obsessive-compulsive person always to be aware that he is a 'this' or 'that'. This awareness of and interest in establishing his role is an essential step in the transformation of whole

> areas of living into his characteristic mode. Once his role is estab-
> lished in his mind, it becomes a general directive for behavior, one
> that is often capable of including even the details of facial expressions,
> ways of speaking, and the like. Compulsive people are usually espec-
> ially aware, in this way, of their professional role — the compulsive
> doctor plays the doctor — or their marital or parental role ... It is
> this awareness of 'role' and acting always under its directive that fre-
> quently gives the behavior of these people a stilted quality or a stuffy,
> pompous one[43]

But the key attraction of role theory is its promise to fuse subjective and objective testimony, to light up the inter-face of personality and work, shuttling between the actor's conception of his part, and others' valuations of it — and his performance.

It is only really in the last ten years that writers have set themselves to describe role performances with this strategy in mind. And even so, ext-reme styles of work — the very good and the very bad — have captured disproportionate attention. On the one hand, we have styles that evoke admiration to the point of biography, and on the other, styles that strike observers (and even the person himself) as awkward or uneconomical or plain ruinous — in people who seek psychiatric help and appear unwit-tingly in technical journals and case-books. But we will find that, even if it is inconveniently scattered and discontinuous, a reasonably promising stock of testimony exists, especially in biographies; there is at least enough to give Lasswell's main hypotheses an initial trial. After all, the prime aim of the biographer has always been to pin down and account for what is admirable in his subject's style. Both tasks, however, are much more dif-ficult than they seem at first, and it is hard to keep them distinct from other but lesser tasks, such as following the outward trappings of a career or sketching the assumptions and moods of an era.

Let us turn now to Lasswell's grand scheme.

Agitators, administrators, theorists
Lasswell's scheme

Political types differ in the essential functions they perform, and wish to perform, and they attract personalities appropriately organised and shaped. Agitators, administrators, and theorists exhibit distinct needs patterns and developmental histories. An exceptional man may progress to (or even combine) work along more than one line, but most actors specialise, not merely because of the taxing requirements of each role, but also because the inner appeal of each is distinct, and a pattern developed in childhood confirms an individual in the incentives, gifts, and 'modes of dealing with the world' necessary for superior accomplishment in each.

The mark of the *agitator* is the urge to win an emotional response from a public; he over-values verbal formulae, gestures and single acts of innovation. *Administrators*, focused on the manipulation of the efforts of a fixed group, work in the short term, and show impatience with abstraction. *Theorists*, though they may attach themselves to particular activists whom they hope to influence, deliberately choose the abstract and impersonal, and prefer to deal with problems, and people, at one remove.

Whether the *agitator* attacks or defends social institutions is secondary: it is above all his own agitation that he must communicate and spread. He lives, in effect, to shout or write —to be noticed, to provoke and to leave his mark. A prey to rhetoric and moral fervour, and quick to derogate opponents, he becomes frustrated and confused in the tangled mass of technical detail on which successful administration depends. Landed in a responsible post, he longs to desert his desk for the roving freedom of the platform and the press.

Agitators are strongly narcissistic. They are encouraged in this by 'obstacles encountered in . . . early love relationships, or by overindulgence and admiration in the family circle. Libido which is blocked in moving outward toward objects settles back upon the self.' The search for response also involves an element of latent homosexuality.[44] The *oratorical* agitator, in contradistinction to the *publicist*, seems to show a long history of 'impostorship' in dealing with his environment, and those who, like Lasswell's Mr A., have been consciously attached to their parents and have been 'model children' seem peculiarly disposed to choose remote and general social objects for their assault, their thought-systems becoming rounded and finished. Those who have been conscious of 'suppressing serious grievances against the early intimate circle', and who have been unable to occupy the impostor's role, like his Mr B., are inclined to pick more immediate and personal political targets. What the displaced affects will be displaced *on* depends upon models offered when early identifications are being made. With the latent homosexual trend goes an assaultative, provocative relation to the environment; with a stronger impotence fear, grandiosity.

In the 'Afterthoughts' to the 1960 edition of *Psychopathology and Politics*, Lasswell further distinguished 'enthusiastic' from 'persecutory' agitators.[45] The demand for response in both is a drive to obtain affection and respect promptly from large audiences, but some enthusiasts are so seductive in their approach that they cannot be classed as power-centred personalities in any strict sense, while many persecutory types, preoccupied with censure, condemnation and the maintenance of standards, are evidently driven by guilt and self-condemnation and hope to obtain relief by projecting their weaknesses onto others.

Some *administrators* are full of ideas; others are seldom attracted by novelty. Some do their best work under an indulgent chief; others fall to pieces without strong pressure from above. While some derive their influence over subordinates from the authority of their positions rather than from their personalities, others may be depended upon merely for the conscientious performance of detailed tasks; still others neglect details and prefer to think in terms of general policy. Three sub-types emerge: the hard-driving, the cautious-conscientious, and the balanced.

Viewed developmentally, it appears that a first group — which includes most of those who show imagination and drive — is remarkably akin to the agitators, differing only in that, bound more closely to particular individuals, they displace their affects upon less generalised objects and are free from the compulsion to 'get a rise out of' large numbers of people. This ties them more securely, however, to the members of their own environment whose relations they seek to co-ordinate. Their specific differences from agitators rest principally on the cultural patterns available for identification at critical phases of growth.

A type often met with in the public service is the conscientious, over-scrupulous official, whose 'touchiness, fondness for detail, delight in routine, and passion for accuracy at once preserve the integrity of the service and alienate the affections of anybody who has to do business with the government'.[46] Their failure to 'achieve' abstract objects is due to excessive preoccupation with specific individuals in the family circle, and to the correlative difficulty of defining the role of the self. Deeply concerned about particular people, and about their own failures in relation to many of them, administrators of this type cannot emancipate themselves. The case of Judge Y. in *Power and Personality* (1948) illustrates the bureaucratic trait of avoidance of responsibility.[47] At first sight resembling compliance and identification with authority, this really covers unconscious hostility to routine authority, which emerges as an unending crop of doubts and queries about how rules are to be understood. Compulsiveness quite generally undermines competent work and its basic postulates. The 'Afterthoughts' (1960) adds the suggestion that, for some, the predilection for red tape is connected with the struggle to keep destructive impulses under control. Such cases, in which the demand to coerce is close to full expression, show greater affinity with power-centred, than with more permissive, types.

Another group of administrators is recruited from among those who have passed smoothly through their developmental crises. They have not over-repressed powerful hostilities, but have either sublimated these drives, or expressed them boldly in the family circle. They display an impersonal interest in the task of organisation itself, and assert themselves with firmness, though not with over-emphasis, in professional and private life. Their lack of interest in abstractions is due to the fact that they have never needed them as a means of dealing with their emotional problems. They can take or leave general ideas and have no compulsion to use them to arouse mass emotions. Tied neither to abstractions nor to particular people, they are able to deal with both in a context of human relations, impersonally conceived. Their affects flow freely; they are not affectless, but 'adjusted'.

The *theorist* is not described at length or illustrated by example. His leading features are, however, implicit in contrast with agitator and administrator. Indeed, it is not impossible that Lasswell began with the elements of this type, and built the other two mainly by contrariety. Remote and highly rationalised targets attract the theorist, where the raw agitator picks more immediate and personal substitutes (for his parents) to attack. Agitators attack with the polemic, theorists with the system. Agitators assault or provoke the environment; theorists, more fearful of reprisals, tend to grandiosity. Theorists, in contrast to administrators who take or leave general ideas, need abstractions in order to deal with their emotional problems. Theorists are unable to assert themselves firmly in interpersonal settings (as administrators delight in doing); they suffer (as administrators do not) from a crippling lack of affect.

Indeed, a rather severe if not neurotic detachment is seen as a characteristic feature: all affects admitted to consciousness are tamped down and drained of intensity.[48] They lip-read emotion in others, cut off brutally from their own. Lasswell posits the childhood trauma of crises in which love, rage and fear ran simultaneously at peak levels, leaving an enduring 'stasis'. Detachment may, he notes, contribute to conciliatory and scientific skills, but also to calm, pitiless and destructive conduct in advisers 'who have been able to survive . . . during times of great insecurity', or in intellectual fanatics.

In an essay written slightly earlier than *Psychopathology and Politics*, Lasswell acknowledged that as well as a 'method of collective influencing', agitation was also a phase in the life-cycle of each social movement — the phase in which 'a new system of symbols' is forged, and in which 'a collective ideology is [spontaneously] propagated and accepted'.[49] *The Oxford English Dictionary* tells us that the word 'agitator' was first used in English in 1647 to refer to the agents delegated to act for them by private soldiers in Cromwell's army. Not till the early nineteenth century was it used in the fully modern sense. The first individual so described was Daniel O'Connell, the Irish nationalist, and it was O'Connell's Irish followers themselves who declared that 'agitation' was their chief object (*O.E.D.*). Lasswell noted that agitation is a phase marked by fanaticism, repression, conspiracy, heroism and vivid belief, and that it comes to its consummation in the phase of organisation: 'The tactician substitutes for the prophet, and the bureaucrat for the enthusiast.' When successful, social movements produce 'rather permanent alterations in the practises of society'. Nevertheless, the 'transition from agitation to organization tends to occur even though society has made few of the concessions demanded; the movement's achievement may turn out to be largely therapeutic, compensating for 'the impaired self-feelings of a group'. Hoffer's *True Believer* extends this scheme to full coincidence with the *Psychopathology*, positing in a successful movement an orderly sequence of 'men of words', 'fanatics', and 'practical men of action'.[50]

The types may also stand out in quieter times and in the polity at large. Administering, although it is the central function, may be variously combined with theorising or agitation, and we may wish to explore particular cases of inter-role conflict, or significant instances of role-switching or rigidity. Lucian Pye has already suggested that the politics of developing countries, in particular, is approached more accurately when a second grid — that of modern-minded/traditional — is superimposed on the basic scheme.

> Six types of roles stand out as determining the alternative patterns of political development from traditional to modern systems. First there are the *administrator* and the *agitator*, each of whom stands in one system and seeks to bring about radical changes in the other. Then there are the *amalgamate* and the *transmitter*, who occupy positions in both systems and strive either to keep the two systems separate and autonomous or to cause only gradual changes. Finally there are the *ideological propagandists* and the *political brokers* who attempt to integrate the two systems either by providing a common symbolism or by aggregating the separate interests of people at both levels of the society.[51]

Lasswell's scheme has a sturdy initial plausibility. A 'functional' analysis of political motives and skills, we readily agree, may well require the setting aside of conventional ideas of what is and is not politics, and the replacement of institutional labels like 'President', 'politician' or 'party boss' with new groupings based on inner promptings and gifts lodged deeply in the personality. The three types certainly are distinct, and appear to cover the field. One feels, as well, a subjective assent, a recognition of one's own mode. But a measure of final conviction is withheld while the types and their defining characteristics remain at this fairly high level of generality, and at some remove from the cases adduced in their support.[52] This initial classification of political actors in terms of a few leading 'nuclear' characteristics needs to be steadily refined. 'More complex syndromes of further correlates associated with the nuclear defining characteristics,' or 'co-relational types', will then emerge (Greenstein), and ever sharper distinctions in the developmental paths leading to the sub-types will become possible.[53]

The main theoretical armature of the 'nuclear' types is a Freudian object-relations map. Figure 1 shows how this suggests a continuum linking closeness of ties to parents with the preference for closer or remoter political objects as targets for displaced affect. (It also shows that the 'healthy' administrator is uniquely free from the compulsion to displace.) This central *donnée* is, however, inadequately spelt out, and, since it is quite original, cannot be supplemented from standard Freudian writings. Lasswell is a maddening writer, burying ideas of extraordinary delicacy and strength in a prose that seems at times almost deliberately ugly and imprecise.

A second and deeper source of difficulty is that the type-descriptions draw as well on a second body of psychoanalytic theory. Ernest Jones remarks in his biography that Freud's discovery of the Oedipus complex would alone have ensured his lasting fame, but in fact he went on to a second discovery of roughly the same epic scale — the psycho-sexual stages of childhood development. Lasswell's typology conjures with these as well as with the laconic and flattened-out version of the Oedipus complex at the base of his object-relations scheme. Agitators are, he tells us, 'fixated' at the oral phase, administrators at the anal, and theorists at the phallic.[54]

While there has been considerable work on the personality residues of the individual's path through these character-forming stages,[55] very little light has been shed on the *social* stances likely to be engendered or reinforced as the child passes through each stage. The one project designed to test Lasswell's scheme with a sample, did, however, concentrate on this.

Figure 1.   Object-relations in the political sector (greatly magnified)

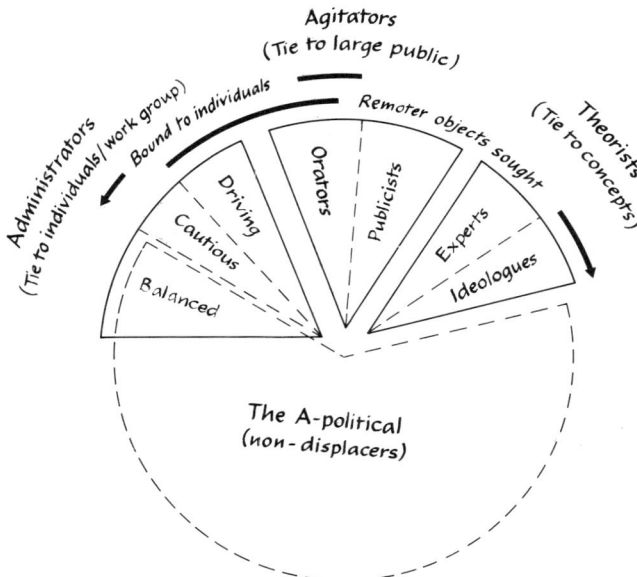

G. E. Swanson, arguing that student politicians should already share, and show, the concerns of adult political workers, set out in 1957 to compare the 'needs systems' of those running the political clubs and newspaper of the University of Michigan with those of their less politically-minded contemporaries.[56] He began with a 'job analysis' of the roles of journalism and speech-making. Leo Rosten, he recalled, had concluded:

> the energies which lead men into newspapers are . . . the desire to startle and expose; the opportunity to project personal hostilities and feelings of injustice on public persons under the aegis of 'journalistic duty'; the inner drives for 'action', plus inner anxieties about accepting the consequences of action . . . There is a sense of invulnerability attached to newspaper work. Journalism represents a world within a world. Reporters derive a vicarious pleasure in experiencing the excitement of events as observers, not participants, without personal risk in the outcome of those events.[57]

Swanson's own expectations were set out as follows:

> First of all, the publicist deals with the controversial. Secondly, he takes a side. He is trying to influence the direction of decisions; not simply to see that they are made . . . [He is] unusually concerned about the problems of power and authority.
>
> Such persons are likely to view the environment as filled with people who want to force their will on the self whether it likes it or not. This world must be controlled. The publicist takes an active rather than a passive approach to this problem of control. Instead of retreating from the world so it cannot touch him, he advances to direct it away from interference with his desires. Such a pattern of attitudes toward the world is called anal expulsiveness in psychoanalytic theory.
>
> Some activists, however, are content to work behind the scenes. They are the powers behind thrones, the nameless, faceless movers of events. The publicist takes no such role. His name will be known. As Lasswell suggests, both orator and publicist are likely to be 'strongly narcissistic types'. They want a public validation of their competence, independence, and virility. This is the need pattern of the phallic character in psychoanalytic theory.
>
> But publicists are not orators. They avoid the face-to-face contact with their audience. In this way, they avoid the approving roar of their audience, but should they fail to persuade, they also avoid the cat-calls of rejection. There is a great need for support that can be satisfied in this way — a great dependency on the approval of others that requires protection. These are sensitive people. Behind the writing desk, they can nurse their rejections in private and gather strength to try again. This is the pattern of oral dependency in psychoanalytic theory.[58]

Using a pencil-and paper test for such 'needs', the Krout Personal Preference Scale, Swanson found that his student editors, indeed, turned in significantly higher scores than a normal control group on anal expulsive, phallic aspiring, and oral passive items. The political club leaders shared the editors' strong phallic and anal expulsive tendencies, but, in line with their lesser need to withdraw from social contacts that would leave them open to audience rejection, had weaker 'pre-ego', oral dependent and anal retentive scores. The less active club leaders scored identically with the most active, and psychologically, political left and right formed a continuous group.

Swanson follows Lasswell's lead in declaring political preoccupation 'immature'.[59] Indeed, he muses at some length on the 'healthy' alternative:

> When one predicts certain 'strong tendencies' among [agitators], he assumes some kind of standard of comparison, some kind of person ... that has weaker predispositions along these lines. The standard of comparison for our theory of the [agitator], and for psychoanalytic theory generally, is the genital character. Genitality involves the expectation that, in most cases, the environment is a supportive, gratifying place that will satisfy many of the individual's demands. It means that the person expects that he is capable of modifying that environment and, if need be, controlling it, but that he does not have to watch it constantly in order to be free of unwanted restrictions and threats. It means that he has the ability to hold up the expression of impulses if the deprivation from their expression would be too great, but to let them pass into overt behavior when the opportunity permits. It means that he can give gratification to others without immediate reward.[60]

He proposes a 'social mode' appropriate to fixation at each psycho-sexual stage, thus:

Oral dependent	Need for security, protection; dependence on approval of others (narcissistic).[61]
Oral sadistic	Sharp demand that environment care for one's needs.
Anal retentive	Protecting oneself from an environment perceived as hostile by withdrawing from it.
Anal expulsive	Drive to active control, moves to direct the world away from interference with desires; overt hostility to others.
Phallic aspiring	Demands public validation of one's competence, independence, virility; active attempts to control.
Phallic resigned	Withdrawal.
Genital	No sense of continual threat, or need for constant surveillance. Can delay gratification if expedient, can give gratification without immediate reward.

Agitation calls, then, on pre-genital drives; and, more precisely, on the *active* alternative in each of the psycho-sexual stages. Swanson's data strongly confirm this for anal expulsive and phallic aspiring clusters (though it is odd that findings on the genital clusters are not reported).[62] Here, far from 'making do', as so often, with a student sample, the use of student politicians and journalists performing their work for no extrinsic reward seems to make an especially pure and strong case.

Other confirmatory work is more marginal. One analyst reported in 1945 that the majority of administrators he had had as patients (some twenty) were obsessional types, a conception roughly equivalent to that of the anal character.[63] Freud's 1908 paper on this subject had observed that some of his patients were 'remarkable for a regular combination of the three following peculiarities: they are exceptionally *orderly*, *parsimonious*, and *obstinate*'.[64] Later papers by Freud himself, Jones, Abraham and Ferenczi added several further traits: self-will, defiance, active insistence on pursuing one's own path, self-importance, procrastination, a

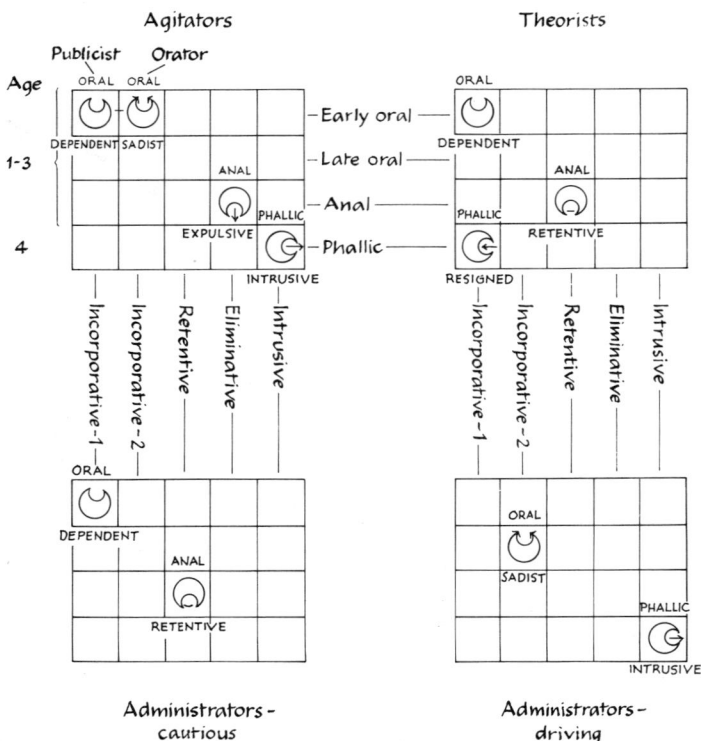

Figure 2.   Pre-genital fixations of political actors
(after Erik Erikson's diagram in *Childhood and Society*, p. 84)

passion for personal autonomy and self-control, punctuality, irritability, cleanliness, and quasi-sadism and hatred. 'In extreme cases [they] become ... parsimonious, stingy, meticulous, punctual, tied down with petty self-restraints. Everything that is free, uncontrolled, spontaneous is dangerous.'[65] These traits in individual bureaucrats match the commoner complaints made against bureaucracy itself: indecision, avoidance of responsibility, waste of time, rigid adherence to rituals which make no sense, and the compulsion to make others conform. The sample also showed a lack of empathy and a desire to punish. 'The chances for improvement are small because so many of the faults of bureaucracy are based on the personalities of the bureaucrats.'[66] The anal character clearly helps to draw much detail in the 'cautious-conscientious' sub-type into a firm pattern. The recent psycho-biography of Frederick Taylor, the prophet of scientific management, is most plausibly organised round the identification of its subject as an obsessive type, *par excellence* : one who not merely fastened finely constraining work and life-habits on himself, but moved actively to impose them on employees.[67] And a 1955 questionnaire study found a strong correlation between student performance on an anality scale and on a political aggression scale (items mostly about forceful opposition to Communism). 'The anal character is apt to express his hostility only indirectly. He is, moreover, often a strict conformist ... [In politics] he will hold rigidly conventional views, but with aggressive passion. This, of course, is the pattern usually called *reactionary*.'[68]

The research thrust, however, is all in the direction of loosening familiar component elements in a search for more powerfully explanatory subtypes and 'correlational nuclei'. The personality-based *skill* is our unit of analysis. It tells in the plainest fashion what resources an individual brings to the political arena, and thus, (given the appetites and recalcitrances of the structures of politics) broadly the tasks he is likely to assume or to be allocated. *Also* (given the limits of these skills and his in-built disposition, where he has a choice, to use one rather than another of them in key parts of his work) it tells roughly how acceptably, and/or productively, he is likely to perform.

2 *Agitating*

We turn now to an attempt to single out key elements in political work. Agitators, administrators and theorists form distinct enough groups, and most of our material — whether testimony or observations — will come from individuals in distinct uniform. But our focus must now shift a fraction from whole persons to *functions* — hence the gerund of the title, since most political actors of any significance have a little of all three sorts of work to do from time to time, and their performance breaks readily into an 'expressive' style (performance in relation to an audience), an 'administrative' style (perhaps divisible into a 'decision' style and a 'colleagueal' style in relation to work-flow and work-group, and a 'cognitive' style (in relation to knowledge and the use of ideas). This is the path taken by David Barber's comparative study of U.S. Presidents of this century.[1] Of each style in each function one would ask: what draws (or drives) him on to give this characteristic performance — for example, before an audience? What skills does it demand? When and how did he learn them? How did his capacity mature; when did it fix and settle; why did it settle in just that mould; did it, perhaps, harden into a carapace with the man and his creativity dying insensibly by degrees behind it? What special rewards or punishments has it brought in his career; how much does he owe his general success or failure to it, and how much of his success or failure on significant occasions?

The *agitating* function involves at least three elements:

There will be preoccupation with speaking (or writing, or both) as an activity that is somehow deeply satisfying or challenging to the individual — as *he* does it (he may have small interest in the activity at large). His speaking bears a message — perhaps, over time, even a number of messages (cf. the remark of a retiring member of the Bundesrat (1972) — 'I think it is time to conclude my twenty-year speech'). But the vehicle itself seems sometimes pre-eminent — the thing is *to be* 'the Speaker' — and the message matters little. (J. F. Kennedy: 'The youth leaders of today are the youth leaders of tomorrow.') Lasswell says of his Mr A.: 'He [is] fundamentally an agitator, and secondarily a social radical.'

However blurred and inchoate the message, there will be some sense of special fitness or 'right' to represent *this* matter, or type of matter, before others, and to thrust it forcefully on the attention of the electorate. There may, for example, be a bias towards good news or bad. Where A. seeks, above all, to be winning, to calm and to reassure (even perhaps as he frightens), B. wishes to shock, alarm, denounce, and spread fear or distrust or hate. Crowd-compellers seek to bludgeon and herd people in a hypnotic ecstasy along a road already chosen by the leader himself (Alexander, for example, or Napoleon); crowd-exponents seek to sharpen and make aware latent fears or grievances, making articulate what is dimly felt (Aneurin Bevan or George Wallace); crowd-representatives find pleasure in voicing known and settled opinion, affirming 'right thinking', putting plainly 'what decent people think' (Teddy Roosevelt, Stanley Baldwin, and the mode endemic at regional levels of government).[2] Even at its most general, the urge is to rouse efficiently some particular affect.

Lying behind the whole performance there will be a sense of calling, of a mission to lead, or of a mysterious destiny.

The lure of oratory

Though the subject of Lasswell's longest case study is an orator, a noted and obsessional one with a distinctive denunciatory style, there is little analysis of his *speech-making* as an activity, or life-based skill.*[3] We turn, therefore, to an author who, though he lacks any theory of political types, has nevertheless the greatest known talent for the case history — Freud himself. Freud's study of President Wilson,[4] written in collaboration with American politician, William Bullitt, in 1932, and finally published only in 1967, after the death of Wilson's widow, was greeted with dismay by American psychoanalysts (especially Erikson)[5] for its mocking and cutting attitude towards its subject, and with condescension, for its old-fashioned and 'clumsy' psychoanalysis. It is nevertheless a brilliantly comic and penetrating study, and it makes a special effort to deal with Wilson as a functioning orator. Oratory was well known to be his ruling passion, and he indulged it prodigally in his successive posts of President of Princeton, Governor of New Jersey, and President of the United States from 1912 to 1919. 'The Moralising President' of history books, he was a man who valued the Presidency above all as a pulpit; he was also lucky, as Freud says, that his moral earnestness happened to be the tone that America, and later the world, was anxious to be spoken to in for so long. Freud notes:

> Throughout his life he took intense interest only in subjects which could somehow be connected with speech . . . His method of thinking about a subject seems to have been to imagine himself making a speech

---

* Mr A.'s world view is set out below, pp. 189–93.

about it. His literary work was speech-making on paper, and its defects were for the most part defects produced by using the technique of oratory in literary composition. He seems to have thought about political or economic problems only when he was preparing to make a speech about them . . . His memory was undoubtedly of the vasomotor type. The use of his vocal chords was to him inseparable from thinking.[6]

Perfectly aware, of course, of his passion, Wilson noted of himself at the age of twenty-eight:

> I have a sense of power in dealing with men collectively which I do not always feel in dealing with them singly. In the former case the pride of reserve does not stand so much in my way as it does in the latter. One feels no sacrifice of pride necessary in courting the favour of an assembly of men such as he would have to make in seeking to please one man.[7]

'He always addressed audiences with this turned-on, intimate warmth', Bullitt recalls. He valued, it seems clear, being a Speaking Man, rather than a man speaking for anything in particular. 'If I had my father's face and figure', he once said, 'it wouldn't make any difference what I said.'[8] Sometimes, however, he saw a particular message, or at least a tone, more clearly, declaring, for example, soon after his acceptance of America's need to go on to a war footing, 'I wish there were some great orator who could go about and make men drunk with this spirit of self-sacrifice.'[9] From 1917, Bullitt notes, he began to be persuaded by his own oratory about the nature of war — and peace — and by January 1918 he fully believed that he could raise the war, by the power of his words, to the plane of a crusade for the principles of the Sermon on the Mount.[10] In normal times, however, as the Georges remark, he committed 'his desire for domination and his ambition for great accomplishments only to reform projects which already enjoyed considerable support and were within reasonable possibility of achievement'.[11]

His style was that of 'a boy immensely impressed by the phrases of a pedantic preacher. Archaic affectations, symbolism, alliteration, flight from fact to generalization, the piling of adjective on adjective, the use of superlatives and words with vague connotations like "counsel" and "process" characterized it.'[12] He was himself aware of his pedantry, but helpless to alter it. It was a style peculiarly remote from fact, which made it easy when necessary to forget unpleasantnesses, which he became more and more prone to do.[13] It was a style that delighted and impressed many, but left others, especially journalists, who had to grapple with it sentence by sentence, deeply uneasy. In fact, one of the first books about Wilson to be published after his death was by an exasperated political journalist, William Bayard Hale, who tried through minute analysis of his speech-patterns to show that the person behind them was cold, weak, anxious and hollow.[14]

'His pleasures', Bullitt remarks, 'were all connected with the use of his mouth' — but goes on to explain that he took no interest in food or drink. His great love of speech, Freud mused, was not necessarily the sign of a strong libido, merely of one 'concentrating its flow into a few channels'. (Lasswell recalls Ferenczi telling him that all the revolutionary agitators he had known were 'noticeably deficient in the intensity of their emotional attachment to objects . . . indifferent to the accumulation of property, and . . . lacking in possessive jealousy in their sexual life. This deficiency in warmth of affective experience was sensed by the revolutionaries themselves, who felt that they were in some way estranged from others.' Their orgiastic indulgence in oratory seemed *an attempt to warm their lives.*)[15]

What lay behind Wilson's extraordinary passion? Freud and Bullitt give an answer in two parts: first in childhood identification, and second in adolescent crystallising of purpose. Wilson's father, a Presbyterian minister and sometime 'Professor Extraordinary of Rhetoric' at a small theological hall, had a most imposing bearing and an obsession with speech: he cherished words

> for their own sake, for their sounds, caring more for the expression
> of a thought than for its substance. He sought unusual words in the
> dictionary and used sumptuous phrases to give splendour to common-
> place ideas. At the deathbed of a parishioner he would remark: 'He
> has no speculation in his eyes.' He wrote his sermons and delivered
> them with rhetorical intonations and polished gestures. To preach
> from the pulpit was not enough. He preached incessantly to his fami-
> ly and to all his friends and acquaintances. In his life he had two
> great passions: words and his son, who was invariably called Tommy.[16]

Tommy, thought to be too sickly to attend school, was educated till the age of thirteen by his father, and coached unremittingly in fluent and elevated verbal expression. Obedience to his father, passivity towards him, became the boy's leading stance: 'His excessive interest in making speeches would be surprising if it were not obvious that he found in the performance outlet . . . for his passivity to his father . . . When he spoke, he was doing what his father wished him to do; but he was also by iden-tification becoming his father.'[17]

The confirmation of his vocation, however, was postponed till his twentieth year, when at Princeton he chanced on an English magazine article lauding the moral power of the orators of the House of Commons. He saw in a flash a career in line with his talents and wrote at once to his father that he had just found that he 'had a mind'.

> He sat in his room at Princeton . . . and wrote out a number of
> visiting cards inscribed *Thomas Woodrow Wilson, Senator from Virginia.*
> The seriousness with which he took his vocation to be a Christian
> statesman can scarcely be overestimated. He continued to do badly
> in those studies which were not connected with speaking or writing,

but in those which had to do with words, he did well. He threw himself into the work of the debating societies and was elected Speaker
of the Whig Society.* He devoured the speeches of Burke and Bright
and the political essays of Bagehot. He walked in the wood at Princeton
and delivered Burke's orations to the trees. He wrote for the *Prince-
tonian*, of which he had become an editor, an article on oratory ...†
He stood in front of his mirror and practised gestures. When he
returned [home] to Wilmington for his holidays, he mounted the pulpit of his father's church on week days and delivered to an imaginary
congregation the speeches of Demosthenes, Patrick Henry, Daniel
Webster, Bright and Gladstone.[18]

Freud and Bullitt show neatly how important Gladstone was as an ego-
ideal of the adolescent. Though his father wished him to become a clergyman, Wilson feared that, if he did, he would never achieve independence.
In proposing the vocation of Christian statesman on the Gladstonian
model, he transcended rather than disobeyed his father, by choosing a
role he would have to applaud — a role which wasted nothing of his
father's coaching or his example or his ideals.

The most impressive part of Freud's biography is the analysis of the
place of speech-making in Wilson's psychic economy. Closely studying
Wilson's illnesses, Freud found a three-way pattern between them and his
speech-making and what might be called the salience in his unconscious
of his father at that moment:

Three months after Wilson's inauguration as President of Princeton
his father died ... In the customary manner, he replaced his lost
father by himself and thenceforth in his unconscious he was more
than ever the Reverend Joseph Ruggles Wilson ... His addiction
to speech-making, which was already excessive, grew to fantastic
proportions. [Several pages then describe in detail an extraordinary
torrent of speech-making to audiences outside Princeton in 1905
and 1906.] His speech-making saved him from one of his ordinary
'breakdowns' but drove him into a more serious illness.[19]

This economic pattern was repeated in 1906, 1908 and 1919.

One of the outstanding merits of this over most other psycho-biographies

* The theme of designing constitutions for debating clubs had a life-long
resonance for Wilson. A baseball club of thirteen-year-olds. the Lightfoot, was,
under his chairmanship, provided with a constitution and formal meetings
governed by parliamentary procedure. His main work as professor of political
science, *Congressional Government*, sought, in imitation of the British Constitution, to make the legislature more powerful within the system, and to make
the orator himself more powerful within the legislature (in such a grand
setting he might himself hope to contribute). The League of Nations was
merely the last and largest of these constructions.
† This mechanism — of having to express actively something one has taken in
passively to complete the experience — may be familiar. 'Imitation' is
altogether a darker and more serious thing than we commonly allow.

is Freud's ability again and again to propose plausible *economic* interpretations (i.e. interpretations in terms of the current balance of mental forces). Freud is extremely sensitive to disturbances in physiological functioning, and his pages on Wilson's speech-making provide the best knowledge we have of the unconscious meaning of particular bouts of political work to the actor concerned, and of the analysis of *a speech* as a unit of agitation. Given this life planned round oratorical competence, what function does each bout of oratory serve? For Wilson's career is punctuated by these sudden active spells. Again and again he becomes bored with what he is doing, and arranges a manic season of speech-making. The active spells, Freud says, are the obverse of his illnesses, which are just as regular (he lists fourteen breakdowns of two, six or twelve months' duration in his adult life: nervousness, dyspepsia, headaches—all involving a complete inability to work).[20] The active campaigning is part of a larger rhythm in Wilson's life:

> To rest until he had subdued his symptoms, then to return to work with a ruthless determination to assert his masculinity became a formula for his life. Thenceforth each of his breakdowns was followed by an exhibition of increased aggression. The cause of this phenomenon is clear. His unsatisfied hostility to his father drove him to escape by his habitual symptoms. His aggressive activity was still unsatisfied. He returned to work determined to satisfy it through the long-established outlet of identification with Gladstone.[21]

Why *was* Wilson unconsciously hostile to his father? Was it because his father always threatened to overwhelm, engulf, un-man him, press him back into an awed, passive admiration? He must have asked himself how he could ever match qualities as brilliant as these. And yet the clearest of his father's commands was *exactly* to outdo him, to surpass his talents and accomplishments, to do great things, be a great man, dazzle him.

Freud puts it in two sentences. His basic conflict was between his femininity and his exalted super-ego, which demanded that he be all-masculine. Whenever current events sharpened this basic conflict, he broke down. He was still caught on the horns of the major dilemma of the Oedipus complex. After each retreat into symbolic passivity, he threw himself desperately into another bout of 'father-like' activity to placate the stern father inside him. Speaking, as an activity, placated the demanding internal father, and subtly allowed Wilson both to identify with him (taking on his manly qualities as he did so) *and* to be passive towards him (since he was obeying him). In this way it quietened both the active and the passive adversary, whose conflict within him was becoming unendurable.

If the mere delivery of an address drained energy from both internal antagonists, the *subjects* he chose for his speeches (and Freud is commenting at this point on those of 1905—6, in which Wilson declared himself an 'available') gave relief now to one, now to the other. If he spoke on politics, he showed himself exemplarily active; if he spoke on religion, as he often did at this time (on subjects like, what Christ would 'have done in our day, in our place with our opportunities'), he was exemplarily passive. Neither alternative is fully or finally satisfied. With the death of his father, when the son was 45, his compulsion to be active suddenly swelled, and he began to develop his 'inclination imperiously to rearrange the world and to hate with unreasonable intensity distinguished men who disagreed with him'. Wilson's imagination in these months swivelled sharply from religion to politics. 'He seemed possessed!' a contemporary noted. 'He devoted to a single address a passion of intensity that would have served half a dozen ordinary speeches.' It was speak or break down. He campaigned to exhaustion.

Certainly, as Erikson has complained, Freud deploys 'old-fashioned' id-analysis, preoccupied with the unconscious side of the story. For a complete account we would certainly want to examine the speeches themselves: their themes, their originality, and the expectations of their audiences. How conventional was Wilson's theology? Was he, in any way, a religious innovator? How commonplace were his reforming ideas, and those of his secretary, Colonel House?[22] How strong an orthodox radical liberal was he? At what pressure of intellectual aspiration did he function best? How important was it for him to effect real change? This is 'ego psychology', and it is certainly skimped in Freud and Bullitt, but it is hardly the more valuable half of the story. The conventional wisdom of political commentary, the *nous* of the ordinary working journalist, though it can, on occasion, give us critical news — as when a politician suddenly changes his strategies, or his allies, or his programme — is, in principle, superficial.

But the surface and the depths are not the only areas open to scrutiny. There is an indeterminate, intermediate area, a 'pre-conscious threshold', comprising the personal resources the actor can call on to carry out the conscious purposes he accepts, or sets himself. Hale's study of Wilson's speech patterns conveniently guides us not to the deep unconscious, but to this area of character traits, defences, and cognitive style — whatever it is that sets limits to the theoretically possible or ideal way in which the job could be done, that makes its performance 'characteristic' and therefore predictable, recognisably just another bit of work of the kind that this man does.

In *The Story of a Style — A Psychoanalytic Study of Woodrow Wilson*, Hale sets out to distil Wilson's character from his language.[23] His writings and speeches over forty years are studied with an exemplary minuteness (there is, for example, a count of 'adjectives of hostility'), and Hale succeeds in proving his general thesis, that it is possible to draw important inferences from a close study of a person's habitual language. Wilson is convicted of having used words in order to obscure the facts of real life. Prone to perseveration and repetition to an extent that indicates a tired or slow-moving brain, he had an inordinately small stock of words and phrases, often meaningless. He liked vague, cloudy expressions, and pompous phrases of a pseudo-scholastic kind. His style exudes snobbishness, romanticism, obstinacy, aloofness, incapacity for empathy, and impatience with any disagreement. A deep, inner sense of doubt and inferiority demanded the cloak of an over-emphatic assertiveness and dogmatism. Ernest Jones, reviewing this pioneering study, summed it up crisply: there are here 'plain indications of God complex'.[24]

The craft of the psychological analysis of particular speeches has developed steadily. Kenneth Burke has several exemplary essays in this mode.[25] The Inaugural Addresses of each President this century have been lightly combed.[26] But the most sophisticated exercise to date is Edwin Shneidman's analysis of the Kennedy—Nixon television debates of 1960. He painstakingly establishes each man's logical style, then what each man must implicitly believe to support such 'logic', and finally the specific psychological traits that the speech gives expression to — and to which audiences unconsciously respond.[27] These traits can predict actual work-style with remarkable accuracy.

It is not clear how psychologically typical an orator Wilson is. Certainly Schumacher's biographer has a similar story to tell about the choice of political work essentially solving problems of uncertain masculinity, though Schumacher had, as Wilson did not, a firm sense of 'constituency'; being champion of the weak and poor was his necessary licence for virile aggression.[28]

Oratory was, of course, more central to politics in an earlier period. In Victorian and Edwardian days, it spanned both Left and Right. 'In the opening days of the labour movement', Robert Michels writes, 'the foundation of leadership consisted mainly, if not exclusively, in oratorical skill', and he notes that in 1909 the socialist students at Ruskin College, Oxford, went on strike against a curriculum giving to 'sociology and . . . logic a more important place . . . than to oratorical exercises'.[29] Contemporary newspapers in Melbourne used to send two men to cover an election 'policy speech' — one for the content, and one for the style of composition and delivery.

The biographer of Alfred Deakin, who was Prime Minister of Australia in 1903, 1905—8 and 1909, has caught the Australian appetite for oratory in this period very well, and has worked hard to convey the flavour of Deakin's particular gift — which was also an obsession.[30] It can best be studied, however, in *A New Pilgrim's Progress*, the eccentric and rather eerie novel the future politician wrote when he was twenty-one; it is entirely about oratory, preaching and lecturing, and the learning of things (mostly vapidly theosophical) to preach.[31] Some dozen rapturous bouts of

the hero's speechmaking are described, all with an intense narcissistic
glee at his uncanny mastery of the audience and his openness to the secret
direction of supernatural guardian spirits. The hero/author clearly wishes
to create a brilliant, theatrical impression, to make a covertly feminine,*
seductive assault upon the audience. Though their response to his exhibi-
tion is orgasmic — partly because the material of his discourse reveals
sexual secrets (hidden parts and forces) — he wished to leave them tearful,
chastened, and inspired. He wishes to be the bearer of good — if fairly
startling — news; but he has a remarkably casual, almost mediumistic,
unconcern for the precise content of the message itself.

When he turned to *political* oratory these characteristics persisted. The
diffuse idealism and vacuously high tone of his theosophy converted
readily into the 'booster' nationalism of his federation campaign; so did
the orator's grandiose image of himself as 'a finer ideal of each member of
his audience'. Certainly his platform manner was becoming old-fashioned
well before his retirement, and it was always, perhaps, a little bombastic
for audiences equally receptive to his contemporary, George Reid, 'with
his absurd obese figure, his purring voice breaking into falsetto, his slang
and his clowning'.[33] But Deakin remarkably resembles Wilson in his
wish to *be* the Orator and to move large masses with indeterminate uplift-
ing fare.†

During the lifetime of these men, the congregation became merely an
audience, and since then the orator's special powers have been altogether
eclipsed by the public address system. But there were still the dictators

---

* Lincoln's biographer writes of his customarily using a 'tender, maternal,
coaxing, soothing' tone, and Leo Abse describes Gaitskell's 'caressing, maternal
tone'.[32]

† What really *was* so bad in Liberal oratory? The answer may perhaps be
suggested by a passage from Empson's *Seven Types of Ambiguity* — about the
badness of Victorian verse:

'Probably it is in this way, as a sort of taste in the head, that one remembers
one's own past experiences, including the experience of reading a particular
poet ... You may say ... that atmosphere is conveyed in some unknown and
fundamental way as a by-product of meaning ... This belief may in part
explain the badness of much nineteenth century poetry and how it came to
be written by critically sensitive people. They admired the poetry of previous
generations, very rightly, for the taste it left in the head, and, failing to realise
that the process of putting such a taste into a reader's head involves a great
deal of work which does not feel like a taste in the head while it is being
done, attempting, therefore, to conceive a taste in the head and put it straight
on to their paper, they produced tastes in the head which were, in fact,
blurred, complacent, and unpleasing'.[34]

Certainly, Deakin's and Wilson's wish to be the Speaking Voice springs from
a massive projective identification with their portentous Reading-and-Speaking
Victorian fathers.[35]

of the inter-war years — above all, Hitler, whose oratory and propaganda campaigns were as thrilling and inexplicable to his contemporaries as they were monstrously successful. Bychowski's early psycho-biography catches the close detail of a typical performance:

> The general character of these speeches is well-known. The fast rising violent passion, the outbreaks of elemental hatred turning into downright rage, vilification of opponents, and the extolling of the services he himself and his movement had rendered, the final solution of all problems and the hoodwinking of his audiences with promises were common ingredients of all his speeches. But if one listened more closely to the words, if one observed the speaker himself, it was striking that the voice gradually became hoarse, changed to a scream, the wild yell of a madman; it was a voice well suited to the vulgar ranting and self-praise or praise of Germany which was his theme. The speaker foamed at the mouth, his forehead dripped sweat, his gestures were violent; they were meant to be forceful and impressive. The pictures of Hitler after his speeches are striking: his face is soft, flabby, expressionless, his hair is pasted to his forehead, his whole figure expresses weakness and exhaustion. The fit of madness was over, the inspired prophet, having spent all his force, returned to his normal self.
>
> Hitler's behavior during his speeches, the graduation of his excitation, and his method of developing his ideas give the impression that he deliberately works himself up to a state of near-madness or ecstasy, as if he were driving or urging himself on, forcing violence upon himself as a manifestation of strength and brutality, a proof of truly masculine self-assertion. The riding crop . . . and the boots worn by a man who never rode horseback seem to have had a similar purpose.[36]

Contemporary politicians, even if still able in crises to fill large halls, now reach their essential audience through television, which may well subtly alter their message, bleaching out certain colours in the emotional range. But the drive to 'win an immediate emotional response from a large public' — to win mass love or respect or fear — clearly continues to be an indispensable part of many political roles; and even in the sedate modesty of local or organisational politics, one readily collects testimony to the 'thrill of playing an audience like a violin', the excitement of 'the cut and thrust of public debate', and to the mysterious invigoration of cynosural verbal performance.

In order to write, Wilson had to imagine himself speaking; Deakin's best writing was 'candid, direct, flexible and fluent . . . [and] permits the reader to recapture the flavour of [his] talk'.[37] Most agitators speak and write with equal facility. We come occasionally, however, on political figures who dislike rhetoric (Hoover, Chifley, Boss Cermak), whose rhetoric is counter-productive (Andrew Johnson, who in winning the rabble lost the Press), or who suffer simply from speech-block.[38] The historian Edward Gibbon, who spent eight ambitious but perfectly silent years in the House of Commons, may be the most famous of these,[39] but Lasswell has clearly warned us that the publicist may be as specialised a creature as the orator (though his case, Mr B., establishes nothing about his writing gift — he was too shy to take the public platform — beyond noting a 'relatively inarticulate' early environment).

A recent autobiography by the French political journalist, André Gorz, testifies pointedly to an extreme preference for writing (see below, pp. 221–5).[40] An extraordinarily shy and withdrawn man, Gorz makes a living as a left-wing weekly journalist, his pieces, 'each containing a discreet dose of poison', speaking out strongly on behalf of oppressed or rebellious groups. 'An agent of contestation', his detachment is icy: he strikes a special vein in demonstrating the absurdity of all politics. He puts the world into files, builds up bulky dossiers on every subject, and can by statistics — whose impersonality he loves — get to the nub of the problems of distant States. Gorz's journal strongly corroborates Leo Rosten's theme of publicists' aggression from safe cover.

The lure of issue-and-affect

What can be concluded, from a still closer study of the business of agitating, about the agitator's choice of the issue to speak out on, about his choice of the tone to adopt towards it, and about the dynamics of the persuasive process itself?

Very often the issue picks the agitator rather than vice versa. As Lasswell noted, the agitator is in the first place a man who is himself agitated; roused by events to an unusual excitement, his normal field of vision usurped by a highly magnified picture of his issue and its ramifications; a man stung into demanding that others *en masse* quail, rage or condemn, too.

The anti-fluoride campaign serves as an example. As each successive municipality decides to put fluoride into its town reservoir, a group of local people suddenly launch an astonishingly sharp and heated attack on the proposal. Few of those who protest have ever appeared before in public debate. Their 'case' is as confused as it is vehement, and tries the patience of even the well-disposed. The judge, for example, who held the Tasmanian Royal Commission into fluoridation complained:

> He had been told that fluoride caused the First World War and the Russian Revolution; that fluoride was a Zionist plot or the nefarious design of some group of international financiers to dominate the world; that water with fluoride in it smelled foul because it was decomposed; that taking fluoride had the effect of a 'chemical lobotomy' producing a lackadaisical attitude with over-indulgence in sex,

alcohol, sleep, food and spending money; that it was responsible for an increase in gross indecency and child molestation cases; that it caused an increase in juvenile delinquency, the failure of elementary school children to pass examinations and that it was an organised attempt to undermine Christian standards.[41]

When this process was first under way on the eastern seaboard of the U.S., an enterprising Harvard political sociologist set out to understand the protesters and interviewed a score of the most vociferous.[42] What was it that sensitised them so drastically to this issue? Were they simply people with strong private fears of being poisoned, aroused by the notion of *anything* in the drinking water? One or two were preoccupied with health routines and bodily integrity, but in general the concern was more ideological than delusional.

> The poison argument is best understood symbolically . . . its plausibility is derived from its metaphorical function . . . 'the principle of saying one thing and meaning another.' . . . The poison argument expresses a set of diffuse but intense ideological apprehensions. The threatening themes of poisoning — deception, loss of control, debility — correspond to themes found in an image of American society . . . The image may be summarily described as follows: There are profound contradictions between fundamental American values and the current condition of American society. Power is dangerously concentrated in distant centers, and enriches itself through the exercise of coercive authority, hidden behind a baffling screen of vast government bureaucracies and giant corporations. Deception has become a practiced art in public affairs: actual motives are rarely revealed by professed reasons. The individual is increasingly manipulated, and the scope of his initiative steadily contracts; the process is moving to an end that will find most men dependent on impersonal agencies.
>
> Fluorides are necessarily administered to all users of a water supply: therefore it is compulsory, depriving the individual of the most intimate right to choose what he will ingest into his body. The advocates of fluoridation do not claim that it will end dental decay, at worst a minor health problem; and further, fluorides are potentially poisonous: therefore there must be disguised motives for initiating a program that is neither urgently necessary nor entirely safe. A government agency developed fluoridation and presently sponsors it, while the chemicals and equipment are manufactured by large corporations: both are seeking to extend their power, whatever the risks to health or the violation of personal liberties.
>
> Fluoridation, the poison argument asserts, is cumulatively poisonous: little by little, day by day, it will reduce vigor and strength, and healthy individuals will be made weak and sick. With all the force of a fine metaphor, the poison argument focuses the concerns of anti-fluoridationists in a luminous image, and by naming the fears that inspire their sense of alienation from the society around them it expresses, and perhaps tempers, their tensions.[43]

Sensitive enough to elicit this underlying 'ideology', the interviews lacked the depth to test the obvious developmental hypothesis — that those agitated by this issue — men 'who hold a stringent individualism at the core of their identity or who have seen their aspirations unfulfilled' — had as children an oppressive sense of themselves as pushed around, hemmed in, made powerless, and manipulated, and that the heart of the current threat was the re-imposition of this paralysing and shameful dependency.

Looking across the array of contemporary pressure groups one sees a good many of them specialising in a predicament in this way, waiting patiently for their 'natural clients' to fall into them, and to become receptive to the remedy they profess: thus proportional representation enthusiasts wait for disgruntled candidates, single taxers for developers, and pacifist groups for conscripts and their mothers (who have, of course slightly different concerns, the resister-sons having concluded that their mothers are, when one gets right down to it, not really worth fighting for: a comprehensible, if bleak, form of resolution of the Oedipus complex).[44]

In many other cases, too, the lure of the issue will lie fairly deep in the personality. For example, a branch of Women's Liberation discovered that ten of their twelve members were the firstborn of parents who would have much preferred a son, and that two, with younger brothers who had died in infancy, suffered from 'survivor guilt'. Clearly, a cause determined on declaring and achieving equal status for the sexes will draw disproportionately on those for whom this is already a life-theme. Again, an observer at an Abortion Law Reform meeting spoke of a 'curious, intangible atmosphere' which he could not pin down, till he noticed the extraordinary number of physical deformities and handicaps in the room, and decided he was attending a gathering of 'those who would really rather not have been born'. One of the group confessed that she had been the eighth child of a Catholic mother who had been warned not to become pregnant again, and who died giving birth to her: the thought, 'it would have been better for me not to have been born than to have caused her death', had made the morality of abortion a life-long preoccupation for her.[45]

At this deep end, where the issue has an existential grip on the agitator, there is perhaps not much question of a *choice* of affect. Issue and affect are one. But beyond cries of fear, hate or envy, questions of organisation and tactics and of co-operation with others before long bring with them alternative ideas of just what the case or remedy is to be, or how it is to be presented to win significant support. Lasswell, reviewing L. Pierce Clark's biography of Lincoln, notes how he won the Republican Presidential nomination from Seward in 1860 because he was 'less ruthless and peremptory, more conciliatory and winning' and knew how to state the principle of anti-slavery so that it alarmed few.[46] And, of course, most of our politics is contributed not by 'birds of one note' but by professionals, who have the chance, within limits, to choose the issues they take up and the way they shape them. (The proportion of political manoeuvring absorbed in single-campaign involvement may, however, be rising.)[47] Many of the issues that preoccupy professionals lie at the rationalistic pole of politics, and are somewhat impervious to individual re-shaping. A personal passion, is, after all, unlikely to underlie incremental school or farm subsidies, or drought or flood relief schemes. Much propaganda also is carried out under the direction of men who have no particular convictions about their work: 'The modern public relations counsel or advertising agency or press agent has the same code as the lawyer, without the restraints ... They accept fees to organize symbols to promote the attitudes desired by their clients'.[48]

The movement of issues across the political field is shown in figure 3. The two extremes are more or less antithetical, and the course of an issue is typically *across* the field from left to right; politics, as Lasswell noted, is 'the process by which the irrational bases of society are brought out into the open'. The issues that most evoke irrational responses are those of 'style' (compulsory school prayer) rather than 'position' (minimum-wage law), of self-expression and taste rather than self-interest, of manner of life rather than of material gain, of religious, ethnic or cultural, rather than of occupational, significance. Rationality is harder to come by in questions which deal with the attraction and repulsion of primary political groups, or which touch on repressed material — sex, aggression, war, criminal punishment, birth control, obscenity, authority, religion — or which conjure with abstract, distant and vague matters — foreign policy or ecology. One may, however, be rational about prohibition and fetishistic about money.[49]

Of course, most professionals have a preferred tone, and will take up most readily those issues or projects which it can most conveniently accommodate. Those who wish to persist in claiming that the country is in grave danger — threat experts — will tend to adopt a fear-based style; those who think the fundamental questions are distributive, will have a style based on envy. They will not find it easy to exchange messages, even in the short run. Our orators, Wilson and Deakin, obviously selected issues that they could fairly comfortably annex to their personae: Wilson can be seen interesting himself only in matters that involve uplift, preaching,

Figure 3.   The movement of issues across the political field

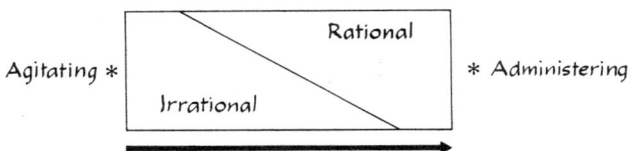

and the high moral tone; Deakin is happiest with consensual, nation-building themes. Lasswell's study of Chicago Communist leaders in the Depression stressed how closely personality was matched with the necessary tasks and style of Left agitation, especially such traits as high anxiety and a disposition to 'externalise rage': if rage pays off

> it is likely to be relied upon in the future . . . and . . . to become a basic feature of the personality structure. If the environment is cowed into submission by means of rage reactions, the personality may develop into an 'externalised rage type'. Such types respond with ungovernable outbursts against deprivation . . . They struggle against their own tendencies to submit and to give up the rage reaction; and they struggle against their own deep craving to give and to receive affection. They react against their submissive tendencies by exaggerated truculence toward the environment, and they center their affections, not upon external objects, but upon themselves.
>
> It is obvious that the possibility of co-operating with others depends upon directing assertive impulses against acceptable goals, and turning love toward common symbols and practices. This involves some relinquishment of rage reactions in primary relationships, and some limitations of secondary narcissism . . . During crisis their fellows become very indulgent toward anyone who takes the lead in expressing and directing destructive impulses toward the symbol of the enemy. When the rage types possess skill in words, they may win . . . admiration . . . their social role is to intensify collective reactions through extreme statement and impetuous action.
>
> Such types are so dependent upon huge and instantaneous supplies of deference that they cannot endure lack of appreciation or criticism . . . [and are easily led into] factional conflict. In disgust they may 'throw the whole thing overboard' . . . such personalities are constantly poised on the edge of proud isolation and of spectacular participation in mass action. Although they are peculiarly susceptible to propaganda for organised radical and revolutionary movements during crises, they heighten the internal conflicts within these movements whenever difficulties arise.[50]

A similar accommodation of style may occur in Lasswell's 'crowd representatives' who tie themselves to a 'constituency' and undertake to register its constitutive affect, or leading tone, and to deliver this as a regular input to the system. Thus the biographer of the Australian Country Party* leader, Michael Bruxner, notes:

> He entered politics at a time when country people . . . were becoming aware of their common identity, and beginning to bridle at the townsman's contempt for their values, a contempt summed up in

* Since the foundation of this party in 1919, most Conservative ministries in Australia, federal and state, have been coalitions between this rural wing (averaging 12% of the total vote) and an urban wing, some three times larger.

the jokes about Dad, Dave, and Mabel, the embodiments of rural woodenness and gaucherie. It was Bruxner's genius to stand the Dad and Dave stereotype on its head, to find virtues in slowness of thought, to discover stability in solidity. In doing so, and in leading a political party whose values these were, he helped to restore the self-confidence of the country.[51]

We reserve till later the discussion of making a career of agitating, since it introduces a set of additional questions to do with the choosing of issues and shaping their presentation, of co-operating with enemies or competing with colleagues, and of working within institutions.

Let us now try to identify the persuasive process. What goes on when the agitator's campaigning (speaking or writing) 'persuades' his audience? First, obviously, the agitator *begins ahead*: he knows the rough shape of his audience's affect (which they may not), and he has a set of ideas calculated to sharpen it. His aim may be to deflect, defuse or aggravate it, but in bringing it into relation with his body of ideas, he sees the promise of annexing some of its psychic force to power his chosen project. He hopes to leave behind a chart where there was only perturbation. He will often be concerned to conjure with the operational affect of his own group or movement — the distinctive affect-mix within which followers find comfort and personal meaning. His task will sometimes be to redirect old staple affects to fresh provocations. He will certainly be anxious to use the demonstrable strength of affect in his audience as *itself* a warning to outside groups of the significance of his ideas or leadership. But the key work seems to lie in making conscious an affect previously only dimly perceived by his hearers, and, after removing barriers to its expression, fostering its growth and its firmer articulation as it is more and more clearly related to the new ideas. (One agitator, of course, will rarely monopolise an issue or campaign; more often he will have one phase or section only in a complex, shifting and unpredictable distribution of influence, a day or two of notoriety, one discrete slice of the audience. Most agitation, we also know, is waste, and much actually counter-productive.)

Are left- and right-wing oratory, then, fundamentally the same? Certainly, many wish to argue that extreme Left and Right currently converge in mood and tone,[52] but the best study of right-wing agitators points up a possibly vital difference in aim: where the leftist generally pushes issues towards a rational solution, winning intellectual assent to an apt policy, defusing the raw emotions of political hurt, the rightist seeks primarily to aggravate the original affect — and his work of persuasion is essentially a seduction, a playing on latent desires to do the forbidden:

> Instead of the specific effort the reformer and revolutionary demand, the agitator seems to require only the willingness to relinquish inhibitions. And instead of helping his followers to sublimate the original emotion, the agitator gives them permission to indulge in

anticipatory fantasies in which they violently discharge those emotions against alleged enemies.[53]

The right-wing agitator's remedy is less a change in the political or social structure than the recognition of an implacable and protean enemy, and the *elimination of people*. The economic, political and cultural grievances he conjures with are diffuse and often contradictory. What is constant is the emotional sub-stratum of distrust and dependence, and a sense of exclusion, anxiety and disillusionment — a complex malaise which he manipulates, crystallises and hardens, while at the same time cheerfully distorting the objective situation. He plays on his public's sense of helplessness and dependence, their ambivalent protest against manipulation while yearning to be protected and led. He portrays a conspiracy to withhold from them their fair share of material and spiritual goods; he feeds premonitions of disasters to come through the erosion of the moral mainstays of social life and revolutionary dislocation; he transforms disillusionment into a full-scale renunciation of values and ideals.

> He can excoriate the others for their seemingly materialistic attitude, since he, on the other hand, has at heart only the nation and the race. He can thus identify himself with any symbol suggesting spiritual spontaneity and, by extension, with any symbol suggesting that he strives to gratify suppressed instinctual impulses. He can appear as the enemy of those unjust constraints of civilisation that operate on a deeper, more intimate level than those imposed by social institutions, and he can represent himself as a romantic defender of ancient traditions trampled down by modern industrialism.[54]

All of his themes converge on one ultimate aim: his followers must place all their faith in his person — a new, externalised, and brutal super-ego.

'Except through translation into their psychological referents, it is impossible to understand modern agitational themes',[55] and Left and Right make a notably different appeal there; both these points are confirmed in a recent deft comparison of the Birchite *Blue Book* with a standard Communist Party tract.[56] Though both deploy a monolithic, conspiratorial Enemy bent on world domination, the Communist author does not feel personally threatened or in 'the last days'. His enemies, though insensately greedy, are all too rational and their moves can be exposed and minutely documented ('the "great conspiracy" is clearly to bore us to death'); the fine head of moral indignation and a pretence of humanistic compassion, however, cover a bleak, lifeless, mechanical deeper stratum where the individual can only survive in the species, mass society, or the machine. In the *Blue Book*, it is fear of death itself — specifically in the form of cancer — that is projected on to the Communist conspiracy, a single malevolent organism relentlessly 'boring from within'. Against such a demonic, implacable foe, the only fitting affect is finally paralysing dread.[57]

The sense of mission

All three of Lasswell's types may be thought of as 'callings' — for which people can feel themselves in some special way chosen, and to which they may dedicate their lives. This somewhat exalted frame of mind has not been adequately studied, despite its subtle flavour of discreet megalomania, half-masked by outward humility or fraternal concern. It seems at bottom to reside in a shaman-like sense of familiarity with the common life, but also with something outside it, that promises to illumine and re-centre. There is no doubt an element of fantasised omnipotence at the heart of most precarious performances — goal kicking, surgery, confidence trickery.[58] But manic assurance in crises seems more a forgivable accompaniment than an actual aid to success. One reason for the unpopularity of political actors is undoubtedly their habit in rash moments of letting this sense of personal destiny show. A clear case of a God complex, Ernest Jones said of Wilson, and this was exactly what alienated Freud, who relates the anecdote of Wilson's shaking off the chairman of the Democratic National Committee, who had called attention to his campaign services, with the words, 'God ordained that I should be the next President of the United States. Neither you nor any other mortal or mortals could have prevented it.'[59]

The hero of Deakin's novel, towards the end as his powers ripen, finds his name changed from Restless to Redeemer; and he meets a Redeemer's fate, trampled underfoot by the mob as he insists on taking the place of seven prisoners about to be executed. That Deakin felt his father's pressure for extraordinary achievement very keenly is shown in the play he wrote two years earlier, *Quentin Massys*. A five-act Shakespearean pastiche, its hero has twice to win a prize against impossible odds of inexperience.

My only hope,
O God, is in my Ignorance, and that perchance,
Beneath the stubble that offends mine eye,
Some seeds of His great harvest hidden lie,
And I must search, and will, until I find,
Though I run Ruin's plough through all my mind.[60]

The winning of approval from a father whom he rapidly outstrips is the central theme of both works — the object, indeed, seems more precisely the double one: of winning public acclaim *as a result* of forcing a father's submission before superior gifts and accomplishment.

It is well known that leaders who come to the fore in national crises tend to be psychologically unlike quotidian leaders.*

* Heinz Kohut notes that charismatic leaders are 'often splendid in a crisis, when groups can fruitfully identify with their righteousness, firmness and security. They have an intense conviction of the legitimacy of their own wishes and, without shame or hesitation, set themselves up as the guides, leaders and

A sense of mission and identification with the nation sets them apart; they have an unusual disposition to see the world in black and white terms ('splitting') and to believe that Divine providence is discernible in their own careers.[62]

An interview with a Melbourne adolescent who had just decided to become a politician throws some light on this sense of calling in somewhat more routine circumstances. In his final year at an inner suburban High School, he was interviewed in 1968 as part of a metropolitan-wide sample; his interviewer, however, had the good sense to let him amplify his answers to the stock questions.[63]

Evan: the schoolboy agitator

What subjects do you like best at school? Social Studies — it's interesting. I'm interested in politics. There's not so much work — just interesting discussion. *Are there any you particularly don't like?* Eighteenth century history — rotten teacher — boring, too much studying.

Do you have any plans for when you leave school? Think I'll go into politics. But first Law, to have something to fall back on. *Which party?* Labour is closest to my ideas. *Why this interest in politics?* Just a field — the way others want to be a policeman. Initially because I was at a Central School and I was never very interested or good at sports or anything, so I sort of became the intellectual among the Second Formers [age thirteen], I used to concentrate on Social Studies. In the Fifth Grade [age ten] I became extremely interested in the American Civil War and collected Confederate flags and things like that. *When did you first become interested?* Don't know really where it came from. It just always interested me — the whole thing of politics and power. *Do you read the paper every day?* Yes. *Since when?* Since Second Grade [age seven] *Were you impressed by Mr. Menzies?* Yes, very — although I became disillusioned. I was very impressed with the big nobs. I was very romantic. Still am, about people like General Robert E. Lee, fighting for lost causes. And the romantic ideal of power. *Did you like to lead as a child?* Yes, I always liked to be leader. *Were you?* Well, a lot of teachers have said I had leadership potential, although when I had the leadership, I never did anything right. In the classroom I always felt superior because I felt

(Footnote continued)
gods of those in need of guidance, leadership, a target for their reverence.'[61] He distinguishes 'messianics' whose appeal lies in their ideals ('the self is largely merged with the idealised super-ego') from 'charismatics', identified with omnipotence ('the self is largely the carrier of the grandiose self'), but suggests that both suffered 'early severe narcissistic injuries from mother or father, and precociously took over their own 'parenting'; they live in an archaic world which has withdrawn its empathetic contact from them, after having first, as if to tease them, given them a taste of its security and its delights.'

I knew more than all the other kids in the class discussions. Used
to be a loudmouth, virtually. Which I hated because I like to be liked.
How far back do you remember these interests and emotions? State School.
[Example of incredible project 36 feet long in Grade Six (age eleven).]
How do you feel about being told you have leadership potential? Well,
I still don't think it. I like other people thinking it, but I
don't myself. Because I like to make a joke of things.

    How interested are you in politics and current affairs? Very. *What
does it mean to you?* Everything. Interested every day in developments.
Who talks most about politics of people you know? Myself! It's difficult,
because I talk to so many — perhaps my Social Studies teacher. I
also talk to the rest of the class, but on a more basic level. I also
talk to friends. *What do you usually discuss most?* Ideas. General events.
[He has helped to establish an underground magazine at school, and
is active in secondary school political clubs.] *What are your aims
here?* To increase political awareness among kids. The literature is
of a radical nature, because in education one is given only the right-
wing attitude. *What sort of topics do you discuss at home?* [His younger
brother, aged twelve, had claimed that he talked incessantly about
politics at home.] I don't talk about politics usually at home because
it only leads to strife. Mostly because I'm going through a rather
revolutionary phase. My mother's unstable, anyway, and is likely to
make a big thing out of nothing. So I tend to keep my activities
centred away from home. *How do you explain that your brother says
you talk a lot about politics?* Well, I suppose most of my talking is about
politics. My little brother asks me a lot of questions about my room
which is covered in posters: Ho Chi Minh, Mao, Che Guevara, revolutionary activities throughout the world. Mother tells me to stop
indoctrinating him. *Does your father have the same attitude?* Dad's a
realist, but Mum was brought up in the East End [of London] and her
brothers and sisters were members of the Young Communist League
in the 'thirties when the Fascist groups were around. One of my
uncles is still a member of the C.P. Anyway, there was a lot of talking
about politics then; my mother wasn't happy at home and I think
that that's why she has this resentment against politics. *Do you get
on all right with her?* When she's sane. You have to play her. She's
good to get on with, if you keep off certain topics. She's unstable,
but probably no worse than others. Sometimes you aggravate her
purposely. I get on well with my father but he isn't around so much.
[He is an insurance agent]. *Did you have much trouble with them when
you were younger?* Yes. They were always complaining about my
schoolwork . . . Eventually the whole family was led to believe I was
an idiot, whereas when I look back at my reports I realise I was in
the top 25%. There was this myth that I was so lazy — something
always has to be wrong.

    What's your opinion of the Prime Minister [Gorton]? Inconsistent,
unsure, not definite enough, not fulfilling what his backers wanted
him to do. *What are the main things a Prime Minister has to do?* Provide

a symbol of leadership, like Menzies. Has to be able to inject a vitality into the administration. We're a young nation, and shouldn't settle into dogmas already. He should be a Leftist, we need a leader of vitality, who can inject into the public an enthusiasm. Holt, at least, did produce an image acceptable to the public — not strong leadership, but a fair bloke doing his best. *How does a man become Prime Minister?* Machinery or actions? Has to be able to play the organisation's game — sometimes restricting his own ideals so he can get pushed to the top. Has to use his own ideals, but also the machinery to push him there. *Do you see him as a compromiser?* Yes, for example, Jim Cairns . . . if Labour had a communications outlet like in England, he could, I think. [Long monologue on the Press in England and Australia.]

Could you ever be Prime Minister? Anyone can, if they wish — they have the chance; whether they get there or not is different. *Do you think you have the ability?* I like to think so. *Would you like to be?* Yes. *Why?* If I was satisfied as a backbencher, no. But at present, as father says, I'd like to 'grasp at the highest rung of the ladder'. Therefore I probably will go up the ladder a little, instead of just staying on the bottom. *Your father sounds ambitious?* Yes, he is, but he's a noble failure. [Talks about father's defunct business.] We're middle-middle class but could have been upper. Not that I'd want to be, I hate class. I abhor it so much I don't think about it. *Say you were Prime Minister, is there anything you would be specially keen to get done?* Bring an awareness to the Australian public. De-institutionalise the Australian community. Instil a want for change and improvement. Get rid of apathy and 'it's all right', so that people are working for something, and not just the materialistic gains instilled by the 'happiness' propaganda of bourgeois capitalism. Middle class apathy is awful. *What's your general impression of politicians?* Those I don't like are insincere or ignorant, others I admire. It's difficult to generalise: some are there for selfish gains, others for idealistic motives. *Why do you want to be a politician?* I need it. *Why? Security, prestige, income, power?* I don't know if it's power so much, I want to be known. I'm an egotist, an extrovert, an exhibitionist — the whole lot! Also I feel I'm competent — that's probably the main thing. I've never been good with my hands or anything like that. *How would you describe yourself as a politician?* [Given list of 12 adjectives.] This is my idea: conscientious, idealistic, competent. Ambitious, yes, but I'm too lazy. Powerful — not really what I want because I like those who fail, Ned Kelly and so on. Selfish? — materially I am. [Talks about bourgeois capitalism — fact that it has made him what he is. Yet he hates it, feels that people are really not better off.]

One final question: whom do you most admire? A man who is willing to sacrifice his own existence for the benefit of others. I could say Che Guevara but I don't appreciate all his policies . . . *Which?* His dogmatism about the only change that can come is through revolution. He's not my ideal — just an idea of an ideal.

Under its pleasantly joking and self-deprecatory surface, and its avowals that he may well find his level mid-way up the ladder, this interview seems to embody nicely the sense of political mission we are concerned with. Politics is already 'everything' to Evan: he moves in it with a sense of uncanny ease and competence; he has always been fascinated by power-relations and the 'romance' of power. He wants to be seen, known, liked and admired. He practises actual political techniques — speechmaking, journalism — and the oral delight is patent; he identifies experimentally with leaders (Menzies and the poster people), seizing particularly on phallic assertiveness, 'injecting vitality' into civil service and electors; he already has a picture of an inadequate and manipulable 'They' who can, despite their conditioning, be cajoled into healthier attitudes; he is cynically alert to the provocativeness of his (provisional) opinions, and the strategic use of ideals. Like Wilson and Deakin, his open self-assertion evidently follows a loving father's injunction to outstrip him, do notable things, though his mother's suspicion ('resentment') is a slight worry.* If, like Gorton, he 'fails his backers', he has a consolatory myth, already amply peopled, of the noble lost cause.

Yet how little realistic foreknowledge Evan has of what a politician's life would be like, and how little introspective knowledge of himself or his fitness for the work he has chosen. In politics more than in other fields, it seems that the adolescent's anticipation of the quality of his vocational future is destined to be dominated by fantasies.[64]

Agitating as a career

On first coming across Lasswell's scheme, one is inclined to put politicians *en masse* into the agitator group — after all, they do not, unless they are in cabinet, administer to any degree, nor do they theorise. They are before the public more than civil servants or critics; indeed, they *live* before it in a way the others do not. But in fact few of them, over the long term, seem to work primarily with the aim of stirring the feelings of large publics — the essential agitational act — and those who do tend to look imperfectly adjusted to official life. It seems somehow unparliamentary to act in this way, *directly* courting the mass audience. And, as agitators, they still look quite ineffectual beside such resolutely unparliamentary actors as anti-Communist, anti-integrationist, or women's movement leaders.

Certainly individual politicians will often earnestly seek to gain publicity for some predicament or proposed remedy. David Riesman notes wittily that they are, in this thirst for publicity, like clergymen fighting for a diminishing share of attention in the media and the suburbs.[65] But

---

* It has already been pointed out (see note 22, p. 436) that absent or neglectful fathers (and 'overwhelming' mothers) may also spur sons to Phaeton flights.

this is less agitation *per se* than a step in institutionalised reform; and it is not one they monopolise.* Journalists quite independently launch such reform campaigns. So, for that matter, do administrators, who often covertly persuade journalists to 'discover' scandalous conditions in jails or hospitals or schools, in the hope of getting more money, or another boss. But the 'clean up' campaign, the ventilated grievance, the 'hard case' within established rules or values, is *sub*-agitational since it works with token dosages of affect, and introduces no incongruities of perspective. When really strong shock-waves of agitation break, the issue, and the agitator who embodies or personifies it, will be found at the outer edge of settled politics. Marginal men make the social innovations; their appearance is as dramatic as it is unpredictable.

Karl Deutsch noted that the solutions to really serious political problems were

> more likely to be found by some deviant members of the community — persons whose memories, habits, or viewpoints may differ significantly from those of most other groups in their community or culture and who may have fewer habits and interests to sacrifice in identifying themselves with new ideas and new patterns of behavior.

The deviants, misfits, strangers, members of minorities and 'marginal men' who perform this innovatory function will rarely, however, carry through their ideas to the stage of implementation. Prophetic leadership gives way to continuing leadership, and the new ideas are accepted without the individuals and groups who originally propagated them, as in

> the story of . . . Cobden's Free Trade agitation and British commercial policy in the mid-nineteenth century, or the story of William Lloyd Garrison and the abolition of slavery, or the role of Tom Paine in the American Revolution, or the story of Edmund Burke and the actual consolidation of conservative power in England at the turn of the eighteenth century.[67]

Politicians, just because they are clustered about the settled centre of politics, and privy to all its understandings, have as a political group less call to agitate than others. It is as if, after winning their place with a little ritual agitation, it is understood that henceforth their serious work is to be done in a different style. The 'seasoning' of the traditional politician may be observed in the standard twinned photographs to be found in biographies: the 30-year-old firebrand on first election, and the worn 64-year-old Minister, grey wheel-horse of the Establishment.[68] The political recruit will often have some pet notion he is determined to press upon the public, and which he may persist in professing without much enlarging over the years. Parliamentary colleagues tend to respect

---

* That the 'Fabian' public education campaign to convert majority opinion is now a convention of civics, rather than of expedient politics, is argued convincingly in W. H. Whyte's essay on his 1960–4 Open Space Campaign.[66]

such specialisms; a parliament has (like a university or a newspaper) a fantasy of collective competence, and is pleased to see men taking up new problems and neglected fields. Pure agitational work, in short, occupies relatively little of the ordinary politician's time.

We lack studies in depth of real agitators, particularly of how they contrive to stretch their issue or their affect into a life-work, keeping the public attentive, and their own morale and sense of mission afloat.[69] It is clear at least that a critical thing will be their relation to a movement, either pre-existing but peculiarly susceptible to their line, or made up of those they have themselves persuaded and banded together.

The typological 'life-histories' of social movements which seem to be transcribed from one sociology text to another have, however, decided for some reason that agitators are influential (and indispensable) only in the early stages of a movement's career. Herbert Blumer, for example, writes: 'A social movement [develops] its organisation and its culture . . . in the course of its career'; it has four phases, which may be summarised as follows:

> In the stage of *social unrest*, people are uneasy and act at random; they are susceptible to appeals and suggestions that tap their discontent; the agitator is likely to play an important role. The random and erratic behavior sensitizes people to one another and focuses their restlessness on certain objects. There is even more milling in the state of *popular excitement*, but more definite notions emerge as to the cause of their condition and what should be done about it. So there is a sharpening of objectives. The leader now is likely to be a prophet or reformer. In the stage of *formalization* the movement becomes more clearly organized with rules, policies, tactics and discipline. Here the leader is likely to be a 'statesman'. In the *institutional* stage, the movement has crystallized into a fixed organization with a definite personnel and structure to carry its purposes into effect: an administrator is likely to lead.[70]

Agitation, Blumer goes on to say, plays its most significant role

> in the beginning and early stages of a movement, although it may persist in minor form in the later portions of the life-cycle of the movement . . . It is essentially a means of exciting people . . . it acts to loosen the hold on them of their previous attachments, and to break down their previous ways of thinking and acting . . . To be successful, it must . . . arouse feelings and impulses; and . . . it must give some direction to these impulses and feelings through ideas, suggestions, criticisms, and promises.
>
> Agitation operates in two kinds of situations. One is a situation marked by abuse, unfair discrimination, and injustice, but . . . wherein people take this mode of life for granted and do not raise questions about it. [They] are marked by inertia . . . hence the function of the agitation is to lead them to challenge and question their own modes

of living. It is in such a situation that agitation may create social unrest where none existed previously. The other situation is one wherein people are already aroused, restless, and discontented, but where they are either too timid to act or else do not know what to do. In this situation the function of agitation is not so much to implant the seeds of unrest, as to intensify, release, and direct the tensions which people already have.

Agitators seem to fall into two types corresponding roughly to these two situations. One . . . is an excitable, restless, and aggressive individual. His dynamic and energetic behavior attracts the attention of people to him; and the excitement and restlessness of his behavior tends to infect them. He is likely to act with dramatic gesture and to talk in terms of spectacular imagery. His appearance and behavior foster the contagion of unrest and excitement . . . The second type of agitator is more calm, quiet, and dignified. He stirs people not by what he does, but by what he says. He is likely to be a man sparing in his words, but capable of saying very caustic, incisive and biting things — things which get 'under the skin' of people and force them to view things in a new light . . . His function is to make people aware of their own position and of the inequalities, deficiencies, and injustices that seem to mark their lot. He leads them to raise questions . . . and to form new wishes, inclinations, and hopes.

While [agitation] serves to recruit members, to give initial impetus, and to give some direction, by itself it could never organise or sustain a movement. Collective activities based on mere agitation would be sporadic, disconnected, and short-lived.[71]

Other mechanisms, Blumer says, are needed to give solidity and persistence: the development of *esprit de corps*, or morale, of ideology, and of tactics calculated to gain and hold adherents, and to reach objectives.

But this seems altogether too flat a view of agitational work, especially in cases where the agitator stays with, and continues to mould, his issue and his group. Ideology, in particular, cannot be neatly sliced away from agitational appeal. Often, too, the initial agitation sets the organisational affect for the movement and the whole slant of its recruitment. David Truman's brilliant discussion of group leadership — as a problem in maintaining cohesion among members cross-pressured by their other attachments — has prepared the way for future monographs analysing cases where agitators themselves become 'reformers', 'statesmen', and administrators, or at appropriate times recruit or deploy suitable colleagues or disciples to these extra tasks.[72] Where an agitator spends a life-time with his group, the history of their inter-relations is complex. Where the outsider sees only an extraordinary stubbornness and crashing predictability, the group in fact plays a dramatic part in the ideologist's own self-definition — his winning of authoritative support (the nod) and the right to act as spokesman, his skirmishes with rivals hated more than the official foe, his lonely education in his craft, his disappointments in leaders, joys in discipleship, rage at apostasy, struggles against identification with the enemy, the ebb and flow of hope, vitality, and purpose, to the final Eriksonian crisis of integrity in old age, and ultimately, public honours.

We note briefly, too, the deviant case of agitator spurning group or disciples and continuing as a lone figure. Incompetence or the sheer impersuasiveness of the 'message' may be the cause (as with Springheel Jack of Hyde Park[73] or W. J. Chidley of the Sydney Domain[74]), but the formidable New York anarchist, Paul Goodman, exemplifies the deliberately detached agitator, declining all appeals to work with disciples in, for example, free universities, local self-government schemes or communes, in order to continue an agitation at his chosen distance.

If political studies have failed to come to grips with the full-time agitator, they have looked with some care and sophistication at several legislatures and individual legislators. In so far as these tell us about the strains and strategies of pursuing a meaningful career in political persuasion over years, we may think they are not wholly off the point. The best of them is James D. Barber's *The Lawmakers*.[75]

Barber studied the adjustment of all the new members of the Connecticut legislature in 1959: there were 150 of them, mostly Democrats, as that party was returned in a landslide to its first majority for 80 years. A comprehensive questionnaire was supplemented by thirty-odd personal interviews. Reading through the protocols and checking them against members' actual performance, it seemed that two points were critical — activity, and willingness to return — and that these two points were independent of each other. Each type has a characteristic legislative style and pattern of involvement with substantive work, as well as of constituency setting and nomination conditions.

Barber found that two-thirds of new members were not merely ineffectual to begin with, but were unlikely to learn from experience. The more he studied the groups, the more they seemed to be based on the members' characters: a special set of personal needs underlay each political style, and there was a special set of anxieties and defences against them. Briefly, Spectators were preoccupied with their unloveableness, Advertisers with their impotence, Reluctants with their uselessness, and Lawmakers with their achievements.[76] Their experiences in their nomination, in the cam-

Figure 4.   Four patterns of adaptation
(after the diagram in James D. Barber, *The Lawmakers*, p. 20)

| | | Activity | |
		High	Low
Willingness to	High	Lawmakers 34%	Spectators 31%
Return	Low	Advertisers 17%	Reluctants 18%

paign, and in the legislature itself had provoked serious problems of adjustment for each group and sharp feelings of inadequacy in three of them, which in turn led them to characteristic strategies for coping with or overcoming their discomfort.

It is through the activities of the Lawmakers that the legislature functions. They find the actual work of the institution itself, and the active manipulation of its processes, a challenge. They show a pressure for completion, for following through and finishing tasks; they are concerned that the decision process is fully rational; they feel for their fellows an acceptance based on insight. Their personal strengths are an 'ability to perceive the environment realistically without becoming fundamentally discouraged', and a capacity for maintaining a strong sense of personal identity while actually changing and developing. Their most notable gift is for defining what they can best do in a given situation — in linking their personal knowledge with issues, in singling out significant bills and bits of bills to work on, in their realistic sense of what is personally and socially possible.[77] Their difficulties come from adjusting to the need to be 'a public figure', to have to 'campaign' rather than to persuade rationally, and to compromise and accept the philosophy of political trading.

Barber ends his account with a shrewd list of questions for selection committees seeking to identify Lawmakers, and he analyses well why the legislature will only reinforce the maladaptive patterns, that is, why a majority of recruits will fail to learn to perform acceptably or work productively — a peculiarly sad outcome when one reflects on the indeterminacy of the politician's job and on how most of its tasks are at bottom self-defined and self-imposed.[78]

3 *Administering*

General Administrative Capacity

Is there a generalised capacity to administer?

Some notable administrators seem at home in any executive setting, and some are barely conceivable outside the organisation they have themselves created and shaped. Wartime bureaucracies bristled with successful transfers and dramatic enlargements of talent — headmasters turned generals, businessmen and union leaders filled important political and diplomatic posts, routine public servants from legalistic corners blossomed into large-scale managers of emergency plants. And many went on to a third life after the war as company directors, vice-chancellors or ambassadors. Such men and careers strongly attest to a generalised gift for management and administration.

But cases abound, too, of 'field-dependent' administrators. Lord Reith, for example, showed exceptional executive capacity in building the BBC in the 1930s, sustained in his work by a sturdy belief in the cause of popular enlightenment and uplift, and also perhaps by an ability to be his own ideal listener.* When war came, he chafed to be given some emergency task equal to his talents. He got a post in the Ministry of Transport, organising ports, and was so unsuccessful that he was eased out after eight months and never used again, though he continued throughout the war to hope for a Cabinet post and even for the viceroyship of India.[2]

The biography of James Forrestal, Roosevelt's Secretary for the Navy, and Truman's Secretary for Defence, shows how a man who had already demonstrated extraordinary capacity in Wall Street before joining the civil service in 1940, nevertheless found a peculiar appropriateness to the tasks of war organisation in the tense aggressiveness of his personality, in his life-long struggle to appear stronger and tougher than he actually was. 'The compulsion to work, to be grim, to flex the muscles and jut the jaw suited the national temper' in those years.[3] After 1945, however, his preoccupation with 'preparedness' and 'living in crisis' set him increasing-

---

* Just as, in inventing the popular daily thirty years earlier, Northcliffe was, in substance, consulting his own tastes and perceptual and cognitive style: 'Everything counts, nothing matters.'[1]

ly at odds with other Administration officials, till after four years, he was dismissed as a man 'impossible to work with', and committed suicide.

Over-determined striving does not, of course, guarantee success. One of Lasswell's cases, the educational reformer, I., was field-dependent to a dangerous degree.[4] He would perhaps have done better as an agitator in the broad cause of progressive education, but he could not 'shake off his managerial aspirations' — in imitation of his father, a notable headmaster. School after school foundered under him. His interests are fixated 'in a relatively narrow sphere in which the affects are so powerful and at the same time so contradictory that difficulties are assured'. A life-long close-fought engagement with his powerful internal father left him unable to manage 'an impersonal attitude toward his colleagues and superiors'.

We distinguish between 'general purpose' and 'field-dependent' administrators less to catch two firm types (though something very like them seems to crop up regularly in public administration writing)[5] than to suggest the utility of the double question — not only, 'How is it that he is able to administer so well?', but also, 'What is there about this issue, problem or field that draws out his repertoire of skills so fully?' For example, we should ask of Dag Hammarskjöld why he excelled as an *international* civil servant[6] and of Alfred Deakin why he made a superlative Minister *for Irrigation*,[7] and we should be ready to ask of any successful administrator why his particular style was appropriate to *that* phase of his organisation's development.[8] Our review of studies of administering is, in any case, arranged in three descending steps — first, the traits posited of good adminstrators in general; second, the special skills they may deploy with greater or lesser emphasis and relish; and third, their individual styles and drives.

Leading traits of administrators

Lloyd Warner's 1962 personality study of some 250 U.S. civilian federal executives[9] declared their main traits to be these:

They find their work-world demanding, complex, a strong pressure on them. At times they feel it constricting, with its multiplicity of authorities, rules, colleagues and clients, and they attempt to change or modify it; but they rather easily relapse into acceptance when their efforts are not welcomed.

On the whole they view authority in a positive way, look up to superiors who support, direct, set goals, and are sympathetic. They co-operate, and maintain good relations with them. They see the Service as a whole as a valuable, effective and supportive system, and they feel secure in it. There is even a certain sanctification of power, although there is always the nagging doubt that there may be faults in the system. A faint strain of resentment at direction and imposed authority persists (especially over 'unethical' commands). They dislike the seeming omnipresence and omnipotence of authority.

The issue of autonomy and emotional independence is critical. In responding to the demands of authority, they seek to behave rationally, with active and independent intelligence. Although they accept structure, and need it, they seek at the same time to 'go it alone'. These men characteristically defer, receive advice and direction, and move on.

There is an anxiety as well about being dependent — needing something external to themselves in order to act, to realise their capacities fully. These men have, behind their stirrings towards independence, strong needs for dependency, seeking sympathetic care and succour from others, especially superiors.

They have a rather uncertain sense of self, of needs and personal goals. Their achievement drive is often 'second-hand', pressed on them, and accepted as a duty. They accept blocks and obstacles to accomplishment rather readily. Their aspirations and ideals for their career are often very lofty — and cloudy.

Though capable of taking and showing initiative, they tend to react to situations rather than set out to shape and structure them themselves. Demands for solo performance especially unsettle them (at the worst, they become resentful, fail in tasks, or lapse into fantasy and magical solutions). They like working closely with others, and do their best work in a group.

They have difficulty resolving situations in which they are emotionally involved, disliking especially conflicts with authority, and the tension between their drives for autonomy and need for affiliation. The handling of close relations with others is also a constant worry. When they can deflect emotion, however, and deal with situations objectively and intellectually, they act decisively and resolutely.

They are more concerned with the external than the internal, they are afraid to fail and anxious to please. They are far from being cold or impersonal manipulators of others or exponents of abstract systems of thought. They sincerely respect and follow the conventional values. If they sometimes react with hostility, it is largely covert, and rarely expressed outwardly.

Warner and his colleagues see an important difference of emphasis in the autonomy-seeking of older and younger administrators.

> It appears that many of these younger men are deeply dissatisfied
> with their self-image. Possessing lofty ideals and high levels of aspira-
> tion, they are drawn to the service and to the system of authority and
> structure in search of a more successful self-identity. Identifying with
> the system which they firmly believe to be right and good, the young-
> er executives seek the advice and support of the system.
>
> The younger federal executive ... accepts the restrictions of large
> organization, the many directives, and the need for coordination and

cooperation. And given this acceptance he orients himself toward achievement rather then autonomy; he does not fight the system.

> Self-determination ... becomes [for the older executive] a concern of first-order importance. Yet in pursuing autonomy his ways of coping with the situation and with authority tend to be passive. He does not move directly in terms of actively engaging and dealing with authority, but he strives for autonomy covertly or at the level of fantasy ... He does not seek ... advice [from the system of authority] in the same positive way as does the younger; or if he does, he does not feel capable of acting upon it or receiving support. There is more resistance, more negative reaction, more hostility, and less identification. He needs, yet rejects.[10]

Warner's interviews and TATs unfortunately cannot elucidate the developmental paths behind these vocational preferences and aversions: even the three individual cases presented at length — an ambitious mid-westerner, a 'classic executive type' brahmin, and a ritualist-retreatist — have too little childhood detail to offer any analytic purchase.[11]

There is so close an agreement, however, between the character of Alger Hiss, the only administrator besides Forrestal so far to have attracted a psycho-biography,[12] and the Warner administrator-profile, that it is tempting to draw upon Hiss's developmental history as broadly illustrative.* At the same time, we may check Lasswell's hypotheses about the making of administrators (see above, pp. 16—17).

Hiss's career, as it appears in the public record, was distinguished and utterly straightforward.† His success, his biographer tells us, was due to

---

* There is one large objection that we must face squarely: if Hiss did spy for the Russians, at least in the years for which Chambers produced papers — 1934–7 — (as I believe, but Zeligs does not) surely he cannot be in any way 'representative'? I think it is possible to see the traitor-Hiss as a split-off part of the personality, functioning as it were autonomously and in alternation (and according to Chambers 'with a strange savagery')[13] to the dutiful/conventional-Hiss. It is something *extra* to be explained, that does not invalidate the main features of the account of how he came by a conventional administrator's leading traits.

† He was a gifted law student (Harvard Law School, 1929), secretary for a year to Mr Justice Holmes, then a young practising lawyer in New York. In 1933 he accepted a job as assistant general counsel to the newly-created Agricultural Adjustment Administration, a New Deal agency in the front line of politics: 'I accepted on the basis of conscience and civic duty ... It was like enlisting in time of war.' A year later he was lent as legal assistant to the Nye Committee on the private trade in munitions. Then he moved to the Department of Justice to help in cases involving the constitutionality of the A.A.A. and the Trade Agreements Act. In 1936 he moved to the State Department as personal assistant to the Assistant Secretary in charge of trade agreements (an old Harvard teacher). By 1944, working with characteristic diligence and precision, he had become deputy director of the State Department's Office of Special Political Affairs, a specialist in the proposed United Nations

hard, compulsive work, a 'lawyerlike, hypermethodical' deliberateness
and caution, an 'adaptive, formal informality', politeness, correctness,
self-containment, affection objectively balanced, and a flair for attracting
the notice of (and for working to) distinguished seniors. He was a 'proper
and obedient boy grown into the conventional gentleman', restrained and
understated, with a certain aristocratic air, but with overtones of a stilted,
'pedantic sense of righteousness'.

Alger Hiss was the fourth child and second son of a Baltimore importer
and his wife, both of respected middle class families. In 1907, when Alger
was $2\frac{1}{2}$, his father killed himself over a business failure. His mother bore
his final child, a son, a month later, and set about restoring her social status
by extravagant activity in civic, women's and educational associations.
Though she managed the house with executive efficiency, she left the
children unloved. As a toddler and until he was twelve, Alger's main
source of affection and understanding was his Aunt Lila, who had moved
in to help care for the family after her brother died. Her constancy made
up for Minnie's frequent absences and counterbalanced her authoritarianism; in effect she replaced his mother.

Mrs Hiss determined that her daughters would make wealthy marriages, and that her sons would make successful professional careers.
Her social aggressiveness and ambition disturbed her second son: 'He . . .
said that from the earliest time he can remember he knew it was necessary
to resist his mother's will.' He remained, however, a dutiful boy, who had
learnt that rewards come to the obedient, and who never expressed, if he
ever consciously felt, his hostility. He envied his elder brother's rebel-
lious-seductive ways, but cleaved, himself, to the path of containment and
rectitude.

When he learnt, round the age of ten, of his father's suicide, he felt
mainly that his father had let the family down horribly, and consciously
vowed never to do anything of that sort. Throughout his life Hiss showed
pronounced 'caretaker'-like behaviour, marrying a divorced woman with
a son already aged exactly $2\frac{1}{2}$, and looking after a regular stream of relatives, indigent friends and acquantances with exemplary generosity. His
first ambition was to be a medical missionary but in adolescence this
metamorphosed into an interest in the consular service, for which his law
studies were to be a preparation. At Harvard, however, he embraced an

(Footnote continued)
plan, and in March 1945 he was made director. He was an adviser in U.N.
affairs at the Yalta Conference, executive secretary of the U.S. delegation to
the Dumbarton Oaks Conference, and secretary-general of the San Francisco
Conference establishing the U.N. In 1946 he resigned from the State Department to become president of the Carnegie Endowment for International Peace,
largely concerned at that time with U.N. affairs.

image of the reforming lawyer at the service of the poor and underprivileged, and the A.A.A. sustained him in this at the outset of his administrative career.

His biographer deftly sketches the psycho-social interior of the Hiss
household:

> The ... house at 1427 Linden Avenue was small and well ordered ...
> Life at home centered in the dining room. The dinner hour was the
> only time all members were gathered together. Table talk was spiri-
> ted ... There were lively discussions, mostly about music, books,
> plays, with easy laughter and joking. Much of the hilarity and heady
> talk was over Minnie's head ... to her children she seemed like a
> puzzled, slightly bewildered, but very conscientious teacher who has
> just taken over a spirited class whose members constantly quote the
> prior teacher and other authorities whose views are at variance with
> the new teacher's sense of correctness. The difference in ages did not
> restrain a close relationship among the children. All five were of high
> intellectual caliber.
>
> Family life in the Hiss household, though basically ordered, allowed
> many areas of free activity. Certain patterns were fixed and largely
> unquestioned: the children were expected to be punctual at meals,
> come in with their hair combed, hands washed, and the boys with
> jackets on. Once a week, at Sunday dinner, each of the children had
> to report to the rest of the family what he or she had learned during
> the week.

The boys had well-defined chores, including shopping for their maternal
grandmother who lived just down the street.

> Attendance at Sunday school and church at the nearby Reformed
> Episcopal Church was obligatory ... Bible reading at home, in which
> the children shared in the reading of verses, and Sunday morning
> prayers, led by Mrs Hiss, were formal, serious, and highly discip-
> lined.[14]

Alger took eagerly to primary school and followed there, too, the home
pattern of fluent obedience. From a mother efficient rather than loving
and from her regimen of chores and culture, he learnt the rewards of dutifulness and became a model pupil. At the same time he admired his
brother's outgoingness, his quick wit and charm, and especially his early
emancipation from his mother, 'which he managed without strain or
disruption of affection'. Though Bosley's individuality and non-conformity
posed problems within the family, he always remained his mother's
favourite. 'He was the bright elder son who claimed and received most of
the attention during my earliest years ... At times I felt a little overlooked
(not neglected), but didn't resent Bosley's status and didn't envy Donald's
niche, which I considered babyish.'[15] Bosley's freely moving way of life
left an indelible imprint on his brother, but his iconoclasm never found
overt expression in Alger's character.

It was a childhood, we may think, which instilled a tropism for authority, a preference for arranged tasks and for working as part of a team,* a need to be seen to be doing useful and difficult things and to find one's main reward — indeed, one's self — in the appreciation of one's efforts by others, especially by discriminating elders. It was an apprenticeship in reining in the emotions, in the habit of deflecting affect to resolve difficult situations. He 'counters the aggression of others', his biographer states, 'by increasing his "objectivity"'. 'When he is under emotional stress he thinks harder, more logically, and more objectively.' His self-justificatory book, *In the Court of Public Opinion*, is unreadably dull, and he behaved at his hearing as if someone else was on trial.

Coached away from self-expression, he was also trained against any great concern with general ideas: he took them in, he used them, but he did not dwell on them, and did not let them capture him. He was intelligent, Chambers wrote, but 'not a highly mental man . . . Ideas for their own sake did not interest him at all.'[16] Though he sought out editorial positions in college and university, he liked the administration involved, and wrote little — and nothing self-expressive or polemical. Was he kept from agitating by his knowledge that he was an impostor, and not really the 'model child' all thought him?

Lasswell's more general prescriptions do seem to cover the case well. Hiss is, like Lasswell's K., the 'obsessional perfectionist, who carries the scars of parents continually at war . . . and is so concerned about definite people and about his failures in relation to many of them, that emancipation is unattainable'.[17] He resembles also Lasswell's H., the striking feature of whose history is his 'prolonged worry about his adjustment to specific persons . . . Even his administrative ideas were closely tied to the immediate context of the Service. His life was dominated by his relationship to definite people and this meant a prolonged carry-over of early attitudes.'[18] Alger Hiss, unlike Bosley, could not free himself from his disappointment in his mother, or recover from his father's rejection. In his work-life, his defence against unusually strong persecutory and depressive anxiety took the form of a demand for an organisational niche that continually reassured and rewarded and called for ever more strenuous efforts.[19]

While ministries afford a peculiarly pure culture for our administrative types, all organisations except the tiniest create administrative tasks, and many of the more sophisticated, private as well as public, seem indeed to owe their existence primarily to the opportunities they offer for the exer-

---

* The children co-operate, as it were, to fill the missing father's place. He grows into social space that is clearly and firmly layered. Though in the one crisis of career mentioned involving a direct choice between siding with radical peers or conservative seniors, the A.A.A. 'purge' of 1935, Hiss calmly chose the latter.

cise of advanced managerial skill. Is administration one subject, or are business management and public administration separate if parallel enterprises? How closely do the leading traits of successful business executives match those of public officials?

The psychoanalyst William E. Henry, who acted as consultant to the Warner study, had already some years earlier sketched the profile of the U.S. business manager.[20] He found that such men share the following traits:

1. A high achievement need. They see themselves as hardworking and *achieving* people; they 'must accomplish in order to be happy'. They enjoy tangible results less than the continual stimulus of current striving.

2. High ambition − a drive to move continually upwards, and to accumulate the rewards of status. On the job, they work for increased responsibility and greater challenge; outside, for social reputation.

3. Ease with authority. They see authority as 'a controlling but helpful relation to superiors'. They look to them as 'persons of more advanced training and experience, whom [they] can consult on special problems' and for clarifying guidance. They do not see authorities as destructive or prohibiting; they are highly responsive to them. This feeling of personal attachment to, indeed identification with, superiors is buttressed by a certain detachment and impersonaltiy in their relations with subordinates, who are seen as 'doers of work' rather than as people; there is no real feeling of being akin to them.

> It is as though he viewed his subordinates as representatives of things he has left behind, both factually and emotionally. Still uncertain of his next forward step, he cannot afford to become personally identified or emotionally involved with the past. The only direction of his emotional energy that is real to him is upward and toward the symbols of that upward interest, his superiors.[21]

This does not mean that executives are cold, or treat subordinates casually; they are often quite sympathetic, especially with subordinates they can see as 'themselves again'.

4. High 'ability to organize unstructured situations', and bring them into a meaningful and predictable framework. This is a type of intelligence, a skill in linking and testing. But there is a tendency, too, to rely on techniques they know will work, and to resist situations which do not readily fit into this mould. (Writing ten years later after closely observing a similar sample of working executives, Melville Dalton found that the strong managers stood out from the rest principally in their capacity to tolerate ambiguity, and to turn to good account unstable situations not yet covered by rules.)[22]

5. Decisiveness: the capacity, not necessarily for instant decision making, but in the end to settle a question. This goes with an ability to give others a sense of sureness and certainty about things being settled. Abraham

Maslow likewise found in the strong manager a 'trait of directiveness':
'Resolving problems and issuing orders come easily' to him, and he has a
'stronger Gestalt motivation':

> He is more irked than other people are by lack of neatness, lack of
> order, lack of aesthetic rounding out, lack of completeness ... This
> is the kind of person who simply *has to* straighten the crooked picture
> on the wall ... This is the person who needs to perfect the environ-
> ment more than other people and for him, having power to do this
> is a very wonderful thing. As a matter of fact, it may be the main
> reward for having power. Such a person may be willing to take on
> all the nuisances, responsibilities, irritations, and self-abnegations of
> power just so that he can retain in his own hands the power to get
> rid of irritating incompletions, lack of neatness, lack of closure.[23]

6. A firm sense of self. These are men not easily influenced by outside
pressures; they know what they want and have well-developed techniques for getting it. And Maslow's strong leaders attended to the

> objective requirements of the situation without fussing too much
> about the delicate sensitivity of the followers ... [They] have to be
> able to withstand hostility ... without falling apart ... to say 'no', to
> be decisive, to be stong enough to do battle if that is objectively neces-
> sary, to be tough, to fire, to hurt people, to give pain ... The good
> leader ... must [also] have ... the ability to take pleasure in the
> growth and self-actualization of other people. That is to say, he ought
> to be parental or fatherly ... [And] if he is really and sufficiently
> sensitive to the requirements of reality, then he is able to be un-
> popular with his children for the time being.[24]

7. They are active, striving, aggressive. It is hard for them to desist
or be still — to take holidays or to retire.

8. They are somewhat apprehensive of failure, and have a 'sense of
the perpetually unattained'. There is always somewhere to go, but no
defined place at which to stop. They react badly to any blocking of their
mobility or their energy stream (cf. Lasswell's case J., who, blocked by a
powerful boss, took a mistress).[25]

9. They have a stong reality sense; a concern with the immediate present; an overpowering interest in the practical, the immediate, the direct.
Maslow, too, noted the ability of the 'strong personality' to be

> *all there*, to be totally here and now, to be able to pour himself totally
> into the current situation, to be able to listen perfectly and to see
> perfectly ... giving up the past and the future [and] pushing them
> aside from the present situation ... [This implies] considerable cour-
> age and trust in himself, the calm expectation of being able to
> improvise when the time comes ... a particular kind of healthy self-
> respect ... It also implies freedom from anxiety and from fear. This,
> in turn, means a certain appraisal of the world ... which permits
> him to trust it ... Self-respect means that the person thinks of him-
> self as a prime mover ... the determiner of his own fate.[26]

From projective tests Henry inferred some fairly strong developmental patterns. First, attachment to parents.

> In a sense the successful executive is a 'man who has left home'. He feels and acts as though he were on his own, as though his emotional ties and obligations to his parents were severed. It seems to be most crucial that he has not retained resentment of his parents, but has rather simply broken their emotional hold on him and been left psychologically free to make his own decisions. We have found those who have not broken this tie to be either too dependent upon their superiors in the work situation or to be resentful of their supervision (depending, of course, upon whether they are still bound to their parents or are still actively fighting against them).
>
> In general we find the relationship to the mother to have been the most clearly broken tie. The tie to the father remains positive in the sense that [they] view ... the father as a helpful but not restraining figure. Those men who still feel a strong emotional tie to the mother have systematically had difficulty in the business situation. This residual emotional tie seems contradictory to the necessary attitude of activity, progress, and channeled aggression. The tie to the father, however, must remain positive — as the emotional counterpart of the admired and more successful male figure. Without this image, struggle for success seems difficult.[27]

Second, the transfer of dependency feelings to the organisation. Given that for most successful executives the dependency on the mother-image must be eliminated, it is essential that feelings of dependency on the father be transferred to the organisation's operational framework and its established goals. Given the context and broadly guided by this, they can concentrate on their individual tasks and achievement. But there is a sub-group of narcissistic administrators who can do valuable work despite the fact that they demand complete independence, feel loyalty only to themselves, and dislike working in a framework established by someone else.[28]

Setting the vocational profiles side by side, it is hard not to see the administrator as simply the business executive, half-achieved — though administrators themselves would no doubt say that they were 'less technical' and generally operating 'on a higher plane' than executives. Both clearly strive to be independent, decisive, productive, responsible, in control, and to work rationally, objectively and hard, but the administrator is less assertive, more uncertain, conflicted and defensive, and has, above all, less thrust and self-definition. Lasswell seems to have been right about the basic cause: the more cautious administrator is still locked in the disappointments, resentments and anxieties that are the legacy of his relations with his parents, and which organisational situations constantly reactivate.

Forrestal forms this sort of contrast to Hiss, and his biography offers a good view of the personal balance of the hard-driving administrator, its formation and its psychic costs.

> Parsimony and generosity, rudeness and thoughtfulness, above all keeping people 'at arm's length' and reaching out to them — Forrestal's personality was peculiarly dichotomous; it is almost as if he never was able to decide what sort of man he wanted to be ... Did Forrestal understand why he worked sixteen hours a day? ... 'Deeply sensitive, uncertain, afraid of intrusions upon his soul, he solved his dilemma by becoming a caricature of the Rational Man. Functioning almost entirely on a rational level, he could never allow himself to enter the world of childhood, for to do so would have meant shedding the self-woven cocoon by which he protected his vulnerability.' ... The 'rational face' Forrestal chose to present to the world ... was ... 'that of the physical man.' To Forrestal, 'strength of character and body exercised daily, stressed independence, and allowed no contact with his interior.'[29]

Forrestal decided on his own initiative to go to college and build himself a successful career. He chose Princeton, because he wanted to meet 'people who counted for something'. There he became an amateur boxer, joined select clubs, became editor of the daily paper and was voted the man most likely to succeed. He took as little money from his family as he could, stayed away from home, never discussed personal problems with his peers, and left the Catholic Church. Yet he retained many of the family values, respected work and was proud that a 'Mick' had been successful at a rich Ivy League college.

He joined a Wall Street investment banking firm and experienced a meteoric rise — from bonds salesman to manager of a district office, to head of the sales department, to a partnership and vice-presidency of the firm. He was regarded as the 'boy wonder' of Wall Street, engineered tremendous coups — such as buying Dodge Motors for his firm and merging it with Chrysler — made himself a millionaire and became President of the firm. He married at thirty and had two sons, but he wanted no strings attached to himself, saw little of his children, and later was virtually separated from his wife. While he enjoyed his wealth and liked to be with prominent people, he was scornful of the 'useless rich'. In 1940 at the age of forty-eight — immensely able, with tremendous drive, scorning weakness and resenting strength, afraid of emotional attachment — he left the business world for the wartime bureaucracy. His Washington career was almost equally dramatic, starting with the task of organising supplies for the Navy, he became in turn Secretary for the Navy, then Secretary for Defence. He took a particular pleasure in winning the approval of his sea-going admirals — (making himself a real Service-man where his father had been a make-believe one). His interests ran from defence matters into economic and general foreign policy; he had a wide and influential Washington and press acquaintance. He considered late in his career running for Republican nomination for President.

His early home-life as the third and youngest son of an 'absent' builder father and a driving puritanical mother had left him insecure and withdrawn, guilty about a certain passivity in his make-up. He had decided early that his 'weak' father presented no acceptable model, but he could not fall in either with his mother's wish for him to become a priest. In adolescence he struck off on his own, fairly clearly rejecting his family, though holding to many of their values, but by then his personality had set:

> The Forrestal who, as a child, had been deprived of love and understanding would not, as an adult, be able to give much love and understanding to others. The Forrestal who, in his youth, was uncertain of his abilities and lacking in confidence would, in his mature years, work harder and longer than most men, and would also attempt to prove himself by becoming first richer, and then more powerful than most men. The young Forrestal who was often ill, ashamed of his physique, and perhaps uncertain of his masculinity, would, all his life, try to appear 'tough' ...
>
> All his life Forrestal had difficulty relating to and accepting authority. For those in authority whom he regarded as weak he generally had contempt; those who were strong he tended to dislike and resent. The former category may have included his father; there can be no doubt it included certain business associates and a large number of politicians, chief among them Truman. In the latter group were one or two professors at Princeton [he left without completing his degree] ... some of his superiors at Dillon, Read, Admiral King [his first Navy chief], and Franklin D. Roosevelt. Priding himself on his own independence, he regarded dependence upon others as a form of weakness, and he was also inclined to avoid people who were, or would become dependent on him.[30]

Forrestal fills the Henry executive profile quite well: intense achievement drive; grim and humourless concentration on work; compulsive, ever-renewed protestations of adequacy; inability to play, fantasise, or empathise; the kind of ego-strength giving constant, strong self-directedness addressed strictly to immediate, external, material reality. He fits less well into the developmental scenario, which requires that the tie with the mother should either be weak or broken successfully and without guilt; and which requires strong identification with a strong and positive father. (The father perhaps may be 'blamed' as much as the son for this, and it may be one source of the life-long special strain evident in Forrestal's accomplishment.) In any case, his biography, focused as it is on the final dive into psychosis precipitated by his dismissal, is a grim warning of the possible costs of the career of the driving administrator.*

Behind the great satisfactions of the role — the pride of craft, the rewards of achievement — there lurks, it seems, anxious compulsiveness and an inability to rest on accomplishment or to believe oneself finally worthy. The constant show of manly independence may be read as a perpetual denial of persisting passive dependent needs. The lack of empathy for, or emotional identification with, subordinates helps screen the executive's own 'weakness' from himself. The strong pride in masculinity and hard-headedness, bought at the cost of suppressing major parts of the self, is, at bottom, a life-project of disavowing helpless dependence on the nurturant mother.†[32]

In one respect, however, Forrestal departs significantly from the executive profile — and the 'family' resemblance in the functionary profile, too — in his lack of ease with authority. This is so pronounced that it brings him almost to the edge of the third administrative type that recent research has uncovered, the independent entrepreneur as Collins describes him. This is the man who

> cannot accept without reservation authority imposed on him either by other people or by the impersonal organization in and of itself. He cannot live within a framework of occupational activity set by others, and he cannot accept in an uncritical manner the rational and legal rules imposed by bureaucracy ... [From his childhood he carries an image of authority] as demanding obedience and conformance without offering in return the physical necessities and psychological protection which [are] due those who conform and obey ... In [situations of uncertainty] the entrepreneur does not look for solutions within the existing framework of organizational controls. He goes, rather, outside the framework ... his mode of coping with insecurity and danger is never to return — in more than a tentative way — to organizational security, but to go deeper into dangerous territory. Eventually, in his seeking for a world which he can control and which is secure, he begins a new enterprise.[34]

* Despite his toying at the end of the war with 'going public' in a Presidential bid, Forrestal's case hardly supports Lasswell's idea that the active, hard-driving executive type closely approaches the agitator.
    Like Lasswell, we must leave the balanced, smoothly-grown 'genital' administrator unillustrated, though we may note the recent vigorous nomination of Samuel Pepys for the office.[31]
† Forrestal's 'suicide note' before he threw himself to his death from a hospital window took the form of a passage copied from Sophocles' *Ajax* — full of hopelessness, despair and raging fury against the mother. The secret he had kept all his life he brandished at the end in the world's face: the mother was uncaring, cold and hated, and he would destroy her and her baleful presence in the self.[33]

The developmental history of the 'organisation maker' features a mother, deserving and wronged, who needs love and protection, and a little boy who has had perforce to take over as the man of the house because the 'real' man in the family has proved himself inadequate: the father may have died or he may appear

> so weak and incompetent that . . . he 'might as well have been dead'. Sometimes these men recall their fathers as once able and energetic men who, in the face of crisis, failed and suffered an emotional death. Sometimes they see their fathers as inherently lazy and inefficient, as models of ineffectiveness which they must avoid. Sometimes they are confused by the fact that the father turned completely inward on himself, away from his son and other members of the family, often without hope and not even looking for work. Here the father is recalled as a weak, unknowable and strange figure . . . Sometimes we glimpse a father who was present and able to provide for his son, but who was emotionally withdrawn from him.[35]

The entrepreneur, naturally concentrated in the business world, can also flourish in the public sector, particularly at its growing edges. We may take Reith as an example — in his solo success, his failure in 'foreign' structure, and in his deficient father-image.[36]

Lasswell has taught us, then, to see administration as a whole, and his successors have confirmed the value of his stratagem of ranging the personalities it attracts along one spectrum, perhaps now most conveniently named: functionaries — executives — entrepreneurs.

Special skills

If administrative capacity, under psychological analysis on Lasswellian lines, comes to seem at bottom a matter of largely unconscious qualities, such as ease with authority, liking for structured inter-personal relations and collective effort, and drives for certainty and power, there persists an older, commonsense tradition in administrative and management studies, which lays stress on ego-skills like the ability to manipulate and lead, reality sense, or talents for bargaining or for making decisions. Intrinsically interesting, these ego-capacities have in recent years themselves come under psychological scrutiny. Under what conditions, psychodynamic and inter-personal, do they flourish? How are they learnt in the course of normal or abnormal childhoods? Can they be taught, or consciously developed?

The notes that follow, while they do not pretend to exhaust a large and wide-ranging literature, at least sample some of the more interesting projects, particularly those with developmental or training implications.

Manipulation

'The most important qualification of one who is high in the service of the state is his fitness for acting *through others*', wrote Sir Henry

Taylor in 1836; 'since the importance of his operations vicariously effected ought, if he knows how to make use of his power, to predominate greatly over the importance which can attach to any man's direct and individual activity.'[37] The motives for choosing administrative work as a career, a psychoanalyst muses, 'have something to do with deriving a sense of well-being and security from knowing how to get others to do things that one decides are worth doing. Success in achieving this has something to do with finding out in the early years, when dealing with parents and siblings, how to get other people to want to do what you wish.'[38] 'The administrative sense', Kenneth Burke wrote, 'is decidedly that of acting by proxy, and utilising the differences among the agents through whom one acts.'[39]

Since the 1820s, when the word 'manipulation' first began to be used of the management of people as well as of things, it has carried the sense of unfair as well as dexterous practice. The most popular articles in journals such as the *Harvard Business Review* are those that relate with a certain relish the tricks that can be relied on to win organisational games and relieve executives of the oppressive sense that modern teachings on human relations, which advocate mutual confidence, open communication, continuing consultation and participation by subordinates, friendship and an atmosphere of democracy, form a complete and obligatory system.[40]

The social psychologist Richard Christie has been experimenting in small group work for over ten years with a focus on the 'Machiavellian' type of person who effortlessly manipulates social situations.[41] With the aid of *The Prince* he constructed a pencil-and-paper test of Machiavellian views, tactics and morality. The only subject to make the highest possible score was an industrial social psychologist from a top university in his late thirties, who had just founded a successful management consultant firm. The lowest score came from a young woman in a small midwestern town, who was preparing to become a missionary. College students came out well above the national norm; medical students scored higher than a group of Washington lobbyists, and among doctors psychiatrists came first and surgeons last.

In the laboratory experiments, in which the Machiavellians naturally took the lead, it became clear that their prime asset was their relative lack of affect. 'Success in getting others to do what one wishes them to do' is helped 'by viewing them as objects to be manipulated rather than as individuals with whom one has empathy. The greater the emotional involvement with others, the greater is the likelihood of identifying with their point of view. Once empathy occurs, it becomes more difficult to use psychological leverage to influence others to do things they may not want to do.'[42] Their coolness preserved them, too, from gross errors in reality testing. Machiavellians were little concerned with conventional morality. Lying, cheating and other forms of deceit came easily to them — in fact, they relished this side of the experiments. They asked not, Is it wrong, but, Does it work? They were also uncommitted, as detached from their own beliefs and ideology as they were from other people. They concentrated on getting things done, and did not bother about long-range ideological goals. They 'appear to despise inefficiency more than [they] deplore injustice',[43] and are more concerned with 'conning others than with what they are conning them for'.[44]

The fact that they respond so well in the laboratory to the challenge of loosely structured situations, where exact roles or tasks are not predefined and improvisation is required, setting immediately about testing limits, initiating action, and controlling the group and the resources to hand, suggests that in the real world the manipulatively inclined on the whole positively assist stability and order. They are unlikely to command the moral indignation necessary to support gross opposition or drastic reform, though once a new movement becomes powerful enough to disrupt established modes, they may flock to either side to impose structure, or take advantage of its absence, to achieve power and influence, regardless of the ideologies at stake.[45]

Though manipulativeness can be established in children as early as ten years old, little light has yet been thrown on developmental factors. One study showed that the greater the rapport a subject had with his parents and the stricter they were, the less likely he is to be Machiavellian, while the more manipulative are likely to remember their parents as having strongly Machiavellian views and being rather punitive.[46] Another showed that there was a tendency for low-scoring parents to have high-scoring children. What is at work is clearly not simple identification. It may even be that a manipulative bent is learnt at an early age from unintentional rewards by parents, or picked up rather from siblings or peers. Perhaps the 'open' parent is reliably the cool operator's first 'con'?

An American analyst recently published a long, reflective essay on two cases of manipulative personality. One, a mock-modest Jewish business man, who had refused the intellectual career his family had pushed him towards, was a patient; the other was the published biography of the 'playfully grand' English adventurer-impostor, Donald Crowhurst. His joint portrait of these two may be summarised as follows:

> The manipulative personality has a peremptory need to put something over on someone. 'Telling the truth has a very low priority for him. He is not usually embarrassed if he is caught in a lie.' If the worst comes to the worst, he will appear to be 'contrite', thus restoring his 'good image'. With the manipulator, the image is all.
> He is intensely narcissistic, a fact which provides some 'insight into the superficiality of his relationships, his callousness, lack of loyalty, and egocentricity'. His omnipotent narcissism is a defence against threats of frustration, anger, envy or pain that could result from dependence on another for gratification. But it is a fragile narcissism;

his life is 'governed and regulated by the repeated need to repair narcissistic wounds through the mechanisms of purging the shameful introject and reunion'. The 'shameful introject' which he contemptuously purges to restore his sense of omnipotence has 'strong libidinal roots in anality and defecation'. There is in the personality a great need to please (or to appear to), and a preoccupation with the reparative qualities of dramatic speech coupled with dramatic action.

Adolescence is a particularly active time in the life of manipulative personalities: in some cases the consolidating work of adolescence provides sufficient control over the impulses for the individual to become adaptive and even productive in his machinations.[47]

The career and personality of Henry Kissinger have also been taken as a prime guide to the Machiavellian character.[48]

Reality sense

The ability to see things 'as they really are' has often been named as the political leader's chief need. Schumacher's biographer, appalled at his subject's wilful and repeated misreadings of his situation, presses the point hard: an 'outward orientation', an ability to take into account *others'* needs and expectations buoyed up the careers of successful leaders (for example, Franklin Roosevelt and Konrad Adenauer); while the unsuccessful (Wilson and Schumacher) wore themselves out in self-defeating manoeuvres.[49] (A similar comparison for Australians would be that between Menzies and Evatt, the Labour Party leader of the 1950s.) Interestingly enough, two rather different types of realist politician stand out: the stolid representative type who seems only to need to consult his own prejudices to catch the national pulse, and the mercurial actor type (Lloyd George, Mackenzie King) who keeps abreast by flashes of empathy.

Psychologists have little yet to offer in the way of elucidating or accounting for this ability. But a speculative essay on 'Some conditions for development of judgment' by Foote and Cottrell shrewdly gathers 'mainstream' professional opinion.[50] Noting that judgement must always be assessed in context, in total living-situations, they stress its inter-personal character — A.'s reasonableness in a situation is assisted by B.'s, C.'s and D.'s; people can help each other to extend their skill. Parents anxiously watch the development of this capacity in their children — 'Problems of judgment which may terrify a child may challenge an adolescent whilst boring an adult'[51] — but it reaches no reliable peak at any age, and can be developed indefinitely. A person's reality sense, they suggest, will, other things being equal, grow in capacity in such conditions as these: when it is unhurried in its exercise (it is hard to ruminate patiently if parents have punished slowness); with the experience of bearing the consequences of mistakes and the development of self-criticism; with practice in actual or simulated conditions; when responsibilities are expanded to keep pace as one acquires a vocabulary for analysing and assessing success or failure; as one gets close to, and learns by identification with, masters of the art; as the group honours the skill, allows for its autonomous use, and welcomes the use of 'third parties', the *via media* and conciliation. Reality sense, in short, shrinks with provocations to diffuse anxiety and grows with self-trust and confidence.

Psychoanalytic elucidation of the reality sense is disappointingly meagre. Although the 'reality principle' overarches the psychoanalytic landscape and the new 'ego psychology' school promises a quite direct approach, most attention has so far been given to two preliminary matters – the development of object relations[52] (rarely extended to the belief system)[53] and the commoner forms of neurotic distortion of reality testing[54] – and to one rather tangential contrast, the boundaries of irreality – the sense, that is, of what it is like for things to be real to one, as one's ego boundary constantly shifts and takes in or excludes elements of experience.[55] The child's first judgement, Freud noted, was whether to swallow it or spit it out;[56] and perhaps by six months the infant is up to the advanced exercise of forming a picture of himself as his mother sees him.[57] Though Piaget has closely studied the maturational process by which the egocentrism of young children is gradually changed into a conception of a universe of cause, time, space and substance, we know a good deal less about the processes involved in the individual's construction of a picture of social and political reality, and lack any account of the growth of the reality sense itself in this area.[58] Our particular quarry is, of course, the superior grasp of political and organisational realities shown by outstanding practitioners.

Money-Kyrle, however, in an interesting essay, 'On the avoidable sources of conflict', sets out certain standard ways in which political reality tends to be misread, and thus, in a negative way, approaches our problem.[59] There are various situations in which otherwise realistic and reasonable political actors flounder. For example, the external world may be misread through the distorting glass of *depression*, as when the capacity to face up to an unpleasant or onerous reality, a long-term danger, caves in, and the group substitutes the aim of taking action against the anxiety itself instead (for example, it rounds on those advocating rearmament as 'warmongers'); or the group may see the aggressor as more powerful than he is, and puts 'not provoking' him ahead of defending one's friends or oneself. In this case, a 'secondary repudiation of aggression' blurs the difference between its use for good or bad purposes (for example, the 'phoney war' of 1939–40, the early Cold War and, one might add, the Vietnam War).

Situations may also be misread through the *projection of paranoid – schizoid attitudes*, for example, where demands for the control of others' behaviour to this or that good end become so clamant as to suggest that control is desired for its own sake (the demand that there be *no* control is its mirror-image) or where the desire to right a wrong gets swamped by the desire for vengeance.

There are also misreadings due to our ignorance of other people and groups, which 'stems either from an inability to identify with them in some respect, in which they remain enigmatical to us, or from a defensive projection into them of something only in ourselves, so that we . . . actively misunderstand them'.[60] Passive failure to understand is nearly always the result of an unconscious fear of what we might find in them, which corresponds with what we are most afraid of facing in our inner world, figures that arouse either depressive or persecutory anxiety: we substitute a blindness, (for example, the upper class's apathy to the conditions in the new towns of the industrial revolution). Active misunderstanding of others occurs when other groups attract projected denigration or over-idealisation. Where arrogance, contempt, or the envy often underlying them, characterise group relations, rational accommodation of differences becomes very difficult. Exaggeration of the strength and malevolence of outgroups or political opponents, where fear is the basic affect, is part of the same process.

In any of these situations, it is nevertheless possible that a strong and realistic political leader may come to the fore and cut a way through the apparent impasse — as Churchill did in 1940, or Wellington in 1815, resisting demands for a 'hard peace'. How is the creative leader able to escape the incapsulated mania of the pathogenic situation? Either a special history has failed to instil in him the common sensitivities and fears, or an exceptional constitution sets his ego at an unusual remove from his affects.

Reality testing is a complex accomplishment involving many ego-functions, and clearly includes holding in abeyance the emotional factors in perception and correcting distortions of perception in which past and present images are confused.[61] Schachtel's 'focal attention' is also involved — close attention to an object sharply differentiated from all else, and repeated approaches to it from different angles in an effort to assimilate it thoroughly.[62] But reality sense is something more still, since it binds our perceiving, testing and acting to our deepest personal concerns; it 'intuitively appreciates the nature, direction, and purpose of events, in accordance with their libidinal claims' (Weisman).[63] In the context of politics, we deal as well with an unusual talent for the *shared* reality of organisational and public life.* As yet we are ignorant of the childhood

* Speer (*Spandau Diaries*) nominated as Hitler's greatest strength his ability as a *Menschenkenner*. 'He knew men's secret vices and desires, he knew what they thought to be their virtues, he knew their hidden ambitions and the motives which lay behind their loves and their hates, he knew where they could be flattered, where they were gullible, where they were strong and where they

sources of these strengths, but we may note Schachtel's suggestion that it may be the assurance of the mother's constancy that allows 'extensive and often repeated experimentation with disappearing and reappearing objects', and, conversely, that no child is more handicapped than the one whose parents discourage him from seeing them frankly, from all sides, as they are.

Bargaining

Bargaining has been called *the* political skill.[65] Inside organisations it shows itself as an ability to control by negotiating alliances — building coalitions, and generally 'playing the numbers game' — but it is more often practised from one's organisation outwards, on its behalf, so that it is almost by definition interstitial, having its location in the uncertain space between political units, and its greatest scope where no fixed rules or precedents bind their interaction.*[66] In government, however, a solid part of it concerns the discretion that administrators (defined narrowly, but in a sense wide enough to include ministers) may exercise in the application of rules to individual cases. In the Australian system, association heads are probably the group to whom bargaining is most critical, and amongst whom the conscious assessment of this capacity plays the leading part in the processes of selection, recruitment and promotion. Some bargainers are formally specialised out as lobbyists and public affairs consultants. English and Australian politicians, that is, back-benchers, bargain less than their American or French counterparts,

(Footnote continued)

were weak; he knew all this . . . by instinct and feeling, an intuition which in such matters never led him astray.' This gave him an extraordinary power over others (including Speer himself). As a strategist, he showed the same unerring eye for his enemy's inner weaknesses. This knowledge, far from engendering sympathy, left in him a supreme contempt for his fellow creatures.[64]

* All these cuts may be placed differently. Those more interested in analysing organisational processes than personal skills may prefer March and Simon's usage. They define bargaining — crisply and negatively — as *neither* problem solving, nor persuasion, nor politics — but as the fairly unusual and often final thing which occurs only *after* people have *stopped* assuming that they share relevant goals and criteria and can jointly work out an acceptable course of action (problem solving) *or* that differences in their beliefs, goals or criteria can be adjusted by reference to agreed touchstones (persuasion) *and* when they have accordingly formed up into tight factions highly conscious of their relative strength (politics) . . . *then* they are ready to bargain.

'In bargaining, the participants work out their own objectives and strategies privately before meeting together. They assume that their objectives, or at least their immediate objectives, are not shared by the other participants, and that persuasion will be ineffective in reaching agreement. Instead, agreement is reached by exchanging concessions or pretended concessions, with each side trying to gain a maximum and give up a minimum.' In the blur of practice, they concede, much bargaining takes place disguised as problem solving or persuasion, and all four processes are often in continuous oscillation.[67]

which demonstrates that they are less central in the political system, and much of their bargaining is done over style, not substance — with journalists. And, finally, there are in every political system actors with no particular position or constituency, who are merely gifted 'fixers' and who, for usually brief terms, and with a lucky or coincidental circle of acquaintance, are able to bring off extraordinary coups (Beaverbrook, Bernard Baruch).

As well as being interstitial, bargaining is lateral — in clear contrast to giving or accepting orders in vertical authority relations. The gifted bargainer, indeed, is the one who can get furthest with least formal power, or who stretches what material purchase he has on a deal to exceptional lengths. It is a more personal, less structured method of controlling others than accepting a place in an organisational hierarchy. Bargaining roles tend therefore to be filled by a range of personality types rather different from that found in positions where unilateral control is more pronounced, as in straight business or administration. Bargainers by preference differ from others in their essential feelings about the exercise and acceptance of authority. One is tempted to say that it is a peer-oriented or fraternal mode of work, compared to the ineluctable father-son overtones of hierarchy, but there are large exceptions in capital-labour wage negotiations or the relations of a great power and its satellite.* Collins's study of independent entrepreneurs noted their preference for working through a system of interlocking deals rather than assembling a fixed structure of work-associates.[68] The role probably shapes, as well as attracts, the men who play it.

Though bargaining is central to, and continuous in, all politics, it becomes the prime concern of elected representatives in systems like the American or the French, which allow the legislature a significant veto power over the executive. Thus Dahl and Lindblom write:

> The [American] politician is as much the human embodiment of a bargaining society as any single role-player can be.

> The politician is, above all, the man whose career depends upon successful negotiation of bargains. To win office he must negotiate electoral alliances. To satisfy his electoral alliance he must negotiate alliances with other legislators and with administrators, for his control depends upon negotiation. Most of his time is consumed in bargaining. This is the skill he cultivates; it is the skill which distinguishes the master-politician from the political failure. And if the politician frequently neglects the substantive issues of policy in order to maintain, restore, or strengthen his alliances, this is a part of the price a bargaining society must pay.[69]

Their later discussion focuses on the extent to which long-term rational policy-making — especially in economic policy — is jeopardised by a

---

* Even here at the negotiating table it may have a 'lateral feel'.

Constitution ensuring that 'no unified, cohesive, acknowledged, and legitimate representative-leaders of the "national majority" exist'.

The point is succinctly made in the case of France by Stanley Hoffman:

> The structure of the two Republics allows one to present what the French would call a *portrait-robot* of the kind of leader who would succeed best in a system of that sort. One could christen him the nondirective leader, or the perfect broker, and compare him usefully not to executive leaders in other political systems, but to successful legislative leaders in a highly decentralised assembly such as the United States Senate. What is required is a certain indifference to policy outcomes, a tight resignation to letting events impose decisions that can then be 'sold' as inevitable, instead of risking trouble by suggesting decisions which anticipate events, a Byzantine respect for ritual, inexhaustible patience for bargaining with a wide variety of groups, scrupulous observance of the dogma of equality among members of the parliamentary stratum, and of the sacrosanct distance between it and the electorate (that is, no appeal to the people above the heads of the parliamentarians) — in other words, a willingness to isolate oneself and one's leadership within the confines of the 'House without windows' to make sure that, should one be overthrown once, one would nevertheless not be ostracised later — and, finally, the art of manipulating the 'parallel relations', having in one's hand the cards represented by the key men who, behind the facade of impersonal equality, nevertheless possess the levers of influence. Smoothness, unobtrusiveness, procedural self-effacing skill, flexibility, what the French call *astuce* — a somewhat subdued brand of cleverness — these are the functional requirements of 'routine authority': we recognise men like Chautemps, Queuille, Edgar Faure (until he asserted himself and dissolved the Assembly in 1955) and even Briand or Blum.[70]

Bargaining, this reminds us, may be pervasive in our politics, but it is pre-eminently a minority affair — control of leaders by leaders. And we must note that it strikes the idealistic, particularly, as a corrupting activity. To compromise a sincere demand, to do a deal for part now, the rest later, to offer support in a dubious case to win support later oneself, to maintain a public protestation while privately settling for much less — these are all activities that sadden the onlooker and, if they are pursued as a career, may well leave a man not merely with a reputation for deviousness, chicanery and equivocation, but morally marred.

Bernard Shaw, typically, once turned the point inside out, when he commented on a Labour M.P.'s stand 'on principle' which lost him his seat:

> When I think of my own unfortunate character, smirched with compromise, rotted with opportunism, mildewed by expediency . . . dragged through the mud of Borough Councils and Battersea elections, stretched out of shape with wire-pulling, putrified by permea-

tion, worn out by 25 years pushing to gain an inch here or straining to stem a back-rush there, I do think Joe might have put up with just a speck or two on those white robes of his for the sake of the millions of poor devils who cannot afford any character at all because they have no friends in parliament. Oh, these moral dandies! these spiritual toffs! these superior persons! Who is Joe anyhow that he should not risk his soul occasionally like the rest of us?[71]

But the point is taken very seriously by the biographer of Sir Robert Walpole, the Whig Prime Minister; he ends a hundred-page defence of the pragmatic politician, who in difficult days 'shall have "jumbled something" out of' his unextraordinary contentions, with the admission that Walpole 'must be held in some degree responsible for a lethargy of the national spirit which, apart from all moral considerations, had become a serious political danger by the end of his administration'.[72]

Beaverbrook's performance, on the other hand, has prompted in biographer and reviewers a dazed admiration, as if at a conjuring display. Having, as a young Canadian millionaire, entered the British Parliament in 1910

Aitken's interest in the House of Commons ended. He was not a man much given to hearing others talk, nor greatly interested in making prepared speeches to such an audience ... His passion was for political 'fixing', and no eye was more penetratingly turned upon the leading personalities in the political maelstrom ... The first coup, and it was a devastating one, was his role in the unexpected accession of Bonar Law to the party leadership in 1911 ... In the tangled story of the Irish Question between 1912 and 1914 he acted as ... the go-between who attempted to achieve compromise ... [During the war, he] became the virtually self-appointed voice of Canada in Britain and ... the natural publicist and appreciator of propaganda ... emerged. But he remained also the fixer, the go-between, and the one-man liaison team between the Canadian Government and London ... Asquith's downfall in December 1916 was ... he later claimed, 'the biggest thing' he had done ... One result of this crisis was the most strange of all; [he] found himself in the House of Lords ... [and] was already embarked upon his career as newspaper proprietor, having just acquired control of the *Daily Express*. And all this within six years of arriving in England![73]

There is a not dissimilar excitement to be found in Doris Kearns's account of Lyndon Johnson's rise to power in the U.S. Senate. Johnson, too, despised oratory, and set himself from the first the ambition of controlling the Senate. Johnson was

a man who believed that success in any institution depended upon the most detailed possible knowledge of the way things worked

> ... and ... he pursued such knowledge with unremitting, almost
> obsessed persistence ... and ... an almost shocking capacity to com-
> prehend an institution, to become aware of the process through which
> it operated, and to sense the vulnerabilities of that process.[74]

He attached himself at once to the reigning elder, the conservative Richard
Russell, modelled himself on him, extracted his encyclopaedic lore and his
favour, and won the grudging respect of the 'inner club'. He seized, when
it first became vacant, the small job of Minority Leader; two years later,
a change in the party balance made him Majority Leader, a position still
largely a formality — but Johnson was a master at miraculously stretching
the power-resources of formal posts. The 'challenge was to increase his
resources without seeming to threaten those with established power'.
He did it by what seemed a minor procedural reform — giving freshman
senators at least one good committee — but it turned out to be Johnson
who allotted the assignments. He also came to be the man who allotted
office space, and special campaign funds, and prestigious outside appointments, and overseas jaunts. 'In all this', Kearns notes,

> Johnson managed to recreate the earliest world he had ever known
> ... allowing him once more to perform the role he enjoyed the most
> — the role of the exuberant child with an endless supply, indeed
> almost a monopoly, of things to barter.

> Johnson was also developing an incomparable system of intelligence,
> through which he sought to learn the wants, the needs and the
> desires of each of the Senators ... From facts, gossip, observation
> ... he shaped a composite mental portrait of every Senator: his
> strengths and his weaknesses; his place in the political spectrum;
> his aspirations in the Senate, and perhaps beyond the Senate;
> how far he could be pushed in what direction, and by what means;
> how he liked his liquor; how he felt about his wife and his family,
> and, most important, how he felt about himself.

> As Johnson's mental portraits ... became more complete, his poli-
> tical touch became finer ... his entrepreneurial spirit encompassed
> not simply the satisfaction of present needs but the development of
> new and expanding ones ... Johnson's capacities for control and
> domination found their consummate manifestation during his private
> meetings with Senators ... What gave the most effect to these indi-
> vidual sessions was the wondrously exact fit of the appeal to the man
> at whom it was directed.[75]

By the end, of course, he had greatly changed the character of the institution — distrusting oratory himself he had moved the locus of decision
from the Chamber to 'places where he felt most at home — the cloakroom,
the office, the hallways'. Yet, Kearns muses, there was something about
the Senate itself remarkably appropriate to Johnson's gifts:

> That institution — with its style of gentlemanly behavior and its

substance of realistic maneuver — provided Johnson with an opportunity to accommodate, for the time being, the split between his
public and his private self; he was at ease with both the genteel
world of the Southern committee chairmen and the hard-dealing
world of Western gas and oil men. For Johnson, the polite, polished
conduct on which the Senate prided itself had a familiar ring; these
were the forms cherished by [his mother] Rebekah Baines and her
father. And if the facts of life in the Senate belied the fiction, so had
they in his home. Not only was Johnson able to accept and work
with both the fiction and the fact, as does every successful Senator;
he relished their coexistence, which was both reminiscent of the
trials of childhood and annulled them: now he was in control — his
was the authority to bestow and withdraw — and he was receiving
more than he had to give.[76]

The glimpse of how these unusual gifts were shaped and sharpened is
perhaps inevitably tantalising, but she leaves (as did Beaverbrook's biographer) a sufficient sense of a whole personality called jubilantly into play,
to make us sceptical of the theorists of bargaining associated with the
Journal of Conflict Resolution, who wish to comprehend its processes in a
utility calculus borrowed from economics.[77]

Decision making

When the student shall have attained to four and twenty years of age,
more or less, the sooner he is in office the better; for it is there only
that some essential processes of his education can be set on foot, and
it is in youth only that they can be favourably effected. An early exercise of authority is, in the case of most men, necessary to give a
capacity for taking decisions. It may be thought, perhaps, that
whether he be a member of the government, or in active opposition to
the government, he is still acquiring experience and practice in affairs.
But a long experience of the latter kind, by habituating a man, not to
taking decisions, but to taking objections, — to finding difficulties, and
not resources, — is apt to be fatal to his effectiveness as a statesman in
the exercise of power. Men thus practised and otherwise unpractised
become timid from foreseeing all that can be urged against any
measure they might adopt, and not feeling fertile in expedients. There
may be a converse disadvantage in men entering upon office without
having been practised in opposition; but prudence is much more
easily learnt than decisiveness: the former may be taught at any age,
the latter only to the young. Also the drudgery of an office should be
encountered early, whilst the energy of youth is at its height and can
be driven through anything by the spur of novelty. (Sir Henry Taylor,
1836)[78]

More than other administrative skills decision-making has been
thought teachable. It falls readily into a personal part and an inter-per-

sonal part: the former includes things like intelligence, decisiveness*
relevant knowledge,† a gift for finding apt analogies for new problems,
or for hard, rapid work at high levels of abstraction; the latter concerns
the ability to relate fruitfully to the information and control-systems of
the organisation, to get presented with the decisions that need to be made,
and to see that a decision is implemented — in short, to work with others
who have apt knowledge and interests at stake, and to win and keep their
support for agreed plans. In a sense, the ur-administrative decisions are
those about the shape of the decision-making processes themselves in the
organisation, and there are strong analogies between administrative
design-processes and individual problem-solving. Only a small fraction
of the administrator's time, of course, is spent in actually choosing between
courses of action that have been presented for selection. Much more work
goes into intelligence activities, 'searching for situations and problems that
call for attention, and filtering and interpreting incoming information
about the changing environment that might signal such situations and
problems'. And even more goes into designing the various 'action
alternatives' themselves.[81] The striking thing, however, about organisational action, as Chester Barnard pointed out, is the degree to which it
strives to be perfectly rational.[82]

There is by now a library on decision-making — the work mostly of
American business schools in the last twenty years, and to a large extent
the product of dissatisfaction with the older economists' model of rational
entrepreneurial choice. In a recent article reviewing the field, Herbert
Simon, the doyen of organisational theorists, warns that in real life
administrators 'exhibit only *bounded rationality*' and that the decision-
theory models of rational decision-making — even though extended now
to take some account of 'uncertainty of consequences (statistical decision
theory), of time and cost involved in obtaining information (sequential
sampling, search theory, theory of teams), and of opposition of interest
among rational actors (... oligopoly, game theory)'[83] — leave unsolved
the problem of real life limitations of knowledge and skill.

---

* Taylor saw a basic temper of decisiveness, energetic and overleaping, which
needs to be 'curbed or indulged in different degrees at different stages in the
consideration of a question'. A *'couchant* attitude of the mind' is best at first —
'or (to transfer the metaphor) ... the wheeling survey which precedes the
stoop. But when the time comes to stoop or to pounce, the energy ought to
be in proportion to the previous abstinence.'[79]

† This term includes the capacity to remember; cf. this note on Secretary
McNamara: 'A critic warns, "People are taken in by his computer-like recall —
they think it's intelligence." This certainly is the thing people seize on — his
memory for facts and statistics and his use of them to deflate opponents. "He
can recall things from two or three years ago that everyone else would have
to scurry round and look up," a Ford executive who once worked closely with
him recalls.'[80]

> The central phenomenon to be explained [remains] how organisms
> are able to behave in a relatively adaptive, goal-oriented fashion in
> an environment whose complexity is grossly disproportionate to their
> information-processing and computational powers.[84]

Simon takes some heart, however, from computer simulation, which has
enabled a much closer approximation to the administrative behaviour
of middle managers or the decision-processes of, for example, a bank trust
officer or a department store buyer, and looks forward to the development
of self-improving computer programmes which will enable moves based,
not on an exhaustive scanning of each possibility, but on rough hunches
and appropriate ploys.[85] He warns, though, that there are further intractable problems in the fact that it is rare for individuals concerned in
administrative decisions to share fully the same goals, and that they will
also selectively see (or fail to see) certain problems as problems, according
to their position in the organisation and their personal interests.

The thrust of logical and statistical devices to increase managerial
rationality has by no means ceased. Operations research, P.P.B.S., the
Delphi system, and corporate strategy all find eager clients, since they do,
indeed, help to clarify choices on which failure or success may depend.
In general, however, such devices help at the lower levels or outer edges
of managerial concern. In management studies as well as political science
there are signs of a swing back to Boswellising — in the hope that the study
of the actual practice of reasonably successful administrators, and perhaps
modest improvements to this, may yield more than the most intricate
modelling. The psychologists Joseph de Rivera and Irving Janis have
recently analysed several portentous foreign policy decisions. De Rivera
has studied the Marshall Plan, the 1950 Arms budget, the National Security Council's challenge to this, and the U.S. entry into Korea, and Janis
has examined Roosevelt and Pearl Harbour, Truman and the invasion of
North Korea, Kennedy and the Bay of Pigs, Johnson and the Vietnam
escalation — and, on the success side, Kennedy and the Cuban missile
crisis, and Truman and the Marshall Plan.[86]

But the project of catching administrative decisions 'on the hoof' quickly
runs up against such difficulties as the implicit decision, the decision *not*
to act, the purely formal decision, the decision that must have been made
but leaves no trace, and the impossibility of sorting real-life administrative
acts into orderly text-book sequences like agenda-building, search, commitment, implementation and evaluation.[87] Arranging a run of decisions
into consequential sequence — identifying problem A, and deciding to
tackle it, creates problem B which, when tackled, creates problem C, and
so forth — may very well over-rationalise the administrator's behaviour:
what is the organisation doing in between these sequences of decision-
making? In fact, the fate of whole 'decision sequences' is often bound up
with the competition for the time and attention of leading executives.

While 'critical' decisions, those raising questions about basic purposes, will be the analyst's prime quarry, they may sometimes require no different patterns of organisation or modes of analysis from routine decisions: the two can often not be told apart until their outcomes are known. The extent of disagreement about desirable alternatives and possible outcomes will influence the strategies organisations use to decide critical questions: is this matter one for computation, a study group, a vote, a sage judgement or a brainwave?[88] There is, it has been suggested, a Gresham's Law in decision-making, which ensures that routine activity, with its immediate deadlines and explicit rewards and penalties, drives out innovative planning activity.[89] Incrementalism is the instinctive creed of the administrator, and his natural tendency is to avoid decisions which threaten to disrupt the customary workings of the organisation.[90]

'Conflicted' decisions are intrinsically interesting — their neglect in traditional economic theory guaranteed its shallowness — and seem urgently to invite psychological analysis.

Irving Janis has demonstrated a fruitful scheme for this which applies whether the conflict is pre- or post-decisional.[91] His focus is intra-personal — it is not just a small-group problem, although presumably small-group conflict predicates individually conflicted members — and his preferred context is foreign policy making. But his hints on the teasing out of unconscious and pre-conscious factors in the making of demanding public commitments can be carried into many other fields.* Here, local government supplies an apt case.

The following narrative is adapted from the Melbourne *Herald* of 5th April 1970, where it was accompanied by a photograph of a bald, smiling, pyknic businessman in his shirtsleeves, picking up walnuts on his lawn:

> 'It's been a helluva Easter', Sir Maurice said, 'The worst I've ever had. For a long time, I'd a feeling in my heart I was alone in the wilderness. I have suffered considerable pain and anguish. My wife and I have been nervous wrecks.'
>
> But the pain eased yesterday when Sir Maurice Nathan somersaulted over the leaflets by-law under which war-resisters were being fined for distributing leaflets in a city square. He admitted he was wrong.
>
> 'On the Tuesday before Easter, my City Council general purposes committee decided *not* to repeal the by-law. That, I thought, was that. I'd made my decision. I've always been a man of decision, my father died when I was 24. I had to take over the business. I learned early to make decisions and stick to them — I can't stand people who pro-

* Related studies concern themselves with the stress of vocational and marriage decisions (Freud's Dora makes a most convenient case) and decisions to undergo surgery.[92]

crastinate. Then I began to have doubts. Nobody agreed with us, we were all alone, without friends. But for a start I just couldn't believe that these other people were right, and I was wrong. But it started to nag me, deep down.

I spent Good Friday thinking about it. I began to have a horrible fear I might be wrong. On Saturday I went to the football, purely to test public opinion. I spoke to people in the social club, I spoke to people in the outer. They all said I was wrong. I tossed and turned on Saturday night. I couldn't sleep. The nagging pain got worse.

Then on Sunday, I went to communion at St. Paul's. I spoke to Dean Thomas, he saw I was worried. We had a half hour talk. Then the Dean wrote me a letter, offering further advice, and hand delivered it to my home that night. The nagging persisted.

Then on Monday morning, I made up my mind. I *was* wrong. It took me that long to make up my mind. But once I admitted to myself I was wrong, I started to move. I sent urgent telegrams to all members of my committee to attend a special meeting on Wednesday morning.

Then I went to the races, and talked to all sorts of interesting people. They all said the by-law should be repealed. On Tuesday, I took further advice all day as to whether my reversal was correct. I asked all sorts of eminent people about it. But, by then I was beginning to feel better.

Yesterday, to my surprise, pleasure and gratification, I found out that all of my colleagues had also had second thoughts. I found extraordinary unanimity amongst us. So we reversed the decision. Later I got up and reported to full council. It was a hard speech to write, I spent a lot of time over it. Thank heavens it's all over.'

I asked him if the threatened union boycott of his brewery and his furniture store had influenced him? 'Never. It didn't sway me a bit. But I believe the threat of industrial blackmail against my two companies was a wrongful act.' Sir Maurice said he couldn't remember the last time he'd made a major mistake like this. 'I don't make mistakes too often.'

Some obvious features of the case are the unusual pain of indecisiveness to a man for whom being decisive is a vital part of his self-image; the shock at massive disapproval, not just from the Press, but from his friends and even from the common men in the outer ground; the shame of having to announce a reversal, first to fellow committee men, then to Council and the public, for a man who 'doesn't back down' — a shame that still outweighs the value of his new-found intellectual conviction; the compulsive way that, even after he has changed his mind, he goes on collecting opinions to support him.

Janis proposes a nine-cell score sheet for diagnosing such quandaries. Is the problem about *utilitarian gains* or losses for the self or significant others; about *social approval* or disapproval of the self: about *self-approval* or disapproval? Then in each case, what is the weight of *conscious, pre-conscious* and *unconscious* factors? 'The chart can be visualized as having plus and minus entries in every cell, the pluses representing ... [the] tendency to *accept* the given decision ... and minuses representing ... [the] tendency to *reject* the given decision. The pluses and minuses would have to vary in size to show the relative *magnitudes* of the various sources of ... motivation.'[93] Where the large minuses are located is the best clue to the individual's choice of mode of resolving the crisis.

This decision to repeal an archaic by-law, that is, to allow war-resisters to continue to make speeches and hand out leaflets in the square, fairly obviously resulted from social disapproval. The reporter, however, thought that the man's own story altogether underplayed utilitarian losses to the self in the form of reduced profits from the unions' boycott. He enquired about this, and was rebuked. Let us speculate in more detail about what actually happened.

At the time of the original 'wrong' decision, the single conscious argument for repeal may well have been, 'We are supposed as a democracy to allow, even to encourage, free speech and dissent.' Against this, however, were thoughts like, 'We will be putting down disaffection and disorder; preventing violence; cutting off the agitators' free newspaper publicity for teasing the police; generally asserting and endorsing decent, right-minded values ... and anyway, there are better places for agitators, like the Yarra Bank [a public park].' Utilitarian considerations at the preconscious level may have included, 'We're removing scruffy louts from clean, commercial streets; they could deter overseas tourists and visitors; we particularly don't want housewives pestered and confused.' (This would be the paternalism of a true City Father.) At the unconscious level, the pacifists are cowards, unmanly, and in effect Communists, the Enemy, attacking national values at the root.

Our councillor seems originally to have imagined that all these ideas were shared by the Establishment, colleagues and friends, and the public generally. The only groups possibly out of step were the Press, the universities and the unions — three excellent parties not to agree with. The Church, of which he took unusual stock, unsettled him, but he was already reeling from his repudiation by his circle of influential acquaintances, and even by the common men of the outer, to whom he had incredulously repaired. Some secure sense, deep down, that he could rely effortlessly on the basic decency and representativeness of his spontaneous reactions in public matters had been badly bruised.

Finally, as his account vividly attests, he wrestled with deeply contradictory feelings about himself. At first, he could comfortably organise his self-esteem round the idea that he was just the sort of man strong enough to uphold an unpopular law and one who did not shirk tough decisions — in fact, people looked to him for such decisions. The very great salience in the unconscious of the demand to avoid cowardice and weakness, to be a real man — against which the resisters' despicableness was calibrated — made it, of course, peculiarly difficult for him to admit his error. The man who takes a deep pride in not backing down is forced, in public, to do just that. But he recovers fast and characteristically — acting decisively to formalise his change of opinion.

Diagnostically inert, the real promise of Janis's score-sheet lies in the prospect of assembling comparative data on each type of conflict to highlight patterns in the 'choice' of mode of resolution. He is particularly interested in the unfruitful 'rationalising' reactions to conflicts rooted in social disapproval, which may take the form of ignoring or avoiding information which points to potentially undesirable consequences, discounting or intellectually denying it, forgetting or unintentionally misinterpreting it, or inventing new reasons to support the old decision. Alternatively the actor under strain may try desperately to re-persuade his critics, to 'prove' by compensatory gestures and acts that, despite his error he is still a worthwhile person, to condemn privately the 'wrong' decision and blame it on others, to seek the approval of at least a few people among the ranks of the critical, or to disaffiliate altogether from the disapproving group. In his reaction to guilt, as well as to shame, the individual follows out character-based paths laid down in childhood. To some extent these will be culturally derived, but they will also follow institutional patterns and traditions — the administrator in this bureaucracy or that will be encouraged to some reactions to crisis, and discouraged from others, according to its special 'operational code' (Leites).

One question Janis asks is what sort of information or psychological preparation could render national security decision-making less brittle, and performances less vulnerable. He summarises the procedural proposals so far recommended, but acknowledges that their testing is still in the future.[94]

It is clear that decision-style — of which conflicted decision-style is a sub-set — forms a key part of the individual style of administering. Decisions draw on capacities and predispositions (and repetition-compulsions) that go down deeply into the administrator's character. Perhaps this is another way of saying that they raise important moral questions. Chester Barnard thought the administrator's most important work was to set the ethical tone for his organisation; and Edward C. Banfield notes that the administrator

> decides what state of affairs the organization will seek to bring about (what its 'mission' is), he reduces its ends from higher to lower levels of generality (translating 'purpose' into 'goals' and 'goals' into 'objectives' and 'targets'), and he decides the terms upon which competing

ends are to be compromised (what is to be given up when something must be given up) . . . He decides what it is the 'duty' or 'obligation' of the organisation to do, what its 'institutional character' ought to be, and what is 'fair' and 'just' in particular cases.[95]

This is one reason, perhaps, why administrators cannot be purposefully trained for their work. The administrator must learn good judgement, that

mysterious faculty . . . which enables him to draw correct conclusions more often than does the 'average' person. To the extent that this skill can be learned or developed, it must be . . . as other skills are – by doing, and especially by imitation. The [administrator], if he is to learn at all, must learn in much the same way as the swimmer learns to swim and the cyclist learns to ride. He must be put in a position where he has to make judgments and to bear responsibility for them. He will no doubt benefit from serving an apprenticeship . . . with a master craftsman in the art of judgment, but the benefit will come not from learning the craftsman's wisdom . . . but from acquiring his 'feel of the situation' . . . [and from gaining] experience of the *specific realm of affairs in which judgment is to be exercised* . . . The [administrator] must have profound knowledge of the ways of his particular tribe – its language . . . customs, modes of thought, and mystique . . . This is very different . . . from being trained to use technical [administrative] knowledge as the basis of decision.[96]

The preponderance of genetic or historical elements in the individual administrator's behaviour sets a fairly low ceiling to what all but the most ambitious programmes of 'executive development' are likely to be able to achieve.[97]

The culture of administration

Administrative roles and interactive styles

Organisations proffer their administrators a range of roles which may more or less closely match their preferred modes of working. These preferences – for autonomous tasks, say, or for working anxiously on colleagues' morale, or for assaulting the environment on the group's behalf – will be closely related to the roles that individuals have carved out in the nuclear family. Abraham Zaleznik has evolved over the last ten years an instructive typology of principal administrative functions – homeostatic, mediative, proactive – and of administrative personality-types – person-, task- and fusion-oriented – which may or may not coincide in real organisations. He has elaborated this scheme (see table 1) through the use of experimental interaction methods,[98] projective tests,[99] and the dogged Boswellising of notable administrators,[100] and, with increasing assurance, the outlines of the distinct developmental paths behind each.

His monographs, however, go well beyond this typology to tackle such

Table 1. *Three administrative personality types*

Patterns of emotional investment	Person-oriented	Idea/task-oriented	'Fusion'-oriented
Defining concerns	Warmth, intimacy; seeks lateral, peer-like, friendly relationships; passive, incorporative style	Achievement, mastery; task comes first; blunts consideration for others' feelings; keeps tenderness for private life	'Organisation'; work flow and processes
Aptest executive functions	Homeostatic (maintaining the internal stability, 'steady state' of the organisation)	Proactive (actively seeking out environmental possibilities, enlarging scope for organisation's creative potential)	Mediative (procuring internal changes in response to environmental pressure)
Ego qualities	Toleration of closeness, caring; dependent on others, unable to take aggression in self or others; conformist, conservative; low self-confidence	High work performance: vigorous, energetic, aggressive; intolerance of warmth, closeness; likes competition, aggression, vertical relations	Can work *and* wait; accept intimacy, aggression, vertical authority; anxiety about responsibility; being at odds with others, falling behind arouses dread; 'once-born'; tends to conventionality, superficiality, optimism
Development history			
Identifications	Mother-dominated; feminine passive identification	Mother affectionate, nurturant; father distant, cold but influential (not laissez faire); strong identification with father	Both parents showing love, exercising control
Expression of talents	Opaque: valued more as friend than as leader, work exemplar	Strong sense of competence; history of individual work	Secure sense of worth Excels in group activity, sports, not necessarily to the detriment of schoolwork
Energy use	Drain from maintaining defences against conflict and aggression; conscious attitudes altruistic: identification with the under-dog	Drain from defences against intimacy, tenderness and deeply rooted passive wishes	Less rigidly constructed defences: accepts responsibility and guilt; but can be depressed and immobilised by mal-performance

Adapted from A. Zaleznik, *Human Dilemmas of Leadership*, New York, Harper and Row, 1966, Ch. 9.

questions as the psychic costs of working against one's bent (for example, the 'ideas man' who takes up general administration),[101] the way executive roles cluster for subordinates into a reinforcing 'family' constellation of authority (for example, paternal-assertive, maternal-nurturant, fraternal-permissive); the way executives half-consciously dramatise their subordinates' assimilation of these displays; and, above all, what goes into the individual's role-task work, his sustained conscious effort to synthesise his own needs, interests and aspirations with the organisational requirements of his position and to implant his particular value preferences into the organisation's working shape.[102] His portraits of 'Dr Cadman', 'Dr Asche' and 'Dr Suprin' in *The Executive Role Constellation* are the fullest and most acute clinical studies we have of administrators at work.

Carl Edwards, in an independent attack on the developmental antecedents of 'interactive style' (preferred method of approach to social situations) reported in 1973, in effect extends the Zaleznik scheme beyond the managerial elite to the population at large.[103] With the help of a simple, self-administered quiz, he shows, first, that a typology distinguishing *co-operational, instrumental* and *analytic* styles is able to order behaviour in a great many experimental and real-life contexts; then, turning to a sample of sixty-odd adults, who as children had been subjects in the *Patterns of Child Rearing* study,[104] he shows that each style has its roots in a distinctive type of upbringing — roughly: conventional, mother-dominated; conventional, father-dominated; and 'modern', respectively. Edwards is particularly strong on sex differences in details of upbringing and style.

This agrees very closely with the Zaleznik scheme, and Edwards happily acknowledges the actors of *The Executive Role Constellation* as 'carriers' of his styles. But there is some loss of grasp: the sense of Zaleznik's 'fusion' mode is rather lost, and 'idea-orientation' becomes split off from 'task-orientation'.[105] (Indeed, most of Edwards's comments on the 'analytic' style bear more directly on Lasswell's *theorist* class. And this becomes quite explicit, when he discourses on the hesitations of 'analysts' in practical contexts, such as the special disabilities of Adlai Stevenson and Eugene McCarthy as presidential candidates.)

Compared with R. F. Bales's more finely-meshed scheme (see below, pp. 123–30), Edwards' categories seem rather simplistic, but Graham Little's searching study of university learning and teaching has shown its value, deftly adapted to deal with *organisational climates*.[106] Just because people have preferred interaction styles, they will approach a strange institution such as a university with a powerful implicit demand for an indulgent or training or cultivating experience — and will come up against staff themselves habituated to responding to students mostly in one only of these ways. This can obviously be extended to acclimatisation in large groups of any kind.

There is one other advantage of looking at contrasts in preferred interactive style — in suggesting broad patterns in the vocational performance of people much less sophisticated and highly specialised than Zaleznik's managers. Smith's Lanlin, for example, whose world view is analysed below (see pp. 164–7), is presented as having, as a sales manager and a staff association man, a notably 'conformist' style. Seeing him also as an Edwards *co-operative* * adds at once several new shades — the fact, for example, that this style has overtones of somewhat conventional femininity. Let us consider a summary of Smith's analysis.

> Lanlin's job is selling appliances to customers of the store he manages in a lower middle class section. He feels secure and safe working for a large, well-established company, guaranteed seniority and retirement pay. And the job offers opportunities for recognition and a sense of accomplishment. Selling gives him great satisfaction, and plenty of opportunity to 'softsoap' and cajole, tricks that had once proved very effective with his mother.
>
> For many years his previous job (with the same company) was clerical and boring, but he had built an elaborate second 'career' as employee representative on the firm's labour relations committee. This work, and his experiences as delegate to state and national union gatherings, afforded solid satisfactions: display and recognition, a speaking role, acknowledged status; the opportunity for self-improvement, getting out of his 'mental rut', meeting all types of people, 'learning the way the company was set up from the inside'; and being in a position to help straighten out grievances, 'set things to rights'.
>
> It seems, then, that most of the drive keeping Lanlin active in unionism for nearly a decade, was diverted into the functionally equivalent job of selling, work which provides equal or greater opportunity for display, recognition, nurturance, and which, moreover, is more congruent with his basic social philosophy.[108]

The case shows convincingly how an individual's work-performance, analysed so that we are able to make its own organic style, can get us pleasantly close to the heart of both personality and 'project'. Here, two apparently very different occupations are revealed as attempts at the same ideal or, in Smith's phrase, 'functional equivalents'. The assorted component skills of implementation present themselves in characteristic *bundles* — as general as these interactive modes, or as particular as individual administrative styles.

* Emphasises 'receptivity to and understanding of the needs of others, and resolution of social conflicts through personal sacrifice'; offers help, cooperation and understanding and assumes others will reciprocate — 'Can't we all be friends', 'Let's keep the peace'; dwells on sociability, popularity and affection.[107]

Learning to administer
Cultural learning

Although the exact paths to the acquisition of particular administrative skills must apparently remain obscure, it has not escaped notice that the general thrust of socialisation in contemporary society is towards the inculcation of norms and habits germane to bureaucracy. Miller and Swanson in *The Changing American Parent* (1958) remarked on the way parents were coming, partly unconsciously, partly systematically, to build into the child's personality aptitudes which would reliably fulfil the demands of large-scale organisations. They distinguished between an old middle-class or 'entrepreneurial' pattern of child-rearing, which demanded a rather extreme self-control and self-denial and an active, manipulative ambition, and the new, 'bureaucratic' family mode, which relaxed these demands in favour of greater ease with authority, warmth and supportiveness to peers, general accommodativeness and readiness to seek direction and, indeed, 'conditional love' along family lines — from the large organisation.[109]

A 'bureaucratic orientation' scale which discriminates well between those young recruits to large organisations who will resign early, or remain but unhappily, and those who adjust smoothly has recently been designed.*[110] It measures traits of the functionary rather than the executive, and correlates well with authoritarianism and dogmatism and negatively with Machiavellianism. In an effort to trace the roots of this disposition, a junior version has been developed to study the preferences of children in relation to school arrangements, and this has been found to work as far down as early primary grades.[111]

Keniston's reflections on the personality-mould that his Harvard drop-outs were refusing are perhaps the most acute we have on the inculcation of administrative values. Society, he notes, may prize the 'ego virtues', concentrating on 'the development and primacy of the ego over both basic motivation and conscientious inhibition, encouraging qualities like adaptability, skill, rationality, efficiency, independence, impartiality, tolerance, autonomy, fairness and neutrality. It may approve of men and women who are controlled, rational, efficient, realistic and unsentimental.'[112] One side of the ego in particular is cultivated; playfulness, fantasy, relaxation, creativity, feeling and synthesis (regression in the service of the ego) take second place to problem-

---

* The sub-sets of this scale are: self-subordination, a willingness to comply fully with a superior's stated wishes and to have decisions made for one by higher authority; impersonality, a preference for impersonal or formal relationships with others on the job, particularly with superiors and subordinates; rule-conformity, a desire for the security that the following of rules and standard operating procedures affords; identification, a pleasure in one's organisational identity and conformity to in-group norms.

solving, cognitive control, work, measurement, rationality and analysis —
the 'technological ego', core skills necessary to operate advanced
technology — which also fit the rapid change and rootlessness of our time:

> Continual social change ... requires extraordinary flexibility and
> adaptability to a changing environment, and further demands the
> ability to make highly selective and partial identifications ... the
> fragmentation of traditional roles and the shattering of intact com-
> munity pushes the individual toward a cognitive outlook, toward
> the subordination of feeling, toward the dissociation of private and
> public life. All of these social stresses bear most heavily on a few
> specialized ego functions: rapid adaptation, selection, discrimination,
> choice, reality-testing, cognition, and dissociation. In a society where
> cognition takes priority over feeling, where questions of 'how' are
> given precedence over questions of 'why', and where fantasy, ideal-
> ism, and the Utopian spirit must be subordinated to the 'practical'
> world, the cognitive, instrumental, and practical sides of the ego must
> dominate.[113]

Most desirable positions in our society require

> advanced and specialized training and, with it, high levels of
> dispassionateness, ability to remain cool under stress, capacity to con-
> centrate, to maintain long-range goals yet to adapt rapidly to new
> conditions, to deal with remote and distant situations, to abstract, to
> co-ordinate complex operations, to synthesize many recommend-
> ations, to plan long-range enterprises, to resist distraction, to persevere
> despite disappointment, to master complex conceptual assignments,
> to be impartial, to follow instructions.[114]

How is this specialised 'ego functioning' learned?

> Unless parents consistently teach and reward such skills as post-
> poning, concentrating, waiting, manipulating, and conceptualizing,
> these talents develop slowly or not at all. A middle-class mother, by
> teaching her child that waiting will be rewarded, lays the basis for
> a later ability to concentrate in school; and parents who reason with
> and explain things to their children encourage them to deal with the
> world conceptually and verbally... Parents who combine dependency
> with demands for achievement, who make their love and approval
> conditional on the child's accomplishments ... [and who] push
> children toward independence and autonomous self-control ... lay
> the basis for virtues which will enable the child to 'do well' in
> school and in technological life ...
>
> American education is the further expansion, development, and
> rehearsal of social and cognitive skills whose foundations must
> have been laid in the home. Social skills involve the capacity to 'co-
> operate', 'to follow the rules of the game', to 'be a good loser', to
> 'wait one's turn', to subordinate personal needs to the interest of
> a group ... But even more fundamental are ... the ability to con-
> centrate, conceptualize, analyze, abstract, organize, schedule, defer,

arrange, measure, and co-ordinate. The successful finished product of such an education ... has the capacity to concentrate for long periods on assigned tasks, to remain cool, dispassionate, accurate, and object-ive in work, to undertake and carry through unaided complicated and long-range projects, to operate at high levels of abstraction, to work for long periods on tasks with no relevance to his everyday needs and experience.[115]

Keniston's drop-outs, the 'uncommitted', are refusing exactly, and *en bloc*, these demands, and their refusal has authoritative support (for example, Philip Slater's *The Pursuit of Loneliness*).[116] But among those to whom they *are* congenial, we shall find the outstanding administrators of our day. (Jules Henry's splendid *Pathways to Madness* has the closest account I know of a child's — in this case, a six-year-old girl's — domina-tion by the conventional need to achieve, and its intimate warping of the intellect.)[117]

The notion that different cultures adapt a basically standard organisa-tional imperative, the bureaucratic form, in the light of their peculiar values and needs has been most fully worked out in Michel Crozier's classic, *The Bureaucratic Phenomenon*. Through a detailed study of two large French bureaux where impersonal rules and routine bound individual behaviour to a stifling extent, he diagnosed a national need in organisations to evade face-to-face relationships and situations of personal dependency, whose authoritarian tone they cannot bear.[118] (His lead has been followed in later studies of Burmese, English, Turkish and Japanese organisational cultures, pointing up their mirroring of authority patterns in the family.)[119] One expects to be led in the way one has been fathered.

Learning the craft

He had an earnest persuasiveness founded on a command of the situation as a whole, and he tended to view politics in much the same way as he had for so long surveyed the Australian bush from horse-back or from an elevated trig station. After spending twenty years in the field with compass and theodolite he also tended to think that political solutions were easily discovered if the correct levels had been taken and the right angles had been measured. If things turned out the wrong way, then he started again.

(Frank Crowley, *Forrest*)[120]

Political biographers regularly face the task of describing what it is that their man has learnt in his pre-political work-life that gives him special strengths in office. Sir Henry Taylor is at his most engaging when explaining why naval officers make better statesmen than soldiers do — their 'profession combines more than any other, a life of solitude with a life of emergency' — and why business and the law are somewhat disabling.[121] David Barber is at pains to trace the lineaments of Franklin Roosevelt's style in his early navy work and Truman's in his army command.[122] There must be some validity in this, but a certain cheapness of plausibility* in the enterprise leaves some uneasiness: we feel we know neither the theory of such translations of skill, nor the units of exchange — and it is curious how little political actors themselves directly testify on the subject. Certainly one can think of a great many routine or unsociable jobs which are unlikely to nourish political confidence or *nous*.

More remarkable though, is the scarcity of information about the way in which leading administrators assemble their craft. Their memoirs look outwards: they see themselves as characters in someone else's film.

> Q.: *How do you explain the fact that you have become almost more famous and popular than a president? Have you any theories?*
> Dr Kissinger: Yes, but I won't tell you what they are. Because they don't coincide with the common theory. Intelligence, for instance. Intelligence is not all that important in the exercise of power. . . My theory is quite different, but, I repeat, I won't tell you what it is. Why should I, while I'm still in the middle of my job?. . .
> Q.: *I expect the root of all lies in success. What I mean is, like a chess player you've made two or three clever moves. China, first of all. People admire a chess player who makes away with his opponent's king.*
> K.:   Yes, China was an important element in the mechanics of my success. And yet, that isn't the main point. The main point. . . Well, why not? I'll tell you. What do I care after all? The main point stems from the fact that I've always acted alone. Americans admire that enormously. Americans admire the cowboy leading the caravan alone astride his horse, the cowboy entering a village or city alone on his horse. Without even a pistol, maybe, because he doesn't go in for shooting. He acts, that's all: aiming at the right spot at the right time. A Wild West tale, if you like.
> Q.: *You see yourself as a kind of Henry Fonda, unarmed and ready to fight with his bare fists for honest ideals. Solitary, brave.*
> K.:   Not necessarily brave. This cowboy doesn't need courage. It's enough that he be alone, that he show others how he enters the village alone and does everything on his own. This romantic, surprising character suits me, because being alone has always been part of my style, or of my technique if you prefer. Independence too. Yes, that's very important to me and in me. And, finally, conviction. I am always convinced of the necessity of whatever I'm doing. And people feel that, believe in it. And I attach great important to being believed. . .[124]

It is not that there is a lack of memoir-writers among administrators — indeed, we are already confronted with the appalling richness of the day-by-day diary of a working life[125] — but that people are not good at

---

* Not that we are always told the expected. The reflection that 'revolutionary training [on campus] is perhaps the best training a youth can get for a career in the establishment' can startle the reader slightly.[123]

attending to their own learning processes, and are worse, if anything, at accounting for their skill than for their knowledge. It is hard to see why 'professional socialisation' studies should have concentrated on declining professions like medicine and should largely have ignored administration and management.* A perceptive essay sees *apprenticeship* as the vital learning relationship, and advocates the deliberate pairing of 'high flyers' among neophytes with leading practitioners, as well as more strenuous efforts to turn administration into a self-educating and self-analysing profession.[128]

It seems useful at least to distinguish between the learning process in tall and flat organisations (see table 2).[129] Tall organisations have many levels and, at each level, a short span of control; flat organisations have few levels and a broad span of control at each of them. Tall organisations

* The medical studies noted the importance in the neophyte's development of the first encounter with clinical responsibility.[126] It may be that for the young administrator the depersonalising of his literary style is the equivalent rite of passage. Sir Henry Taylor's notes on this, 'Of Official Style', seem to me still quite illuminating.[127]

Table 2.   *Tall and flat organisations*

Tall organisations	Flat organisations
Supervision	
Close. Detail of subordinates' work felt to be of great interest.	Loose. Operations tend to be technically simpler and individually more challenging.
Need for tight discipline in very complex, intricately co-ordinated operations.	
Subordinates are seen as a team, judged on personal relations with the supervisor; unconscious desires to please carry the main burden of competitiveness.	Subordinates are judged on individual standards of performance measured impersonally and objectively.
Close administrative controls — especially on individual's communications (to keep channels clear and open).	Fewer rules and regulations; more permissible variation in behaviour; more informality.
Promotion	
Promotion is gradual, by nicely graduated steps in increased responsibility. Individual is close enough to his superior to understudy him, and succeed him without too much strain.	Promotion is sudden, by large steps; the individual is on his own.
Supervisors help subordinates prepare for it, and can be appreciated for this.	Everyone is self-made. No gratitude to superiors.

predominate in government (including defence) and production; flat organisations predominate in sales, service, party political and religious fields. Administrators learn their trade in an always shapely if not always slow climb, politicians quickly, if at all, in flushes of promotion and over-promotion. It may be that flat organisations are, in general, on the increase and that hence men from such backgrounds are becoming disproportionately active in politics. In no field of political work have we more to learn.

Individual administrative styles

There is no agreed approach to the analysis of individual styles of work in administrators, and no reason why there should be one. It would be pleasant, nevertheless, if one could sense, behind the row of proudly isolated fresh starts which comprise the field, that something in the nature of a craft was building up.[132] Biographies tend to ignore the practical side of politics, and, where they do go directly to what is strongly personal in their subject's style of administering, seize principally on some

Table 2. *(continued)*

Tall organisations	Flat organisations
Leaders	
Leaders emerge who have been repeatedly evaluated in the many choice points in promotion. However, individual insecurity about status persists right to the top.[a]	Leaders emerge more as surprises, and may suffer from the over-confidence of the successful.
Leaders are very much at home with rules and the paraphernalia of a highly rationalised organisation — often with financial, legal or technical backgrounds. They talk of the 'science of management'.	Leaders tend to be 'inspirational' — often with a sales or marketing background. They may be hero-worshipped.
Optimum organisational affect	
Contentment.[b]	Enthusiasm, morale.

[a] At the highest reaches, however, there are rather larger steps in responsibility and special doubts arise about the fitness of individuals who have been moved along very gradually. This is the realm of training programmes and agony. The trauma of the 'last step up' has also struck observers of private business. The patterns of the higher levels of organisation restrict aggression: 'The man who is a specialized manager has learned to function within a very confining set of rules ... to control himself ... The head of a firm is more often than not a man of extraordinary aggression. In conformity with other stereotypes he is often cocky, self-confident, loud, domineering, sometimes even a tyrannical egomaniac.'[130]

[b] Ghisetti and Johnson conclude that flat organisations better satisfy individualist needs (such as autonomy and self-actualisation), but that tall organisations better satisfy *dependency* needs.[131]

Table 3. *Four U.S. Presidents* (after Neustadt, *Presidential Power*)

	Roosevelt	Eisenhower	Truman	Kennedy
Methods of personal leadership				
Intelligence	Massive unofficial network. Incredible grasp of details	Employed a complex staff system, and was the last to know tangible details	In theory committed to tidy charts, 'completed staff work', but improvised arrangements round problems: accessible, informal. Grip of relevant detail	The personal command post in major issues — deliberate reaching down for details, hard questioning of alternatives, drive to protect options from foreclosure by sheer urgency or *ex-parte* advocacy, close watch on follow-through. Even in secondary (to him) issues, he constantly looked for men and means to set up this personalised pattern with its stress on open options and close control. Criticised as 'indecisive', produced side-effects of bureaucratic frustration and bafflement
Autonomy	Kept choices in own hands as much as possible. Overlapping delegations, competitive advisors	Staffs, inter-agency committees, massive delegations of authority. Preferred to let subordinates proceed on lowest common denominator of agreement than have their quarrels and issues and details pushed up to him — last to come to grips with acts of choice	Let others' initiatives time his choices — dealt with next thing on his desk. Lack of bureaucratic 'feel'. Loyalty to subordinates	
Decision style	Liking to defer, have maximum time to apply personal perspective, choose strategic moment	Disposed to keep away from them, have them made 'below'	Welcomed them in the line of duty; decision-machine: fast, firm on the spot	

Power sense	Unmatched insight and sensitivity. Long and relevant experience; 'Uncle Ted'	Blunt. Expected orders to carry themselves out and others' self-interest to work in favour. His army command was no preparation for politics. Neither liked the game, nor gained much understanding of its rules	Uneven—quick and self-protective when he felt he was protecting his Office. Less relevant experience, but fast learner	Strong urge to master the machine, especially after Bay of Pigs. Poor with Congress: excellent with foreign heads of state; superb at public relations
Sense of purpose – incentives	Unmatched hunger for power; found its exercise challenging and exhilarating, and was completely at home with it (the White House being a family seat)	Wanted to crown a reputation, not to make one. Seeking duty – and *status* not power	Position unsought; expected always to be loyal lieutenant	Family implanted competitive drive. No group links. Dispassionate, fascinated by the technical side of politics
Direction	Feeling for policy direction – New Deal, internationalism	Purposes too general and imprecise to direct policy	Inherited, somewhat inflexibly defined, dealt only in specifics	No ideology, but developed several major commitments: to disarm, to integrate negroes, to streamline economic policy. Much in domestic politics bored him.
Sense of confidence – self-image	Extraordinary faith in own competence. No conception of the office to live up to – he *was* it	Saw himself as the good man above politics, the hero bringing national unity. Self-confidence slumped when faced with hard, divisive issues	Separation of self and office: 'A million could have done the job better, but I had to do it.' Loved his image of the Office. Confidence came from his ability to live up to this. Calmest in crisis	Confidence matched challenges of office. In crisis, cool, collected, courteous, terse – 'the stance of a junior officer in the second war'. A 'schooled' temperament, dry view of fellows and self. But belief in his 'mission' – twice saved from death; having 'impossibly' won the Presidency

odd, defensive trick or ritual.* Few biographers have had the stamina even to answer Lasswell's basic catechism (see above, p. 13), let alone the ambition to pursue the matter exhaustively. Three approaches, however, do show some disposition to systematise.

Richard Neustadt's careful comparison of the 'personal leadership' of Roosevelt, Truman and Eisenhower came out in 1960 with an air of distinct originality.[133] He maintained that to make an autonomous contribution to events, a President needed to be able to reach out and down for the critical choices, time to seek and apply his own perspective to them, and ways of supplementing official advice with those 'odds and ends of tangible detail that ... illuminate the underside of issues put before him'.[134] Where this presidential 'self-help' was minimal, so was the creative contribution. Neustadt saw the two extremes in Roosevelt and Eisenhower, with Truman somewhere in the middle. Where Roosevelt let his channels and advisers become orderly, Neustadt says, he acted out of character. When Eisenhower could not work through a set procedure, or when his channels failed him, or when his associates quarrelled openly, he grew either disheartened or enraged. Truman's methods followed forms somewhat like Eisenhower's to results somewhat like Roosevelt's.

Table 3 sets out Neustadt's main points of stylistic contrast (shorn of much delicate and acute accompaniment) and adds his later reflections on Kennedy.[135] These differences in methods of work are to be understood, he suggests, in the light of each man's 'personal resources'. But beyond noting that Roosevelt's ambition to be President was lifelong, he does not seek the source of any of these adult habits and stratagems in childhood experience — though he has a good deal to say about the benefits of Roosevelt's experience in the bureaucracy and the drawbacks of Eisenhower's in the Army and Truman's in the Senate.

Neustadt's contribution — which Kennedy carefully studied — was to link the analysis of critical (usually 'poor') decisions with the 'structural' problems of relating fruitfully to the information and control systems of the Presidency. He was altogether less interested in the personal qualities of his subjects as they bore on their methods of work — Burns or Galbraith, for example, is much more illuminating on Kennedy's cast of mind. But his scoring-categories do spell out the elements most relevant to a rating of presidential performance. I have also found them a most convenient way of approaching the two studies of Australian ministerial

* Examples from Australian biography include: Bruce's behaviour when made an offer; Deakin's when his leadership was questioned; Page's way with a file — attacking the pin and strewing the papers round the room; McLachlan's compulsiveness; Chifley's ruthless self-effacement and avoidance of unprofitable emotions; and Bruxner's superlative performance of secondary roles.

style that bear detailed examination, Ellis on Page[136] and Heydon on Pearce[137] — and Neustadt explicitly welcomes comparisons with the problems of 'office holders in other political systems'.

Two ministerial administrative styles

Sir Earle Page

The second son of a coach builder in Grafton, New South Wales, Page trained in medicine at Sydney and returned to establish his own private hospital there in 1903. After army service in the First World War, he entered Federal Parliament in 1919, and was elected at once to leadership of the new Country Party 'for his fighting qualities, political sensitivity, wide knowledge and constructive ideas'. A combination of dreaming idealist and intensely practical man of affairs, he was Federal Treasurer 1923–9, Minister for Commerce 1934–9, 1940–1 and for Health 1937–8, 1949–56.

He was associated with the Commonwealth Bank Rural Credits Department, the reform of the science research authority, the National Health Scheme, the National Health and Medical Research Council, various primary marketing schemes and 'co-operative federalism' generally, including the central funding of States' debts, the Agricultural Council, and federal aid roads. Only devolution (New States) and the Clarence River dams eluded him.

He was physically strong with great endurance — 'with a stocky, powerfully built torso and blacksmith's arms ending in small, delicate hands'. His political style, like his tennis style, showed 'reckless energy, native cunning and a certain contempt for the orthodox rules of the game'.

The public style: Intelligence. 'His main driving force was ideas, and they were legion.' Bruce, in his biography, defined his main job in the nineteentwenties as arguing Page out of nine out of ten of them. He could absorb ideas from others 'regardless of their rank, race or political philosophies, so long as they contributed to the achievement of his own political ends'.

Throughout his life he maintained interests in newspapers, farming and timber milling; and he never lacked a local cause — the New States Movement, dams, roads, power-lines, ports, river dredging, irrigation, tourism.

'In every phase of his national activities Clarence Valley development was his guiding star and his dominating interest. To him it was a microcosm of rural Australia, complete with all its merits and disabilities. Among his colleagues there was always subtle suspicion that whenever he propounded a national policy he was visualizing its effect on his own home territory.'

Autonomy. Page had patience and persistence. He knew what he wanted in form and content, and strove for it. Either he would convert his most stubborn opponents, or they would tire or die. He was quick to seize the initiative and having prepared in detail in advance, would overwhelm the unsuspecting. He was invulnerable to external criticism, insulated by an unusual puckish egocentric sense of humour. His personal charm and irresistible persuasiveness won over sceptics and opponents. He could be cunning, ruthless and the soul of beaming amiability all at the same time.

Decision style. His office work-habits were chaotic. He tore files to bits, lost vital papers, slid quickly off the subjects others raised and could not be brought back to the point, and prevaricated as deadlines approached. In short, he was adept at escaping control of any sort. He would innovate in his own way, at his own pace.

Personal resources: Power sense. As a high tactician he had few peers. He triumphed in ministries marked by extreme divergences of interest and temperament — steering nonchalantly between them or blatantly ignoring them, while he drove on towards his own objectives. He anticipated others' reactions minutely and looked in advance for possible reactions in every quarter before he acted. He moulded the Country Party as a fighting force and set its broad tactical path especially in relation to other parties.

Sense of purpose and direction. He was self-centred to an extraordinary degree — the universe revolved around him and his plans. He sought to subordinate everyone and everything to his ends, personal and political. He pursued all his projects with singleness of purpose; they gained coherence and drive from having a concrete local application.

Self-confidence, self-image. Never a modest man, Page entered parliament to be Prime Minister — he had hoped to succeed Hughes, but he soon became convinced that subordinate ministerial rank did not preclude achievement and in fact, offered certain opportunities denied to Prime Ministers preoccupied with overall control. He was wholly optimistic, with an unswerving faith in himself and his ideas.

George Pearce

George Pearce was almost permanently in the Australian cabinet from 1908 to 1937, mostly as Minister for Defence, but for eight years with Home and Territories and for four with external affairs. He had been a carpenter and union organiser before his election as a Labour Senator from Western Australia. He left Labour with Hughes in 1917. A stolid, cautious man, essentially shy, he looked like a country solicitor. He was stiff, if not priggish, always had his day's work under command, and spoke clearly but colourlessly. He wielded his greatest daily power from 1915 to 1919, when he was in charge of all war supplies. Patient, phlegmatic, practical, judicious, he lent strength and calm to successive ministries; he had, Menzies said, 'the gift of synthesis' and 'constructive opinion'. It was the very simplicity of his methods that intrigued a new secretary in his last years and provoked his biography.

The public style: Intelligence. So long a minister, Pearce became something of a superior bureaucrat, first in his mastery of detail and, secondly, in his detachment from the underside of politics. He rather drastically misled his colleagues on three issues where they looked to him for 'inside' guidance – on union opinion on conscription in 1916, on arbitration in 1925, and on support for secession in Western Australia in 1933. He had a firm – and formal – partnership with his senior officers, but saw too little of those in the layer below.

Autonomy. A rule-addict, he made the mastery of procedure his path to party leadership. He respected accurately the boundaries of his colleagues' preserves, and expected the same courtesy in his own field. He kept the upper hand in his dealings with his permanent heads and it was his own fault that he was seen as a 'routine, commonplace, reliable, well-organized tool in the hands of experts'.

Decision style. Practical, orderly, controlled, purposeful, consistent, 'he had a well-developed sense or knowledge of what was within settled policy, what was referable to a colleague or determinable by him under legislation, what required consultation with colleagues or with State governments . . . and what needed to go to cabinet – either for specific authority or to get what he called a free hand'. He was discriminating in seeking, taking – and rejecting – advice. From his middle years, after a heart attack, he always scrupulously *under*-worked. He delegated consistently and intelligently, but not enough. He had great liking for and trust in civil servants, and took the blame for and defended subordinates. He gave speedy decisions – at most a day's deferral for consultation – and had simple rules for prompt and clear communication in his department.

Colleagues and subordinates at many points in his career drew on his flair for conciliation – in inter-union differences, cabinet disputes and inter-service rivalries. In cabinet discussions he showed a remarkable talent for succinct and judicious synthesis.

Personal resources: Power sense. He rose rapidly to the top in Perth unionism and parliamentary Labour, but retentiveness more than ambition marks his career as a whole. Securely based in the West and in his own competence, he held firmly to secondary power and avoided the full heat of leadership. He had a canny wariness with clever or powerful people, edging away, for example, when Murdoch, the press magnate, showed a disposition to groom him as crisis leader in the depression. Early filial relationships with the Labour leaders, Watson and O'Connor, gave place to fraternal ones with Prime Ministers Hughes and Bruce.

Sense of purpose and direction. The militancy and aggression he showed in his early campaigning and in the Senate — 'he never wasted time on small names, he attacked the leaders' — rather soon disappeared. The 1917 break with Labour was perhaps less significant ideologically than his throwing in his lot with Bruce five years later. Thereafter he 'never quite gave the impression of conviction of the earlier years'.

Sense of confidence. He knew he did his job well, and behaved not unlike the 'captain of a team' who 'often gave the impression that he would be captain for a long time'. There were touches of megalomania about his wartime administration — a 'sense of infallibility' and a tendency to be 'blunt and unreasonable with visitors'. The only story of his childhood he recounts in *Carpenter to Cabinet* is about bringing home a cartful of drunken workmates as a lad of twelve. It is in character with his whole career.

A second approach to personal administrative style — also through President-watching — is that of David Barber.[138] His recently collected essays on the Presidents since Theodore Roosevelt deal with each man's real power situation and the climate of expectation in which he took office, but concentrate on the elements of style in oratory, work-management and personal relations that bear the clear impress of personality. In broadest terms, he distinguishes productive-adjusted (F. D. Roosevelt, Truman), passive-compliant (Taft), withdrawn-dutiful (Coolidge, Eisenhower) and compulsive-insecure (Wilson, Hoover, Johnson, Nixon). The individual profiles are quite elegant and propose a theoretical novelty: there is, Barber argues, an identifiable formative period, that of 'first independent political success, in which the major elements of presidential style are exhibited — the period when a young man, drawing together themes from his past, present and anticipated future, answers for himself the question, 'What works for me?' The relationship between the style of this period and presidential style is direct: in rhetoric, business management and personal relations, presidents tend to behave as they did when they first found a way to succeed with these tools.[139]

Barber is convinced that the compulsive-insecure President is an identifiable menace that 'gatekeepers' must learn to bar.

> The active-negative character is . . . an accumulative personality, one which tends to experience compromise as an erosion of the ego, and achievement as a reason for escalating the demands of perfectionistic conscience. . . The frustrations of power pile up slowly but steadily, until the temptation to reassert one's integrity and manhood by some adamant stand becomes irresistible.[140]

His analysis of President Nixon's style — and temptations — is first class, particularly his thorough exposition of a 'compulsive crisis' pattern — a predictable process of 'fastening, tensing, release and let-down' illustrated from *Six Crises* and the events of Nixon's first term of office.[141] The compulsive-insecure administrator is liable to adhere fatally to a failing line of policy, his energies so taken up with the resolution of internal conflicts that his judgment and sense of larger purpose desert him. Eli Chesen's independent analysis of Nixon's work-style is also a splendid model of such work.[142]

A third approach stems from Nathan Leites's studies of elite 'operational codes'. The tactic here is to extract from documentary or interview material the organising assumptions of political actors, the unspoken 'givens' defining the spirit and calculation that lie behind high-risk political work, and then to appraise them as a psychological system. Leites perfected his craft on exotic political cultures, Russian and French.[143] English M.P.s[144] and several individual politicians, especially U.S. Foreign Secretaries and Senators interested in foreign affairs,[145] have now been tackled in this way, with considerably smaller yield. Cultural familiarity is clearly a handicap; in any case, Leites's brilliant eye for microscopic detail, as well as his firm psychoanalytic grasp, make him a hard act to follow. Edwin Shneidman's approach through 'personal logics', though quite independent, is nearer in spirit to Leites's work.[146]

4   *Theorising*

At some time almost everyone working in politics feels a need for theory – at the least, for some sense of context – and thus ventures on our final class of work. In systems as pragmatic as ours, however, more theorising than other political work tends to be contracted out and given over to full-time specialists. Demands for theory arise only occasionally and tangentially. Theorists themselves rarely stray into agitation or administration. The Leninist demand, that theory and practice should be one, seems unrealistic. Much as we might wish, therefore, to concentrate on the activity rather than on the person performing it, it seems sensible to ask first about the personal sources of the capacity to theorise.

The capacity to theorise
Those who choose to approach the political world as theorists seem to share at least these defining traits:

Intellectualisation. They deal with anxieties by turning them into words, propositions, and statements, which they then work on and manipulate; they build and maintain a system of ideas. Though deeply concerned with originality, intellectuals strive to relate themselves to a theoretical tradition, and often make themselves, in effect, the son of some dead and famous man (often enough childless) on whom they lavish the love with-held from their real fathers. There is an element here of piety, a concern with passing on and preserving certain freely-adopted, high values.[1]

The intelligence necessary for an individual to turn to intellectualisa-tion as a prime defence is partly innate: yet it can be sharpened by disting-uished mothering and certain family constellations and crises. Language, analysis, and writing are the theorist's ruling passion. Gorz's case (see above, pp. 34–5, and below, pp. 221–5) shows how the affair with language may be a troubled one, and failure with early plain speech may stimulate compensatory tastes for abstraction and the written word.[2]

Passion for Judgement. The theorist has a passion for judging – com-positions, performances, people. He delights in vivid, vehement assess-ments, and discriminates in many fields, well beyond personal competence or practical utility.* He is concerned to judge things consistently and on clear grounds. Very often, and especially in politics, his judgements are negative; indeed his basic social stance may be 'oppositional'. A trick of 'trying it again with a not in it' tends to cut the ground from under any commitment, and to put in hazard attachments to any group or enterprise.[4] Often this impulse towards negativism and detachment fosters a capacity for utopian thought, for imagining the world radically changed, which may become a resource in social criticism. One might guess that the passion for judgment, whenever it emerges in the child's life, presupposes parents who judge the child vigorously.[5]

Poverty of Affect. Behind the vehemence of the intellectual's judgements may be sensed a protestation of concern. Lasswell saw a rather severe, if not neurotic, emotional detachment as a characteristic mark of theorists.[6] All affects admitted to consciousness are tamped down and drained of intensity (the defence of 'isolation'). Cut off brutally from their own affects, theorists lip-read emotion in others. Detachment may contribute to conciliatory and scientific skills, but also to calm, pitiless, destructive conduct in 'advisers who survive', or intellectual fanatics.

Lasswell posits the childhood trauma of crises in which love, rage and fear ran simultaneously at peak levels leaving an enduring stasis, as the precondition for emotional isolation.

Suspension of Action. The forswearing of immediate action necessary to 'think the situation out' is often carried to extremes. The playing with ideas becomes so pleasant, or so complicated, as to be an end in itself, and the commitment to action lapses. Consider the research groups that come back after years with bold plans for further research, or the stereotype of the professor as full of splendid ideas but without the least notion of how to interest others in carrying them out. Indeed a flight from people to ideas seems basic to the theorist's stance, a search for safety in being cut off from a world that can be treated as a spectacle. We would expect to find much physical illness in the childhood of those who so much dread exposure to social contact and conventional occasions, as well as a recoiling from the example and precepts of a 'too public' parent.[7]

Lasswell offered no case to portray the theorist type: he may have assumed that readers of a book like his (or this) would have merely to study themselves to check and assent to his characterisation and develop-

---

* As Konrad Kellen points out in his introduction to Jacques Ellul's *Propaganda*, intellectuals are 'virtually the most vulnerable of all to modern propaganda, for three reasons: (1) they absorb the largest amount of secondhand, unverifiable information; (2) they feel a compelling need to have an opinion on every important question of our time, and thus easily succumb to opinions offered to them by propaganda on all such indigestible pieces of information; (3) they consider themselves capable of "judging for themselves".[3]

mental story. But I believe we have in Henry Adams a brilliant and suit-ably rueful volunteer. His full-length self-portrait, *The Education of Henry Adams* (1905), is not only centrally about failing to make a mark in politics, when from the first there had been no question of any other métier, but is written with an undercurrent of wistful bitterness and indeed sad rage that might be thought endemic in those fated to be mere critics of politics, but which they are normally careful to hide from others, and even, for long stretches, from themselves.[8] It is a mystery story then, and the mystery is, 'Where did I go wrong?' For young Adams had set himself the goal of being President — not 'unreasonably', since his grandfather had just stopped being that, and *his* father had been President, too, in the early days of the Republic. Henry Adams's father was a national political figure and later Ambassador to Great Britain.

> Probably no child, born in the year [1838], held better cards than he ... As it happened, he never got to the point of playing the game at all; he lost himself in the study of it, watching the errors of the players.[9]

He looks in four main places for the flaw. The first in his constitution. 'A certain delicacy of mind and bone' may have unfitted him from the beginning for a basically coarse and violent pursuit. This was exacerbated by sickness in early childhood, which meant that he

> fell behind his brothers two or three inches in height, and proportion-ally in bone and weight. His character and processes of mind seemed to share in this fining-down process of scale. He was not good in a fight, and his nerves were more delicate than boys' nerves ought to be. He exaggerated these weaknesses as he grew older. The habit of doubt; of distrusting his own judgment and of totally rejecting the judgment of the world; the tendency to regard every question as open; the hesitation to act except as a choice of evils; the shirking of responsibility; the love of line, form, quality; the horror of ennui; the passion for companionship and the antipathy to society — all these are well-known qualities of New England character in no way peculiar to individuals but in this instance they seemed to be stimula-ted by the fever, and Henry Adams could never make up his mind whether, on the whole, the change of character was morbid or healthy, good or bad for his purpose.[10]

Secondly, proud as he was of the family tradition and culture, they had their darker side, and were hopelessly out of tune with the times. 'The Adamses ... had preferred the national service'; they were no part of the Boston social or political hierarchy. 'They were statesmen not politicians', he loftily remarks, and goes on to note cheerfully that he was the third son and fourth child: 'The boy had a large and overpowering set of brothers and sisters, who were modes or replicas of the same type, getting the same education, struggling with the same problems. . . They knew no more than he what they wanted . . . but all were conscious that they would like to control power in some form' — in politics or literature. Even the servants colluded in the family myth: 'You'll be thinkin' you'll be President too', says the Irish gardener. All this seduced the boy into thinking that the world of the Boston 'upper-class *bourgeoisie*' was 'the world which he was to fit', and that his ideas, 'alone respectable, would be alone respected'. Bostonian intellectual culture, epitomised in the smug Unitarian clergy, believed it had 'solved the universe . . . The problem was worked out'; it stifled all anxiety — and interest, and it strangely denied flux. The family's particular inheritance was fatally 'eighteenth century' or even 'Cromwellian': they had

> viewed the world chiefly as a thing to be reformed, filled with evil
> forces to be abolished. . . The New Englander . . . in his long struggle
> with a stingy or hostile universe, had learned to love . . . the pleasure
> of hating; his joys were few.[11]

Thirdly his apprenticeship to his father may, on balance, have been a disability. We should note the boy's precocity: he was ten when his father ran for Vice-President on behalf of the new anti-Slavery party, and this 'would have dwarfed for the time every other excitement. . . This political party became a chief influence in the education of the boy Henry in the six years 1848 to 1854, and violently affected his character.' Shouldering his way past his elder brothers, he attached himself to his hero-father and for two winters, from his 'little writing desk in an alcove' in his father's study, he eavesdropped enthralled on long nightly discussions of politics by the Free Soil leaders. Yet he was to realise that his father, though a thoroughly estimable man, was too conventional, too dogmatic, too uncomplicated to serve him — 'restless-minded, introspective and self-conscious' — as a model. What sufficed his father as a political agenda not only built nothing forward for his son, but, perhaps unwittingly, sacrificed him.

> His father's business in life was to get past the dangers of the slave-
> power, or to fix its bounds at least. The task done, he might be content
> to let his sons pay for the pilotage; and it mattered little to his success
> whether they paid it with their lives wasted on battle-fields or in mis-
> directed energies and lost opportunity.[12]

Henry brusquely dismissed his own formal education as hopeless. Learning Latin and Greek at secondary school, 'he was condemned to failure more or less complete in the life awaiting him'; he should have learnt mathematics, French, German, and Spanish, or just stayed at home with 'half an hour's direction every day' from his father. Harvard, if enjoyable, was no better; and two years of living in Berlin and Rome put him 'in a fair way to do himself lasting harm', when his father suddenly offered him a job as his secretary, and saved him. After a year in Washington, this transported him for a decade to the U.S. Embassy in London; but

even the close and privileged view he gained of English politics seemed
dross to him in the end. In his restlessness he even tried Marxism, but
settled for Comte. His most serious work was as economic journalist for
the *North American Review*.

Finally, he returned to Washington, aged thirty, full of idealism still,
although sobered by the apostasy of old friends ('a friend in power is a
friend lost') and the Free Soilers' deals with Democrats, to join a set of
intellectual young men grouped round the Secretary of the Treasury and to
await the new dawn of the Grant administration.

> When he looked round him ... on the men he was to work with – or
> against – he had to admit that nine-tenths of his acquired education
> was useless, and the other tenth harmful. He would have to begin
> again from the beginning. He must learn to talk to the Western Con-
> gressmen, and to hide his own antecedents.[13]

This plan broke down over the character of Grant himself, under whom
Adams had hoped to serve: Grant had (as Adams said of the whole country
at that time) 'reverted to the stone age', and the lesson that one could not
trust him was like 'the kick of a mule. The lesson it teaches is only that of
getting out of the animal's way.'

> To the end of his life, he wondered at the suddenness of the revolu-
> tion which actually, within five minutes, changed his intended future
> into an absurdity so laughable as to make him ashamed of it. He was
> to hear a long list of Cabinet announcements not much weaker or
> more futile than that of Grant, and none of them made him blush,
> while Grant's nominations had the singular effect of making the
> hearer ashamed, not so much of Grant, as of himself. He had made
> another total misconception of life – another inconceivable false
> start... After such a miscarriage, no thought of effectual reform could
> revive for at least one generation, and he had no fancy for ineffectual
> politics.[14]

And so he went to Harvard, to teach mediaeval, and write American,
history. But he bought a house in Washington facing the White House, and
observed the Presidents closely and balefully for the rest of his life. Does his
book solve his mystery? We note how the blame is progressively externalised, but he does have a firm conclusion. What he should have done
was the one *'thoroughly unreasonable'* thing, the thing that never entered
his mind – he should have 'gone West, and grown up with the country'.
For to belong only in high-minded New England was to belong nowhere –
and he did not even belong properly there. As a child he recalls feeling
always estranged, and looking out to sea from his Quincy holiday home,
envying the line of departing Cunard steamers.

The most rounded and satisfying account of the intellectual's psychic
economy is Ronald Fairbairn's 1940 essay, 'Schizoid factors in the personality', which highlights attitudes of omnipotence, isolation and detach-

ment and pre-occupation with inner reality, and relates these back to fixation at the early oral phase, following disappointment and frustration by the parents, but particularly the mother, in subsequent stages.[15] Intellectuals, he notes, are prone to treat others as less than persons with an inherent value of their own, and to fear emotional loss and exhaustion in personal relationships and social contexts generally, and to use, in defence, techniques of merely 'playing a part' or of 'exhibitionism', substituting showing for giving. They also tend to heap up their values in the inner world, to libidinise the process of thinking, itself, and to fall in love with intellectual systems. Politically, he notes that in despair of loving, and convinced that their love destroys, schizoid intellectuals may elect to make a (largely unconscious) compact, as 'revolutionaries', to let outright hatred direct their actions.

Lasswell saw phallic arrest as the critical thing in the developmental history of theorists, and the clue to their strain towards abstraction, impersonality, grandiosity and incapacity to act. J. S. Mill's breakdown in his nineteenth year, which he engagingly represents in his *Autobiography* as the culmination of his isolated, arid and polymathic education at his father's hands, is rather better explained as an inability to keep up any longer a life as his father's slave.[16] That he must wish his father dead to open a path ahead for himself was the thought that prostrated him and, in time, he effected an ingenious cure by happening upon a fictional representation of his guilty thought.[17] Woodrow Wilson was able to love the father who was stifling him: Mill felt principally fear.

> Mill's melancholy in 1826 was the result both of the nature of his education and of his relation to his father. A child who grows up in an environment of which he is afraid develops the habit of passing all emotions through the analytic filter of his intelligence before expressing them, in order to determine if they are 'safe' emotions to own to. Often the effect of such a procedure is the development of a split between the emotions and the intelligence and a general, progressive loss of energy, and interest in life: the schizoid personality.
>
> If Mill, governed by a father who would have despised the spontaneous exhibition of the natural feelings of childhood, developed this type of mental filter for the emotions — a secondary judge, or second personality — unconsciously in his early life, the nature of his training was such that he consciously continued to consider emotions objectively and to direct his course of action to produce the emotions he desired.
>
> The crisis came as he approached maturity, when the inner director, or inner intelligence, became aware of the superficiality of the connection between actions and the considered emotion which was to be the result of those actions. That is, Mill became aware that he had no genuine emotions, because a rational plan to produce them had preceded their appearance. Emotional exhaustion was the result.[18]

More general psychoanalytic studies of intellectualisation, obsessional thinking, and the urge to write, offer further suggestions about the personal sources of the capacity to theorise. Several writers who point out that the passion for abstract thinking masks a flight from unwelcome emotions also stress the central importance of precocious intellectual (including super-ego) development, and a relative slowness of instinctual development, in children affected. However, they nominate various phases as critical — battles with anal-sadistic tendencies in the second or third year, or later conflicts about ambivalence towards parents or about passivity or sexual identity.[19] Children observing sexual phenomena, which they register intellectually but cannot cope with properly in terms of their feelings, also turn to abstraction. Howe, as well as Lasswell, has seen the root of compulsive thinking in castration-fear.[20] Identification with parents, themselves markedly cool or obsessional, plays an obvious part.

Anna Freud demonstrated the critical place of intellectualisation in normal adolescent development; with the sudden access of instinctual energy, the youth becomes not only moral and ascetic, but more intelligent and intellectual.[21] Speculation on love, death, religion, politics and the social order serves a double purpose, grappling covertly with conflicts between instincts, conscience and reality. A daydream quality in adolescent thinking, however, reveals that the mere process of speculating or discussing is more gratifying in those years than any application of conclusions to actual behaviour.

Edmund Bergler found that 'a spiteful desire for *oral* independence' underlay the urge to write in several cases. These men 'seem to say: "I need no one, I am self-sufficient, and I can do everything alone"', in an aggressive way making the mother unnecessary and declaring that they have overcome their disappointment.[22] MacCurdy saw, in cases of obsessional system-building, the cultivation in fantasy of an idealised mother-infant relationship, covering grudges and actual disappointments.[23] Envy of a pregnant mother's creativity may be a further spur to a small boy.

Sartre's *Words* gives perhaps the most penetrating testimony about the origins of the urge to write. He describes very beautifully his mother reading aloud to him, his grandfather handling the books in his library, his grandmother reading her romances and Flaubert in her winged armchair, and the slow rise of the wish to provide the occasion for their pleasure himself. The decision to adopt the writer's vocation came at eight in a long and intense colloquy with his grandfather that juggled desperately with their mutual but diverging estimates of his genius.

> I accepted, in obedience to [him], the dedicated career of a minor writer. In short, he flung me into literature by the pains he took to steer me away from it: to the extent that sometimes, even today, when I am in a bad mood, I ask myself if I have not used up so

> many days and nights, covered so many sheets of paper with my
> ink, dumped on to the market so many books that no one wanted,
> in the sole and mad hope of pleasing my grandfather. That would
> be a joke: at over fifty, to find myself embarked, in order to fulfil
> the wishes of a man long since dead, on an undertaking of which
> he would certainly have disapproved. In fact, I am like Swann cured
> of his love and sighing: 'To think that I've spoiled my life for a
> woman who wasn't my type!'[24]

His earliest 'novels', fragments of melodramatic adventure, alternated
with fantasies of the birth of a sister and of incest. He writes at length on
the link between the urge to write and the denial of death.

Of course, only a fraction of those with a head for theory will finally
turn in the direction of human or social problems. What determines
whether the theoretically-inclined person chooses social studies rather
than science or literature? In a bold attempt to settle this question at one
blow, Ann Rowe in the early nineteen-fifties interviewed matching groups
of a score or so of eminent American physical, biological and social scientists.[25] The sample, she found, was overwhelmingly formed of first children or eldest sons, with both a very strong need to achieve, or to keep,
independence, and a great curiosity.

Future biologists were frequently bereaved early (death making life
the problem); physicists, as children, tended to be social isolates with
an uncomfortable body-image; social scientists were often in severe conflict with parents whom they saw as socially superior in the district. The
social scientists' earliest interest was literature; they disliked mathematics
from the start. Their TAT stories featured 'general helplessness in the
face of severe problems', strong dependence on parent-figures, and much
rebelliousness, often accompanied by guilt feelings; they were the most
aggressive group. Their childhoods were very much more sociable than
those of the natural scientists, and their interest in sex more precocious;
on the other hand, a dominant mother may often have hindered their
achievement of a masculine identification. They divorced much more
often — perhaps because they asked more of marriage.

In England, Liam Hudson presides over a series of studies exploring
the constitutive differences (which can be established well down the
schools) between the science mind and the arts mind.[26] Both the 'convergent' and 'divergent' styles of intelligence he dubs defensive, though
the former are likely to seem 'closed' and the latter 'open'. The converger
concentrates on the impersonal aspects of his culture, strikes for the one
right answer, is cautious in expressing his feelings, and goes in for ego-
restriction. The diverger attempts a synthesis of the intellectual and the
personal life, but is weak at close, impersonal, technical argument: he
achieves emotional freedom at the price of hollowness; he is concerned
with people, but at one remove.

> The convergent parent ... shies away from all expression of strong feeling ... [and] may guide the ... child into less embarrassing spheres by offering approval whenever he masters some safe, impersonal skill ... Or, as a reaction to the embarrassment the child has caused them [the convergent parents may] become critical. Either way, the child realizes that security lies both in choosing an impersonal field within which to work, and in being right ... the child latches on ... to his parents' distaste for 'gush'.
>
> The diverger's mother ... binds her child to her by disregarding his practical, logical accomplishments (or even by ridiculing them) and by holding out a promise of love which she may or may not be able to fulfil. The child grows up addicted to people: he sees them as the source of his security, and fears impersonal logic as a guillotine which could sever him from them. He tries interminably to mine comfort from the discussion of personal relations, although unable perhaps to relax into them at first-hand.[27]

He has pursued the first images schoolchildren form of science and arts work and particularly the double image of scientists as 'more masculine, but cold'. And recent comparison of the dreaming habits of the two groups suggest that convergers' identity crystallises in the latency period, when rationality and internal control are paramount, while that of the divergent child 'sets' later, and less firmly, in adolescence, when emotional considerations are again more pressing.

> If a child fixates early, one would expect him to choose work that is impersonal; to show a limited capacity for introspection and emotional response to people; to be conventional; to be dissociated in his expression of sexuality; to separate clearly his working life from his private life; and to work harmoniously in groups. In contrast, one would expect the child who fixates relatively late to choose work involving people; to show greater capacity for introspection and emotional response; to have relatively little reliance on social conventions; to show a freer, and more integrated, pattern of sexuality; to separate his private life from his work relatively little; and to have difficulty in working in groups.
>
> The converger, though conventional, is more capable than the diverger of *authentic* emotional response. In contrast ... the diverger will tend to have recreated his impulsive life in intellectual terms, and to respond, especially in crises, in ways that are at once florid and hollow. One would also expect that the divergent child, being less clearly formed, would experience more turbulence in adolescence than the converger; and that he would be more likely than the converger to throw himself into social life in a disruptive way, pursuing his autobiography at his institution's expense.[28]

More recent reflection on the differential fertility of the two groups led to these further propositions:

> Where the action of the 'aggressive' principle predominates, the individual will primarily concern himself with issues of law-making and control. He will also tend to deal with inanimate nature, or with people as if they were inanimate. Whereas if the 'sexual' principle predominates, the individual's approach will be more exploratory and evocative. He will tend to work with people, to concern himself with human emotions and human relationships, and to approach inanimate nature in anthropomorphic terms.[29]

Thinking where the 'sexual' principle predominates, Hudson argues, is 'associated with a greater degree of access than is the "aggressive" principle to "primary process" thought'; with weaker boundaries between one sphere of thought, or life, and another; and with lack of adherence to socially defined conventions. The tendency is to think 'in a diffusely "eroticised" way'.[30]

Hudson's 'arts-minded' group carefully links social science people and humanities people. We, however, would happily exchange the latter for a third group, political ideologists, whose divergent proclivities are untested, but to whom we must nevertheless now turn.

Ideologising

The theorising relevant to politics can be divided into 'ideologising' and 'providing expertise'. In Western democratic politics there is rather less demand for the former, but we may ask where what demand there *is*, is situated, and where it might be located in the future?

There is a dialectical relationship between ideologising and providing expertise. Societies have a rhythm of change and consolidation, of ideology and organisation. In an era of nation-building or in active periods of social change, ideas are thick on the ground, and intellectuals have their best opportunity for intervening in practical politics. Attention shifts, in times of consolidation and calm, of low-pressure politics, to the details of running the machine; men are occupied in thinking of new things for the machine to do, so that designs for a better one lapse, and experts, not ideologues are in demand. Ideology, in times of large upheaval, works to give people at large a common understanding of what is wrong with the system which is about to break down, and therefore a common set of expectations and hopes for the system which should succeed it. (Mannheim chose to call the critical and forward-looking theories 'utopian', and reserved 'ideology' for those that justify the *status quo*.) The individual 'theorist', depending on the point at which he arrives in the cycle, will be proffered work as an expert or as an ideologue. Ideology never quite dies though — there is always room for honest doubt about where we are in the cycle.

Similarly, at the next level down, individual social movements call for different intellectual inputs at each stage of their development.[31]

Theorists' ideas, at first little noticed, are made serviceable by agitators, who are in turn supplanted by administrators once the movement is successful. On the dull plane of routine politics, there is a perpetual tug-of-war between idealists and functionaries. But in group settings, ideology works to move people in fair numbers from one social perspective to another; it is *the* way of indicating the moral superiority of new ideas.

> An ideology is the product of man's need for imposing intellectual order on the world. The need for an ideology is an intensification of the need for a cognitive and moral map of the universe, which in a less intense and more intermittent form is a fundamental, although unequally distributed, disposition of man.
>
> Ideologies arise in conditions of crisis and in sectors of society to whom the hitherto prevailing outlook has become unacceptable. An ideology arises because there are strongly felt needs, which are not satisfied by the prevailing outlook, for an explanation of important experiences, for the firm guidance of conduct, and for a fundamental vindication or legitimation of the value and dignity of the persons who feel these needs . . .
>
> Ideologies are the creations of charismatic persons who possess powerful, expansive, and simplified visions of the world, as well as high intellectual and imaginative powers. By placing at its very center certain cosmically and ethically fundamental propositions, an ideology brings to those who accept it the belief that they are in possession of, and in contact with, what is ultimately right and true.[32]

We are still ill-equipped to answer questions about why ideologies succeed, though, as Clifford Geertz has argued, literary criticism may well be our main guide: the theory of ideology, Geertz says, remains 'crude, vacillatory and evasive' because of the absence of

> anything more than the most rudimentary conception of the processes of symbolic formulation. There is a good deal of talk about emotions 'finding a symbolic outlet' or 'becoming attached to appropriate symbols' — but very little idea of how the trick is really done. The link between the causes of ideology and its effects seems adventitious because the connecting element — the autonomous process of symbolic formulation — is passed over in virtual silence. Both interest theory and strain theory go directly from source analysis to consequence analysis without ever seriously examining ideologies as systems of interacting symbols, as patterns of interworking meanings . . . It is the absence of [a science of symbolic behaviour] and in particular the absence of any analytical framework within which to deal with figurative language that have reduced sociologists to viewing ideologies as elaborate cries of pain. With no notion of how metaphor, analogy, irony, ambiguity, pun, paradox, hyperbole, rhythm, and all the other elements of what we lamely call 'style' operate — even, in a majority of cases, with no recognition that these devices are of any importance in casting personal attitudes into public

form, sociologists lack the symbolic resources out of which to construct a more incisive formulation.[33]

A small clue may lie in the similarity of mind between those who manufacture ideology and those who consume it with particular avidity. Both may need a clearly-ordered picture of the world, firm rules for right and wrong, a way of explaining everything that happens, and a 'mission in life' — in short, a powerful intellectual and moral drive to 'be in direct contact with the sacred'.*[34]

When the thing is done on a historical scale, however, the problem becomes that of explaining the improbable transmutation of the ideologist's private struggles into a world view that speaks to the needs of his age. When a whole culture is disordered or overturned, the new message will be eagerly received, not only by those who are temperamentally attuned to it, but by the whole society. How did a Luther, a Rousseau or a Marx come to say just those things that were needed to usher in a new age?

Erikson has tried to find an answer for the young Luther.[36] He makes him understandable, if not sympathetic, and shows clearly enough how *ideological work* finally resolved his 'crisis of identity'. Luther's father — cruel, sentimental and ruthlessly ambitious — emerges as the fatal conjurer: the whole performance required 'a father and a son of tenacious sincerity and almost criminal egotism'. Erikson also shows that Luther's historical following was fortuitous, and that he was followed not for what he taught, but for what he said parenthetically people might give up. As must often be the case, only part of his message was taken up.

When I read Rousseau I thought I saw that his impact, too, was somewhat beside his doctrine; *The Social Contract*, which philosophy schools still prescribe, seemed to be a shambles of a book.[37] Rousseau's appeal rested — and still rests — as much on his having fused the main romantic values (autonomy, subjectivity, emotionality, simplicity) into a single sensibility, as on anything in his programmatic working up of them. To minds in tune with his, the legitimacy of established authority snaps like bamboo. He dispensed with Original Sin — and so writes like the first modern man.[38]

Nathan Leites has tackled the problem of how Marx came to turn Russia upside down in his brilliant and neglected *A Study of Bolshevism*, which

---

* A twenty-year-old is much more likely to be an ideologue than an expert; a fifty-year-old, the reverse. Ideologies give 'simplified and yet determined answers to exactly those vague inner states and those urgent questions which arise in consequence of identity conflict. Ideologies serve to channel youth's forceful earnestness and sincere asceticism, as well as its search for excitement and its eager indignation, toward that social frontier where the struggle between conservatism and radicalism is most alive. On that frontier, fanatic ideologists do their busy work and psychopathic leaders their dirty work, but there, also, true leaders create significant solidarities.' (Erikson)[35]

approaches Lenin's political mind through a content analysis of his collected works.[39] Lenin demanded, above all, a non-Russian, non-Liberal, political code: his brother, through sheer niceness and ineffectuality (their father's legacy) had been cut down by the Czar when Lenin was twelve. Bolshevism became the obverse of idealist, worthy, impractical Russian reform, and it triumphed in the very land where Marx had given it no chance.

Turning from the history of ideas to political sociology, we can ask what ideological services the primary political groups active in our own society demand? Functionalism and group theory put forward familiar (and somehow comforting) propositions, such as that it is really the social group of similarly situated and agitated ordinary folk which produces ideology; or that ideology is the product of social strain and discontinuity, with victim-groups demanding to have their plight put in strong words;[40] or that politics is a miscellany of causes — mostly small. But these propositions do not explain why those directly involved in the predicaments do not develop their own ideological theories. After all, the process by which social irritation is turned into a political demand accompanied by a case (that is, rationalisation) is habitual in our politics. Why should intellectuals be called in to help?

Often enough they are not. Farmers' groups, for example, are content to bargain for subsidies, or unequal electorates, without seeking a physiocratic justification of the primacy of life on the land. But if the ordinary practices of group bargaining and administrative accommodation go on at sub-ideological levels, the case changes when there is a public to convince or a serious problem in the morale of the group itself. Aitken's assessment of Bruxner's achievement, for example, although it is — in the usual Australian way — sub-ideological, stresses how Bruxner met the existential demand for group ego-enhancement.[41] Deakin, in a similar subdued way, served the federalist cause by looking attractive *and* native, thereby making nationalism seem nourishing. Lang, too — the only Australian Labour leader to be genuinely idealised by the rank and file — built up working-class self-esteem in Sydney in the 1920s and 1930s by populist rhetoric of a vivid kind. His biographer shows, however, how negative his ideology was — he stripped the validation from the rich and educated, but identified, in fact, with the poor, rather than the working class.[42] Australian 'ideology' has, indeed, been notably derivative and second-hand[43] or else implicit.[44]

Theorists, where they are involved, bring certain nuances to ideologising. Within the group, they pin the predicament down and more accurately represent it in symbols; they cultivate an awareness of it, and make the demand less raw, if not actually palatable, to outsiders. In some steady and successful causes we may see the development of two sets of ideological symbols, one for the members themselves, and one for public consumption, and there may even be functionaries specialising in each.

Intellectuals get their general skill as 'brokers' from sheer language-gifts, from their customary biographical ties to the group they choose to serve, and from the fact that they have grown beyond the group and have an outside view of it. Mannheim has shown how the modern university works to forge a common language and a mutual understanding between the youth of the main groups into which society divides. That ideological brokerage is a trade is shown by men with ideologising talent who move from cause to cause.

Future public demand for ideological services seems scattered and declining. The day of the gifted amateur critic of politics has passed; we have moved on from nineteenth-century prophecy to *The American Political Science Review* — although it may yet be rather too early to talk of 'The Knowledgeable Society'. Political factions, stock or developing, will continue to offer agitational openings for in-group intellectuals, but we no longer expect such men to enlarge notably our moral sensibilities, or even our policy-options.

There remains the self-demand for ideology. Erikson has written at some length on how, for the young person, the formulation of an ideology and the forging of an identity are one and the same thing.[45] His studies of Shaw, Hitler and Gandhi — all of whom left useful autobiographical testimony — show prolonged, isolated and strenuous work to achieve a 'second birth', to slip from the niche their family and small society had trained them for, and find a vocation and a message that would do justice to their singularity. That they happened to be nearer forty (Jung's stage of 'individuation') than fifteen when they found their 'line', led their biographer to develop the concept of the *adolescent moratorium* to describe those close-mouthed and inward-turned years during which the youth bides his time and refuses serious social roles. Murray, Keniston, Lane, Helfaer and Little contribute instructive cases of young ideologists self-formatively at work.[46] The most sophisticated theory of the function of ideology — not yet matched by case studies — still remains Willy Baranger's.[47]

But ideology sometimes bursts in like a flood. Some sudden scare or trauma, an impulse, call, or word dropped, may trigger a shift of values.[48] Ruskin, for example, discovered politics because of his divorce:

> The private fact was that the son of an eminent Victorian had
> suddenly measured his length on the gritty high road at the time
> when his stride was most swinging and assured. The public fact . . .
> is that the eminent son got to his feet, knocked his father down,
> and proceeded from street to street hitting out right and left at the
> passers-by and pulling down the houses in a heap behind him.
> The extraordinary thing is that he did this in the most benevolent

of tempers, with the sincere conviction that the society that had produced his father and himself was rotten and needed to be reconstructed.[49]

While the sudden conversion may mark the adherent rather than the ideological innovator, the change in the personal emotional state that ideologies effect shows clearly why they are valued. Self-hatred, resentment and hostile self-destructive attitudes are transformed into peace, energy, joy.[50] Several writers, for example, have analysed Malcolm X's conversion, in the last months of his gaol sentence, to the Nation of Islam.[51] Like a blinding light, it promised escape from his own 'whitened mind' and allowed him squarely to hate 'the Man'. American whites, he learned, had tricked the enslaved blacks into accepting a white God, and thus an ineradicable sense of inferiority; in fact, blacks were the Chosen People of the older and stronger Allah. Ideology lifts the burden of personal guilt, projects it and licenses a righteous anger and aggression. It is little different with the current Women's Liberation or Gay Liberation broadside:

> Coming out as a homosexual has been a truly mind-blowing experience. I don't think it took much courage — only about ten minutes' worth ... Certainly I have never had such an overwhelming feeling of liberation. Nor have I ever known a time when my set of values and my ideology changed so rapidly and radically. The terms 'deviant', 'perversion', 'sickness', 'abnormality' no longer worry me because they are totally irrelevant to my situation. And the problem of being stigmatised has completely disappeared. For, by coming out, I have not *accepted* my homosexuality (which still implies an apology): I have *chosen* it ... The discovery that I have nothing to hide, and that I have nothing to lose, makes me invulnerable.[52]

Ideology justifies, energises, and politicises. It replaces insight. It may cure nothing, but it can make a wasp of a grub.

The collapse of ideology is correspondingly deflating, paralysing and deadening. Whittaker Chambers, who broke with Communism over Stalin's purges, after twelve years' devoted service, found the metaphor for this in Kafka:

> The important thing to those who survived such breaks was that their lives were henceforth stripped of meaning and purpose. They ... would hold with themselves a daily colloquy much like that between the Mayor of Riva at the bier of the Hunter Gracchus in Kafka's parable ... :
> 'Are you dead?' asks the Mayor.
> 'Yes,' answers the man on the bier, 'as you see.'
> 'But you are alive, too,' says the Mayor.
> 'In a way,' says the man on the bier. 'In a way, I am also alive.'
> In life, the man on the bier explains, he had been known as the Hunter Gracchus. Hunting one day in the Black Forest, he slipped

among rocks and broke his neck. 'Then came the mishap.' He found himself neither quite dead nor yet living. 'My death boat went off course . . . All I know is that I remained on earth and my boat travelled earthly waters. So that I, who wished only to live among my mountains, travel, after my death, through all the lands of the earth . . . Nobody . . . will come to help me.'

'A terrible fate,' says the Mayor on reflection.[53]

Consulting

Although Western democratic politics favours 'theorists' who provide expertise over those who dispense ideology, and social scientists over social philosophers, separating the two is not entirely straightforward. First, they are alike psychologically: the keen concern with politics in those who seek detached-adviser roles is intertwined down to the root with unconscious anxieties about getting hurt, shamed or worsted. Fear of exposure may well itself have led to the acquisition of this sort of knowledge.

Secondly, through all the social sciences there is a perennial debate about priorities in detachment and intervention, in theory and practice. How important is striving to know what would help the hard-pressed policy-maker, compared with theory-building? And *can* knowledge that is relevant to policy be better acquired through work centred on the issue or the client, than through patient, and apparently unfeeling, system-building?[54] How much should taking the problem as the power-holders see it be regarded as itself an inherently conservative position?[55] How powerfully do the conventions of academic and professional career-building implicitly reward the non-interventionist social scientist and hamper the radical?[56]

Each social science discipline, of course, works individually as a miniature social system to recruit, socialise and reward certain preferred styles of intellectual performance — and those only. Some supply precision in work, or a sense of contextual support, or opportunities for deductive or mathematical reasoning, and each of these qualities is critical to the appeal and self-image of that discipline. Compared, say, with clinical psychologists, sociologists have rigid and statistical notions of proof; compared with historians, their style is loose, cursory, and divergent. Sociology has been seen to cater for seemingly contradictory beliefs in the power of reason and the primacy of the irrational; for the desire to hunt for the causes of the largest possible human system, and for indirect reform — without a direct, damaging clash with the prevailing order; for demands for distance from one's object of study — a 'modest yet arrogant' stance, protesting that one is outside, above, or in advance of, one's setting; and for a chance to unmask and to trace the *unanticipated* consequences of action.[57] The central, energising question for the sociologist may

be 'Who am I?' and his discipline merely a long, roundabout way of finding out.*[58]

It seems that the crucial matter for the individual social scientist is
the selection of his appropriate subject — and the key thing in this is the
critical distance he can set up with it. This partly depends on the intellectual situation inside the discipline he has chosen to approach it from, but
he also needs in one way to be over-close and over-concerned — his interest must be over-determined — in order to draw on appropriate energies,
and yet remain distanced enough to lift him above raw feeling and involvement. Not only will the 'proper' distance differ subject by subject,
but conceivably at different points in the researcher's life. Psychiatrists
and anthropologists are so far the only social science groups to have taken
seriously the idea that the key to their understanding of their material
lies in the scrupulous study of *their own reactions to it*, (the analysts' 'coun-
ter-transference').

The *work style* of the individual theorist presents as large and clear
a field of study as administrative or agitational styles, but has so far aroused
little systematic, let alone psychologically informed, interest. For many
years we had only Coser's light sketch of Simmel's 'style of work'.[59] Then,
in 1970, his pupil Arthur Mitzman contributed a masterly and resolutely
Freudian analysis of the family situation of the young Max Weber as it
illuminated his initial choice of intellectual problems to attack, and his
own sense of skill and indeed of his calling as a social-political analyst.[60]
Mitzman focuses on Weber's twenties, the years he spent as a jobless
post-graduate, cooped up still in his father's house, contemplating marriage and various legal and university careers, and writing an unending
stream of tracts on the political and economic problems of the day. And,
wonderfully, it is through the minute analysis of this neglected juvenilia
that Mitzman reaches into Weber's inner cast of characters and the feelings inexpressible in his daily life that politics could, as he increasingly
found, commodiously stage at one remove.

The family background Mitzman describes is tense and bleak. The father, a senior bureaucrat and political notable, tyrannised his wife, a
solemn, pious martyr who, from very early on, made her unhappiness
miserably clear to her eldest son. There were constant rows over finances

---

* I should like to report here an impression of my own from the first national
  conference of Australian sociologists in 1964: a sense of the social cost of
  establishing a new discipline. These gentle, modest folk were all 'twice-born':
  pulled up several times by the roots, on their second or third profession (they
  included people who had been clergymen, teachers, probation officers, social
  workers) and their second or third marriage and, often, country, sufficiently
  shaken out of the routine life to have developed a somewhat wry and cagey
  detachment. Behind much dull and cautious conjuring with subjects like
  deviancy, religion or class lie personal victories in forging a language in
  which to speak coolly about topics that had once been electric.

(the money belonged mostly to the wife) and about her religious friends and enthusiasms. Weber senior was an atheist, a cynic and a snob. Weber took the mother's part, but was quite unable to stand up to the father. He despaired of mediating between them, though he felt he understood them both very well; he was simply torn between their completely divergent perspectives. He could not bring himself to accept his mother's religious beliefs, or to deny the strong attraction of his father's political power and public authority, though he was contemptuous of his lack of idealism and his subservience to higher authority.

It seems clear that for a time Weber dreamed of himself succeeding Bismarck — his pamphlets would prove him the young man with the answers. (One national question, for example, that he 'solved' was the riddle of falling agricultural production in East Prussia: tenant farmers were leaving, and being replaced by inefficient Polish farm labourers, because they rejected the *subservience of tenancy*. What young critic was better placed to write with conviction about a burning desire for independence? And his attack broadens into a general critique of Bismarck's policy, his supporting groups and so on.) He saw himself as a national leader in embryo — but where was his constituency? He looked for some emerging group in German society embodying a new spirit that he could wholeheartedly make common cause with, but could find none. He toyed for a time with Christian socialism, but settled for imperialism. Only by Germany's taking on some bold new civilising mission (over the Poles, for example) could his own generation of young people find something worth doing, a way forward from the political stasis of their parents. And, making this the theme of his inaugural lecture as professor of economics at Freiburg in 1895 (aged thirty), he helped usher in the epoch of German liberal imperialism.

So much for the young man with a profound sense of political mission. The next year, in an act of manic assertiveness, he threw his father out of his house. The father died of a heart attack before they could be reconciled, and Weber sank into a twelve-year 'breakdown'. When he eventually resumed university teaching (now very much *historical* sociology), all political ambition had been put firmly behind him. Indeed, he settled down to prove exhaustively that there was no way out of the 'iron cage'; and, although in his last decade he allowed himself some pleasure in his private life, his social pessimism remained unrelenting. His basic knowledge of the unreconcilability of his parents' worlds became, in his sociology, a programme of 'value-free social science', under a heaven, however, in which the gods were for ever at war: 'The genius or demon of politics', he notes in *Politics as a Vocation* (a late work), 'lives in an inner tension with the god of love . . . This tension can at any time lead to irreconcilable conflict.'[61]

Mitzman's account sharply underlines two elements in our general model of the theorist: he is a man basically afraid of his own aggression; and he is a man many of whose problems stem from 'having no group'. (Weber mused, in a late confession, 'I am . . . not really *quite* securely at home anywhere. It is as though I could (and wanted to) pull myself back from everything, and completely.')[52]

The demand for expertise

Government agencies collect in the normal course of business nearly all the knowledge they need. Tuned alertly to its particular client-ele, constantly refining its practices, each builds a staff of lifelong special-ists in the problems of the office, and a collection of data unmatched outside it. Administrators watch their counterparts in richer countries for practical hints or novel devices, and set their own research units to hunt out critical local information. Why should they ever call on out-siders?

Sometimes they strike some hitch in an outside technicality, or one too intermittent to justify a staff specialist. Technical consultants on con-tract work are quintessentially 'expert', but their work will not often be central to policy, and they will rarely be intellectuals. Sometimes, how-ever, by setting up a committee of inquiry or an advisory panel, officials will intimate publicly that they are looking for new policy ideas. Those asked are mostly representatives of interested groups with predictable views, but sometimes they will be a little more detached or wayward — independent specialists, foreign visitors, or academics.

It would be risky to take at its face value the sudden or massive interest of officials in being advised. They pursue their careers in a hazardous environment, and more important than the meeting of minds in co-option may be the averting of threats to their office's stability or existence. An advisory council can popularise the agency, shelter it in the performance of unpopular acts, make it more appealing in certain quarters and/or more generally respectable. At one blow, it opens client groups to view. Poten-tial critics, tempted to share the burden of power, are disarmed. The committee of inquiry can buttress a jurisdictional claim, strengthen a point of view not quite viable internally, and justify bold, or modest, ac-tivity. And, if the worst happens, reports can be pigeon-holed, and com-mittee meetings not convened.

Social scientists answering the call to advise officials will find that a good deal depends on how early in the problem they have arrived. They have the most chance to be influential when they are asked to help identify or redefine a problem, decide what data are pertinent, and what the main policy choices are. But they are more likely to be set to weigh relatively fixed alternatives, to find means to carry out a policy already decided upon, or even to assess the effectiveness of an existing programme. They may also be harried for quick answers — the official wants to act now, and is impatient with any wish to explore all the evidence first — and for solutions depressingly close to present practice. For all these reasons — and sheer initial mis-selection — consultancies are very often uncomfortable and unfruitful.

Yet the programme-professional — the theorist in flexible relation to administration — is a rising type:

> In many a corner of the bureaucratic machinery of modern society, one finds . . . the 'program professional' — the specialist in depth (e.g., experts in social insurance, rehabilitation, public assistance, public finance, housing, race relations, labor disputes settlement) whose professional competence and commitment are beyond question, but whose commitment to particular programs and policies (e.g., health insurance) is just as strong. By virtue of his technical prowess, he makes himself indispensable as a policy adviser. In his job moves — between government and private agencies, civic organizations, foundations, universities — he follows the programs to which both his skills and his social philosophy are bound . . . End products of broad movements of social reform, these men combine professional standards of work with programmatic sense and constitute an important link between professional culture and civil culture, the man of knowledge and the man of power.[63]

Daniel P. Moynihan, himself an outstanding representative of the type warns, indeed, of the danger of the professionalisation of reform, as researchers increasingly monopolise the identification, characterisation and treatment of problems.[64]

Occasionally theorists of an older stamp, philosophers, historians or literary men, still project themselves into administration — Malraux say, in France, or Theodorakis in Greece — and turn in performances more divided than synthetic.*[65] Henry Taylor, long ago, in his somewhat autobiographical chapter 5 of *The Statesman*, warned of the perils for an administrator of literary or philosophical pretensions. Commoner still, however, is the situation of the young theorist, letting go of his discipline, and turning himself laboriously into a career administrator. It *is* possible to combine both roles, but it is a heavy extra load and requires a capacity for ruthless detachment. The paths begin to separate as soon as the young graduate stops thinking of himself and his work in relation to the state of knowledge in his discipline, and accepts the performance principle:

---

* Nehru 'read General de Gaulle's letter outlining my credentials, put it on the table and said with a broad smile: "So now you're a minister . . . " The phrase did not in the least mean: you're a member of the French government. In a slightly Balzacian, and especially Hindu sense, it meant: so this is your latest incarnation . . . "Mallarmé used to tell this story", I answered. "One night he was listening to the cats talking in the gutter. One inquisitive black cat asked his, a venerable tom: 'And what do you do?' 'At the moment, I'm pretending to be the cat at the Mallarmés . . . '"' (Malraux, *Antimemoirs*)[66]

is his work satisfying superiors, getting the business done? Alternating spells of practice and reflection — criminologist to prison governor to criminologist — may become more common as careers become less institution-bound. Meanwhile there is little besides fresh, professionally organised knowledge of a more or less technical character that social scientists and other knowledge-workers can bring to administrators' assistance.

If theorists continue to desert ideology for expertise, and if consulting increasingly renders them half-administrators, we may see political work in the future much less as Lasswell's three-panel fan (see figure 1, page 19) and much more as one *Images of Class* subject put it: a giant balloon (administration) with a small bubble (agitation and theorising) on either side. Lasswell, himself, meanwhile has warned us:

> An end to animal miseries, primitive social issues, and stupid controversies will be won at the price of a decline in the moral exhilaration of public affairs and at the risk, as enlightenment, resources and skill combine, of a minocracy of power.[67]

Much in earlier pages may suggest a view of politics as a regressive phenomenon that ought to be outgrown, and of political workers as perpetually on the edge of, if not well into, neurosis. Another analogy seems preferable: politics as the symbolic projection of collective psychic tensions, doing for society what dreams, say, do for the individual.[68] The political figure is then his culture's instrument of selection, detection and creative expression. He must dive 'in' and 'down' to tap the accumulating pool of collective feeling which has not yet been properly channelled into intellectual or political conceptions; then, reversing direction, he must strike outward, press into service the technical skills necessary to portray vividly the condition revealed. His advance sensitivity to cultural determinants is his prime gift, and his stature depends on his ability to embody not merely proximate 'group' but also 'master' tensions in his culture. What work matters more?

PART TWO

Outlooks

We never think that what we think conceals from us what we are.

Paul Valéry

5 *The classification of world views*

The Bales typology

Robert Bales, of the Harvard Social Relations Department, published in 1970 a massively deceptive book called *Personality and Interpersonal Behavior*, which, with its modest 'do-it-yourself' format, seemed to be addressed only to those hardy souls wishing to start a particular sort of experimental small group — the cerebral self-analytic group in a university setting.[1] And that is the way all the reviewers have received it. In fact, it offers for the first time a possible basis for what one can only call comparative biography.[2] Along the way, it provides the scaffolding for that definitive classification of world views which political psychologists have long been seeking.

The book outlines, indeed, *four* interlinked schemes (or one basic plan overlaid with three transparencies). First of all, there is a top layer of 26 characteristic ways of behaving in group situations, or 'inter-personal styles'. Secondly, there is an interlocking classification of 26 world views (or belief stances or value positions) which go together with, and elucidate, each of these styles. Thirdly, there is a further matching classification of 26 personality-types, complete with leading traits, and drives and defences in graduated measure, each organised around a central 'project' or life-plan. Fourthly, there is a scheme setting out the kind of early childhood upbringing that leads to and shapes each character (this includes family climate, family theme and disciplinary style, as well as parents' characters and their ties with the child and the ways in which the child accepts or fails to accept them).

The history of the development of an intellectual scheme of such magnitude and complexity is of very great interest, and we must be grateful to the author for a reasonably full account of it. Political psychologists will find of particular moment the fact that it was a specially mounted attack on the problem of the classification of world views, conducted as far back as 1958, which afforded the key break-through in the whole analysis. To summarise drastically: Bales had started accumulating data on small-group interaction in 1944; by 1958 he had a mountain of observations and meticulous measurements of such things as agreement and conflict, liking and antipathy, success and failure in problem solving, low and high participation, coalitions, splits, deadlocks, withdrawals — observations, above all, of types of leadership and followership in groups. This data was supplemented and given substance by concurrent personality-testing of every participant. In sum, he had the histories of several hundred closely-watched small groups, and rich personal files on all group members.

The aspect on which most data were available was leadership. Bales had early distinguished 'task' and 'social' leaders. By 1958, he had, in addition, clearly singled out autocratic leaders, conservative, cult, dramatic, extremist, guilt-inducing, inspirational, managerial, outlaw, popular, prophetic and receptive leaders; he had also distinguished various types of followers and recusants and, indeed, scapegoats. But what did being, for example, an autocratic or outlaw leader in a small group amount to as a 'project'? He decided, in a move that would have delighted R. G. Collingwood, to attend more closely to what each type said they were about, to their most general value-statements. 'One seeks the realisation of certain values,' Bales reflected, 'primarily because the realisation of one's values affects his self-picture. The reward comes (mostly) because, if one realises the values, he is awarded a certain kind of group role or group position by others ... The rewards, so far as they exist, are mainly a product of maintaining that group position.'[3] Even though the expression of strong beliefs was very rare in the groups (it accounted for some 2–3% of all recorded 'acts'), an examination of just which beliefs subjects would own to promised to go to the heart of group-performance. So in 1958 he made a collection of 250 of the most controversial general opinions he could find or devise, put them to a sample and found that 144 of them *did* arouse significant disagreement. He factor-analysed them, and found three largely independent factors, which accounted for nearly all the pattern.[4] Then — and here is the breakthrough — he mocked up an alignment of these as axes of a hypothesised value-sphere. Setting Axes 1 and 2 at right angles (see figure 5, stage 1) gave, with half-way points, eight initial value positions, the principal combinations of the two independent values. As it was clear from small-group work that each of these predispositions could present itself 'ascendantly' or 'submissively' as well as in 'average' strength, an upper tier and a lower tier were added, giving 24 hypothesised positions. The final step in constructing the value sphere was to select the alignment of Axis 3, which, after careful thought, was set not at a true vertical to the others' horizontal, but at an angle of 45°. Each of the positions was now describable in high, low or medium quantities of the three values, and, between first principles and the stimulus of his twelve dozen sample sentiments, he could give substance to each with a rationale and representative opinions.

Upon this basic frame of 26 world views or personal projects, — 'ways of being in the world' — he was soon able to construct 26 matching inter-

Figure 5.

STAGE 1

Axis 1

Opposed to conventional authority
Allied with conventional authority
B
F

crossed with Axis 2

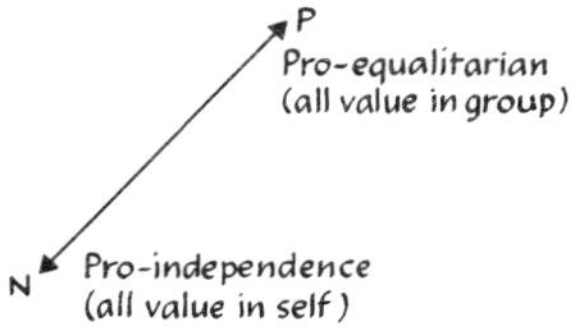
P
Pro-equalitarian (all value in group)
N
Pro-independence (all value in self)

yields

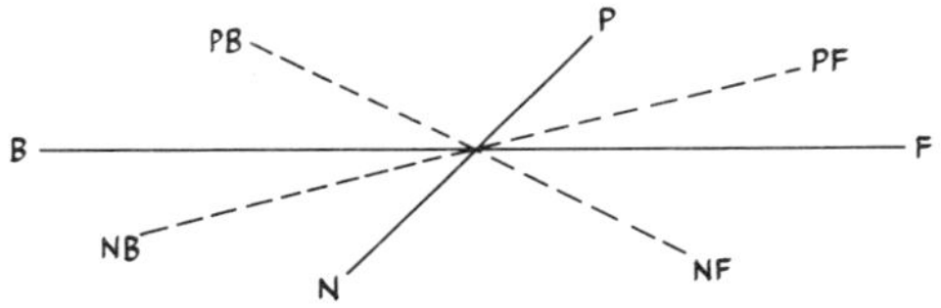
PB
P
PF
B
F
NB
N
NF

eight basic value positions

STAGE 2

Allow that each of these may be taken up also at double-or half-strength, i.e.

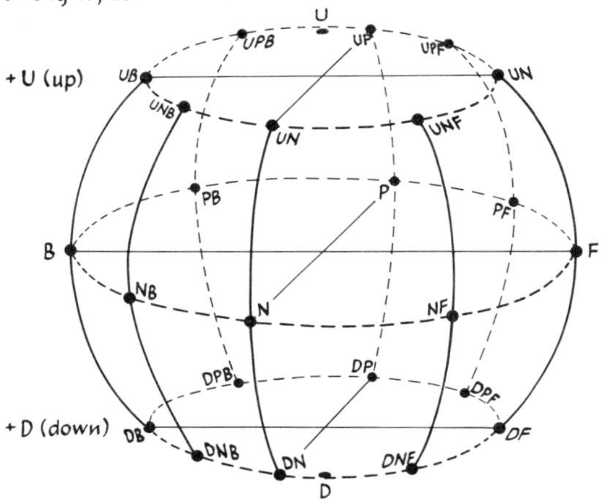
U
UPB
UP
UPF
+U (up)
UB
UN
UNB
UN
UNF
PB
P
PF
B
F
NB
N
NF
DPB
DP
DPF
+D (down)
DB
DF
DNB
DN
DNF
D

(which, with the addition of a theoretical North (U) and South (D) pole of pure 'dominance' or 'submission', gives us 26 positions)

Figure 5 continued

STAGE 3

Axis 3

is inserted at a 45° angle to the vertical, to run from UPB to DNF

(An epicentre 'A' at mid-point on all 3 axes makes a 27th-perfectly colourless-possible position)

personal styles, and once these were conceptualised, could devise schemes for allotting group members empirically among them, whether by gathering others' views of their role in the group, or by examining the frequency of their performance of different sorts of 'consequential' group actions. Then, with a sample population representing each of the 26 possible group styles, it became feasible to feed in the data from personality tests, and subjects' testimony about the sort of upbringing they had had. (These last two, the most empirical moves, produced incidentally the weakest and least compelling reaches of data.) Table 4 gives an outline summary of types.

That so many data on each 'position' could, following these procedures, be as it were mechanically delivered, should not conceal from us the considerable originality and artistry* that Bales displays in making of each a coherent, understandable whole — so that the childhood does plausibly set the cast of personality, the 'project' reflected in the world view and the preferred role or position in the group (a position, as he puts it, that 'rep-

---

* Nor should we overlook his fidelity to, and resourcefulness in extending, basic psychoanalytic personality theory. With the excuse that he has found psychoanalytic terminology off-putting, he is at pains to avoid it — at the cost, perhaps, of failing to reach his most natural (and useful) audience.

resents the best one was able to obtain, all things considered, in one's family'). I do not wish, however, to exaggerate either the richness or the finish of the 26 type portraits, averaging seven to eight pages each. That Bales envisages future small-group members actually reading about themselves makes his type descriptions both over-cautious and, sometimes, over-kindly. My students complain that they are 'bland' or 'American' or 'read like astrology', and claim not to recognise themselves in any of them, or to be spread about through at least a dozen.

But for the student of world views, there is an exciting sense of spaciousness about the Bales value sphere. It is liberating to be finally free of the constricting linearity of the conventional Left-Right political spectrum.[5] It is stimulating to be encouraged to see social movements from their outset as somewhat provisional 'federations' of less than wholly compatible temperaments. And, not least, it is good to have politics fused again with morals and religion, from which it should never have been academically detached. The spatial metaphors of the scheme are themselves informative: they help one to conceive a tug of liking, of affinity, between 'neighbouring' positions, or a fascination between antipodes – so that one may define any position as, in a sense, a defence against the unconscious attraction of its polar opposite (which introduces a touch of dialectical thinking into the analysis, as well as realistically reminding us of those odd, awkward, apparently contradictory bits that one regularly finds in otherwise tidy outlooks). And it is satisfying, finally, to see that over-studied type, the authoritarian personality, filling just one neat slot out of 26.

Certainly, some adjustments, such as *ad hoc* magnification of certain reaches of the sphere, may be necessary in order to analyse the consequences of new issues; work with cultures somewhat different from our own, or sub-cultures or social movements which deliberately set themselves against the cultural grain, may call for reversed signs, one or more new axes, novel spheres. But for now and for us, Bales's projection has an air of encompassing sturdiness.

But his gift, of course, is richer than this. Far from being merely a chart of society's ideological surfaces, Bales's scheme grounds each main value-position in a carrier personality-type, and that, in turn, in a constitutive childhood. How can political psychology best use this powerful magazine of new techniques? In a macro-political direction, the tempting prospect opens up of a resolutely psychological attack on problems of social aggregation and political leadership. What are the latent patterns of alliance and enmity? How fully do established political formations harness these energies, and how well do they steer them? How do new movements, stressing new values, mobilise types previously inactive and in what different ways, for that matter, do they reward and employ them? Which social plights demand which type of leader? How do leaders fare as they strive now to stretch their appeal, now to narrow and 'purify' it?

Table 4. *A summary description of the Bales character types*

Ego strength	Idealisation/optimism	Affection missing	Pervasive anxiety — fear of crumbling defences
UP Friend to all	UPF Head Prefect	UF Loyalist	UNF Authoritarian personality
Social success	Social solidarity and progress	Group loyalty and co-operation.	Autocratic authority
Identification with idealised parent	Identification with authority/group members, through idealised father	Identification with 'larger plan'	Identification with aggressor/protecting entities
Denial of negative feelings/objects	Denial of dislike; sex-drives harnessed to social forms	Drives securely harnessed to action	Repression of feminine submission/masculine facade; denial; projection
Extrovert, over-expansive self-picture			
Parents warm, concerned, optimistic — sweeten their discipline		Deficiency of affection in upbringing	Bad parent who depends on power of aggression
P Comrade	PF Idealist	F Conformist	NF Voice of conscience
Equalitarianism	Altruistic love — believes in power of goodness	Conservative group-beliefs	Value-determined restraint
Identification with good parents (or refuses identification and remains a child)	Abject identification with idealised parent, and through him, society	Identification with local institutions	Identification with the aggressor
Denial of negative feelings/objects; 'false positive' defence	Denial of negative feelings/objects; repression of aggression; affection harnessed to group tasks	Conditional-love-type upbringing	Denial of material/social reality; isolation; insulates himself from dangerous objects. Grinding, unfriendly, guilt-inducing Disciplining parents
Parents united, harmonious, their warm concern builds secure self-image	Maximum parental idealistic optimism		
DP Kindergartener	DPF Faithful servant	DF Fag (obsessional — compulsive)	DNF Martyr
Trust in goodness of others	Salvation through love	Self-knowledge and subjectivity	Self-sacrifice for values
Parents dependable models to trust	Abject identification with idealised father	Identification with tasks	Identification with the aggressor — out of desperation, to prevent being devoured by anxiety. Blames mother
Denial of tough-minded assertiveness; most successful harnessing of drives; 'false positive' defence is possible	Devalues sex, aggression, power, wealth — sorrowful, a moralist	Inhibition, feminine masochism; involvement minimised; disassociation of parts of self	Denial of sacrificed parts of the self, associated with sex and aggression; and of positive traits in others
Self-protective introversion			
Most indulgent upbringing		Conditional-love-type upbringing	Coldest parents

Aggression main drive	Pessimism/cynicism		Affection plentiful: Growth ethic
UN Lone wolf	**UNB** Law-unto-himself	**UB** Mocker	**UPB** Youth champion
Tough-minded assertiveness Identification with aggression; difficulty in identifying with father	Rugged individualism and gratification Identification with the power to defy authority and rise above/outside the law	Value relativism and expression May copy parent or be the joke' that reconciles/unites them	Emotional support- iveness and warmth Identification with warm, protective parent
Masculine facade; re- pression of affection- ate feelings; anxiety disowned Maximum discipline upbringing	Parental inadequacies force a child to develop pattern of self-reliance	Humour/cynicism	Sex sublimated in affection; bends rules for growth; love cures anxiety Maximum family warmth
N Independent	**NB** Delinquent	**B** Disbelieving rebel	**PB** Mother, herself Permissive liberalism
Individualistic isola- tionism Identification refused. Anxiety disowned	Rejection of social conformity (Mother-centred family.) Identifica- tion refused — identifies instead with 'bad examples', trouble makers	Rejection of conserv- ative group belief (Mother-centred family.) Identifica- tion with mother- and-children	Identification with mother-and-children; champions mother against authoritarian father
Parents unadmirable and not identified with; precocious autonomy	Sex-role rebels; cynical, lost.	Attacks the system of punishment	
Maximum parental cynical pessimism			
DN Resentment man	**DNB** Beat	**DB** Passive resister	**DPB** Underdogs' ally
Rejection of social success Identification refused with parents, with whom nothing can succeed; espouses failure	Failure and with- drawal (Broken family)	Withholding of co- operation Identification with mother-and-child- ren; wish to show how wrong the punishments/aggres-	Identification with under-privileged Wish to be cared for like an infant
Repression and denial are the main defences. Envy is the leading emotion	Denial of positive feelings	sion of a rejecting father were. Wants to unmask others' aggression	Trust in goodness of mother. Neglected by parents
		Rewarding mother but no (or rejecting) father	Blames father who does not care for his child- ren

This study takes an opposite, and inward, tack. It is less ambitious, but perhaps a necessary preliminary. Before Bales's scheme can be confidently used in large-scale analysis, we have to be sure that it accommodates individuals sensitively, and does, in fact, encompass the contemporary variety of salient world views. We propose, therefore, to sort some 35 classic and/or accessible political psychology cases by means of the Bales frame, asking if, indeed, each confirms the type-links hypothesised between opinions, personality and upbringing. Our concern is equally with how much is lost in individual uniqueness by subsumption into types, and with how much the types themselves are capable of enrichment by telling case-detail.

Testing the types

The questions we shall ask are whether the Bales types are clear and distinct, and whether their spread is comprehensive. The thoroughly miscellaneous case studies of individual outlooks assembled by political psychologists over a generation and a half offer an excellent basis for a test. They are not impractically numerous: only two or three score of real quality have followed Lasswell's pioneering study of Mr A. in 1930, and they tend to follow a fairly standard form, which, although it may rather skimp 'inter-personal style', fixes firmly on the links between outlook, personality and upbringing.

To launch the trial, I have chosen to present in abbreviated form four cases from the splendid set Henry Murray published in 1944 of eleven young Harvard men facing war service with reluctance.[6] A somewhat neglected resource, never published in book form, their penetrating quality as portraits is rather obscured by a topic-by-topic rather than a person-by-person format, and these cases are remembered, if at all (I have found few working citations in later political psychology writings), as being rather Blimpishly about the psychology of morale. I believe them to be the best studies of outlook we have, and regret that I cannot reproduce them all here. I have chosen a 'representative' four who best demonstrate between them the political sense of the Bales scheme by taking up its polar positions: P and N, F and B — or in this case actually DB. (See figure 5, stage 1.)

Ingle as comrade — P

Ingle, a notable student politico and 'revolutionary socialist', is on excellent terms with his eminent parents, who are currently working in public capacities out of Washington. Under their guidance he has embarked on a rather original career linking anthropology and biology, 'biology, socially-applied': 'My chief interests are in genetics, the human body, population, birth rates, the effect of diet on metabolic rate, climate on human constitution, and various racial and genetic strains that contribute to the difference in races.' To his mind, this splendidly combines his scientific and political ideals:

> The creation of a new society is close to my heart. It is also close to my nature ... I, as an anthropologist, will have ideas and know where ... things are really going, and I will be able to push. I will be part of the wave of the future.

He seeks revolutionary progress towards better social conditions in food, health and housing throughout the world, and has already brought off a neat piece of research in physiology. In the U.S. after the war he expects,

> Government ownership, a changing state, with the same ideals of social and even revolutionary progress that were born with this nation, with a more complete democracy than it has ever enjoyed, both in the sphere of education and politics.[8]

His political interests go back to preparatory school where a master introduced him to Marx and stimulated him to think on a global scale with sociological concepts. He was fascinated by the Spanish Civil War — 'If I hadn't been so young I might have enlisted and gone over to fight' — found the Communists alone admirable in it, spent his freshman year reading Lenin, Marx, Engels, Pareto and Veblen, but has now moved away from official Marxism to social democracy, although he continues to admire Russia (especially for its 'nationalities policy') and to insist that dialectical materialism is a powerful aid to thinking about biological problems.

As well as being an accomplished agitator, who has mounted several highly successful political campaigns on campus, he is a *theorist*. Murray at once complains of, and oddly defers to, a 'mind that is a veritable maelstrom of concepts', the 'steam-roller way he flattens [one] with the heavy volume of his thought' and the unusual scope, precision and readiness of his ideological knowledge. This recent devouring and digesting of the social philosophy shelf is actually his fourth such voracious intellectual foray. At primary school he read his way, with his parents' approval, through the physiology of sex and the literature of comparative religion; at secondary school, he read science (he thinks of himself as a scientist). He deals with anxieties, Murray says, by a flight into objectivity, and at the expense of a loss of contact with his feelings ('isolation'). But he emphasises how dedicatedly Ingle holds to his world view, and how he has subordinated his egocentric ambitions to the achievement of its hopes.

What especially concerns Murray, however, is the contradiction between Ingle's fervent and sincere anti-Fascist convictions and his disinclination to join up. In fact, he is at this time quietly exploring his chances of war research work in domestic food and nutrition or military adjustment to foreign climates, both centred in Washington, where he could rejoin his parents. Murray diagnoses, especially through TATs where heroes seem fated to violent ends, an unconscious fear of mutilation and being wounded — a residual castration complex — the outcome of a submerged revolt against his father.

Certain other qualities of Ingle's political outlook stand out. He is completely positive, absolutely sure of the value and realism of his goals; he throws boundless energy into his work and plans; 'growth and change [are] the center of his philosophy'. He has a keen intellectual curiosity: he wants 'to be awake to everything', to 'know enough to be right'; intellectual success, he says, is as important as anything else to him. He has broad sympathies: racial equality, the brotherhood of man, the elimination of oppression, the classless society, are concepts underpinned by extensive travels with his parents who were always concerned that he should understand the lives and attitudes of other peoples; he finds much in Harvard constricting. He gets on well with people of all sorts, and

> While he has little sensitivity for ordering personal relations, he enjoys and is invigorated by the manifold intellectual attitudes of everyone he meets, especially those attitudes which he accepts as a possible challenge to his own. He is eager to test all men's beliefs against his, and this testing cannot be fully enjoyed if he does not give opposing points of view their full measure of value ... He acquired early the habit of comparing diverse ideologies and beliefs.[9]

Finally, he is extraverted and materialistic; man's welfare can best be served by improving his environment — his body, his physical surroundings, the social system; the personal core is irrelevant or invisible to him:

> His feeling function being undeveloped and his respect for religious imperatives being nil, he has little basis for moral certitude. Consequently, his apperceptions of good and evil, his valuations of himself and others are insensitive and unreliable. His judgments of men are marked by a tolerance that borders on indifference.[10]

Ingle considers that he has had a richer background than his friends in many things. Murray agrees that Ingle has been exceptionally fortunate in his parents, and in fact seems to know them — they are both intelligent and cultivated people with a wide range of intellectual and artistic interests, who have pursued independent careers and yet maintained a harmonious and cohesive family life.

> My father and mother are supremely happy together. His intellectual force and executive ability complement her artistic intuitions and individuality.[11]

The family is a 'micro-democracy with a prevailing atmosphere of liberality that exemplifies differentiation and integration to an unusual degree': the parents have given him such continuous and judicious support that he has always felt confident of himself and of his own views. On the other hand, since they are intelligent and up-to-date, he has not had the experience of developing beyond them, or finding their views too narrow to contain his own. He has always felt that they are moral models, devoid of hypocrisy, and feels he has learned from his family 'appreciation of co-operative life, solidarity of group living, working together, sharing responsibility'. Finally, their political preoccupation and sophistication implicitly encouraged him to welcome social and civic responsibility in his turn.

He enthusiastically admires both his parents. His mother, an art historian and climatologist, he says, has 'a very affectionate nature, and might easily have spoiled me, if she had let her impulses overcome her good sense': 'we have ever had the closest intimacy'. He considers her a real companion and 'excuses' several absences and seasons of physical punishment (both parents taking an equal part) when his hyperactivity and temper tantrums made him unmanageable – at the age of five and between the ages of seven and nine.

Of his father, a successful business executive turned government ad-viser, he declares:

> I have envied my father his gifts, but we have always been very con-genial, and I have never admired any other man more. We share a great number of interests. Intellectually I resemble him more than I do my mother ... His range of friendship is perfectly enormous. He has great personal magnetism, enthusiasm, and character. His literary style, with its humor, charm, and simplicity, has always been my model. He is thoroughly at home in English literature and economics, and has taught me a little of his wide knowledge of nature study and plants.[12]

Ingle enjoys as much as anything arguing political and social issues with his father; discussions, he says, are always rational and objective, never rancorous. (If this is true, as Murray observes, it shows considerable mag-nanimity on the father's part.) Yet over the years, he has evidently permit-ted his son complete freedom of speech, and even some sense of triumph, since his own political position has moved from staunch Republicanism to a willingness to assist a Democratic administration in 'social reconstruc-tion'. He has been, Murray says, a rock of strength to his son, a magnet pulling him back steadily into the central American tradition.

Yet these debates, and behind and beyond them, Ingle's erection of a fully-fledged ideology running directly counter to his father's, seem to Murray, a 'displacement to the intellectual level of infantile hostility', thoroughly enjoyed because unpunished. Ingle's TATs abound in rebellious aggression: the hero in 40% of the stories is either a revolutionary or militantly opposed to the party in power; conflict between parent and child – in quarrels, wars, murders, sudden deaths – occurs in 30%. One TAT, echoing *Don Giovanni*, has a father dying 'of disappointment' over a dissolute *and radical* son, then tearing the son's 'soul away from his body' and dragging him 'down to Hell'. Despite this massive residual unconscious hostility, which is undoubtedly the source of his radicalism, the relationship with the father on the conscious level is stimulating and rewarding, perhaps because the 'son's hostility has never been directed against the father as an individual personality but against the father as a Rôle standing between him and his mother, or between him and complete freedom'.

Ingle as P. One cannot pretend that Ingle is a perfect example of P. Indeed, he exemplifies Bales's rule that adjacent positions exert steady attractive force. There are elements of PF, UP and UPF in Ingle's personality. His idealistic optimism, his great admiration for his parents, and his work on the foundations of a notably altruistic career, all point strongly to PF, but his identification with his parents is hardly abject, and there is a marked absence in the record of other admired persons. Ingle shows a distaste for self-interest, competition, and the idea of 'the individual as of primary value' (N), but (unlike Lake below) he insists on a programme of *equalisation,* and he broods not only on how much science will be needed to achieve it, but also on how much force. His career as a student leader, his sense of himself as well-born (he tells Murray he thinks he will have five children 'because the preservation of the superior genetic strain is the duty of educated people') and his intellectual and professional ambition, all point to UP. But he aspires to a *team-working* life and subordinates his egocentric ambitions to his ideology: to be part of the 'wave of the future', to act in the historically required and astute way, is the comrade's central demand. UPF — the Head Boy — is also not implausible (if American social change had conceivably been more collectivist in the 1950s and 1960s). Ingle, Snr, certainly wishes to give his son the sense of carrying on the essence of the American programme, but it is Ingle himself, with an energy of whose roots he is unconscious, who insists on the generational break, the new agenda and the new men. Nevertheless, it was the strength of these ascendant and forward tendencies that made card-carrying party loyalty first uncomfortable and then impossible for him.

As Bales describes him, the P — 'moving towards equalitarianism' — Comrade type, is an altogether gentler, more modest, simply affectionate, and middle-of-the-road person than Ingle. He does not *espouse* equality, make it programmatic, imperative or 'radical'; he has instead a personal warmth, a tropism to people. P is essentially 'an appreciator of others', who associates the ability or power to dispense affectionate concern most closely with his self-picture. Nevertheless, 'share equally', 'satisfy everyone', and 'the value is in the group, not the individuals', are propositions at the core of P's value-position, as they are of Ingle's. In principle, the *universalist* values (as distinct both from the localist F and the particularist N) are the property of the P position, and as these are certainly the nub of Ingle's outlook, his placement seems inescapable. In short, Ingle provides

Bales with a fully political, 'ideologised' case, and one not of the centre but of the far Left.

The personality traits of the P type — predicated on 'near-optimum conditions for personality integration'[13] — fit Ingle's case. First, he has high ego-strength — a well-organised, intellectually efficient personality based on the harnessing of drives in an integrative way; secondly, he has personal flexibility, an unusual 'freedom from socially negative traits that suggests either a happy endowment or a successful process of growing up'.[14] There is no type-hint of Ingle's extraversion, his 'objectivisation of intellect', or his blindness to the moral surfaces of individual behaviour. On the other hand, a tendency to the 'false positive' — the compulsive denial of negative feelings or objects — *is* listed as a minority option, for 'those who manage, though under considerable strain, to keep their aggressive drives suppressed even though they are basically higher than their affectionate drives'.[15] Certainly, Murray saw lots of covert hostility — and anxiety — in Ingle.

Finally, the developmental pictures match most satisfactorily: the parents are united and harmonious, 'high on optimistic idealism . . . emotional supportiveness and warmth',[16] able by affection to cajole the child out of negative phases, and by warm concern lead him to form a secure and valued self-image. It is not so clear that they are 'low on inhibitory demands and discipline'. While one hardly expects Bales to lay down for the type what is uniquely strong in Ingle — a sense of special privilege in having uniquely effective and talented parents — it might well be borne in mind as a minority option. (There are, after all, several plausible biographical essays on people who have become socialist out of a sense of over-privilege.)[17] The Ingle family style of 'micro-democratic' functioning* — practice in shared responsibility and in equal-but-different treatment within the family — may very well buttress adult equalitarian preferences. There is, finally, a hint (no more than a hint) of *refused* identification, of remaining the Child, remaining against the forward leadership, and of choosing to forego leadership in his turn, and this hint answers to some of the inner nuances of Ingle's story. The essential point that the case adds, however, is that, if P's equalitarianism is to be fully ideologised, then covert aggression against the father is the likely carrier.

Couch as independent — N

Couch, a physically frail Southerner with a 'touch of nascent literary genius', is the least patriotic of Murray's subjects. He hardly notices the war's existence and does so only in a tone of lofty disapproval; the rare allusions to the war in his TATs paint it in terms of cruelties inflicted on

---

* The family style is too briefly described; Murray does not tell us if there was one sister or two. Ingle's two spells of ungovernability suggest that there were two.

civilians. His physical disability disqualifies him from war service, but Murray notes that 'detachment … aloofness … lack of concern' and 'solipsistic isolation' were well established in his personality much earlier, and adds that this 'formidable cluster of basic sentiments' leaves him invulnerable to social issues. A writer, Couch explains, is in principle uncommitted to society; he is certainly uncommitted to the nation:

> The artist or writer does what he must do. He isn't very important anyway. He doesn't effect anything. There are lots of other people to take care of the world.[18]

But in some moods he has twinges of conscience, and complains of an 'autism or extreme egoism, extreme ambition, and self-interest'. In fact, it is partly to discipline such tendencies that he currently studies sociology, in which he has already assimilated the standpoint of Pareto. Politically, he is an arch-conservative, hostile towards the masses and the idea of a classless society, and the problem of Negroes and racial equality. He has no trust in the common man and no expectations of a better America or a better world society after the war. He is quite satisfied to leave government and society as they are, as long as they do not interfere with his 'ambition to perfect himself as artist and gentlemanly *connoisseur* of culture'.

It is in religion and aesthetics rather than politics that Couch is in full revolt against his devout and conventional parents, and he devotes a large section of his autobiography to tracing his steps in apostasy (a development which owed much to three stimulating intellectual friendships at school). He explains that he is not an atheist:

> Morally I am more remote from my parents than they realize, yet essentially only in the one respect, the recognition of religious authority. I am no longer a Christian, but I am or am about to be a man of good will. If I forsook their faith irrevocably it was without undue cynicism, bitterness, or a lapse into the equal and opposite error of atheism, or that of abandon.
>
> To relate my total perspective to theirs as simply as possible; the elements of their conception of virtuous character which I have retained in mine I have bereft of religious meaning, and given a new context in a total conception of the superior secular man. I have added two entire systems of value, that of intellectuality and that of culture, which open realms unimagined and inaccessible to them.
>
> Morality for me is the strategy of self culture, [Couch speaks of this elsewhere as 'a veritable "culte de moi"'] … My major experiences have lately centered about the discovery of *higher* culture and art, and intimate almost mystical emotional experiences of prolonged introspection, music, drugs or drunkenness.[19]

His ideal, the superior secular man, he further defines as 'a man who has achieved cultural superiority':

> Whose thought attests a mind of great clarity, vigor, depth, subtlety,

precision, originality, whose feeling moves between exquisite sensibility and the depths of joy, pride, and melancholy. His conversation is astute, felicitous, urbane, witty. In matters of culture his flair is impeccable, yet catholic. *Voila un homme!*[20]

However, he admits that the 'metamorphosis' which has benefited him so greatly has also cost him a good deal: sometimes the detachment of his whole system of values frightens him and he complains of the 'enormous pressure of an unconscious burden of sin and guilt feelings', indeed, of a 'neurosis'. Murray notes that, in addition to a relatively standard and clear-cut obsessional neurosis, Couch has a hysterical inability to speak on occasion, and sketches a two-level structure of internal conflict: near the surface, a struggle between the ego and the super-ego, initiated by the 'attempt of pride to deny and repress conscience', and, on a deeper level, a conflict between the id and the super-ego.

These conflicts cast their shadow in his intellectual style. Murray notes his 'neurotic habit of confronting himself, when caught between two opposites, with each choice of action equally weighted with reasons, thus bringing his will to a state of complete paralysis'. Couch's

> determination not to commit himself to any definite standpoint is unrelenting. Only indirectly can one arrive at what would appear to be his more basic sentiments on each question. Asked for his opinion face to face, his answers are usually balanced and rebalanced by a series of limiting and qualifying phrases, a practice reflected in his free associations by the plethora of opposites, suggesting schizoid intellection, such as

> Radicalism — Beneficial, harmful.
> War — Evil, horrible, glorious.[21]

Couch himself remarks that he has a 'great urge to master and control' — and, therefore, 'peculiar sentiments *against* authority and control'. Murray calls him 'proud, lacking in respect for his superiors, addicted to vainglorious masquerades', and doubts his sincerity. Aristocratic in his social sentiments, he has no secure moral standards, no interest in any social enterprise, no group loyalty or sympathies. He is an 'extreme intraceptor', concerned with the quality of self-culture, of becoming as opposed to being or doing, and remains stubbornly true to his own subjectivity and individual truth — a solitary. His aim is to be a writer, to 'dominate by the wit and subtle brilliance of his language, to display his very soul to a select and discerning auditory'. Allied to his strong need for recognition is a powerful streak of exhibitionism.

Couch's substitution of the cult of sensibility for religion has involved a complete disruption of sympathy between himself and his parents. Although he consciously excuses their shortcomings and their failure to understand or nurture his creativity, a TAT story of a young man returning from college, gives the true picture of the present sad state of their relationship:

> He quickly loses the sentimental glow, and a tension begins to infuse the scene. He sits there staring at his family with hostility. He realizes that they are ugly, noisy, crude, loud, stupid. He realizes that he hates them, but also realizes that he is very like them in most respects — appearance, mannerisms, and speech. He feels a hatred, a very deep hatred of the family, which is essentially a hatred of himself.[22]

His autobiography vividly sketches his development — and grievances — in childhood.

> My parents are intelligent, religious, middle class people. They have little sympathy with the world of the 20th century, as one finds it, let us say, in the social life of academic circles. But if they are not very sophisticated, they are intelligent, refined, relatively to their associates, and have commonsense almost in overplus ... Perfectly matched, [they] get along beautifully together. I never heard one angry or cross word, never any conflict at all.

> I had a very salubrious childhood ... We had a comfortable house, full of antiques, good food, sweetness and light, Sunday School literature, — a very wholesome and cheerful home ... [My parents were] affectionate and over-solicitous, but not overly over-solicitous.

> First and foremost with my parents is the Christian life, which for them amounts to sincere conformity to the recognized practices of church going, church work, bible reading, prayers, tithing, charity, and the sincere cultivation of the Christian virtues of faith, self-sacrifice, good will, purity, probity. Closely allied to this Protestant ethic is the bourgeois one of industry, thrift, hard-headed wisdom, the traditional family life, and the rest. And if these be considered *ideals* ... my parents attain them admirably.[23]

At first without complaints, and then helpless, passive, and unable to resist their influence till his later adolescence, he is now bitter that his parents were so limited and incapable of encouraging his gifts, and he feels that twenty years spent in 'banal, mediocre, callow, and provincial' surroundings were a grave handicap. 'My parents gave me too much affection and not enough understanding.'

> When I was five I began to draw. My parents did not discourage my enthusiasm, yet I was left to my own devices ... They never thought to provide me with decent paper and brushes, or with good pictures as models ... They could have had no comprehension of what the artist-personality *means*, psychologically speaking, and no genuine knowledge of art itself ... Finally they were beyond a doubt consciously unwilling to encourage *serious* interest and ambition lest I eventually become unshakeably set upon art as a career, with all that that prospect conjured up for them of Bohemianism, ethereal impracticability, nude models, garrets and starvation ... I began with enthusiasm for stories and words at the same age that I began with

enthusiasm for pictures. My parents neither obstructed nor sped my progress. From them throughout I had no meaningful supervision of my reading nor careful, stimulating instruction ... So up to the age of fourteen I stood without solid grounding in anything, without dignity, without indoctrination in the processes of clear and penetrating thought, nor indoctrination in the traditions of the world, in discrimination in the social graces.[24]

His father was in commerce — a stern man, 'harsh, intolerant, and inconsiderate'. He overburdened his son with commands, requests, and injunctions. Couch was often fearful of discovery in wrong-doing—he still has a tic of turning his head slightly to the side when talking to an older man that dates from a sudden blow from his father when he was aged nine. The father expected more attention and affection from the son than he ever got. Couch never idealised him or wanted to be like him, and indeed was often ashamed of him. In his dreams, Couch says, his father is 'alternately the object of hostility and of presumably homosexual feelings'. Antipolarity of sentiments, Murray observes, is all-pervasive in Couch's personality, and it is probable that its roots lie in an early love for both his parents, which turned to hate.

Although Couch never accepted his mother's sentiments as his own, never admired her or wanted to be like her, he nevertheless sometimes feels that he *is* like her. She is more affectionate and solicitous than his father. She tends to spoil him, she over-praises him, and often complies 'quite deferentially' with his wishes. This deference gives him a peculiar satisfaction, since his erotic impulses are linked with narcissistic exhibitionism and sadistic dominance.* He is as ambivalent towards his mother as towards his father; he dreams of her as a sexual object and at the same time feels that she is repulsive.

Couch aims to uproot in himself all his parents' qualities, both inherited and acquired, and has constructed to this end an exactly contrasting ego-ideal — an ideal so lofty, however, that it plunges him either into painful inferiority feelings or grandiose fantasy. As his sense of frustration grows, so does 'the elevation and distance', as he calls it, 'of my expected trajectory'. So too the cleft between his parents and himself grows wider, and his resentment and contempt increase in proportion.

---

   * Murray also detects a strong element of bi-sexuality — often found connected, as he notes, with a high degree of narcissism, as well as with creativity. 'It is the interplay of the male and female elements in himself, indeed, which gives rise to his most ecstatic experiences. Actual woman does not appear to him to be necessary to his creative life. In fact, she constitutes a direct threat to it, because it is only by the development of extreme narcism [sic] that he can heighten those aesthetic feelings which are to him the culmination of delight. This, as well as his homosexual tendencies and the exhibitionistic erotic fantasies of which he is ashamed, account for his devaluation of heterosexuality to the point where the act itself appears to him to be absurd.'

Couch as N. Despite the rich idiosyncrasy of Couch's case, Murray holds a very firm view of him as a type — the artist as 'romantic genius', a type that has for generations pursued a path of 'insulated individualism'. Indeed, he rounds off his discussion with the reflection that it is exactly such parents as Couch's, representing 'the marriage of puritanism and commercialism', who, with their profound fear and loathing of art, are responsible for the 'compulsive egotism and subjectivism of the majority of great uncompromising artists in this country'.

It is a shock, therefore, to find that Couch is not altogether easy to place in Bales's scheme. The rejection of social conformity (NB) is one clear way of summing up Couch's project; so also is the pursuit of self-knowledge and subjectivity (DF). One has to read some way into the fine print to appreciate that Bales reserves the former position for the relatively mindless, delinquent gang-member, and the latter for the Faithful Servant. Another aspiring novelist among Murray's cases, Yawl, whose scheme it was to pillory his parents' 'puritanism and the profit motive' can certainly be placed comfortably as a Law-unto-himself — UNB (see p. 156). We have settled on N — 'towards individualistic isolationism' — the Independent, first because it exactly catches Couch's attitude to the war; secondly, because it fits his strategy as an artist reasonably well; and thirdly, because it fits too the essence of his childhood project, which underlies his artistic strategy — the project of proving his differentness, separateness and ability to think and act perfectly independently — that is, his refusal to identify with his parents.*

The ideological core of the N position is that all value is contained in the self — and that the self needs, for its own health and growth, to be isolated and protected from the group.† The N type values privacy, time to himself, freedom of movement, going it alone, *autonomy*. Contact with others threatens and debilitates, and he fears and rejects group-inclusion on any basis of affection or solidarity, and especially on grounds of 'mere' equality. Others in turn are apt to describe him as unfriendly, aloof, self-concerned, detached, unsocial, defensively secluded, negativistic (he 'specialises in disagreement') and alienated. Having struck out on his own,

---

* One must justify, however, denying him 'promotion' to the more ascendant UN position, especially in view of the fact that Murray appears to rate his expressive abilities — and certainly his abilities as a connoisseur — very high. He undoubtedly has the ambition and *scale* of life-project to warrant an ascendant placing, but he seems dejected at times by the way he has still to go, and there is also that paralysis of mind before value-conflicts. Anyway, he lacks the sheer head of aggression for UN, and the directness of aim; Couch's parents will be *indirectly* shamed, forced to acknowledge their undervaluation of him by his future public fame. (His invalidism — the suggestion perhaps that he *works lying down* — seems, from the choice of name, also to have weighed with Murray.)

† Bales notes dryly that isolation may in some cases really help, since it cuts down the level of stimulation — something he handles with difficulty.

he is determined to show that he cannot be brought back by affection, reward, or even seduction.[25]

Bales foresees in N a degree of neuroticism — anxiety, suspicion, hypochondria, dependence, or guilt, indecisiveness and doubt (as in Couch). He also predicts a cognitive weakness — an over-estimation of intellect and understanding (perhaps just because 'ego strength' has been such a prolonged issue) associated with an ambition to control one's life completely by intelligence and rationality. (Couch, for his aesthetic ends, however, dabbles in non-rational, ecstatic states.)

Aggression is posited as N's main drive, although 'it is neither consistently controlled or targeted, being sometimes turned outward, and sometimes inward in depression'. Bales also sees a blocking of drives by an internal division of the personality against itself, exemplified in Couch's endlessly qualified rhetorical style. The principal defence is the 'disowning of anxiety and drivenness by their projection on to others', which is hardly Couch's charge against his parents.

There is one darker strain, however, in Bales — N as the spoiler — from which we must exempt Couch:

> The N type of person is one who, for whatever reason, feels he has been denied love and acceptance and has 'decided', as it were, that what he cannot have he will hate and destroy. His feelings of insecurity, worry and suspicion, and perhaps of jealousy can be understood as manifestations of his basic distrust. He feels he will not receive the rewards of love, no matter what he does, and he wants revenge. He becomes a 'spoiler'.[26]

It is a large omission, too, that N as described holds out no prospect of the creativity that Couch seems to possess in unusual measure (Bales, with only cursory discussion, nominates as the sole potentially creative sites, D, DB and DP) and that it misses the central narcissism.

Finally, the childhood picture, as we have mentioned, is illuminating and broadly accurate: the child sees his parents as unadmirable, cannot identify with them, and is set at an early age on differentiating himself from them, and achieving autonomy. But this picture, although it is correct in its general outline, is wrong in almost every one of its specific details (see table 5).

We may conclude that the main assistance the case brings to the type is the notion of an *occupationally* standard — if rare — mode of defining the interior requirements and justifications of isolation, independence and self-concern. The artist, preparing and protecting the creative space for his work, calls to his aid 'silence, exile, and cunning'.

Lake as Conformist — F

Strong, stocky, phlegmatic, and seriously short-sighted, Lake is from Kansas and, in second-year Arts, just getting over the 'vast impersonality' of Harvard. His bad eyesight eliminates the possibility of active service;

if he is drafted, he hopes to get into the Business School's Quartermasters' course, which will help his later career. His sentiments 'seem to be in entire conformity with parental teaching and tradition'. 'He stands by the great middle class from first to last'. His analysis of the present crisis is 'simple and reasonable, uncomplicated by the corrosive subtleties that embarrass some of his more sophisticated classmates'. He is willing, he says, to do what is required of him in the war, but he has no moral or ideological commitment to participation, and his personal sense of loss and privation

Table 5. *Couch as N: Parental traits*

Bales's N	Couch

Both parents:
  * Sharp discrepancies between parents, in the form *either* of exaggerated male/female role-differences, *or*
  of confused or ambivalent sex-role pictures, leading to difficulty in adopting conventional sex-role
  The father especially is rejected or feared, yet makes heavy demands on the child for manly behaviour or qualities; the son can neither accept nor completely reject him, or his model of the male role
  * Moderately high on inhibitory demands and discipline
	Both parents:
	  * High degree of marital harmony Conventional sex-roles
	
	There is some puzzle certainly in Couch about narcissistic exhibitionism, revulsion from women, and bisexuality
	Murray thinks that it is the mother's *late* attempts at affection and closeness which most threaten Couch
	  * The father is certainly seen as stern and punitive, but Couch's deeper complaint is of 'too much affection and not enough understanding'. Murray says shrewdly: 'Had they been less affectionate, Couch might have found a sterner vein in himself, but as it was he felt helpless, passive, and unable to resist their influence until his later adolescence'

* Moderately low on emotional supportiveness and warmth
  * Moderately high on pessimistic cynicism
	* Moderately high on emotional supportiveness and warmth
	  * Moderately low on pessimistic cynicism

In sum: the resources of the parents for bringing about a conventional socialisation of the child are low. The parents do not agree well with each other, hence do not present consistent norms to the child; they are rather cynical about values in general, or ambivalent about conventional values, and they have neither the power of rewarding and stabilising the child through affection, nor that of arousing his admiration. Hence he is left on his own, to work out his psychological destiny as best he can.

is strong. After the war, he hopes for a world more or less socialist, but embodying as many liberal democratic qualities as possible. He greatly admires businessmen such as his father and hopes himself to become one.

The quality of his mind saddens and exasperates Murray. He is distressingly sane, following the rule 'forget about yourself, escape into normality'. He is 'two-dimensional', a 'bland sociocentric extraceptor' with little self-knowledge, and no private feelings uniquely his. A nominal Episcopalian, Lake is uncertain about, though distinctly favourable to, religion; he sees it as 'unifying' to society and 'stabilising' to the individual – it 'gives strength'. His parents, though highly moral, were not church-goers, and his present religious ideas centre round aspirations to selflessness and benevolence, and a compulsive optimism; he does not discount active church membership sometime in the future.*

Besides extreme conventionality, Murray notes his other-directedness (he functions most happily when he is incorporated in a group); his lack of emotional intensity or depth ('not easily aroused by anything'); what looks like emotional stability but which is perhaps just an 'activity level ... below average'; conscientiousness; a slow thinking style, 'arguments being based on very simple and commonplace assumptions', together with 'an inability to think of specific problems in relation to general ideas'. Most remarkably, he has a 'compulsive determination to look at the bright side of life', which is built into the ego-ideal, the conscious ego, and the unconscious ego:

> Optimism is the right and happy attitude, and one should concentrate on this. No matter what happens there is always a good side and one should keep thinking of this. . . Deep inside I am really very much of an optimist. . . It is a part of my nature to ignore and forget all those things that are disheartening. I use terrific logic sometimes to make things seem right.[27]

This 'philosophy' of positively negating everything unpleasant or disagreeable Murray likens to Christian Science, in which Lake's mother was briefly caught up.

Lake's feelings about his parents are extremely positive. In the play-test he creates a scene of a happy family with the parents presiding over it; in the argument-completion test he scores highly on arguments favourable to parental and traditional standards; he and his parents stand together as a unit. (Lake is the second son, with three younger siblings.)

> In all my attitudes, my parents and I are in agreement, both father and mother. I admire them both very much, and I want to go a little farther, to show them that I appreciate what they have done for me. I also want to have their friendliness, discretion, and honesty.

* Nor does Murray, who, finding his TATs 'seething with melodramatic robberies, violence, accidents, and sudden death', predicts that joining a church would ease the strain on 'overburdened repressive mechanisms'.

Their philosophy 'is to do everything in moderation' — an ideal which Lake himself cherishes.

> The policy my parents adopted in bringing us up was one of making us all partners in the family and teaching us to reason out our problem and then follow a course of our own discretion. Of course, they were always on hand as council.

They showed no favouritism among the children: they

> were always fair to us and we to them ... Our parents were always extremely interested in things we did, and always encouraged us in constructive ideas. They taught us to be ambitious and to go farther than ourselves. We were always confident of their love, but they never embarrassed us with affectionate demonstrations.[28]

He has always had the greatest admiration and respect for his father, most of whose standards he has taken over himself. He prefers him to his mother, and was always pleased when people said he resembled him. He describes him as 'a happy fellow' who 'gets the most out of life', energetic and masterful. His discipline, though, was not at all severe. This whole-hearted approval carries through the TAT stories as well.

His mother is also described as 'ideal': lady-like, tactful, active, just and — the one negative note — 'rather haughty'. She

> is small, heavy, not demonstrative, just. She doesn't get angry, is very practical, and has a good business head ... She gets along well with people, is respected and admired by every one I know ... She was teacher, being at home all day. From her I learnt altruism — doing unto others — and equality.[29]

She did most of the disciplining with even-handed justice. Physical punishments were rare; 'good word whippings' were the rule. He denies ever feeling rebellious after punishment. His TAT stories bear out a warm early relationship with no trace of oral deprivation, weaning trauma or oral aggression, but contain an astonishing amount of aggression, some of it directed to objects symbolic of the mother's body. Stories of collisions and eye injuries point to a traumatic primal scene experience, and Lake confirms this. Fantasies of ripping open the mother's body evidently relate to resentment of the mother's pregnancy and a wish to destroy the new rival.* Three babies in succession kept these preoccupations vivid in Lake's childhood, but it seems that, after each birth, his aggression was almost immediately repressed under a strong reaction-formation of nurturance. He remembers, however, being excessively 'curious' as a child, and it is possible that the impairment of his eyesight,

* Corpses are mutilated in these fantasies, and bodies are torn open; there is a trunk murder and a Caesarian operation. One TAT recounts how two American brothers, interned in Germany and converted to Nazism, become pilots and, on a mission to their native land, bomb and utterly destroy their own home.

which was first noticed when he was about eight or nine, was the result of guilt engendered by his voyeuristic tendencies.

The bizarre unconscious fantasies laid down in these years connect with nothing in his present life. He genuinely and spontaneously admires and respects both parents and shares in large measure their assumptions and sentiments. There is no trace of aggression in his social attitudes. Although the developmental record, Murray concludes, contains no evidence of mutual enjoyment of intimate companionship, his parents have been unusual in their lack of possessiveness and exploitation, in not using their son as an agent for upward mobility and in imposing on him 'no obligation . . . to fulfill the thwarted ambitions of either one of them'.

Lake as F. Though Lake's 'extreme conventionality' comes to us rather pre-packaged, so that we cannot independently taste its quality, there can be no doubt whatever that he fits comfortably into Bales's F, the conformist type — moving 'toward the conservation of the best in group beliefs and precedents' — whose essence lies in a 'willingness to sacrifice the self to some degree for the sake of social role definitions or social norms'.*[30] Murray marvels at the degree to which 'uniqueness and individuality are all but obliterated' in the man.

He comfortably fills out the leading traits suggested: a 'will to believe'; 'fastening and confining his conscious attention and will to the desired goals' as the mode of adjustment (his thinking is 'based on very simple and commonplace assumptions'); unusual lack of understanding of repressed tendencies; ineptness with 'fantasy, freedom, humor, or expression' — although it is salutary to appreciate that what the conformist represses is, above all, aggression; sexually, he may be quite active and aware.[31] Some minor details in F are strikingly evident in Lake's case: matter-of-factness, practicality, literalism; fairmindedness; responsibility and conscientiousness; strong will; stability of character.

He fails to testify on — though he by no means falsifies — predictions that he will be fascinated by deviance and local in his pieties; although Murray stresses his immersion in 'old-fashioned middle class standards', he is in the process of tempering Kansas with Harvard conventions. One prediction alone he contradicts — that of being deductively rather than inductively inclined — since he starts out by being over-impressed by the rules: 'He lives "by the rules" and will stand or fall by the rules.'[32] Murray notes Lake's 'inability to think of specific problems in relation to general ideas'.

Developmentally, too, the case bears out the type: both involve an upbringing of the 'conditional love' type, producing an ambivalence or

---

* Several touches — the compulsive optimism, the 'equality' mother taught, the 'sociocentrism' — might suggest PF, but the optimism lacks any *idealistic* quality, and is comfortably subsumed under the F trait, the 'will to believe'.

balance between positive and negative feelings in the child:

> The parent gives conditional love when he gives love only as a reward
> for conformity to desired patterns of behavior, and withdraws it as
> punishment for nonconformity. The child is thus taught to control his
> wishes for love and also his tendency to give love. At the same time
> he is taught to tolerate a certain amount of punishment and to
> administer it himself in the 'training' of others. This mode of control
> may be applied so exclusively and literally by some parents that the
> child is trained to ignore or bypass other normal modes of control
> through integration within his own personality: the higher mental
> processes of reflective thought; fantasy; the involvement of the self
> and the evolving self-picture; the introduction of variation; testing of
> reality limits; experimentation and creative re-combination.[33]

He identifies less with either parent than with the compulsions and
constraints placed on action by common values and social norms,
although he tends to become like his parents, and is proud of having taken
over his standards from them. (For details of predicted and presented
parental traits, see table 6).

The major novelty, and it may be an important one, that Lake's case
throws up is the suggestion that conformism, and especially its *cheerful*
variety, may be a painfully and laboriously *constructed* position, following
a murderously hostile episode, whose very extremity frightens the child
back into submission as the only bearable course.

Table 6. *Lake as F: parental traits*

Bales's F	Lake
Both parents:	Both parents:
* Are alike, and have similar effects on the child	* Full attitudinal agreement. But the father is notably preferred — indeed, identified with
* Use conditional love; they are low on resources for overcoming negativism and anxiety; they give approval rather than love	* They *may* use conditional love, but at the warmer end of the category
Father:	Father:
* High on inhibitory demand/discipline	Low on inhibitory demands
* High on optimistic idealism	* Insufficient information
* Low on emotional supportiveness/warmth	* Moderate emotional warmth
Mother:	Mother:
* High on optimistic idealism	* Insufficient information
* Average on inhibitory demands/discipline	* Seems moderate to high on inhibitory demands
* Low on emotional supportiveness/warmth	* Moderate emotional warmth

Grove as Passive Resister — DB

Grove, a third-year Harvard medical student, is a political liberal, 'highly in favour of *Labor, Classless Society*, and *Communism vs Fascism*' and strongly negative on *Businessman* and *Capitalism*. He is, however, apathetic and indifferent towards the war and its issues, and his political and religious sentiments are low-key and unworked — 'Only in rare instances,' he says, 'am I so strongly convinced of any belief that I would be willing to argue it with others.' Incapable of moral indignation, he 'hates' Nazi ideology, but 'can't get up enough spirit' to wish to enlist, and inclines to the judgment that Hitler is no worse than many another leader. He dislikes *Americanism*, 'super-patriots and rabble-rousers', but is concerned that his pacifist stand is isolating; he feels implicated in 'whatever happens to this country ... this mess, which is my fault as much as anyone else's', and fears that, if he does not fight, he 'will not have contributed to the organism to which [I] belong', and will not find — or deserve — a comfortable place in post-war society. He confesses, however, that he cannot conceive of anything except his family for which he would be willing to risk his life.

His leftist sentiments are casual and shallow. Although mildly in favour of socialist reform, he does not seek, or even seem to miss, a coherent world view. He simply negates or inverts the opinions of his Republican father, a successful Californian businessman, who has been antipathetic to him from the beginning. He has little taste for ideological thinking, no disposition to identify himself with any cause, and, indeed, little capacity to view the world from an impersonal standpoint, sociological or political. He dislikes philosophy and scholarship, and is sceptical of the power of thought to settle, or even illuminate, anything. He applauds imagination, intuition and spontaneity. He is mildly interested in psychology and psychiatry, but his approach is reductionist and deflating, devoid of idealism. He has no personal interest in religion, but believes it socially useful: 'It's a unifying force. It's something people can fall back on in time of need, in time of emergency. It explains a great many points that government can't explain... It is all embracing. It is an international thing, an organization above governments.' His parents did not attend church or discuss religion at home, though his mother, a convinced pacifist, 'always talked of the evil of killing anything', and taught him that war was 'primitive and barbaric'. His own Episcopalian contacts proved, if comforting, 'rather barren... There [was] nothing to fear or worship in the mystical and emotional way that a child seems to relish.'

Murray is brisk about Grove's character. His main trait is passivity — 'behind his personable exterior and friendly manner is an aversion to life born of an inveterate inertia coupled with timidity and ineffectiveness'. 'I hesitate to make decisions,' he says, 'and prefer to let things take their course ... to let others take the initiative.' 'I seem to be afraid of life. At the present time I show signs of confusion and helplessness.'* 'I have a not unpleasant preoccupation with death.' Insecure, dependent, incapable of aggression, the character is built on mother-fixation and identification.

As long as he can remember, Grove feared and dreaded his father†; he dilates on capricious discipline, severe punishment, insult and rejection, maltreatment of mother, irascibility when drunk, brutal frankness and vulgarity. His TATs show much bitter father-son conflict and keen desires for revenge. With a large part of his personality, Grove wishes his father dead, but his aggression is so mixed with anxiety that, even in dreams, he cannot imagine injuring his father, or anyone else for that matter, with his own hands; the enemy must be killed by a machine, or by someone else, or by accident. Once he was less inhibited, and made two spirited attempts on his baby brother's life in his first months — by cramming him with food and dropping him — but this raw drive has long been buried under anxiety and passivity. (The brother soon outgrew him to become a sports hero and the apple of his father's eye.)

Yet there survives some residual affection and admiration for the father, and indeed some elementary dependence on him. 'Especially in the last three years I've realised what a fine man he is essentially... When it comes to the big things, you can rely on his being a big help.' The pattern they have established is based on the father's always assertive prescriptions. The son impulsively opposes his authority with passive negations (*passive resistance* is his life-skill); one of two results will follow. *Either* Grove is worn down (the father's case always weighs heavily) and gives in, thus reserving the right to blame his father if things go wrong, *or* Grove wins, and thus defeats himself, since the end result of passivity is lack of achievement and loss of self-esteem.

'My mother is one of the most perfect women in the world, and I have always been devoted to her', Grove says, and his TATs show no trace of un-

---

* He reported a grave anxiety-attack on hearing the news of Pearl Harbor. Walking back to his room that evening, he became aware of severe palpitation of the heart. He felt the earth falling away from under him and he thought of his mother miles away on the California coast. He went to bed but the anxiety persisted. He could not sleep. In desperation he woke his roommate and begged him to sit up with him for the rest of the night. He could not bear to be alone. The following day similar sensations recurred and it was a week or more before he became tolerably composed... Claustral anxiety and deep fears of unsupportedness also occur in a dream of that time — of floating into a cafeteria and through a round air-vent into the kitchen, and then back again, passing through the same hole into the outside air.

† For six months or so around the age of eight, he led a group of neighbourhood children in 'worshipping' a fearsome idol ensconced in a 'temple' in an old garage on a vacant lot (in 'fascinated fear of the dark and dangerous power which he sensed in his father').

conscious hostility. 'I retain a childish desire to be with her whenever I am in trouble or have to make a decision.' He has never felt she was unstable, unjust, domineering or interfering. Although she praised him 'a lot', she has never been physically demonstrative and never demanded much outward affection from him; as he grew up he had the sense that his love was freely given.

Their strong attachment is founded primarily on the dependence of babyhood, and on fears of the strange and threatening world outside the region of her protecting presence.* The attachment exhibits a pattern of succour and nurture with the parent and the child taking alternating roles, each sympathising with the other when circumstances seem to justify it (the parents have spent years, and remain, on the edge of divorce). This hardly nourishes, Murray tartly observes, an independent, courageous confrontation of life's difficulties and dangers.

Grove as DB. Grove very snugly fits the description of the DB character — the Withholder of Co-operation: the 'male who . . . wants to be a mother', who, identifying with mother and children, wishes to show how wrong the punishment and aggression of a rejecting father were. Indeed, Bales actually predicts pacifist sentiments for this position, or membership of some radical religious sect; the psychological point of this is 'to unmask others' aggression'. He foresees the DB world view as often not highly elaborated.

The DB type also 'contains more of his aggression than do others'; he devalues the self; he is cynical and disillusioned, given to day-dreaming and, above all, is steeped in depression. Having become convinced the role of 'positive, creative, mothering, [and] nurturing' is unrealisable, he is disconsolate. (The actual early loss of the mother may be expected in some cases.) His sexuality, aggression and anxiety are all locked in depression, if not actually low to begin with.

Potentials in the character that Grove conspicuously does not take up, however, are (a) integrative harnessing of the drives in 'creative dreaming', actual creativity and, in groups, leadership of a prophetic type, and (b)

---

* His current romantic fantasies have a quality of backward-looking: return to the mother, the womb and death. In one TAT story a man goes to the graveyard to talk to the dead. A young girl answers him from the grave and asks him to join her. The apparition of the young girl rising out of the tomb so overcomes him that he dies.

As a child, Grove says, his favourite book was *The Black Arrow*, and his favourite incident in it, the hero getting off his horse to embrace his love as she dies. It is a matter of interest that no such death takes place in *The Black Arrow*: it is the hero's wicked guardian who dies in the hero's arms. Did Grove misremember the book, or did Murray mishear him? No doubt Grove would find the fantasy of the hated father's abdication quite as affecting as that of a 'dying together' with the beloved mother.

the courting of others' aggression: he may make a dramatic show of his willingness to receive punishment. 'He is a natural victim or scapegoat... Other more active types are probably more often the scapegoat. But in a certain context, he "interposes" himself... The relevant context is one in which aroused aggressive feelings of group members are moralistically bound by a task-effort for the group as a whole (as in a war effort), and the DB member tries to show that their expression of aggression does not deserve moral legitimization.'[34] His dragging his feet symbolises the

Table 7. *Grove as DB: parental traits*

Bales's DB	Grove
Mother:	Mother:
* Moderately low on inhibitory demands and discipline	* Very low on inhibitory demands and discipline: 'Mother would never spank us. First she'd start to, and then she'd get to thinking how funny she looked and start laughing... It's lucky that my mother didn't have charge of bringing us up entirely'
* Average emotional supportiveness and warmth	* Unusually deep and stable relationship
Father:	Father:
* So antipathetic as to make assumption of the adult male sex-role difficult	* Perhaps antipathetic, but the son retains residual admiration, affection and elementary dependence
Both parents:	Both parents:
* Moderately pessimistic/cynical	* Father may be inferred to have been cynical. Otherwise no evidence
* Non-idealistic	* Mother pacifist
* Rather passive non-conformists	* Father a good deal more colourful
* Inhibited and internally divided	* Mother's nervous breakdown
* Interact little with each other or children	* Constant discord — and, on the positive side, the son sees the family as 'close': 'our family had a great deal of pleasure together'
* Standards poorly developed, non-consensual; neglectful rather than disciplining and rewarding on performance	* Father, although capricious, keeps up solid pressure for adequate performance
* Much plain chaos in relations with children (too many of them, separations, ill-heath)	* Framework of resilient routine accommodates mother's ill-health and absence, father's drunkenness, and the divorce that is always in the air

reservations of half or more than half of the group under task – or con-servative – pressure. 'So far as he succeeds, the aggression in others is left unbound, and it is displaced upon him instead of the enemy for whom it is prepared.'[35] Self-immolation, by fire or starvation is a possibility. A minor feature which one does not much see in Grove is that of the gullible lamb 'unprotected against [the] wolves of the radical left'[36] – partly because of his high intelligence and partly because of his sceptical aversion to moralism and ideologising. ('There is probably some connec-tion between the fact that he holds to no abstract ethical principles and the fact that he dislikes his father', Murray notes.)

On the other hand, Grove considerably enriches the description of the DB type with, first of all, a number of aphorisms, where 'no actual examples of value statements which express this direction are available from factor-analytic studies'. (For example, 'few beliefs I'd argue for', 'family [properly, mother] only object I'd risk life for', 'thinking settles nothing', 'have a not unpleasant preoccupation with death'.) Grove provides too a strong hint that the mother-identification may direct voca-tional choice into work that ministers directly to her expressed or imputed needs. (Grove's mother had a long neurotic illness ('caused by the father') and left her son with the fear that she might die of heart disease.) And, most importantly, he presents the possibility, within the general rubric of the position, of an alternative nucleus of passivity and inertia instead of depression (although, of course, the two are linked). In Grove, we have 'feet-dragging' on a scale that amounts to an 'aversion to life'. Where the central fantasy is of a lost Eden, every way forward must seem to lead downhill.

The family constellation that throws up the DB type, Bales says, is the 'rewarding mother but no father', or 'the father ... rejected as a model of positive identification'.[37] He posits also moderately high discrepancies between the parents. The minor-trait predictions are less firmly fulfilled (see table 7). What Grove contributes to the nexus of family possibilities are: first, the crossed-identification two-sibling family pattern in par-ticularly sharp form, with the parents actively cultivating the children's bias – to the point where the father is envious of the mother's attention to Grove (although Grove insists that she treated both sons perfectly even-handedly); and second, the passive containment of even very strong anti-authority impulses when the father is accorded the residual moral edge.

Murray's other seven cases

Murray's remaining seven cases were all described in a plausible and enlightening way, and each of them fitted neatly into a different niche in Bales's scheme. The process of sorting can, however, become tedious, and I therefore deal summarily with the remaining cases, which extend our sense of the scheme by approximating a position already sketched, but in an appreciably more 'ascendant' form.

Hawk, a young man with a 'God complex',[38] wants eventually to become a politician, after training in commerce and law. A Democrat with socialist learnings, a 'New Dealer plus', he has an outstanding record as a leader of his peers, an unusually strong reality-sense and an air of creative promise. He is the second son of upper-middle-class Prussian parents who emigrated to New York soon after their marriage. The father, now an invalid, was slowly defeated by business reverses and has turned in on himself. The mother, to whom Hawk feels closer, is 'nervous and emotional' and 'over-solicitous', and has passed on her own unfulfilled ambition to her son.

Hawk fits the UP — Friend to All — prescription rather loosely; he is less interested in 'social success' or 'popularity' than in tangible power. He is not clearly 'group-identified', nor out to lead in the 'good and benign parent' or 'receptive' style. Though he is certainly 'extravert' and 'exo-cathective', his principal defence-mechanism is hardly 'repression of negative feelings'. What fits best, however — and this is central to the personality — is 'an over-expanded self-image' and a disposition to 'over-rate his value to, and status in, the group'. Hawk presents a veritable Kohutian 'grandiose self' in search of its social mirror, and indeed (following Lasswell) 'deference' seems to be his prime demand: a migrant child who (as so often) in unfamiliar terrain has come to father his parents; a younger son in a family where a flight to autonomy is seen as the heroic path; a second-born who has somehow made himself the cynosure of the family and overtaken not only the first-born, but the father as well. In choosing politics as a vocation, he is essentially proposing to widen his circle of admirers from the original family to the community at large. In this ambition he has been confirmed by his effortless dominance over his adolescent peers; this gives his ambition a thoroughly reasonable appearance.

With much the same forensic ideology* as Ingle, we judge Hawk to be slightly more ascendant. Ingle, though hardly modest in his intellectual

---

* Why should Hawk, whose parents are conservative, and who has his own eye on business success and a name in the legal world, wish to speak for equalitarianism? One feels that in his zeal for advancement he would espouse whatever is in vogue with the New York Democratic Left. But it is possible that some element is personal — the legacy, perhaps, of brief years of inferiority.

Table 8. *Location of Murray's cases in the Bales frame*

UP	UPF	UF	UNF	UN	UNB	UB	UPB
Hawk	—	York	—	Shea	Yawl	—	—
P	PF	F	NF	N	NB	B	PB
Ingle	Nack	Lake	—	Couch	—	—	—
DP	DPF	DF	DNF	DN	DNB	DB	DPB
—	Finch	Dunn	—	—	—	Grove	—

powers or ambitions, cheerfully envisages a career as policy adviser; Hawk wants to be out there in front, publicly acknowledged and acclaimed as the policy *maker*.

York also foreshadows a political career like Ingle's as an international civil servant, but the man to compare him with is Lake, for he too is conformist, a conservative with no equalitarian impulses or labour sympathies and an individualist taste for 'ambition and initiative and everything'. He is, however, an articulate and principled defender of non-conformity, and a warmer conservative than Lake; his perspective, both global and domestic, is broader, and tinged with optimistic idealism. He is studying German, intends to enlist on graduation, and, after the war, hopes to help in the reconstruction of Europe.

By far the poorest of Murray's subjects — the son of a parcel deliveryman in Boston — he lives at home and has earned his own way through school and college. Both parents are the children of Lutheran pastors, but his mother, a college graduate and ex-schoolteacher, is the dominant partner, and the pressure of her unrelenting ambition for him has been 'like a whip daily driving him to do his utmost'. He admires his mother's drive and realism, but judges her somewhat unloving and her discipline both mechanical and over-strict.

York fits the UF Loyalist prescription — 'moving towards group loyalty and co-operation' — most precisely in his attitude towards the war: he is the most simply patriotic of Murray's men. His personality also broadly fits the UF position; we may contrast his strong sense of self and of transcending his origins with the carefully acquired stolidity of Lake (plain F). His ideology fits, too; he is robustly and durably conservative in politics and religion. Yet he does not quite take the high ground of the UF position as Bales describes it: that is, identification with the 'larger plan'. Some leading traits match up with those predicted: his belief in holding negative feelings in check and 'smooth conventional control of a rather high level of aggression'; his will to achieve and to move impulse rapidly into action; his seriousness and humourlessness. But he disappoints other predictions; for example, that of being 'internally conflicted . . . not very well put together', that of specialising in mediation, and that of being sophisticated. Yet we do find in York's case the UF type's vital spur: the parents are so unsatisfactory, and even so discordant, as models with which to identify, that some generalised higher authority (or wider external group) is pressed into service as the focus of the individual's strivings. (A schoolmaster, not his parents, was the source of his plan to train in German.) Bales predicts the crucial deficiency of affection in York's upbringing, and its legacy: the same deficiency in the adult self. The family constellation, Murray says, has created such a strong need for achievement and recognition, such a strong ego-ideal, that the affectional capacities have been outbalanced.

Shea, a monomaniac and highly gifted young biologist, demonstrates that even Couch can be surpassed in egocentric isolationism. Shea has turned his back not only on the war, but on human society itself: 'The world, even in a social sense, is to me, inanimate.' He works obsessionally and aggressively, one of his strengths as a scientist being this very drive to shatter the false beliefs, proofs and premises of others. (He thinks poorly of Harvard teaching and of Harvard in general; Murray, in his turn, votes Shea the most unco-operative Clinic subject ever.) A lone wolf, his character is a wall of resistance and protectiveness; his sentiments are stubbornly negative and defiantly opposed to what others most value. A 'furious ego drive', 'rigid repressions', and 'a poverty of emotional and imaginal development' are Murray's summary.

His childhood was 'never happy'. His father, an embittered, and finally paranoid, journalist, largely ignored him. His mother, possessive, hard-driving, cold and stern, herself from a background of stark poverty, 'holds him to the iron rails of her ambition' by a 'bitter and relentless compact'.

Shea admirably exhibits the key features of the UN character—organised for cold assertiveness: these features are ambition, determination and will; total concern for the self and disregard of others; provocative tough-mindedness and absorption in the practical and the material; readiness to hate, scorn and ridicule; in short, identification, openly and proudly, with the power of aggression. These are already welded into a *vocational* purpose and style. As predicted, his main defence is repression of the polar type DP — characterised by tender, affectionate and 'feminine' feelings — until he reaches a chilling degree of what Murray calls 'anti-intraceptive-ness'.

His childhood background is one of exactly that maximum coldness hypothesised, where high demands outweigh limited affection, punishment is preferred to reward, and the harsh, intrusive and threatening promptings of the parents (and their lodgement in the super-ego) take on a somewhat persecutory quality. The Oedipal conflict is resolved by precocious independence, an early and stable devaluation of both parents, and an ego-autonomy built on rage and disappointment.

A fourth case, again primarily to be compared with the stolid Lake (F), exemplifies a more submissive and defeated conformist stance. Dunn is, in fact, a moderate socialist, but, cautious and personally depressed, he looks forward a little glumly to a career as a Government official. His political line is some way to the right of his father's, although Dunn is still closely attached to him. The father is described as a liberal Democrat manager, who was 'a struggling, upward-mobile optimist until the Depression came to strip him of all his earnings' and left him a bitter suburban 'revolutionary'. Dunn came to Harvard to do Arts with a business career in mind but, under his teachers' influence, he has switched to the project of reforming bureaucrat.

Outwardly popular and successful — he is a notable athlete — he is privately depressed, bitter and deeply dissatisfied with himself, complaining of half-heartedness, paralysis of emotion and will, a congenital pessimism and a corrosive scepticism which allows him nothing to admire. Hyper-correct in appearance and manner,* dutiful, and somewhat obsessional, he is given to ruminative and permanently inconclusive theorising, and has something of a 'purity complex'.

Bales describes DF — the Obsessional Compulsive — as '"plowing ahead," like a ship in heavy seas, persistently, even obsessively, on the task'.[39] DF is serious, work-oriented, indeed, a compulsive worker. Ever self-examining,† he is deadlocked between a drive to settle his thinking once and for all and a compulsion immediately to unpick the product, an urge to uncover his basic feelings but simultaneously to bury them deeper — he is deadlocked in a paralysis of motivation. Inhibition of aggression *and sexuality* lies at the root of the personality, underpinning the very archetype of the 'cautious administrator' (Lasswell): most docile in accepting authority, affectively neutral, fearful of disapproval and guilt, and (on the positive side) stable, determined and responsible.

Dunn, who so far fits best with his Bales type, also exhibits an upbringing exactly in line with that predicted — the 'conditional love' kind (see above, p. 146), where reward and punishment have been 'impartially meted out according to his degree of conformity with parental requirements'.[40] Inhibited and introverted themselves, the parents interact little with the child; they punish perhaps by silence or withdrawal, but above all they punish impulsively and without explanation, reacting 'to a compulsive pressure toward inhibition whenever the offending wish, act, or impulse' springs up in the child.[41] The child realises he has done *something* wrong and must inhibit, but precisely what it is he is left to wonder.

> The motivation for self-awareness, self-analysis, the spreading uncertainty about what to do, the pervading sense of doubt, the urgent need

* One is reminded of the young Hiss (see above, pp. 54–7) by Murray's description of Dunn striving assiduously for conspicuous success — in sports and club membership as well as study — as if 'to regain, if not to surpass, his family's former social status by "making good" at school and college'. Outstandingly conformist in manner, his need for social approval runs hand in hand with an unconscious and denied over-valuation of conventional standards. Another unpreferred son, he resembled Hiss also in the sharp split between his public and his private selves; practised dissemblers, they move rapidly between a correct and dutiful exterior and a secret, resentful and hostile core.

† Bales's position-tag, 'Towards Self-knowledge and Subjectivity', is somewhat misleading if it suggests that we are dealing here with the foundations of philosophical or psychological creativity: the DF project is joyless, typically unproductive, something merely plugged away at — in short, neurotically self-questioning.

to look to some other for leadership, to ask for suggestion, all may
have some such base.[42]

Even behaving correctly may bring little or uncertain reward. The parents
do not provide enough love to overcome their negative images, and leave
the child half-loving, half-hating, uncertain and inhibited. He may hold
hopeful and idealistic ideas in the conscious part of his mind, but he will
be unable to keep entirely repressed the crawling hostilities and negative
feelings from which his parents have failed to rescue him. (Murray notes
that Dunn's TAT stories contain more implicit blame of parent-figures
than any 'in the entire collection'.)

But Dunn has even more than the standard 'conditional love' ambivalence. He reads his mother's preference for a younger brother as a *betrayal*
making his own life-project barely worth-while. Bales sets at the core
of the DF type an inability to win through to a sense of the self as an
'exerciser of voluntary control' and purpose, and remaining, therefore,
a life-long *agent*. Dunn's central complaint is a shade darker: it is that
of deadened feeling, aspiration cut off at the root, depersonalisation of the
personal core — a depression strikingly like that of the DB type, Grove,
above.

> The most salient opposite figure to the DF [type] is possibly the DB
> [type], who is similar to him in degree of inhibition but takes an
> opposite solution by hanging back from task commitment instead of
> plowing into it . . . They are very visible contrasts and dramatize . . .
> the difference between the 'faithful servant' and the 'reluctant' one.[43]

Pitching in, instead of hanging back, seems developmentally related
to father-identification. Grove shows no identification, while Dunn is
quite positively identified, although his father's vocational collapse has
caused him serious difficulty.

Our last three cases open two new meridians, PF and NB, and offer a
glimpse of an antipodean relationship between two positions, UNB and
DPF. We start with the most ascendant case.

On his eighteenth birthday, Yawl threw up his course and enlisted as
an Air Force pilot. He is a would-be novelist — emotional, impulsive and
powerfully attracted to the prospect of change, sensation and excitement.
His outlook is militantly egocentric; as a schoolboy he idolised Byron —
the current model is D. H. Lawrence. He is diffusely radical, although
social issues barely engage him, since his interest is focused very sharply
on the psychology of character and personal relationships. Murray dubs
his temperament profoundly Rousseauian, 'preoccupied with his individual sensibility and individual will', with the tension between them and the
fixed order of society, and with the eager accumulation of aspects of experience that are conventionally denied or devalued.

The product of a long-standing father-son conflict, much in Yawl's
outlook is shaped by explicit and violent recoil from his businessman

father's ineffectuality, his bland Rotarian conventionality and his Babbitt-like preoccupations. The son rebels against all forms of authority, and, intent on 'self-expression, and the living of the good, free, uninhibited life', plans in due course to write novels that will relentlessly expose the hollowness of conventional life.

The eldest of five children, Yawl resembles his mother in appearance and temperament. However, they have been locked in a prolonged struggle over his failure to contain his aggression and 'furious temper'. There is evidence of trauma from weaning and from the birth of siblings, 'with felt deprivation of love (i.e. partial rejection by both parents)', leaving repressed passivity and dependency needs. The reaction-formation, based on pride and narcissism, is compounded of basic needs for rejection, autonomy, aggression and recognition — the boy having learnt that the only way to attract notice in his family was to do something startling or provoking.* Although he has some residual affection for his mother, he is doing his best to sever himself from all that his parents stand for and to look in precisely the opposite direction for a way of life.

Yawl makes a first-class UNB — 'towards rugged individualism and gratification' — the Law-unto-himself type, whose central project Bales defines as becoming identified with the power to defy authority and rise above and outside the law. The position 'fuses ascendance, both of social role and instinctual gratification, with a negative attitude toward social conventions, as well as toward others as a group'.[44] He is aware that he is regarded as an outlaw, and likes to be provocative about it; he champions the free expression of tendencies that are normally repressed, particularly those that involve sex and aggression. Developmentally, the UNB project takes shape as the counteractive rejection of the polar DPF path, that of 'the good boy' who has allowed himself to be deprived of his masculinity and has submitted in a loving and feminine way to the demands of the autocratic father. Unconsciously tempted to take the 'slave's way out', UNB consciously cultivates his 'eccentricity' and unconcern, while certain 'paranoid' tendencies testify to the survival — and strength — of the disowned temptations and to signal feelings of threat that they may yet break through. Murray, indeed, finds a core of 'passive fatalism' in Yawl, the 'shadow self of a rebellious individualist'. *Pride*, he insists, is the key to him: 'the desire to maintain self-respect by action (when not doing the thing would signify lack of courage and so provoke contempt of self)'.

---

* Murray pursues this trend further into his 'Don Juanism': Yawl reacted to the usual infantile traumatic situations with pride, narcissism and the need to reject. 'His feeling, however, remained attached to the mother image. The longing to return to her, coupled with counteraction against his own passivity, has forced him to look elsewhere for his ideal. He is searching for a lost feeling connected with woman. This accounts for his interest in subjective values and for the particular emphasis which he puts on erotic love.'

His upbringing is also reasonably in line with that predicted for the type — though Bales himself seems uneasy that a parental picture apparently so mildly alienating should produce so alienated a type; this includes discipline slightly outrunning love, and parental traits, inadequacies or mistakes which teach or force the child 'to develop a pattern of reliance upon himself'.[45]

If the breadth of Yawl's alienation sweeps him impatiently past any political concerns, a degree of embeddedness — in vocation and filial relation — seems in the case of Murray's last two subjects to have prevented their even sighting the political realm: it is religion that draws them.

Nack, a pacifist medical student, simply ignores the war's existence and gets on with his work. Medicine has long appealed to him for two reasons: before her marriage, his mother had planned to study medicine, and during his childhood she herself was often sick. If he were forced to declare his politics, it would be the rural conservatism — individualist and isolationist — of his Vermont farmer father, but the deep piety of his religious stance stems from his closer, indeed reverential, tie to his mother. His pacifism Murray attributes less to fear of being hurt than to fear of hurting and performing 'sadistically' like his father.

An excellent illustration of Bales's PF type, the Idealiser — 'toward a kind of dedicated, quiet, altruistic love' — Nack does, indeed, see himself as the 'good child of a good parent'. Having experienced the power of goodness in his own life, he believes in its power to make things right in the world. Optimistic idealism pervades his thinking, which at times borders on the 'false positive', the dangerous tendency to 'overlook, deny, or beautify the negative and the ascendant when it is associated with parental figures, with group norms, and with symbols of higher authority'.

The upbringing hypothesised is accurate enough in broad plan, requiring a loved parent who is identified with an abstract symbol of higher authority (for example, religion, the law or the nation) and who is thus able to bring 'the powerful forces of affection and identification to the service of abstract ideals'.[46] This is essentially a training in the ability to idealise. But the hypothesis goes astray in details: the spur is *not*, in Nack's case, 'an easy and successful process of identification . . . with the parent of the same sex' and 'a relatively unproblematic taking-over of . . . the masculine role by the male child'.[47] Nack's mother, not his father, is the significant parent. The parents, too, are not alike and of one mind, but 'as different as black from white'. And Nack's mother not only loves, but binds and drives her son.

Finally, Finch, an eager, timid Arts student, who is so frightened of being called up that he enrols in theological school to be exempt, even though he is not sure of his religious belief. He is abjectly identified with an imposing clergyman father. Without political convictions and particularly 'any view that might impose participation [in the war] as a duty', Finch's social views are humanitarian and vaguely liberal: 'He sides in general with the upper middle class.' At the age of twelve he had a mystical experience in church: it seemed that 'for one instant God appeared to him in the guise of his father'. And his picture of his father remains astonishingly idealised. In one sense he has never really differentiated himself from this 'wonderful' being; they have the same sentiments, the same calling. However, he openly dislikes his mother, an aggressive disciplinarian and intrusive worrier; the females in his TATs are dominant, coercive, restraining or undisguisedly malicious. There is no trace in his fantasies of overt heterosexuality; in fact, oral homosexual preoccupations point to a classic inverted Oedipus complex.

Finch rather splendidly exemplifies Bales's DPF — the Faithful Servant (or, more sharply, Castrate) type, the good boy who has allowed himself to be deprived of his masculinity, and has submitted in a loving and feminine way to the demands of the autocratic father. Finch seems to 'depend for his self-picture on the power to be both good and submissive'.[48] In outlook, the DPF is on the side of authority, sublimation and the control of impulse; he is very faintly equalitarian. Bales describes in more detail the beliefs of the 'tender-minded conservative':

> He tends to downgrade the importance of power, aggression, and material wealth in human affairs. 'Our present difficulties are due to moral rather than economic causes.' His moralism, though definitely present, is submissive and positively oriented to other people — even toward those who transgress and may actually be threats.*[50]

Finch's upbringing is exactly that hypothesised (although Bales, in deference to readers' susceptibilities, softens the part of his text which might be found too unflattering, and speaks only of experiences of copious, undeserved and unconditional love from the parents — experiences which exact close identification with the parents, and also prodigies of dutiful inhibition). The reader may care at this point to recall to mind Yawl, our antithetical UNB type.

A review of the test
Ideally, to absorb case material and learn from it, one may require a certain superfluity of detail, leaving room for impressions and imaginative efforts somewhat independent of the case-writer's. The need to be concise (especially in the last seven cases) has meant a painful jettisoning of detail that

---

* These phrases imply something very close to the point made by Ernest Jones in his celebrated essay, 'The psychology of Quislingism' (1941).[49] The refusal by Finch, here, to make enemies of or to see as evil the Germans or the Japanese makes Jones's point exactly. We shall see, however, that such a refusal is rather more centrally the impulse of DNF, a variant of the authoritarian personality.

is not only intrinsically interesting, but also perhaps vital to the reader's full imaginative understanding of each subject. It would be ironic if this exercise in ruthless filing, designed to allay the anxiety that political psychology cases must inevitably ramify in unending miscellaneity, had merely reinforced some such sense. However brief these lives, they at least put a face to eleven of the conceptual boxes of table 4. In sorting them, I have been impressed and delighted (in a way my text may not reflect) not only by the frequent exact correspondences — suggesting even at times that Bales must have had, for example, Lake, Dunn, Nack or Finch in mind as he wrote — but also by the way that cases *in the process* of being considered as possible instances of these types take on a trimness and definition, a manipulability and readiness to be compared and filed.

It also helped, I think, that the cases were a set, a collection of near-equals. While one might, in the abstract, hesitate in deciding whether Ingle was P or UP, Couch N or UN, they were plainly less ascendant than their fellows, York and Shea. And each, by his reaction to the common ordeal of expected war-service, took up a characteristic 'self as national' stance, which was not only starkly diagnostic, but stood in for Bales's indispensable category of 'style in the group'. Indeed, several of these men (Yawl, York, Finch and Couch, for example) declared their character *at once* in their attitude to the war. It was impressive, too, how choice of vocation in each case linked up with and refined the basic value-position. A casual reading of Bales may have left a picture of N, for instance, in terms of his occupation, as a run-of-the-mill individualist entrepreneur (like Collins's men; see above, pp. 63–4). Couch and Shea show us how militant egocentricity can be intricately bound up with careers in science and the arts. Yawl finds in writing a way to pillory his parents; Finch finds in the ministry a career 'sweetening the yoke'. Our three would-be administrators (Ingle, York and Dunn) show how scripts which are frankly personal can be accommodated by that comprehensive frame; in Hawk we are lucky to net an accomplished agitator — although somewhat opaque as to issue and affect.

If the test report has skimped case detail, it has also pared down the type-descriptions. I have merely given the general 'feel' of each, skipping many of the alternatives they contain, as well as much listing of traits, and much of the full (and rather mechanical and fallible) predictions of childhood circumstance.* It may help, all the same, to imagine Bales placing

* Just as the value sphere is predicated on the three value axes, Bales has a supporting 'childhood climates' sphere, using the axes: discipline — indulgence (UN — DP), warmth — coldness (UPB — DNF), optimism — pessimism (PF — NB); each childhood setting (with separate predictions usually for each parent) has determinately high, average or low quantities of each. Auxiliary assumptions are: that a surplus of discipline over warmth produces anxiety, and that the level of anxiety determines 'whether the basic sexual drives are released

at the centre of each of his types as he constructs it a frozen moment, as it were, of socialisation — a crucial moment around which the style of that type coheres. I think the Dunn material (p. 146 above) most clearly catches this artful projection, although it is to be found in every type, and remains the best assurance that one has properly seized the point of each.

It is difficult to know how much a single case can, or should, disturb the balance of a type. I have therefore not made much of discrepancies. But Murray's cases do demand both additions and subtractions. Through Ingle, for example, one could add to P the option of a fully-wrought equalitarian ideology, fuelled by covert aggression against the father; through Couch, one could add to N the choice of independence *for creativity*; through Lake, one could add to F the sub-type of the compulsively cheerful conformist who has passed through a childhood episode of murderous hostility; through Grove, one could add to DB the sense of a reluctance to become engaged graduated by the strength (though it is always low) of positive identification with the father; through Hawk, one could add to UP a more manipulative and power-seeking and, as it were. professionally pleasing sub-type; through Dunn — and Hiss — one could add to DF the burden of a failed father, the project of family-status reparation and the traitor's split between dutiful front and secret, hostile core.

One hesitates even more about subtracting from types. However, Nack, a perfect PF, identifies with his mother, not his father; the PF prescription ought therefore to be enlarged to include this possibility. The case of Dunn, a plain DF type, suggests that the tag 'towards self-knowledge and subjective completeness' might be more prosaically rewritten as 'neurotic self-questioning'. Finch, the DPF type, shows that 'willing submission' can be adopted in an extreme form without the melodramatic rescuer-and-salvation fantasies which the type-description at present includes.

More generally, the cases suggest that the image of the parents in relation to other siblings — a matter on which Bales is silent, and even Murray a little lax — may be almost as fateful as the image of the parents as spouses. Thus Dunn and Grove harbour grievances about maternal betrayal, while Hawk treasures the sweetness of maternal preference. This point seems more informative, and perhaps easier to settle, than the question of whether the parents are harmonious or discordant, similar or discrepant, optimistic or cynical, which is so emphasised at present. It would be helpful, too, to know if narcissism is as unrelated to position as intelligence is said to be.

Bales's scheme, having passed a first test for inclusiveness and clarity,

(Footnote continued)
into the derivative and sublimated forms of affectionate feeling, or whether they remain anchored in more primitive forms of expression'; that parents on the P side are regularly described as similar, on the N side as discrepant; and that parents will be (described as) much like the subjects themselves.

may now be used for a more ambitious and specifically political exercise in cumulative comparison.

Politics down the meridians

A special feature of Bales's scheme is his nominating fifteen positions as intrinsically political ones, following the clue that much in the politics of small groups closely mirrors the national political stage in cast and plot, throwing up groupings that demand to be called, for example, Far Left, Far Right, Liberal Centre, Conservative Centre, and so on (see figure 6). Political psychologists may be wary of turning exclusively to those who might be thought of as the regular consumers of politics. Political psychologists are, after all, interested from time to time in events whose reception is near-universal and in the immunity of many to particular agitations. There is, however, an obvious economy in electing to work first where the soil is believed to be richest, and setting aside for the time being positions possibly too dejected or withdrawn or too ruthlessly self-absorbed to have much energy left for public affairs.

In this part we therefore present a further 24 cases, grouped about Bales value-positions, for detailed and thorough comparison. The cases are simply the classic political psychology cases, which have long challenged us to make something systematic of them without giving clues that would help to build such a system, and some new but accessible cases done

Figure 6. Political positions.

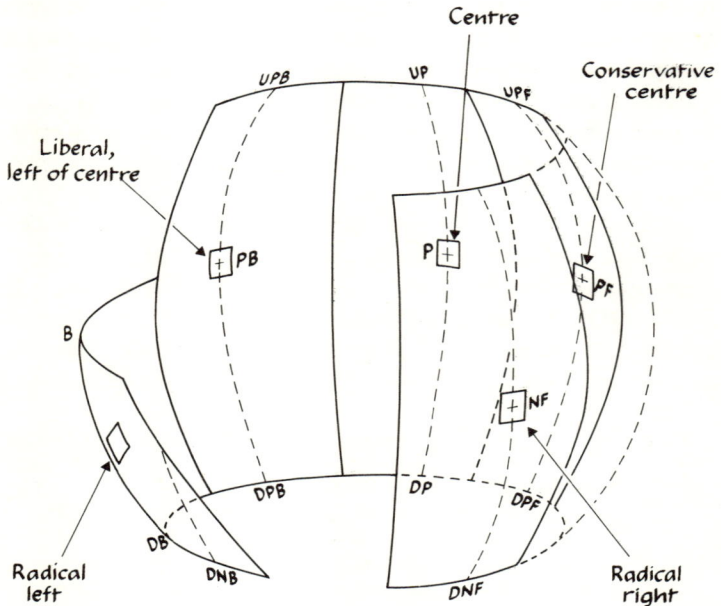

on traditional lines. The clusters into which they group, after being individually submitted to Bales's scheme, turn out to be at once like and unlike Bales's 'party' expectations. His Radical Right, the NF meridian, indeed comfortably contains our Authoritarians, but our Centrists converge on his F meridian, which is supposedly non-political, rather than the PF or P predicated; and we have had somewhat to re-group the Left half of the sphere, distinguishing Radicals centred on B from Alienates on DB, DNB and the supposedly non-political DN, and from the Liberáls or Democrats on the P and PB meridians. Disagreement, however, on these 'party' boundaries (presumably because small-group politics does not exactly correspond with national politics) is of small account compared with the opportunity that the Bales scheme affords of finding a precise place in a comprehensive scheme for every sufficiently-studied outlook, and of encouraging a richly discriminating comparison of apparently similar outlooks, by leading us beyond forensic into latent ideology, and beyond that into character, personality and general life-project and into the formative matrix of chidlhood.

The Conformists — the F meridian

Although Bales, as we have seen, does not think that F — the conventional conformist — is 'political', his scheme challenges us to make something psychologically of types we tend to take most for granted: the decent, limited, almost wholly predictable people who gravitate 'naturally' to positions of responsibility in community groups (churches especially, perhaps) and to office in local and regional government. The Murray cases we have already looked at — York, Lake and Dunn — afford a nice sense of sweep from hungry ambition through bland stolidity to rather glum conscientiousness. They provide a fair taste of lives, as it were, *in harness*, task-bound, literal-minded, and effective at the high cost of suppressing the personal. Their childhoods illustrate in concrete terms an upbringing in the conditional-love mode. However, as students — two of whom plan careers in public service (one vaguely socialist, one progressive conservative) while the third (blandly entrepreneurial) is aimed at a business career — they could hardly tell us much about the social processes or contexts of mature conformity, nor could they illumine Bales's important maxim that F is *orthodoxy in strictly local terms*.* Bearing in mind that conventions, for the conventional man, depend wholly on context,† and

---

* 'The spectrum from P, through F, to N, then, is the spectrum of complete universalism to complete individualism. Type F, in the middle, is presumably "particularistic" in a social sense.'[51]

† This is a simple point, but one which, when forgotten, is enough to vitiate a good deal of earnest social-psychological scale-building. One thinks, for example, of the New Zealanders in the *British Journal of Social and Clinical Psychology*, locked in a dispute about whether their fifty-item conservatism scale, when applied to members of real-life right-wing groups, does, or indeed

are therefore subsidiary to the tropism to conform itself, we turn now, for some light on the way in which conventionality is espoused, and the style in which it is embodied, to cases of Conventional Men offered by recent writers. (For further discussion of clinical and laboratory studies of conformism, see pp. 410—12.)

Smith's Lanlin as F

Interviewed at the Harvard Clinic over a long Cambridge winter in 1947, Charles Lanlin, a 41-year-old Boston Catholic salesman, came up as a notable conformist.[56] Smiling, sleek, smooth-fronted — given to light, double-breasted suits and bow-ties — he thoroughly enjoyed his inquisition. Although he had little enough to say about politics, which was hardly a leading interest, he enjoyed dilating on the pleasures of 'selling', and of being father to four children. He had been approached as a union activist and, indeed, had been one for eight years, but it turned out that he had recently given up that work when he became manager of one of the retail outlets of the household appliance firm he had worked for all his life. He was also the proud owner of three nearby shops — 'the property' left him by his father, rent from which, bringing him in about as much as his salary, firmly buttressed his lower-middle-class position. He was, in fact, about to become a leading figure (as his father had been before him) in his local chamber of commerce. 'I love my community', he confessed, and over the years he had served on numerous other neighbourhood associations.

His political ideology, largely subliminal, was that 'good business' — the reasonable pursuit of gain in a community of reasonable, like-minded men — 'meant the good life for all'. Government, especially, had to be kept running on sensible business lines to avoid natural tendencies to 'waste, foolishness, and inefficiency'. A good President — of the nation as of the company — assured contentment and drive. He supported social

(Footnote continued)
should, measure one thing or five[52] — or, more memorably, Herbert McClosky's first attempt to relate conservatism and personality, which found that high scorers on a 'Burkean' conservatism scale were alienated, hostile, suspicious, obstinate, compulsive, timid, submissive, and with a strong sense of personal worthlessness.[53]

On the other hand, in a much more promising attack, Berkowitz and Lutterman, working with a Wisconsin adult sample, found that those most active in local community affairs, though politically conservative and culturally conventional, were more altruistic, trusting, optimistic, and even, perhaps, more inner-directed than the average.[54] And McClosky, in a second and spirited attack, defined 'conformity' as holding beliefs adhered to by more than 70% of fellow citizens, and in national and Minnesotan samples found high conformers to be more optimistic, more altruistic and more at home in their society; more perspicacious and intellectually active; higher in self-esteem; 'well-integrated, candid, and willing to take risks'; more tolerant and trusting, and less rigid, anxious or paranoid.[55]

legislation for the working man, but as a 'business proposition'. He saw no conflict between business and labour that could not be worked out 'reasonably', by sitting round a table: most strikes are unnecessary. American business was the envy of the world; there was not one country that would not adopt 'our way of life' if it had the power to do so.

The investigators pressed him hardest on Russia — the focus of their study — but he could manage little more than the notion that it was a backward country of great resources and ignorant people, dominated by leaders of evil intent, whose motive was world domination. He thought that its threat to the U.S. was, however, of a kind that could be contained by firm action. Lanlin's Russia is basically an unruly, obstreperous child, really dependent on 'us', but nonetheless making 'unreasonable' demands. Firmness, 'education' and 'engineering know-how' will, however, eventually bring it up to scratch, for Russians basically admire us. Asked what he would do if he were head of the Russian government, Lanlin replied that he would 'Let them have religion. Let them have fair newspapers. Let them have education. Let there be an exchange of students ... Their boys will see how Americans really think, and when those boys grow up and become leaders, they'll be broader people for their visit to America and Russia will broaden.'

As Smith analyses his personality, Lanlin is intelligent, but at sea with abstractions: he performs best in detailed, concrete, ordered situations. He has a massive desire to please and be liked. He is always tactful, appears warm and interested, and has many pleasant acquaintances, but few, if any, friends. He holds a tight rein on his anger and hostility in the interests of smoothly flowing relationships and social approval. He is a man under firm — and gratifying — self-control, determined to be a 'good guy' and knowing exactly what this requires. A dependent person, for whom environmental support is crucial, he greatly enjoys having other people in turn dependent on him. Trusting, optimistic, conscientious, determined to be 'constructive', Smith yet detects in him a deep underlying tendency towards passivity.

Lanlin's father, a frugal, hard-working man, who had left school early, worked up to be manager of a suburban food-store, and, after a life-time's austerity and saving, finally acquired the freehold of a block of shops. Lanlin's energies, as far back as he could remember, were geared to reaching this rather reserved and (to him) awesome figure, and 'staying on the good side' of his more emotional, somewhat mercurial mother; he developed, he boasted, techniques of 'soft-soaping' her that usually got him his way. A highly dependent, passive, only child, he learned early to master and repress his aggressive and destructive tendencies by a form of reaction-formation that has 'reasonableness' as its motto. The decisions and the main thread of Lanlin's life were in his father's hands. He regrets, however, that his father did not push him further educationally than a year's business school. Even now, he feels that much of his good fortune is less his own than his father's doing, and as he grows older, he feels he is growing more and more like him. Certainly his 'business' outlook is a replica of his father's.

Smith suspects a strong fear of rejection by the father: 'My father never punished me, perhaps because, when he told me something he did not want me to do . . . [his] tone of voice was enough.' In Lanlin's TATs father-figures play a restrictive and threatening role, especially in regard to aggressive impulses. (In casting the U.S. as a strong man, and Russia as an unruly boy, he replays this childhood 'first reading' of basic relationships.)

He was much closer to his mother — confidant and comforter to her — and in her company developed his confidence in the efficacy of being a gradualist and a negotiator. Yet his mother could still punish and flare up in anger. She rarely did, yet the degree to which Lanlin avoided provoking his parents to hostile rejection attested his fear of it. Why did Lanlin give up so early any form of struggle and rebellion against his parents' authority? Why did he not assert himself more? It seems probable that rebelliousness was not stamped down ruthlessly in his earliest years, but rather eased out of him by degrees in a situation where, as an only child, he enjoyed and did not want to lose high gratification from his parents. His parents gave him enough, but his father was sufficiently distant to buy conformity gradually, outbidding the rewards of rebelliousness. Being his mother's confidant, too, though it was rewarding, may have developed in him an added feeling of responsibility. In asking for his sympathy, his mother was also asking for his support and help in 'keeping things going'.

The adult Lanlin continues to identify strongly with quietly powerful figures, now transformed into the image of top management. These figures now stand behind the system of values he takes to be the actual state of things and against which he sees the Russians fraudulently making their unreasonable demands. Reinforcing his tendencies to conform to the perceived demands of his parents were the understandings of the larger society: the roles of agitator, rebel, trouble-maker and Communist ran in the mould that Lanlin had early and decisively rejected.

> An early and unterminated dependency relation with his parents . . .
> left [him] with a predisposition to accept loyally the economic and
> religious order of the dominant society around him: a fusion of
> middle-class and Catholic values.

Smith, thus concerned to demonstrate the primacy of the personal roots of Lanlin's conformism over mere other-directedness or conscious design to adhere to beliefs of prime acceptability only, was perhaps lucky that a key sliver of ideology — the U.S.–Russia relationship — turned out so neatly interpretable in appropriate familial terms. But the real highlight of the case (already touched on above, pp. 84–5) is the analysis of how the present-day performance of the *ur*-conformist roles of *staff-association man* and *salesman* robustly satisfy the leading needs of the adult personality — needs for display, recognition and nurturance — within a master-frame of deference.

One could have wished (as ever, but especially here with the intensity of the research attack) for a richer account of Lanlin's childhood. Is it, one wonders, full enough even to reject for lack of confirmation the modest hypothesis that Lake (above, p. 146) gave us: that cheerful conformism

> may be a painfully and laboriously *constructed* position, following a murderously hostile episode, whose very extremity frightens the child back into submission as the only bearable course.

Unfortunately, we are left guessing.

Davies's Webb as F

The epitome of the 'delegate',[57] local member and parliamentary 'spectator' * this methodical and cautious Australian Country Party politician, aged 55, heavily lined, muscular, just under medium height, had been in Parliament for six years when first interviewed.[60] Sixteen years later, he still holds his seat. A perusal of his contributions to Hansard yields these principal ideas:

> First and foremost, a sense of special hardship — sometimes unnecessary and unjust hardship — facing country dwellers, not understood in the administration, or in the capital generally ... Present farm affluence was precarious — railway policy, for example, threatening it from one side, a rash immigration policy from the other. Only constant vigilance could prevent things slipping back. Science had somehow to be brought solidly to the land.

While he believes in the 'full reward for enterprise and initiative', he invokes the remedy of 'public provision' almost without limit.

---

* 'Spectators' are defined as 'low in activity and high in willingness to return'.[58] Superficially, Webb is more of a 'reluctant'[59] — rural, retired, with a thick network of local contacts; pushed into nomination, rather than seeking it; educationally limited, dutiful, eager to be of service, lacking social skills; but does not participate much in parliamentary work, and tends to silence and ritualism. Yet his determination *to stay there as long as possible* exculpates him, and requires the 'spectator' model. He does, indeed, enjoy the prestige and honour and privilege of admission to the Elect — and this may well 'assuage nagging doubts about his worth as a person'. However, although he contributes little to debate or legislation, he is no superficial 'socialiser' or 'tension-reducer'; there is in him a strong streak of implicit denigration of his fellow MPs, and his own energies flow rather into tireless electorate work and, every two years or so, quixotic stands as 'the man who says No'. He has also long aimed to be an MP; he tried first in his mid-twenties in the city.

> Only his party really stood for decentralization — in the sense of a
> really decisive shift of power and people and production from the
> city to the country-side. He praised voluntary service as a principle
> of civic life, local government set the best example. Leaders should
> remain alert to their 'stewardship'. Many things, perhaps the most
> important things, were, and had always been, 'above party'.[61]

He also shows unremitting opposition to 'permissiveness' or any departure
from the strict canon of Methodist rectitude. He is a tepid partisan, uneasy
with point-scoring, scornful of rhetoric, believing that each party, 'representing, as it does, a different section of the community', and made up
in the main of likeable, decent and co-operative men, has a right to a
turn in office. Indeed, he is less interested in law-making than in attending
to the concrete demands of his constituents, which he has made into
a taxing and anxious, yet deeply satisfying, routine. He is the sort of M.P.
who is never entirely happy about a proposal unless he can be taken and
shown on the ground some material thing on which it is proposed to spend
money. He emphasised that his seat was pressed on him rather than stri-
ven for, a reward for years of faithful support for older men in the party,
and service in many church, sporting and civic organisations in the district. But he accepted with alacrity.

Underlying his sober and circumspect narrative of unexceptionable
motivation and modest achievement, there glint some wilder themes.
First, he has a sense of mission. He feels himself to be a 'natural leader'
— 'It's a sort of flair for the public life, really . . . if it doesn't take a political
turn, it comes out in [civic leadership]' — elected less by voters than by a
Calvinist God, and now fully consecrated to the work to the near-exclusion
of all private concerns. Like his father before him, Webb is a lay preacher
and, for a time in adolescence, contemplated a minister's, or preferably
a missionary's, career. There was never a time when he did not see it
as his duty to teach others how to live. Secondly, as a background to his
stands of principle on matters of social morality, he has a lurid sense of
galloping decadence, and a proud sense of himself as a lone crusader
licensed to righteous anger. He bears easily the discomfort of others' scorn
and of being thought 'unbalanced'; he is assured of an ultimate, if posthu-
mous, vindication. The sense of things of value silently and relentlessly
slipping away carries over easily from the moral to the economic and
social terrain; in his father's day all these matters were somewhat better
arranged. Thirdly, his ego-ideal, as M.P., is that of the affluent man, the
man leading from strength, the giver. He detects in himself, and in many
of his fellows, a reparative urge. Having done uncommonly well in their
private exploits, now, in late middle-age they somehow owe it to their
fellows to repair the imbalance, even perhaps the damage, caused by
their acquisitiveness; they are resolved to give something back.

Further light is thrown on Webb's general ideas and his way of being

an MP by a glance at some leading traits in his personality. He is outstandingly deferent, and seems consistently to over-estimate authority-figures
– praising his father, his teachers, his early bosses, some leading politicians
he has come to know. It is a pleasure to him to rehearse their virtues,
their kindness to him, and his indebtedness to them – to do them honour.
He seems to steer himself gyroscopically by attaching himself to admired
elders, and recommending himself by his deference, correctness and
hyper-activity. He is, of course, strongly identified with his father, thinks
of himself as very like him – 'active and clean' – although a shade tenser,
and neither as big a man, nor as valuable. He adopted without question
his father's conservative views and appetite for local politics, his active
Methodism (somehow he, youngest of the four sons, was the one who
inherited the family Bible), and, informing the whole, the father's spirit
of zeal, of working to the limit, of the imperium of scruple.* His project,
we might say, was to 'become superior by resembling a superior'.

He has a deep aversion to the subjective, and arranges his work so as
to lose himself in long spells of continuous activity. He avoids situations
that may become too personal, and becomes anxious at the irrational in
his clients, or in himself. What he dislikes most about his job is having to
deal with the 'personal messes' of the inadequate or delinquent; moral
indignation quickly chokes sympathy. He seeks 'plain dealings with
plain people', and a concern for the material colours even his approach
to his favourite 'social' questions. He talks unwillingly of his childhood,
reads no fiction, admits no experiences of awe. The one passage of fantasy
in the record occurs in his maiden speech, where he summoned up a
picture of the gallery at the opening of Parliament, lined with Members'
children looking down on their fathers, agog with pride, a moment indelible in their memories. To be seen as admirable is vital to him: he enjoys
the satisfaction of performing a great many small actions all of which are
right, and he hoards tangible evidence (letters, presents) of others' gratitude and approval.

Rigidity and narrowness of outlook are linked to a need for order and
deliberation in thinking. Indeed, his whole routine of life and work is of
an extreme orderliness amounting to rule by detail, which may be partly
understood as an attempt to outwit and confute basic feelings of inadequacy and deficiency. It is perhaps because he so often has the feeling of
acting with barely sufficient resources that he must break tasks down

---

* Though in many respects he has surpassed his father's achievements – a
successful farmer where his father failed, a successful father settling *his* son
on the land, an M.P. where his father did not make the local council, lay
preacher in demand by other denominations – Webb does not allow himself
much comfort from it. This would seem to be one severe penalty of conformism (the adoption of another's exact pattern of goals): whatever the effort,
the trophy is withheld. The unease is generalised; the generations lose at
each change.

into little manageable units to be done at his own pace, scrupulously (cf. Lanlin above). The strategy has abundantly proved its value, and he has become thoroughly adept at it — at the cost, however, of its becoming 'second nature'. He is, as it were, permanently the tortoise who races the hare or the servant in the parable given only one talent who must take special care to do well. Hence much of the strain — and pathos — of his attempt to live day by day up to his ego-ideal of the nurturant M.P., the dealer from strength.

We note, finally, his preoccupation with control and self-control.* Parliament and the Church draw him partly because they control, and he, by his membership, files in as a Guardian. He is fascinated with the ability to say No — both with the strength and virtue of those who can, and the weakness and shame of those who cannot. He is fascinated with how, when it is a plea for help, not a temptation to indulgence, the good man *cannot* say No. Indeed, there is a self-abnegating, duty-addict quality about his determination to do everything his constituents ask of him (incidentally, showing up the laziness and ineffectuality of brother M.P.s). In his compulsive self-control, he relies astonishingly on projection — the single most striking thing about his political style — and, indeed is unable to recognise as a serious political problem anything other than the sort of family problems that were painfully prominent (as we shall see) in his own early experience — those of difficulties in schooling, an inadequate breadwinner, the family threatened with breaking up, and having to sell up the farm.

The youngest of a family of four boys and a girl, Webb's father was a gold-miner in a small mine in a remote corner of fields that had been worked out in the Gold Rushes of the 1850s, in which his grandfather, by now a successful small farmer nearby, had taken part. Webb's mother was the daughter of another (German) gold-fields family. When Webb was five, the mine began to give out, and his father bought a small dairy farm. Within four years, he was ruined by the big drought of 1914, and had to sell up and get off the land. 'He went timber-getting round about for a while, but didn't seem to be making a go of that, so they got him to go to Melbourne to his sister's for a holiday; she found him a job locally as a carter, which he kept till retirement. He suffered much from a lung complaint caused by his work underground, which 'put a tremendous strain and anxiety on [him] and mother'.

Close to his mother in these anxious years on the farm, Webb clearly caught the full force of her anxiety and doubt about the father's ability to cope, though he consciously remembers only the sadness of selling the farm and leaving his bush school, and the shock of the meanness of life in the poor city neighbourhood they settled in. Projective material, how-

* He chooses self-control first of the Morris Paths.

ever, hints at a searingly rebellious undercurrent in these years, when the boy struggled with almost overwhelming emotions of hate and scorn, and suggests his exaggerated dutifulness and deference can be understood as a reaction-formation — a denial in the strongest possible terms of these rebellious impulses, a denial that doubts about his father had ever been entertained or necessary.

Setting the father up as an ideal figure, and adopting wholesale his views and values, Webb incorporated many realistic elements of his character. That he was not fully appreciated by, indeed consistently under-estimated by, those surrounding him, left him both with a scepticism about public success, and an implacable ambition to win it with exactly those values. His virtues set the pattern for Webb's 'ideal leader' — a 'doer not a talker',

> quite small, retiring . . . never pushes himself forward, but with terrific knowledge — a committee-man, who'll go to endless trouble, yet will be the last to talk and so modest that no one will ever know how much he contributed to the final thing.

Webb made a poor attempt at recreating his childhood in the interviews but, in an aside on a visit to a guide-dog training school, offered with almost a child's awed empathy, a view of a 'conditional love' system of upbringing, which may echo his own.

> Many dogs are offered, but the rigid instruction and training given means that at most, only one dog in ten ultimately qualifies as a guide dog. The dog must show a complete willingness for his work — if that is not the case, the dog is immediately rejected. Even when a dog has almost completed its training, it may be rejected outright because it does not meet the temperamental requirements of the unfortunate individual who will acquire it.

The parents' demands for goodness and obedience — and we may be sure they were high — seem to have been at least matched by Webb's determination to press model behaviour on them, devotedly, doggedly, forever fearing rejection, on the lines of the formula: 'I feared my father, but I also loved him. My whole life has been geared to discipline, and I feel terribly fortunate that it has.'

The similarities between Webb and Lanlin are obvious: their lives lived from the outside in, not an opinion out of place, and to a second-hand plan (their fathers'); their lugubrious piety and self-discipline; their awe of authority; their patient subdivision of tasks into small units; their tireless willingness to load themselves with local chores — in short, their passionate pursuit of lower-middle-class conventionality. Both Webb and Lanlin are fortunate in having found apt vocational solutions to their needs for display and recognition (and, to a lesser extent, nurturance) within a master-frame of deference. It is true that Webb's stubborn puritanism makes him closer to what Australians call a wowser, a public kill-joy;[62] his complacency has a pessimistic edge, where Lanlin's was optimistic; but both contrive to feel lodged close to the estimable heart of their society — 'the Property' being for both a kind of tangible attestation to this. Their pieties are pieties *of place*. They would, however, hardly get on in person. Webb hates Catholics, is ambivalent about big business and has no interest in the U.S.; Lanlin would find Webb glum, rigid, and *far-fetched*.

Little's Bond as F

A third-year Law/Arts student at Melbourne University, when interviewed in 1967, Bond was the leading light of the campus conservative ('Liberal') club and already firmly determined on a professional political career.[63] Charming, self-deprecating, clever, but an activist and extravert rather than an intellectual, he happily labels his politics 'conservative' but adds immediately that he is also 'pragmatic and flexible — biased towards reform'. Respect for what is, for what has already been achieved, for the older generation, for parents and teachers, is the corner-stone of his outlook. 'The university,' he says, 'should make students fully aware of the traditions and values of our society as well as the views of the critics of our society.' He himself criticises rarely and gently, and is concerned rather with constructive order and organisation. Where 'unfortunates' *can* demonstrate needs, 'generosity' is called for. His spur to change is sentimentality. He is an active Anglican adherent.

He is most surprised at how congenial, even welcoming, the university environment has turned out. It has given him scope for perfecting his organising talents, and brought him into genial contact with like-minded peers, gifted young politics lecturers who strengthen the philosophical basis of his views, and even future Labour activists. He speaks of discussions giving you 'even deeper and better reasons for a thing that you believe'. As a priggish, identity-foreclosed schoolboy he had imagined the university as a hate-filled, leftist hot-bed in which he and his friends would be pariahs:

> I thought university students were radicals or left-wingers or sloppy dressers . . . I was determined that I was going to be different . . .
> It seemed pretty awful some of the things that people would wear, do, say, speak about up here . . . They seemed to unnecessarily try and buck things, buck traditions. They seemed to go out of their way to shock . . . I thought students were terrible cynics and . . . cynical for cynicism's sake.

(He had argued hotly with his Matric. English master over *Hamlet* — it was *not* inevitable that every adolescent had to have his ideals shattered to achieve a mature tolerance of life. If you could see the end result, he thought, you could be clever and skip that stage, and avoid the symbolic orphaning, the solitude and fear when guides and restraints have been discarded.) He drew his menacing image of the university not only from the media, but from his elder sister's friends, and her own dropping out to a 'hippie' life-style. Now he looks back on his fears with some amusement. What he had taken for cynicism were 'sincerely-held idealistic beliefs that don't happen to coincide with mine'. The campus norm was not protest and shock, but something more like a silent recoil from that expectation; making himself spokesman for this silent majority, he had seized the chance to help set a new, more muted style of student politics.

Bond's father is a business executive, but neither he nor his wife is a graduate. 'My mother is far brighter than my father', Bond says, 'but my father is far more broadminded.' It is part of Bond's picture of them that the weak father missed his opportunities through dullness, while the dominating mother lacked the money. Their ambition for Bond always included university, and with this in mind, they chose his expensive private school (to which he is determinedly loyal) with its emphasis on high achievement. Bond says nothing about his early childhood, but is anxious (as with his images of the university) to disentangle a school-boy view from his present view of his parents. As 'child', he gave his parents 'unquestioning obedience' and fully accepted their aspirations for him. He was the white sheep to his sister's black — 'they've never thought *I* was going to be a flop'. His parents' outlook then seemed an 'unsplittable monolithic block', though he saw rather more of his mother, her 'strictness' and her rigidly conservative moral and political views. Now, he notes,

> increasingly I disagree with my mother ... the older I get the more
> I seem to be inclined to go towards my father's views on what is
> good to strive for, and say, and what moral values and so on.

The father, no longer obscured by his brighter, more opinionated wife, can now be explored: he is easy-going, broad-minded, experienced in things that have come to interest the son. However, a respectful, and above average, closeness and continuing dependence still mark the son's relationship with both parents: 'I still think my views would be more or less precisely the same as theirs.' He basks in their warm support — 'I think they still think fairly highly of me.' 'The sort of life I want [that is, a political career] is what they're keen for me to do.' And a new-found ability to admit his political ambition and competitiveness to himself makes it easier for him to manage his short-term trimming and adjustments. (He contrasts his flexibility with the plight of 'cast-iron' conservative contemporaries, who are forced under radical pressure into hiding their party allegiance and remaining silent, or into drifting slowly to the right.) Nonetheless, in some vital way politics and 'warmth' seem to have become separated out in Bond's life: he has a very wide acquaintance ('thousands of people drop into my room'), but few, if any, friends. Indeed, his 'friends' are mostly strategic, and

> are going to be active in the Labor party ... it'll be rather good be-
> cause I hope that I'll have a rather different outlook from many
> other people in the same party as me ... I feel I've got an advan-
> tage.

More independent, more sophisticated, more tolerant 'these days', he is still basically submissive and deferent — and rather timid. With his mother, as a child, he 'looked out on the world of men and saw that it was dangerous' (Little). That view persists.

We reserve leading features of Bond's case to sustain our student pair, but some contrasts with Lanlin and Webb stand out immediately, stem-ming from the difference in age; Bond was born some forty years further into our century, and several rungs higher up the social scale. Bond's mother's 'strictness' and intolerant moralism, real enough, no doubt, in their time and place, are a pale shadow of a 1905 regimen of piety ('seen but not heard') — just as, in the same way, today's Anglicanism is almost empty of content, a drastic dilution of strict, turn-of-the-century Methodism. Where Lanlin and Webb are preoccupied for the greater part of their adult lives with the small details of material accumulation, Bond has launched at once into symbolic manipulation — and by his prowess in this will press his claim for future promotion. Half-playfully putting together the 'principles' of his politics with his student peers, Bond has the look of a *free spirit* beside Lanlin and Webb, locked in the static pieties of the previous generation and their narrow and all-absorbing neighbour-hoods (though twenty years on, the 'understandings' of Bond's student peer-group may well come to seem confining enough).

And it may also be because of class and generation that Bond's mother, far from colluding in a family myth of the father-as-hero, seems subtly to undercut the father, and imperiously to demand superior *and public* attain-ment of the son, as if to compensate for the waste and frustration of her own unused gifts.* Though Lanlin's and Webb's mothers complain about money troubles to their sons and impress them as 'special helpers' in difficult straits, they stoutly preserve in them a sense that they will be doing very well indeed if they come up some day to their father's mark.

One further odd family detail exemplifies the type. Schiff, in an exemp-lary piece on campus conservative converts, notes:

> The desire to appear as the dutiful son is extremely pronounced in
> many of the young conservatives. More than half of the college-age

---

* We have seen this already in the UF type York, and incidentally it is almost
standard (together with an idealised *grandfather* figure, strong man, founder)
in the family background of Australian politicians of the Right.[64] However,
it was already anticipated in Plato's brilliant sketch of the making of the
'*timocrat*',[65] and, if it must have a name, we could perhaps do no better than
call it, after Coriolanus's mother, the *Volumnia syndrome*.

converts with siblings (and two of the more deeply involved non-converting conservative activists) appeared in this role in their families. Some of the siblings in question actively defied their parents, adopting religious, political or career lines that directly conflicted with parental wishes. Other siblings were chronic failures or play-boy, disobedient types. In every instance where there was sharp contrast or complementarity between siblings, the totalistic convert emerged as the 'good boy'.[66]

Bond's 'black-sheep' sister — long in danger of being a 'flop' — in choosing to drop out and be a hippy rebels and rejects parental values for both children; in the same way, Bond fills the role of 'good child' for them both.

Walter's Dianne Ellis as F

In 1971–2, in delayed imitation of U.S. campus 'events' of the 1960s, a group of student 'revolutionaries' at La Trobe, one of Australia's newest universities, mounted a running confrontation with the administration, which almost paralysed it. Dianne Ellis led a 'Moderate Students' Alliance', and was for eighteen months their principal student antagonist.[67] She did not take on the radicals in open debate, but manoeuvred behind the scenes in student government, issued a stream of rebutting leaflets, and acted as a key and trusted adviser to the administration. A fourth-year Politics and Sociology student, 'nicely' dressed, forceful in manner, fluently spoken, her voice takes on a hard edge of asperity as she talks of her opponents, whom she sees not only as paid agents of international Communism, but as 'psychologically unbalanced . . . in need of treatment' and, in several cases, 'certifiably schizophrenic'. Behind such leaders, student mobs in crises became violent and ugly:

> People were really mad at that time . . . [storming a Council meeting]
> . . . you could hear them screaming and ranting and raving . . . and
> they had stones, cans of petrol and iron bars . . .

The radicals, she explains, wanted not only to demonstrate that 'every-body was nasty and the authorities were cruel', but to seize complete control, pervert the university's working and 'churn out hundreds of students yearly in their own image'. She sees herself and her friends standing sanely aloof from this Gadarene stampede, preserving 'institutional integrity' and the university itself as a welcome haven from the crass politics of selfish factions in the larger society. The basis for the radicals' success, she felt, was the trendy counter-cultural ambience — free thinking, sexually-libertarian, drug-taking, pacifist and anti-authoritarian — which was dominant on campus, and which she had already confronted and 'got through' at school.

Both in her studies and in her political struggles, she has had ample opportunity to think out her position, and she admits she has moved somewhat to the right over her four years at university.

> When I came up here I would have said I was a 'small "L" liberal'.

> Now I see more clearly what's behind the Left, I oppose them more strongly than that. I think my ideas are much more solid now.

However, she prefers to stress the unchanging character of the 'basic principles' of her politics — 'an unbiased legal system, free enterprise working alongside government . . . freedom of the individual, freedom of speech . . .'. She believes, above all, in 'legitimate institutions', established procedural forms, strong people and logic, and has little interest in political ideals or reform. Indeed, accepting and working to maintain the given, she acts mainly to curb and stave off the initiatives of the Left. She and her parents are still of one mind politically; they approve her line in student affairs, but deprecate her 'over-involvement' and her association with lower-status peers. 'Due process' and 'rationality' may have marked the Alliance side in the 'events', but Dianne herself is not beyond the reach of political emotion:

> Sometimes, you know, when there are strikes on, I could scream. I get livid and jump around the kitchen floor yelling to get the frustrations out. I hate . . . not with a vicious hate . . . but I *intensely* disagree with certain unions and union leaders, and certain people politically, and socially, too.

Walter sees a strong strain of projection in her politics. She values *controls* so much because of the urgent need to keep her own destructiveness in check. She 'abhors', but is preoccupied with, others' violence and irrationality, their sinister power and ruthless ambitions. Her lurid fears are a way of disowning such qualities or wishes in herself. In fact, she is self-centred, attention-demanding, self-aggrandising — a 'professional' in student politics. She boasts of her contacts, experience, power and achievements: 'I've had, you know, quite a major effect, here.' She catalogues her family's possessions in some detail (they include a hobby farm and a beach house) and these evidently give her a secure sense of a favoured position in society. Her 'first memory' is of her own first possessions, and she plans, she says, to marry a man with a 'middle to upper income'.

'It was a funny sort of background', Dianne says, describing her childhood.

> It's been close . . . but day to day, within school or business, you're independent . . . once you go out of the house, you're on your own . . . I love my parents very much, and I've got no complaints about my upbringing. I reckon I had a pretty stable one . . . very affectionate. And we were always seen as individuals, encouraged to go out and do our own thing. But at home we work together, co-operate automatically, because we love each other.

Her father, an engineer with his own successful business, is the decisive parent, although Dianne feels, and resents, a certain distance between them.

> He was often away on business for days at a time, so I came closer
> to my mother. I'm a close friend, as well as a daughter to her, where-
> as with my father, it was more father-daughter. On some occasions
> it wasn't — we used to go riding together, and then we were very
> close.

Dianne seeks to dismiss her brother, '10½ years older and married' — 'I've
been almost an only child.' But he did play a part in her family scene,
entering into discussion and enjoying a relationship with her father,
which she envied:

> When I was very young, my brother was old enough to talk about
> issues so there would be often a two-way conversation through my
> brother and my father — my mother would pop in her bits. She has,
> strangely enough, become more vocal and opinionated over the
> years. I remember up to the age of six or seven or even older, I used
> to storm out of the room and take my tea into the lounge-room and
> not eat with the family, because they wouldn't let me say anything.
> But since the age of ten or twelve, I've either yelled over the top of
> them and they've had to listen, or then they started to listen to me
> and we'd all discuss things.

A 'masculine' competitiveness seems to have been engendered. Dianne
wants to assert herself in order to gain her father's attention, yet at the
same time she wants to feel 'very, very close' to (submit to) him. This
struggle between independence and submission runs through her narrative. There is a 'safe home base' from which family members individually
'venture out' — *pushed* a little, perhaps, to be independent and achieving
— and then a return to a rather cloying, undifferentiated family warmth.

> She must assert her independence in competing for 'deference values'
> from powerful masculine figures; but this very assertiveness creates the
> danger of alienation from the very figures she seeks to impress.

Impressing and winning favourable attention from 'strong' people
has remained a leading preoccupation, and she values hierarchy, since
within it she can carve an assured place and identity. Rigidity and idealisation of authority are the legacies of ambivalence denied in the father-
daughter relationship. By her aggression, her driving manner and her
vocational aspirations, she transcends the secondary status of her
childhood 'feminine' identification, and so surpasses her mother. (She
is slightly defensive about still living at home in her fourth year, but explains it as simply cheaper, and 'my mother's really a kind of flat-mate'.)
But she has made no break — even on an intellectual level — with her
parents; indeed, her differences of opinion with them 'grow narrower with
time'.

In campus politics she has found, with remarkable economy, a way at
once to assert herself, to be legitimately aggressive and power-seeking,
to win the attention and recognition of powerful figures — and to do all

this for *principles* her parents heartily applaud: she has found, in short, a way to be both strong and obedient.

Before comparing Bond and Dianne Ellis, it will be helpful to glance at an American study on typological lines.

Schiff's composite college conservative converts as F
In 1963, L. F. Schiff interviewed some thirty conservative activists on nine New England campuses, who had gone through something like a conversion-experience.[68] He found, first, that these were solitary conversions, involving no idealised seniors or exciting contemporaries. Secondly, no programmatic issue sparked them off; it was conservatism as a system that they seized on. Thirdly, the essential thing seemed to be to find a personal label, an ideological cloak, which asserted a desirable moral and political identity — desirable, above all, as cutting one off, once and for all, from the negative identity of the amoral, deviant liberal. What invariably precipitated either a sudden crash 'reading up' of conservative doctrine, or a collapse back to parental views previously resisted or rejected, were 'shocking' discoveries about the moral and/or political climate of their new surroundings, which then began to seem sinister and to threaten in some way the heart of their self-image.

As children (all but one are only or eldest sons) all these young men had a domineering parent (or parents) with very definite and ambitious expectations of them. Under enormous pressure to measure up to their demands, each found himself in his own way — always covertly, and at times involuntarily — veering away from the course lovingly mapped out for him. Unable completely to fulfil expectations, but unwilling openly to defy them, each young man arrived at the point of conversion bearing the weight of this unacknowledged conflict. The turn to conservatism magically resolved this: 'obedient rebellion', a *repudiation of repudiation*, either transformed, or effectively disguised, overt rebellion. In the simplest transformation, enhanced obedience to parents enjoined rebellion against potentially disobedient impulses projected upon university peers (and/or staff).* *Over*-obedience most effectively disguised rebellion (from both self and parents) allowing the son to appear to be acting zealously to extend parental precepts.† Indeed, obedience and rebellion become in large measure fused in these men. Turning 'conservative' aligns the son with his parents' values, implicit and explicit, so thoroughly (sometimes, indeed, to the point of caricature) that he is able to use the political front as a cover for a certain amount of otherwise unacceptable 'hell-raising'.

* These disobedient impulses were, however, still kept alive. Thus the 'obedience' in one student's *conservative* campaigning sanctioned the rebellious satisfactions inherent in his bringing out long-suppressed *activist* and expressive tendencies.
† Thus a turn to hyper-orthodox religiosity both reproved lukewarm parents and allowed the son more freedom to differentiate himself in other spheres.

(Agreement between these parents and sons on moral questions is remarkably high, some sons lamenting even, that their demanding parents had not been strict enough with them.)

Personality tests administered with the interviews disclosed much self-restriction and a tropism for the conventional. Conservatism appealed because it was 'mainstream' and the done thing, but also 'high-status': the sons had introjected the parents' avid status-seeking. It conveniently rationalised deference to authority* and conformity to traditional morality, with which they were already psychologically at ease. It made risk-taking and achievement goals that were romantic *and public*, allowing them meanwhile to pursue characteristically low-risk, private career-plans and virtuously to disavow 'materialism'. It comforted and reassured young people 'whose self-esteem had been transitorily disturbed, those for whom "identity foreclosure" rather than genuine personal change was the way out of a developmental crisis', by its intellectual simplicity, its close and deductive nature, its pessimistic outlook on human possibility, and its self-consciously hard-line attitude. It made a sense of resignation, of inevitable compromise, of reduced hopes, feel right. In consciously becoming 'hard' and 'pessimistically realistic' (and at the same time repudiating idealistic and radical assaults on their complacency) these young men fell back on a rather narrow concept of the self — a concept which was essentially white, American and middle-class — and on conservatism's legitimation of self-interest as a basis for political judgment. Compared to their liberal peers, they are prepared to concern themselves primarily with selfish and parochial matters. A need to exercise tight control over anxiety, to maintain a high level of self-esteem, makes this path especially attractive to them. Finally, as all ideologies do, conservatism permits the displacement of otherwise unacceptable hostility on to public objects.

Schiff's text sustains a running contrast between his 'converts' and a control group of 'natural' conservatives, which we have skimped in summary, but which accords well with the broadly different feel of the Bond and Dianne Ellis cases. Dianne, though reporting no sudden emotional shock or illumination, is a convert, in that she reports a definite movement to the Right in her time at university. Converts, as more extreme, are more aggressive, more rigidly allied to conventional authority (since they have more ambivalence to overcome), are more tightly self-controlled, and have more brittle self-esteem. Bond is a sunnier activist — more open, more flexible, more trusting — as well as an activist on a sunnier campus.

* Schiff notes a 'Young Americans for Freedom' style of 'passive, though frequently enthusiastic, obedience to duly constituted leaders, strict hierarchical social organisation and a general dependence on adult figures to provide both programs and direction', and a 'proclivity toward posturing rather than program'.

Schiff's merit is to direct our curiosity, in the case of Bond as in the case of Dianne, to the covert rebellion smuggled in behind the zealous obedience-project. Dianne, as a militant, exacts family pride and approval not only for much 'masculine' competitiveness and assertiveness, but also, in fact, for a largely independent choice of studies, friends and life. Behind Bond's maintaining views 'more or less precisely the same' as his parents, and championing them in a somewhat sceptical environment, he too is laying a slow siege to his dependence, and paving the way to a situation where what he does as a student 'heavy', or a young lawyer or political figure, largely escapes parental examination behind a bland uncritical approval of his exemplary broad espousal of such roles.

Conclusion
Two fifty-year-olds and five students (or six, if we count Schiff's composite convert as one) — what have these cases done to modify or extend the F type-description?

Family background. Bales expected parents (see table 6 above, p. 146) to be alike, low on emotional supportiveness and warmth, and high to average on inhibitory demands and discipline. In short, he expected them to co-operate in imposing a regimen of 'conditional love'. This was true in all cases. Dianne went further to evince mild fear, and Lanlin and Webb, marked fears, of rejection by the father; Lanlin feared rejection by the mother as well, as did York; Dunn was convinced that his mother *had* rejected him in favour of his younger brother. 'Deficiency of affection' — the meridional mark in upbringing — is thus amply confirmed.

Bales's general rule that parents will tend to have been much as their child is now, and his specific prediction for F, 'high on optimistic ideal-ism', * point towards a complacently conformist home from which the child goes forward to an uncritical, even eager, acceptance of the social, political and moral *status quo*. This, again, is largely the case. But there are arresting variations, of a scale and intensity to suggest sub-types. For example, Lanlin and Webb show a simple positive identification with an idealised conformist father, while Lake and Bond identify with a parental amalgam. Also, F types may identify less with either parent than with the compulsions and constraints of common values and norms, though tending to become like the parents and proud to have taken over their standards. York and Dunn both have broken fathers, while Dianne has outstripped her mother. (We have already touched on the mother's critical part in the creation of the father's status in family myth.)

---

* Taken strictly, only one of the parents (York's bustling mother) comes up as an optimistic idealist. They seem, indeed, generally a rather dour lot — and one, Dunn's bankrupt father, is a bitter suburban 'Maoist'.

Cutting across this division, but equally marked, is a contrast between parental conformity and parental ambition: on the one hand, parents expect their children to lead the same sort of lives as they have (although the children may surprise them) and exert little pressure for achievement — this may be seen in Lanlin, Lake and Dunn, and possibly in Dianne and Webb; on the other hand, there are parents who exhibit an ambition so hard and driving that it constitutes a major problem for the child — this may be seen in Schiff's men (ambitious father and/or mother), York (ambitious mother) and Bond (possibly ambitious mother).

Implicit in Bales's reservation of the tag 'identification with idealised parent' for the PF position (the optimistic idealist), there is, I think, the assumption of a certain sensed weakness or *falling short* in F parents; their children turn to the 'local God or his representative', to a local form of authority, in order to fill out the inadequacies and shortcomings they experience in the home. Thus supported, they are extremely secure.

The cases also offer sub-types, which we have already discussed. First, Lanlin, Bond and Dianne exhibit an apparently smooth and steady assimilation of type-characteristics. Secondly, there is an urgent reaction-formation against ambivalence and/or hostility — a *repudiation of repudiation*, in Schiff's useful phrase — which is seen in its adolescent stage in Schiff's men, in its Oedipal stage in Webb,* and in the pre-Oedipal stage in Lake. There is also the variant in which hyper-conventionality is fuelled by rivalry for the role of the good child in a sibling pair (for example, Bond, half of Schiff's men, and possibly Dunn) or in a group (for example, Webb).

The most solid novel contribution which the cases make to our sense of the type is their uniform testimony to an 'unterminated dependency relation with the parents' (Smith) — the initial and continuing great regard for the parents' model and their good opinion.

Social stance and style. Cases which are unhesitatingly recognised as F types will hardly cause surprise by scoring consistently well on the several constituent indices of conformity, but they have, perhaps, helped to clarify what these indices are.

First, the F type makes sure that his life-project is in close alliance with conventional authority: Webb is, and Bond aims to be, a conservative politician; York wants to be an administrator helping to reconstruct Europe, Dunn as U.S. federal administrator. Lanlin has distinguished himself as a staff association man in his company, and serves it even more eagerly now as a sales manger. Webb is also a lay-preacher in his church.

---

* We may recall, too, Lasswell's vignette of the 'compulsive conformist', Mr L., whose political opinions exactly parallel those of his father and mother, who is consciously preoccupied with conforming to the parental pattern of belief and occupation, and, indeed, has the strange premonition that, if he goes his own way, something terrible will happen.[69]

Authority is held in respect, even in a certain awe. It is pleasant to work in its service — to set others, as it were, an example — and there is a special pleasure in having one's service recognised. Doubters and deviants* receive short shrift, and subversives are frankly hated. The F type tries to help to get the right things done, to persuade others to recognise needful tasks, and to keep them serious, co-operative and hopeful.

Secondly, the F type is willing to accept a 'work-horse' role, to load himself with unpopular chores and difficult assignments, and to go at them patiently and with full attention; he leaves to others, with relief or scepticism, the business of pondering abstract principles or long-term goals. Hierarchy suits the conformist. We even begin to make out from Webb and Lanlin a conformist style of work, which guarantees a modest success — and perhaps no more than that — in many different work situations. It is a style that avoids unstructured situations; it is built round 'nice, exacting and clean-cut' tasks, and concrete, if small, achievements; it makes the most of any opportunities for approval and prestige, though shying away from close competitiveness or open conflict: in short, it seeks recognition on the basis of tangible results. Although the conformist

> is relatively low in generating hypotheses on his own, he is better in elaborating hypotheses suggested by others. Having listened to others and being alert to what he can learn, he is quick to pick up their ideas and think of ways of putting them to constructive use.

He plays his cards 'close to the chest' and takes care to prevent his boundaries from becoming too permeable. The reverse of impulsive, his moves are cautious, long-considered and held back for maximum strategic effect. Continuous activity is demanded, and there is a compulsive quality to the performance, as if any relaxation would disturb a strict conscience. He is

> a thorough worker ... He sees each [task] as a unit with many ramifications which he covers before he is through with it ... He strives for closure with a great intensity, for in achieving it he has demonstrated his capacity to master the situation, gain the recognition he desires, and leave nothing with which others can find fault.[70]

Thirdly, F types experience atrophy of the personal core; as Bales puts it, 'fantasy, freedom, humour and expression' are denied or repressed by the super-ego. Here, the sense is of lives lived from the outside-in, of self sunk in role (Bales), of 'hand-me-down' life-plans, of 'identity foreclosure', of a somewhat lugubrious piety and earnest self-discipline, of an extravert flight to activity and possessions, of a passion for the ordinary. The personal shallowness that horrified Murray in Lake is an obvious feature in all eight cases; these are deliberately plain, stripped-down, workmanlike and safety-seeking folk.

---

* Only Dianne and Webb, in fact, exemplify Bales's 'fascination and preoccupation with deviancy'.

Personality. Bales sees the conformist as having a stable character and a strong will; he sees him as responsible, practical, and perhaps sociable and persistent. Our eight cases add a number of characteristics to this basic sketch.

All eight cases are conventional and/or conformist:

It is likely that all of them feel the need to flatter their self-esteem; they have a strong need to feel important.

All (except possibly Dunn) are extraverts and/or activists.

All of them exhibit a cognitive style that could be described as slow, rigid, obsessional, and confined to concrete terms; they are compulsive and inclined to break tasks down into little fail-safe sub-tasks, which they can prove they have performed correctly. Bond and York exhibit this trait least.

All except Lanlin, and possibly Lake, are ambitious.

York, Dianne, Webb and Lanlin all have a rather high level of aggression kept under tight control.

Bond, Lanlin, Dunn, and Schiff's men may be described as timid, safety-seeking, dependent and submissive.

York, Lake, Dunn and possibly Bond have a low sex-drive.

Lanlin, Webb and Dianne are property-conscious.

Dunn, Webb, and Schiff's men are pessimists; Lanlin and York are optimists.

As Schiff noted, the master-themes are self-restriction and the search for strength and security through obedience.

Opinions. Lanlin and Webb admirably illustrate the localism of the F type. This was blurred in the case of the students, but Bond, York and Dunn had all bent somewhat to conform with campus orthodoxy, while the socialist among them (Dunn) preserved us from lazily conflating conservatism and conformity.

The most useful idea thrown up was that maintaining an orthodox outlook might well be less the preservation of a static pose, than a dynamic process of repudiating ever recurring impulses to repudiate: F thrives on subliminal fascination with B, and protests its deference and rectitude only by, and in, quelling impulses to rebel. The drama is not less keen for being overwhelmingly pre-conscious.

The Rebels — the B meridian

Again, we glance first at a celebrated case from *Opinions and Personality.*

Bruner's Sullivan as B

Sullivan is a large man, aged 48 when interviewed in 1946; plump, greying, with a pink complexion, large mouth, and indistinct eyebrows that make his blue eyes seem small, he has the over-all appearance of a jolly piggy-bank.[71] He is a Communist, though not a party member, and earns a precarious living working on weekly newspapers and doing occasional publicity jobs. He is married to a second wife, his first having divorced him ten years earlier for his alcoholism. He is now an abstainer. He talks volubly, with expressive facial emphasis and awkward, outsize gestures, and plays up the paradoxical qualities of his views.

He is delighted to be quizzed on Russia, about which he is massively informed, and all-positive. For him, Russia is, above all, a promised land, living testimony to the possibility of a better world. He admits the police-state features of the regime, but thinks they are justified by 'encirclement', and merely temporary. Apart from some minor mistakes in planning (unspecified), the Russian experiment is proving an all-round success, demonstrating a viable, alternative way forward in social welfare, cultural progress, industrial technology, and treatment of minorities. The proof is in Russia's war record, and in the violence and malevolence of the opposition to her in the rest of the world — above all, in the U.S. Press. He believes that capitalism is dying, and fated to be replaced, after an inevitable interval of Fascism, by Soviet-type socialism. He broods over scenarios of fatal collisions between the U.S. and Russia; if war breaks out, he says, it will certainly be America's fault, but it is pointless to blame those fulfilling their historical role. He thinks that Britain may yet side with Russia and stave off 'vaporisation'.

Although he has helped support various Communist causes, and although Russia engrosses his reading, his talk and his reveries, he prefers the role of independent radical (like his idol, Scott Nearing) to that of party member. He feels flawed by 'the pattern' of his culture and upbringing, and unable, finally, to bring the necessary intellectual integrity, vigour and courage to the tasks of the time. He does what he can in a modest way — at least, he says, his life has *purpose*. Brought up a Catholic, he gradually fell away from the Church in his twenties, but he has no animosity against the faithful: he has simply decided that, for whatever reason, he lacks 'the religious instinct', and looks back a little condescendingly on his earlier beliefs as a 'crutch', and on the Church as a somewhat illusory source of forgiveness and hope, and an object of dependence. The high point in an unsettled vocational career (which consisted of much unskilled labouring interspersed with journalism) was a stint after 1933 with the Works Progress Administration Writers' Project. It was then that his radicalism took shape and increasingly became the centre of his life. His present work is neither particularly interesting nor remunerative, but he takes considerable satisfaction in being a semi-professional man, and a free-lance, for the most part his own boss. He is a keen amateur painter, omnivorous reader of books and seeker out of intellectual discussions, and a part, with his friends, of a loose-knit, radical cultural circle.

Bruner begins the analysis of Sullivan's character with the paradox of his describing his whole life as a search for security and affection, and his contriving, despite his high intelligence, to achieve so nearly the opposite. He finds the answer in a defensive, *minimal* defining of security ('I never use the gold standard; I always use the hamburg standard'), having learnt in the thorny bosom of his family that the fruits of a responsible quest for security would be taken away from him, and that only immediate pleasures were safe. Accordingly, he narrows the scope of his preoccupations, his hopes and fears in his personal life* — which indeed has about it a rather desperate, blundering, even self-punishing, quality — to avoid confronting immediate and seemingly insoluble anxieties. In the past, drink has helped him gloss over the uncertainty and excessive modesty of his aspirations; currently he resorts to passivity and inordinate sleep. His TAT stories have a Pagliacci-like tone: behind a light-hearted, out-going, worldly-wise front there is a tense, frustrated, anxious and sadly serious man, who has developed a careless, 'knowing', clowning exterior to hide his weaknesses from others.

There is also considerable hostility in Sullivan's make-up. His humour, as well as his politics, has an aggressive edge,† and is used to shock people and disturb their complacency. As a revolutionary in fantasy, he casts himself as Samson, poised to bring down capitalist society in general ruin. He is also determinedly autonomous — a defence against what he has found to be the dangers and frustrations of staking much on dependence. What sort of childhood lies behind a personality organised in this way?

Sullivan was the first son and second child of poor Catholic parents in a Connecticut textile town where his father worked as a knitter. His mother was born in Ireland, where she had had some education; his father, native born, had only primary education, but showed unusually broad interests for his background. There followed six younger children in the next twelve years, three of whom lived to maturity. Home life was not pleasant; the mother sought to control the family by playing off the children against each other and against their father, showing traits that have recently contributed to her admission to hospital as a paranoiac. Sullivan worshipped his father, who died of tuberculosis when Sullivan was fifteen. Sullivan had thereupon to leave school and find work. His father, whom he fondly remembered after thirty years, 'didn't have any

---

* His marriage is one of 'intellectual companionship' only.

† All the same, he goes rather further than most 'Marxists' in disavowing hatred of individuals. People, he claims, are basically 'trustworthy and when they let you down, there's an economic reason ... I've always believed that and I always will.' Even Republicans 'are good men, you know, according to their lights ... Now this J, he's a splendid fellow. Marvellous fellow. He sees Communists under the bed ... but he's a likeable fellow ... he's got integrity ... Well, gee whiz, just because they don't agree with you ... your social and economic beliefs ... There're other likeable things about them.'

faults, except being ill, of course, always having a little touch of T.B.' He was the

> finest looking man I ever saw ... just handsome. A gentle person ...
> One of the earliest memories is of him entertaining us with all kinds
> of sounds of birds and animals, and songs ... Going up to meet him
> when he came home from work, and he'd take the youngest on his
> shoulders and two or three piling on to him.

In a family of much confusion and disturbance, the father was the centre of peace and serenity:

> I'd say his strongest point seemed to me to be that he had a kind
> of kindly, calm philosophy. For example, when my mother was
> blowing off her top and sprinkling holy water on everybody from
> top to bottom in the house, raising Hell, my father would sit calmly
> and look out of the window. And he'd sort of try to calm things.

Sullivan clearly got from his father a kind of warmth and comfort that children more usually find in their mothers. The 'minstrel type of Irishman', sensitive and humorous, he figures in Sullivan's recollections as a vivid, talented person of broad and contagious interests. He was a great entertainer who could do imitations, recite Shakespeare, play semi-professional baseball and act in amateur plays, as well as being a radical who tried once (unsuccessfully) to organise his factory and who read and quoted 'in great gobs' from socialist authors.

Mother, on the other hand, was all villain. As matriarch and disciplinarian she commanded no respect. She was given to constant harangue and 'mental punishment', 'rubbing it in' that they were poor and that the children were 'bringing disgrace to the family'. The chief ideal in the home, Sullivan said, was 'to be smart, so as not to bring shame on the family'. The mother, in short, exerted a cold, relentless pressure to conform, to maintain appearances, for which she offered little recompense.

First the Catholic Church, then the church of Communism, provided him with a haven of security that was not to be found in his mundane affairs. To Russia, the tangible guarantee of his faith, he attributes the same total perfection that he ascribed to his father, the only solace of his turbulent childhood. Both have been too important to him, and his inner resources have been too precarious, for him to admit the slightest flaw. To the seemingly unfair attacks on Russia in the mass media, he reacts just as he had learned to respond to his mother's attempted defamation of his father, with utter denial of the criticism.

To his miserable relationship with his mother may be traced both the apparent lack of emotional depth in his marriages, and some tendency to reserve his stronger emotional ties for men. His frustrated need for dependent well-being (perhaps at the root of his alcoholism) springs from the same source, and, at the heart of the burden of anxiety he has carried throughout life, lies, no doubt, the guilt and conflict that his childish hatred of her must have aroused. She left her mark, too, on his attitudes, impressing him with their poverty and 'under-dog' status, and maybe pre-figuring the exploiter (in the *dramatis personae* of Marxism) to his father's role of working-class martyr and his siblings' union of the oppressed.

But her largest legacy was his anti-conformity project. As a 'Communist and intellectual', he can finally show his total contempt for the frugal respectability and petty ambitions that his mother epitomised; the time for all that has passed. As a shrewd and well-informed man, with some knowledge of the *realpolitik* of world affairs, he can pour scorn on euphemistic bourgeois respectability. He now enjoys a 'career' of shocking people and disturbing their complacency, demonstrating forcefully that he is not their man, but his own — and a person of consequence. He has the comfort, too, of joining the big battalions; in aligning himself with the coming Power, he comfortably contemplates the day of final reckoning and the settling of scores. Marxist 'determinism' further absolves him of much of the pressure of responsibility in his personal life: these are not the times to seek to build solidly, and if he fails, or breaks down, this is merely in the pattern which is in store for millions.

Sullivan as B. His views make Sullivan a perfect B type — 'rejecting conservative group belief— the Disbelieving Rebel:

> He completely rejects the whole fabric of traditional religious beliefs, traditional localism, traditional concentration of wealth, and traditional political arrangements, which form the core of the conservative, local community ... He does not feel a part of the traditional local community, and he does not feel bound by its values ... [he] does not want to be coerced by God ... society, or the government.[72]

He disbelieves in the ideas used to justify the social norms which control behaviour — and in the whole system of social control itself. 'He wishes to install another form of society, or perhaps a different mode of existence, in another place and time.' He cleaves, beyond the letter, to the spirit: his 'disbelief' signalises his ability to repudiate any lingering hold the old ways may have on him, and he works as hard to root out the last unconscious traces of conformity as his polar opposite (F) does to prove himself incapable of putting a foot wrong (or even wishing to).* And 'disbelieving' exhausts him. He does not go on to live really differently, but remains frozen, 'lost in the fantasy of wildly improbable ambitions, unable to decide anything, or to actually strive for anything far in the future'. It is misleading to think of Sullivan as a 'Communist journalist'; he does not write Left-wing journalism, but is a hack reporter with a private fantasy world of Communist pieties.

---

* Bales stresses that, in rejecting *local* pieties, B types are necessarily led to embrace *universalistic* values. He notes, too, that B 'all the more strongly rejects' in that he 'still partly believes'.

Little is clearly posited about the personality of the B type, beyond a tendency to retreat into impersonality, to over-value rationalistic argumentation, and, generally, to timidity. B rests content with a declaration of independence; he does not go on to give demonstration of it. Sullivan manages broad Marxist rhetoric and has strong intellectual curiosity, but Bruner judges his capacity for organised and abstract thought 'limited': he 'rambles', is 'careless and superficial', 'over-generalises', and is 'incapable of long-term perspective'. Nevertheless, his 'highly developed world-view in the realm of safely impersonal ideology' manages remarkably to compensate for the feeble aimlessness of his personal striving. Sullivan is impulsive, with strong emotions, 'rather inadequately controlled'; above all, he has a high level of manifest anxiety (including claustrophobia and feelings of de-realisation). Faintly aggressive, clowning in conservative company, he approaches the UB type's use of humour and dramatisation as a significant element of style.

The B type's family background shows an absence of suitable conventional models who, in being loved and trusted, can sweeten the assumption of conformity. The father is moderately low in inhibitory demands and discipline; this may suit the B type, who is likely to be disappointed in his father, and reject him. The mother, though higher than the father, is still only average in demands and discipline. Possibly the father's status in the local conservative community is low or insecure, and the mother has assumed additional status and power within the family. Indeed, the family may be mother-centred, and the child more strongly identified with her than with the father. Both the mother and the father of the B type are relatively high in emotional supportiveness and warmth; this affords a basis for identification with their personal traits (their attitudes perhaps to class or status) but not with conservative values, since they are predicted to be somewhat pessimistic and cynical, and are unlikely to hold them. Thus in so far as the child does identify with one or both of them, he will automatically assume a heretical or extreme Left-wing attitude. Even if he is negative or ambivalent towards them, he is unlikely to be led away from the B direction.

The father, therefore, is suspected of being disappointing — not good or strong enough to inspire acceptance, or simply 'bad', or 'desired but absent'. This last phrase fits Sullivan's case exactly. The general scheme, however, hardly prepares us for a father abjectly idealised (in the PF manner), or a mother hated almost to DN pitch; Sullivan's recoil against her is the main impulse in his personality. (It is significant that Sullivan does not much read the organs of the Left, but prefers to build his picture of events by obsessively denying, disbelieving, and putting a *not* into, the pronouncements of the conventional media; the truth lies not in what father says but in the never-ending, point-by-point repudiation of mother.)

In the search for a label for this position, 'Utopian rebel' first presented itself. Utopianism turned out not to be as central as the idea of disbelief, but it did point to two key features of the B 'repudiation' of conventionality: first, it is less enacted than projected on to a distant and cloudy landscape; secondly, it is 'totalistic' — that is, only a 'root and branch' renovation of social life is seen to be able to extirpate the evil and error in the world that one had been sentenced to. We pass now to the original, classic case study of a disbelieving rebel.

Lasswell's Mr A. as B

A crusading Leftist Churchman in his sixties when interviewed in Chicago in the late 1920s, Mr A. has a thin face, a Van Dyck beard and a scholarly stoop. 'His eyes twinkle with good humour, and he is gentle, responsive, and anxious to impress.'[73] On the public platform, however, or writing in support of one of his 'causes', he is truculent, sarcastic, abusive, and cutting:

> He confesses that he has taken an unmistakeable pleasure in 'rubbing the fur the wrong way.' He enjoyed nothing better than accepting invitations to lecture on social and economic subjects before conservative audiences, and scandalizing them by declaring that 'organized business and organized crime are hard to distinguish from one another', 'corruption and capitalism are one and inseparable', and 'capitalism . . . means war'.

Suspected of unorthodoxy in theological school, he has been expelled from one denomination and disowned by several congregations. He has crusaded in the local community against alcohol, vice and municipal corruption, and for labour unions and socialism on a State-wide basis (once as a congressional candidate). Most recently he has been a national campaigner for pacifism, and against America's involvement in the First World War.

Since his views have so largely *been* his career, we may quickly sketch their joint history. Already at high school, converted to evolution and free trade, he 'began to develop a feeling that intellectual brilliance meant dissenting from the convictions of middle-class people like his own relatives'. At college he was impressed with a teacher's remark that 'Every man who was intellectually honest and independent would sooner or later discover that he questioned his own dogmas, and a period of bitter anguish would ensue', and he came to anticipate 'doubts' as a mark of intellectual keenness and honesty. At theological school, he debated questions concerning the authority of the Bible so hotly that he was several times in danger of expulsion. He left his first congregation when the othodoxy of his beliefs was questioned, and, moving to the city, threw himself into the agitational work of the infant socialist party. Expelled from his denomination, he took up lecturing at an independent Ethical Society with precarious finances. He had just started work with a third congregation when war broke out in 1914, and his denunciation of it cost him that post. When interviewed, he was still dependent on the support of his family and several wealthy radical sympathisers.

Lasswell discerned certain 'private motives' informing leading features of Mr A.'s agitational career, and saw them first of all behind his espousal of brotherhood:

> He ... identified himself with the workers and with humanity at large, serving a poverty-stricken congregation, spending his own money on the work of the church, adopting the socialist dream of a brotherly state, and demanding the abolition of fratricidal war.

In this Lasswell saw a strong repressed hatred of his own elder brother, of whom he steered clear in adult life. Guilt over this animosity, which had been so powerful in childhood, and which he had never frankly faced, was dealt with by finding generalised brother-substitutes to love, extending his own prohibition against brother-hatred to all society, and buttressing his position with elaborate ideologies of brotherhood (reaction-formation).

Second, behind his espousal of a rigid and censorious puritanism, Lasswell saw a constant struggle (dating from intimidating prohibitions of infantile masturbation) to repress his sexuality.* Only partially successful, this struggle left him with a sense of sin, an uneasy conviction of hypocrisy, and profound feelings of insecurity, which he found might be alleviated

> by publicly reaffirming the creed of repression, and by distracting attention to other matters. A.'s rapid movements, dogmatic assertions, and diversified activities were means of escape from this gnawing sense of incapacity to cope with his own desires and to master himself. Uncertain of his power to control himself, he was very busy about controlling others, and engaged in endless committee sessions, personal conferences, and public meetings for the purpose. He always managed to submerge himself in a buzzing life of ceaseless activity; he could never stand privacy and solitude, since it drove him to a sense of futility; and he couldn't undertake prolonged and laborious study, since his feeling of insecurity demanded daily evidence of his importance in the world.

The mask of rectitude, which his concealments, as well as his abstinences, kept successfully in place, was highly important to him. Indeed, his narcissism was well-marked.

> He had unbounded confidence in the brilliance of his mind, and this intellectual arrogance was nourished by the easy ascendance which he won over the poorly educated people among whom he worked. He was careful to keep in environments where his mind would not

---

* He did not, in fact, marry till he was over fifty, and struggled with fears of impotence, as well as of failures of repression.

be put to the test of keen competition. [He] didn't compete with the
clergymen who had the largest posts in his denomination, he struck
out for himself in no hazardous business or professional enterprise,
he took up and finished no piece of investigation ... After the days
of his scholarly ascendance in high school and college, [he] fell out
of competition in academic pursuits.

And he valued very highly, as if to offset the lack of warmth in his object-
relations, his capacity to produce words.

Finally, ambivalence to his father, both directly and as reflected in his
sexuality, vitally influenced his outlook and style. Since his mother died
when A.'s sister was born, and the children were cared for thereafter by a
succession of elderly, unmemorable housekeepers, Mr A.'s father, a somewhat uncouth and domineering rural parson, was especially significant
for the boy. Though he succeeded in identifying to a large degree with
his father, particularly in choice of profession and distaste for money-
making, he carried much unconscious hatred and resentment over the
price he had had to pay to become and remain his father's favourite —
sexual abstinence. The hostility which was denied personal expression or
even conscious recognition was displaced on to remote symbolic objects,
such as the dogma that required acceptance of the Scriptures by faith, or
the endorsement of the capitalist system or of an imperialist war.

These family circumstances also left A. with a strong latent homosexual
trend. On first meeting a stranger, he would be 'winning', over-personal,
anxious to charm and impress, but if the affection too quickly volunteered
was rejected, or if he sensed opposition, he would quickly veer into an
'over-reaction of jibes, flouts and sneers' to salve the wound to his narcissism. In his public campaigns, he exceeded the bounds of convention,
and became recklessly provocative. Lasswell suspected also that 'struggles
with the feminine component' informed A.'s care to keep away from close-
working subordination to a powerful personality; he stayed in environments where his authority was unchallenged — in the church he was both
the financial pillar and the pastor, and among the socialists he bore a
halo of moral and cultural prestige.

A denunciatory oratorical style and programme thus caught up and
harnessed with remarkable economy a whole cluster of powerful personal
'motives'.* Lasswell's final note is, however, of an unmistakable *artificiality*
about the whole performance: for this man the tasks and personal rewards
of agitating and getting others agitated far outweigh the objects of the
crusade, if indeed these are clearly seen at all. He espouses rather than
embodies rebellion.

Mr A. as B. The main impediment to classing Mr A. as B is his hereditary

---

* And others we have not the space to detail, especially the 'early oral' traits
of optimism, generosity and easy dependence on female coddling.

and continuing belief in God, in a vocation as His 'vicar', and in the strict Puritan code. One may urge that A. seems to have lived permanently in the purlieus of doubt; that, by the end, he had run himself out of any institutional, indeed congregational, context; or that puritanism had, over his life-time, developed into an 'oppositional' rather than a conformist stance. We cannot deny that his 'rebellion', such as it is, issues from a carefully-secured, if narrow, *highly conventional* base. However, once given this minimum stake in the game, as it were, it is entirely plausible to represent the unfolding (radicalising) of his outlook — rationalised as a steady disenchantment with 'white collar' reforms, and a 'realisation' that political democracy 'required' economic democracy — as, psychologically, a steady widening of the conventional understandings to which he was eager to lay siege. His project, we may say, was the B type's project of becoming ever more deeply unsettling to middle-class convictions and established authority. (His fervent equalitarian sentiments might seem to argue for a P placement, but Lasswell has underlined their quality of 'protestation', and he clearly wished among his working-class 'friends' to be taken less as a brother than as a mentor and benefactor.)

He fulfils remarkably one of Bales's DB requirements (see the case of Grove, above, p. 150) — the courting of others' aggression and making a dramatic show of willingness to receive punishment, to demonstrate vividly (maybe by starving) that the community's mobilisation of aggression in support of the war is morally repugnant. Mr A. has, however, too many ascendant characteristics to lodge for long in the DB position — his very pacifism is truculent and aggressive (cf. Grove's mute and reproachful stance).

As we have already noted of Sullivan, denying F and the local pieties has led to a progressive widening — a 'universalising' — of A.'s sympathies. But he is like Sullivan, too, in being *exhausted* in denial; nothing personally new or constructive for the group follows from his running up the rebel flag — and one senses that it is more important to him to be distanced from, and defiant of, conservative opinion, than allied with fellow radicals. He protests his difference, too, like Sullivan, in a blatant disregard for money.

Lasswell thought A.'s personality, with its orality, narcissism and latent homosexuality, a splendid model for the *agitator* political type, and he quite brilliantly used A.'s testimony to tease out the peculiar satisfactions and compulsions of the trade (see above, pp. 24–5), Mr A. fulfils Bales's expectation of over-valuing rationalistic argument: a most striking instance, not mentioned in our summary, is his siege by post of Church leaders whose published views he is convinced can be shown to require pacifism in present circumstances. Bales's prediction of timidity or impersonality he fulfils less well. He echoes Sullivan in being highly anxious. However, in binding much of his anxiety in a Puritan regimen, he, in addition, both 'earns the right' to censor others, and accumulates the head of frustration and aggression to do so with gusto. In pouring self thus into role, a fine intelligence is used in a blunt way.

The family background, while not at all the mother-centred one predicted, is starkly sufficient: it involves a domineering and largely admired father, who exacts an over-severe Obedience project, behind which, however, is smuggled a Rebellious intellectuality, which progressively makes over what is outwardly a conformist role into a finally truculently repudiatory one. (Keen sibling rivalry for the 'good boy' slot in a conditional-love setting intensified both the pains and rewards of early obedience and, subsequently, of late rebellion.)

Little's Compton as B

With a cynical 'private' smile, long bushy black hair and full beard, and studiedly inexpressive clothes, Compton, a final-year Science student at Melbourne University, has an air of aggressive self-containment.[74] He gives a grudging interview. In a questionnaire on the 'university experience', he has written that 'Students should learn that it is possible that this is not the best of all possible worlds.'

He is deeply interested in politics — above all, in the current issue of whether young men should continue to be conscripted for the Vietnam war. As a 'deferred draftee', he stands a good chance, unless the policy changes, of being sent himself when he graduates. He has this year joined a Left-wing club and done some anti-war demonstrating and campaigning. He looks forward to a future Socialist party to replace the trade union Labour party, and to a society where rational public planning will supersede the random 'accidents' of private capitalism. His other main concern is that he is losing momentum, and not doing terribly well, in his Science course — it seems unlikely that he will be able to tackle post-graduate work. Should he, even at this late stage, switch to Arts, in which he did notably well at school?

Compton's political style, which Little dubs 'oppositional', exhibits three main traits. The first of these is *self-reliance* — individual and generational. He is a lonely critic, who could be described as Fabian, and not at all in tune with the ethos of the contemporary New Left. But he has a strong sense of belonging to a generation of students whose fathers have left them a mess ('things are in a bad way ... it's pretty lousy, for many people at least'), and who must seize the initiative to reform and rationalise (students are 'supposedly the intellectual elite of the community ... An intellectual person has got to do something'). They have only themselves to depend on, and will have to build from nothing. The second trait is *radicalism* — in the broad sense of a total disrespect for existing structures. It is important, he says, for people to realise that 'the world we live in isn't here because of divine grace or something'. There is no God, and there is little health in social authorities either. He doubts the efficacy of teachers at school or university; the Church is bankrupt; no political leaders at home or abroad excite his admiration. The third trait is *rationalism*. A belief in the efficacy of applied intelligence, a hypostasising of the sheer processes of rational planning, stands out in, because it so nearly exhausts, his 'socialism'. He has no generous social sympathies, no deep moral indignation or utopian visions. He looks forward, himself, to a career 'in computers' or simply 'rationalising companies'. All in all, a politics epitomising an unwillingness, indeed, refusal, 'to celebrate the given'.

These traits also infuse Compton's personal style as a student. In the questionnaire he ticks 'opportunity for individual development, training in independent intellectual work, the encouragement of energetic scepticism' as proper university aims — all stress reason and self-reliance — and puts last the item which suggests that 'social needs should strongly influence what the university teaches'. 'Teaching social traditions . . . and professional training . . . are next in *un*importance.' He has wide, extra-curricular interests and, despite his indifferent grades, has found an 'unofficial' niche as a jokey member of a clever, intellectual set. He speaks contemptuously of pompous law students — 'houndstooth sports coats, with a tome under their arms . . . *they're just old before their time*' — who should instead 'freely accept their own generation, coolly appraise their elders' achievement', and apply themselves to repairing the damage. He advocates radical reforms in teaching methods, but is uninterested in the organisational and social sides of the university (beyond his own small circle). The university has given him, above all, he thinks, an assurance of his cleverness:

> Going straight out of school having been . . . crushed and sat on by everyone . . . I would have remained . . . very much a timid small fry all my life . . . I think I can stand up for my rights a lot more . . . I know I can sort of stand up and scream at someone in a job, and if I don't like the ways they do things I'll tell them so.

As Little judges his personality, the *independence* on which Compton so insists has several layers. Compton is, in fact, rather abjectly identified with his father ('people say I'm like him'); the father is the one who demands independent resourcefulness in himself and his children, rather beyond their ability comfortably to supply it. Compton's dilemma is that to interest his father he must seem not to care for his regard, while, if he seems to need him, he will lose his only chance of having him.

The father, a business scientist, is himself 'fairly left-wing' — a long-time Labour voter, snorting critic of the bumbling Establishment, and a rationalist. In being 'oppositional', Compton is partly being obedient and conformist. Yet Compton's own anti-authority stance is weakened at the core by wistful hopes that his father may yet take him up and give him his approval. So he drifts, rudderless, between a view of the world as 'a lousy mess', and a view of it as *possibly* not the best of all possible worlds. As Little observes, this is a precarious foundation for any resolute radicalism, and it may even be that the note of stridency and protest in Compton's scornful critique is a tacit admission that his forthrightness and independence cannot really compare with his father's.

Other personal traits, although they still strain after likeness to father and father's approval, seem also to conjure with mother's model — only to push it indignantly aside. His mother, who also has a degree,* comes a-cross as fussy, old-fashioned, not serious — the unthinking *religieuse* and ceremonialist of the family. Compton's impatience with female company, intimacy, sentiment and ritual — his general 'masculine protest' — seems designed to separate himself from her qualities, which are embarrassing, intrusive, in themselves, but dangerous in that they could undercut his identification with his father. Little judges the resulting ego-restriction to be severe: 'Compton is good at analysis and at opposing, but lacks a sense of the concrete, the human, the felt.' His cognitive style is notably deductive, and he posits, by preference, highly abstract solutions to problems. He is not a co-operator: hyper-individualist in what he demands from the university, and happy in his in-group precisely because it cherishes individual sharpness.

Little leaves the resolution of Compton's outlook rather open. Is there sufficient guilt for his cold rejectiveness to fuel some future destructive and self-punishing act (in the Samson tradition)? Is there enough basic self-doubt and self-contempt, enough fury at father's ineluctable superiority, to mount a cold and intense siege on authority, from motives of envy and resentment? Or is Compton's 'oppositional stance' a shallow, attention-getting façade of provocation, behind which there is merely a sad eagerness to be noticed, to be instructed, to yield, obey and fall into line? If either the first or the third of these possibilities should actually occur, then Compton moves even nearer to B placement.†

Conclusion

These three case-studies — voices from the late 1920s, the 1940s and the 1960s — may now be drawn together and compared with Bales's template, in the hope of making it more comprehensive.

First, all three, however finally weak and unproductive their rebellion, are unquestionably *anti-authoritarians*, with a total disrespect for existing

---

* Compton's Science-Arts dilemma is that he must do Science to be like, or to impress, or possibly to outstrip, his father, and must therefore do it well — as he could, if he were really his father over again. But perhaps if he is *not* like his father, he could do Arts better — although that would be to give up his one sure model. This is complicated by the fact that an elder sister, the father's favourite, has already done exceptionally well in Arts.

† In fact, re-interviewed some years later, when Vietnam conscription was no longer an issue, Compton was, politically, a much depleted figure (personal communication from Dr Little). This suggests that the third possibility has come out most strongly.[75]

structures; they are united in a refusal to celebrate the given. Other features of their disobedience include:

A wish to install an entirely new form of society. All are, as it happens, 'socialists', but, when it is applied to three generations, the term conveys only a sense of the scale of difference required. (Compton demands, on behalf of the new generation, a 'clean slate', the older generation having left nothing worth carrying forward.)

A tendency to a 'universalising' of sympathy as a consequence of rejecting (and transcending) local pieties; this is least marked in Compton.

An ideological window-dressing of their repudiation — 'over-valuation of rationality' — and a preoccupation with the denying of abstractions.

Despite a wish to go beyond the disowning of false principles to root out the last trace of emotional attachment to present arrangements (for example, A.'s and Sullivan's disregard for money), a sense overall of their *being exhausted in the very effort of repudiation,* and unable to go on to any decisive action or different life.

Their retaining in their rebellion strong touches of conformity. Sullivan and Compton, with 'radical' fathers, base a good part of their oppositional stance on filial pieties; Mr A. keeps the conformism of his 'model Christian boy', but uses it as a base for ever-widening denunciation.*

A lonely rebellion — in which coldly marking one's distance from conventional belief outweighs any forging of new fraternal links. Sullivan draws back from party membership; Mr A. condescends to lead 'the brothers'; Compton is an accomplished non-co-operator, uninterested in the New Left.

A predominance of negative over positive affects in outlook, especially hate, scorn, bitterness and cynicism. Sullivan shows this least of the three.

Secondly, in regard to personality, our cases suggest that, beyond Bales's 'over-valuation of rationality, retreat into impersonality and timidity', there is anxiety (apparent in all), leading to 'minimised hopes' in Sullivan and Compton (remember that Compton is downwardly mobile — Little talks of his 'somewhat grim readiness to take responsibility for himself'), a strong head of hostility (apparent in all), and arrogance and/or superiority in Mr A. and Compton. All are of high intelligence. A. and Compton are happiest with abstractions, but Sullivan cannot manage them. Compton and Sullivan cultivate a clowning humour that also bites. All have a fear of, or distaste for, women.

The family stories they tell do not agree with Bales's prediction, except in the very broad and possibly tautological sense that none of the parents were suitable conventional models, who, in being loved and trusted, could sweeten the assumption of conformity. The father was the more important

---

* This may explain their failure to conform with Bales's expectation of a sub-theme: rejection of limitations on impulse-expression, a sense of 'no rules needed' as a recoil from a repudiated 'system of rewards and punishments'; and a preference for fantasy and feeling over logic and argument.[76]

figure in each case. Mr A.'s father (the mother died early) was ambivalent-
ly loved, and imposed an excessive regimen of obedience. Compton's
father (the mother was simply disregarded) was abjectly identified with,
but he rejected his son, and set a stiff independence/achievement project.
Sullivan's father providing sanity, warmth and gaiety for fourteen years,
preserved Sullivan from the mother's cold manipulative paranoia.
Sullivan's and Compton's fathers were themselves 'somewhat radical'
(though *not* pessimistic/cynical) and even Mr A.'s highly conventional
father 'disliked the rich'. Sibling rivalry fuelled A.'s egalitarianism, a trait
weakly marked in the others.

The Alienates — DB, DNB and DN

If the Rebel, the B type, appears to show almost a natural bent
for ideologising and to have an aptitude for politics, it seems characteristic
of Alienates that they cannot easily harness to politics the equal or greater
pressure of hostility and pain they feel. Their negativism seems at once
more total, and yet less easy to focus on. However, some Alienates do
exhibit a fierce and narrow politics almost entirely split off from the main
body of their concerns. There are many shades in it, as we might expect in
a cluster of positions distributed across three meridians. In any case,
whether or not they take concrete ideological or political form, these outlooks express alienation, rather than rebellion.

We may start with a glance backwards at Murray's Grove — the mildly
leftist medical student who somehow could not 'take hold', and was
hanging back from work, the war, politics and life in a state of hopeless
inertia, unconsciously preoccupied with a Lost Eden. Grove, we said,
elevated 'feet-dragging', and a feeling of reluctance, to the status of an
aversion from life, and though a frank father-hater, he could summon up
no more than a token and passive resistance to him — or to social authorities. To confirm our grip on the DB, the Passive Resister type, I present here
another case from *Private Politics*, a case I now see as remarkably similar
to Grove, but only after the exercise of testing them both against the Bales
typology had cut through much apparent difference in ideology and style.
This most co-operative subject was interviewed immediately after an
uncharacteristic but intense flirtation with political activism.

Davies's East as DB

East, an Australian public servant (an archivist) and Catholic minority-
party activist, in his middle thirties, is, at first glance, strikingly different
from Grove: a pragmatic Centrist instead of a hostile Liberal; a Christian,
pious to the extent of a shot at the priesthood, instead of a comfortable
agnostic; would-be philosopher and scholar with a Natural Law cast of
mind, instead of a self-indulgent anti-intellectual.[77] At the emotional
core, however, their world views are hauntingly similar.

It is surprising to see the passive resister as a political *activist*. In fact, we caught East when he was depressed, disillusioned and cynical, after five years' hard work for the new Democratic Labour Party, culminating in a parliamentary candidature and massive defeat. He was retiring hurt, with the feeling that he had wasted his time, been made a fool of, swept by an eddy of history out of his depth and out of character. The party leaders had simply had no strategic sense, just a vulgar propensity to be combative and assertive. Not liking the limelight, he was relieved to be resuming his customary posture of inaction and waiting in the wings 'doing nothing, but going on talking and discussing', turning over ideas which might be wanted some day for a politics of 'progressive moderation'.

How had he come so to miscast himself? First, there was his considerable frustration: he had long been fascinated by politics, but felt roughly equal distaste for the major parties, and there had seemed no way in. Then, having just abandoned training in a religious order after four years, he was 'fed up with being a spectator . . . on the side-lines all the time', and wanted to become involved. Secondly, he felt directly called to help the Church with his political talents — a sober sense (coached by his father) of political realities, and (transcending his father) a gift for Utopian scheming about, for example, 'decentralization of power' or the 'regime of *agape*'. Above all, the challenge to help *build* something at once new and historic, with people and ideas, attracted a man denied the hereditary constructional occupation of the family males. And, if he made a success of it, his mother would be thrilled (and perhaps vindicated) and his father finally forced to admire him.

Indeed, aged 35 and unmarried, his emotional dependence on his parents seemed remarkable, the obverse of a crippling lack of self-assertion. 'I recognize my failings and therefore wish to restrain whatever is aggressive and self-assertive in me' (reads his preferred *Path of Life*). Diffident, self-deprecating, depressed, emotionally paralysed, he volunteered a story of a mysterious neurosis which has lasted 25 years, and which he fancied might now be just about to lift:

> At about ten, I'd say, I became a different person. I don't know that
> I ever *felt* different, but till then I was good at everything. I was even
> a good runner. After that my work began to fall off progressively.
> People were always saying I should be doing much better. But I took
> to doing things as an obligation; I got no personal pleasure out of it.
> It had been different before . . . I saw so much of [my parents' quar-
> rels] — I was always the one for some reason who got involved . . .
> that I . . . developed the habit of putting off deciding about things —
> deciding what I *felt* — almost indefinitely . . . I was somehow dead-
> ened — it didn't seem worthwhile or possible [developing my own
> ideas, making my own discoveries]. I just did what was expected
> of me — I was always, I suppose, a 'good boy' — never because it
> meant anything very much to me personally.

The onset of this automaton-like state in which nothing seems worthwhile or possible coincided with the birth of his second sister, an event evidently long dreaded, and which finally dashed his hopes of remaining closest to his mother. But we must set the context.

> There was a tremendous clash in my family right from the beginning [he explained] about who was to run things. My father's family was the usual patriarchal English model, and he was quite sure about the man's role of being master in his own house. On the other hand, my mother's grandmother (her father's mother) had been, as far as I can make out, a real Irish matriarch . . .
> Well I think what my father did was to clear out from the start – at least from when my brother [born 3 years before me] was little. There were constant rows about how to bring him up: my father wanting, as usual, his pretty authoritarian methods; my mother objecting violently; and he just gave it away altogether and refused to have anything to do with the children.

A self-made industrialist with strong conservative political affiliations, the father was a cold and lonely man, isolated in authority, aloof from ordinary folk, given to sudden whims and rages. Damned in advance by his mother's favouritism and indulgence, and undermined by his elder brother's relentless scorn, East's early efforts to impress his father met with little success, if they were not flatly repelled. Turning his attentions back to his mother, East's problem became how to do what pleased her. The birth of his second sister, and the discovery that his mother really put his father first, and/or really wanted another *girl*, annihilated him; they reactivated in extreme form the jealousies of his fifth year, the doubts about whether his mother was any longer worth his love, and his revulsion at sexuality. By the age of ten, he felt that he had exhausted every possible model of behaviour to draw special love from either parent – to no avail. This restless changing of direction persisted in his efforts to settle to a vocation. He thought that law would please his father and the priesthood his mother, but he was perpetually in doubt, half-hearted, unable to bring himself to believe unqualifiedly in any of them. Yet, under this drift of abortive schemes, lending them, indeed, a certain pathos, lay a sombre resolve finally to impress.

His main defence against authority-stress is passive resistance – evasion, mulish inaction, or flight. He also 'understands', opening the way to resigned acceptance; he nags in a wifely way, or urges transcendence – 'Couldn't we raise all this to a rather higher plane?' He is congenitally uneasy with superiors and inclined to question the legitimacy of their commands; he sees certain faults in all of them – especially arbitrariness and coldness. He calls himself 'a bit of a rebel' (and he has been one at home, at school, in the Order, at work, in the Democratic Labour Party), but he has always been a lonely rebel, disliking possible co-rebels almost as much as the enemy. It is, of course, from his father that East adduced the standard defects of authority — he was remote, isolated, coldly manipulative and peremptory in command, and it was against him that East perfected his characteristic defensive strategies. It is nevertheless intriguing that the gravamen of his charge against Santamaria, the architect of the D.L.P. — that he will not fully identify himself with the party, or declare his permanent involvement, and that he would betray it or kill it off at a moment's notice, if he decided it had served its purpose — encapsulates his worst infantile fear: that his father would abandon the family. And it is striking how, even when East had decided that Santamaria's policies were fatal, he was unable to bring himself to move to the attack, as if Santamaria, though quite wrong, remained somehow the better man.

We do not finally tether East's political outlook, however, until we see both the father's 'active intent shrewd-dealer' view of politics, and the cloudier Christian Democrat or future 'Progressive Moderates' model that is nearer his own taste, as mere islands on a sea of 'female' scepticism. Women need not concern themselves with politics, he says: 'they have better things to do, and . . . in all important matters they already rule'. Adjudicating as ever between 'paternal' and 'maternal' claims to pre-eminence, he cannot conceal his bias towards the 'real world' of children and home and the 'simple life of the parish' that his father spurns and belittles. Male triumphs have to East an air of make-believe; the world of men and affairs is at bottom hollow. The original identification with his mother thus provides the basis of his world view. His later sharp disappointment with her generates his pessimism, his automaton state, and his romantic identification with lost causes. But he has dealt with both, too, by preserving her ideal qualities beyond cavil in a transcendent Mother Church, a memorial to that first brief but perfect symbiotic union.

East as DB. What East most usefully contributes to the type description is, I think, his first-hand account of the 'automaton-state', of deadened feeling, of aspiration cut off at the root, of the depersonalising of the personal core. He had lived only so as to win favour in his mother's eyes — and she had turned away. He also corroborates Grove's brother-pair with crossed-parental identification, and Grove's passive containment of even very strong anti-authoritarian impulses where the father retains the moral initiative.

The main difficulties he presents as a stock DB case are threefold. First, there are his periodic, courageous efforts to break out of a passive-with-drawn routine into something else (including his current declaration that he is on the point of overcoming his long neurotic stasis). As a student late in the war he joined the Navy; as a candidate for the priesthood near the end of his training, he rejected demands for unquestioning obedience, and left; as a party stalwart, he made a stand on several points of principle, and resigned; as an archivist, he volunteered for a challenging post in a new nation. These are perhaps *evasive* assertions, but a true DB type should be more inert. One suspects that East's father — and his activity/achievement orientation — continue to weigh more with East than the type-model.

Secondly, the father looms larger than he ought, if he were truly or finally rejecting, in the conservatism of East's politics. Far from being a 'gullible lamb unprotected against the wolves of the radical left', East has shown himself the dupe of a notable wolf of the radical right, Santamaria. East strives, in fact, to incorporate all that is usable in his father's pragmatic centrist position; his tactic is not to contradict but to *transcend*, to lift it to an altogether higher intellectual and moral plane, to give it tone and polish. In outsmarting his father, he incorporates him, compels his (unwilling) admiration and co-operation, and shows himself the larger and more complex mind. But the old man declines the part written for him.

Thirdly, as an honours History graduate and long-time philosophy and theological student, East has an unusually developed and *conventional* ideological position. In this he is siding with, and *celebrating*, his mother's piety against his father's agnosticism, and one may read much of it as 'reproof' to the father. But in partly transferring his identification with his mother to an identification with the Church, he assumes, in value terms, a conservative and conventional position, that of the F type.* He does indeed make gestures at European Christian Democracy, and 'a middle way between socialism and capitalism' (and his religious beliefs seem perfectly orthodox), yet he is characteristically inept and ineffective in harnessing ideals to tasks.† He is also notably less interested, himself, in the mainstream Catholicism of the suburban parish than in Fr Courtney Murray, a rounded philosophy of history, rural communes with religious overtones, and dreams of a future Catholic party ruling by moral superiority and wisdom. Indeed, his sense that Utopian dreaming is his special strength recalls Bales's nomination of 'prophetic leadership' as an outside-chance DB option.

Still his mother's confidant, East has unusual trouble investing the world outside his original family circle (though he never came to terms with the idea of his younger sister) with meaning. Apart from the Church, he finds nothing in society at large to arouse strong feelings: his tone is an even, ironic, debunking pessimism. Lasswell posited in 'cautious' administrators this quality of remaining closely bound to the first little cast of characters, preoccupied with one's 'adjustment to specific persons'. East, however, has cleared the hurdle into abstract interests: his problem is rather to keep these interests earthed.

---

* He is certainly not a Martyr (DF) and, like Grove, does not in the least court aggression.
† He is frankly sceptical of the value of archival work.

DNB — Beat types
Keniston's Inburn as DNB

Tall, thin, polite, bespectacled, nice-looking, hesitant in speech but with a deep, actor's voice and rich syntax, Inburn, an English Literature student at Harvard in the early 1960s, was intensively interviewed after scoring top marks in a campus alienation survey.[78] The interview took place just in time, for half-way through his second year he suddenly threw up his studies and decamped to Haight-Ashbury by motor-bike.

His political outlook was not probed in detail, perhaps because he seemed so massively anti-political, incapable, certainly, of any political or other long-term commitment. But in broad plan his outlook epitomised alienation: 'The idea of trying to adjust to society as now constituted fills me with horror.' Mistrustful, pessimistic, resentful, anxious, egocentric yet self-contemptuous, rejecting American culture, conventional social groups and values (particularly 'everything, and everyone that's complacently middle-class'), he feels himself an Outsider, estranged and distant from others, rejecting happiness as a goal, and viewing the universe as an unstructured and meaningless chaos. Asked how he would reform the world if he could, he says, 'I guess I'd like to have us all go back to the womb.' He has no plans for his life, no ambitions — 'Nobody strives for ideals any more. It's hard enough just to strive' — though perhaps in the distant future, after a life spent 'accumulating the most varied, the most valuable and most significant set of sense experiences it is possible to take in' and cutting through the social superstructure of 'tin and shit and kite-paper' to 'the bedrock of sheer existence', he might *as a writer* pass on the 'truest possible picture of this world' before he dies.

This gives the shape and flavour, perhaps, of Inburn's world view, but it is possible to say more about its leading cognitive and affective qualities. First, there is an unconscious reification of early infancy as the model for all later satisfactions, and against which all later relationships are to be found wanting — lacking its passivity, its claustral security and its effortless gratification. Secondly, he is fixated on the modes of perception, and experience generally, of early childhood, and makes a conscious effort to cut through conventional, 'normal adult' categories of perception to heightened sensations and to modes of experience more direct, immediate, naive and whole. Thirdly, he is suspicious of all social appearances, and probes anxiously for flaws and underlying chicaneries: not till he has demonstrated others' basic sham, hypocrisy and deceit, does Inburn feel that he has struck bottom (and striking 'rock bottom' is his prerequisite for building a viable identity). He therefore has an intellectual style of 'unmasking' and reductionism, and a programme of intense and total repudiation, which lie against a backdrop of existential pessimism: religion, conventional values, social institutions, culture itself, Inburn feels, are all arbitrary games played by the conventional and fearful in order to 'blind themselves' to the deeper absurdity of the world. True intimacy is impossible, as individuals are separated by their self-centredness and their inability to understand each other. Social relations generally are based on mutual exploitation and appropriation, restrained only fitfully by fears of punishment. The universe is inherently chaotic and unpredictable.

Finally, Inburn shows a failure of repression and, indeed, flaunts socially unconventional and taboo feelings, fantasies and impulses — leaving a sense of drivenness, or unreality, and of being flooded by unwanted feelings and ideas. (Unlike the self-punishing neurotic, however, Inburn projects his blame outwards, and universalises his own state into the human condition.)

Inburn's project, therefore, is in essence one of denial and estrangement —withdrawal to a small sub-society of fellow-alienates, agreed on the futility of endeavour and the emptiness of love, believing merely in the intensification of life and/or in the role of detached observer, the camera-eye: Inburn rejects, more or less completely, 'adult values, groups, institutions, and roles as conventionally defined'. He thinks of himself as 'deliberately choosing a deviant outlook'; and although he is 'deeply and openly unhappy', he avers that 'others would be unhappy, too, if they but saw the same things with the same honesty'. His

> alienation fulfills many simultaneous functions: unconsciously, it
> is a description of [his] own felt condition as [an] outcast ... from
> Eden; it provides an ideology for attacking apparently authoritative
> ideas ... and principles which might prove untrustworthy; it reflects
> a fear of commitment to an adult male role which, as instanced by
> [his] own father ... has ... proved inadequate and inconsistent.[79]

Inburn describes his father, an ex-schoolteacher from a poor midwest farming family, now a Detroit company executive, as a 'phlegmatic, deliberate, steady-minded Welshman' and 'pretty much of a failure in his own eyes. He's done pretty well as far as the world is concerned, though.' He is 'a pillar in the community. (Small pillar. Small community).' He feels there is and always has been a great distance between his father and himself.

His mother, the daughter of a Greek restaurant owner in St Louis, is also an ex-schoolteacher, but socially and culturally highly ambitious and mobile. Volatile, passionate, yet delicate, his mother was, he says, 'particularly good looking when she was young — black hair, a good nose, strikingly large eyes ... and a delicate yet hard, vibrant, vivacious body'. She rose to an extraordinary position among her contemporaries, through sheer will and hard experience. His TATs show that he feels, indeed, too close to her.

We have, then, an only child, 'destined to feel more intensely about his parents than would a child with siblings'; parents of strongly contrasting temperament — the mother sensual and driving, the father drab, acquiescent and, as we shall see, fatally *absent*. As Keniston reconstructs Inburn's developmental history, the mother is

> emotionally seductive, seeking from her son a kind of emotional
> fulfillment he could not provide and unconsciously attempting to
> use her attractiveness to bind him to her. Thus, even as a small child,
> Inburn probably felt torn between his dependency on his mother
> and his enjoyment of their extraordinary closeness on the one hand,
> and on the other her unwanted possessiveness and her unconscious
> needs that he be more to her than a son.

Further, by leaving the son in no doubt that she found the father dull and disappointing,* she intensified Inburn's rivalry and wish to supplant him. When Inburn was five, the father did suddenly depart — for the war — and remained away for four years, an absence the boy must unconsciously have considered a token of his own triumph. His autobiography celebrates these years as an idyll of closeness and understanding, indeed, as an infant-mother symbiosis restored. The father's return abruptly shattered the idyll, but, a resigned man, 'failure in his own eyes', who has given up an idealistic career for money and routine, he proves incapable of offering the son anything better, and thus becomes the object of a double grievance.

Keniston, describing the hollowness of Inburn's victory, memorably catches the central emotional state of the Oedipal 'Pyrrhic victor'. What Inburn most deeply longed for, Keniston argues, was total fusion with a maternal presence, and he wished to remove whatever stood between him and his mother. But though in some psychological sense, he believes that he succeeded in vanquishing his father, he simultaneously lost the goal for which he strove. In place of the surrounding and comforting maternal presence, he won a mother, whom he now sees, at best as controlling and limiting, and at worst as devouring and murderous. The intimacy he wanted with her is replaced by her stringent limitations of his initiative; by her possessiveness; by her efforts to make him unsexual, unaggressive and conforming. And furthermore, by defeating his

---

* In a later, much longer look at the grandparents and the parents' childhoods,
Keniston uncovers strong grounds for the couple's mutual dissatisfaction.[80]
The mother, an emancipated woman of the late 1920s and early 1930s, with
artistic, radical career interests, identifies with her father. The father, in revolt
against narrow, practical parents chose an idealistic, cultural job. Both were
looking in marriage for qualities in their partner that would strengthen what
they thought best in themselves. But undercut by old ambivalencies — a real
wife is surely less manly, a real husband surely more so — their mutual
support fails. The wife buries her talent; the husband takes a 'paying' job.
The birth of the hero staves off divorce, but when the wife proceeds to enthrone the son, the husband lights out, devotes himself monomaniacally to
work.

father he has lost his right to a father he can admire: instead, he now sees him as psychologically absent, not worthy of respect or emulation, 'phony' in his appearance of respectability, underlyingly weak, controlled by a woman. The real victor — the one who alone retains the capacity to affect, move and change the world around her — is the mother. Ironically, both father and son end up in the same boat — her victims.

The legacies of this state are a debased image of conventional values and authorities. Inburn is left with a conviction that adulthood in general is disastrous insofar as it means becoming like his father; an excessive fear of his own aggression (believed to have once been so effective); a split image of both men and women — men are either archaic, pre-Oedipal, unassailable destroyers or post-Oedipal, passive weaklings (with whom Inburn resolutely refuses to identify)* and women are early bountiful nurturers or late binding, limiting castrators (who bar the way to full masculinity); a paralysis of sexuality, torn between simultaneous desires for passive incorporation and phallic assertiveness; and, colouring all, a powerful regressive nostalgia for a lost Eden, and an outcast's self pity.

Inburn as DNB. After Inburn, Bales's sketch of the DNB Passive Alienate type — organised for withdrawal after conviction of failure — seems a little pallid. This is partly because Bales's DNB is observed still clinging to the group, wishing fervently, maybe, to cut loose, but too enfeebled and low-spirited to try, so that the principal colours of his portrait are dejection, passivity and unreachableness, a sense of being a failure, unviable and disliked.† Inburn, while at the deepest level fully validating the position's central set of qualities — denial of positive feelings, cynical pessimism and the cult of failure — has an energy and bitter *élan* arising from the depth and thoroughness of his repudiation of the conventional, which contrast sharply with the hypothesised reproachfulness and joyless air. Bales does, however, note in an aside the chance that a certain pride may be invested in the 'power to hate and escape'; this fits Inburn, and helps to illuminate his case.

Because of this general presumption of *silent* reproach, Bales expects little from the DNB type in the way of finished ideology. Bales wonders if the DNB may simply have no clear characteristic set of values; after all, he lacks any vital motive to persuade others, having no projects for them

---

* In determining *not* to let what happened to his father happen to him, but to be radically different, Inburn perhaps shows an attachment to his fantasy of what his father might have been, had he followed through his youthful aspiration and retained his early dreams: he identifies with his father's lost idealism.

† This sense is elevated, indeed, into a neurotic 'delusion of dislike' (from which we must emphatically exempt Inburn).

or belief in their possible aid. (On the contrary, as himself a black sheep, as well as a lost one, he makes a uniquely attractive potential recruit to all manner of other good causes, including tender-minded conservatism – the DPF position – and tender-minded radicalism – the DPB position.) Bales suggests, for lack of specimen opinions, that DNB believes that the real substance of life consists of a process of disillusionment, with few goals that are worth the effort spent in reaching them. This, too, catches Inburn at the deepest level, but quite misses the fluent torrent of his hyper-critical and systematic contrariness. Bales says that DNB 'does not wish to make a moral point of his failure or that of the group'.[81] Inburn *does* (and he carries Keniston some little way with him), despite the fact that he is deeply attached to a self-image of the 'camera-eye', the non-judgmental stance, transcending and reproving the *bourgeois*. 'To establish . . . an ideological position out of failure and withdrawal, he would generally have to form or join a still smaller alienated subgroup', Bales adds. And while that, again, is what Inburn does, we must note that his ideology is perfected beforehand (and in isolation) at Harvard.

Little is clearly predicted of DNB personality traits. On the ego-id front, he is said to be 'without adequate modes of expression of instinctual drives', unlikely to have 'completely accepted or integrated into the personality' the 'appropriate conventional adult sex role', and to be liable to 'splits and confusions between masculine and feminine conservative role traits'. All this is true of Inburn. However, predictions on the ego/social-identity front – that the DNB type may have a 'split and poorly organised' self-picture, only partial acceptance or knowledge of ordinary social norms, and few friends – do not stand up so well. Inburn, it is clear, lacked neither the social nor the intellectual equipment for outstanding conventional success: he simply *chose* to brand it as chimerical. Contrary to type – 'withdrawal *after* failure' – Inburn chose not to *go on* 'succeeding', but to deviate and rebel. He thus answers always in a special key to the type attributes: withdrawn, alienated, hostile, depressed, eccentric, immature and, perhaps, chronically sick, guilty or indecisive.

The family background picture, following the clue that the parents are likely to be out-of-touch and the child's upbringing so ineffectual or inadequate about the requisites of conventionality and success that it amounts to a 'training in failure', answers even less satisfactorily to the case. Again, we would expect the story of a person who samples success and declares it unacceptable to be different from stories of born losers. The remarkable thing is that, entered from up or down stage, the psychological landscape of failure and withdrawal should be so unvarying and uniform.

Keniston himself takes up the question of the psychological and especially the developmental differences between his Beat or 'Uncommitted' type (he examined in detail a further eleven cases from among Inburn's alienated Harvard contemporaries, without adding significantly to the clinical picture)[82] and other apparently contiguous types. After observing that 'the mother's idealisation of her father, accompanied by a specific denigration of the relative worth of her husband, occurs more frequently and more intensely in "alienating" than in ordinary families', he continues:

> In its broad outlines, the basic family constellation and develop-
> mental history that I have linked to alienation also appears related
> to a number of other conditions in adolescence. Thus Lidz, Fleck,
> and their associates, in their studies of the etiology of schizophrenia
> in adolescence, often find among middle-class male patients a com-
> parable although more extreme picture of a mother-son alliance
> against the father, a confusion or reversal of sex roles within the
> family, and a father who is unable to be 'psychologically present'
> in a paternal role ... A similar picture of family dynamics emerges
> from the work of Irving Bieber and associates, *Homosexuality*
> (... 1962), who describe the most common pattern in families with
> psychoanalytically-treated homosexual sons as a 'close-binding
> intimate' mother plus a 'detached' (ambivalent, distant or hostile)
> father. So, too, Erikson ... describes a similar family pattern in the
> etiology of acute identity diffusion among adolescents ...
> The students studied here appear to differ from those described
> in the aforementioned research studies in several ways that may
> be crucial: one, in their ability to 'intellectualize' successfully;
> two, in the frequent signs of a covert identification with a fantasy
> of what the father was like when he was young, before he was
> 'broken by life'. Impressionistically, it seems that the degree of
> psychological disturbance in these students was closely related to
> their *inability* to maintain a positive image of a father who existed
> before they were born. Students who had no such image appeared
> to be most disturbed; those who had an active fantasy of their youth-
> ful father seemed to be the most articulate and outspoken critics of
> American society ... It may be that the capacity to express aliena-
> tion in ideological, political, or revolutionary forms is related to
> an implicit identification with the lost idealism of the father.[83]

But, four years later, after a close study of a dozen leading student radicals (unfortunately yielding no case remotely comparable in quality to Inburn) he abandoned this promising theme.[84] His set of explicit contrasts there, between Radical and Beat *types*, retreats to a position which merely accords Radicals a healthier and more normal upbringing on all counts than the Beats, who are left locked in personal neurosis and undifferentiated — and unapproached — in ideological potential.

Wienecke's Katie as Beat

Fortunately, a new Australian case has come forward which may further confirm our sense of the type. Katie, a twenty-year-old Arts student, was first interviewed in a psychiatric hospital after a suicide attempt.[85] She had dropped out of her course at Flinders University, after a successful first year, to spend almost twelve months drifting about the country taking casual jobs and hitch-hiking from city to city. Her suicide bid came early in her second year of resumed studies, after the perfectionist demands she made on herself had precipitated a panic loss of ability to concentrate. She transferred to Melbourne the following year.

Describing herself as shy, idealistic, austere, insecure, and 'inadequate — in every way, you name it', she disclosed a personal landscape both cold and bleak. Having perfected a lifelong project of self-sufficiency and *withdrawal* — 'my highest demand on myself was to be unaffected by the world' — she is now alarmed that she cannot give love, make friends or find a purpose in life beyond mere academic success and perhaps a dimly-glimpsed aesthetic quest. Indeed, she persists in her studies and her aim of being a 'perfect student', for reasons almost exactly as pessimistic and disillusioned as led Inburn to drop out — she cannot imagine herself doing any useful work in the world outside or after she graduates, so that she may just as well stay where she is. She suffers from incapacitating cycles of severe depression — '*monthly* cycles, and it's not related to femininity or anything' — and has a nightmare picture of her future as 'Just growing on ... 25, 30, 35, 40 ... haggard old dame ... still in and out of hospital ... oh God ... hating my job like my mother hates her job ... dragging on'. In more cheerful moments, she imagines some impetus for social change 'filtering down' from academic studies and the new generation slowly accumulating power. Like Inburn, she too has, at the edge of her plans, the notion of an eventual book of discomforting truthfulness.

She owned to a season of keen interest in politics and a conventional array of New Left and/or Maoist views, but protested that she was 'basically not interested in politics, anymore'. She saw her early radicalism as hopelessly idealistic: 'Most people will never be happy, regardless of the social structure'; the change necessary in human nature in order to produce a better society, 'to stop craving after material things, and this idea of possessing somebody, and possessing children', made it almost inconceivable. But she saw her early radicalism not only as idealistic, but as psychologically suspect, as a hothouse growth.

> My more Communistic-type thoughts were just an escape hatch, really — a private fantasy world I could escape into. I never did anything about them ... It doesn't seem the end of the world, now, that I don't have to think about social ideals all the time.

And, she added, she was currently finding her personal programme of 'purity and stoicism' so engrossing that she had no energy left over for politics. The mysterious thing, she said, was the depth of her father's influence on her politics, given how little she has had to do with him.

She describes her father, an itinerant building worker in Western Australia, as

> Very aggressive, very hostile, very mixed-up, very lonely. Very intel-
> ligent and sensitive, and a very good mind – if you can reach it . . .
> but it could all be my imagination, as there's always disillusionment
> when I see him.

Politically, he is 'a raving red Communist' and he has been since his youth.

> But he did his thinking in complete isolation – with nothing but
> a book – and no one around who knew anything he was talking
> about. He's entirely destructive in his criticism – he really raves on.
> His extremism has also led to his sickness . . . When he talks about
> 'our' people coming down, he means the Reds, and he looks forward
> to the end of our world, *our* people.

His 'sickness', paranoid schizophrenia, together with alcoholism, led
to the break-up of the marriage when Katie was twelve, amid scenes of
violence and terror, with Katie deeply ambivalent in her feelings and
often thrust into a mediating position.

She finally blames her mother – 'a very shy, introverted, self-effacing
woman – everything's got to be her fault . . . if a tree falls down three
miles away, she thinks she's to blame' – for the failure of the marriage,
for failing to keep things together, or to help the father, whom she sees
as too sick to cope. But she has a more fatalistic explanation to lessen
the pressure of blame:

> My mother always found it difficult to get close. She had terrible
> problems with boys and going out – didn't get married till she was
> about 31 – and then to my father! – put in a Catholic orphanage at
> 3 and raised there – who had the same problem . . . What a vicious
> circle! Even before they separated, it was never a very normal type
> of marriage or relationship. He was always away building in the
> bush or something . . . flitted in and out of our lives. In fact, I don't
> think he ever formed a relationship with my mother.

Katie reacted to the divorce by plunging into a fantasy world peopled
by Red Indians:

> I needed something after my parents broke up. Something about the
> American Indians drew me, and I began to copy them – all their
> ideals and their stoicism and fire – they were romantic . . . The
> Indians in my mind were perfect: exciting, stoical, able to be cruel
> and to take cruelty, and be proud and dignified, not weak . . . My
> heroes were always killing white people, and having savage mur-
> derous attacks upon their women and children, the innocents, and
> I was always preoccupied with their pride and nobility.

Racing home from school where she would talk to no one, she read avidly
about Indians, wrote reams of stories about them, drew and painted and
sketched them, dreamed about them – and hallucinated them: 'I could
will to see them there actually in front of me – their feathers and their
coats, the wrinkles in their faces, the crinkles round their eyes, and how

they'd sit on the front seat and everything.' Her mother thought it was a precocious intellectual interest in anthropology. When she was sixteen, her father on a visit said, 'Why are you so interested in these Indians? You ought to be interested in what's going on in the real world — in China. That's where it's all happening.' This miraculously sparked off her political period, when she found she could, indeed, endow Third World people with the very characteristics that she prized in her Indians.

But Katie's project of self-enclosure and withdrawal was launched well before secondary school. Dragged about in the wake of her father's search for work, she was sent to kindergarten and seven primary schools, all of which she hated and found a torture. At kindergarten, she screamed and was inconsolable at being left by her mother. School, she generalises,

> was the bane of my existence. It was the most loathsome experience. I felt that I was up there for examination by the whole world. It was absolutely shocking — something I had to prepare my whole anatomy to resist. When I went there, I had to wear this expression on my face, walk in a certain way, dress in a certain way, and do every-thing in a certain way, because it was the most terrible place to be in. It was like a burning incinerator. All those horrible people . . . I had to shut myself up so they wouldn't get at me. *My mother didn't know any of this.*

The mother was 'too preoccupied, no doubt, by her problems with my father', Katie now rationalises, but then Katie chose to bear her burden alone, keep her almost overwhelming feelings of hatred and despair from her mother, and to perfect at school an icy composure, an expression of stony severity, a programme of purity, hardness, pride, 'an austerity that is pulling me back towards suicide all the time'.* This is the same cluster of ideal/fatal qualities that she was later to bestow on the Red Indians. They were a means, too, of holding on to a part, at least, of the lost father.

She feels strong resentment at her mother's present inadequacy, her inability to help her, just as she was inadequate in the days of Katie's school ordeal, and as she was unable to help her husband during his break-down; indeed, the mother is failing once again to notice that her daughter is in difficulties. Yet the strength of her identification with her mother approaches the point where she finds it hard to conceive of herself as a separate person:

> My ties with my mother restrict me. I feel bound to her. At times I get to thinking we're almost the same person. I get really worried. I identify with her worrying, her frantic panics, her inadequacies . . .

She identifies, too, with the mother's fate of just 'dragging on' joylessly

---

* 'When I was about 11 or 12, I was desperately confused about whether I wanted to have friends or not . . . I mean, it seemed I just couldn't make them . . . Later on, I resolved it: it wasn't *right* to have friends — they would just be impure and frivolous.'

(the same phrase that Katie uses to describe her father's present life). Her
mother's control over her, her inability to let her daughter go, her wish to
live through her — '*Of course*, we're very close, I'm all she's got!'* — are
compounded rather than cancelled by an apparently equal and opposite
helplessness and wish now to be looked after *as a daughter*.

One step in disidentification is Katie's refusal of the female role. 'My
parents' split made me lose faith in marriage, and see horrible badness
in my father and mother'. She herself will, certainly, have no children —
'it is unfair to them to thrust them into life', at least the life that would
await them as *her* children.

> —I never wanted to be feminine, wear dresses and that sort of thing.
> I thought it was corrupt.
> —Do you feel attracted to men?
> —Oh yes. It depends — I can switch on, and then switch it off
> again. I can disillusion myself with anybody. And I usually do, in
> order to stop hankering after them or something . . . I didn't ever
> want to be anything of either sex . . . I don't think sexual inter-
> course achieves anything . . . When anyone seems to be coming
> close to me, I just withdraw . . .

She holds fast still to her adolescent vows of 'puritanism, purity — no
make-up, old clothes, disdain for other people, self-sufficiency'. 'My problem is,' she says, 'staying within myself and presenting a front to the outside world — just not coming out of myself at all.' When asked why, she
replies, 'Because I think basically, there's nothing to come out to.' She
has a recurring dream of *emerging from a tunnel and sitting on a brick wall
and looking over a town, and 'there isn't anybody I know — there isn't anything
at all'*.

Katie and Inburn

> He scored among the highest scores on every index we then had
> of alienation — on distrust, pessimism, resentment, anxiety, egocen-
> tricity, the sense of being an outsider, the rejection of conventional
> values, rejection of happiness as a goal, and a feeling of distance
> from others. And had other subsequently developed measures of
> alienation been available, he would have scored high on them —
> on self-contempt, interpersonal alienation, dislike of conventional
> social groups . . . the view of the universe as an unstructured and
> meaningless chaos.

This description of Inburn exactly fits Katie; she is also a 'perpetual stranger', doomed to eternal disappointment, who gives as her reason for
keeping going, 'fear of death, I guess — and false hopes'. She is as taken

* In her suicide scenario, her mother, on hearing of Katie's death, having
nothing now to live for, would herself commit suicide with pills Katie would
send her. This would also prevent her from feeling guilty for long about
Katie's death.

as Inburn with the Existentialists' demonstration of the purposelessness of existence, has the same sense of 'seeing through' the consolations of weaker folk, the same intensity of repudiation of conventional props. Like him, she avidly collects extreme ('bad', 'weird') experiences, but with an extra streak of masochism he lacks — as if it is through pain, above all, that she breaks out of stagnation and numb unfeelingness. She is more conventionally political in her interests (though inactive), with a fully developed model of an alternative society, at present put away as a dream, and she gets a good deal of nourishment and orientation from the literature of the women's movement ('*The Female Eunuch* was me!'). She persists, as he does not, with intellectualisation; it is a low path, but the *only* one, and the threat of that failing her is the most dangerous thing of all. Compared to him, she is solitary and self-punishing in her withdrawal (which is based in the super-ego, not the id), but not less obdurate.

We cannot (apart from the last lines of the case) really confirm in her the lost Eden theme so central to Inburn's case, and what there is of it seems foetal rather than oral. The Oedipal picture is, however, strikingly true to type: she is an only child of mismatched parents deeply disappointed in each other; the father is psychologically (and physically) absent; the mother is too close and binding, turning to the child for excessive supplies; both parents in their turn are fatal models for identification, but particularly the parent of the same sex. The stages in Katie's shifting views of her parents before they fell to open fighting, when she was nine, are not clear. But at the age of five, she was taken to a psychiatrist for bed-wetting in protest against the father's disruption of her sharing the mother's bed, and there are other things that broadly fit the 'Pyrrhic victor' pattern. She *does* get the mother to herself (though she would have preferred 'getting close to' the father 'more than anything'), and the mother, when won, is constricting, castrative — 'she passed on most of her hang-ups to me' — and depressing in her inadequacy as a model.*

* It may be instructive to note one path from the Oedipal Pyrrhic victory which may be counted 'positive', and which, binding the personality to a particular ideology and style of work, seems almost the 'royal road' for those entering one particular vocation — the clergy. Philip M. Helfaer reports a common pattern in a sample of liberal theological students:
'There is not only a strong, prolonged relationship with the mother, but there is a quality to the relationship that gives it a very special aura. The father is not only more or less devalued, and this usually in terms related to the family religion, but he is in some manner and to some degree edged out by the son in relation to the mother ... A variety of other circumstances ... add to the specialness of the mother-son relationship. [Two sons] are only children; and in their cases the birth may have been particularly difficult ... In [another's] case there is his prematurity and his feeling that his mother lived out with him the Samuel story. It seems clear that ... the mothers [in every case] turned to their sons for gratification that an absent or supposedly inadequate husband could not provide. The ... sons were all trained

(It is interesting that it should be the grandmother, otherwise not much mentioned, whom Katie most credits with keeping the idea of a career for her alive.) Finally, in charting her own course, she gets what mileage she can from identifying with the *young* father and his lost idealism. She sees herself as a student building more sanely and constructively forward from the young man's lonely, romantic and ruthless ideas, and as a person subduing or reversing those weaknesses of character that made him a certifiable drifter instead of a hero.

Katie as DNB. 'DNB — Denial of all positive feelings' is a perfect tag for Katie's organising principle. She is also, true to type, pessimistic, dejected (with mild delusions of dislike) and unreachable; she has very few friends or acquaintances, and has refused the conventional sex-role. She is not, however, notably passive — there is in her style a taut pressure of intellection; nor, most importantly, is she straightforwardly *cynical*. Certainly, she holds a low view of most other people and, consequently, of what societies might achieve, but she has a score or so of highly idealised characters in her cast (including most of her mother's family) and she thinks of herself as fatally idealistic. Indeed, it is the perfectionism of her ego-ideal the history of which she makes the core of her autobiography and which demands extraordinary achievement, that can make small set-backs totally disruptive, plunging her into the depths of suicidal depression. Her carefully planned over-dose is in the familiar pattern of adolescent idealistic suicide.[87] Short, regular cycles of elation-depression sweep thoughts and feelings now into an optimistic-idealistic trajectory — the PF position, now into a spin towards abject disappointment/disillusion — the NB position. Cynicism, in comparison, is a low-keyed, sour, stable state. Here too, as with Inburn, 'withdrawal *after failure*' has to be read in an individual sense.

Was her upbringing, for that matter, essentially a 'training in failure'? Although the family amply fills Bales's sociological requirements of lost status, brokenness and social marginality, it seems, on the contrary, far more remarkable how smoothly a disrupted home, rough bush schools and arid frontier-town life delivered this gifted girl to university. Far from 'the problem centering on the inability of the parents to transmit

(Footnote continued)

in one way or another to have the virtues, emotional sensitivity, or whatever, that the husband did not have. To the sons, the predominant and most influential parent is the mother. The strongest identification is with the mother, and the sons become religious through their closeness and identification with her.'[86]

This variant, in short, accepts 'castration' and a celebration of permanent union with the mother *on a higher plane*. Even here, some partial identification with, or finding of some strength in, the father, gives the project a sounder prognosis.

the conventional culture', the wonder is rather the steely serenity with which, against such odds, the maternal grandparents' upper-middle-class expectations prevailed.

The agreement between Katie's developmental history and that sketched paradigmatically for Beats by Keniston is, with suitable changes for sex and with the exception only of the father's unpredicted radical extremism, extraordinarily close. One notes again (as with East, above) how exposure to fierce and protracted conflict between parents competing for the child's support can leave the individual drained of the power to invest normal cathexis in objects in the outer world ('there's nothing to come out *to*').

DN — Resentment types

The passage from the DNB climate of dejection and denial of the positive to the DN climate of impotent hatred and envy is only a short step. The move across to DN, however, lands us among Alienates with a massive disposition to displace their affects into the political realm. Their politics is as characteristically short-winded as it is hysterical — and it has, as does so much else in their lives, a somewhat masochistic and self-defeating quality. The New York analyst Henry Hart has contributed a study of six male patients, second-generation New York Jews from Eastern Europe, in or on the fringes of the American Communist Party in the 1940s, which splendidly exemplifies this type.[88]

Hart's composite Jewish radical as Resentment Man
These men were not, Hart warns us, fanatical Communists, but they were sufficiently earnest and like-minded politically to encourage systematic comparison of their personalities and upbringing. Three of them — a dainty opera singer, an impractical if original chemist and a Madison Avenue hack with a private career as a sensitive, child's-eye short-story writer — are presented in reasonable detail; the others — two minor bureaucrats and a failed academic — are only lightly sketched. We shall use Hart's 'composite fictional personality', drawing more on qualities common to all six than on telling individual detail.

The six men exhibited, first of all, self-dislike, and a sense of personal incompleteness or inner inadequacy 'as if they could not assume any dignity in their own right':

> None had a sense of basic integrity and honesty, but [all] felt a great
> deceit in themselves, as if their bravado concealed an emptiness, a
> weakness that must never be revealed. It was as if they were to
> say, 'Who am I anyway? I'm not sure. It doesn't matter who I am,
> since I cannot really let myself be known for what I am or think,
> since I cannot be proud of the name I inherited.'

(Four had actually changed their surnames by deed-poll.) Hart found the roots of this self-depreciation and need to camouflage in ambivalence to and in the father, which, displaced on to politics, underpinned the 'subversive and revolutionary attitude which seeks to destroy under cover of respect'.

Next, Hart noted a passivity and inability to compete — the product of conspicuous 'spoiling' by mothers in childhood. The mother, in every instance the dominant parent — 'over-protective, over-solicitous about health, authoritative, inhibiting, [expressing] her love largely in terms of food and anxiety' — did her best to instil in her sons the idea that this is a dangerous world and that 'fighting was more dangerous than having a weak character'. Constantly complaining of her husband's inadequacies (real enough), she nevertheless encouraged her son's abject dependency on her ministrations. Forced by default, as it were, to assume parental authority, she had a deep mistrust of and contempt for men and, by spoiling her sons, she rendered them unfit for vigorous competition with others.

Subjects' political expectations inevitably carried over these discoveries about parents:

> Father was only the nominal head of the family, and his governmental authority was laughed at. He only seemed to be strong and sensible . . . He can be put aside in order to win the infantilising dependence on mother who is the real government because she provides food and solicitude, and demands no work or responsibility in return . . . The ruling class must be turned out because it was weak and ineffectual, and [the new generation] were to be taken care of by a bounteous government.

Finally, subjects carried self-defeating and self-sabotaging tendencies, in their work and their domestic lives, to a near-masochistic pitch.* Indeed, this seemingly deliberate 'destruction of opportunities' was the quality which first marked them out in Hart's eyes as a special group. Here, then, is a novel triad — masochism, passivity and radicalism. What binds them together? Hart reflects:

> By unconsciously increasing one's own suffering by self-defeating tendencies, one gives oneself greater freedom to hate and offend others. An outlet free from guilt is provided like war, for one's aggression, since if the whole world is persecutory, one is liberated from the necessity of careful, mature planning and responsibility. The passive dependence of the child on the mother can be reinstated without guilt or loss of narcissistic equilibrium. In all three [masochism, passivity and radicalism] there is a return to the magical expectation of childhood. 'I can hate and hurt others as much as I like and they will still love and protect me, because, see how much I suffer.'

---

* Passive homosexual and overtly masochistic trends were, indeed, a marked feature of subjects' sex lives — 'the expression of the longing, in disguised form, for the love of a father who was virtually absent from their lives'.

And the suffering is, indeed, none the less real for its being in large measure self-provoked by subjects' own policies of hatefulness and hurtfulness in their personal circle. When the magical expectations behind such policies, however, are disappointed, the hate is deflected away from the family and self, and loaded on to social and political targets.

The Oedipal hatreds in these men are unusually powerful and dispersed. In a sense, the Oedipal situation is never worked out, since the incest tie to the mother is more or less permitted by the combination of a weak father and a possessive, protective mother. The father is despised and pitied as a castrate; the mother is admired but, because she is blamed for the father's castration, is also deeply mistrusted and feared. Both are repudiated as usable models and are felt to have betrayed their son, and sown in him the seeds of inevitable defeat. And, in a final extraordinary turn, it appears that

> All of these six men were younger brothers, subject to the bullying
> and physical submission to older brothers, in a sort of Jacob-Esau
> relationship, in which the younger brother gets mother's love and
> cooperation in defeating the father and the older brother not by
> brawn but by brain.

These elder brothers, outwitted with mother's tacit approval, bear a large share of the Oedipal burden, since they so plausibly replaced such weak, passive and amiable fathers as the hated tyrants who must be overthrown.

In filing Hart's composite radical as DN — 'organised for rejection of social success' — the Resentment Man type, we anticipate less a firm click than a rustle of approximations. Certain other positions seemed plausible at first: with regard to ideology, the Comrade (P), the Underdog's Champion (DPB) and the Rebel against Convention (B) were all possibilities; with regard to family constellation, the mother-centred B, DB and NB, or the father-blaming DPB were possible; and in terms of personality, the DF Masochist, the DPF Castrate, or the DPB Infantilist are not unlikely. None of these categories, however, has more than a very limited applicability. Clearly, the triad of masochism, passivity and radicalism affects many different positions in Bales's scheme. One feels, also, that so stark a family constellation as 'castrating mother — castrate father' deserves a position to itself. The solution, I think, is to propose Hart's men as a sub-type of DN; two of its levels they at least approach, and they fit one of them well.

The basic impulse in N (as in the case of Couch) was parents with whom it was impossible to identify, and the painful and anxious project of constructing *de novo* a perfectly independent (and reproving) aim and world view. The DN type's position is essentially the same, only one shade more forlorn: it comprises a weak ego, a sense of fated defeat in the air, energies immobilised by powerful inhibitions and a regressive tug towards passive dependency, with impotent hatred and envy as the leading affects.

The parents Bales posits — 'silent accusers', sour, asocial, defeated, negativistic, neglectful, basically not taking receipt of their children, and raising up inexorably their own replicas — are highly plausible. Yet, after Hart, they seem cardboard cut-outs, altogether missing the furiously misdirected energy and passion of these men's trapped mothers, and the pathos of their own 'fatherless' condition. Hart's subjects' path to 'their own devices' lies through the thickets of the mother's dominance and the massive handicaps this imposes. Yet since the essence of the situation is in their *refusal* of identification, it seems more reasonable to include them as sub-types rather than to re-classify them.

The key, in terms of personality, is repressed aggression (aggression being the main drive down the whole N meridian); it is sometimes turned outward in resentment, sometimes inward in self-dislike.* Bales sees the DN type moving to isolate himself from the successful and from all reminders of them (defence of repression/denial) and indeed from people in general, although, at the same time, he uses his failure silently to accuse the successful. One of Hart's cases, 'destroying his opportunities', passed up all chances of exercising additional responsibility at work and dreaded becoming in any way conspicuous. Defeats (and self-defeats), which bring with them vague feelings of distress, depression, guilt, suspicion and envy, tend, however, to become routine.

Beneath DN's conscious aim of demonstrating independent self-sufficiency lurk strong dependency-needs. He is likely in times of dejection to seem to be asking to be taken care of, but he will still most probably reject and resent efforts to do this. The type-description catches well the masochism and passivity in the cases, though it puts greater weight still on *withdrawal*:

> The DN member tries to cut his contact with popular people in
> order to avoid the pain of feeling himself unpopular, unloved and
> unloving.[89]

The cases illustrate this less dramatically. The type-description also emphasises the *splitting off of the hopeful part of the self*, which accords well with Hart's imputed 'sense of personal incompleteness/inner inadequacy' and self-hatred, which bind together the masochism and the passivity in his cases.

Bales, following the 'silent accuser' metaphor, sees DN, by and large, as too negative, too self-absorbed (if not actually depressed), and too misanthropic, for ideology or politics. At most, his pervasive envy may

---

* Sex drive is also notably weak. Hart describes one patient's need 'to have
a deep pity for the women he loved, as he had for himself, a repetition of
his relation to [his] mother who not only pitied him but exacted pity from
him ... It was a definite step forward ... when [he] learned that one could
win the love of a woman without having to be castrated.'

throw up a bitter rhetoric of disparagement: 'I have very little in common with most of the people I meet', 'People are no damn good', and so forth. Without ideological initiative himself, he may, however, succumb to *conservative* conversion to 'introverted' work (work sufficiently non-competitive to avoid the risk of shame or envy) or to *radical* identification with the under-privileged, since they (like him) have been beaten by the system, and so appear as a 'far out prospect for the party of the far left'.

The radicalism of Hart's cases is rather more ego-syntonic and more a response of the whole personality (Hart notes that the healthiest man got least personal satisfaction from his radicalism). Family experience has taught them — through the father — that authority is hollow, powerless and a sham, yet it hangs on, keeps them sons still; through the mother, they have learnt that an alternative nurturance of 'each according to his needs' can be organised ('The habit of looking to the State for protection comes easily to young sons in a matriarchal family'). They have also caught the notion of a phobic social environment* from mothers dubious not only of their husbands' general worth but of their sheer bread-winning capacity. Finally, ruined for competition, they are ripe for an ethic of co-operation.

Hart's cases work valuably, I think, to erode Bales's emphasis on *social* success as the dominant, if soured, concern of those in the DN position: these men are consumed with anxiety about where, *in any way at all*, the self may be confirmed and asserted. On the other hand, Bales's type-attribution, of envy and resentment as the position's focal affects potentially organisable for politics, is not only perfectly compatible with Hart's story, but seems to add some deeper missing shades.

We leave a question mark over one final feature of these DN cases: their touching the edge of the well-known Oedipal 'Pyrrhic victory' scenario — sketched most vividly in Kenneth Keniston's *The Uncommitted* — which lies at the root of the adjacent DNB Beat character. What, we must soon enquire — since none of these men, despite their distress, ever showed the slightest sign of dropping-out — turns some 'winning' sons this way, some that?

Krugman's Jewish radicals

A year after Hart's paper, Herbert Krugman reported on a canvass of New York, Los Angeles, Washington and New Haven analysts for details of patients who were, or had been, Communists.[91] The 35 cases on which he obtained briefings — all middle-class intellectuals, and nearly all with Jewish migrant parents — amply confirm Bales and Hart on the repressed-

---

* cf. Hart's parenthetical comment on one patient's demeanour after he had left the Party: 'The fear of being attacked never leaves a revolutionary, even when he has become a conservative reactionary and has replaced the father.'[90]

aggression character, and Hart on the 'castrating mother, castrated father' family constellation, as a seed-bed of radicalism.*

Krugman, however, sought to differentiate between recruits who used the Party for 'masculine' and those who used it for 'feminine' purposes, and, concentrating on the ten and eight cases in which this could be unequivocally demonstrated — 'cases with the most pronounced history of confusion and conflict in self-image' — proceeded to spell out its implications for membership-style and depth of commitment. The 'masculine' style, involving 'defiance of authority', 'energetic assertiveness' and frank hostility to others, was espoused by those who turned to Communism because of a 'need — largely unsatisfied before joining the party — to indulge in ruthless and hostile behavior *without feelings of guilt*' (my italics). Five women, three of whom were dubbed 'fanatics' by their analysts, were among their number. The 'feminine' style, involving acceptance of authority, passive dependency and solicitude for others, characterised those seeking a protector and a chance for martyrdom and needing a pretext for submissiveness without guilt. Five of these were men. Krugman's hypothesis is that working for the Party gives more unique and robust satisfactions to 'masculine' women and 'feminine' men, who are therefore apt to work harder and remain members longer. Those with more conventional needs find alternative sources of satisfaction easier to come by, while males, particularly, find demands for abject submissiveness to party leaders onerous, and so are likely to be less committed and to drop out more easily.

It is in his description of the group of five 'feminine' men that Krugman most recalls Hart's cases:

> The self-images of the five men ... feature dual, conflicting, and extreme attitudes toward their ability; they think of themselves alternately as superior and as worthless people. They are also good, nice people — too nice to be aggressive to others — and in some cases martyrs.
>
> These men fear being aggressive — that is, challenging authority. They also fear aggression — that is, punishment for perhaps wanting to challenge authority. And ... they fear awareness of the feminine component in their submissiveness. The party gives them compelling reasons for being good, submissive, nonaggressive members, and at the same time offers them the bittersweet role of the martyr as a way of handling the aggression which they expect towards themselves.
>
> Another defense which these men use is the avoidance of areas of competition and hence of possible defeat; thus, the party frequently

---

* And of homosexuality: there were 1 overt and 12 latent (strictly defined) cases in 20 males, 5 overt and 3 latent in 15 females.

serves as an alibi for almost deliberate nonachievement. Still another common defense . . . is hypochondriasis . . .

The fact that they are passive and are afraid of being aggressive does not mean that they do not have hostility; nor does their being masochistic mean that their hostility is resolved by being turned against themselves. Rather, it means that the men in this category have an ability to *postpone the discharge of hostility* . . . They can be martyrs not because they love people, but because being martyrs allows them to look forward with pleasure to the day of revenge. This is the bittersweet essence of martyrdom.

Noting that emotional problems of mother-domination and sex-role conflict are relatively common, Krugman concludes that recruits to Communism are special only in the way that they defend themselves against these problems — that is, through intellectualisation and displacement on to politics: 'With the aid of the party, he exploits his intellectuality in such a way that he can give guilt-free expression to his hostility'. This 'seems to suggest that, because of the guilt-free nature of his hostility, he can be more hostile than other people'. In the light of the paucity of well-studied female political cases, it is a pity that the comments on the women recruits are so brief — the 'fanatics' seem, in Bales's terms, almost certainly UN types, and we get no real hints about the dynamics of the passive women to match his account of the men.

Lindner's Mac as DN
An individual case report centring round painful conflicts over dependency and aggression focused on Communist Party membership is Lindner's analysis in the mid 1940s of Mac, a minor Communist functionary in Baltimore.[92] Mac, tall and sandy haired, was not Jewish or intellectual or middle class, but a runaway, Ohio Dutch farm-boy, who had found his way into the Party in his late teens and given it almost twenty years' service. He sought treatment for impotence and depersonalisation, and he strenuously denied any ideological stress. Lindner, however, discovered that it was, in fact, his desperate resolve to remain loyal to the Party after he had come to doubt its worth and hate its leadership, that was the cause of his symptoms. Orphaned early, and brought up by a patriarchal grandfather and his sullen, hostile, ex-servant second wife, Mac had run off at the old man's death, because he feared he might murder 'Ma'. The Party permitted him to redirect this great accumulation of hatred and aggression, to channel it fruitfully and contain it. It also again allowed him ('underneath all, a wholly dependent type whose primary longing was for ever to be a kind of suckling as he once was to his wet-nurse') the status of dependent infant, as he nestled into its all-embracing discipline. During the years of industrial strife and the war, while policy demanded and gave latitude to his hostility, he was compliant and ful-

filled, but in the early post-war years, 'when for a time there was no one
to hate or fight', he began to chafe badly under party discipline, which
became 'burdensome and nagging, resembling the régime of his grandmother'. Despite his best conscious efforts to disown his mounting frustration and anger, to 'give nothing away', he was simply unable to remain
compliant under the new conditions, in which the Party had ceased to
serve its purpose for him.

Unfortunately, we do not have enough detail in the case to argue strongly either for a DN placing, or against it (despite the strong positive identification with the admired grandfather); it is merely not implausible.

André Gorz as DN
In his book-length intellectual self-portrait, *The Traitor* (written in his
early thirties), the Paris political journalist and critic, André Gorz, presents
himself as a prime candidate for DN placement and splendidly lights up
the position from within.[93] His text, in the form of a journal kept over
nine months (he is 'giving birth to himself'), probes present moods, chronic
attitudes, political and philosophical convictions and their psychological
and developmental underpinnings, and shows us with remarkable
candour how his particular way of being a critic can yoke together violent
aggression and massive timidity. He is the poet of Bales's 'withdrawal'.
Yet he has a strong sense of himself as a representative type — the radical
intellectual, isolated, aimless, weak, despairing, self-hating — and imagines that such readers, especially, might profit from his confession. Perhaps, he muses, even his appearance is representative:

> a thin fellow with hollow cheeks and eyes, receding forehead and
> chin, a long neck poking forward over his slightly hunched back,
> with the gait of a heron and parsimonious gestures, as if he were
> trying to contain his being within himself.[94]

He is an obsessional writer — a man 'condemned to write in order to feel
he existed' — who has no other life, for whom everything besides thinking
and writing is boring, a waste of time. He persists with his two pages a
day 'for fear of leading a commonplace life, of dissolving into anonymity'
and the bourgeois condition. Though trained as a chemical engineer, he
operates now as a literary all-rounder, seeking, he says, to create — in
philosophy, fiction, politics, autobiography — non-criticisable, wholly
admirable things. Marxist journalism, however, provides his livelihood,
and fruitfully deploys his unusual gifts for statistics and economic analysis, for contesting and controverting conventional opinion, and for speaking out for all oppressed and rebellious groups (see above, p. 34).

In his personal life he is totally unassertive. He is meek, obsessional,
scrupulously obedient to authority, asking always for less than he needs.
His possessions and, indeed, his acquaintances are stripped to a minimum,

and he attempts to 'reduce to a minimum the lived contact with reality', to escape, retreat and hide away.* 'Out there', the demand is always 'Show what you can do', and he hates to be tested or judged; 'in here', safe, his own man, he creates in fantasy whole new worlds, and holds readers at his mercy.

And, indeed, his writings, as well as grandly negating the environment, assault and provoke it; his fantasies are full of aggression. He 'writes against the world in order to destroy it', to show it as 'desperately in excess' and inauthentic; he dreams of finding a way of writing that will make itself 'a bomb annihilating everything by its explosion, including itself'. At the same time, the soul of prudence, he wishes to 'offer . . . no surface to attack' and to take refuge in a perpetually shifting, ironic stance.[96] He recalls for some years as an adolescent *putting himself to sleep* by imagining that he was firing a cannon out of his window, or even through the walls, or that he was in a car, or a tank, running down great crowds of people.

Bored, depressed, self-pitying, he complains that he belongs nowhere, to no group, no enterprise. He is exiled from groups and enterprises and marginal to society and history; he is refused purpose. Whenever he is tempted to end his isolation by integrating himself with some cause (such as Communism) the reasons quickly become transparent, bad, a betrayal of himself. He rapidly moves to abandon all groups that seek to apply constraints to him – he is a 'natural traitor'. He is naturally nothing; he can never be integrated or whole, must always question, contest and doubt.† He has always felt miserable, without a future, indeed, hardly viable. His earliest memories were of being the victim in playground fights, and of hiding – under couches and tables, under the piano, behind curtains or in closets:

> He would huddle into dark corners and make believe he was a
> tiny animal, a solitary captive fallen out of someone's hand or pocket,

* He is married, but owns to the 'agreeable' fantasy that his wife will die, thus enabling him to retire to a tiny attic. He altogether lacks phallic assertiveness, and sees himself as a man 'whose tenderness was . . . furtive, who even in his way of making love seemed to ask forgiveness for his own existence'. He confesses to necrophiliac fantasies – 'impotent with available women, [I] even started a story about a man who, in order to make love to a girl, first anaesthetizes her with a wad of cotton soaked in chloroform and wrapped, so as not to burn his own skin, around the outside of a napkin ring' – and recounts other fantasies of killing or anaesthetising women *to escape their paralysing gaze*'.[95] A mother, whose 'gaze' arouses only to wither, clearly stands at the head of this female line. His father, officially declared null, always seems to have lacked the status of a rival, while envy of an elder sister, 'more loved', seems further to have sapped his masculine identification.
† He expresses a special sense of futility about his obsessional, yet always inconclusive, philosophising, and bemoans his habit of 'flight to abstraction' to evade life's difficulties.

whom no one wanted, and then he would cry to himself quietly, comfortably, full of self-pity, and after he had mourned his exile, he
would harden himself by knocking his head against the wall until he
saw stars, and then, to punish himself . . . he would do the things
that were hardest of all: pull out his hair and eat it, lick the soles of
his shoes after walking over dogs' refuse, or not drink water for three
days.[97]

Gorz was the second child (there was a daughter eighteen months older)
of an ill-assorted Viennese couple, a timid, Jewish small-businessman
well into his forties and the bossy young typist who talked him into marriage. A resigned and humble man, he must have been attracted, the son
speculates, by the energy and assurance of this confident young woman
'who never hesitated and seemed ready to swallow the whole world'.
During the first years of the marriage, his mother used her new wealth
to dazzle her own family, and propelled her husband into business initiatives and quarrels with his relatives. With the birth of her son, she turned
her whole attention to making him a prodigy, 'the decoration of the
family', the virile, aristocratic Aryan she would like to have married.
She named him André after a local actor who played just such parts and,
when the boy was seven, she had her husband baptised as a Catholic,
paid a bribe for new birth certificates for the children and changed the
family name to Gorz — a weighty non-Jewish name. She monopolised the
boy, ruthlessly denigrated the father in the eyes of the son, and made
him, 'in his own house, the "poor relation" . . . continually harangued,
shoved, nagged at'.[98]

Gorz found little to admire in his father; he saw him as a humble man
with plenty to be humble about — spineless, deferent, narrow-minded,
ignorant, eternally reproachful and trying pathetically to put on a good
front even with his son. Caught thus between incompatible parents, the
boy was unable to find firm ground. He envied others with identities
very different from his own (as an adolescent he put in a spell with the
Nazi youth), but which were, above all, *clear-cut*. He felt that, at bottom,
he was simply inadequate as he stood and that, under the sustained pressure of parental reproaches, he was an ingrate for not giving them more
satisfaction. But he puts the core of his problem back in pre-Oedipal times,
in the years when his mother sought totally to shape his character and,
in particular, to monitor his every utterance. As far back as he can now
remember, even to the age when he was beginning to speak, he had always
been afraid that he would say something wrong, something more than
he meant. He describes his voice even at the time of writing as low, indistinct, monotonous and easily unnoticed. 'Language', he says, 'was the
exclusive property of his mother. She ruled over words in order to rule
over men by cascades of talk, holding her disconcerted interlocutors
paralyzed, as if in glue. Language was her kingdom', in which he had to
say what she thought, or wanted to hear.[99] These inevitable, repeated

failures in communication led him always to expect to disappoint others – being never the person he should be: 'unable to free himself from her verbal ascendancy', from the flood of words that greeted his slightest murmur, he could 'escape only by a stubborn silence'.

Indeed, there were long struggles with his speech. He lisped, he stuttered, and his mother attacked the problem vigorously, correcting his lisp with a metal loop and his stammer with mechanical exercises (a squint, too, was fitted with glasses); 'He spoke perfectly, but with a voice so low and so fast that his mother was forever complaining, "What are you saying? Talk louder! What are you mumbling about now?"' They nicknamed him 'Mumbler', and 'even hearing the dreadful word kept him from wanting to speak'. He proposed as an image for one long part of his childhood an endless hedge of adult faces leaning over him, which suddenly burst out laughing – at his stammering, his mistakes, the accidental witticisms he was made to repeat *ad nauseam*. He became for others an Odd Little Person. His mother made him feel that all encounters with people were a test he had to pass, that all grown-ups were judges. She would endlessly instruct him, 'Stand up straight. Don't forget to take off your cap. Don't look self-conscious. Look people in the eyes when you talk to them. Don't mumble, open your mouth. Look like a little man.'[100] When, however, he sought in naive boasting or play-acting to make some real show of himself, his mother stamped out such attempts in the name of 'sincerity'. Many leading features of Gorz's history can, indeed, be traced back to this crucial early inability – in the face of maternal 'mirroring' so distorting and malign – to weld his ego, his speech and his external self into one secure identity, which left him with an oppressive sense of his fatal singularity and unfitness for ordinary life. His decision as a student, for example, to think and work henceforth in French instead of German, rid him of some part of his mother along with his mother-tongue; with foreign speech he felt much freer, since what he said was not 'part of him', but merely a public currency. His taste, too, for abstraction and philosophy – meta-languages denying or transcending ordinary speech – clearly sprang from the same root. His oppositional stance of perpetual contestation guaranteed an identity in sworn enmity to his mother's idols of status, propriety and conventionality. Lastly, his passion for writing allowed him imperiously to be himself, since 'to write is to speak in the absence of others and to refuse them speech, it is . . . to forbid another person to tell me what he means . . . constantly obliging him to ask *himself* if he understands the meaning of the text'.[101] It leaves a man 'anonymous and invisible', and able to choose his own times and occasions.

A Resentment Man *par excellence*, Gorz embodies the focal DN conflict between an intense aggression and a dread of expressing it, and the defining nullity of the parents as models for identification. Somewhat against Bales's expectation, but like our other cases, he uses *politics* above all, as a lightning conductor. He finally denounces his mother ('traitorously') in his journal and then, in print, is as directly aggressive as he can be. This, he claims, is therapeutic: 'Instead of keeping the world at a distance like an enemy who must not be allowed to get a grip on me, I am learning to yield to it.'[102] He also illustrates well (like Shea, the UN type, and the N type, Couch) an eminently successful project of tightly harnessing occupation to personality type in defiant individualistic isolationism.

Gorz's castrate father and overwhelming and intrusive (though not Jewish) mother splendidly embody the pattern set by earlier cases.[103] Gorz himself epitomises the DN life-strategy of *withdrawal* and throws up *poverty of affect* (or at least, protestation of affect) as a new* and plausible, DN trait; this is in line with Lasswell's notion of it in 1930 as a characteristic mark of theorists, based on the childhood trauma of crises in which love, rage and fear ran simultaneously at peak levels, leaving the victim burnt-out and incapable of strong positive emotion.

The most novel thought that Gorz leaves us with, however, is the irony of the very common association of extreme individualism of tempera-ment and life-style with the bleak orthodoxy of radicalism. Gorz might well have wondered, in Shirley MacLaine's words

> Why was I so attracted to the collective way of life when, above all, I wanted to reserve my right to be an individual?[104]

The question is a good one, and misleads only if it is thought to require a psychological answer, when the speaker has arrived there instead by the simplistic situational logic of 'My enemy's enemy is my friend'. When one cannot identify with one's parents' bourgeois conformism, one first adopts its flat ideological opposite. That this is so psychologically make-shift, however, contributes powerfully to the ambivalence and ineffect-uality often found in Western socialism. As Arnold Rogow has noted, 'an extreme emphasis on social justice and an end to inequality may mask intense aggressive, competitive strivings and an unconscious need to lord it over others' — it may mask, indeed, 'an unconscious wish to keep things as they are'.[105]

The Alienates: Conclusion

The Alienates' camp (see table 9) is clearly the camp of neurosis. Personal defeat prevails: *self*-defeat, certainly, but a malignity, too, of fate, as if, for the hubris of a little extra intelligence and sensitivity, each as a child had been allotted an unplayable part. The political movements to which they are attracted and which they try to help will suffer much downward drag in consequence, but we should mark implicit strengths as well — for example, Inburn's counter-cultural *élan*, Gorz's bitter spirit of contestation and East's Utopian dreaming.

* Poverty of affect was, however, one of Lindner's Mac's presenting complaints.

Table 9. *The three positions of Alienation*

DN	DNB	DB
Identification refused	Identification with father's lost idealism	Identification with mother and children, in reproof of neglecting, rejecting father
Oedipal Pyrrhic victory	Oedipal Pyrrhic victory in extreme form	
(Absent father, castrating mother)	(Absent father, castrating mother)	
	Lost Eden	Lost Eden in extreme form
Destruction of opportunities — but perseverance in routine	Withdrawal and failure	Passive resistance/ joyless feet-dragging
Hatred and envy	Dejection. Denial of positive (or possibly suppressed hatred)	Depression possibly, and certainly passivity and inertia

The Democrats — the P meridian

Though Murray provided two exemplary cases of Democrats — Ingle (P) and Hawk (UP) — they were, in a sense, too strong and too professional for our needs. Hawk, it will be recalled, proposed, after a brief law career, to become Democratic Congressman for New York, and Ingle seemed already an incipient U.N. adviser or administrator. Both had elaborate and practised ideologies of equalitarianism, rooted more (we suspected) in the head than the heart. Yet a certain amount of sophisticated speculation about the essential qualities and developmental requirements of the 'democratic character' has built up over the last twenty years. It needs to be substantiated by examples. We quickly sketch the theorists' expectations, then glance at a test case.

The Democratic character

The authors of *The Authoritarian Personality* themselves posed the question at the end of their labours: Is there a *contrary* type—a person who is psychologically a democrat? And, from their accumulated material on 'low scorers', they claimed indeed to discern a 'democratic pattern — affectionate, basically equalitarian, permissive in interpersonal relations' which carried through a person's outlook from 'matters like intimate features of family and sex adjustment, through relations to people in general, to religion, and to social and political philosophy'.[106] The 'genuine liberal' was compassionate, morally courageous and had a strong sense of personal autonomy; he could accept guilt and blame and often had aesthetic interests. They confused the issue, however, by pointing to certain sub-

types who scored speciously low because of compulsive anti-conformity
or anti-authoritarianism.[107] Things were hardly advanced by Levinson's
near-tautological demonstration that the more strongly anti-ethnocentric
people were, the more urgent they thought it to do something to correct
ethnic inequalities.[108]

Thus matters rested in 1950 when Harold Lasswell took up the challenge.[109] He proposed freedom from anxiety as the critical component, and
an ego unweakened by moralism, fear or aggression — for it is anxiety that
propels the individual into negative and mistrustful projections about
others, and generally deforms outlook. One comes by this only through
early trust in a good mother, an experience which also informs the chief
democratic convictions: an expectation of rich rewards from close human
fellowship, a disposition to share the good things of life with others, and a
confidence in human potentialities. He coined the term 'open ego' to
suggest the democrat's ability, indeed his drive, to transcend his cultural
origins and reach out to a sense of common humanity. And he stressed that
the democrat is 'many-valued', that is, not preoccupied exclusively with
the pursuit of virtue, love, knowledge, wealth or power, but partly with
each — although with power least of all.

Inkeles, ten years later, dusting off the Lasswell prescription, found an
'extraordinary degree of agreement' about the traits of the democratic
character, who should be

> accepting of others rather than alienated and harshly rejecting; open
> to new experience, to ideas and impulses rather than excessively
> timid, fearful, or extremely conventional. . . ; able to be responsible
> with constituted authority even though always watchful, rather than
> blindly submissive . . . or hostilely rejecting . . . ; tolerant of differences
> and of ambiguity, rather than rigid and inflexible; able to recognize,
> control, and channel his emotions, rather than immaturely projecting
> hostility and other impulses on to others.[110]

He also judged some basic feeling of obligation to society and an eschewing
of self-centredness and 'privatism' to be part of the model, the 'rough
first approximation', whose refinement by empirical research he urged.
And, to a degree, this was forthcoming in Lane's and Martin's studies.[111]
Martin found 'tolerance' a demonstrable syndrome and charted its links
with other traits like 'empathy' and 'insight'. Lane's discoveries were more
sociological; his dozen Eastport men, interviewed in depth, were
gratifyingly non-projective (anti-Them), mostly because they were non-
identified, with no sense of belonging to any substantial Us.

Levinson in 1964, also advocating fuller analysis of equalitarian
syndromes, noted that 'equalitarians' disliked rigid hierarchy and preferred
'self-expression, self-understanding, and affectional mutuality in human
relationships. . . They tend, on the average, to be more insightful, flexible,
autonomous, unvindictive, love-oriented and change-seeking. They have,

Table 10. *A comparison between Beats and Radicals* *

Radicals	Beats

Mothers

BOTH: unusually strong tie in early childhood

Less intense. Mothers strongly encouraging achievement, independence, initiative. Genuinely fond of, grateful to, mothers	More intense, less adequately resolved. Intrusive, over-protective, close-binding, mother-son relationship. Mother-son alliance against father. Mothers sensuous, seductive, neurotic

Fathers

Affection for fathers. Whatever their weaknesses, fathers had important strengths, especially in convictions and ideals. Conscious ambivalence towards them. Fathers described as expressive, warm, sympathetic, highly involved	Little affection for fathers. Perceived as weak, detached, absent, distant, remote and sometimes totally uninvolved in the upbringing of their children

Parental Relationships

Parental united front	Schism between parents, plus mother-son alliance against father, leading son to believe/suspect he was preferred to husband

Family culture

BOTH: highly permissive

Combined with extremely high standards and expectations, and strong support of son's individuality and autonomy	Considerable parental confusion over principles, and mothers reluctant to see son become autonomous and independent
Oriented to responsibility, independence, social involvement, expression of feelings, service to others, self-fulfilment	Oriented to conventional goals of success and social status

Childhood experience

Characteristic active involvement in school, local community, life — with strong parental support. Precocious moral/political sensitivity	Characteristic withdrawal into inner life: greater involvement with parents, pre-adolescent isolation

BOTH: intellectually precocious

Leaders in peer-groups	Small participation in peer-groups

BOTH: considerable conflict

But often outside home, in larger community	But always within home — between parents
Conflicts within home either hidden from children, or uninvolving	Mothers actively solicit sons' sympathy

Adolescence

BOTH: considerable turmoil, especially about sex

Problems of moral scruples — and of reconciling own moral code with peer-group practices	Avoidance of active, initiatory role

Table 10 continued

Radicals	Beats
	More preoccupied with incestuous fears/anxiety.
More overt, vehement, direct rebellion against parents — turning their own principles against them	Less direct and pointed — since parents' principles confused. So rebellion more pervasive, long-lasting
Willing to assume positions of leadership, initiative	Aesthetic, literary interests; detached 'camera-eye' style
Personality	
Energy applied in service of ego and superego. Freer to act in line with their own principles and better grip of reality. Focus on inner life more than balanced by immersion in activity. Psychic conflicts largely resolved; major energies focused on change in the outer world	Energies locked in internal conflicts — especially attempts to regain simple, direct relations like mother-child symbiosis. More prone to symbolic acting out of childhood conflicts and themes. More depressed, rebellious. General inhibition of relationships, withdrawal from potentially gratifying social/work involvements, active emphasis on inner life. Strong, diffuse hostility — and neuroticism. Highly creative/aesthetically imaginative

* Summarized from Kenneth Keniston, *Young Radicals*, New York, Harcourt, Brace, 1968, pp. 349–58.

by and large, come farther in the direction of moral integrity and personal maturity' — although one cannot identify equalitarianism with 'maturity or mental health or total freedom from irrationality... For example, in contrast to authoritarians, relatively equalitarian persons may tend unrealistically to idealize the disadvantaged and to reject the legitimate authority.'[112] However, Keniston attempted in 1968 to draw up a developmental table to predict which students at university would drop out spiritlessly, like Inburn and the Beats, and which, like the leaders of the Students for a Democratic Society, would stay on and rebel fruitfully (see table 10). He expected both types to come from mother-dominated families, but he thought that the radicals' mothers would be less binding and manipulative, and their fathers more concerned and admirable. Keniston set out, in fact, to study a whole conference of student radicals, but failed to work up a single pertinent case. Helfaer, however, has produced an exemplary case, which bears directly on the matrix of the democratic personality.

Helfaer's Eyman as P

Aged 25, Eyman is a Unitarian clergyman in his first parish and just married.[113] Quite tall, lanky, slow and deliberate in his speech and movements, he talks very seriously, but 'with a twinkle in his eye, and conveys the feeling that he is sharing something quite personal in . . . cosy intimacy'. He is an activist, involved in civil rights, urban renewal and Vietnam agitations. In fact, he comes fresh from a week in gaol (for demonstrating) in Selma, Alabama, where he went to help Martin Luther King and the Southern Christian Leadership Conference. Such activity — 'this form of witness' — is very near the heart of his religion, his 'prophetic ministry' as he calls it, and he pictures himself as a 'man growing out of the soil of his people, their traditions — but rising above them — proclaiming the great, simple verities that undergird life'. He speaks of his Selma experience as personally enriching, and, indeed, he works on his open-mindedness, striving consciously to be flexible, open to new forms of experience and ideological perspective. His theology is diffuse and tenuous: God is a 'dimension of the universe' and of human experience — an unfolding of creativity in which we can all share, that is, not a being external to the ego. For Eyman, all experience is the result of the ego's action, or interaction with others, or of forces completely neutral and impersonal with respect to human life.

If his humanism, his 'reverence for life', enhances his concern with minority groups, the underdog, and pressing social issues, it grows naturally, he feels, out of an upbringing in which he was expected to 'take care of my things and of people', and was rather chivvied towards maturity. A sensitive, thoughtful child, Eyman developed a strong capacity to recognise and respond to feelings, and a distinct talent as a mediator. He is, however, relatively unoriginal in his thinking, as the bland and limited quality of his Rorschach responses attest, though he shows a special interest in abstract and extremely general concepts (he hoped at one time to become a physicist). His TAT stories present heroes either struggling manfully against large external forces, 'the power and might of the world — the force of impersonality, the force of entrenched ways, the force of thoughts that have been enshrined and made sacrosanct', or else living as if they were held down and controlled by some inner pressure, particularly in 'mundane daily life, the life of the business or professional man', which he sees as depersonalising and isolating, as if 'to be a man in a man's world is to be . . . out of touch with all that is warm, nurturing, meaningful'. Special qualities of his relation with his mother have also left their mark. He seems to have been over-stimulated and overburdened by her closeness. Yet he was the one who had to learn to take an early responsibility for controlling the feelings of both of them. This has left him with an emotional and instinctual apparatus under excessive control, indeed almost stifled.

Halfaer makes much of the fact that he found his own way to religion and did not finally fix on the ministry as a vocation until a great many realistic evidences for its appropriateness to his gifts and interests had accumulated. The contrast with *conservative* theological students, who normally report conversion experiences (and precocious identity fore-closure) at ten to twelve years of age, is striking.

Eyman was born and raised in a major Middle Atlantic states city, and had the status of an only child for a long time. His sister, M, was not born till he was $9\frac{1}{2}$. His father, 'a quiet, self-contained, gentle, but athletic and self-assured man', made a career in the insurance business after an Ivy League education. Mother is described as emotionally labile, rather irri-table and not as thoughtful as father. Forbears in the U.S. go back on both sides to the time of the Revolution.

Eyman grew up in a stable and secure family, where the parental bond, if strained at times, was strong. He had a particularly close relationship with his mother; his frequent illnesses claimed her special care, and she would confide her problems to him, including her complaints about her husband. Her irritation was apt to flare up easily, and he became adept at reading the signs, reining in his own anger, and allowing things to cool down. He felt 'some distance' between his father and himself when he was young — his father was often away on business or out at Socialist Party or Urban League functions — but he felt great respect and affection for him, and, as an adolescent, found his gentleness, his calm and his quiet convic-tion admirable, although he thought him perhaps too 'withdrawn' and slow to act. He seems to have reacted to the birth of his sister by relinquish-ing his claim to a child role, and throwing himself into that of 'third parent'. Particularly in the period just before and just after M's birth, however, Eyman shared a relationship with his mother from which in part father was excluded — and by which he was, to a degree, devalued. Eyman was drawn into the role of family mediator, with the sense of specialness and mission which that encourages, and which was to find later expres-sion in his ministerial vocation. Though highly moral and concerned with ideology, both in politics and child-rearing, the parents were not religious, and Eyman takes great pride that it was he himself who, in the seventh grade, first got his family involved with the Church.

There was also, however, a darker side to Eyman's childhood, which Helfaer brilliantly detects and elucidates as central to Eyman's whole ideological enterprise. When he was about four, he developed a phobic fantasy which frightened him, but in which he also indulged as a kind of anxious game:

> Well, there was — I believe I referred to him as 'Killer-Man' who was
> on this bus going by the house. And . . . I thought he would kill me
> if I was visible to the bus through the front windows . . . two or three
> different windows in a room looking out on the street. Or perhaps

> I'd have to move across the room to be not visible from the bus.
> This all depends. Sometimes when there were other people in the
> room, I decided . . . 'I'm not playing now.'

The Killer-Man fantasy symbolised in a concrete way a more diffuse sense
Eyman carried through childhood, a sense that

> Beneath a nice, placid surface, where things were basically fairly nice,
> there was something diabolical going on . . . Several times . . . it
> occurred to me quite consciously that it would be possible that the
> world was a façade put there — all the people with whom I came in
> contact, merely acting out a role, all built up to fool me.

When, at about thirteen or fourteen, Eyman became consciously preoccupied with the question, 'What is God like?', he saw two alternatives:
a theistic God who could intervene directly in one's life, and a deistic one
who set the world working in an orderly manner but then remained aloof.
Eyman very much preferred the second alternative — which, after all, with
his 'divine dimension', he has closed upon. But if, as he was in times of
particular stress inclined to think, there was a God who could 'do something for me and to me', then there must be a corresponding supernatural
evil underlying the placid facade, too.

> The deism, and later the humanism, defend Eyman against the phobic
> anxieties [of his infantile neurosis] and the totalistic personality
> organization the phobia has the power to bring about. And ultimately,
> it is as if Eyman maintained an unconscious belief in a supernatural,
> theistic God, who like the God of Barth [and the conservatives], is
> all too capable of intervening in the affairs of men; so that the lib-
> eral rejection of conservatism may, in part, represent his defense
> against his own underlying conservatism and the form of personality
> organization that would entail.

Eyman's quest soon led him into active involvement with the liberal
Church, and ultimately to sophisticated versions of his preferred beliefs —
and to a sense of nascent leadership. He considered other careers which
would have drawn on his social concerns, but chose the ministry as the one
with the most openness, flexibility and freedom of self-determination.

The Killer-Man 'game' symbolised Eyman's age-appropriate 'castration
anxiety':

> At a time when Eyman was competing avidly and aggressively with
> his father for his mother's attentions, it must have been less painful to
> create, by a series of projections, a retaliative figure outside the house
> than to see his [calm and peaceful] Father aroused to angry retalia-
> tion with it.

It symbolised also his chosen response to this anxiety, which was to withdraw from phallic competition with father, and renew his investment
(within the enclosed, protected house-space) in the maternal relationship
and its corollaries.

Eyman's early relationship with his mother was intense and prolonged; its effects pervade his belief system and character at all levels.

> The concept of God, for example, as a 'divine dimension of the universe' may be seen as a symbolization which preserves and expresses the tender, hopeful aspects of the maternal relationship as well as the wish for fusion with the mother ... Similarly, Eyman's concept of the divine dimension unifies, brings together within one symbol, the essence of all that is good, valuable, and meaningful within the universe. It tends thereby to focus and re-create that original sense of global hopefulness and oppose it to all the possibilities for opposition, hopelessness.

His TATs attest to the continued fantasy of fusion, the hero in several of them having incorporated the maternal, caring functions. One story simply offers the 'memory' of being held on mother's lap, looking up, and being 'a person' through the reflection of her gaze. He now enacts in his professional and social concerns the tender-minded, highly empathetic, sensitive style he perfected with his mother. (And a certain covert tendency to view daily life and 'daily people' with contempt represents both his rejection of his father's life-style and his ambivalence towards his mother.)

However, there is a dread of fusion as well. The 'immobilising' of entrenched ways, the vocational depersonalisation, in the TATs first quoted, the impersonal threatening forces, which now play a fixed part in his belief system, are the heirs of the 'diabolical evil beneath a placid surface' (the sequel to complete fusion). In fact, Eyman has two concepts of action. Action is possible in the religious context, even in the face of strong opposing forces — indeed, struggle against inimical social forces is the essence of the ministry as he sees it. It is in the day-to-day institutional context of his professional duties that he feels confounded, and fears drabness, failure, and 'getting stuck'.

Finally, and most interestingly, Helfaer dilates on Eyman's use of the programme of an 'open ego' as a leading characteristic of his ideological and professional style. He is proud of his uniqueness, which he sees as the foundation for a critical moral stance, and of his ability to be challenging, because he is different from others. But he also has a sense of himself as potentially heroic — *in so far as* he can expand the boundaries of the self to contain a 'conception of the whole'. If he can mature so as to weld an extreme self-awareness to an awareness of what global responsibility requires, then his ministry will, indeed, be fruitful. Helfaer points out that this high ego-ideal and emphasis on the ideal development of the self both maintain and draw on the fantasy of fusion with the mother, but also defend Eyman against it, since he is, after all, becoming more and more his own man all the time.

Eyman as P. Eyman does, I feel, add significantly to our picture of the P meridian as Ingle and Hawk left it. For a start, he is no mere acquiescent equalitarian (in fact, we noted his contempt for routine and for stodgy folk who are not disposed to press toward the 'creative dimension'), but a man striving, consciously and unconsciously, to stretch his 'identifications' and sympathies — to get 'a conception of the whole'. (We might recall here Murray's remarks in Hawk's favour: 'his preoccupation with self-becomingness is continuous and sincere'. 'His new ideal . . . is a multi-sided man who has experienced everything and sees the world as a totality.')* Lasswell's 'open ego' pressing towards full human range does not seem too far from this.

But there is an extra twist (caught, indeed, in Bales's UP expectation of the fully expanded ego, 'the over-expanded concept of the self')[114] where the democrat in Eyman seems to wish, like Rousseau, to make himself the measure of all things. 'The most important thing in life is to fulfill one's own nature . . . the only way to benefit society is to benefit oneself as a member of society', Hawk asserts. And Eyman's whole altruistic programme is based on his passing everything through his own sensibility to arrive at a sense of what is to be done. (If such a quasi-experimental use of self as political touchstone should prove type-characteristic, we may doubt the cohesiveness and longevity of movements that attract P types in numbers.)

Secondly, Eyman challenges the bland, single-layer model democrat of all theorists. His present and conscious insistence on a world which is trustworthy, rewarding, steadily improvable and human-scale, is at the same time a denial of a past (and unconsciously still attractive) view of it as a battle-ground for supernatural forces, both good and evil, where the outcome is quite obscure and may possibly be wildly unjust. (Bales's phrase, 'false positive', however — as instanced, for example, in Ingle's 'boundless enthusiasm and optimism' — certainly hints at some hollowness of this sort.) And, of course, Bales's scheme sees all positions as, in a sense, a defence against the unconscious attraction of their polar opposites (though here the phobic theism would fit the F or NF positions better than N).

All three subjects score well on democratic convictions. Murray was impressed with Ingle's 'subordination of his private ambitions to larger ends' — indeed, he comes out as the best 'team-worker' of the three (the others do not provide much competition). All manage in their plans, however, so generous an accommodation of the public to the private, that one is in doubt how to assess the 'sacrifice'.

All three are also ideologists rather than plain folk with warm hearts. They are all upper-middle-class, schoolboy and college leaders, 'sensitive' symbol-manipulating sons steering a course away from the already 'soft'

* Ingle likes well enough to listen to new points of view, but only to exercise his system.

business careers of the fathers. All have, as Bales foresaw, 'high ego strength'; they are well-organised, intellectually efficient personalities based on the harnessing of drives in an integrative way; they have unusual personal flexibility, and the social adroitness to operate at all levels of the status hierarchy.

They add little, however, to our model of the democrat's personality. Ingle is a rampant extravert, 'out of touch with his feelings', launched on a 'flight/into objectivity', with no moral or psychological sense; Eyman has a powerful moral sense', and Hawk falls somewhere between Eyman and Ingle. Eyman's 'stifled impulse-life' surely runs counter at some serious level to Lasswell's 'freedom from anxiety' or Inkeles' stance of 'self-acceptance'. All are 'universalistic' in focus and values, and tolerant — though Ingle's tolerance 'borders on indifference'. But it is not clear whether or not they have compassion or moral courage or the ability to accept guilt and blame.

The lines re-form, however, as we move back to childhood. All three grew up in unusually harmonious and cohesive and possibly child-centred families, where there was a strong parental bond. They were assured of their parents' constant affection and interest, discipline was gentle and 'tender-minded', and they were treated early as 'responsible' and 'mature' and encouraged to take an adult's place in a family of equals. The parents were admirable moral models, and, though none was religious, their political preoccupations in each case were sufficiently serious and sophisticated to have impressed assumptions of civic responsibility on the sons. Each was the 'favourite' child of the family (Eyman and Ingle had younger sisters, and Hawk had an elder brother), but, more importantly, each was the mother's 'closest'. All are mother-identified.

The fathers are held in high conscious affection and regard* — and have left the sons little problem in assuming confident masculinity. Eyman and Hawk are convinced that (with mother's strong approval) they are going on to careers very much more important and worthwhile than their fathers'; Ingle wishes more to carry on a tradition, though in a new and wider field. Ingle has massive residual unconscious hostility to his father, which spurs him on to radical extremism, and an unresolved castration anxiety that unfits him for active service. (Eyman's 'castration' crisis similarly affords the hook on which his ideology is hung.)

One arranges them conveniently enough down Bales's P meridian according to their (unconscious) relationships with their fathers. Hawk (UP) is confident of having won the phallic contest, and it has left his sense of what he might attempt somewhat without boundaries; Ingle (P) is still grimly intent on its pursuit; and Eyman (DP) has withdrawn, in effect, to be a 'man' in a female world.

The key thing in each case seems to be that the parents, and particularly

---

* And Ingle is proud to have moved his father politically to the left, Eyman his to religion.

the mothers, gave the child in the early years a very solid basis for self-esteem; so that when it became necessary for the mothers to detach, each child had a valued self to turn to and develop. All three currently have powerful ego-ideals around which they have imaginatively projected their altruistic life-projects.

The reader may now care to turn back to table 10, Keniston's contrast between Radicals and Beats, the left-hand side of which gave his prescription for the 'psychological democrat'. It will be seen that Helfaer has provided Keniston with the exemplary case that he himself failed to assemble in *Young Radicals*.

Adjoining meridians

Bales dubs the PF meridian the 'Conservative Centre', and the PB the 'Liberal Left of Centre'. We have already glanced at two cases of the PF stance, Murray's Nack and Finch, who perhaps sufficiently illustrate its defining tone of altruism and optimistic idealism, its conservatism in politics and religion, and its family matrix (deep identification with parents themselves identified with some abstract symbol of higher authority). The embeddedness in their filial position and their vocation (medicine and the ministry, respectively) alerts us to the essential quality of the PF project in social terms — eager service within established structures. Indeed, one is tempted to see the professions, at least in their ideal self-image, as the social sub-systems specifically designed to harness and organise the talents and energies of persons so formed. It is unfortunate that we have no representative case for UPF — the position taking up the meridional stance not only with 'ascendant' force (task-bound ambition and aggression), but also, perhaps, with characteristically broader sweep and some sense of taking system-responsibility (guyed a little in our tag, 'head prefect'). In terms of political work, this is the probable site for Lasswell's 'balanced/driving' (genital) administrator (see above, pp. 16—17 and 63n).

If an essential rung of PF eludes us, it must be confessed that the accepted case-file of political psychology offers no help at all with the whole PB meridian.* We are lucky, then, that a small Melbourne drive to collect *women's* outlooks, should have recently netted a splendid UPB, who not only graces that position, but provides us with a novel view of the whole P quadrant.

Considine's Anna N. as UPB

Aged 56, the mother of four grown children and widow of five years' standing, Anna is currently employed as tea-lady on the Commissioners' floor at Victoria Police Headquarters, Melbourne.[116] (She was subsequently

---

* A possible exception is R. J. Lifton's Hiroshima peace-worker, 'Angel', who, if less fanatical and exotic, might well exemplify DPB.[115]

promoted to a better-paid, superannuable post with the same organisation.) She is regarded there as 'refreshing' and a 'breath of fresh air', not only because she effortlessly assumes the social management of the floor, but because she 'does battle' with her patrons over their authoritarian views. 'I go in with what I hear from the kids around here [her children's friends]', she says, and she taxes the police leaders with their lack of understanding and rapport with young people — their harassment of young drivers, for example, 'just because they are young and poor', and their overbearing treatment of marijuana users. 'It stimulates them,' she says comfortably, 'because they're shut up all day with people who think just the same as they do.'

Accustomed to finding the assured liberality of her views provocative and stimulating, Anna is a classic Lazarsfeldian 'opinion leader', effortlessly dominating a large and miscellaneous circle of relatives, neighbours and friends of the marriage. (One young girl begged to see Considine's transcript, because she felt it would be 't'riffic to have Anna's ideas about things written down'.) Her affirmative counsel and reliable tolerance are valued, it seems not only because they appear 'hard won', but also because they are inextricably intertwined with a life and opinions of the strictest conventionality. She is quite curious, herself, about the source of her power as a moral teacher. 'I think that I'm a victim of an early environment, but I'm not sure if it's a hang-up ... [or a great resource].'

> I come from a very bawdy, down-to-earth Italian background, and
> I think I was fortunate in being able to pick from it the things that
> were useful and throw out what was of no use ...

Her migrant parents had come independently about 1915 to rural Victoria, where they met, married, and raised three children. Anna, the eldest, grew up in a large country town.

> We were the only Italian family in W—, so we grew up with Aust-
> ralians — merged in easily. Although we had that bit extra because
> of the Italian insight into food, art, music. And, once again, I accepted
> all the things I wanted to, and chucked the rest over my shoulder.
> And that's the way I lead my life ...

If Australians in general were easy to get along with, the Irish Sisters running her convent school induced extraordinary anxiety and stress in their dutiful pupil — at first over her father's non-observance:

> Round 8 or 9 I had this great project of getting Dad to Mass ... and
> yet somehow he wouldn't and I prayed very earnestly — I used always
> to say, 'Please God, don't reject my father' ... As a girl of 11 I'd re-
> solved on Christmas Eve, This is the day I can get him to go to Mass,
> and I said, 'Tomorrow the greatest feast of the Church is going to
> happen!' And he said, 'Oh no, it's not. That's the Resurrection.'

This was followed by anxiety over the personal demands of a truly pious life:

I was terribly impressionable as a child, because Sister got up — it was
the time of the Mexican Revolution against the Catholics and Father
Pio had been persecuted and shot — and she said, *'You are all going
to die for your faith before the year is out* because look what's happening
in Mexico.'

Well, it probably didn't hit anyone in that place except me ...'
I went out, and I was sleepless for three months — my mouth broke
out in ulcers. My mother got the doctor down and he said, 'Now
Anna, I know something's bothering you ... ', he could tell it was
nerves, and I looked at him, he was a Catholic, and I thought, 'Well,
you're not going to deny your faith, but I am, because I haven't got
any courage' — and I knew I wasn't going to be able to withstand
this persecution, which Sister said was going to come ... so, anyway,
I couldn't confide in Dr Walsh because I felt he would have laughed
at me, I suppose.

I was so mixed up in all of it — felt like I was looking down a
lion's mouth all the time ... Anyhow, I must have got to the end of
my tether, and I was walking to school with my uncle (who's now
the parish priest at F—) who was only 3 years older, and he stopped
still in the middle of the street and said, *'Look, what is the matter
with you?'* and it all spilled out, that I was going to deny my faith,
and I wasn't going to see God, I was going to the Devil ... And we
got to the end of the street, and one school was on one corner and
one was on the other, and he said, 'You silly bunny, don't you know
that if you want to die for your faith God will give you the grace
to die?' And, in 24 hours, my mouth cleared up and I was cured.

In the course of time — but it was a long and anxious process — she came
to a grateful recognition of the health and sanity of her father's relaxed
religious views (which she sees now partly in terms of *national* character):

He said that God had made him, and that He understood him, and
that therefore he didn't have to go through all that gafoofle of proving
himself the whole time ... He believed in God all his life — and saw
Him in Nature. Seeing things germinate — he used to tell me — made
it impossible for him not to believe in God.

Some tension remains, however. In the middle of these mature reflections,
she revives the little girl's rationalisation that, if her father did not go to
Mass, it was not really because he did not want to, but because 'someone
had to cook the dinner', and she tells an affecting anecdote of the day of
his death, when she was with him, *'as I'd always prayed'*, so that she could
get him to make his act of contrition.

Religion continues to be a leading preoccupation, and, apart from the
story of her marriage, fills up the greater part of the interview. Though
pressed hard, she has nothing to say about politics — 'I don't really get
involved in anything except my own sort of situation,' she apologises. Yet
'her own sort of situation' covers a very generous area of moral concern,
and she can be seen in her reflections on the Church to be teasing out

resourcefully the 'useful things' in the Sisters' teaching, and tempering them with the honest scepticism that she found first in her father, and now finds in her sons and daughters. That the Church, like the Police, might be profoundly mistaking the young, is her great fear:

> I still believe, certainly, as I did as a child, in a Higher Being — and I think it's good to belong to something whereby you can express this, and identify yourself as one of these people . . . I believe in the *future* of the Church, but not entirely in it in its present form. It's been a man-made thing, and you can't deny that there's a great drop-out of young people. The kids have just for some reason walked away from Mass . . . But I don't believe, just because they've done that, they've stopped believing in God.

Though zealous in her own observance, she is critical of the Church's teaching on contraception, sex before marriage, marijuana, divorce and compulsory Sunday attendance.

> I think the Church in its efforts to make people do the right thing has lost the sense of them as people . . . Of course, I belong to the old school, but I realise now that when I was young I was constantly seeking new things and looking past old rules, just like young people are doing today.

In her determined empathy she seems to contrive a somewhat exaggerated picture of an essentially restless younger self. She is in no awe of 'the theologians' and expresses vivid personal convictions about God being 'in people' and about the Holy Spirit's manner of working, as concrete findings of her own experience. She is most interested in the new currents in Catholicism that would emphasise the congregation 'as a community . . . as one', but feels 'too individualist — too Italian' to want to give up her 'insular communication' with God. 'I don't believe,' she concludes, 'my church is any better than anybody else's, but I do believe in it, and that it will somehow someday *do* something.'

The story of her marriage, which we will give entirely in her own words, is also notable for its focus *on the children*:

> I suffered greatly through marriage. From the moment I married, I married insecurity . . . The thing was, I married a gambler, and I had to live a hand-to-mouth existence . . . went 12 years with the same overcoat. But, in actual fact, marriage with the love of my husband with all his failings, I valued more than the previous security, because I became a woman fulfilled in being a wife and mother. And I was always a wife before I was a mother, and I remained like that throughout the whole of my marriage, and I think that's why the children are as [confident and independent] as they are . . .
>
> To belong to someone is the richest thing in the world — that has never changed for me — I knew that as a small girl. I wanted to belong to somebody, and I was never left unfulfilled in that way — but I paid for it in other ways . . .

Did we struggle! Three months after we were married, he fell sick, and from then on I think each year I put him to bed about five times a year ... And I had to placate sales-managers — he was a wonderful salesman — extraordinary, but, like all salesmen, he 'dried out' on his products — got sick of them — and trailed from firm to firm ... This left *me* with a permanent sense of insecurity, but somehow it never rubbed off on to the children ... Although we had rows — big ones — I don't think that I ever stood up against *the father* — and that, of course, comes from the Italian heritage — that the father is ... that to *make the father* the head of the family, gives the children the security they need (whether, *as wife*, you like it or not). What's important for them is that they know their parents love each other ... so they're not afraid later to risk loving other people.

I was always ten jumps ahead of my husband's schemes ... Because I came from a very affluent home — and I don't think he could forget that — he tried to give me what he thought I didn't have — and I didn't want what I'd left behind. It took me 18 years to get that through to him ... I think I paid off his debts three times — and that was principle (and protecting all we had, the house) ... But in marriage you reach a point of crisis — and only when you face that, and fall back in love — have you really got the ideal thing: you have accepted that person with all their imperfections ...

My husband and I respected and loved one another, and we always (all of us) talked things over. I think the children would value that ideal love — and, if for some reason they didn't achieve it, I think they would divorce.

The transcript is studded with vivid self-descriptions and disclosures. She sees herself as *deviant* ('As an Australian-born Italian, I'm one from the start') but she wishes to distance herself somewhat from 'that image of slight dishonesty'. She is more Australian ('there's a lot in the Australian way of doing things — as I learnt from my husband') but she is also proud to report that 'They tell me up in the Office, I'm very much a Continental woman.' She is *deeply emotional*; *very happy* ('relatively, I think, I'm a very happy person — though still heartbroken over the loss of my husband'); *capable, adaptable* ('In 20 years, we had something like 12 shifts of house — you have to learn to live with insecurity, rather than security'); *confident, enthusiastic, easily inspired; moral* ('Actually, I haven't gone off the rails all that much'). She is also *self-accepting* ('My problem [in re-marriage?] is somehow to find a way to go on being the person I am': 'I need a highly sexual partner — I think I still will when I'm 90); she is *wise* (for example, 'When we start talking about acting through principles, we mean we don't really know why we're doing it'); and, in her own strongest word, she feels *fulfilled*. Asked if she ever regretted not having a career, she said, 'As a matter of fact, I feel great pride that I've been able to do what I have — I left school [at 12] very badly equipped.' But we only see her fully in the round as she talks of her parents, lovingly cataloguing her father's qualities, which she feels she has by and large appropriated, and, as firmly, differentiating herself from those of her mother, whom she trusts she resembles as little as possible.

Family background. For six years, Anna enjoyed the undivided affection of her parents. 'My early life was very secure', she reports, but adds at once, because of my *wonderful father*, who, 'because of the luck of his job, was always at home'. The mother, for whatever reason, was not admired. Maybe she is blamed, in a projection of guilt, for the 'loss of a little sister when I was 20 months old'; more likely, her permanent readiness (and perhaps inclination) to bear little rivals and supplanters is the cause. But Anna remains passionately convinced that 'My father wanted only me — that was enough for him. He thought: "One will do. Give her everything"'. However, through 'mistakes' and/or her mother's malice (the couple, against Church precept, practised contraception), a sister, Vennie, arrived when she was six (of whom Anna has never really taken receipt), and a brother, Louie, when she was ten ('who was loved by the whole lot of us').

The father worked as a chef in W——till 1929, and then bought a Continental foods business in a fashionable Melbourne suburb which began to falter badly with the Depression. He then returned to W——in 1932 in the reckless project of opening his own restaurant. Anna alone in the family supported him in this, if she did not, indeed, originate the idea. She left school, aged twelve, to help him full-time, and the business succeeded spectacularly. Nevertheless, she continued for nine years to work selflessly to establish the family fortune. In 1941 (when Anna was 22) they moved to Melbourne, and the father opened several similar ventures with ex-employees as managers (of whom Anna's future husband was one). Anna, still living at home, went to work at a hairdressing aunt's, and spent seven years fending off importunate, and often rich, suitors, before making her final, gambling choice.

Anna's account of her father takes on mythic dimensions, but there is a solid sub-stratum of fact: he was a remarkable man. 'My father was . . . one of the most full Christians I ever knew . . . I'm quite certain that if one goes to a place of eternal happiness, then my father, when he died, was there *instantly*; 'dynamic and organised, dominant, a leader', he was 'extremely intelligent though uneducated. He could, I think, have been a fine surgeon.' He was a remarkable amateur sculptor; he was 'always an inspiring person, and also, like most Italians, he turned things for his own ends — he was one of the few who made money during the depression'. 'A man of honour', in his own phrase, a man who paid his debts punctiliously, he was yet conspicuously charitable, and a 'soft touch' for drunks, 'swaggies' and anyone down on his luck.

From an early age, Anna consciously modelled herself on her father: 'I had such great admiration for him. He was full of common-sense. Yet he came from an island that was full of superstition, and he'd kicked the lot by the time he was nine!' She identified herself with the exceptional youth her father had been:

> I helped my father because I saw him as this young kid of 15, who'd come all the way from Italy — walked into this strange land to make his life. I found him inspiring, and I'm the sort of person who *is* inspired like that — and I stuck by him — wouldn't say it was without some form of resentment - *because I had to.*

Indeed, in the extremity of her devotion, she seemed not merely to identify with him, but to seek to be a mother to him. This left her mother with the somewhat residual functions of a drudge.

> Momma was always a hand-wringing sort of person . . . and I was always placating her, and trying to do what would shut her up. Not that she didn't work — she certainly worked! But she loved it, you know: she was dragging in the money . . . Ar, it drove me mad. But poor Momma always got on my nerves — she really did. She dominated me by whingeing, you know! And she's still that sort of person today.

The contrast between her parents never ceased to amaze Anna ('From the moment they put their feet out of bed, they were fighting like Kilkenny cats'). Her father was so intelligent, decisive and dynamic, while her mother was 'fractured', 'disorganised — and still is'. She has a 'very disordered mind (that rubbed off on me, too; though I must say my years with [my husband] restored me back to what I should have been)'. As a child, Anna was never in the least worried about her mother's failure of religious observance — it was father alone she wished to redeem; when, late in life, the mother turned strongly to religion, Anna rather held it against her, as a predictable, craven trick common on that side of the family.

In the romantic rush of her tale of helpless infatuation with father and their miraculous partnership together, we should not lose sight of her glinting sense of having been 'used' — her devotion, all those years, taken for granted, denied any life of her own, driven to whistling Beethoven symphonies to herself as she cooked '1,500 pieces of fish every Friday night . . . He really was a tyrant' — and, after nine years, she had 'absolutely had it'.

> I feel they demanded too much of their children — that you should be eternally grateful to them for what they had done, achieved . . . When my own children were born, I remember thinking: 'Well, you don't owe me a thing!'

In her current search for secure work, she is determined, above all, 'not to be a burden' to her children. Indeed, she wants nothing but their love and bright futures, and the recognition that she has — with her special gift of 'choosing the good things and chucking out the rest' — found in her childhood experiences all that she needed to become, in her turn, a wonderful parent.

Anna N. as UPB. Bales names the UPB project 'towards emotional supportiveness and warmth' and expects to find such people swelling the liberal centre of politics. Their strategy in society as in the home is 'encouraging the young, allowing them to develop, and changing the hampering effects of tradition for the sake of growth'. They are against punishment (Anna says it 'only makes them aggressive'), and believe that 'Love cures all', and that the fewer restraints on impulse expression the better (UPB is the pole of this axis). They are equalitarian and somewhat sceptical of 'authorities' and 'tasks'.

As people, they are 'ascendant and expressive, open, warm, friendly, affectionate, nurturant . . . and rewarding to others'. They can praise. Their strong sex-drive is sublimated to a capacity to work powerfully with affection: they can feel it and elicit it in an unusual degree, and consciously direct it to reduce feelings of anxiety in others. They espouse the 'growth ethic', and go to great lengths to protect and champion the 'backward-tending' young (half-expecting, however, in this to be finally ruled against). Their self-image is that of the 'good parent who depends upon the power of love'.

They come from homes of maximum family warmth, where unconditional love and praise is the rule. (Bales's expectation, however, of *identical* — or identically perceived — parents gets a heavy jolt in Anna's case.)

I feel that Anna, while principally breathing life into each detail of the type-description, most interestingly shows the degree of *correctional amendment* (and cross-sex identification) that may be necessary to transmit this invaluable temperament from one generation to the next. And still following this generational clue, I believe further that her case helps us achieve an overall view of the whole P quadrant. All of its people are warm-hearted, forward-looking and healthy, but they perceive their place in the chain of generations very differently. PF types are pious, epigonistic, fashioning their burgeoning projects in faithful imitation of admired elders. (Finch will follow exactly in his father's footsteps; Nack will become the doctor his mother has needed and might have been herself.) P types, though grateful enough to good parents, are self-starters, peer-oriented and determined on novel projects. (Hawk will be his own kind of politician, Ingle his own kind of U.N. adviser, Eyman his own kind of clergyman.) PB types, the most far-sighted and nurturant, set themselves to shape and champion the *next* generation of achievers, and thank their parents, above all, for the good-parent model, itself.

The Authoritarians — the NF meridian
Jones's Quisling-like patients
In the first year of the Second World War, Ernest Jones in London saw two patients who wanted Hitler to win: their disease, he judged, was a 'peculiar inability to face, or even to recognise, an enemy'.[117] That there were, Jones reflected, so many such people in every country menaced by the Nazis,

was exactly what Hitler meant when he spoke of his 'secret weapon'.

In these cases, Jones decided, an inverted resolution of the Oedipus complex paved the way for an identification of Hitler with an archaic image of a supremely powerful, indeed irresistible, father. The thing could take two paths: the serious aggressive intent behind the irresistibility could be denied, fear repressed and all danger denied; or the irresistibility could be frankly admired and identified with. Either way, the desperate project was to convert the image of the evil father into that of the good one, by equating gross preponderance of power and inevitability of success with 'goodness' in some final sense. Underlying this dubious, indeed fatal, equation was an archaic identification of sadism with sexual potency.

> Our starting-point in any constructive analysis must surely be the fear of the dangerous Father or of one's dangerous impulses towards him. If one is unable to face this situation then there remain only two alternatives: to submit to him or to ally oneself with the dangerous forces through the mechanisms of acceptance and identification. These alternatives are not so mutually exclusive as they might appear; often they are both operative in the same person . . . Both are *exquisitely homosexual solutions*, there being always some complex emotional relationship with the enemy in place of an attitude of *aloof opposition*. The fear is both sexualized and moralized.

In the first path, submission depends on 'a secret hostility that cannot be accepted' — it is the *passive* homosexual 'solution'. Passivity and masochism are linked with the guilt that underlies the moralisation. One patient maintained that

> Hitler's very insistence, and the enormous energy he has devoted to achieving his aim, in itself put him in the right . . . Insistent 'wanting' of that degree could only mean 'wanting back', so that Hitler had a right to demand the return of what had been taken from him, all this being of course rationalized in terms of Germany's reactions to the treaty of Versailles. The analytic point is that *primary* aggressive wanting was so repressed as to be inconceivable, though its existence was after all implied in the idea of the Father demanding back the penis of which he had been robbed. That this cannot be an isolated reaction is shown by the inactivity of the Allies for so many years under the illusion that Germany's conduct was a more or less proportionate response to the aggressivity of the Allies immediately after the last war and therefore need not be supposed to betoken any innate aggressivity of her own. Such is the revenge of bad conscience; it tends to paralyse the power of resistance.

In the second path, in which 'the idea of aggressivity is denied and the hope entertained that it should be possible to appease the enemy by making suitable concessions', we see the faint beginnings of a positive admiration.

> The admiration may be somewhat masochistic and accompanied by

the hope of obtaining a kind of protective security through coming to terms with the enemy. Politically this may go with a fear of 'Bolshevism', i.e. of a chaotic mob, which may afford grounds for identification with the powerful dictator. Perhaps this was the characteristic attitude in Denmark and Norway and it may be likened to that of the younger brother. The most complete forms of identification, however, occur where the homosexual trends are of a more active kind. With such persons tyrannical tendencies are already present which render an identification easy. One imagines this to be so with the well-known Fascist leaders in the various countries. It is probable, however, that when the alliance is complete, even the most active of these types is forced to regress to the deeper level of passive homosexuality. Mussolini will probably yet follow the path of Seyss-Inquart, Henlein and Quisling himself.

I would suggest that the people who are most subject to the wiles of Nazi propaganda are those who have neither securely established their own manhood and independence of the Father nor have been able to combine the instincts of sexuality and love in their attitude towards the Mother or other women. This is the psychological position of the homosexual.

Sanford's three first steps towards the Authoritarian Personality

Vito as NF. At the very time Murray, at Harvard, was resourcefully tackling the reluctance to fight Fascism, Sanford, at the University of California, set out to probe local problems of poor morale, the passive character and American softness in students, and had some 300 of them fill in lengthy questionnaires just three days before Pearl Harbour. Familiar with Jones's article on potential Fascist sympathisers, Sanford was quick to spot a general pattern in responses:

> Those who report temperamental likeness to their fathers ... are not so sure of their strength. They admire maleness and tend to identify social values with softness; their generally hard-boiled and materialistic attitude works against ... liberalism, tolerance and idealism.[118]

And shortly after, in a detailed portrait of the least pro-war man in the sample, he moved a decisive step nearer the delineation of the celebrated Authoritarian Personality.[119]

Vito, a student of criminology, aged 21, is of Italian extraction, born in California, and a 'good attending' Catholic. An only child, whose father is a bank clerk, he is frankly interested in prestige and status, and ambitious for professional success. He is politically conscious, impatient with the humanitarian 'softness' of New Deal liberalism, and scornful of existing American institutions and democratic ideals. A rabid isolationist, whose heroes are Lindbergh and Wheeler, he believes that the victory of Germany will have no serious consequences for, and that no one has aggressive designs against, the U.S. As Sanford paraphrases him:

> We are safe unless we resist or behave provocatively, and to do either
> of these things would be quite foolish in any case because by now the
> Axis powers are much too strong. And, furthermore ... since our own
> ideals and institutions have nothing to commend them anyway, it
> might be a good thing if Hitler [or some American of equal strength]
> did take over.

To submit to such a man, 'powerful enough and plausible enough', would
be no disgrace. Indeed, Sanford interjects, it would gratify Vito's deepest
wish — he 'has the soul of a Fascist' — and allow him to give up the elaborate system of personal defences he now so painfully maintains.

A drive to have power over people seems a leading trait in his personality. To the TAT picture in which a man lies on his back on a couch and
another man is seated beside him with his hand held above the first man's
chest, Vito responds:

> Mandrake, the Magician. Lando, the cruel magician, had Mr X. under
> his hypnotic spell. In such a condition Mr X. was completely sub-
> servient to Lando's will, with the result that a series of crimes were
> committed by Mr X. Mandrake, the Magician, was called in to break
> the spell.

As well as preoccupation with power, the story suggests some of Vito's
vocational fantasies: he will stamp out crime, using (magical) powers to
overcome evil forces whether they be within himself or others, and so
essentially right are his views, that his use of power over others will be a
service to mankind. Other projective material discloses an open aggressiveness — a contempt for weakness, affective inhibition and avoidance
of intimacy, paranoid/megalomaniac tendencies, and a homosexual trend.
The self-assertiveness, hostility and lust for power cover an underlying
weakness, submissiveness and possible passive homosexuality.

> It may be further hypothesized that out of this deep-lying affective
> disturbance impulses essentially criminal in nature have been gene-
> rated, and these he seeks to control by paranoid mechanisms. His
> special hatred is reserved for those who by their actions or by their
> ideas threaten his conviction of his own rightness, for upon this
> conviction depends the integration of his personality.

The father appears to have played the dominant role in the family and
to be the central figure in Vito's life. The mother's influence seems to have
been negligible. The father's discipline was more feared, and more effective: he set family standards. Vito claims to resemble his father in appearance and temperament, but seems to have taken into his personality both
the mother's pattern of weakness, timidity and dependence, and the
father's of boldness, aggression and strength.

> Fear of the aggressive father not only inhibited the disposition to love
> and protect the mother but gave rise to an attitude of passive sub-
> missiveness and a need to be loved by the father. These latter

tendencies conflict with pride and the greater fear of emasculation and must themselves be held in check — by the constant assertion of masculinity.

Mr Q., an American Quisling

Seen as a psychotherapy patient with marital problems, Mr Q., a tough-looking, 35-year-old mechanic, turned out to have the personality and world view of an extreme authoritarian.[120] Though he had spent the war working in a defence plant, he had sympathised throughout with the Axis powers. He believed the Jews in Germany 'went too far and abused too many people', that the Nazis had in many ways a strong case, and that 'Secretary Hull got us into this war by provoking the Japs until they were desperate'. Thus, far from accepting the Axis powers as legitimate ene-mies, he directed his hatred at those American leaders and groups, the 'Warmongers', who most vigorously opposed them, and his anxiety mounted as the U.S. mobilised more and more effectively. He admired Lindbergh, but also Henry Wallace, for he had some radical economic notions and a 'highly dramatized solicitude for certain underdogs'.

A cold and cynical man, he saw all human relationships in terms of dominance and submission, and liked to present himself as a victim of injustice and misunderstanding. He had a hero-worshipping attitude to his father (a successful small-town dentist), the Standard Oil Company, and Henry Ford, but little capacity for affection — 'Genuine warmth of feeling was reserved for his tropical fish.' He was preoccupied to a large degree in guarding himself against repressed (passive) homosexuality — he shunned, for example, all-male company. 'His fear of homosexuality was a fear that he would be turned into a *woman*, in his mind something utterly wretched and powerless.' What was particularly striking was the way in which a kind of primal-scene imagery had come to dominate Q's view of the world: 'somebody is brutalized, somebody is on top and somebody on the bot-tom, there is a persecutor and a persecuted one.' He saw all relationships in these terms, being at the same time attracted and repelled by each role.

In describing his childhood, Q. put his mother for a long time in the role of tormenter (he constantly spoke of her 'holding a stick over his head'). When the true picture finally emerged,

> it could be seen that the admired father was in reality a mean and
> brutal man who tortured his wife by telling her, in front of the child-
> ren [there were two younger brothers], of his sexual adventures,
> and who was given to sudden fits of unrestrained physical violence.
> [Q.] lived with the conviction that to oppose this man was to be
> annihilated. Instant and complete submission was his only recourse.
> When the mother refused to submit to the father, but seemed by
> continued yapping about to provoke him further, [Q.] was filled with
> terror — and this was stilled only by taking sides with the father and
> convincing himself that his mother was in the wrong.

Submission, For Q., was not only a means of avoiding annihilation; it
came to stand also as a means of attaining mastery, for, by submitting to
the father, he could participate in his power. (Even if Japan should win the
war, he said, American businessmen would still run everything.) At the
same time, however, he was afraid of the feminine position in relation to
a powerful man, for this was to court the greatest danger of all — castration. So he endowed his mother (and, later, his wife) with masculine characteristics and cast her in the role of oppressor. It is doubtful if aggression
against the father ever even took firm shape — the impulse was no sooner
formed, than it was instantly deflected towards the mother. But he had a
capacity for sudden violence — whenever it seemed that his best efforts
to submit and be passive might still not save him from castration — 'then
he was prepared for the desperate all-out destructiveness of the pogrom'.

At the deepest level, Sanford judged, Q. was identified with his mother
and America. This made him feel that he was in the greatest danger of
being conquered and oppressed, and he was 'forced to re-arrange the
world in order to free himself from anxiety'. He turned things around in
exactly the way he did in childhood, when he sought to ally himself with
the father against the mother. The German and Japanese militarists were
made to appear as victims, even while they were viewed as strong and
irresistibly violent. 'He projected onto them his own persecution complex.
The warmongers and the Jews, like his mother, were hated primarily
because, despite their weakness, they refused to submit or keep quiet and
so foolishly provoked the strong enemy.* The idea that the mother, the
Jews, and the warmongers were the oppressors was secondary.'

Mack, an Ethnocentric man

A 24-year-old ex-Army clerk and officer-trainee, Mack is studying law
at the University of California under the G.I. Bill of Rights: he wants to be
either a corporation or a criminal lawyer.[121] His other main preoccupation is whether to get married now or wait till he finishes his course. His
origins are small-town 'rural'; he grew up in sight of the Rockies and
feels sentimentally Irish, though the links are by now tenuous and he has
no connections with Catholicism, or any religious denomination. His
politics is rather conservative (but comfortably contained within the
moderate wing of the Republicans) and complacently 'prejudiced'; it
includes some mild anti-Semitism. It takes its shape from an over-all

* 'A tendency to identify with the oppressed was never far below the surface.
Relatively late in his treatment [Q.] joined a picket line in protest against
a store's refusal to hire a Negro, and he dreamed that there was a Jew in
his family and he was preparing to defend the house against the Gestapo.
In his world of oppressed and oppressors, different groups of people could
at different times have one or the other role; and this Quisling, this anti-
Semite, was close to being, and at the same time almost hopelessly distant
from being, a champion of the oppressed.'

respect and admiration for power and authority, and a determination to play some significant role himself in the Establishment. Feeling securely that he is a member of the decent, 'average', in-group majority, he is apt to underline the hierarchical arrangement of social groups, and to distance or be mildly contemptuous of certain ethnic and other out-groups. He believes in the need for a strong but 'streamlined' Government executive, shorn of New Deal sentimentalities and excesses. His two years in wartime Washington — during which he suffered a mild conversion to conservatism — have left him with some 'inside-dopester' traits. He wishes, above all, to be thought practical and a realist in politics.

It is Sanford's considerable achievement to have demonstrated that behind this rather commonplace stance, which might perhaps be described as straight F in Bales's scheme,* lies a theoretical potential for political menace under conditions of some future great lurch to the right in national politics. He does this by showing that to scrutinise very intently this outlook, personality and childhood brings out the unmistakable outline of the Quisling as already present — if only faintly. Sensitive critics like Edward Shils have protested that this is to 'over-interpret the material'.[122]

Mack's father was a lumberman and timber concessionnaire, deeply introverted and retiring (Mack speaks of his 'not wanting to meet people'. 'He used to spend his winters alone in the mountains'); he was 53 when Mack was born. Mack's mother died when he was six, and an aunt, living near by, and a sister four years older, helped care for him thereafter, although the father, semi-retired, devoted much time to the household. Sanford divines through Mack's almost completely positive testimony, that the father was a defeated man, incapable of understanding or affection towards his son, who in 'a strict and authoritarian manner held up conventional moral standards to him, without being able to show that adherence to them actually led to worthwhile ends'. The mother had also been strict as well as loving, and her long illness may have made her love seem insecure and clouded. Her loss, which he took hard, may well have given later discipline a tinge of special harshness and unfairness.

Prominent in Mack's personality are strong (maternal) dependency needs, which he 'tries to suppress because they do not accord with his ideal of masculinity' — as well as later father-dependency needs focused on direction and advice, and upon fears of parental rejection. Repressed hostility against the distant and moralistic father is also strong, but it is never allowed to surface because the father is conceived as too strong and dangerous. Aggression is therefore disclaimed, redirected or smothered,

---

* It may be salutary to reflect that Mack is possibly less conservative and certainly no more authoritarian than Walter's Dianne Ellis (see above, pp. 175–8).

and he allies himself with restraining authority. Submission to, and admiration of, authority thus become his project, enabling him to 'gain a sense of adequacy by participating psychologically in the father's power. This, in the last analysis, is the homosexual solution of the Oedipus problem.'

> There would seem to be no doubt that Mack has longed for his father's love ... He has tried to replace the imagery of a bad, dangerous father with imagery of a good father who would spend '*all* of his time with us'. But Mack is not able to admit this need. Even while *acting* in a submissive and deferential manner he seems to cling to the belief that he is very manly and self-sufficient ... For [Mack], to submit to a man and so to gain his love has definite sexual implications. It may be connected with very primitive imagery of passivity and emasculation ... Mack's homosexuality, repressed in childhood in a setting of sadomasochistic relations with the father, has remained on an infantile level; insufficiently sublimated, it cannot find gratification in friendly, equalitarian relations with men but, instead, it determines that most such relations have to be on a dominance-submission dimension.

His repressed homosexuality is mainly responsible also for his fear of weakness and the need at all costs to conceal any signs of it. A sickly child, it must have been hard, indeed, for him to close with a father who seemed by comparison so strong and dangerous. And behind his blanket association of weakness with femaleness, we may see the terrifying 'lesson' of his mother's illness and death.

> It is very likely that he regards his dependent needs as signs of weakness ... and ... this is another reason why he cannot freely admit the existence of these needs. It is as if accepting help or love or comfort from a woman meant being somehow identified with her, and hence open to the dangers with which women have to contend. Accepting help or love or comfort from a man suggest being treated like a woman by that man, and hence threatened with the loss of masculinity. But because in his innermost self Mack would like to be treated in just this way, the sense of weakness is constantly stimulated, and no amount of counteractive striving can entirely dispel it.

From these basic trends in personality — dependence, hostility against the father, submission, passivity and homosexuality, and above all, fear of weakness — the leading features of Mack's political stance can be recognised as 'defence derivatives':

Denial. He 'attempts to conceal weakness by verbal denial and by presenting a façade of toughness ... All through his interview he [protests] that he is not weak but strong and that if at any time he has appeared to be weak, then this was entirely justified by external circumstances.' To this end he exaggerates the power and misreads the intentions of out-groups, such as the Washington bureaux, the New Deal and the Jews, according to the formula, 'If I appear to be weak, it is because they are so strong, and out to take unfair advantage of me.' Unable to behave aggressively, he can at least be tough-minded, and his general 'anti-intraceptiveness' can be understood as primarily an attempt to ward off any suggestion of softness.

Projection. "'I am not weak, they are." It is not so much that he sees weakness where none exists; rather, he thinks of people and groups in rigid categories of weak versus strong, and if any weakness is actually there it is what first strikes his eye . . . His main concern is not to be in any way identified with weakness.' Religious people, Jewish refugees and women — these he must at all costs set apart from himself.

> If one asks why he cannot have pity for weak people but instead actually hates them, the answer is twofold. In the first place, they remind him too much of his own weakness and all the dreadful fear with which it is associated. Second . . . he believes weak people to be dangerous.* When he says that Jews 'should not resent' their persecution we can readily infer that he believes they *do* resent it and will seek revenge in time. Women and Negroes [and oppressed people generally] are regarded in this same way.

Counter-action. Mack's striving for power and status to 'raise' himself, is largely over-compensatory. For him 'going up' means going up a steep hierarchy: it is 'natural' that there should be extremes of powerfulness and powerlessness and, far from wanting to challenge this, he seeks a place at the very top. As in relation to his father, he argues that the strong ones are the good ones, and even in admiring and serving† them, he overcomes weakness through a sense of participation in their power.

In sum, Mack attempts to allay his sense of weakness by aligning himself with powerful individuals and groups. Yet he 'submitted' to his father out of fear, and with a considerable residue of hostility. His conformism now is strict and rigid because he has not fully integrated conventional standards with his ego. His repressed hostility is displaced on to out-groups, who are hated for being selfishly and ruthlessly aggressive, as well as weak:

> The frustrating, punishing, persecutory features which had to be denied in the father were seen as originating in outgroups who could then be hated *in safety*, because they were not strong in actuality, and *in good conscience*, because the traits ascribed to them were those which the ingroup authorities would condemn.

If ethnocentrism is Mack's principal outlet for his aggression, his cynicism

---

* He projects acquisitiveness and resentment as well.
† At the same time, of course, authoritarian submission guards the adherent against his underlying homosexual submission and passivity; but when the strong man or the strong group is *strong enough*, then his homosexual submission and passivity are also secretly gratified. (Mack's dislike of Roosevelt centres on his being *weak*, in comparison, say, with Churchill or General Marshall.)

should also be noted. His surrender to his father is a nagging reminder that he *is* weak: in trying to separate himself from this thought, he projects his 'contemptibleness' on to mankind.

Returning to 'anti-intraception' — Mack's crippling inability to empathise — Sanford's last word is on 'ego restriction'. Mack 'cannot reckon with the psychology or the sociology of other people because he cannot — out of fear — examine the conditions or determinants of his own behaviour'.

> The problems with which he was faced as a child — problems centering around the loss of his mother and the necessity for making an adjustment to the 'distant' father — were ... more than the undeveloped ego could handle. Primitive defenses, chiefly repression and countercathexis, were necessary; and since that time, the ego has had to devote so much energy to maintaining these defenses that it could not develop normally. It remains narrow and constricted, in danger of being overwhelmed by emotional impulses from within or authoritative commands from without. Since the inner impulses are more to be feared than the outer authorities there is rigid adherence to the standards of the latter, but since these authorities are not accepted in any fundamental way this adherence could be given up altogether in circumstances that made it safe to do so. Since the traumatic experiences of childhood have not been integrated with the ego, the categories with which the child structured the world have persisted, in more or less unmodified form, to dominate contemporary thinking. Since there is little that is truly *inside* the personality, there can be little tolerance of inner conflict and little self-criticism; instead there is an attitude of hostile watchfulness toward a world that is largely alien.

Discussion

The triumph of *The Authoritarian Personality* was to show that Quisling and Ethnocentric are conjoined: that the processes ensuring ready submission to the strong leader also instil a watchful suspicion and potential hatred of scapegoat groups. In the course of this proof, Sanford and his co-workers accumulated much rich and plausible detail on associated traits — conventionality, aggression, superstition, punitiveness, tough-mindedness and preoccupation with dominance and submission* — and the 'character' took on a specious familiarity — so much so that Bales, faced with des-

---

* Later work that Sanford summarises in 'The approach of *The Authoritarian Personality*' has, equally plausibly, added these traits: 'relative inability to accept blame; a tendency to view interpersonal relations in terms of power and status rather than in terms of love and friendship; a manipulative attitude toward other people; the inability or the unwillingness to deal with the indefinite, the ambiguous or the merely probable; tendency to treat property as an extension of the self; tendency to see the real self and the ideal self as essentially the same, and signs of self-contempt underlying this self-overestimation;

cribing the UNF ('towards autocratic authority') stance, is able simply to say, 'That's him.'

Politically, the position involves identification 'with something large, strong, moral, and protective. Often this is law and order, strong leaders, the nation, religion, or God' and demands for the urgent punishment of deviants, scapegoats, and out-groups. Personally, it involves a masculine façade (and repression of feminine submission), a tough-minded approach to the world, and a strong belief that at bottom people are no good.[124] The principal mechanism is identification with the aggressor, with the bad parent who depends on the power of aggression. The parents' discipline, especially the father's is stern, and the child suffers from overriding anxiety, relies heavily on denial and projection, and carries a permanent fear of crumbling defences — in all, 'a personality-type precipitated by an emergency in socialization'.

In the excitement of unravelling the dynamics of authoritarian aggression and submission, however, it seems that its economics have been skimped. The authors of *The Authoritarian Personality* had themselves no sooner erected the full summary portrait, than they dismantled it again into a confusing set of hastily sketched *sub*-types (surface resentment, conventional, sado-masochistic, tough guy, crank and manipulator). Adorno, in his 'sociological' chapter, argues that it takes many types to make an authoritarian *movement*; indeed, Adorno's steps retreating from the clear-cut Authoritarian resemble hauntingly those of Sanford approaching him. Let us now see, not how they converge (that has perhaps been sufficiently obvious), but how they continue obstinately to strain apart.

Access to aggression. Jones's patients are spectral enough, but they do have an air of frozen immobilisation before the Great Dictator, 'fixed beneath the shadow of terror like a hare'. Vito, on the other hand, about to push people around for his splendid career and their own good, has the look of at least a small shark. It is true and important that all our NF cases share an inner climate of sado-masochism, a blend of vicarious approval of the principle of using force and a tearful sense of self-pitying weakness — an eroticised and moralised father-fixation. But they are spread over an extreme range of potential aggression. Mr Q. has 'a capacity for violence',

(Footnote continued)

self-pity; rigidity in adjustment; constriction of fantasy; concreteness of thinking; less differentiated emotional experience; undifferentiated conception of the opposite sex; relative absence of a value for achievement for its own sake; ego-alien dependency; tendency in emotional crises to emphasize somatic rather than psychological complaints'.[123] This is enough, Sanford reflects, to design a totally new and convincing replacement for the worn and nearly transparent F scale.

but only in the remote contingency that his ultimate in obeisance will not avert 'castration' — in real life, he continues over four years to make arms for a war effort he thinks can only provoke final defeat and occupation. Mack is *'incapable of* aggression' — except in cynical, ethnocentric revery. These men, surely, are comparable to the DPFs immobilised in castrated reverence before the charismatic figure of the wonderful father.

This, more than anywhere, is where *The Authoritarian Personality* fell down: it predicted chilling mass acquiescence in Fascism, and failed altogether to identify the cadres. To do justice to this range of aggression in our cases, the whole NF meridian may be needed. Only those 'authoritarians' able actively and aggressively to ally themselves with established or usurping authority, those with 'tyrannical tendencies' (Jones), should be UNF.

Pressure of anxiety. Our NF cases abundantly show that extra pressure of anxiety over F which is the whole rationale of the meridian. *Conforming* is (and was) simply that much harder, more painful, and more important for them. Mack's childhood, for example, was demonstrably colder, and his father harder to like than Lanlin's or Webb's (see above, pp. 164–7 and 167–71). Sanford rightly makes much of his incapacity to take blame, to be self-critical, to show insight — but what as much as anything keeps him a 'mild case' may be this very penchant for converting anxiety and aggression to somatic illness. But the capacity of *politics* to evoke these men's central anxieties is highly variable. While the Quislings are all highly involved with their good/bad or bad/good leaders and their fateful actions, there is no evidence that Mack's views on Jews or deviants or criminals have, or ever have had, any substantial emotional charge, nor, for that matter, his images of any of the Washington figures that he is happy to gossip about. Indeed, if it is read carefully, every line in Mack's portrait, though touching on some true detail, seems inexorably overdrawn.

Established and usurping authority. Sneakingly, like Jones's men and Mr Q., or openly and defiantly, like Vito, the Quislings declare the national enemy their hero and the national leaders villains and 'warmongers'. They find it easy to controvert conventional wisdom and to disown established authority. This is certainly authoritarian submission, but, more importantly, it is submission to a bad father who is desperately to be wished good. Conventionality, however, altogether outweighs authoritarian submission in Mack's modest hope that Mr Dewey, who is out, will be voted, this time, in. There is no desperation and little ambivalence, and it is the authors, not the subject, who have mistaken pseudo-conservatism for conservatism.

Mack, in short, is an excellent 'authoritarian', *only* if by that is meant a project of placing the trust of the self and others in conventional external authority in a very marked degree, and consistently preferring coercion of the self and others by conventional authorities to equalitarian, flexible, social relationships. He is not an 'authoritarian' if the project is essentially one of over-assertive support for a pseudo-conservative cause occasioned by a need to alleviate feelings of personal inadequacy on the one hand and diffuse mistrust of conventional leaders, on the other. (This distinction informs Adorno's 'conventional'/'sado-masochistic' sub-types, but, more significantly than he realised, it goes to the heart of the syndrome.)

Bales seems to wish to stress, above all, the *moralism* of the less assertive authoritarians. He makes NF 'the Voice of Conscience', the man who, in a grinding and guilt-inducing fashion, reminds others of what the rules prescribe, and he makes DNF 'the Martyr', the man who strips his life of all colour and spontaneity — indeed, individuality — in an effort to avoid in any way at all infringing accepted standards. Such people certainly exist, although I have not so far found them in the political psychology case-book. What is important is that the issue of correct behaviour is made the important frontier between Authoritarians and lesser Anxious types; the former are free to indulge a moral aggression, the latter need 'the Rules' as a desperate assurance that their lives are on the right lines. The developmental switch-point between these two paths needs, at the least, clarification. Here we have merely drawn attention to another under-discussed but even more politically vital boundary, that between F and NF.

Other cases

As we might expect from the general climate of politics, ethnocentric cases have proved more interesting and rewarding than sado-masochistic ones, and the focus of ethnocentrism has been Negroes rather than Jews.

We turn, first, to the only child in our gallery.

Frenkel-Brunswik's Karl, an eleven-year-old Ethnocentric

> Negroes . . . make trouble, start wars. I wouldn't mind having all the Negroes in Oakland [California] and all the white people in a different state. I would like to have a couple for good fighters. They are good fighters when they fight with a knife. Like somebody starts a fight and you have a gang with some Negroes to fight with you on your side with knives and guns . . . Jews . . . think they are smart and go anywhere they please. They think they are hot. They dress up in all kinds of jewelry. Some just kidnap girls and boys and use them for slaves . . . [The Chinese are good fighters, and so are the Filipinos:] They are good fighters and definitely good to go through jungles with . . . [*Will there be wars in the near future?*] I think so because there's always going to be a war . . . We won the last war because of the atom bomb . . . Hitler . . . was a little bit O.K. Sometimes he got a little bit too mean and did dirty stuff like putting lighted

matches in the toenails of Americans ... We should put all the Germans and Japs on an island and put an atom bomb to it. [*What is America's biggest problem?*] A lot of people are getting mad because everybody is starting war against each other ... [Strikes?] If grocery stores go on a strike, we won't have no food. Farmers can go on a strike and there will be no food, and we will have to grow our own food ... *How would you like to change America?* I would like to have a filling station every couple of blocks or so and palm trees and grass along the streets and lawns in front of people's houses and have the back yards all cleaned up and flowers growing. Every store should have all kinds of candy and bubble gum. They wouldn't have no fights in the neighborhood. The cops would take them all in. At Fleishhacker's [an amusement park] have nice warm water [in the swimming pool] and the zoo cleaned up. Every day there would be hay for the animals that eat hay and the lions would have lots of meat every day for breakfast and lunch.[125]

This is a sample of the social opinions of an unusually fat and passive boy with a history of many illnesses. It shows a concern with cleanliness and external beautification, with the removal of aggressive groups, and with having a constant flow of supplies. Animals rather than people concern him, and his emphasis on rigid order and regularity in the appearance of streets and so on sharply contrasts with his emphasis on, and even open advocacy of, turmoil and chaotic aggression. These are, of course, not necessarily the views he will have as adult, or even as a fifteen-year-old — indeed, it is precisely the overcoming of such immaturities that is the task of the teen-age years. But they disclose a pattern of personal needs and preoccupations which are less susceptible of amendment, such as rigid dichotomisation, aggression, fear of imaginary dangers, fear of threats and deprivation, and exaggerated adherence to conventional values such as cleanliness and order.

Karl clearly believes in fulfilling the requirements of submissive obedience (though he is in practice pretty inept). He believes that children should be punished for 'talking back to grown-ups' and for breaking windows ('You should go to Juvenile one year for that'). His interest in teachers centres on their strictness, and this attitude fits within a general hierarchical conception of human relations in which the weak are expected to exhibit a self-negating surrender to the strong. He has a rigid conception of sex-roles, disliking girls who are bossy or 'butt in', and an extreme 'externalisation of values' — that is, he exhibits opportunism, conventionality, status concern and explicit condemnation of those who do not conform. He also showed, in ingenious tests, marked intolerance of ambiguity.

Behind the aggressive facade, Karl has a feminine identification. In his bloodthirsty TAT stories neither the aggressive nor the passive man makes out. The man who is passive and in possession of some fortune is usually attacked in some surprising way (from behind or while asleep) and destroyed. The aggressive man is regularly caught by the police and sentenced to life or more often the 'chair'. In one story, the 'crooked place' is turned into a Safeway store, revealing his deep-seated longing that all the dangerous men will be removed, and he will be allowed to be passive and surrounded by food, without fear of aggression and the ensuing necessity for being himself aggressive. This is the way he imagines girls to be: in the stories they usually manage to be safe and to get food and money.

Karl does not look very favourably on his parents: he would take neither of them with him to a desert island, but would take instead, predictably, 'food, water — and a girl' to feed and be fed by (his recurrent dream is of *going with a girl to dinner*). He expresses hostility towards his mother more directly than towards his father; he opens his account of how he would like to change her by saying, 'To make her nice'. His greater concern with his father seems a factor of the father's greater power, ability to protect and to provide goods — Karl sees authorities as above all 'deliverers of goods'.

Frenkel-Brunswik (for only the second time in these cases)* had the parents themselves interviewed. They both turned out to be violently anti-Negro; both are from broken homes, with foreign-born parents; they are still entangled in the process of assimilation, and are downwardly mobile. Apparently, as a counterbalance, they stress their 'belonging' in somewhat extravagant social aspirations, on the one hand, and in the rejection of the 'socially inferior' on the other. As parents, they are sticklers for obedience (perhaps even 'revengefully' repeating their own bleak upbringing) and seem not to realise that the children (Karl has a brother a year older) are 'overtrained, and welcome the more severe punishment of the father'. They are determined that the children will adhere fully to conventional and rigid rules and stereotypes, but they do not sweeten the task with much affection.

Concerning Karl's future, Frenkel-Brunswik makes brief play with the idea of 'a social upheaval of a major order which might bring such an individual to the fore', but predicts for Karl, more prosaically, 'an inconspicuous, unsuccessful life, ridiculed and baited by his fellows, and possibly even passing over into a state of disintegration'. In short, he might be described as DNF.

Coles's John, Louisiana racist
Coles encountered John in 1961 on a New Orleans picket-line protesting at the admission of black children to parochial schools.[126] Aged 47, a garage-proprietor and devout Catholic, John was currently spending

---

* The first was Murray's assistant's interview with Ingle's parents (see above, p. 132).

much of his time in segregationist agitation, and had run several times for local office:

> Up and down he walked, picketing, tall, husky from the rear, an incipient paunch in front. He wore a brown suit, slightly frayed at the cuffs, and on its right shoulder rested his sign, wrought and lettered by himself:'Fight Integration. Communists Want Negroes With Whites.' His shirt was starched and he wore a tie. He had brown eyes. He was bald but for the most meager line of black hair on his neck ... His face was fleshy and largely unlined ... He would talk [to passers-by] if they showed the tiniest interest ... and seemed to be in charge.

He is a passionate segregationist, who advocates deporting most Negroes to Africa (keeping perhaps a sterilised few for heavy labour), all Jews to Russia 'where they came from', and generally clamping down on foreign immigration. He has taken part in two lynchings (nothing else 'keeps them in their place'), and threatens to shoot any black who tried to buy a house nearby, and even his own twenty-five-year-old son, if he persists in attending integrated church functions. 'This is a war,' he explains, 'between God and His Commandments and the Devil, and we may lose.' God, indeed, may wish to 'punish us' for, among other things, 'nigger-loving'. President, Congress, New York, Hollywood, the Press, the Banks, the Stock Exchange, the U.N., the Supreme Court — all threaten the true America with Communist subversion. The U.S.A. had been right to fight the Japanese, but it was hard now to see why we had fought the Germans. The racist journals he eagerly reads prime him on the 'biological inferiority' of blacks, the world Communist plot, the menace of fluoridation, and the coming Armageddon when God and Country desperately confront the dark forces of world atheism.

These views crystallised when he was in his early thirties. He had returned from four years' army service in the North, only to fail at T.V. repair work (he had done radio repairs before the war) and spend some months on relief. Then he landed a boring and poorly paid clerk's job in a state office, from which a chance political contact had only just rescued him. There are a number of incitements to hold these views at their present pitch; they include his success as a candidate in recent polls, the fact that Church authority is now taking the wrong side, the decay of his once-genteel, inner residential district and his loneliness as his marriage disintegrates (his wife is emotionally cold and crippled with stiff joints) and his family dissolves. Coles hints that the oddly keen provocation of his son's exposure to mixed-race marriage-guidance classes run by the Church reactivates episodes in his own life of tempting but frustrated 'nigger-loving', firstly as a pre-school boy, and later as a returning veteran, when Negro maids cared more effectively for him than his mother did, or, later, his wife.

There were, in fact, dramatic 'colour' differences in his immediate family; he and his father were short and black-haired (the French Catholic strain); his mother and brother and sister were tall and fair (an English Baptist strain). His parents favoured the fair ones and he was overlooked, and worse. His mother, nervous and ritualist, simply neglected him (despite his frequent illnesses and truancies). He failed sadly to get along with his father, a simple but hard-drinking motor-mechanic, who had been at the French front for the first two years of John's life. Indeed, John took the brunt of his father's frequent but unpredictable rages. He learned early that it was dangerous to speak his mind; 'Perhaps his life, as we now see it, has been a quest for that very possibility', Coles muses.

Coles's account stresses the strong support in his local community for these noxious opinions: 'though we may consider his beliefs delusional, they are held in common with thousands'. It is hard to call him mad; he works, has a family and friends, is not shy and withdrawn; in fact, he talks winningly and responds quickly to others' feelings. Yet he is fanatic, where his neighbours remain morose or querulous. Once an active child, now a fighter, he goes out to do battle with the forces of evil as he sees them for 'a world as white and shadowless as possible'.

Active as he is, and extreme as are his views, he seems to me exactly the case we need to show, in the NF position, the Warrant Officer, as it were, of the radical Right crusade.

Further studies

We have noted the 'specious familiarity' which, by dint of classroom repetition, came to overlay the 'authoritarian personality' as an embodiment of the characteristics of the F scale. Yet an unaccountable excitement overcame most of those researchers in the 1950s and 1960s who actually identified an authoritarian, and they hastened to report how very true to type in fact they were. Several such accounts, indeed, involved authoritarians 'turning themselves in'. In 1949, an ex-corporal studying psychology at the University of Texas under the G.I. Bill of Rights recognised his personality and attitudes as 'fascist' and put in a 'self-analytical' term paper partly boastful and truculent, and partly asking for help.[127] Robert Lane, keeping a special eye out for 'anti-democrats' in his analyses of working-men's and students' political outlooks,[128] reported the case of 'Novak', an Adams student, who in a political autobiography acknowledged, and asked for relief from, his masochistic identification with a cold, stern father (this time neither lower-middle-class nor socially marginal, but a professor of law).*[129] A discursive review of biographies of near-

* The most interesting detail of this case was a painful 'double-bind' resembling the one already noted in Little's Compton — the father saying: 'Do as I say, but don't be so damned compliant' and 'Be aggressive and hard like me — but not against me.'

authoritarians in the early 1970s included as an appendix a further stock American student case.[130] Reports like these, content to tick off the items in the Sanford check-list, add little to our understanding of the type. There is, however, a recent English study, reflecting on the likely preponderance of authoritarians in military formations, which goes on imaginatively to detail the probable impairments in organisational 'reality-sense' that this selective recruitment could exact.[131]

The *left-wing* authoritarian theme[132] has produced a good deal of unprofitable polemics, poor F scale correlations, and no well-studied case. This has led some text-book writers to declare the concept unjustified.[133] I would suggest, however, that Curle's case, Gwenneth — the bitter, ruthless, but hollow and anxious student leader — though a lightning sketch, does at least keep the question open.[134]

For the next new step in thinking about NF, however, we have to go back to Nevitt Sanford, who returned to the root of the problem thirteen years after the California study.

Sanford's Pat

A short, somewhat plump and plain but hyper-active Drama student, Pat scored highest at her College on both the F scale and a scale to measure 'impulse-expression'.[135] She is less 'emotionally free', however, than impulse-ridden, and Sanford judges that the energetic promiscuity which is her main pursuit is based on unconscious self-contempt as well as on a 'primitive super-ego' that is 'fairly well out of communication with her conscious self'. She has, he reports sadly, 'little or no inhibition of impulse through the action of inner moral conviction, little or no inclination to blame herself for moral failures, no sensitivity to moral issues'.

> She denies guilt and anxiety through her near-delinquent behavior ... By acting, often enough, in a way that would ordinarily arouse guilt she may prove to herself that she may do so with impunity ... She cannot bear consciousness of guilt or conscious anxiety or depression, but must act in order to ward off these feelings.

Unable to control her own impulse-life, she is nevertheless highly censorious of others' behaviour, and of out-groups generally. She seeks external agents to keep her in check — a Strong Man to put her in her place and keep her there — and demands, in society, a firm hierarchical ordering of authority. Although politics is the least of her interests, she is predictably anti-equalitarian, and opposed to all radical notions in child-rearing, family relationships, women's role and status, and social-group relations. Her acceptance of a relatively low status for women in society, and for herself *vis-à-vis* a future husband, no doubt rests on her unconscious self-contempt; this helps to explain her striving for social status and the benefits of economic security (she is determined to become a star). 'These strivings seem mainly behind her anti-Semitism and anti-Communism. She could not do anything that would threaten her social class membership.'

Sanford attributes her failure to develop a 'social' super-ego to her rich but uneducated parents, who could not supply consistent discipline or stable patterns worthy of identifying with. The mother was 'generally ineffectual' and the father was a 'rigid traditionalist unprepared for life in the modern world'. She was left in the care of the servants and an elder brother, who introduced her precociously and actively to incestuous relations, and left her with a deep sense of hopeless inferiority.

In all, she presents a picture of marked ego-weakness. She has little insight and very little empathy for other people. She has lurid fantasies but no intellectual interests. She has strong narcissism but no vocational plans beyond being 'discovered'. She has, indeed, been clever (or lucky) so far to have found so serviceable a vehicle as drama school in which to act out her fantasies — but the prognosis is not good.

There are difficulties in the Bales scheme in maximum scoring on both pro-authority and impulse-expression axes; DNF, after all, is the pole of restraint, and it is hard to see Pat, socially and politically, as more than a submissive authoritarian. But the larger question, I think, is whether admirers of *The Authoritarian Personality* will be content to see the concept stripped down to mean little more than a primitive and 'split off' super-ego.[136]

As relief from a future which may have come to seem too uncertain I close this discussion with a backward glance at the sureties of the past, in an inspired piece of psychological forecasting that is little known, but should be celebrated wherever literary or political criticism is done.

Lowenthal's Knut Hamsun as future Quisling
The Norwegian novelist Knut Hamsun, in his first book, *Hunger* (1890), states themes that he was to repeat almost endlessly in his later work. These include the abandonment of any participation in public life, submission to the stream of incomprehensible and incalculable forces, distrust of the intellect, flight from the city, and escape to Nature. In the 1920s and 1930s his work not only enjoyed an excellent international reputation, but was regarded — even by liberals and socialists — as politically above reproach.

Writing in 1937, well before Hamsun's sympathies for the Hitler movement became public, Leo Lowenthal, who had been alerted by the fact of Hamsun's unusual popularity with German readers, argued that a liking for his mood and themes should presage an acceptance of political authoritarianism:

> The pagan awe of unlimited and unintelligible forces of nature, the mystique of blood and race, hatred of the working class and of clerks, the blind submission to authority, the abrogation of individual res-

ponsibility, anti-intellectualism, and spiteful mistrust of urban middle-class life in general

— all these themes Hamsun celebrated could, Lowenthal argued, find their enactment only in Fascism.[137] And, under the threat of invasion by Hitler in 1940, Hamsun, indeed, proudly filed in with Quisling.

Authoritarian aggression and submission are inextricably intertwined.

Further work

What has our combing of the case-file of political outlooks yielded? At the least, I hope that it will provoke some sympathy and admiration for the craft of case-writing itself. Although they are very uneven, and in some respects disappointing, the cases tell us vital things about the structure and processes of belief that no other approach can. It is remarkable, too, how cases, which naturally tend to be unique portraits (even if they are *explicably* unique), control this tendency every time by revealing a certain social representativeness. Further, they can be summarised and standardised without losing all their virtue, and subjected to quite elaborate exercises in comparison; indeed, we begin to see how it is precisely the accumulation of instances that provides illumination. The five broad groups into which we have divided them, although in themselves unsurprising, do bring out the uneven spread of research effort across them, which few readers will fully have appreciated. Case-writing has been undervalued in political studies; it is tedious, time-consuming, and of uncertain immediate use. It has tended to follow in the wake of new political fads and currents. This must surely give way soon to attempts at a more systematic coverage.

All this was, no doubt, if not agreed, at least demonstrable before Bales. What difference has his scheme made to outlook analysis? Although our sampling of the political psychology cases has not exhausted even the most obvious aspects of the scheme (five of the positions are vacant, and eleven have only one occupant), its general serviceability is patent. We have established, I think, three main points. First of all, cases take on a new potential depth of comparison, now that we have this more finely meshed classification. In setting Eyman beside Ingle, for example, or East beside Grove, or Gorz beside Hart's men, we cut through distracting surface differences to reach the foundations of psychic structure.[138] Secondly, we now know more clearly where new testimony is needed, not just on types, but on sub-types as well, because, thirdly, we have learnt that as cases cluster about their position, they invite an expansion of the central type-concept in order to take full account of the main differences disclosed.

People encountering the Bales scheme for the first time tend to make one standard manoeuvre of resistance. 'Is everyone,' they ask, with an edge of hostility, 'supposed to be able to have only one world view, and to be saddled with it for the whole of their lives?' To this, I am afraid, the answer is substantially, 'Yes', although Bales himself speaks deferentially of 'education, re-education, and therapy' as devices that can assist individuals to overcome handicaps that have kept them D, N or B. Indeed, his own devotion to the small-group movement attests to his belief in the special opportunities for benign growth that it affords.

For the moment, we can merely take the point that, usually, it 'doesn't seem like that' to people who are reflecting on their own ideological experiences — especially perhaps to students, who are earnestly and consciously building up, testing and remodelling their structures of belief. And we are certainly obliged, as Bales was not, to treat *shifts of belief* (including the high drama of conversion and de-conversion) as a major question to be confronted in the psychology of political opinion.

I do not wish to attempt here any summary of our substantive findings — we have still to review the study of outlooks from a quite different angle. The classifying exercise has, however, left us with several questions and reflections which may be set down briefly at this point.

How thickly populated are the various positions? Are the positions for which we did not find instances (UPF, for example) really so uncommon? Could one, in principle, estimate (by attitude-scale survey, for example) what percentage of people in Country A, City B, Organisation C, or Movement D were, say, democratic personalities (P types) and monitor this over a period of time? Bales has investigated the density of population across ten of his groups: group members

> are not typically distributed at random or equally throughout the space; more are found on the positive side of the space than on the negative side, and the tendency to be on the positive side is very marked for women as compared to men. More [group] members are found in the forward part of the space than in the backward, and this tendency is more marked for men. On the average, women are further downward, considerably more positive, and slightly backward from the men. Men are about equally distributed between the upward and downward parts of the space, with a few more in the downward part, but women are definitely found more frequently in the lower part of the space . . .
>
> The distribution of points representing the positions of all persons in all groups resembles a spiral with the lower end reaching around backward toward the DNB region. The main body of points curves positively forward and upward, reaching its largest concentration in the UPF region, then trails off thinly into the UNF region. The N, UN, and UNB regions are thinly populated, and even UB and UPB are rather low in number of points. The regions DN and DNF are very sparsely populated indeed, but with a few more males than females.[139]

According to Bales, then, most functioning small groups appear to have roughly four clusters in them: the largest is centred on UPF, the next largest on PF and P, the next on PB, and the smallest on DN and DNB. (In missing a UPF, then, we have had extraordinarily bad luck.)

One wonders about the representative quality of Harvard students. The institution itself seems to suggest the UPF position. But Bales's opinion is that our everyday assumptions about the political 'spectrum' are fairly accurate; that is, most of the people most of the time are somewhere near the political centre (the P meridian) or a little to the right (the PF meridian) or to the left (the PB meridian), while only very few are to be found on the far right (the NF meridian) or the far left (centring on DB and B, with a few DNB).

It is not immediately clear how we might move to classify large populations into Bales types. The short questionnaire used in the groups presupposes some reasonable exposure to, and reflection upon, other members' group performance and style. If, however, we concentrate on outlook-measurement, it is possible to administer Bales's condensed list of the most critical 'value statements' (forty items, *Personality and Interpersonal Behavior*, pp. 506–10) in door-step interviews (indeed, pilot tests in Melbourne have been most encouraging). To be quite confident about each placement, however, one feels that some second call-back instrument of finer diagnostic texture may well be needed in addition. There is clearly great scope for a standard inventory form which enquires simultaneously into outlook, social self and family background, since the cases have shown these can all be decisive in placement.

The power of vocation to bind personality to project was perhaps the single largest novelty our cases brought to the aid of classification and type-description. Preoccupation with students and their intra-group involvements led Bales to overlook this powerful resource; yet most of Murray's men and our other student cases showed an acute awareness, not only of what they wanted to work at in their maturity, but of the very style in which they wanted to approach it. With our older subjects (Gorz, Mr A., Lanlin, Webb) the vocational style *was* the man. (Of course, in many routine jobs the incentive – and the scope – for personal definition in work will be much less, but it is rarely entirely negligible.)

Intrinsically political positions. Our clutch of cases – they cannot in any way be thought of as a sample – showed discrepancies with Bales's sub-scheme of political positions (see figure 6, p. 162); they were of two main sorts. First, we found instances of strong politics in types who were presumed to be apolitical. All our DN cases were protesting radicals rather than mute withdrawers; most of our F cases were politically highly concerned and ideological; our UNB anarchist pointed up a possible *meridional* political outlook. (DNB was anarchist as expected.) Secondly, in some cases the political outlook was more radical or less conservative than had been presumed. All our P cases were leftist militants instead of relaxed centrists; two NF cases were orthodox conservatives rather than radical rightists.

One is tempted, indeed, to see F rather than P as the political centre – or rather, to see the F – B axis as the one with the highest charge of intrinsically political current (if not the most clients), with the flanking NF – PB and PF – NB axes carrying most of what is left. In this view (see figure 7), both N and P would be largely heterogeneous, politically inert and unfocused. The mere fact that P is quite possibly the most densely populated position, and undoubtedly politically benign, is not sufficient reason in itself to make P the fulcrum of the political system. More work is clearly needed on the analogies between small-group and national politics.

The political homogeneity of positions. In 'party' group terms, our cases in each position showed a gratifying homogeneity, drawing much the same political conclusions from the shared world view. In sorting cases according to the Bales scheme, however, we enter character at the level of the *project*, and this is a good way below the level of conventional political affiliation (at which Grove and East, for example, look so different). Having noted that, strictly, F meant conformist, not conservative, we were not surprised by the appearance of a socialist DF; indeed, there is the case reported by Riesman of a Californian schoolboy Communist DF dutifully carrying out his mother's fanatical prescriptions.[140]

Two methodological points emerge from our survey. First, efforts to match case- with type-childhoods were so uniformly approximate that some redefinition of basic childhood categories seems in order. The idealist-optimist/cynic-pessimist axis, in particular, seemed to have little interpretative value. Relations with siblings, barely considered in the present scheme, were quite frequently a decisive factor in a case. Secondly, although an analysis of parental identification is a useful means of assessing the effect of upbringing on personality (a more effective means than the analysis of the 'economics' of aggression, sex or anxiety, or the 'dynamics' of the (choice of) defences, although these could indeed, at certain points, be quite decisive) it turns out to be only approximate. I found myself at times in my transcriptions moved to adapt attributions of identi-

Figure 7.

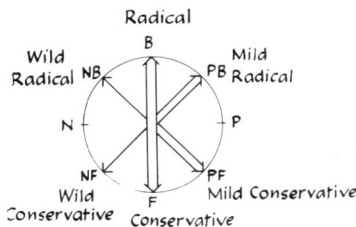

fications to fit my own sense of the case, although this is obviously a dangerous exercise on such interpretative ground. Many subjects themselves might well disagree with attributions of identification or, more generally, simply not know how to sum up this portentous relationship.

So far we have only considered the structural 'outside-in' aspects of familial relationships, personality and outlook. In chapter 6, I shall attempt to examine the phenomenological 'inside-out' aspects.

6   *Attending to an outlook*

What is an outlook?

After so much classification which is, of its nature, 'outside-in' and more absorbing to professional students than to outlook-holders themselves, we now turn briefly to what it means and what it *feels like* to set up, maintain, trim, reconstruct — in short, inhabit one's own outlook.[1] We are concerned with what might help an intelligent, reflective person to see his individual career as consumer or critic of politics in a new light, and, above all, if that is possible, to see his political thinking in an insistently *psychological* light.

Two things about outlooks are immediately clear, and they cut across each other. First, one has a sense always of knowing only a determinate part of one's own outlook; what is out of reach often seems portentous, and one feels that there is little chance of getting a comprehensive view of it — or of getting one that is trim enough to convey effectively to someone else. Conversely, we accept that our own view of another's outlook, which may be quite neat and adequate for our explanatory purposes, will probably not match up at all closely with his own.[2] Perhaps a rehearsal of the onlooker's difficulties will lead us to a closer view of the subjective ones.

Outlook and onlooker

How does the eager field-worker, attempting even in prolonged and empathetic conversation to elicit an informant's outlook, cope with the subliminal, the unworked, and the incoherent on any large scale? It is a problem anthropologists have long faced, and met with implicit rules of craft. But here is a rare direct reflection on the problem: the problem arises

> of the effect of informing or of stimulating information about world views on the intellectual structure of the world view. An outlook on life is a construction . . . No man holds all he knows and feels about the world in his conscious mind at once . . .
> Protecting deities, the need to keep one's account with the gods — such things come easily and often to [the Maya villager's] mind.

Further details, deeper relationships, emerge to awareness during the
ceremonies when the meaning of things is dramatized before him,
and if the native is induced to sit and reflect, if he finds it interesting to arrange his thoughts so as to communicate them to someone,
perhaps an ethnologist, the structure of the world view grows and
develops. Every account of a world view is therefore a temporary
construction, a precipitation of a crystal from thoughts that from
day to day are carried in the flowing solution of life's doings.[3]

In modern society, the problem is compounded by social mobility
and the periodic reconstructions of 'self-image' that Peter Berger has
described:

The course of events that constitute one's life can be subjected to
alternate interpretations ... As we remember the past, we reconstruct
it in accordance with our present ideas of what is important and what
is not ... Thus we have as many lives as we have points of view ...
One cannot ... understand Greenwich Village without understanding
Kansas City. [Greenwich Village] has served as a socio-psychological
apparatus through which men and women pass as through a magical
retort, going in as nice Midwesterners and coming out as nasty deviants. What was proper before is improper after ... What used to
be taboo becomes *de rigueur*, what used to be obvious becomes laugh-
able, and what used to be one's world becomes that which must be
overcome ... One now realizes that the great emotional upheavals
of the past were but puerile titillations, that those whom one thought
important people in one's life were but limited provincials all along.
The events of which one used to be proud are now embarrassing
episodes in one's prehistory ... Thus the glowing day,when one was
class valedictorian makes room in one's reconstructed biography for
a then unimportant-seeming evening when one first tried to paint,
and instead of reckoning an era from the date when one accepted
Jesus at a church summer camp one does so from that other date
... When one lost one's virginity in the back of a parked auto-
mobile ...
Greenwich Village may later become but another phase in one's
life, another experiment, another mistake even ... The conversion
experience in the church camp may later turn out to have been
the first uncertain groping towards the truth one has now realized
fully in becoming a Catholic ... [Or] one may discover in one's
psychoanalysis that both conversion and sexual initiation ... were
part and parcel of the same neurotic syndrome ... We stumble like
drunkards over the sprawling canvas of our self-conception, throwing
a little paint here, erasing some lines there, never really stopping
to obtain a view of the likeness we have produced.[4]

Though collectors of political outlooks have not, as yet, worked with
patience and delicacy on a sufficiently extended time-scale to catch many
such autobiographical shifts, they certainly endorse the prevalence of

the subliminality Berger stresses. Indeed, they report that the very act of setting up their 'nets' regularly throws informants into a kind of self-disillusioning spin. Robert Lane writes that asking students 'What are your political ideas?'

> often uncovers what seems at first to be an extraordinary poverty
> . . . What each of these men took to be a belief system marked by
> the richness of a political philosophy turned out on examination
> to be a set of undigested and unreflected-upon labels: conservatism,
> liberalism, internationalism, inadequately illustrated by examples
> from current events. Almost without exception, these highly intel-
> ligent and educated men had failed to give much thought to what
> *they* believed, though they might have done a creditable job reporting
> the beliefs of Thomas Hobbes, or John Stuart Mill, or Karl Marx.
> Thus they are at first as surprised by the quick exhaustion of their
> store of [propositions] as by their lack of self-knowledge . . . if their
> motives were buried in the unconscious, their politics were lost in
> the great unawareness.[5]

And I had myself noted earlier, in conversations with adult activists, that

> There was something almost comical in the contrast between the
> alarm and hopelessness with which subjects took up the task of
> describing their politics — a task that seemed enormous, impossible,
> like the ones given to little girls by gnomes in fairy tales — and their
> complacent satisfaction several evenings later as they sat with folded
> hands over the completed work, with nothing further to add. Out-
> looks . . . are shallow — and unworked . . . Even the brief and casual
> exploration of the sources of their outlooks provoked by the con-
> versations was for each of them a new and somewhat painful exper-
> ience. The image suggests itself of outlooks as something people
> build behind their backs, every now and again passing a beam or
> strut or plank backwards on to a growing pile, which makes in due
> course some kind of habitation, but one they never squarely look at
> — an edifice of the night.[6]

Yet it may have been simply naive of field-workers to have expected so much 'system' in ordinary men's outlooks in the first place. People may be right to regard their capacity for political response as something which, because of its complexity (as well as the 'shroudedness' of its prin-ciples of organisation) is massively 'beyond' them — and this is not at all gainsaid by the idea of 'propositional poverty'. It is rather like one's con-fident sense of recognition on hearing an almost-familiar piece of music (remembering, perhaps, in a rush, something of its shape, mood or pro-gress — or scenes in fantasy, maybe, that it reliably evokes — occasions when, and companions with whom, one has heard it before). Yet if one were asked about the piece, one would be unable to describe the recapitu-lation, the second subject and the shift to the minor key; one might even be hard put to whistle the principal tune. Even (to choose a less technical analogy) if one were asked some question such as 'What do you look for in music in general?', one would have difficulty in finding an answer that did not use trite old labels and very bare and obvious propositions. There is so much experience that one cannot find words to express.

For whatever reason, the characteristic amateurism that music-lovers are readily allowed is oddly begrudged to politics-watchers by many social scientists. Yet ordinary readers, carried along in the flow of someone else's exposition, fill up effortlessly and without compunction even glaring gaps in a political case-record with inferences from subjects' views, tastes or stances in quite other areas of their lives. Anna N., for example, whom we may agree was the strongest liberal in the case-file above, could hardly be brought to talk about politics at all; her 'liberalism' we cheerfully read into the case from her views on young people, the police, the Church, and, above all, the way she talked about herself.

But in fact social scientists, divided sharply, and in ways that mould their whole working lives, over the question of 'cognitive ideals',[7] are nowhere more clearly split than on their view of outlooks. The social scientist of the type we may call *phallic*, who believes that the dominant feature of an outlook is the idea-set, argues that the best sort of evidence for a person's outlook is that person's own explicitly formulated statement of it. The social scientist *resigned* to the weakness of developed ideas and their disconnection from the general temperamental matrix argues that these statements are distorting and that it is better to look at dreams and TAT stories. P and R therefore disagree over the role of the unconscious. R is very ready to put forward explanations in terms of unconscious motivations and P is very loth to accept them.

P believes that an outlook is a heuristic device, shaped by the student for his own (usually comparative) purpose, preferably in as explicit a form as possible. R argues that *subjects* possess their outlooks, each one distinct and palpable, requiring analysis on its own terms. He believes that individuals are more or less prisoners of their outlooks — that although superficial changes in outlook are possible, the core of the outlook is deeply buried and largely incorrigible. (A minority of R types, however (cf. Bales above, p. 263) believes that one *can* come to recognise what one holds (or what is holding one) and, through insight, free oneself from it, and rise above it.) P, however, believes that a person is free to change his outlook. Outlooks are 'aids to navigation' and will only be adhered to as long as they are seen to 'work'. Faults, when detected, will be remedied and the necessary changes made.

P tends to see the study of outlooks as a last resort, something one turns to if, after everything in a situation that can be explained through material interests, group membership, exposure to the media, and so forth has been explained, one is still left with some puzzling residue (as, it might be, with the 'floating voters' in an election study). Then, if they must be studied, it should be with the focus on structure, and with the use of distinct, determinate procedures (attitude scales, for example) which are fully replicable and yield unequivocal results.* R, on the other hand, believes that the study of outlooks is immensely important in its own right, and, indeed, that everything depends on it.[9] He wishes ideally to experience each outlook as the subject himself does. He considers that the focus of study should be the solid material detail and texture of the individual outlook, and that the approach to this personal pattern should be holistic and empathetic. (While P does 'science', R does something more like art or literary criticism.) There is, in short, a radically different evaluation of self-consciousness between the schools.†

The R-type social scientist characteristically finds his *own* outlook problematical, and is perhaps as interested in explicating that, as in explicating other people's; indeed, he rather merges the two enterprises, hoping for reciprocal shafts of illumination. In contrast, P rather insists on his distance and detachment from the object of his study — it is out there and unmistakeably *not him* (note, in the Berger piece on alternation above, the tell-tale phrase 'nasty deviants', signalling a feat of 'knowingness' on the part of author (and colluding reader), safely removing both from any movement of self-understanding). This seems very similar to the dichotomous 'diverger' and 'converger' styles already found dividing our theorists (see above, pp. 107–9).

It is conventional to regard these 'school' disputes in social science as perhaps amusingly stubborn but eventually capable of settlement, and even fruitful in the short run, as problems are taken up by those with the most appropriate methods. In the long run, of course, the hope is that scholarship will afford us all a true and final view of what outlooks amount to. It seems quite as likely, however, that, far from working to correct and educate the naive biases of ordinary understandings, such polemics will merely appropriate and enshrine them. Certainly it is not at all hard to make out among everyday outlook-holders prototypical, and similarly sharp, contrasts between 'phallic' (P) and 'resigned' (R) modes of relating to one's personal belief-system. P is able to offer a viewpoint directly ('Here is — just give me a moment — my line on that') but R is less

---

* It is noticeable that P types, when depressed, are apt to become extravagantly cynical. cf. Abelson's 'theory' of 'opinion molecules', which holds that most of an individual's opinions are just conversation lollipops made up of a fact and a feeling about it; their purpose is to give him something to say when a subject comes up — as statements, they do not *mean* anything, do not need to be connected logically one to another, and cannot really be argued about.[8]

† Of course, not all social scientists belong to one school or the other, but it can be uncomfortable in the middle. The rather flat reception accorded, for example, to Robert Lane's valuable *Political Thinking* may have had much to do with the fact it was too P for R types, and vice versa.

assertive ('How do I know what I think till I see what I say?'). In place of
P's phallic assertion ('My principles, of course, would make that impossible for me') R merely says, 'To think (or feel or do) that would somehow be . . . not quite me.' The phallic thinker regards his inner picture
of the world as being true or false according to how it corresponds item
by item with 'real experience'.[10] R, on the other hand, considers that his
intellectual processes are secondary to his practical involvements and
sympathies. In short, P assumes over his outlook a proud and aggressive
proprietorship, while R's stance is tentative and rueful. P is showily logical, militantly rationalistic (believing, for example, that he can prove the
correctness of his opinions, and force the assent of third parties) and he
is invigorated by the challenge of intellectual difference, probing, testing
and comparing, R is simply turned off by propositional and especially
syllogistic discourse, and sees argument as pointless; he is tolerant, non-
obsessional and intuitive.

P and R are no mere heuristic cyphers — we have already met them as
people in the shape of Ingle and Grove (above, pp. 130–5 and 147–51),
and these are views about their views that they have actually expressed,
or could be inferred to hold. Their substantive opinions, in fact, were not
so far apart: both were politically left-wing, equalitarian, and against
authority; they were quite irreligious, and vocationally bent on careers
of exceptional altruism and nurturance, which they regarded as tragic-
ally imperilled by the war. Ingle, however, wanted eagerly to systematise his ideas, to subject them to an all-embracing discipline and order,
where Grove not only failed to seek coherence but hunted up proofs of
its illusoriness. Ingle's stance before his idea-set was dynamic; Grove's
was static.[11] Grove was indifferent to what others think. These styles,
finally, were developed to confront quite different preferred orders of
fact. Ingle, extraverted and in poor contact with his personal core, placed
all the problems *out there* in a flight into externality and objectivisation
of intellect; Grove, for whom only the personal was problematic, saw
himself and everyone else locked in the prison of their individual characters. Liam Hudson sought the genesis of the Phallic and the Resigned
styles (convergent and divergent, respectively) in the crystallisation of
the ego at different ages, and in mothers who were either emotionally
gruff or clinging, either intent on and rewarding the precocities of their
'little scientists' or ignoring or even mocking them. Our Harvard cases
bring the father into focus. Both Ingle and Grove 'hated' their fathers,
but Ingle, seeing an attractiveness and power in his father's ideas (and
his expounding them) sought to *compete* ideologically, to harness aggression to theorising, and compel admiration — and he found the product
fascinating. Grove, judging his father's ideas to be as deplorable as his
conduct and character, mutely 'ignored' them, while manufacturing his

own ideas by simple negation and lazy inversion. However, he could take no great pride in the result.*

In the general population, Groves outnumber Ingles by perhaps twenty to one. And because the working-face of 'resigned' outlooks is almost as opaque to their owners as to outsiders, we are forced into approaching the phenomenology of outlook for the most part indirectly through 'methods of observation'. How does it happen that sometimes some part at least of outlook undeniably *shows*?

But problems for outlook-analysts and discomforts for outlook-holders themselves are acutely felt on the 'phallic' side as well. The typical phallic qualities — the over-rationalisation, the intellectualising out of raw feeling, the concealment under a flurry of *reasons* of the motives of thought — stand equally in the way of seeing belief-system, temperament and personality in their true relation or holding them in constructive balance. Intellectuals with a mild psychological bent (and usually a rather urgent wish to straighten their record — for example, Henri de Man, Arthur Koestler, Whittaker Chambers, André Gorz, Michael Harrington)[12] testify in a kind of unending penitents' queue to the chagrin and humiliation which follow over-investment in idea-sets that are too external, too explicit, too extended and too taut — and which, when they break down, seem ridiculous. It seems there is a contradiction at the heart of the ideologising project: while its purpose is to simplify, to spotlight the enemy, to prescribe the obvious course of action, its serious pursuit into the further reaches of more finely-spun theory inevitably increases ambiguity and the 'openness' of solutions. In short, it leads away from, and not towards, concrete prescriptions.

Interestingly, two minor academic enterprises seem fixed in this same 'phallic' trope. Attitude psychology, in obsessive pursuit of 'cognitive consistency', has reached intellectual stalemate,[13] as the close-reasoning mind it models has no real-life counterpart. Political philosophy, too, is marked by phallic qualities as obstinate, massive and proud as anything in behavioural psychology; all curiosity about the personal roots of such thinking is turned away very sharply indeed.[14]

We must admit that we lack both sophisticated models to imitate in the analysis of one's own outlook, and work on personal views or changes of view at even the general level of studied 'subjects'. The upshot is that anyone resolving to attend to his outlook is still very much a man on his own. Some small help comes from two main directions. First, we may

---

* It is worth noting that Yawl, the other Murray man who can be placed in the Resigned category (above, pp. 156—8) — 'I came to the final realization that I couldn't convert other people to my point of view … opinions depend … upon people' — was also in notable father-revolt; his project was to ridicule his father *whole*, in fiction. Bales posited the quality of resignation in a marked degree, not only in the DB position (Grove's), but also in DN.

examine suggestions about odd contexts and sites in which some usually implicit part of an outlook may be relied on to make a brief showing; the bulk of our remaining space in this chapter is devoted to rehearsing these 'outlook outcrops'. Secondly, we may experiment with classificatory schemes. Our slow circuit of Bales's types was intended to give readers this experience. But what, in generic terms, one might conclude from accepting a type-label may show up a little more vividly from a simpler scheme. Joan Evans's delightful *Taste and Temperament* sorts out four types of art-lover: quick and slow extraverts and quick and slow introverts; 'Tell me which painters you like', she offers, 'and I'll tell you which you are . . .'[15] Studying such an exercise, one does become aware of patterns hitherto unconsciously but ruthlessly ordering one's responses and is coaxed into fruitful experiments in re-ordering such preferences ('Can I really like Gainsborough and be faithful to my *slow* introversion?', 'How can I have overlooked Chardin, who seems something of a touchstone?'). We are concerned here, of course, with schemes which make a special claim to illuminate the *political* aspects of an outlook (although readers, unfamiliar with them, may also find something of interest in one or more very general schemes)[16] and we divide them merely into those which can be approached directly, and those which require a little specialist — or detached — help.

Direct schemes include:

W. T. Jones's scheme of cognitive 'vectors', 'dimensions' or 'axes of bias', which underlie and rule our preferences for certain styles of solution to problems (for example, static/dynamic, continuous/discrete, and mediate/immediate).[17] The categories 'phallic' and 'resigned' derive from this scheme.

R. K. White's content-analysis scheme for drawing out an individual's leading themes from small samples of his writing.[18]

Rokeach's account of outlooks as constrained, indeed hierarchically organised, by half-conscious values — specifically, eighteen 'terminal' values (or ideals) and twelve 'instrumental' ones.[19]

Schemes which need specialised help include:

Edwin S. Shneidman's approach to personal 'psycho-logics', and in particular his thirteen characteristics of thinking-style of psychological significance. The strategy here is to ask what would have to be true about the world to make it one in which this man's logical errors in thinking could be not only explicable, but justified. To use this scheme, one needs the co-operation of a formal logician.[20]

Norman Holland's procedures for extracting 'identity themes' from written material, via the submerged, infantile psycho-sexual fantasies apparent in it; the writer's style is viewed as compromise formation between these fantasies and the preferred defences against them. For this scheme, one needs, if not Norman Holland himself, an improbably co-operative psychoanalyst.[21]

All these schemes, in summary, offer help in grappling with the 'Resigned' category in outlooks. Given that the questions we are asking ('In what sense is there system to X's views?' and 'What binds his outlook together?') cannot readily be answered in terms of content, the focus switches to style. What he will think or feel about events yet to come is to be gauged less from past or present beliefs ('*owned* propositions'), than from the mechanisms by which he regularly processes input — the cluster of strategies, that is, with which, only half-consciously, he approaches the whole range of the problematic.

Establishing, maintaining and reconstituting an outlook

We review here sites where from time to time the individual may glimpse, and perhaps be moved to investigate, outcrops of a belief-system otherwise buried.

Intake shocks

Comfortably distanced and familiar, politics is normally absorbed without taking any particular notice — as much seeking reassurance that it is all quite as it was before, as to appraise or respond to novelty. In crises, however, it may flood in and totally swamp the whole individual. A leader will desert, perhaps, and one's politics will suddenly stand revealed as a device to hold off the fear of mortality.

> — I came out of the gate of Dr S.'s large house and down the stone steps . . . I felt as if I were thrown into white air . . . it was an indescribable emptiness . . . which almost made me dizzy, as if I were on a high mountain. It was as though I were walking in a mist where there were no other people, and my legs trembled. My body was so shaky I found it difficult to walk.

> — I've never known such panic and chilling, paralysing fear and profound depression . . . The fear was monumental . . . I thought I had gone crazy . . . I felt completely disoriented. I would literally shiver from nervousness and fear . . . I suddenly felt totally vulnerable.

In the first quotation a Japanese woman poet has just heard the Emperor's surrender speech;[22] the second is a confusion of voices from the New York 1961 fall-out shelter scare.[23] The whole security of all these people, as Japanese and as Americans, has been shattered. The deaths of Kennedy, de Gaulle and Nasser have in recent times thrown whole peoples into similar inexplicable despair — not so much grief, as it is customarily called, as shock at losing a 'bulwark against death'.[24]

At the opposite pole to the collapse of this 'shield' of political order, and the flooding in of external terrors, we have autochthonous movements of guilt and self-esteem needling the individual into some new relation to politics. A writer, for example, grows more and more dissatisfied with his celebrated cynicism, tries to inject a little genuine idealism into the conclusion of his current novel, throws down his pen, and spends twelve months in a restless public search for a cause.[25] East (see above, pp. 197–201), released at last from his seminary, becomes aware of a hunger for politics, and finds himself rising early to bring in the newspapers. They have only to become a little keener, and such appetites will shade over into the morbid self-dislike which prefigures the conversion experience.

However, most of the intake-shocks that shake up settled assumptions about politics fall well short of either the 'internal' or the 'external' extreme. Odd, special issues, surfacing publicly, suddenly galvanise *this* particular individual, to his great surprise, out of an amiable, trusting doze into some flurry of response. Issues, as it were, choose among people and strike unpredictably and challenge those who think themselves well out of the way. Recruits to protest campaigns — anti-fluoridation, say, or others mentioned above (see pp. 34–40) — are drawn into play by a kind of affect-matching process. Sometimes it is a solitary affair, like the crusader for mercy for baby-stealers (see below, p. 389) or my own anger at bomb tests (see below, pp. 308–9). Although reflection tends to be brushed aside in the rage to *act* on such occasions, they do allow one a little to investigate the roots of a passion.

The study of such provocations is known as 'microgenesis', which means the exploration of the assumptions of an idea-system by seeing what it makes of a single new item of intake, and of what is organised there to 'receive' it. To 'microslice', as it were, at the juncture of the new event and the structure which determines its meaning is an exercise which outlook-holders themselves may practise, as well as, if not better than, onlookers.[26]

Outlook and system

People may also come to see part of their outlook as problematic — usually a part that is fairly well-developed and explicit — when it happens to jar with elements of some public belief-system with which the individual is normally happy to identify, and on which he leans. These public systems are of two sorts: the forensic ideology such as Marxism or John Birchism, and the looser understandings of particular sub-cultures, social strata or roles.[27] There is, of course, much room for overlap between these two sorts. For example, we can see that Coles's John's anti-Negro views (above, pp. 257–9) largely embody dutifully the 'defensive beliefs of the White caste' which John Dollard masterfully analysed in 1936,[28] and yet are perceptibly sharpened up by his current reading of the nativist press. He is set a heavy problem, however, when he finds himself at odds with local Catholic sentiment over integrated church functions, since he wishes to be a good Catholic as well as a good hater.

One sees the prescience of Paul Schilder, who noted early that trouble can arise for the individual when his various adopted ideologies — group-bound, by nation, class and even family — conflict, and when the rigidity of his ideology trips him up.[29] Something a little more complicated, however, seems to be going on where we find, as in Couch (see above, pp. 135—42), a determined attempt to free oneself from the groups one was 'dealt', by constructing a wholly self-made ideology — in his case, an aristocratic conservatism, contrived in the teeth of the weightiest local conventions. As well as loosely accommodating leading notions to group-memberships, the individual normally tacitly adjusts at least the outer layers of outlook with occupational and social promotion or decline.[30] They must nevertheless occasionally open up to reveal fissures where undissolved and now inappropriate earlier opinions persist. Perhaps after our chapter on the F meridian, we understand a little better the rewards and satisfactions of close conformity to local understandings.

The trials of the would-be loyal follower of a forensic ideological system have been rather more carefully studied — or at least testified to. The fact is that the devotee can only hold the doctrine by distorting it, yet a prime demand of the victim of an over-valued idea is usually that he uphold it against the strongest signs that it is in any way at fault. It seems inevitable that even the most carefully 'deduced' selection and rationalisation of the current 'line' on a particular situation will periodically come into conflict with more deeply-lying but inchoate assumptions among the individual's core-beliefs, and that something clearly theoretically called-for will rouse the strongest instinctive antipathy. Indeed, almost the first thing we may wish to know about someone's identification with a system is how well it fits him *personally*. The better the fit, the greater the likelihood of a long, and satisfying association with the public idea-set; we are uneasy when we see, as with Hawk (above pp. 152—3), an ideology apparently assumed primarily for its acceptability to *others*.

The best work to date on the burden of the quest for intellectual orthodoxy is in the field of religious, rather than political, belief; Philip Helfaer's *The Psychology of Religious Doubt* splendidly elucidates not only the fundamental psychological differences between liberal and conservative Christianity as belief-systems, but the role of *doubt* in each. The liberal has learnt to live with — even to turn to positive use — recurrent and pervasive doubt; the conservative structure is monolithic but shakier — admit one tiny doubt and the whole is in danger of collapse. Nevertheless, there is a substantial literature on the struggles of Western intellectuals to persist as orthodox Communists, and it is clear that the psychological intensity of their struggles with doubt and faulty intellection has been as severe as that of any Christian. Admissions of backsliding, heresy or apostasy act for the still faithful as 'awful warnings' — and yet carry a burning fascination: Whittaker Chambers described

> the fever with which I decided to read my first anti-Communist book. I mean fever quite literally; and furtiveness as if I was committing an unpardonable sin, as I was. For the fact that I had voluntarily opened the book could mean only one thing: I had begun to doubt.[31]

There has resulted a lively and largely successful effort to build a full-scale psychological theory of ideological conversion and de-conversion to encompass both political and religious testimony, which anyone who has been through these straits will find richly informative. The maverick star of this enterprise is Kenneth Burke, who contributes not only a splendid book on St Augustine's conversion, but, drawing on his own brush with Marxism in the early 1930s, a brilliantly generalised phenomenological account of what it is like to go through a massive ideological *bouleversement*.[32] The American analyst Leon Salzman, building firmly on William James's foundations, distinguishes 'progressive/maturational' conversions from 'regressive/psychopathological' ones, which involve deep self-dislike and a critical redirecting of hatred to external targets, now legitimised; they occur typically in authoritarian religious or political settings.[33] Most later writing, both critical and autobiographical, can comfortably be annexed to this master-scheme.

Such intellectual and emotional crises cause the individual more excitement over, and more emotional investment in, his beliefs than he will experience at any other time, and are accordingly very often described in exact, even gaudy, detail, but practically always *without insight*. Bertrand Russell's description of his conversion to pacifism at the age of 28 will illustrate the point.

> Suddenly the ground seemed to give way beneath me, and I found myself in quite another region . . . At the end of those five minutes, I had become a completely different person. For a time, a sort of mystic illumination possessed me . . . Having been an Imperialist [it is 1901], I became during those five minutes a pro-Boer and a Pacifist.[34]

And he launches into a vivid recital of a storm of odd thoughts and feelings that rushed through his mind at his friend's wife's deathbed — yearning sympathy for others, a reverence for all life, and so on, without seeing that he was re-experiencing very much in their original form the wild surmises, omnipotent wishes and dreads that he had felt as a two-year-old at his mother's death. It was a double dread, since her dying shortly afterwards dragged down his inconsolable father as well (as he feared his friend Whitehead also would succumb to *this* grief). His storm re-enacted not only the original raw affect — at bottom, rage at abandonment — but his courageous defence against being overwhelmed by it. He resolved to lead a totally unaggressive life.[35] It is certainly ironic that our central beliefs at their very peaks of illumination should still in essence be obscured from us: Veléry's lines on p. 121 catch the paradox well. But it has been left to the Uruguayan analyst Willy Baranger to spell out in full the case that the principal purpose of a belief-system is to shield the individual from the true springs of his motivation.[36]

We will come finally to the subject of the impingement of insight on outlook, but it may be politic — keeping to the conscious and outward layers of outlook a little longer — to sketch first the steps by which political views are customarily assembled and yoked together.

Outlooks and the standard cultural package

Field-workers have got surprising mileage out of asking outlook-holders to describe 'any recent major changes in their views' or to consider 'how their present opinions have evolved'. An intellectual is perhaps self-defined as one insisting on a *history* to his opinions, but many others can be found with tales of ideological 'phases', 'fresh starts' and 'turning points'.[37]

Political socialisation, a scholarly specialism almost on the scale of attitude psychology, has flourished over the last fifteen years.[38] What help does it now offer someone wishing to rehearse the development · of his own political ideas?[39] Principally, I think, it provides a rough guide, against the background of an epigenetic scheme of progressive maturation of cognitive skills,[40] of the normal course of sophistication of political thinking with age. One may not recall learning about the policeman, the Queen or the threat from the North when one was four, or about foreign policy, the lower middle class or how to read an organisation chart when one was twelve, but for an Australian child this would be about average. It is less the sheer information about politics that the child steadily acquires that is important than the actual ability to think complex thoughts about what he knows. A twelve-year-old has almost the full range of adult political 'objects' — liked and disliked, maybe, in as many different ways — but he cannot justify his views or, for that matter, say where they came from. It is during the secondary-school years that this randomly accumulated detail becomes articulated and given causal and moral texture; between the ages (roughly) of seventeen and twenty-two, it becomes infused with *personal* meaning as outlook crystallises.[41]

Socialisation writers, preoccupied with the accumulation of information about the political order, have been notably less informative about the acquisition of broader cultural beliefs and assumptions which make up the set of lenses through which we view politics, and which account for most of the meaning we see in it. But recent advances in method — for example, Fred Greenstein's semi-projective story-telling or Jeanne Knutson's intriguing picture-cards[42] — enable even young primary-school children to be used as direct informants about such matters as implicit attitudes to authority, assumptions of equality or independence, co-operation or competition in social life, acceptable ways of expressing strong feelings in public, the amount and quality of trust, and the relation between the private realm of personal and family life and the secondary environment. Our inquisitive autobiographer could at least learn from such work where he leans away from the stereotypes of his culture — but he would hardly find out exactly where he parted company with them, since the P-type assumptions and procedures of such work hardly direct him to the personal sites of critical divergence. Set to describe, say, the 'stages in the development of my social ideals', our autobiographer would still be pretty much on his own.

However, the political psychology case-file does at least suggest one or two sites to check. *The all-absorbing fantasies of 'latency'*, like Wienecke's Katie's imaginary world of Red Indians, constitute an important lode of proto-political thinking. Standing at the edge of his first little kingdom, the child, unwilling to embrace the ordinary social world on the terms it seems to demand, builds an ideal commonwealth in fantasy where things are properly done, thus reproaching the parents for their example and performance,[43] while exciting their admiration for an ambitious intellectual performance. The runaway 'genius', Barbara, described by Harold McCurdy, invented a commonwealth of this sort around the age of nine, in her Fable of Farksolia (a planet twice the size of the Earth, inhabited by people twice as intelligent and good).[44] Many less inventive children may recall a particular book they 'read to pieces' in these years, whose central fantasy will no doubt have been doing much the same work: adumbrating *a world without the adults*, comfortably thickened by the presence of objects that the child would like but does not, in ordinary life, possess.

The twelve-year-old religious phase has been described magisterially by Anna Freud in 1936[45] and in vivid detail by many writers in their autobiographies. The intellectual operations involved are slight; the child takes over hungrily and uncritically the prevailing notions of the proselytising group, which are often enough quite marginal or foreign to the parents — Catholic in the case of Mary McCarthy,[46] Anglican in the case of James Agee,[47] and Evangelical in the case of James Baldwin.[48] The child seeks to procure an experience of 'truth' and acceptance transcending the everyday; he turns ascetic, and goes into training for the illumination with pure thoughts and good deeds; and, more boldly than in the latency fantasies, he conjures with hatred of the parents, bringing it almost to the surface (this is beautifully caught in Agee's novel), but, at the last moment, he finds it is magically diverted and put aside with a great lifting feeling.

(Katie's original fantasy proved sturdy enough to permit a wholesale revamping in terms of the new ascetic ideals.)

The adolescent crystallising of outlook. Erikson's lesson — epitomised in his maxim that the achievement of identity and of ideology are two aspects of the same process — has in our time accompanied, if not provoked, a revaluing of adolescence. From the conventional view of it a generation ago, as the pre-serious, 'half-strong' phase, the years of being disoriented by sex, or simply the time for intoxicated dreaming,[49] we have been led to hail it as the heroic life-stage, pregnant with the seeds of historic change. Erikson has admitted — and sensitively elaborated — the autobiographical basis of his 'discovery',[50] but he has left us to notice how flatly this controverts one of the most heartfelt essays by his own analyst, Anna Freud. There is a decidedly mocking tone to her treatment of this period in *The Ego and the Mechanisms of Defence*: physiological changes, she notes, sharpen the adolescent's intelligence, making him think; but what he thinks is tawdry, ineffectual ('The intellectual work performed by the ego during the latency period and in adult life is incomparably more solid, more reliable, and, above all, much more closely connected with action')[51] and, though it purports to grapple with the great questions of history, morality, life and death, it is entirely self-centred and conjures blindly with unconscious conflicts. Her essay leaves the sense even that the very form of the resolution of these conflicts is predestined — it is simply the second time round the Oedipal track — and this crisis will be resolved in exactly the way it was between the ages of four and six. Erikson has taught us (in his essays on Shaw and Hitler perhaps more clearly than in his books on Luther and Gandhi) to take the adolescent's conscious preoccupation with outlook in these years very much more seriously: faced with the necessary vocational and marriage choices, he earnestly summons up all his resources, searches each one of his roots for its value, and each possible major model for its true worth. Eriksonian notions casually produced in case-comparisons have gained grateful acceptance,* yet there is a hollow at the centre of the enterprise. No auxiliary concepts are presented to analyse the central intellectual and cognitive tasks of ideology-construction.† Lack of these concepts is hardly concealed by

---

* These notions include the *negative identity* (all that one has been warned not to become — which therefore fascinates); *ego diffusion* (the 'reckless', 'thoughtless' unfocusing and drifting that looks dangerous, but does no real harm, and indeed educates); the *adolescent moratorium* (the close-mouthed, stubborn years when the young person declines to link up with public groups or restlessly changes from one to another); and *totalism* (wild swings between the mood that everything is possible — our social reservoir, perhaps, of idealism and cultural regeneration — and the mood that, in an irremediably spoiled world, nothing is).

† 'Concepts [in adolescence] undergo organization of increasing order, rank and level, and become components of organized conceptual constructs whose grammar and syntax we do not know yet.' (Arieti)[52]

making a virtue out of falling back each time on the subject's own words for his predicament.[53]

Writers on later stages of the life-cycle have made light of any likely tie with politics. It hardly figures in Jung's account of 'individuation' at the age of forty, or in recent essays on the mid-life crisis, or on the last Eriksonian crisis, that of 'integrity'.[54] This throws us back all the more urgently upon the earliest site of all, the intra-familial years up to the age of five. This sketch, looking for *rememberable* accretions to outlook, has quite ignored it, but we turn now to what these years lay down — and to the ways in which the substance of one's core-beliefs may be modified by becoming aware of part of this as an adult.

Outlook and insight

How would the subjects of chapter 5 have reacted to reading their case reports?[55] Does Inburn, for example, dread anyone discovering his case-history in *The Uncommitted*, or does he leave the book lying about as a short cut for new friends? Does he refuse to recognise the accuracy of the description because it describes a former self? If one were to go as a volunteer to the Harvard Psychological Clinic and procure a 'standard' analysis of one's own outlook, would that herald a great turning about in one's views? Would one's politics notably change, if one were psychoanalysed?

How we are disposed to answer such questions is already built into our personal outlook — and, so far as it runs to 'phallic' or 'resigned' assumptions, has perhaps already been foreshadowed in attitudes to the malleability of world views (see p. 270 above). But there is a little testimony, at least in general terms, on how one's politics can change under psychoanalysis, and we should look at this before resigning ourselves, in the absence of data, to our (various) hunches. Can we clarify a little the *kinds* of matter about which insight has a capacity to unsettle? What sort of new knowledge, and about which aspects of oneself, would dispose one to rethink some unquestioned and cherished conviction?

Psycho-analysis, Ernest Jones assures us, is rather unlikely to disturb our political opinions:

> Mainly because of the time consumed, an analysis is customarily brought to an end when the unconscious conflicts have been re-solved ... There is no motive as a rule to make use of the work done by applying it in detail to the conscious (and pre-conscious) layers of the mind. An impartial observer cannot fail to be struck by the disconcerting fact that analysed people, including psycho-analysts, differ surprisingly little from unanalysed people in the use made of their intelligence. Their greater tolerance in sexual and religious spheres is usually the only mark of a change in the use of the intellect. In other spheres they seem to form their judge-ments, or rather to maintain their previous convictions and attitudes, on very much the same lines of rationalised prejudices as unanalysed

people do. Fads and cranky attitudes, of course, one can count on being altered by an analysis, and opinions on subjects directly connected with analytical problems, such as mental responsibility in crime, are sure to be modified. But I am thinking rather of the main mass of opinions on current topics and events of the kind that make up social life and conversation, opinions which are demonstrably far from objective and which there is every reason to think are extensively influenced by the distorting effects of unconscious complexes. Here it is striking to observe how little advantage is commonly obtained from psycho-analysis in comparison with what one knows must be potentially available. Analysts and other analysed persons often continue to hold heatedly the same convictions and to employ in support of them the same rationalised arguments as unanalysed people in such matters as political controversy ... I have no doubt that it would be an extraordinarily interesting experiment, and one of great profit socially, to conclude an analysis by applying its findings to the various conscious and pre-conscious convictions of the kind just mentioned, to elucidate and estimate the part played by the unconscious in forming them.[56]

A generation later, the 'experiment' remains untried, an 'extraordinarily interesting' possibility still.[57] although analysts nowadays do seem a little more frequently to grapple with religious, philosophical or political convictions, where these are extreme and so closely tied in with central character-problems that they cannot be ignored.* However, few such cases have been reported at any length;[59] Lindner's Mac (pp. 220—1 above) is a rarity; more typical are Hart's men (see pp. 214—18), who stubbornly refuse to see their politics as in any way a symptom. Certainly Jones's notion of a voluntary, purposeful ransacking of an outlook to the very corners remains a therapeutic — and autobiographical — ideal.

One case, however, may be noticed, where a decisive change in political outlook occurred during — indeed, was wholly fuelled by discoveries and work in — the analysis. In Bales's terms, a movement from NB through P to PF, it caught the analyst's eye, not only because from the outset the patient insisted rather boringly and sententiously on parading a home-made 'social theory', but because, as one who was disposed to cavil at Freud on aggression, the analyst saw a chance in the case to turn Freud against himself.

West's Mr C.

The world view expressed by Mr C., a forty-year-old, unschooled engineer, apparently successfully and equably lodged in the middle management of a large manufacturing firm, is distinctly Hobbesian (or, West thought, 'Freudian'): it is a gloomy view of mankind, 'selfish and hating,

---

* In discussions of the effects of therapy, analysts report that, even if patients' political opinions remain largely intact, a good deal of the heat seems to go out of them in the course of an ordinary analysis.[58]

"forced" into co-operations from which it for ever seeks the escapes of destructive group warfare'.[60] Mr C. had, in fact, a 'state of nature' theory, which served the purpose of throwing a critical light on social relations from two sides — showing how 'unnatural' they are (compared, say, to the world of the lower creatures) and how much toll they take of individuals constantly forced to conceal and repress their natural impulses. His views* are, indeed, notable for their anxious individualism and pessimism — he would like to be kindly, friendly and trusting, but society is a jungle of selfish, even merciless, predators. The survival of the fittest may work beneficially in the animal kingdom, but in social institutions it rewards the very worst; he himself is painfully out of place with his 'compulsion to be kind'. He comes gradually, however, to recognise considerable aggression in himself, at once fortified and kept in check by his fear of others. Of course, others are 'just as bad', but his own aggressiveness (no less than the restraints he accepts on it) becomes distasteful to him, and he begins to feel inferior and unworthy.

He then discovers that his adult fear of women derives from an infantile fear that his mother's passionate love would suck him back into the annihilation of the womb. There is a sudden revolution in his marriage, which has hitherto lacked any great warmth; this is accompanied by a revaluation of his sense of the loveableness and proneness to love of people in general, and he 'sees' that he has been so excessively aggressive himself (and has projected this on to others) out of a fear of loving.

However, he is by no means yet free from mistrust; other people are still likely to harbour malice and have hurtful designs on him, and it is hard indeed to know how much faith one should have in them. Then, in his analytic explorations, he finds that, in his early closeness to his mother, he had taken over *her* lively fear of his father, and he recovers clear death-wishes towards him, and 'the nightmare conception ... that both his passionate love for his mother and his passionate desire to be loved by his father threatened his own existence, the former by his being sucked back to the annihilation of the womb, the second by his succumbing to an assault combined of love and anger, such as young children too often imagine their mothers to suffer in the dark hours of the night'. He revalues his father, his colleagues, his analyst and, again, the world at large.

In sum, C.'s misconceptions of both his mother and his father had led him to endow human nature, male and female, with aggressive qualities, which were the product of entirely irrational fears, and had led him to

---

* Mr C.'s social opinions are retailed in copious detail: three dozen from the first 140 hours of analysis, a dozen from the next 20, and a dozen from the final 10; they are not narrowly political — for example, government is barely mentioned, and party never — but Mr C. roams widely over generalised, moralising 'nature of man' pastures.

develop an aggressiveness of his own, far in excess of his social needs. In everyday life, he painfully repressed this in order to secure social approval. But he retained his fears — and his conviction of the harshness of the world and the aggressiveness of men.

> The significant matter for social psychology seems to me to be that here is a man whose view of natural life was similar to that of Hobbes and Freud ... But when he discovered [the reasons for his fear and aggressiveness], those symptoms too were immediately and durably lessened ... In the end C. held the view that most of our aggressiveness is due to fear arising in the fantasy life of childhood, and that fear and aggressiveness are built up both in the individual and in the social group as a vicious circle of distrust and determination not to be beaten.

Taking West's word for the lastingness of the 'cure',[61] Mr C. stands, for our purpose, at an extreme of revision through insight; the whole set of his outlook swings round from watchful mistrust to optimistic idealism in consequence of his liberation from the (quite unconscious) infantile images of the parents as threatening and voracious. And the case illustrates well the Janus-like character of insight: first, looking backwards, there is the experience of recognition (a theme burdensome in the present is traced back to its childhood roots); secondly, this recognition is then 'worked through' (as opposed to being merely glimpsed, as it may be in the case-anamnesis) in a period of double living, refining and matching the affect-contours in the revived corner of the childhood world *and* in the stressful present; and finally, with luck, there is some alleviation of mechanicalness of response and the compulsion to repeat.

From such lonely peaks of self-reconstruction, the impact of insight ranges rapidly down to the lower slopes where the yield is little more than the ability to retreat from a neurotic preoccupation, an over-heated position or an over-valued leader or idea. There is possibly some interest even in the 'insight-withheld' site, where the individual, feeling sadly weighed down by some element in his outlook, hovering on the very edge of comprehending the distorting element in the situation, nevertheless misses his moment. An old example of a dispute between academic colleagues over Indonesian 'imperialism' — it could have been East Timor in 1976, but was, in fact, West New Guinea in 1958 — may serve.[62]

X. and Y., two young university teachers, who until now believed themselves to have almost identical outlooks, suddenly find themselves in a violent dispute about West New Guinea, the news item of the day. X. says that the Indonesians should take control of it at once. Y. says that they should never take control, that they are incapable of governing themselves, and that they would be grotesque in charge of anyone else. X. says that this cannot be known until they have been given a chance. The argument becomes detailed — and the more it does so, the more they find themselves in perfect agreement about the state of affairs in Indonesia and in West New Guinea, and about what needs to be done in both places. Their disagreement about what Indonesians are capable of continues, however, to grow, and becomes total. By now the argument has become painful to both of them; each is as embarrassed and astonished at his own heat as at the other's. No one else takes sides or offers a distraction, and X. and Y. cannot stop, although all they now say amounts to 'Trust them!' and 'Don't trust them!'

An unconcerned listener, who has no opinions in jeopardy whatever course the dispute might take, who knows both disputants well, and who attends more to the rough shape of the argument than to its finer grain, and to certain turns of phrase, might deduce that what is also taking place is an argument about the existential status of 'younger children'. X. (the youngest of three children) is pleading urgently, as in childhood, that 'Good children share.' Y. (the eldest of four) clings to his own hard-won knowledge that 'It's stupid to give things to kids who'll only break them — who're too young to understand.'

Dealing with a remote political issue (but one which they nevertheless find oddly interesting), the disputants have recourse, as we usually do, to an infantile prototype — and, although they both have much real information about Indonesia to deploy, they find it, in the end, to be beside the point. What counts is their unshakeable 'knowledge' of what younger children deserve — a subject on which they happen to be diametrically opposed. Both are embarrassed that the argument has got out of hand — that it has, indeed, come to sound infantile — but they are far from disposed, in the heat of the moment, to reflect on the unconscious shadows* obscuring and distorting their case. Suppose they were to accept, grudgingly, something resembling this interpretation — it is difficult to know in what ways they would be either willing or even able to amend their case.†

Their story, at any rate, alerts us to the fact that insight engages with core-beliefs essentially by recognising prototypes; we may conclude our coda with a brief attempt at classifying them.

Outlook and prototype

For what aspects of adult outlook are we seeking to find childhood prototypes? First, let us consider position on the leading value-

---

* *cf.* Freud's striking simile comparing original categories ('prototypes') with the ghosts in the *Odyssey*, Book xi — 'ghosts which awoke to new life as soon as they tasted blood' — the blood, that is, of the present-day instance.[63]

† Those engaged in debating (a prime 'phallic' activity)[64] are prone vastly to over-value their ability to settle matters by propositional coercion; but they *rationalise* (as in the case above), rather than reason, when gaps open in their line of argument precisely because they stumble upon a reason which cannot become conscious.

axes — attitudes to authority, benefit and control — or Bales's B-F, N-P, and UPB-DNF axes.

Authority values. Beyond exacting a steady disposition to be insubordinate or deferential in degree, an outlook (here merging unabashedly with inter-personal style) encapsulates a stance before authority justified by one's private 'knowledge' of what authority is like — and what it is worth. East (see above, pp. 197–201), for example, knows authority to be remote, isolated, coldly manipulative, peremptory in command and liable to desert at any moment, and has adopted a mixed strategy of evasion and flight, moralistic nagging and psychological understanding leading to resigned acceptance. Webb (see above, pp. 167–72), who consistently overrates father-figures, steers himself gyroscopically by attaching himself to admired elders to whom he recommends himself by a dutifulness and deference so marked that one suspects reaction-formation.

An outlook will also contain a preference for certain authority styles in leaders (and anathematise others), a disposition to look in certain quarters and not in others for leadership, and characteristic ways of behaving as a superior oneself — when given the opportunity. Bales has concerned himself particularly with leadership proclivities in small groups. Obviously one seeks the prototypes of such concerns in the child's relations with family authorities, especially in the first five years of life.

Benefit values fix upon 'who gets what, when, how'. One outlook (P) embraces egalitarianism, champions the underdog, and sees the community as a whole as the repository of all value. Another (N) endorses the man standing alone, the value of competition and rivalry, and the waste of schemes for welfare and coddling. Where A. sees a desperate struggle for supplies, in which he is grievously handicapped, B. sees a calm, orderly ladder of differential comfort and advantage. Where C. would like to bring down the mighty from their seats, D. covets a quiet and prosperous place, arousing no envy in those below, while E. seeks tirelessly to demonstrate that he is 'a cut above' the large mass of ordinary folk.

Politics constantly raises problems of fairness and distributive justice, and people react along well-established, unconscious fault-lines, opened up principally by experience with siblings. My *Images of Class*[65] showed how the same quality of feeling — usually a complex blend of emotions — that originally applied to this or that older or younger brother or sister can often be found to inform adult attitudes to particular present-day classes. For example, the man who felt mostly scorn, but a little grudging sympathy for his younger brothers, feels the same now for the working class. The crackling hostility of a working-class housewife towards the privileged few who 'give themselves airs' is founded on ancient knowledge of her 'wicked' elder sisters.

Images of foreign nations also conjure in symbolic form with private conclusions about how material possessions and status (which have taken the place of love) should be claimed, won, accumulated or shared. X., as we have seen, wishes to succour the Indonesians, Y. to starve them. Some espouse aid for the Third World, others are completely isolationist; some wish the government to 'give leadership' to smaller powers, others fear becoming 'too close to' or 'too dependent on' great powers, or foreign capital or culture. And groups in domestic politics, too, including the political parties, can draw deeply on these original categories. Political debates about benefit do not merely re-harness raw and awkward *childhood* feelings of scorn, say, or envy, but necessarily also call up the individual's whole apparatus of defence against these feelings in a response that derives from the character.

Control values. In his early practical experiments in indiscipline and autonomy under the parental roof, the child is forging lasting patterns of (and sentiments about) impulse expression and restraint, which will direct his conduct in many problematical adult situations and distinctively colour his mature social outlook. West's Mr C., for example, has both a righteous sense of how tightly others need controlling and an aggrieved sense of how much it is costing him to hold himself in to seemly levels of aggression.

Feelings about control and self-control, both of sex and of aggression, tend to be connected by one's taking the self as model for the 'ordinary man': he who doubts his powers of self-control welcomes external restraints generally; he who abhors strictness, and trusts himself without it, wishes to free others also. At one extreme, the psychology of kill-joy puritanism (DNF), and at the other, that of libertarianism (UPB). The F type, while particularly troubled by aggressive drives, is relatively unconcerned with sex; with PB it is just the opposite. The DP type is least troubled in restraining either; DNF is most troubled with both — to the point of stasis. Siblings seem at times to pair off as 'controlled experiments' (rarely, perhaps, without parental collusion) — one taking the broad path, and one the narrow, like Dunn and his brother (see above, pp. 154–6) and Bosely and Alger Hiss (see above, pp. 55–7).

Attitudes to the relative seriousness of particular crimes (especially, perhaps, crimes 'without victims'), to the question of personal responsibility for crime, to the purpose, or the proper severity, of punishment, or to the separation, if any, allowable between public and private conduct, will be pre-formed — although on highly personal lines — by this element in the outlook. The most direct focus of private 'knowledge' in this realm is, of course, in parenthood, and, though precept is regularly undercut by unconscious irruption, views on the proper way to bring up children should run in clear parallel to social views. Joined with opinions about acceptable authority, one's preferences for autonomy or discipline in inter-personal environments or at work will set much of one's course in groups and organisations (and, as Bales has shown in his experimental groups, like-minded people, on this axis as on others, tend to stick together).

At discrete points along our central axes, the history of a child's conflicts is preserved in the form of his values. This is what makes his adult outlook unique — and dignifies it.

Yet we may suspect that if readers, in their browsing among the cases in chapter 5, have been provoked to personal recollection, it is less likely to have been along these structural lines, than *beside* them, on surfaces we have yet to sketch. The axes give altogether too spare and diagrammatic a picture of outlook — a builder's plan of the edifice rather than an artist's (or fond owner's) impression. We move towards the complexity and picturesqueness we want by acknowledging, first clutter, and then confusion.

What we might see as the sheer miscellaneous contingency of the child's home contributes not only the surface appearance, but much of the solid structure of the adult outlook. de Grazia may be right in thinking that about his fifth year the child turns autonomously towards a belief-system in shocked realisation of the limits to his parents' powers, their existential smallness and weakness, and launches on an anxious contemplation of the powers in society and the world.[66] But long before (indeed, from when he can speak) and long after this, the parents surround the child with their own beliefs — many of which, in unquestioned detail, will never leave him,* and whose largest themes are almost certain to be portentous, and even project-setting. For example, a family such as Ingle's, say, establishes politics from the outset as challenging, fascinating, fun; but in the sort of family where feminine identifications hold sway, the child learns that religious language and symbols are especially apt for dealing with prohibitions, ideals and covert hostilities.[68] In a third sort of family, the child discovers that the mother is the real ruler and learns to be indifferent to politics, because it is the realm of hollow men like his father; in another, very similar kind of family, however, the child determines to teach his father how it should all have been done and to compel his mother's admiration.[69]

More-constrainingly, families may establish — often over several generations — unique focal concerns, such as exhibitionism and self-display violence or futurelessness, disconnection or incestuousness.[70] These concerns, transmitted collusively as 'understandings', may colour and direct large parts of a life. With family themes go family styles — of perfectionism, perhaps, or spontaneity, misanthropy or narcissism. In the parents' cognitive styles (which often contrast, so that the mother might be practical and the father a dreamer), the child has first models that he

---

* Of course, the child is no passive sponge to soak up these beliefs; he actively works over what his parents offer, including that especially fateful category of experiences which are 'utterly inconceivable' to them.[67]

may quietly absorb, or patiently or angrily unpick, for his own eventual arrival (after what further work we do not yet know) at a style all his own. And while this may be readily classifiable on Will Jones's or Shrieidman's grids,[71] it will seem to its owner invisible, by and large automatic, showing perhaps just a little in the form of ego-ideal (summed up as 'firmness and brightness' or 'smooth-flowing grace' or 'why not the best')[72] but coming under notice usually only when and where it works least well.

Dollard's celebrated 'autobiography of a five-year-old' catches all this very well, as well as exploring the child's first deep stock-taking of the local community — the social divisions and levels and different customs and life-styles within half a day's walk of his family home.[73] The child's discovery of the social groups 'we' identify with and define ourselves against, of the meaning of father's work and social place, establishes the basis for lifelong patterns of essentially *political* loyalty, sympathy, distance and enmity.

We salute, finally, the inconsistency and incoherence of outlooks. A prototype, once formed, may be used with a positive or negative sign. We may swing from hating a certain object to loving it, but we cannot ignore it or leave it alone. Elements of naivety may be intricately preserved in outlooks of some sophistication, as Shea (see above, p. 153) retained a simple Catholic piety in the shadow of his aggressive scientific materialism. As Bales showed, we are often fascinated by what we defend ourselves against most strongly. Under conscious avowals, unconscious disavowals may lurk; cf. Eliot's confession, 'Intellectual belief was easily come by, emotional belief was the work of a life-time.' A current political object may be annexed to prototype A or prototype B, to become in the one case applauded and in the other deplored — as in the courts an usher may determine the sentence by assigning a case to this bench or to that. This is why we so often find ourselves contradicting opinions we thought we had just secured. Even the same opinions waver and warp as the surface of the outlook responds to variations in the pressure of inner anxiety or, as with Wienecke's Katie (see above, p. 207), the force of inner idealism or hope. And, in the inexhaustible wastes of our ambivalence (which we understandably prefer to see as the ambiguity which inevitably accompanies the presentation of novel events), we contrive to keep our reach small, and our outlooks narrow, partial and blinkered.

PART THREE

Passions

'The emotions are not skilled workers
(Lenin)'

Ern Malley

7   *The neglect of affects*

The third part of this book attempts to catalogue the affects invested in or aroused by politics. It is a task for which oddly little has been expressly prepared. Certainly Hobbes, Hume, Bentham and many older political philosophers prefaced their entry into political discourse precisely with their own catalogue of critical emotions, but, in pre-psychological times, these signalled a courteous redefinition of the agenda of political thought rather than any sharpening of analytic capacity. While modern political critics have scarcely denied emotions their importance, they have contrived so rarely to look directly at them, that emotions constitute a whole missing dimension, as it were, in conventional analysis. What has monopolised attention — for reasons we shall have to seek — is the ideational crust of politics, the demands, rallying-cries and rationalisations that are produced by strong social feelings.

Yet political passions are, surely, very often the nub of what we set out to understand. The individual is tied into politics by its capacity to draw deeply on his feelings and his readiness to dispense adequately robust responses; social movements take their whole shape and force from their constitutive and binding affects; political leaders are like sculptors — whose medium is public emotion. It is only because people momentarily feel in common that they can for a while think alike. As Namier protested:

> What matters most [about so-called political ideas] is the underlying emotions, the music, to which ideas are a mere libretto, often of very inferior quality; and once the emotions have ebbed, the ideas, established high and dry, become doctrine, or at best innocuous *clichés*.[1]

Publics possessed by fear or hatred, groups in the grip of envy, resentment or moral indignation, leaders systematically aggressive or cynical, will act in predictable ways. Affects are taken as causes of men's acts in common speech. Why not by scholars?

The two poles of this debate in contemporary political studies were defined in the same year, 1908. Graham Wallas, in *Human Nature in Politics*, proposed that students drop the 'intellectualist fallacy' that political activity is all calculation, and explore the ramifications of sympathy, fear,

293

hatred and boredom in public life.[2] His discussion, however, hardly gets beyond naming these avenues of promise. Arthur F. Bentley's *The Process of Government*, a much more sophisticated work, exuberantly and at length attacked the habit of treating feelings as causal.[3] To say, for example, that sympathy moves the Samaritan or provokes a child labour law is to delude ourselves that we now understand what remains as mysterious as before. Why are *these* victims pitied? By *whom*, and why *now*? If, indeed, we must 'specialize the feelings' each time to fit the particular case, we get nowhere.* Let us, Bentley concluded, clear out the 'soul-stuff' and 'spook' talk and set out to study directly the acting groups themselves. As befits a behaviourist, Bentley's metaphors betray a suspicion that the world of feelings is not merely slippery and flickering — 'irresponsible and unmeasureable' — but, in fact, positively menacing: he writes of 'deep water', 'hotbeds', and even 'this pit'.

No later political student has fruitfully developed Wallas's lead; and Bentley's, only really taken up in the late 1950s, found a readership already solidly habituated to leaving emotions out of account† —less, indeed, from methodological scruple than from puzzlement at how they could be sifted in. The few brave tries at affect-analysis in the interim — which we will review shortly — occurred at the more eccentric perimeters of social science, and attracted little notice.

It might well have been different if psychology, which still — in the lay view — exists to explain our feelings to us, had in the meantime developed some theory of the emotions. Were such a thing to prove possible, Bentley's objections, of course, would fall away. But psychology, even before the tradition of rough-neck behaviourism established its dominance, had shown marked signs of wishing to be excused so hard a task. William James's treatment of the topic in 1892, for example, was notable for a crassness unique in his writing — 'We feel sorry', he asserted, 'because we cry, angry because we strike, afraid because we tremble' — emotions, that is, are the mere shadows of action. It is remarkable, too, for its positively peevish tone — 'I should as lief read verbal descriptions of the shapes of the rocks on a New Hampshire farm as toil through [another "scientific" descriptive catalogue of the individual emotions].'[6]

A glance at any current standard text shows how little relish later workers have developed for the task. 'We must turn to the poets, the playwrights, and the novelists,' say Krech and Crutchfield, opening the

---

* Bentley had an important second ground for scepticism: so much in politics worked 'automatically', indifferent to feelings of any kind — 'the actual working everyday organisation of our political society . . . goes hammering along in its great features undisturbed and uninfluenced, unprodded by specific Spencerian feelings of any kind'.[4] If true, this would, indeed, be a serious objection.

† The admirable *New International Encyclopedia of the Social Sciences* (1970) contrived to commission only one article on any affect — sympathy.[5]

review in their *Elements of Psychology* (1969)[7] of some notably jejune studies of the affects — a list of 507 things that annoy, a tally of toddlers' tantrums, envy as red and grief as green, the deciphering of facial expressions, fear and dry skin in rats, and so on. One contemporary alone, Sylvan Tomkins,[8] wishes to end the exile of conscious feelings from psychology and to see affects, as in ordinary speech, again treated as the 'primary motivational system'. However, he is still comically entangled with the human face as the site of likely discoveries.[9]

While there is such disagreement about the way forward, Krech and Crutchfield conclude, there is no early likelihood of a satisfactory theory of the emotions. Lacking the security even of agreement about what is problematical, the scattered essays by psychologists and psychiatrists on particular *public* feelings — 'the social psychology of fear', 'the psychodynamics of loyalty and treason' — tend to put idiosyncratic questions to their material, and so to remain notably discontinuous. Affects, it is clear, are only studied against daunting odds. Let us see if we can isolate some of the principal obstacles.

Difficulties of definition

These exist, but they are hardly critical. An adequate vocabulary of the feelings is the legacy of a normal upbringing. We can readily and accurately name, identify and distinguish them as they crop up in ourselves and others, and in works of art. The question whether something is a feeling or not is not ordinarily a puzzle, although it can perplex those erecting or policing a technical language for mental states or 'faculties'[10] (cognition, conation and emotion, for example, or 'moral' as compared with 'ordinary' feelings), and although national vocabularies regularly produce small but intriguing discrepancies[11] to plague translators.*

To decide what we feel, we merely turn the experience about to see what label from some appropriate cluster of 'feeling' words we can comfortably plant on it. Most verdicts are instantaneous, but often in order to identify the feeling we follow a process of thumbing through familiar lists of near-synonyms, as if in a thesaurus, until we hit on the right one.

In fact, the catalogue of the affects that Dr Roget compiled for his *Thesaurus* is still acute and serviceable. Set alphabetically, and ignoring

---

* For example, the German *scham* (shame) and the Italian *preoccupazione*.[12]
  'There are gaps between the words for the dispositions or movements of the soul. The cuts could be made at other places. Different languages cut differently' (Kurt Riezler). Both English *shame* and German *hemel* derive from a Gothic word *skama* meaning to cover, to hide (the French derive *chemise* from it); French has two words, *pudeur* and *honte*, to denote shame felt before an action, warning one against it, and shame felt afterwards — and Greek has a similar pair: *aidos*, shame from awe, and *aiochyte*, shame from dishonour.

simple negatives, it reads:

The Common Affections (Roget 1825)[13]

1. Amicability	21. Humility
2. Amusement	22. Indifference
3. Approbation	23. Jealousy
4. Benevolence	24. Love
5. Calmness	25. Malevolence
6. Cheerfulness	26. Misanthropy
7. Contentment	27. Modesty
8. Dejection	28. Penitence
9. Desire	29. Philanthropy
10. Dislike	30. Piety
11. Envy	31. Pity
12. Excitement	32. Pleasure
13. Fear	33. Pride
14. Forgiveness	34. Relief
15. Gratitude	35. Resentment
16. Grief	36. Respect
17. Guilt	37. Sorrow
18. Hate	38. Vanity
19. Hope	39. Weariness
20. Hopelessness	40. Wonder

Evidently, some fifty-odd headings comfortably embrace what we would agree to regard as the main families of feeling or affect.* We sort experiences in practice with little sense of strain and high agreement, though an occasional complex instance may hang balanced between two categories, or require a fusing of several to exhaust it. Serious disagreement, however, begins as soon as we seek to take the first step towards simplification. Fifty categories are just too many to conjure with — is it not possible, as in the colour spectrum, to divine the primary hues which tacitly order the whole?

* With the aid of Joel R. Davitz, who has recently worked over this ground with a group of Columbia graduates,[14] we may suggest a few modernisations and improvements. 'Boredom' is a fresher term for 'weariness', 'cynicism' for 'misanthropy', 'regret' or 'remorse' for 'penitence', 'depression' for 'dejection', 'malice' or 'spite' for 'malevolence', 'sympathy' and 'loyalty' for 'philanthropy'. Feelings which were regarded as subsidiary by Roget, but which now perhaps deserve their own categories are: 'anger' (subsumed in 'resentment'), 'anxiety' and 'suspicion' (in 'fear'), 'surprise' (in 'wonder'), 'contempt' and 'disgust' (in 'dislike'), 'greed' (in 'desire'), 'admiration' and 'affection' (in 'approbation'), confidence' and 'trust' (in 'hope'), 'impatience' (in 'excitement'), 'disappointment' (in 'discontent'); and 'pleasure' could well be unpacked into 'gaiety', for example, 'delight', 'enjoyment', 'happiness' and 'elation' (which is eccentrically filed under 'vanity'). Missing from the affections and placed elsewhere are 'shame' (under 'disrepute', a social category) and 'frustration', 'determination' and 'obstinacy' (under Will headings). Missing altogether from Roget's list, and so presumed to be new, are embarrassment, self-confidence, self-hatred and such other ego-feelings as confusion, inspiration and nostalgia.

Difficulties of classification

First, we must allow that several classificatory devices do succeed — by their very lack of ambition. Undeniably, there are Positive and Negative emotions and they may well be firmly ordered in this by degree.[15] (A more melodramatic variant wishes to speak of masochistic or sadistic emotions.) There are also, no doubt, self-concerned/other-concerned, and very generalised, emotions.[16] We shall have, of course, to look with special care at the political/personal division.

Slightly more analytic is the distinction between tension-build-up/tension-discharge affects — fear or frustration, say, as against rage or grief. A connected scheme contrasts signal-scanning/drive-discharge affects — confidence or shame, say, as against anger.[17] Both sets link fairly closely with the more obvious positive/reactive sets, that is, those that are sparked off from within or from without* — though projection and externalisation dismantle great stretches of this boundary. The intent behind such schemes is to net physiological correspondences, but they manage less to sort feelings into solid classes than to show their alternative points of physical entry.

There is merit, too, in Fenichel's idea of two bites at an affect — the idea that an affect first comes into view as a signal (or signal of a signal), then gathers strength and threatens to overwhelm the ego, at which the ego girds itself in response and considers how to deal with it.[19] This certainly seems to be the basic dream plot. Another classification contrasts those affects induced by tensions between ego and id (fear of the id, disgust, shame, pity) or between ego and super-ego (guilt, depression) with those internal to the id (sexual excitement, rage) or internal to the ego (fear of reality, or of pain, object love or hate, enduring sentiments).[20] But we need to be careful here, for to talk of the ego experiencing emotion or mastering affect, neglects the fact that emotion is of the essence of what we speak of as the ego.[21] Affects go to the heart of us; indeed, they are, as dreams show, still active while we are asleep.

Franz Alexander's 1935 essay, '*The logic of the emotions*',[22] is still the most original of modern attempts to reduce affects to a very simple order. He proposes that all the emotions, when their idea content has been stripped away, can be seen as expressions of three fundamental biological tendencies or vectors — intaking, retaining and eliminating. Erikson appropriated this idea in his well-known epigenetic scheme of infantile sexuality in *Childhood and Society* (1950).

Drastic clarification is also the ambition of more conventional schemes which sort affects into primary/secondary or simple/compound; these

---

* Note, too, Paul Federn's distinction between staple or idling affects, lurking in wait for situations which provoke them even lightly — and reactive affects.[18]

schemes have a long history.* We may take the matter up with McDougall's *Social Psychology*.[24] What made an affect primary, he argued, was its tie with a principal instinct, that is, its being organised both to respond to certain stimuli and to pursue certain ends. Thus fear is linked to the instinct of flight, disgust to that of repugnance, wonder to curiosity, anger to aggression, elation to self-assertion, 'subjection' to self-abasement and 'tender emotion' to the parental instinct. Compound emotions either mix the primaries, such as awe, reverence, gratitude, admiration, scorn and envy, or the primaries and the sentiments, such as jealousy, vengefulness, shame or remorse. Joy and sorrow (and, for that matter, hope, anxiety and despair) were *accents* rather than true feelings, since they were bound up with the fate of particular projects rather than themselves project-setting. Surprise was merely the suspension of affect.

Shand at once contested this account, although he welcomed the new stress on the active side of the emotions.[25] It 'has not shown that the stimuli that arouse these instincts are always and necessarily connected with the excitement of an emotion'. Besides, there were other instincts like the appetites of hunger and sex and 'impulses connected with exercise and repose', which were as 'basic', but lacked set affects. Joy and sorrow *were* primary, 'manifested very early in child-life' — indeed, focused on feeding, and underivable from other feelings. Self-assertion and self-abasement were impulses, not instincts, and tied in only loosely with the sophisticated feelings of pride or shame. There was no parental instinct. And he wished to add 'Repugnance or Aversion', a sort of negative joy, to the primaries.

Shand took the primary/secondary issue lightly; in his view it was better to be full than neat. But we see at least in this exchange the kinds of matters jostling as criteria for 'primariness'. The order *in time* seems specially important — the earlier the more portentous — either phylo-genetically or ontogenetically. McDougall and Shand watch their pets and babies, and make use of stories of wild animals and primitive tribes. In the sixty years since, great strides have been made in evolutionary physiology, ethology, the psychology of development and the craft of infant observation, but somehow the ambition to weld the new findings into a master theory of the affects has lapsed.† Primariness has simply ceased to be a

---

* Descartes, for example, posited as primary emotions: admiration, love, hatred, desire, joy and sadness, claiming 'all the others are composed of some out of these six and derived from them'. He did not, however, spell out the criteria for 'primariness'. Spinoza, in a bravura deductive flight, 'derived' some 45 'subsidiary' affects from a primary three — joy, sorrow and desire — with a minimum of additional props. His definitions, though always neat, are usually somewhat strained, and never psychologically informative.[23] Adam Smith, Alexander Sutherland, Bain, Darwin, Herbert Spencer and Ribot all submitted revised lists.

† Erikson, for example, is content to make the mastery of a focal negative affect the crucial 'task' of five of his eight life-stages: infancy, mistrust; early

contested issue — and there is even a tendency to insist on the irreducibility of certain compound emotions.* Certainly, there is general agreement that one meets only very rarely a pure affect, long-sustained.

Difficulties with unconscious feelings

We are moved, often in important matters, by affects of which we remain unaware; we project on to others urgent feelings unacceptable in ourselves; we sift and reshuffle our thoughts to disown and dislodge the awkward emotions that inhabit them. Our conscious feelings, we periodically caution ourselves, represent the mere 'tip of an iceberg'. Unconscious feelings, and defences against them, pose three main methodological problems — of presence, of layer, and of time.[31]

Of an affect precariously 'there', we may need to enquire whether it is, in fact, present, or only pretended.† If the affect ought to be there, but is not, *why* is it not? Has it, perhaps, gone into somatic symptoms —the migraine for unacknowledged anger, the envious sore throat — or is it present, but unconscious? The mind baulks at 'unfelt' feelings, but we often substitute a milder for an alarming feeling (boredom for anger, perhaps) or bleach it right out (in isolation or denial), or permit ourselves

(*Footnote continued*)

childhood, shame/doubt; play age, guilt; school age, inferiority; old age, disgust/despair.[26] However, he abandons affect terminology without apology in his analysis of adolescence, young adulthood and maturity. More seriously, the English Kleinian school of psychoanalysis, which has done so much to uncover the realm of early anxiety — both paranoid-schizoid and depressive — and early envy, guilt and feelings of omnipotence,[27] has so far shown no more disposition than orthodox analysis to move towards a fully-fledged theory of the affects. Kleinian work has, however, made clearer than ever the intricate relation between the affects and the early development of the ego — in line, indeed, with Edward Glover's suggestion, 'It is ... plausible that there are as many primitive affects as there are primitive ego-nuclei',[28] and has underlined the portentous '*self*-constituting' power of early affect experiences, in, for example, the formation of the greedy or the envious character.[29]

* Indeed, Glover says that
    'The phenomenon of ambivalence is ill-described as a rapid alternation of love and hate affects or as a simultaneous experience of love and hate attitudes towards ... the same object. It is much better understood by ... postulating an actual fusion of affect.'[30]
Depression, he adds, which looks 'primary' is actually a cluster of compounds — at the least, 'a feeling of impoverishment due to internal loss of love, [a] feeling of deadness due to the action of internal anger directed against the love-object (with which the ego is partly identified) together with reactions of anxiety, guilt and remorse' — whose lesser known components are the best clue to its early history in the individual case.

† As in the droll psychiatrist's parry:
Patient: I feel so terribly guilty about this...
Doctor: Yes, you certainly feel something very strongly. Let us see if we can find out what it is.

to take it out on a substitute object instead. Or is it merely delayed and kept sternly battened down for minutes, hours or days, but bound to flare out in some moment of inattention?

Next there is the problem, first tackled by Ernest Jones, of double cover, or affect guarding against affect — a morbid anxiety may disguise a deep guilt, which may itself be based on fear. These reactive, or double-bluff, structures may be contemporaneous:

> Hate . . . is one of the commonest covers for guilt. . . Hatred for some-one implies that the other person, through his cruelty or unkindness, is the cause of one's sufferings, that the latter are not self-imposed or in any way one's own fault. All the responsibility for the misery produced by unconscious guilt is thus displaced on to the other, supposedly cruel person, who is therefore heartily hated. . . We know that behind it there always lies guilt, but further analysis still shows, in my opinion always, that the guilt itself is dependent on a still deeper and quite unconscious layer of hate, one that differs strikingly from the top layer in not being ego-syntonic [*i.e.* something that the individual can comfortably own to].[32]

Finally, it is often difficult to establish of an affect whether it is old or new, fresh or archaic, or a blend of the two.[33] It is also difficult to establish its real stimulus. The situation may be misperceived along habitual lines. As one analyst put it: 'A person's whole life is a single psychological context' — a view, he noted, which contradicts

> our usual common-sense impression that behavior is predominantly a reaction to present situations and recent events. . . Problems in the present cannot profitably be distinguished sharply from the similar problems in the past. Every reaction to a present situation is based on patterns acquired by past experience.[34]

Pondering these difficulties tends to produce a sense of intellectual defeatism: it seems so clear that there will always be significantly more to our feelings than we can fathom.* But we may still set sensible limits to our frustration and gloom. It is not that our feelings can never, like the rainbow, be grasped; it is more like working on a task with constant distractions. The feelings we are unconscious of do not, when we are un-aware of them, billow out, liquefy or merge; they remain their peculiar obstinate shapes just as when they are in full view.

To the difficulties inherent in the subject matter, we must add one un-fortunate intellectual handicap that most recent workers on affects

---

* Hence, too, the common sceptical doubt that feelings can ever properly be put into words. (Curiously, the same sceptics often overrate the power of infant expressiveness and raw empathy.)[35] Descriptive difficulties are most acute in regressions to very early — that is, pre-verbal — states. It might be truer to say, at least of those with developed vocabularies, with R. G. Collingwood, that an affect not accurately put into words is not accurately felt.[36]

have clamped on themselves. This is the idea that the affects form a system — that they basically register disturbances to a stable state, and, by this very registration, work to assist in its restoration. If they are regarded primarily as communicative devices (forged in the long course of evolution and honed in the mother-child dyad) then they are seen essentially to communicate loss of control. If they are studied as by-products of physiological states, then they evince threatened physical disequilibrium. Some extraordinarily powerful but deeply buried cultural aspiration towards stasis seems to be at work. It sets a very low ceiling, indeed, on the achievement of understanding in this field. The temperament that chooses to see depression, for example, as a biological response to energy-depletion and hence restorative and reorganisational, is not one that will accommodate the idea of tragedy, individual or social.

In sum, the direct study of affects has scared off first-class minds. Those who have persisted fell back rather soon on indirection or forgot their original questions. The great majority have preferred to drive either 'up' or 'down' from affects: up to the ideas with which affects are most closely associated, or down to the instincts, drives or needs that 'underlie' them, as experimentalists measure, for example, hunger, frustration, and fear in laboratory conditions, or as psychoanalysts juggle with the meta-psychology of libido, aggression and the death instinct. We learn a lot as a result, but not about affects, since they have been set indefinitely aside.

Conclusion: one or two first steps

The guiding idea in this essay — it belongs to Alexander Shand — is that while it may be impoverishing to see affects as a whole as 'equilibrating', each leading affect may quite profitably be taken as a system in itself. 'A system as applied to emotions and sentiments', Shand explains, patterns our behaviour with some regularity: there is 'an impulse and an end, in relation to which other constituents tend to become organised'. In particular classes of situation, in the presence, for example, of certain predisposing objects, we are tipped into fear, anger, joy or sorrow, and, while in their grip, are led to seek to respond in certain limited, fairly predictable ways.

An emotional system comprises not merely feelings and impulses, but also the conscious thoughts that help define the situation and choose among the appropriate responses. Unconscious feelings also play a part. We do not need to stay angry to remain in an anger-system — indeed, to operate successfully we may need to put our feelings aside to calculate calmly, or to disarm opponents. An affect may crop up in a variety of 'foreign' emotional systems — fear in joy, for example, or anger in sorrow — as a tincture to the basic affect-state. A final part of each system is 'organised in the body': the part that draws on instinctual response or patterns of impulse. We may or may not know that we are in an emotional system; those watching us may sometimes be wiser, and sometimes mistaken or duped. They will often have to infer the affect state from its derivatives, from metaphors or symptoms, from the 'rigidity of the opposing behavior', or from the 'general weariness' that betrays 'the consumption of energy in the unconscious struggle over the affect'.[37]

The peculiar merit of Shand's approach is that, while maintaining his base in solid affect state, he reaches out cheerfully into the realms both of ideas and drives. We hope, chapter by chapter, to demonstrate its utility, but clearly it meets our prime methodological demand that a way be found to talk increasingly carefully of affects as direct causes of behaviour.[38]

Shand was not satisfied by his large book *The Foundations of Character* (1912), a detailed phenomenology of the primary affects, and he had projected a second sortie built round the 'improved' notion of sentiments, but unfortunately this plan fell casualty to the First World War. Shand saw sentiments as the larger integrative systems that governed the smaller, shorter-lived, centripetal, emotional ones, but had not in *The Foundations* gone much beyond some notes on love and hate. The object of his analysis was the individual as private man; he nowhere sought to tie him in to history or to politics. Yet it is surely in these contexts that the concept of sentiments — emotional dispositions organised in *systems* about the various objects that excite them — promises most.

At almost the same time, in Germany, Max Scheler projected a very similar venture. After his essay *Ressentiment* (1912), he published *The Nature of Sympathy* (1913), which was to have been the first of a series called *Die Sinngesetz des emotionalen Lebens*, to include studies of the sense of shame, the sense of honour, and the emotions of fear and reverence; his aim was 'to treat all the more important *derivatives* of the ... emotion in question. .. ; to give detailed attention to these emotions ... with regard to their *order of development* in the individual and the species; and to assess their importance in the formation and maintenance, the ordering and specifying, of social groupings among men'.[39] None of these was found among his papers when he died in 1926.

Since he was looking for uniformities in personality organisation, Shand felt free to set aside the problem of individual differences.[40] The political psychologist cannot. Everyone has a character, and, maybe, a character uniformly constituted; but few people are politically concerned or knowledgeable, let alone politically at one with others, so that their differential susceptibility to the objects of politics must be a prime concern.

People differ markedly in their average level of affect:

> An ego which shows insufficient control over a rather small quantity of excitement can be called weaker than one which has mastery over larger quantities.[41]

People also differ in their stance towards the affect stream. The volatile hysteric, for example, who is set always at 'high', bobs like a cork upon the slightest ripple; the dull obsessional, whose spirits are permanently 'low', plays Canute at the water's edge.[42] How generalised are such stances? It is plausible that those cool or irritable in ordinary life will be cool or irritable in politics, too, but we all know highly disciplined intellects who keep politics as a kind of bear garden of the mind.*

Personal styles of emotional response to politics are tied closely to individual hierarchies of affect. Our personalities are organised to exact a steady diet of 'necessary' or staple emotions from our surroundings, and it is likely that the angry man is tied into politics, too, by his rage, the envious man by his sense of disparagement and ill-treatment, and the anxious man by his fear. But leading affects form a complex pattern, and a highly personal one. We might describe one man as above all benevolent, but less so from fullness of heart than from earnest conviction, next as prey to all manner of nagging fears and doubts, next as set on a declining plane of disappointed pessimism, and finally as prone to disgust. Or we may credit another man with the leading affects of indignation, misanthropy, vanity, and excitement.

Some way must be found to link public provocations and individual predispositions. We wish to know under what conditions in politics who is led to feel what with what consequences.

---

* cf. David Riesman: 'Since people do now grow up evenly or all at once, they may respond quite differently in different spheres of life. Politics ... may represent the highest reach of a person, or the lowest, or any level between. And the very contradictions between spheres may be the person — and may keep him going.'[43] cf. Emerson's comment (rather like a Saul Steinberg drawing), 'Politics is the cigar-smoke of a man.'

8　Affects in politics

Does politics engage the same feelings as personal life? Does it draw upon them in the same way? Yeats warned that 'The only two powers that trouble the deeps are religion and love, the others make a little trouble upon the surface',[1] but in so far as politics makes a world, it must implicitly offer the full gamut of emotion. At least to a degree, somewhere in it someone must be able to feel almost anything. Yet, like all society's part-systems, politics seems almost bound to 'specialise' — as crime peculiarly conveys excitement, religion awe, and art wonder. Mindful that a different tale may need to be told for spectators and for actors, what is the characteristic affect-mix for politics?

No sharp or final line of division between personal and social affects is to be expected, since all affects are borne by persons, and even very private feelings involve some social context. Yet one set of essentially *domestic* feelings does seem to stand out. Love or grief, for example, must surely relate to some long-standing, private relationship, as individual as nostalgia. Gratitude, shame, pride, hope, with much the same character, also seem positively difficult for politics to call up. And when it does, with a leader mourned, or in sudden feelings of group pride or national shame, there is often the accompanying tinge of surprise, as that the proscenium arch could suddenly dissolve during so 'trivial' a play.

From the other side, it seems impossible to find any staple political feelings which are largely unknown in personal relationships. Hate, for example, which Lasswell, following Henry Adams ('Politics has always been the systematic organisation of hatreds'), plausibly nominates as the leading political affect,[2] is familiar enough in face-to-face dealings. While art or religion appear to demand affects relatively rare in personal relationships and transcend them, building a separate edifice,[3] politics seems to select only the most common emotions and to render them commoner still.

If, then, the affects in broad plan cluster away from politics rather than towards it, our problem is to explain its concentration and over-reliance on some few coarse affects and its use of them in a way possibly uncharacteristic of personal life.

How politics uses affect

The question has been little pursued; indeed, two slender psycho-analytic essays, independently written but mutually balancing, Lasswell's 'Politics of Prevention'[4] and Zilboorg's 'Affects, Personal and Social',[5] almost exhaust the discussion. Both nominate 'second-handedness' as the leading quality of affects directed to political objects; and, as with consumer durables, there are strong overtones of inappropriateness, dilapidation and deserved looseness of treatment. The most general formula, Lasswell wrote, which describes the developmental history of political man

> would employ three terms. The first ... stands for the private motives of the individual as they are nurtured and organized in relation to the family constellation and the early self... Primitive psychological structures continue to function within the personality long after ... infancy and childhood... The prominence of hate in politics suggests that ... the most important private motive is a repressed and power-ful hatred of authority, a hatred which has come to partial expression and repression in relation to the father...
>
> The second ... describes the displacement of private motives from family objects to public objects. The repressed father-hatred may be turned against kings or capitalists... Harmonious relations with the father of the family may actually depend upon the successful deflec-tion of hatred from private to public objects.
>
> The third ... signifies the rationalization of the displacement in terms of public interests. The merciless exploitation of the toolless proletariat by the capitalists may be the rational justification of the attitude taken up by the individual toward capitalism.[6]

So familial grudges are made over into public causes, and, in notable actors, a whole life is moulded 'in such a way as to give an opportunity for the expression of these affects'. Both displacement and rationalisation are beyond the apolitical (although crude half-outlooks may at least displace feelings — though they cannot rationalise them), and the fully successful political figure can quite dispense with the original 'motive', and bury it. The displaced affects, though usually of early origin, are sometimes con-temporary — for example, *current* father-hatred may be dispelled by radicalism.* But there are no conclusive answers to the questions of what the dispositions to externalise and to rationalise do themselves depend on, and what triggers them off.

Lasswell in the above passage was concerned with the dynamics of affect in highly active, highly political men, and thus preferred the term 'motive', with its stronger connotation of action, to 'affect'. But he later touched directly on the arousal of political emotions in the rank and file.

---

* This chimes in nicely with the old story of Freud remarking of his secretary, Otto Rank: 'Rank disposes of the negative aspect of his filial love by means of this interest in the psychology of regicide: that is why he is so devoted.'[7]

'Political movements ... derive their vitality from the displacement of private affects upon public objects.' The affects which are organised in the family are redistributed upon various social objects, and political symbols are particularly adapted to serve as targets, because of their 'ambiguity of reference', their remoteness from daily experience and their general availability. Affect concentrated about a particular symbol increases its competitive power as more and more elements in society are led to read their private meanings into it.[8]

It is a spacious* scheme — of which we have given only the outline — which allows for the sudden release of affects from customary objects with social disturbance, their conscious (and competitive) manipulation by leaders, fits of regression to infantile modes in times of crisis, but, above all, a generally poor match between perceived political needs ('demands') and real tensions, and a more or less constant level of emotional discomfort in society, with politics merely substituting on the symbolic plane one largely irrelevant project for another. Basic to the interpretation is massive unawareness of the real springs of our motivation in politics and the grave inappropriateness of our seeking, as adults, primary domestic satisfactions from the secondary environment.

Two major riders to the thesis drive down closer to the particularities of politics. First is the necessity for ideology — and its warping effect:

> People who are emotionally bound together are not yet involved in a political movement. Politics begins when they achieve a symbolic definition of themselves in relation to demands upon the world. . . Acts cease to be merely private acts; they . . . become related to remote social objects. The conception of self has new points of reference . . . which interlock with those of others. Political acts depend upon the symbolization of the discontent of the individual in terms of a more inclusive self which champions a set of demands for social action.[10]

We take politics in by enlarging the boundaries of the ego, and identifying our own fortunes with those of an external group: this involves a redefinition of identity, of the sense of self and of relevant ties. The individual consciously 'owns' his political opinions; he is, indeed, oddly *proud* of them. As Zilboorg notes:

> The man who states his social feelings and reactions has an absolute need to idealize them, to formulate an allegedly rational and ethical ideology. His ideology is indispensable. The neurotic and the normal are rather humble about their purely personal feelings [and do not set out to 'explain' them — indeed, they are not infrequently baffled

---

* It is also a relaxed scheme, allowing for much slippage and looseness of fit: laden with the emotional charge of such miscellaneous private motives, the political symbol may rapidly accumulate irrelevancy.[9]

by them].... The social affect carries with it more than a tinge of
megalomania; it is something felt and thought for the common weal;
it is a conviction; it is something one is ready to defend even at a
considerable personal sacrifice.[11]

The social affects, in this light, seem less like personal affects displaced
than 'programmes' implanted by competing groups, which capture
and make over the minds of adherents.

A second special feature of political emotion is the prominence of
enmity and combativeness:

Politics ... is the sphere of conflict, and brings out all the vanity and
venom, and narcissism and aggression, of the contending parties.[12]

The appeal is to a particular group of negative emotions, those mobilised
by the 'call to arms', and

a combative loyalty; the social reaction is that of a person who always
stands ready either violently to defend the rights and interests of the
specific group to which he belongs, or to combat the rights and
interests of another specific group whose fundamental aspirations
happen to be contrary to those of his own.

It is not so much the harmony of individual interests within the
group that matters, but the disagreement with other groups ... it is
not solidarity based on love, but cohesion based on hate of the
'external enemy', which is supposed always to be present and always
ready to strike.

Affects operate [in politics] in an atmosphere of watchfulness: they
are ready-to-shoot sentinels; they are marked by hate... Members of
the same class in our culture love one another by way of narcissistic
identification. There is deep ambivalence in this love, with hate as a
major partner of the symbiotic love-hate. The moment one 'betrays
his class', one is dropped and subjected to complete ostracism ... the
ideal must be defended against assailants.[13]

Politics, then, conscripts the affects, puts them in uniform, rigidifies and
coarsens them. Political man simply drops to a lower level of performance.
His reality-testing, his morality, his sense of his own self-interest even, fall
away. The affects characteristically called out by politics — hate, aggression, destructiveness, drives to power and to accumulation, the urge to
punish — depend essentially on the 'gratification of all or of most of those
pregenital libidinous drives which the personal affects [in the interests
of virtue] are always thwarting'.[14]

Although they agree on so much, the two authors draw a different
moral. For Zilboorg, it is the 'groups' who plant stale and inappropriate
affects in their members — economics and culture 'capture' the individual
psyche, and make free with its 'libidinal equipment' for their special
purposes: one cannot, and should not try to, reduce politics to individual
neurosis. Lasswell sees individuals half-blindly grouping themselves

behind delusory symbols and aberrant leaders: the moving groups are constructed in the massing of displaced individual feelings. For one, politics misuses men; for the other, men misuse politics.

The truth of the matter surely lies in the unexplored bonds between individual and primary political group, in some *balance* of testimony. Both Zilboorg and Lasswell may be largely right, particularly if the problem is put in a two-generational setting. Clearly we *are* 'landed' with some groups which, it will seem pointless, dangerous, even suicidal, to desert; we *choose* others, often with some enthusiasm, for reasons that may be highly individual and not fully conscious. And, beyond the relatively static group assumptions, a whole swirling cloud of personal fantasies links us with the incidentals of public life.

Either way, the 'appropriateness' of political affects seems almost permanently in question.* We no sooner identify the feeling that politics arouses in us than we wonder if it is, in fact, justified. The regressive tug of the group tie causes over-reaction as much as the eccentric personal displacement: both, if we stop to test them, dispense emotion that tastes stale. In doubt, we use our immediate circle as a rudimentary way of checking. Of course, *under*-reaction may be more inappropriate still. Ideol ogy, as well as giving stability and direction to our strongest feelings, also preserves us from excessive surprise and 'unrewarding' emotion generally.

Riesman, in one of the few later discussions of these matters, denies that all political affect is displaced, and claims that one can make out much that is 'aroused directly by political events'.[16] These reactions tend to be enthusiastic in tone and easily called forth from people sharing the common emotional temperature of those about them. Displaced feelings, on the other hand, tend to be aggressive, sadistic, the product of life 'in a slightly paranoid and autistic world'; they are characteristically 'explosive', with little real staying power. Appropriate feelings, are more likely to be concerned with human ends than with institutional means; with personal and concrete, rather than impersonal and remote events; with a self-and-others, rather than a self-against-others scheme; with what is *not* in sharp focus as distinct from what is in focus only in a coterie or in the media. Appropriate feelings evince a critical, rather than a submissive, stance towards authority.[17]

Is it so easy to distinguish the two? As an example, let me recall this personal case. In Alberta several years ago I was rather surprised to find

---

* 'To feel "appropriately" ... means primarily being freed of that surplus of unconscious affects which either inhibits or intensifies one's conscious 'intellectual' processes and attitudes toward life ... [So] emotional insight means ... the subtraction, the elimination of the affect which (unconsciously) does not let the individual feel what he feels and see what he sees. To the psychoanalyst it is a matter of making the patient give up or lose something' (Zilboorg).[15]

myself shaking with anger over a tiny item in the *Edmonton Journal*: the French Government had rejected various protests and would go ahead with nuclear tests that spring in the South Pacific. I enjoyed my indignation briefly, and wished I were back in Melbourne where I could at least join some protest; then, perhaps because after all I *could* do nothing, I began to find the vehemence of my feeling itself puzzling. I should perhaps explain that I am normally quite stoical about nuclear testing, and, indeed, about the non-consultation of Australia by the Powers. Two days before this, I had been typing part of my wife's thesis about the early days of Australia's foreign affairs department, concerning the efforts made around 1910 to get the British government to take up with the French government the grievances of British residents of the New Hebrides; the New Hebrides was supposed to be a condominium, but the French were running it to suit themselves, particularly in the matter of land titles. I had typed fast, making a technical task of it, not bothering about the sense of what I was typing. What I had particularly not thought about was that my grandfather, who was a Presbyterian missionary in the New Hebrides at that time, was one of the minor figures caught up in this drama. My mother had, when I was about six, rather thoroughly explained his struggles to me, leaving me with a profound impression of French arrogance, greed and high-handedness in the Pacific. In short, here I was in 1968 gripped by a piece of anti-French affect, which I did not know I possessed, which I had apparently acquired in 1930, and which was appropriate, if ever, to the conditions of 1910.* But does this take us into Riesman's 'paranoid world', the 'autism' or the 'sadism' he speaks of?

Perhaps we should not hope for too clear a line between direct and displaced feelings.† Our political feelings are surely apt to be a variable yet characteristic mixture of the archaic and the appropriate; and whether our affects are 'authentic' (or 'authentically ours') is likely to remain a matter for daily determination in face of what Jung called the 'terrible ambiguity of immediate experiences'. Lasswell's suspicion that political affects are massively second-hand is, after all, only an extension of the general

* This story incidentally illustrates the vestibular function of the 'preconscious' rather well. The anger on grandfather's account, raised from the unconscious but denied recognition on the typing day, stayed on the threshold of awareness, and poured over on to the first even conceivably relevant stimulus — clearly an 'idling affect', lurking in wait for a justifying stimulus (Federn).[18]

† At bottom Riesman's scheme, laid out in *The Lonely Crowd*, part II, and in *Faces in the Crowd*, focuses on appropriateness of affect to character, rather than to the group-situation or to the realistically perceived stimulus. He can therefore conclude that 'on the whole ... only those who are autonomous in character will be found to manifest an appropriate political style' (the 'autonomous' man being not only free of the group, but also psychologically perceptive).[19]

psychoanalytic finding that we meet and interpret all present stimuli on the template of our habitual 'internal organization of the instances'.[20]

Of course, those deeply involved in politics — those for whom it is a second life — will separate personal from social affects only with a wrench. Because they live in politics, because it makes a rounded world, activists will have the capacity (or even the overwhelming temptation) to annex every emotion to it, particularly the self-regarding ones. Churchill's physician noted in his diary in 1945, on the eve of the election:

> Winston told me this morning that he had had an unpleasant dream:
> 'I dreamed that life was over. I saw — it was very vivid — my dead body
> under a white sheet on a table in an empty room. I recognized my bare
> feet projecting from under the sheet. It was very life-like.' He mused:
> 'Perhaps this is the end.'[21]

The ordinary man's repertoire will be considerably more modest.

The political wheel of fortune dispenses great rewards and crippling disappointments; it can bring sudden fame or failure, and it can tantalise for decades on end. Politics has its moods and seasons — now a maelstrom, drawing everything into its depths, now a mill-pond, smooth and still. Camus quotes a certain oriental master, whose daily prayer it was not to have to live in an interesting age.[22] Our age is certainly interesting, but perhaps not so fated to chaos as the years that Lasswell and Zilboorg reflected upon, the years that led up to the Second World War. What is politics currently exacting? The following chapters will consider how affects are harnessed nowadays by politics, and will draw on a survey of the political affects of a sample of Melbourne university students.

A sample's testimony

Seventy volunteers from the political sociology class at Melbourne University kept a diary of their political affects for a month in 1974.* When the entries were brought together, what immediately stood out was their solidly negative cast: subjects recorded two negative reactions to events for each positive one. In politics we are evidently hard to please, disposed to blame ('Politics is simply the largest possible blame-object'), adept at finding ourselves angered, disillusioned and pained. There was no single day on which positive affects outweighed negative ones.

Much of the disappointment and grievance was fairly light, even routine — flip reactions to the activities, as delivered by television or newspaper, of standard 'villains' or 'fools' — but it was sobering to find that the group's personal experiences of politics (which accounted for a

---

* The next three paragraphs derive from figures 8 and 9 below. Entries were scored 'subjectively', that is, as pleasant or unpleasant for the individual to experience. Anger and moral indignation, which may sometimes have been enjoyed, were, however, scored negative, as were pity and sympathy (unless robustly identificatory); glee at opponents' discomfiture, etc., was scored positive.

healthy fifth of the entries) at work, in associations, in social encounters, private talk and autochthonous fantasy, had exactly as negative a ratio.*
Assumptions of some small 'real' world of face-to-face politics, less shallow, less sour, more sunny and rewarding than the manipulated and stereotyped 'secondary environment' of the mass public, are evidently unwarranted.

The Australian nature of the sample showed itself most strongly, perhaps, in the spatial distribution of disapprobation. In the first place, attention to politics as disseminated by the media was divided: national politics 49%, international 35%, and home city 16%. World political events, however, were disapproved of almost 9:1 and local city occurrences 8:5, but a new, active and popular Australian government caused national politics almost to break even for the month.

When the special quality of each recorded experience was attended to (increasing the entries — by double scoring and so on — by a third), three affect-clusters accounted for three-quarters of the total: anger and moral indignation for 33%, pleasure, etc., for 25%, and cynicism, etc., for 18%. (See figure 8, disposing the 1,660 entries, from which the next six paragraphs derive.) The sample's traffic with each emotion is considered in detail at appropriate points in later chapters; but a glance now at the broad terrain disclosed may help to justify that chapter-plan itself.

Hatred, the dominant political emotion, also had the widest range of intensity — from 'dislike', 'annoyance', 'impatience' and 'irritation' at the light end (where entries tended to cluster), through 'frustration', 'anger' and 'indignation', to 'rage' and 'fury' — and most subjects were careful to indicate these shades. It proved difficult, however, clearly to separate out moral indignation, theoretically desirable as this seemed, since the additional elements of revulsion, moral affront, envy, and the urge to punish were often not fully spelt out. Joint reports — of anger and indignation, for example, 'hatred and contempt', and 'disgust and fury' — were also common. Its count, therefore, is almost certainly an underestimate. What was assigned ran at a uniformly high pitch and focused mainly on foreign politics.

Pleasure in this sample's politics came mainly in the form of light flickers of approval and was much directed by ideology. It embraced the style as well as the content of leadership, and, as we have seen, was preoccupied with the activeness and radicalism of the new Australian Labour government. 'Spite', 'glee' and 'gloating' at opponents' mistakes or weakness, were, however, a significant component. The most intense pleasures were the quite personal ones, such as finding that one could be competent in

---

* Politics is not the only major activity to engage more negative than positive feelings. Calvin Hall informs us that, in the dreams of normal adults, 'the ... emotions of fear, anger and sadness are twice as frequent as the ... emotions of joy and happiness. Dreaming on the whole is not a pleasurable pastime.'[23]

authority, or being warmly accepted by some group. Of the allied subsidiary emotions, amusement, relief and astonishment seem by their nature fairly low-key, but curiosity, which was active almost entirely in the personal sphere, was usually quite strong.

Incuriosity, on the other hand, the disinclination to know, lay near the heart of the third largest, the *sour*, group of affects — cynicism, powerlessness, boredom and depression. World politics attracted cynicism and boredom disproportionately; both occurred rarely in the personal realm, where, however, feelings of powerlessness and depression were sadly prevalent. National and local politics carried a relatively light load of this negativism. It became necessary, in sorting these feelings, to open a further

Figure 8. A sample's affects

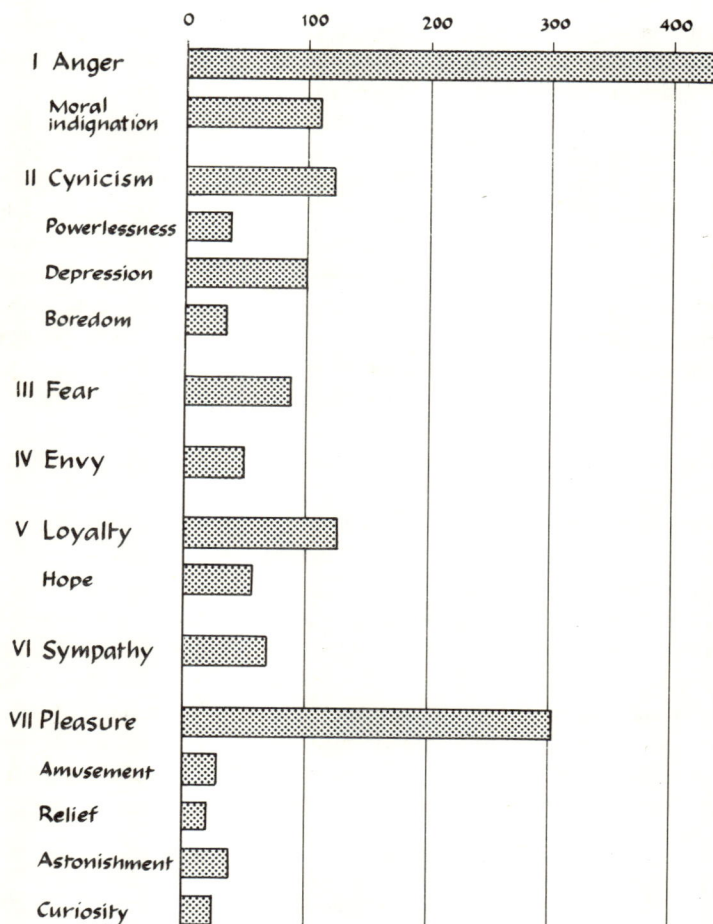

Figure 9.   Distribution of affects*

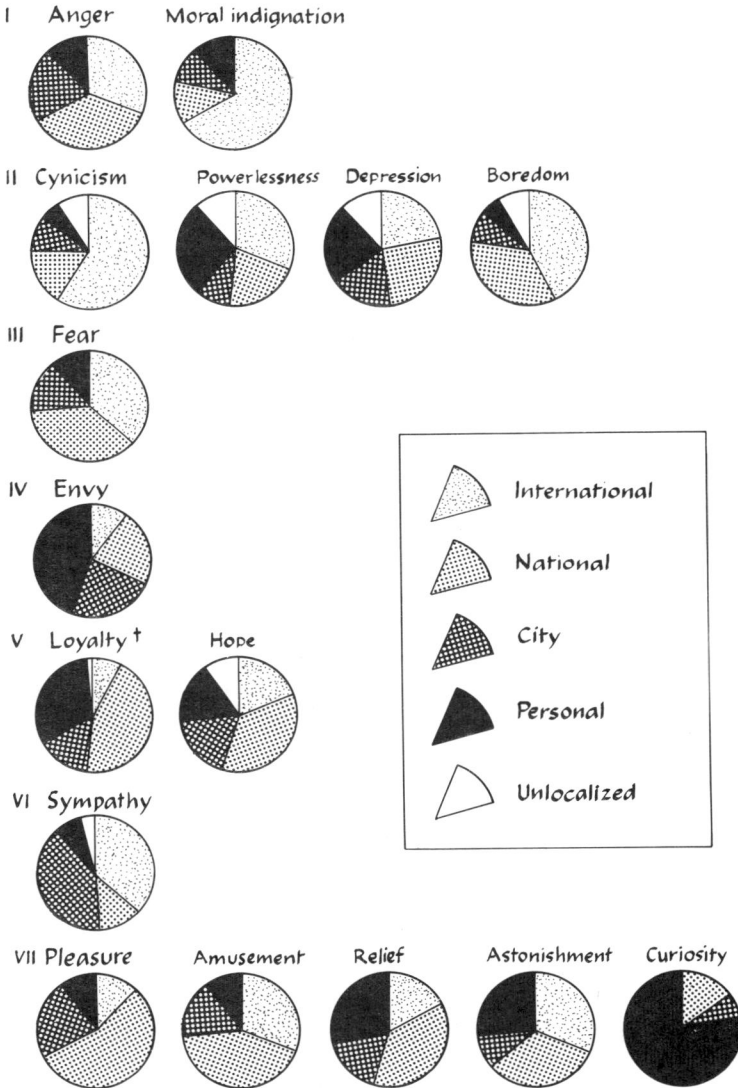

I   Anger   Moral indignation

II Cynicism   Powerlessness   Depression   Boredom

III Fear

IV Envy

V Loyalty †   Hope

VI Sympathy

International

National

City

Personal

Unlocalized

VII Pleasure   Amusement   Relief   Astonishment   Curiosity

* Of the less widely reported affects, Guilt received 14 mentions; Competence received 11; Confusion 9; Incompetence 5; Sense of Obligation 3; Embarrassment 2; Humility 2; Conformism 1; Alienation 1; and Tolerance 1.
† About a quarter of the total for Loyalty in the City and Personal categories was attached to public rather than to private figures.

category of 'unlocalised' provocations; 'politics in general' or 'capitalism' or 'materialism' or 'selfishness' became blame-objects as diarists brooded on their dissatisfaction.

Although we have now accounted for 75% of the diary entries, the remaining clusters, despite their smallness, seem resolutely political. Fear was, in this remarkably secure sample, the emotion most evenly spread territorially, and was frequently linked with depression and power-lessness. Sympathy and pity, after boredom and cynicism, show up as the most media-dependent feelings — a dozen instances attested to the power of a single photograph to move the observer deeply. The groups pitied tend to be either very local or very distant.

Envy was owned to in a mere handful of entries — it is a painful admis-sion. But it seemed inviting to recognise in many more the presence of an 'envy system', when strong reaction to one individual's or one group's acts implied a steep gradient of inferiority or superiority, or the clear framework of an invidious pair. The 3% count is very rough — indeed, it might, with more detail, have been trebled — but it is enough to establish a sharp and indispensable political affect. Envy comes in many forms; commonest here was the 'projection of envy': the attributing of 'pettiness' or 'greed' to individuals or groups with which no sympathy was felt.

Loyalty, too, must be largely inferred — overt declarations of 'pride' or 'trust' in persons or groups account for only one-sixth of our total. One got the keenest sense of it from reading whole diaries, and noting, first, the *enemy* groups whose actions were deplored, and then the subject's own group-ties and sympathies. Hopes were so closely tied to this as to seem merely one wing of the system. Declared group-affiliations fix the indi-vidual's political bearings, especially in domestic politics; indeed, we have here to elide the 'City' and 'Personal' categories, since loyalty is so often given first to a particular group in the local community. It was much harder to net implicit patriotism.

The sample also offered useful testimony on individual affect-styles, the 'careers' of particular affects under observation, and the relation between the flow of political affects and daily personal mood.

Affects as political bonds

If the diarists' affect-experiences represent the smallest particles, as it were, from which significant political structures are built up, what are the main patterns of aggregation?

In their month's vigil, subjects functioned for the most part as a public, an audience to one set of media, informative principally about the recep-tion of secondary events — and the irregularity thereof. Only two or three large items in those weeks managed on any one day to reach emotionally a full quarter of the sample. The average lead story won a 10 to 15% response and, for the rest, events rarely caught 2 or 3%. Furthermore, reactions varied: a thing pleased some, angered others, amused some and left others cynical.

A massing of common response is, in any case, the simplest political *pre-group* pattern: it may be accidental in origin, as sympathy for the victims of fire or flood; it may be deliberately engineered, as by a shock threat or disclosure; or it may (more usually) be a mixture, caused perhaps by a sudden devaluation or the enmity expressed by a foreign government. But it requires both considerable numbers and a common rallying-point.

Some diarists themselves complained that their emotions went for nothing; they and politics survived the month unchanged.* It was fashionable in the group to berate the 'dull' month, but even an audience keeps its books — over the month, the stocks, as it were, of Australian leaders slightly rose, while those of French and American leaders fell sharply — and on ceremonial occasions (for example, at elections) the audience may declare these ratings.[24] (There seems, in fact, to be an odd numerical correspondence between the 2,000 good or bad feeds that empirically establish basic trust or mistrust in the infant and the number of 'impressions of government' registered between elections by concerned voters.) Further, spectators in their daily audit maintain and renew their social stereotypes and ideologies with fresh but reassuringly confirmatory instances.

The *affect lunge*, if we may use this term for the large shift in raw feelings, is normally contained by the customary political forms. Established leaders receive and register the movement of emotion and say, next day, on our behalf, what 'ought to be said' about the event that provoked it. Half their success, indeed, lies in how accurately and truly on important occasions they manage to represent the feeling of the group, and on occasion convey its strength, to outsiders. Debate, dialogue, and more complex dramatic forms of colloquy between representative persons keep people generally satisfied, if not with the result, as least with the process by which issues are being handled or even resolved.

Leaders are only half reactive: they try independently to rouse, sharpen or re-direct feeling among their followers by linking that feeling with explanations and programmes of action. They accept the duty of discerning the accumulating pools of affect in their group and of shaping them to some outcome that will provide relief.† The job is done with much approximation.

---

* The sense that one's affects, however strong, will have no reflection in, or impact on, events, lies at the root of political cynicism — in our sample an intermittent, minority stance.

† James Davies, indeed, thought *the* political affect was the sense of grievance and the will to get it dealt with.[25] Functional analysts of politics underestimate the interweaving of 'citizen input' and 'leader aggregation' of wants. What people find they want is more than half-shaped by the symbolic discourse set up and maintained by public figures themselves. Ordinary citizens adopt

We assume the existence, in society at large, of reservoirs of latent affect — indignation in the old, hope in the young, anxiety in the marginal, and suspicion in the uneducated. We also recognise the special drawing power of each field of policy — fear in defence, sympathy in health, envy in housing and education — and in the institutions that each will naturally erect. People do indeed choose jobs, where they can, for their affect-opportunities; and jobs exact in their turn unlooked-for emotional toll, as servants fall into resentment, policemen into cynicism, and monks and academics into accidie. In politics, leaders make their way largely because they are felt to have the special capacities required to cope effectively and predictably with their group's emotional terrain. (It is not just that they fully share the common affect-mix, but that they profess as well the group-preferred defences against it, that is, they are suitably aggressive, concilia-tory, stoical, or whatever.)

Though always with an eye both to their own following and to the public at large, leaders are normally rather more concerned about their own following. They continually channel the old, staple affects to fresh provocations, sharpen cohesion by the telling evocation of central symbols, and manipulate the operational affect of the group within which followers find comfort and personal meaning. Freud, in *The Ego and Group Psychology*, explored the psychology of the group-tie, an affect-bond more vertical than horizontal, in that it has more to do with identification with the leader, the incorporation of ideology and the forging of a new, group-inclusive sense of self, than with the recognition of fraternal similarities, plain likeableness or human warmth. By this affiliation, one delegates auxiliary ego-functions to the group.

Those who become active in politics encounter a unique set of associa-tional vicissitudes and their accompanying emotional shocks, and the identifying of such stock predicaments helps us to understand their careers — the exaltation, for example, of ideological conversion, the candi-date's 'delusion of success' (which may be a reactivation of primary narcissism), the weariness of sustained campaigning,[26] and the bitterness and emptiness of losing a cause. The diaries provide, on a modest scale, instances of all these — as well as registering, more agreeably, the sense of confidence won from small tasks competently despatched.

But on important occasions in politics, large new affects, affect-shifts, or the slow accumulation of tensions go unaccommodated by existing structures. If they are intense, prolonged and sharpened by propinquity or

(Footnote continued)
admired politicians and grow tall with them by projective identification; they partially delegate control of their affects to public persons ('I won't scare on this till Senator Button does'); and, by putting up for years with ineffectual leaders who merely pass muster and look vaguely right, they ensure that politics will for long periods quite pass them by.

feats of leadership, such affects may become group-constitutive, and a new movement is born. The novel affects may be the product of new life-stresses, a change of ideals, an intellectual discovery, a relaxation of scruple, or some dense amalgam of these,* but the movement has the shape of a storm: it impends, blows up, rages and dies out. Once under way, the constitutive affects become tempered and complicated by considerations of strategy and timing, factions form under rival leaders, and a gulf opens between bureaucrats and enthusiasts.[27] The surge and decline of such great novelties constitutes the largest object of political curiosity; if the tale to be told is not throughout a story of affects, it can never depart too far from them without the sense of losing the central thread.

We now leave such generalities for the testing examination of particulars, but it may be prudent, after these last pages, to remind ourselves of the main injunction we carry forward from the pioneers of the study of political affect — we must never forget 'the *notorious disproportion* between responses and immediate stimuli in politics', the clue to which is to be found in repetition compulsion and our vast and extraordinary amnesia for what happened in our own childhoods.[28]

---

* How, for example, would the reader classify the predisposing factors in the 'spirit possession' movement in Salem, Massachusetts, in the 1690s — in which children and servants momentarily inverted the power structure by claiming privileged access to the spirit world?

9   *The principal affects*

Moral indignation

This affect has its poet, Juvenal, and its sociologist, Svend Ranulf, the author of two considerable and original books of lasting interest, *The Jealousy of the Gods* (1933) and *Moral Indignation and Middle Class Psychology* (1938). In the first of these, he asked why systems of crime and punishment differ so notably from one society to another, especially on matters like capital punishment, theories of deterrence and the so-called 'crimes without victims' — alcohol, contraception, incest, abortion — where opinions differ not only from country to country but among different classes and groups in one society. He put as his principal question: 'At what intensities is the disinterested tendency to inflict punishment correlative with what other phenomena?'

He chose first to study the origin of the urge to punish in relation to the rise of the criminal law in late Athenian society:

> The study of this community may be expected to be particularly
> instructive because it is possible to observe there how the disinterested
> tendency to inflict punishment arose out of nothing. Before the time
> of Drakon, the Athenian state seems to have assumed a perfectly
> neutral attitude towards acts of violence or outrages committed
> among private citizens. Everybody had to defend himself to the best
> of his ability with the aid of his kinsmen. Nobody came to his assis-
> tance if he and his family could not manage by themselves. After
> the time of Solon, the State was to interfere and punish . . . first a few
> and later on a greater number of such encroachments at the request
> of any citizen, even if the sufferer neither defended himself nor comp-
> lained of the wrong he had suffered.[1]

He noted that the new habit of punishment coincided with the rise of the theme of the jealousy of the gods in Greek drama. Common to both, he suggested, was the tendency to envy. The people who had become sud-denly envious were the rising lower middle class, who were particularly jealous of the rich and powerful, and whose moral indignation was a kind of resentment caused by repression of the instincts in a group uniquely forced into strict self-restraint and frustration of its natural desires.

Durkheim had remarked, a generation earlier, that punishment was altogether a more serious affair for the upright than for criminals or would-be criminals,[2] and G. H. Mead had added that moral indignation against criminals helped law-abiding citizens to affirm their solidarity with convention and to inhibit their own delinquent feelings.[3] Ranulf's argument, however, comes nearest to that of Franz Alexander, who said that the demand for punishment is addressed primarily to the pressure of our own forbidden impulses, and that the punishment of any offender compensates for the restrictions we constantly put on our own aggression, and alleviates it.[4]

In *Moral Indignation and Middle Class Psychology*, Ranulf extended the analysis to English Puritans, and, briefly, to German Fascists, again endeavouring to establish the mood of moral indignation from the contents of the media of communication to which large numbers of the community were voluntarily exposed — in the Puritan case, principally pamphlets and sermons — and to trace its culmination in a general programme of repression. Lasswell, in his penetrating introduction to the American edition,[5] objects that Ranulf pays too little attention to upper-class initiatives in coercive legislation in Athens and London, and to their defensive indignation at their threatened decline.

A work that usefully extends Ranulf's concerns is J. R. Gusfield's *Symbolic Crusade* (1963), which makes the onset of a mood of moral indignation the critical thing to be explained in the history of the American Temperance Movement. In its first thirty years, he explains, the leading affect of temperance workers had been sympathy and pity for the victims of alcohol, and their strategy had been one of 'assimilative reform', an invitation to the drinker to follow the reformer's example and lift himself to middle-class respect and income. In the mid 1920s, however, both strategy and affect changed dramatically. The temperance advocate now principally felt anger and hostility towards the non-conforming victim; he no longer saw him as someone to be pitied and helped, but as an intractable defender of another 'culture', who rejects the reformer's values and does not really want to change. The thing then was to force his compliance, legally to proscribe alcohol, and so to affirm symbolically the legitimacy of the temperate life-style, and its social dominance.

Ranulf, he observes, would attribute the onset of moral indignation to resentment caused by repression of appetite and a condemning of what is envied. But this does not explain how assimilative reform was possible in the earlier period when the victim was pitied rather than condemned, and why the main target of the Dry's indignation was not members of the same class or local community — who were greater threats to his 'tenuous system of internal controls' than the Catholic urban lower class or the urban upper-class Church member against whom he *did* campaign.

Gusfield's explanation is in terms of status-loss. In the earlier period, abstinence was the public morality, the dominant way of life of the professional and business middle class, and this class was the culturally dominant one, although the rural pattern of life was increasingly giving way before urbanisation. In such conditions, the attempt to 'cope with' the problems of the poor, the alien, the downtrodden and the conditions in factories and urban slums affirmed the reformer's sense of special status — indeed, he could also roundly denounce the rich for their excess. To be abstinent was above all a claim to respectable middle-class status, which embodied the national ideal of thrifty and prudent behaviour.

By the mid 1920s that ideal was seriously in question, especially in the urban middle class, and the Drys began to sense that history was passing them by. Status, or life-style, conflict of this kind, Gusfield says, is endemic in politics — and of the highest importance:

> Discontents that arise from the status order are often as sharp and as powerful as those that emerge in the struggles over income and employment. In a society of diverse cultures and of rapid change, it is quite clear that systems of culture are as open to downward and upward mobility as are occupations and persons. Yesterday's moral virtue is today's ridiculed fanaticism. As the cultural fortunes of one group go up and those of another group go down, expectations of prestige are repulsed and the ingredients of social conflict are pro- duced ... Most movements, and most political acts, contain a mixture of instrumental, expressive, and symbolic elements. The issues of style ... have not lent themselves well to political analysis. Those issues which have appeared as 'matters of principle' now appear to us to be related to status conflicts and understandable in symbolic terms.[6]

But it is hard to see why Gusfield so strictly separates 'status' from 'psychological' explanation. Surely conditions in which the status advan- tages to be gained from abstinence rapidly evaporate are exactly those to exacerbate envy, and to make the burden of restraint seem heavy indeed. And the fact that the 'scandalous' behaviour of the urban poor is made the justification for prohibition by no means proves that the project of confiscating at the same stroke the pleasures of the cheerfully drinking middle-class neighbour went entirely unregarded. In the case of an Australian 'wowser'[7] politician I studied some years ago, I felt the roughly equal pull of the secular decline in the status of Methodist rectitude and the stress of maintaining a personal system of 'tenuous' internal controls.[8]

In recent days, Gusfield informs us, the American Temperance Move- ment has merged into the general pool of American political and religious fundamentalism constituting the Radical Right, but he has little here to add to Riesman's classic analysis, in *The Lonely Crowd* (1950), of the politics of the 'moralist-in-retreat' (which also draws on Ranulf's categories). In Riesman's account, envy of the successful and powerful is compounded by the sense of being denied a place and of falling increasingly behind. 'Politics, like ... character,' he says, *'curdles* when lack of success reveals and renders intolerable [a] lack of understanding.' The typical 'curdled' indignant's experience of life

> is ... disappointing; he is deprived of a feeling of competence and place ... neither his character nor his work is rewarded. In that situation he tends to turn both on himself — for he is vulnerable to lack of worldly comprehension even more perhaps than to lack of worldly success — and on the world. In a last desperate effort to turn the country back on its inner-directed course so as to make it habitable for him, he is ready to join a political movement whose basic driving force is indignation ... Indignants have hold of one of the great traditions of American politics. This is the tradition of asking the government to govern more than it knows how to govern — as in the case of prohibition ... In line with this tradition, the indignants of today can strive to 'get the law' on those movements in culture — in literature, the movies, the universities, the libraries — that symbolize urban sophistication and tolerance.[9]

Definition

What is the difference between *moral* indignation, and ordinary indignation? First, there is often an added element of *disinterestedness*: the reformer is usually not directly or personally affected by the conduct he condemns. This contrasts with the anger caused by, say, physical injury or economic want or loss. The individual's feeling of *righteousness*, and his sense of his claim to be listened to, is augmented by this personal 'distance' to which he can point with pride. Gusfield, indeed, notes that 'The object of indignation has not only violated *my* norm; he has violated the socially dominant norm and I have a legitimate right to indignation.'[10] And Strawson defines moral indignation simply as 'resentment on behalf of another'. 'One can feel indignation on one's own account, but [moral indignation is] essentially capable of being vicarious.'[11]

Secondly, the transgression is primarily moral, though it may be mixed with other forms of distress, loss or pain.* Because of their ideological inclinations, however, people tend to turn most severe pains almost at once into moral questions — an offence against property speedily becomes one against propriety. Moral indignation, in a word, is typically felt by the conventional for the unconventional.

Further, the target of hostility in politics is more likely to be a conceptual group than real individuals with whom the individual comes into close and regular contact — such targets call up elements of social distance and

---

* Being overlooked, neglected, or treated with indifference or condescension may, however, be a reliable enough spur to moral indignation, in politics as in ordinary life, to be specially noted.

malign stereotypy. In personal life, Strawson suggests, moral indignation is expressed differently in situations where the offender is seen as a morally responsible agent (and *guilt* is in order) and in those where he is not (situations which give rise to questions of 'intellectual understanding, management, treatment, and control').[12]

Ordinary and moral indignation are alike, however, in that both involve a sharp reaction to a provocation or piece of unjust treatment (though moral indignation may tend to be more easily sustained because of its link with some enduring ideology or value-system). Both involve singling out a target victim or group as the cause of one's trouble. Both carry a desire to punish (at the very lightest, to demand an apology or confession of guilt), to degrade or symbolically to demote.

One cannot insist on too sharp a distinction. An aesthetic outrage, for example, falls somewhere in between. But it is important to see in the background the possibility that the personal life-space of the moralist may, indeed, in the long term be directly threatened by the condemned group, in the sense that its success may very well erode the framework of conventional living, which gives comfort and meaning to the indignant.

We regularly test for cant or hypocrisy in the 'moralist'; we listen more courteously when we can spot no publicity motive or personal advantage, or when he is 'sincere', and so forth, in his advocacy. On the rare occasions when we detect envy behind the condemnation, the case collapses; and it weakens whenever we spot 'undue' interest — the anti-pornographer's concern with forbidden matters — or signs of personal over-sensitivity to the issue.

Moral indignation is a relatively pure and raw affect: one can be fairly precise about what is provoking it, how strong it is, and what action it prefigures.

Objects of moral indignation

We may be as curious about the way moral indignation is put aside as about how it is acquired. What remains of the Temperance Movement continues to deplore the brewer, the publican and the common drunk, but Gusfield notes that in these last days the prime target of hostility has become the sherry-drinking Church member. Political groups are indeed prone, when their main assault has collapsed, to turn on their nearest ally—as the Communist party reviles the Socialist party of Australia, or student radicals abuse the liberal staff.

The contemporary thrust of Protestant rectitude — and it is joined in this finally by Catholic opinion — is against the permissive society. Drugs are a more spectacular provocation than alcohol. But the central issue is the management of sex, and war is waged along a very broad and ragged front, which takes in the censorship of pornography, the availability of contraceptives, abortion law reform, divorce law, and the status of homosexuality. The metaphor of 'laxness' unites for crusaders the campaigns on the various fronts, and they are apt, in pursuit of this central, undermining tendency, to involve themselves also in attacks on progressive education and economies in defence. Like the Drys in their militant period, current anti-permissives are less interested in assimilative reform, the sympathetic and patient re-shaping of victims along ideal lines, than in symbolic affirmations and denunciations — the putting down of evil. In saying that it is too late in the day for pitying groups who do not wish to reform, they also protest against their declining cultural status and the spreading neglect of their values.

There is less the sense of one common struggle among the permissive reformers. Dennis Altman has mapped the antipathies between homo-sexual and women's liberation groups, as well as black campaigners for racial equality,[13] and Leo Abse's progress-report on English reformist legislation illustrates the patchiness of even vivid enthusiasm.[14] But these groups are, if possible, even more indignant in temper than the crusaders — indeed, on occasion, they reach record levels of intensity — for example, the New York radical lesbian slogan, 'A lesbian is the rage of all women condensed to the point of explosion.'[15] Recruits are coached in hate — 'consciousness raising' is in fact training in affect-pitch and stamina — encouraged to abandon self-deprecation, and to project maximum aggression on to the stigmatising other. Within the liberation movements, politics centres very much on intensities of affect: a militant 'left' cannot find acts too extreme or aggressive, while a reluctant 'centre' continually recoils and fears the back-lash this attitude will bring. Rival leaders offer alternative strategies, but they work in a public climate which is, in this area perhaps, permanently cool, mistrustful of protest and new claims on attention, and which has a strong disposition to store up outrage.

Other style-of-life issues generate sporadic heat, nationally and in local groups: these include conservationist, anti-pollution, and 'ecological' protest, and anti-bureaucratic agitation — including the anti-fluoride, anti-medical-establishment, right-to-privacy, and anti-data-bank lobbies — an intriguing mixture of new radicalism and threatened comfort which reminds us that indignation is the special property both of the tight-laced new man and of the sagging Establishmentarian. It is striking, too, how indignation has ebbed away from the old 'positional' issues of politics, such as socialist control of production (the multi-national corporation, 'selling the farm', carries what indignation remains) and inequality of living standards — although pensioners, or single mothers, or (in Australia) aborigines, may win special sympathy. (Oddest of all for Australians is the transmutation of the narrow, materialistic Country party into a life-style group, its supporters' economic security having been achieved at the same time as a general subsidence in esteem.)

Our sample registered a clear 7% of its political response as moral indignation. This could, perhaps, be doubled with less laconic entries, and ordinary anger reduced proportionately. The fact that about 1 in 10 of these entries concerned the activities of common criminals (we urged the widest possible definition of politics) alerts us to the enduring value of Ranulf's insight — moral indignation's prime function is still that of branding crime. Additional political outrages spread out from this core in five main directions. First, some 40% charged political groups or figures with sadism, undue aggression or ruthlessness in their actions (Watergate was the principal item, closely followed by American bombing in Cambodia). The indignation was sometimes raw and powerful:

> — Nixon! Completely disgusted. Could hardly read . . . so upsetting.
> — Diffuse political anger: local Right merger proposals; Agnew; 'accidental' bombing of Phnom Phenh. Couldn't someone accidentally bomb New York?
> — Disgusted, horrified, passionately angry with the U.S. and the American hypocrisy which condemns Hitler but creates Vietnam — three times the bombing of world war two! . . . and the corrupt puppets of the South Vietnam Government.

Secondly, another 40% made accusations of lying or fraud. The Press itself frequently came under fire, but the principal target was leaders who falsely represented themselves as stronger, wiser or more caring than they really were; for example,

> — Anger, scorn and contempt for Santamaria [a Conservative Catholic publicist who had attacked state aid for church schools]! — the first extreme political affect for the month.

Obstinacy and disobedience made a third, small category — for example, doctors resisting a health scheme for which the government had a recent mandate, the French persisting with nuclear tests despite a ruling by the International Court of Justice at the Hague, and Nixon stalling over Watergate. In a fourth cluster of entries, moral indignation was the obverse of a stronger sympathy with some deprived or disadvantaged group, and was directed against the hated but nebulous 'They' who were held responsible. Finally, in a small burst of *identification* with the criminals, anger was turned on those 'mistreating' them (policemen, gaolers, advocates of hanging).

A good or bad thing?

The genital character is able to act forcefully in politics, but entirely without moral indignation.

(W. Reich)[16]

We hold in uneasy suspension in our minds two perfectly contradictory hunches about moral indignation. On the one hand, something in us assents to Reich's judgment; moral indignation *is* a kind of 'noise', in no way helping us to find faster or more efficient remedies for abuses or to clarify aims — on the contrary, it impairs reality-testing, especially perhaps the sense of an opponent's real character. One would like it, from this point of view, to be totally banished, or used only as a signal affect, a sign that we still had work to do adjusting our feelings before arriving at a sense of proportion in a piece of politics. On the other hand, there are certain pro-vocations (cruelty, torture, slavery, genocide) about which a person must be able to feel indignation if he is not deeply sick.[17] We may feel, too, that people are in general so hard to rouse that appeals to moral indignation may well be indispensable in change and reform. The natural condition of moral indignation is a short flicker (then unconcern closes over again), but to get political *action* — through agitation and the disciplined pressure of concerted demands — this original, raw affect must be refined into a dependable, even economical, fuel. Sometimes, then, we see moral indignation as all bad,* and sometimes as the only humanly fitting res-ponse. Significantly, on the issue that most succinctly epitomises the choice between renouncing and indulging moral indignation — the aboli-tion of the death penalty — public opinion currently breaks even, for and against.

Is it impossible to expect agreement on judgments of how much moral indignation is appropriate in particular cases? It certainly seems difficult. For example, a criminologist recently offered findings to show that police-men are more authoritarian than ordinary citizens, demanding heavier punishments for most types of crime. At once a critic protested that the police response was perfectly understandable and not necessarily 'authori-tarian';† they simply had closer dealings than did the public at large with the suffering of victims of crime, and greater sympathy with that suffering. One feels some pull towards both interpretations, although it is probable that an initial over-concern with punishing crime has influenced recruit-ment.

Could we not, perhaps, start at one end with extremely idiosyncratic cases — anti-fluoride protests, for example, or doctors' opposition to health insurance — where most would agree that the 'threat is being wildly over-stated, and contrast them with, at the other end, cases like Watergate, where we may legitimately be as indignant as we like, and then work in from these extremes towards the debatable centre? Yet the crusaders are hardly put off by our scepticism. They 'know': they simply see the matter

---

* We see it sometimes, more finely, as depressing. One diarist complained that he 'couldn't stand reading the Letters to the Editor columns, because they were all from persons temporarily beside themselves with rage and struggling to fit their outrage into 300 words'.

† 'An unusual appetite and capacity for moral condemnation of wrong-doing and of out-groups generally' is a leading element in the classic authoritarian syndrome.[18]

more clearly and in proper, ominous context, and feel that their anger is perfectly in keeping; and it may even be sensible to deplore the gloating* character of the U.S. Press's hounding of Nixon.[20]

We may do better to start out from the observation that the morally indignant person has *ipso facto* taken up a stance *denying empathy*. Does this not build in a probability of inappropriateness? If we ignore whatever the object of our dislike attempts to tell us, because we *know* the nature of the offence, or the real truth of his aims and character, we, in effect, pre-empt intelligent compromise, understanding and learning. Riesman was very right to stress the link with ignorance. There is also a link with sadism — the tendency of the morally indignant person is to see the social atmosphere permeated by foulness, and to conjure with images of inferior, dirty and evil-smelling enemies, which leads in the end to treating opponents in outright fury as moral or material refuse.

We warned ourselves at the outset that the question of the appropriateness of political affects would be central and terribly hard, and we need not perhaps feel too discouraged at our failure to clarify at once the bounds of legitimate indignation. Several more affects at least may need to be looked at before we see a path of any real advance. But a small practical test for the propriety of the individual's moral indignation does suggest itself: how free is one to adjust it by at least a notch or two after, say, reflection, discussion, and further enquiries. One suspects that it is above all in rigidity of posture that we find the underpinnings — based in ideology or in character — of neurotic performance.

Rising or falling levels?

Where are the reservoirs of moral indignation to be found in present-day politics? According to Gusfield, they are to be found in the *losing* groups — the aged (politically, rather firmly thrust aside); the depressed middle-aged, especially the parents of rebellious adolescents;[21] those with a primary or 'secondary only' education (who fall behind in sheer understanding and basic political skills); the 'stuck' manual or white-collar worker; the lower-income suburbanite resentful of inflation and the Welfare budget (the 1972 Nixonians);[22] and the 'wowsers'. Secondly, these reservoirs can be found among groups of somewhat ambiguous status: farmers (a rich but now 'stupid' group); doctors (the first profession to be hit by the consumer revolution); and the 'welfare

* Here cartoonists, as they do so often, expose the basic fantasy at work — in this case anal reaction-formation. In the standard Watergate cartoon (at least in the critical month when our sample kept a diary) little Nixon clings terrified to a thin pole just up out of reach of a swelling tide of black, evil-smelling filth. The public takes up the exultant mocking position of the three-year old pointing out a younger sibling's failure of bowel control (his own so recently and precariously achieved). He *gloats* because now not just 'I' but the Rules declare him inferior and a disgrace. The French bomb obstinately tested in the Pacific which aroused our sample was also importantly a 'dirty' one.[19]

and creative' professions,[23] especially sharply nipped by 'incongruities of status'.[24] Thirdly, they may be found among the rising groups: young people, acutely preoccupied with the moral sleaziness of middle age; the new sexual radicals — protesters for homosexual or women's rights; and so forth.

In the perspective of a single generation, is the level of indignation in these reservoirs on the whole rising or falling? Lasswell, writing in 1964, says it is falling:

> In complex industrial civilizations deep moral indignation appears to be a diminishing element in the total system of control. Industrial societies provide many highly diversified environments in which norms vary somewhat from one another. Under these conditions the conscience (superego system) is likely to become less uniform or peremptory.
>
> When destructive impulses are less subject to the inner discipline of conscience, both public and civic order find protection in calculated expedients rather than in deep moral indignation. 'Criminal law' is assimilated to other prescriptions in the legal system and sanctions become more corrective and less punitive.[25]

He argues further that with the development of science and our increasing reliance on 'disciplined calculation ... contextuality and expediency' in social affairs, much of the need for moral indignation as a support for the social order is removed. 'In fact its erratic course under rapidly changing reality conditions can undermine public and civic order. Society learns to play it cool.'[26]

Against this it could be urged that the steady replacement of 'position' issues by 'style' issues multiplies opportunities for, and indeed incitements to, moral indignation in public affairs. As the permanent, somewhat disciplined, and reasonably predictable political party declines in importance, more and more of the action is initiated by 'single-issue' groups. Frank Parkin has shown, for example, that at the height of its power in the mid 1960s, the British Campaign for Nuclear Disarmament drew less than 40% of its members from the Labour party; almost half of those who did generally support Labour nevertheless said that they would probably prefer a straight C.N.D. candidate in a poll; and 80% of C.N.D. members urged that 'the Labour party should put principles before power', i.e. espouse unilateral disarmament even if it meant losing the next election. On the other hand, C.N.D. members had an impressive record of serial or concurrent membership in groups dedicated to the abolition of capital punishment, opposition to Apartheid and racial discrimination, homosexual or abortion law reform, and abolition of censorship.[27]

It is a good deal easier to get worked up about race, peace, abortion or hanging than about the price of barbed wire or postmen's wages, and a large and growing middle-class group, centred in the 'welfare and creative' professions, seems to be refining a view of politics as an expressive activity, where protests and demonstrations are worthwhile for their own sake, as an affirmation of principle, whether or not they achieve concrete results. The burgeoning local community permanent-protest lobby has a similar social composition and emotional core. A succession of 'this year's causes' provides the rallying point and symbol for earnest radical endeavour, and, since success is not the overwhelming concern, such energies can be rapidly switched from one topic to another — each typically providing a focus beyond the scope of any major political party.

Either way, we should guard against simple, direct extrapolation. The new incremental, middle-class moralism may, indeed, be a mere eddy in a tide generally going out, but, as Riesman reminds us, social fashions in moral strictness tend to spiral — 'Congreve, living in a reign of postwar tolerance, might have been surprised at the recurrence of moralization in the Victorian Age.'[28] However, we should not be surprised to find that tastes in moralism are basically generational; Plato, after all, in the brilliant Ch. 8 of *The Republic* taught us to see in the sons' recoil against the fathers' shortcomings the basic source of change in social and political régimes.[29] And, in recent times, explicit theories of child-rearing have so influenced parents' practice as to provoke, as it were, collective controlled experiments in the shaping of the super-ego.[30] The personality-types of the 'wowser' and the authoritarian are now widely recognised as the product of minority, indeed, deviant patterns of parenthood. Lane subsumes both in his category of the 'moraliser', the man with an exaggerated need to feel moral, whose anxious message is: 'I am not sinful.' Such men demand clear rules and strong authority, and, Lane says, 'may indeed be better off in conservative, moralized societies'.[31]

The 'moralisers', we suspect, are those exposed as children to repressive discipline, [32] but, where it takes a sharply political turn, we may discern the special marks as well of the 'displacers *par excellence*', the odd brave men able to stand up for conscience in difficult circumstances,[33] or the 'rage-type' (Lasswell).*[34]

Our discussion may inadvertently have exaggerated the amount securely known in these matters. It may be salutary, then, to reflect briefly

---

* Arthur Koestler, re-telling the story of his conversion in 1931–2, aged 35, to Communism, paints a vivid picture of himself on these lines:

'It did not require much persuasion to make me into a rebel. Since my childhood I seem to have lived in a state of Chronic Indignation. When this state reached its peak, I joined the Communist Party ...

This type [the chronically indignant] seems to depend on a specific quality: the gift of projective imagination ... which compels one to regard an injustice inflicted on others as an indignity to oneself; and vice versa, to perceive an injustice to oneself as part and symbol of a general evil in Society ...

The event that roused my indignation to a pitch never reached before, was the American policy of destroying food stocks to keep agricultural prices up ... at a time when millions of unemployed lived in misery and near starvation ...

Woe to the shepherds who feed themselves but feed not their flocks! Indigna-

on our own poor knowledge of the springs of, or the targets of, our personal political indignation. *Half* of it, perhaps, we may predict; the rest astonishes us as much as it surprises our friends, and in a further, awkward corner are the not too rare occasions when we cannot pump up the indignation all those about us feel. Much about moral indignation — not least its erratic quality — remains to be understood.

Anger and hatred

Introduction

Unlike moral indignation, anger is *not* disinterested. It is brought on, Shand says, by painful blows, overt or threatened attack, insults, deceptions, thefts, neglect, interruptions at food or sex, and once provoked it takes regular forms. These include the impulse to destroy — we bite, break things or dash them to the ground, slam doors, strike, pursue, attack, maim, and kill; the impulse to overcome opposition when obstructed, to threaten or warn off when an attack impends; the impulse to revenge a past injury; the impulse to discipline the disobedient or insubordinate, to protect dependants and the defenceless. We also find it in more complex forms. Mixed with pride or hatred, we get cruelty — the impulse to inflict pain; mixed with love, we find punishment in order to reform (and threats of punishment, withheld love or righteous anger); mixed with pride, we have the project of humiliation in return for humiliation — the 'cold anger of pride', often unconscious.[1] All varieties involve some aggression, and are thus binary with fear, which seeks essentially to avert danger in some pacific way.*

Seneca thought anger was always useless: by being

> over-hasty and frantic, like almost all desires, it hinders itself in the attainment of its object, and therefore has never been useful either in peace or war ... No man becomes braver through anger, except one who without anger would not have been brave at all.[2]

(Footnote continued)
tion glowed inside me like a furnace. At times I thought that I was choking from its fumes; at other times I felt like hitting out, and shooting from a barricade, or throwing sticks of dynamite. At whom? It was an impersonal fury, directed at no individual or group in particular ... My seething indignation ... was directed at the System in general, at the oily hypocrisy and suicidal stupidity which were driving us all to perdition. In my rage-fantasies no people were killed but huge buildings burst open and their walls came tumbling down as if in an earthquake — Ministries, editorial offices, radio stations, the whole *Sieges Allee* with its hideous statues of princes and field-marshals ... My political latency period had come to an end'.[35]

* Shand devotes a whole chapter to the question whether fear and anger are mutually exclusive, and notes that they do often seem to alternate, as the individual hesitates and alters course in relation to his predicament and his response. But fear can be bound into the anger-system, and vice versa: both are present in jealousy and in the care of the young, and they become altogether fused in cruelty.

Anger *is* rash, capricious, unstable, impulsive, comes suddenly and leaves us when we could still use it; it stubbornly eludes us sometimes when our need of it is greatest. But it has its advantages, Shand urges: 'It brings to us a force of a peculiar kind, carrying with it a sudden accession of energy, preventing us from succumbing to fear and cowardice, making us, at least, momentarily brave'; and it is serviceable, setting at our disposal so many pointed weapons for a great range of purposes: it can be used 'not only against material, but also against spiritual opponents, making us angry with our own weakness, indolence, despondency [and] lack of spirit and perseverance'.[3]

By itself, the flash of anger — which tends to exclude ideas, escape control of consciousness and *surprise* us — means little. It becomes significant when it calls into play the anger-system — an enduring organisation of aggressive 'impulses towards a person or class of persons:

> With the growing importance of ideas as causes of the emotion, and of ideas as complicating, prolonging, and directing the course of it, and of the sentiment as moderating its intensity or restraining its irreflect-ive, spontaneous outbursts, the emotion . . . comes to assume a posi-tion of predominant importance . . . But . . . the emotion . . . having once acted as a stimulus to the action . . . often becomes suppressed, while other parts of the emotional system are active. Though the feeling of anger may come back as a sudden throb when we recollect the injury, when some new obstacle intervenes, or yet while we are occupied in avenging it, as in a duel . . . attention is concentrated on the difficult art of the struggle . . . and the emotion is frequently excluded.*[4]

Raw anger contains the moral potential for risking life or for taking it.

The anger-system of most interest in politics is that in the service of hate, and especially 'irrational' hate, or hate of inappropriate intensity.

> Since [hate] is composed of habitual bitter feeling† and accusatory thought, it constitutes a stubborn structure in the mental-emotional life of the individual . . . By its very nature hatred is extro-punitive, which means that the hater is sure that the fault lies in the object of his hate. So long as he believes this he will not feel guilty for his uncharitable state of mind.[7]

The targets of anger

Any political group or actor may attract the hatred of others, and all, indeed, do so. From 'dislike', 'annoyance', 'impatience' or 'irritation',

---

* The anger system can even work without any feeling of anger — when the opponent is so insignificant and our own power so preponderant: 'Thus we destroy a fly or a wasp on the window-pane without a trace of angry emotion' (Shand).[5]

† 'As a mordant fixes a dye in the fabric of a textile, so does bitterness fix hostile aggression; that is, bitterness changes anger into hate.'[6]

the feeling builds up through 'frustration', and 'anger', 'indignation' to 'rage'* or 'fury'. Our diarists, except for some painful personal encounters, directed their most intense anger to world politics. American bombing in Cambodia and French nuclear testing in the Pacific generated between them about one-third of their anger. But, over the month, the governments of South Vietnam, Russia, Singapore, Mexico, Iran, Japan, Belgium, Eire, Northern Ireland and England were also sharply disliked, censure fixing mostly on aggressive words, threats or deeds (few, indeed, directly affecting Australia) or on slow-burning, internal 'oppression'. When aggression was linked with 'criminality', the anger took on an overlay of moral indignation, as with Nixon and Watergate (the largest single item) or a current hijacking. The focus, however, was very much on world leaders as embodiments of their nation.

A rather richer set of properties ordered domestic anger, which was also less intense and less sustained than that projected on to foreign nations. Local groups and actors were indicted of weakness, pusillanimity, flippancy, bickering, narrowness, stupidity, and speaking out of turn, as well as for aggression, arrogance or greed. Questions of style rose to rival questions of substance, and censure extended to the Press which regularly 'disguised' or 'distorted' the meaning of critical events. Subjects' anger, though, seemed somewhat routine, even dutiful, as they deplored checks to the fortunes of 'their' groups, or the gall or good luck of opponents,† and showed, above all, an extremely wide scatter of concern:

> ... meat export levy ... noise pollution ... judge on *Clockwork Orange* ... grant to Showgrounds ... editorial in *Herald* ... defence cuts ... ambulance strike ... young Liberal leaders' style... Right to Life poster ... rise in numbers of 'fat cats' ... radio talk-back views ... doctors' fee rise.

Few of these items stirred more than a handful of subjects.

In personal encounters, however, anger again was stronger. Diarists took offence as citizens at their treatment at the hands of public authorities; they took offence as consumers at poor goods or service; they were annoyed as debaters by the tone or outcome of arguments with family or friends, and as rank-and-file members they were angered by their leaders' performance at meetings or conferences

---

* Implicit in the term 'rage', there may be the fear of 'headlessness', of losing the head (and mind), of being beside oneself.[8] Extreme rage is close to a convulsion. The young Darwin's interest in the expression of the emotions was first caught by Spenser's description of rage in the *Faerie Queene*.[9]

† To this Labour-inclined group, the federal Leader of the Opposition emerged as the 'man you love to hate' — he was disliked almost as often as Nixon. Note the conflicting pull of contempt and anger. 'In contempt, our anger conflicts with a more powerful sense of avoidance. The anger insists on confrontation and concern; the contempt demands distance and indifference.'[10]

('In the [political] club — great fury when someone I resented having authority over me wanted to impose their will on me'). Most interestingly, they were angry as political connoisseurs or critics in protests about 'political climates' at work or in voluntary groups (too much and too little participation were equally deplored), or in revealing, face-to-face meetings with social 'counter-types':*

> — A selfish, rich, old, anti-Government lady infuriates.
> — A drug-addicts' parson smarming on about 'situational morality' — a pretty doubtful helper, I'd say. Thank God, he's not mine.
> — Anger and contempt for Commerce students observed at a party. They're creepy parasites totally equating education and money.
> — A new guy at work, a real live Gordon Comstock, in his shabby, denim jacket. He prizes his worn Maoist thoughts, wants to change the world on totally revenge motives, lacks human compassion, is totally destructive.

However informative on the topology of anger, the diary entries tell disappointingly little about its dynamics. In particular, they fail almost entirely to bear upon the concepts of 'the enemy' or 'the scapegoat' hypothesised in the literature as the two main devices harnessing hatred to politics. Admittedly, half a dozen diarists reported their suspicions that anger provoked in their personal life on a particular day was somehow displaced on to a public figure in the news or on to politics in general; and we catch a glimpse of the 'enemy' rubric in some of the more partisan domestic stances or in attacks on 'world capitalism' or 'U.S. imperialism', and something a little stronger in the 'counter-types' — the sense of political self-definition being achieved and maintained by the elucidation of what one is *not* ('Thank God for mine enemy' ... 'I hate, therefore I am').[12] But, in the modest state of our knowledge of these matters, even very simple illustrations of how enemies are made or scapegoats used would have been welcome.

The Enemy

It is conventional to regard enmities as giving politics its basic structure, and the hatred and mistrust they engender as its leading affects. Individuals are frequently powerless before group pressures to hate and fight; we inherit our enemies along with our loyalties and pieties. Yet we do manufacture some with our own hands. Enemies are those whom we define as such, and this, if we act on it, is likely to prove self-confirming. But to sustain hatred as enmity we need to see an enduring opposition and a continuing, if not cumulative and intensifying, struggle. And we need to believe in *their* enmity towards us — their hatred and their plans to destroy us — which it is the prime task of ideology to reveal.

---

* This may be extended without much strain to include 'para-social encounters'[11] on television.

Once a group has taken on the image of the enemy, we have something of a self-perpetuating system: 'The other party is viewed within the
framework of an "inherent bad faith" model, which itself denies the existence of data that could disconfirm it.'[13] Holsti has explored with some
ingenuity the ways in which John Foster Dulles, in his years as U.S.
Secretary of State, was able to minimise all information tending to dis-
credit his fixed image of the U.S.S.R. as an implacable enemy — essentially
by 'reducing complexities to simplicities, ruling out alternative sources of
information and evaluation, and closing off to scrutiny and consideration
competing views of reality'.

In psychiatry, enemies exist to be explained away: the secret service
agents who continually spy on the normal, dilapidated paranoid are sheer
hallucinations — though the larger idea that his life arouses a good deal
of hostility among neighbours and acquaintances will be quite shrewd.
But in politics, the problem is less to explain the existence of real enmity
between groups, or even the way in which irrational exaggeration and
fixity of the enemy's image grow and survive, than to account for the fact
that the two are nearly always found together, so that irrational hatred
always accompanies and adds additional force to legitimate hostility.[14]
Lasswell put it succinctly in his study of *Propaganda Technique in World
War i*:

> When the public believes that the enemy began the War and blocks
> a permanent, profitable and godly peace, the propagandist has
> achieved his purpose. But to make assurance doubly sure, it is safe to
> fortify the mind of the nation with examples of the insolence and
> depravity of the enemy. Any nation who began the War and blocks
> the peace is incorrigible, wicked and perverse. To insist . . . upon these
> qualities . . . is to make it more certain that the enemy could be
> capable of so monstrous a thing as an aggressive war. Thus, by a cir-
> cularity of psychological reaction the guilty is the satanic.[15]

In a prolonged conflict, normal reality-testing falters and dies, and selective perception takes over. Each side grossly idealises its own cause, the
struggle becomes a moral crusade, a final engagement between Good and
Evil.

The existence of such an enemy strengthens a country's domestic
solidarity and morale. Hitler noted in *Mein Kampf* that

> The art of all truly great national leaders consists among other things
> primarily in not dividing the attention of a people, but in concentrat-
> ing it upon a single foe.[16]

This merely echoes Theodor Herzl's observation, sixty years earlier, that
'A nation is a historical group of men of recognisable cohesion, held
together by a common enemy.'[17] Dr Soekarno's comic confrontation of
Indonesia's 'encirclers' in 1962—3 attempted to reap similar benefits.

In a recent essay reflecting on the broad course of World War ɪɪ,

Shibutani offers a useful supplementary sketch of the domestic processes by which each side in a tense conflict closes ranks, silences dissidents, brands shortcomings as enemy propaganda, rewards the brutal and aggressive, makes the enemy an 'It' (and thus beyond moral care), and passes the leadership progressively into extremist hands.[18] The dismantling of demonic conceptions at the end of the conflict may be astonishingly rapid — or obstinately slow, requiring the demise of the generation that took part in the fighting, as with Australian images of the Japanese.

Enemy pairs tend also to grow alike. It is not just that they find the same faults in each other — thus, during the Cold War, both Americans and Russians declared: *They* are the aggressors, *their* government exploits and deludes the people, *their* policy verges on madness[19] — but they adopt mirror-image postures and strategies of attack. Australians, for example, have watched with interest the anti-Communist lay organisation sponsored by the local Catholic Church speedily take on the discipline, secrecy and phobic attack of its adversary. Anna Freud's defence mechanism of 'identification with the aggressor'[20] has a prime role to play in explaining the dynamic relationship of enemy pairs in politics.[21]

The Scapegoat

Few ancient and powerful ideas can have lost so much definition, in becoming common contemporary currency, as that of the scapegoat. 'Everyone knows' now that when the enemy cannot be attacked directly, either because he cannot be identified or because he is out of range or because there is some conflict about confronting him, hatred will be displaced on to a substitute target, which in some way resembles him, but which is innocent and, if not defenceless, relatively powerless.[22] Indeed, one school of psychologists has attempted, by the systematic teasing of small laboratory groups, to uncover the principles underlying such displacements — but this sort of approach trivialises a basically religious notion out of existence. Restored to its anthropological context, the scapegoat is less a substitute for the enemy than a clue to his nature and to the way in which he must be treated.

In all its forms, the use of a scapegoat is a ceremony, a ritual affirmation of collective beliefs and social cohesion, and it sometimes evokes a fairly flat or shallow hatred, as, for example, in the Moslem ritual of the Casting of the Stones. At Mina on the tenth day of the Pilgrimage to Mecca, pilgrims drawn up at a distance of not less than fifteen feet of three stone pillars (the first called the Great Devil) must cast seven stones at each one, intoning, 'In the name of God, the Almighty, I do this, and in hatred of the devil and his shame' — a ceremony performed ever since the days of Abraham.[23] The hatred is contagious and intense — contemporary pilgrims throw their shoes as well — but 'un-interiorised'. The enemy is out there with a stone face, and 'we' unite in lambasting him. Politics teems with such flat enmities and simple modes of declaring them: the Reds, the Japs, Whitey, male chauvinist pigs, and so forth.

The pilgrims, meanwhile, are unassuaged. On the road back from the Stones, they proceed each to sacrifice a goat, horse or camel (according to his means), and thereby call upon notions of cathartic sacrifice, and sin. The killer is here deeply implicated with his scapegoat: he feels he has within him something that has possessed him and from which he must at all costs free himself; he loads the animal with this and, with its death, is purged and guiltless once more.

In the form with which we are most familiar* — the ancient Jewish ceremony, described in Leviticus, in which the whole community is purified — two goats are required, one of which is slaughtered as a sin-offering (the sins of Israel having been transmitted to the animal) and the other simply driven out. Money-Kyrle has succinctly explained the rite through the notion of the destroying power of sin.

> It was only the goat that was driven away that bore the sins of the people. Thus there was a sort of double purification. First the sins were transferred to one goat. And then, perhaps because this goat was still too nearly identified with the people, or with a son god, another was taken to die in its place.
>
> Those who partook in such rites were aware only that there was something within them that attracted a remorseless and undying hate, and that this something must be removed or they would surely perish. They did not know that this hate was their own hate of their fathers, nor that it had turned upon them because they had gratified in unconscious fantasy their desire to be its object.[25]

Psychoanalytic writers on the Nazi persecution of the Jews, the most appalling modern re-enactment of the primitive ritual, largely affirm this identification of the guilty wish of those who demand a scapegoat.[26]

In ancient rite, the scapegoat purification was a regular ceremonial, and the 'victimage' predictable and token. Kenneth Burke, more than anyone, has insisted that modern societies, despite their loss of the religious faith that would buttress public redemptive rituals, or perhaps because of it, have as great, if not greater, capacity to fall into states of guilty unease and thus to demand human scapegoats for relief.[27] Elements of the ritual remarkably survive extension into modern times. There is nowadays, however, no single, all-purpose scapegoat, such as Tertullian described for late-Imperial Rome:

> They take the Christians to be the cause of every disaster to the state, of every misfortune to the people. If the Tiber reaches the wall, if the Nile does not reach the fields, if the sky does not move or if the earth

---

* Innumerable other varieties of tribal scapegoat practice are catalogued by Sir James Frazer in *The Golden Bough*, and medieval patterns are well-established.[24] We lack a description and codification of modern scapegoats.

does, if there is a famine, or if there is a plague, the cry is at once, 'The Christians to the Lions'.[28]

Instead, there is a demand for a scapegoat precisely fitted to one time and place. In the purge trial, for example, a victim is chosen who will perfectly fit the guilt he is to assuage, and he is coached in his sacrificial role.[29] He must embody a *principle* of evil, so that when he is tortured and killed, a principle is destroyed and not merely a person. Other societies allow a market in scapegoats, where demagogues compete. But trivial scapegoats will not serve, and one cannot appease hunger by distributing blame among many different victims:

> [To] say in effect: Let one fragment of the curative victim be in the villain of a Grade B motion picture, let another fragment be in a radio fool, another in the corpse of a murder mystery, another in the butchery of a prizefight, another in a hard-fought game, another in the momentary flare-up of a political campaign, another in a practical joke played on a rival at the office ... [may simply] add up to a kind of organized inanity that is socially morbid.[30]

The need for a scapegoat always brands some group as the categorical cause of social disorder, marks them down as *evil*, whatever they do, and often before they act at all. Once singled out, the group can be treated as strangers and enemies, and dealt with in ways that would be intolerable if directed towards fellow group-members ('nothing that is alien is human to me'). In war, indeed, we may attribute the irrational ferocity of our hate to the fact that our enemy has become our scapegoat.

Aristotle claimed that we can successfully hate only impersonal enemies, whole classes of people: to hate individuals one knows brings too much guilt — they are too much like ourselves, their qualities too mixed. There is also no 'body-image' of a group to get confused with our own; and we can more readily sustain negative group-stereotypes against reality-testing by making convenient 'exceptions' of the individual members we happen to know.[31] Must we 'generalise the stimulus'[32] to harness our hate to politics?

One diarist, closely involved with Women's Liberation groups, lamented her inability to 'sustain political intensity over anything'. Compared to the radical movement members' 'continual outrage and ready moral indignation, my own emotions keep flagging. My political stereotypes keep turning into men, and fallible men at that.' Another reported a double process. Cheated by a Jewish woman shopkeeper over a pair of expensive boots, she experiences an 'anti-Semitic storm'. She felt 'huge anger — considered writing to the papers, going to court ...' In fact, she wrote to the Consumer Protection Agency, which informed her that since the shopkeeper had agreed to repair the boots, she had no case. 'From an awful sense of frustration — nothing to be done — I fell into an extreme depression — self-reproof for the anti-Semitic thoughts — I didn't know I was capable of that! – then passed to a sense of the futility of life and general mistrust.' Here, hatred for the person was strengthened, rather than mitigated, by being 'generalised' to the stereotype, but that very step aroused still more intense – indeed, paralysing – guilt.

'The Government' as a political blame-object is conveniently 'general': it is powerful, moralising, its great arsenal of sanctions has a permanently threatening aspect, it can equally be assailed for the actions it takes and for those it fails to take.[33] But note the institutionalised hunt for the person to blame or hate when public disaster occurs:

> Let there be a prison outbreak, an escape of a homicidal maniac from a state hospital, or an exposure of graft in the city government, and a hue and cry go up. There are outraged editorials and irate letters from the public. Sometimes these voices name their own scapegoat, sometimes they merely cry for one. Anger wants a personal victim, and wants it now.

In the course of the official enquiry, the onus seems to shift rapidly from one accused party to another.

> As the emotion wanes, the demand lessens, and the final punishment is generally milder and more limited than the initial clamor demanded. One feels at the end of such an episode that one [blame- or hate-object] is sufficient, and that his punishment readily brings a closure to the brief period of distress.[34]

A moment's thought about vindictiveness, however, or about strategies of revenge or that ur-political phenomenon, the vendetta, shows that Aristotle's view of hate is too sanguine. Our understanding of these things at any depth is, for that matter, newly won, and derived from the master concept, narcissistic rage.

We owe this concept to the Chicago analyst Heinz Kohut.[35] He explains its genesis in the politics of a professional association:

> I was at that time President of the American Psychoanalytic Association, and I was puzzling about dissensions within our group, and particularly about the fact that people who seemed to have been friends suddenly turned and became enemies. I learned to recognise that almost certainly, if one looked hard, one could always find some small, but nevertheless undoubtedly important narcissistic injury at the pivotal moment that determined the later inimical attitude of such an individual. It is like the story of the author in *Anna Karenina*, whose book is slammed by a reviewer, and the author remembers that two years ago he'd met him at a party and corrected *one word* the man had said. Now, as reviewer, with the author's book before him, he could avenge that slight.[36]

Narcissistic rage, according to Kohut, consists in

> The need for revenge, for righting a wrong, for undoing a hurt by whatever means, and deeply anchored, unrelenting compulsion

in the pursuit of all these aims which gives no rest to those who
have suffered a narcissistic injury.[37]

He explains that *beneath* it there is always to be found an uncompromising
insistence on the perfection of the idealised self-image, and on the limit-
lessness of the power and knowledge of a *grandiose self*.

> The fanaticism of the need for revenge and the unending compul-
> sion of having to square the account ... are ... not the attributes
> of an aggressivity which is integrated with the mature purposes of the
> ego — on the contrary, such bedevilment indicates that the aggression
> was mobilized in the service of an archaic grandiose self ... The
> shame-prone individual who is ready to experience setbacks as nar-
> cissistic injuries ... does not recognize his opponent as a center of
> independent initiative with whom he happens to be at cross-purposes
> [and] ... cannot rest until he has blotted out a vaguely experienced
> offender who dared to oppose him, to disagree with him, or to out-
> shine him ... The enemy ... is seen by him ... as *a flaw in a narcis-*
> *sistically perceived reality.*

Prime illustrations of a personality so extremely prone to rage and revenge
are, he suggests, to be found in Kleist's Michael Kohlhaas,[38] and in Kaiser
Wilhelm II,[39] but more generally as well:

> In the setting of history, narcissistic aspirations, hurts to one's
> pride, injuries to one's prestige needs, interferences with conscious,
> preconscious or unconscious fantasies of one's greatness, distinctness,
> of one's own efficacy and power, of one's specialness, of the special-
> ness of the group that one identifies with ... are important motiva-
> tions of group behaviour, and can be imbricated with many other
> forces.[40]

The well-springs of anger

If our task were merely to analyse unit-cases of hostile provocation and angry response, we might indefinitely put off looking at the
deeper sources of anger and hatred, since there always seems enough
to go round. But, after a time, this very over-supply — the sense in politics
and social life of legitimate hostility for ever billowing out into hate-
systems of inappropriate intensity — itself makes us curious about the
evident levels of excess capacity in the social reservoirs, and about the
cause of this excess. Hence the excitable writing about naked apes, terri-
torial imperatives, primordial aggression and the death instinct. But
biology over-explains: if our human worst is always perfectly natural,
it becomes pointless to worry at current levels of aggression. Indeed, our
problem becomes that of explaining how, given the in-built bias towards
destruction, societies have for long periods managed to contain it, and
secure civic order and relative peace.

The more manageable model of an anger fund, in principle calculable
for a given society at a particular time, somewhat along the lines of the

classical economists' wages fund, was proposed 25 years ago by Talcott Parsons, in an essay of which the outlines still hold firm.[41] Adapting a scheme devised for use with a single primitive tribe,[42] Parsons suggested that one should add to the sum of frustrations and dammed-up anger generated in adults by their contemporary environment (especially in work relations) the sum total of hoarded hostility and aggression they carry forward from the pain of a conventionally-patterned childhood; the result will give the total of all the 'free-floating aggression' available in that society for all manner of projects and applications.

The notion that particular angers merge and accumulate to provide the potential for protest and violence seems true to our knowledge of individuals, and its extension to social aggregates is eminently plausible. It does seem possible, too, that sensitive observers of a society over several decades might well succeed in identifying the larger movements, the peaks and troughs, in a national anger fund, although unable to be very explicit about their indices. The economic climate is the best studied of these indicators, and the business cycle and terms of trade movements can be readily identified, but *social* indicators for the factors Parsons stressed, such as the stress of competition and the burdens of specialist responsibility and of constant change, are still some way off. He offered no guess at the normal, relative sizes of the childhood and adult layers of the fund — although he did say that 'probably the kinship system has to absorb more strains originating in the occupational system than vice versa',[43] and stressed their mutually reinforcing processes, such as the pressure in both towards compulsive masculinity. The important thing was that both generated much larger quantities of anger than they could absorb and then demanded that the greater part of it be held in repression; and that gross potential aggression could be reduced by reforms in either sphere.

Two themes stand out in Parsons's account of the generation and damming-up of anger in American childhoods: a preoccupation with adequacy, achievement, and being superior, and with fairness and the probability of being 'let down'; both of these are dangerous prototypes for future relations with social out-groups and foreign nations. His analysis turns largely on sex-role learning and highlights the strains and discontinuities for children of either sex in the necessary parental identifications. (One feels that it is nowadays harder for little girls, and that little boys have an easier time.) He altogether misses the pains of the pre-Oedipal phases, the sheer discipline and thwarting that occur in childhood, and the central Oedipal hatreds themselves (which, as Lasswell has shown, pre-eminently seek a political outlet).* But fine psychiatry

---

* Compare this statement of Arnold Rogow's: 'The murderous hostility toward [President] Johnson that existed among youth ... may have derived from the unconscious suspicion that he was not entirely innocent of some connection with the death of John F. Kennedy. In the unconscious of some young people the death of Kennedy at the hands of persons unknown ... but including

is somewhat beyond his purpose of demonstrating the existence of a significant store of hostility, which has been denied expression, but refuses to die, and which can be kindled to multifarious social uses — in practising witchcraft for the Navaho, or (in the case of modern nations) treating minorities as scapegoats, or waging aggressive war.

To know the level of the fund — even that it is dangerously high — would not, by itself, allow us to predict any particular outcome. We need, Parsons warns us, to know just as urgently on what targets the anger is trained, and what possibilities there are of depressing, deflecting or projecting' it elsewhere; in short, what curbs and channels it. We reserve these questions for a concluding section.

While the project of a national summation of angers may seem daunting,[45] if not finally impractical, situations in which the calculation of a group anger fund* is commonplace and crucial to political success, are common. The union secretary, for example, who descends precipitately on a plant in turmoil has, above all, to assess the pitch of locals' anger — and (uncomfortably) often gets it wrong, finding either that he cannot take a firm line with management, or that the terms he has won are contemptuously repudiated by the rank and file. Most bargaining in politics is informed by shrewd estimates of the anger-levels involved, and leaders' cases become 'strong' in the measure that they can point behind them to intense feeling. Unit-angers become the base counters in traditional bargaining politics and seasoned politicians are adept at its measurement in their own and opposing groups.

The special facet of the notion of an anger fund that has attracted most later attention is its quantum character at any time.[47] May it not be that the amount of overt anger plus the amount of covert anger is always equal to unity? May this not also be true of the sum of self-directed and other-directed anger? Lasswell noticed this early on:

> Immobilising neuroses and psycho-somatic illnesses internalise many of the hostilities aroused in everyday life, protecting, to an unknown extent, the social system against reform.[48]

Propositions at this level of metapsychology are difficult to bring to a test, but the idea of the 'functional equivalence of anger forms' (Dollard),

(Footnote continued)
LBJ may have been experienced as the murder of a younger, more virile son (and brother) by an older, impotent father, a father jealous of the son's very youth, good looks, vigor, and greater success.'[44]
* cf. Abram Kardiner on the 'enormous amount of free hatred' in Plainsville, fed by 'suppressed self-assertion' ('Plainsvillers are "against" self-assertion, no matter what form it takes'), and shown in the 'malicious and endless gossip . . . the suppression of free sexual expression, the universal feeling of inferiority, the hatred of progress . . . the low status of women . . . the brutal kidding of children, the universality of stinginess'.[46]

and, for that matter, of targets for anger, is necessary to the fund scheme in order to sustain the pressure towards multifarious release. The theoretical alternative would be to postulate strong dispositions to become angry not because of a general grievance which has been hoarded for years, but only in some very specialised conjunction of form and object, so that the hater will remain unconcerned in any other situation.

The making of the hostile individual

Fromm's description of the 'character-conditioned' hater makes him, indeed, an ideal contributor to the anger fund: the distinguishing trait is 'a continuous readiness to hate, lingering within the person who *is* hostile rather than reacting with hate to a stimulus from without'. What he hates is of secondary importance. It may happen to coincide with realistic threats, but is more often chosen quite gratuitously and then hastily rationalised. 'The hating person seems to have a feeling of relief, as though he were happy to have found the opportunity to express his lingering hostility . . . [his] passion to destroy or cripple life.'[49]

His polar opposite, the personality built round the inadmissibility and denial of his hatred, is the schizophrenic, as described by Frieda Fromm-Reichman, whose primary problem is not his anxiety about others, but fear of his own hostile, destructive tendencies, which he abhors as much as and more than his environment. All his symptoms, she says, and his delusions, hallucinations, catatonic stupor and excitement, persecutory ideas, flow from this.[50]

Between the extremes there is room for a variety of types who are extremely prone to anger. The anal character, for example, is given a special chance by politics, because of his preference for *indirect* aggression. He is typically a 'reactionary'; that is, he holds rigidly conventional views with aggressive passion, and is able to make good use of current frustration in his long-standing covert revolt against authority.[51] The authoritarian projects his hate on to the environment in a diffuse, intense and irrational way;[52] he is especially hostile towards the powerless – the very sight of them makes him want to attack, dominate and humiliate them.[53] The psychopathic personality, bent above all on aggressive action, is of less political interest, but his low tolerance of frustration and his proneness to externalise and project hostility are qualities whose developmental roots urgently concern us.

As well as hate-filled characters, we find those who are merely hate-capped, for whom hatred is a sort of detonator: people so anxious, amorphous, or dejected that only a vengeance-project can draw them into shape.[54] Politicians rejected by the electorate or by their peers have not seldom waged fierce campaigns of narcissistic restitution in this mood. The great lift in most ideological conversions in politics springs from the redirection of hate involved — from self to enemy — and its intellectual legitimation. And neurotics will often set out to be hated a little, among their immediate circle, in order to confirm their wavering sense of self.[55]

In broad plan, the notion of a fund not only suggests that a high, pent-up pressure of anger in a society will mean high levels of overt aggression,* but that the direct expression of anger has a relieving, even cathartic, effect: an overt attack drains away hostility, at least for a time. Yet an anger-*system* may clearly sustain a steady series of attacks, even a series mounting in intensity; and no sooner may one system be 'satisfied' and dismantled, than another may spring up immediately to take its place. The one tight anger-state, then, can bring a single, cathartic, aggressive act, or a dissatisfying one that demands a stronger successor, or no act at all, if hostility is inhibited before the action-threshold. The difficulty of predicting from anger-pressure to outcome has been so copiously demonstrated in laboratory experiment as to raise in sharp form the question of the general rationale of explaining behaviour by means of affect.† The fact that an affect, however intense, may always be 'disowned' and set aside after conscious thought, is only the most acute case in a general situation in which *transformation* is to be expected of affects in the course of their provenance. We should perhaps come to think of *spirals* of affect as our units of analysis, with the expectation of one or more switches of vector as the person is wound (or winds himself) through a full affect-experience. In any case, among the likeliest places to look for these individually comprehensible units of feeling in politics is in the recurrent processes that awaken, harness or curb public anger.

Awakening, harnessing and curbing anger
Awakening anger

In modern China, Lucian Pye tells us, political awakening has largely come as 'a fit of anger'.[58] To become politically aware has been to recognise the nation's humiliations and to suffer a powerful sense of shame driving one directly to a passionate hatred of China's enemies. Under Communism, both the extolling of hate as a positive virtue and the search for enemies have been carried to new extremes. Yet, in Chinese society outside politics, hostility is frowned on; indeed, within the family, it is ruthlessly suppressed. This, then, is what stokes the fires, as it becomes suddenly possible and legitimate for all the accumulating tensions of parent-child relations to be expressed in this one field. And, in 'standing up, being conspicuous, being reckoned with', and, above all, 'exuding hate and

* A recent comparison of English and Italian 'hostility levels' rather dents this assumption: there was no difference in *latent* levels, but a much lower rate of *expression* of them among the English.[56]
† Indeed, in test situations, highly aggressive subjects seem even to have an inconsiderate tendency to inhibit their aggression more than others.[57]

anger', the young political activist is deliciously turning inside out the worst possible emotional experience within the family, that of being brought to book and publicly shamed.

The case is extreme, yet helps us catch in the most ordinary political conversion the intrinsic appeal of the aggressive stance, the somewhat adolescent exhilaration of at last pitting oneself against historic enemies. Salzman's acute study of the 'pre-conversion state' characterises it as a struggle with 'hatred, resentment and hostile destructive attitudes', and shows that drastically to change their target is the basic function of the new beliefs.[59]

The 'awakening' to politics — through anger — of Western student radicals has a similarly standard form:

> Youthful dissent assumes many of the same aspects in many countries ... The first expressions of dissent in action are usually in the form of non-violent civil activity (or civil disobedience) in support of the 'higher ethic' of society. Then these tactics are carried back into the universities by ethically motivated youth from the wider movements in protest against the manifest inadequacies of the multiversity ... The first 'occupations' and 'sit-ins' consolidate the convictions of young people about the problems with which they're concerned and bring them face-to-face in activity with them for the first time. The authorities fail to react at all, or over-react in a punitive way — in either case failing to deal with the youth leaders who at this stage are usually fairly moderate. This creates resentment (students have either been ignored or punished) and it discredits the moderate leadership. As nothing substantial has been achieved the protests continue, evolving an ever harder line — and the protest develops a rationale of its own, as students repeatedly find in their involvement a community of spirit, a feeling of belonging, a shared idea — for a time alienation is overcome. Gradually single-issue-oriented protest (against the draft, the war, the arms race, maladministration, injustice in the multiversity) disappears and the young seek total moral solutions in the adoption of a totalistic ideology in the hope that a concerted attack on the whole structure ('the revolution') will succeed where piecemeal protest has failed — or in the total rejection of the dominant culture.[60]

To what extent is a political leader free to invent new scapegoats? Nkrumah, for example, switched, in about 1964, from British to American imperialism as the main Ghanaian persecutor, and appeared effortlessly to carry his people, long sensitised to the notion of a predominantly malicious environment, along with him.[61] Yet when he went, his successors, of notably less paranoid disposition, managed to dismantle most of the scare paraphernalia and govern comfortably without it. A plethora of extreme right-wing groups can at any time be found competing with their individual lists of improbably-linked enemy groups, and rouse little interest. Parsons stressed that the in-group/out-group pattern into which social hostility is channelled is longstanding and coercive.

But it is too simple to chain anger-arousal to enmity — in politics, as in ordinary life, outbreaks of hatred and violence have a habit of erupting after friendly overtures or substantial success or any sudden increase in pleasurable emotion. Edrita Fried, plotting these occurrences in a large clinical sample, diagnosed a peculiar form of 'ego weakness' in people who

> relate to their environment primarily through processes of incorpora-
> tion and identification. That is to say . . . the capacity for experiencing
> external objects — whether human beings or things — as separate and
> not necessarily unfriendly entities has not sufficiently developed.
> Under the impact of intensified stimulation and increased closeness
> to others, they experience a heightened and threatening sense of
> fusion with the environment . . . and . . . self-differentiation is lost.

They experience a conscious and vivid sense of 'ego weakening', and call in hostility as a remedy, to detach the self from a world that threatens to engulf it.[62] Mannoni, in a study we shall examine at length later, traced the brutal revolt of the Malagasys against French rule in 1947—8 to a marked relaxation of colonial authority, which was received without gratitude, indeed, read primarily as a threat of abandonment.[63] The emotional energy of the Papuan separatist movement evidently has similar roots.

Harnessing anger

Political movements intensify, hoard, refine and bind anger and hatred. They set up circumstances in which conversions are infectious and mutually reinforcing, in which the group's very growth validates its special perception of an 'enemy-mined' environment, and in which particularly aggressive, doctrinaire and self-righteous behaviour and thought are honoured (cf. the Baader-Meinhof gang's slogan, 'Hate 24 hours a day!'). Ideology binds anger by proving that hostility serves a purpose — and can be, and is being, deployed according to some systematic and efficacious strategy. The movement's rules and leadership supplant the individual super-ego, which no longer has to grapple with guilt at feelings of hate; one is now either right or wrong in one's hatred, never at fault for it.[64] The new line encourages hostility also towards one's old beliefs and associates, and the sad consequences of such perspectives. It provides euphemisms for ugly new tasks and actions.

Movement membership also involves complete acceptance of a new and higher authority, one that cannot be hated and must be loved, 'solving' the long-carried strains of ambivalence towards parental authority by splitting and idealisation — to produce a sense of peace, oneness, and even re-birth.[65]

Knowing the rough shape of the members' concerns, the political leader sets out, by bringing them into relation to his scheme of ideas, to sharpen them: he redirects old staple affects to new provocations, makes conscious affects which were previously only dimly perceived; his very rebuffs and frustrations by authority or opponents heighten the wrath of his supporters. In time, the core-memory and calendar of the movement become filled with ceremonial dates and anniversaries, each prompting and reinforcing hatred of the enemy. Fully broken in and harnessed, the movement member reacts at once to the lightest commands of the leader, and the leader can count on practised and eager obedience over a wide emotional range.

Curbing anger

While leaders will often wish to hold the anger of their followers to some optimum that will sustain a particular strategy, and may have to work hard to convince hotheads that patience and restraint in the short term will bring eventual success, there is a peculiar interest in the psychology of the group forced by its circumstances to maintain drastic curbs on its anger over long periods of time.

Abram Kardiner's classic analysis of the Negro personality puts this at the centre of the picture.[66] Constant experience of discrimination undermines self-esteem and builds up aggression, but hostility, because it is socially disastrous, cannot be expressed. A whole set of automatic, unconscious manoeuvres, which 'make things look different from what they are', is thus necessary to replace aggression and restore self-esteem, and to legitimise ingratiation and passivity. Keeping the system going means, however, being 'constantly ill at ease, mistrustful, and lacking in confidence', and severely constricts the range of emotional expression.

> Fear and rage become almost interchangeable. When the manifestations of rage are continually suppressed, ultimately the individual may cease to be aware of the emotion. In some subjects the *only* manifestation of rage may be fear.[67]

Among the techniques for disposing of rage, he lists: suppressing it — by submission, compliance, or ingratiation (in proportion to the amount of suppressed hatred); attenuating it — by resentment; controlling it partially, but with leaks and irritability — or else controlling it successfully for long periods followed by an explosion; denying it altogether and replacing it with gaiety and flippancy; or turning it back on the self in depression or somatic complaints (headaches, hyper-tension). In the case histories, he found all these varieties in all kinds of combinations, but the 'two commonest end products of sustained attempts to contain and control aggression were low self-esteem and depression' — the final results of the continuous failure of a form of self-assertion. Subjects' Rorschach protocols abounded in mutilation responses, and suggested 'a real discrepancy between the stimuli coming from the outer world and the available resources for organised mastery', reminiscent of schizophrenia, which shows that 'the subject feels he is being disintegrated by the onslaughts of forces he cannot ward off'. In the case of the Negro, even simple anger

> must also be checked. Hence, the aggression must be denied, imper-
> sonalized, treated with aloofness, intellectualized, watered down,
> replaced by pollyanna-like attitudes, or made into wish-fulfillments.
> All of these modifications ... distort reality, and, when they are
> carried out repeatedly and habitually, they permanently disturb the
> effective integration of the self to the environment.[68]

While two decades have brought great changes in the social admissibility
of Negro anger, Robert Coles's studies of young children's drawings show
the persistence of the mutilation theme.[69] Australian aborigines conjure
similarly with a 'horrible' and potentially lethal rage and struggle individually to throw off the stigma of blackness as 'repulsive ... an incurable
disease'.[70]

Envy, inferiority and resentment
Introduction

William Winstanley wrote that 'we often make a parade of our
passions, even of the most criminal; but envy is a timid and shameful
passion, which we never dare avow'.[1] The inadmissibility of envy *is* striking. An American professor of anthropology has for several years asked
students in a large undergraduate course

> how many believe themselves to be: (*a*) virtually without envy;
> (*b*) moderately envious, or envious on occasion; (*c*) very envious.
> About 50% of the responses fall in the first category, 40% in the
> second, and only about 10% in the third. Moreover, the 90% who
> deny major envy tend to be vociferous and argumentative: it is a
> personal affront to them to suggest that they are much more envious
> than they care to believe.[2]

And when, in 1955, Geoffrey Gorer asked a random sample of 11,000
English adults to declare their 'worst fault', only two named envy. He
comments:

> This is not due to the employment of faulty categories, for I started
> with the presumption that envy was a major characteristic of many
> English people, and I was constantly alert to any reference to this ...
> The conclusion seems inescapable that either the envy is not recog-
> nized, that it is unconscious, or that it is not regarded as a sin or fault.
> I do not think that it could be denied that in the political appeals
> and actions of the last decade envy has played a major rôle; that
> in the policy of 'fair shares for all' the desire to see that nobody
> has more has been at least as important as seeing that nobody has
> less. Perhaps envy has received so much justification that it is
> no longer felt to be a sin, but is regarded as an aspect of a desire
> for justice ... If this be the case, the remarkable self-knowledge, self-
> criticism and honesty of the English, which I think this study has
> demonstrated, has a blind spot.[3]

Popular denial has been matched by scholarly neglect, as every page of Helmut Schoeck's lively and readable *Envy* (1970) makes clear.[4] (As we shall see, however, poets have rather effectively spread themselves across the disputable terrain.)

What is so painful about envy? Why must we seek to hide even from ourselves this angry feeling that another possesses and enjoys something desirable, and our impulse to take it away or spoil it? It is, of course, socially deplored: Anglicans, at least, regularly pray to be 'delivered from it';[5] parents work manfully to extirpate its grosser manifestations in their children. But why is it purely and simply disturbing and unsettling to experience? There is the sense of lack, of want unpleasantly unfulfilled as we contemplate the other's good fortune:[6] there is the negativism of wishing principally to 'spoil', to hurt, without necessarily having a use for the envied object ourselves, to confiscate, above all, someone's superior enjoyment, (which Horace caught in his defining phrase – the 'very ink of the cuttlefish'). But there is something more, something that is felt as self-destructive and corrosive:

> As iron is eaten by rust,
> So are the envious consumed by envy.
>
> (Diogenes)
>
> Envy and wrath shorten the life.
>
> (Ecclesiasticus, XXX 24)

The Book of Proverbs defines envy as the 'rottenness of the bones'. At its core lies the discomfort of an acknowledgement of inferiority – a narcissistic wound, an ego-chill, if not an ego-eclipse, as we make out that someone else is better endowed and therefore better loved. 'People who are much at the mercy of envy have learned to appraise themselves as unsatisfactory – that is, as inadequate human beings.' Envy is funda-mentally whatever disturbs low self-esteem.[7]

Salzberger-Wittenberg's rehearsal of the domestic and familial occas-ions for envy gives us a somewhat firmer grip on the contours of the affect itself.[8] There is, first, the girl or woman's envy of the boy or man's penis, and the reverse, the boy or man's envy of the girl or woman's organs of procreation:

> Envy relates to the creative functions associated with sexual organs: not just the possession of a penis but male potency ... male asser-tiveness and penetrating intellectual power. Equally, a woman's capacity to grow and nourish an infant and female intuition and sensitivity can become objects of envy.

Men also envy men who are superior in some way, and women envy women. Children envy parents, not just for their strength and knowledge, but also for their partnership, 'the couple who are creative together'. Conversely, mothers may envy the beauty or creativity of their daughters; fathers may envy the strength and youth of their sons. Finally, envy may accompany the jealousy informing triadic relationships:* the husband, as well as being jealous of the wife's relationship with her lover, envies his ability to be more potent and attractive; the young child, jealous of the mother's relationship with the new baby, envies her ability to make and feed a baby, and the baby's ability to command care.† 'Strong feelings of envy lead to despair . . . and a vicious circle arises in which one's inability to love or be lovable makes others still more enviable.[12]

Social occasions for envy cluster, first of all about the obvious disparity of fortunes: the poor envy the rich, the weak the strong, the helpless those who wield power. The child-parent analogy is close — '*I*' feel weak and helpless, '*they*' seem 'all-knowing, in control of themselves, and able to cope with any eventuality'. Secondly, it springs from actual deprivation, a dearth of satisfying experiences. Thus those suffering 'the loss of function, the loss of youth, bereavement, the barring from promotion' feel hostility to those who are better off, who withhold help, who 'cause' the privation. Envy, then, begins with the parents, and passes on later to other adults, 'society at large', or to whole groups like the rich, the upper class and '*Them*' — even, negatively, to the carefree delinquent who gets away with it.

What is envied is at first 'food, security, comfort, relief of pain and all the life-sustaining functions.' 'Klein . . . found evidence that such feelings of envy originated . . . in the baby's relation to the breast.'[13] Later, we envy 'popularity, success, wealth, health, youth . . . freedom, creativity, love, beauty, intellect, integrity', even enthusiasm.‡[14] Individuals are more hated for their non-transferable, admired qualities than for any other reason, a source of hatred that can hardly ever be admitted. Envy can disrupt both learning and creativity. ¶

* It is now common to locate envy in relationships that involve two people, and jealousy in those that involve three.[9] But some writers persist in a simpler reciprocity: envy desires to gain something another possesses; jealousy fears to lose what it already has. One defence against acknowledging envy is, indeed, misnaming it 'jealousy'.[10]

† An anthropologist writes of Egyptian childrearing: 'It is assumed . . . that the knee-baby is always jealous of the lap-baby, and the yard-baby is jealous of the knee-baby ... It is also acknowledged that the youngest child becomes jealous immediately his mother's abdomen becomes enlarged on pregnancy and he is usually told of the forthcoming event.'[11]

‡ 'The objects producing envy are legion . . . In primitive and peasant societies three items — food, children, and health — rank far above others. 'Together these items produce a 'package': 'the survival of the family unit as the basic social and productive unit of a society . . . In more affluent societies traces of envy behavior associated with food, health, and children survive . . . [but] wealth and power, and the good things they are thought to bring (including prestige and status), are perhaps the most common items causing envy' (Foster).[15]

¶ It disrupts learning where the situaton of being dependent, a learner, has to be denied, or the teacher's ministrations are seen less as help than as 'showing

There are, in invidious circumstances, positive alternatives to envy, such as admiration; and, Melanie Klein says, admiration permits gratitude, an affect as hard as envy to allow ourselves to feel, and which is, indeed, its obverse.* Gratitude can only appear when, and to the extent that, envy has been subdued.

A second alternative is emulation, where we set out in some way to acquire the envied objects or qualities ourselves (dropping back again to envy, perhaps, if we should fail). Conspicuous consumption indirectly, and advertising directly, induce competitive emulation. Children's identification with their parents embodies this reaction in its most serious and potent form.

It is this emulative outcome of envy that keeps alive one side of a perennial debate on whether envy is purely 'the rottenness of the bones', or whether it can be harnessed to activity, ambition and achievement:[18] 'A man shall never be enriched by envy' against 'Envy's a sharper spur than pay' (Gay). Others separate or fuse the two strains:

> Envy, to which th' ignoble mind's a slave,
> Is emulation in the learn'd or brave.
>
> (Pope, *Essay on Man*)

> Envy is not an original temper, but the
> natural, necessary, and unavoidable effect
> of emulation or a desire for glory.
>
> (William Law)

A third reading sees the two strains as alternating, so that one strives for a while, and then stops in order to take stock, only to find that one's endeavours have fallen far short; one then falls into envy, and is only able to rise and struggle again when this envy has been mastered.

It is difficult to draw a neat distinction between envy and feelings of inferiority. That one lacks another's qualities or possessions need not, itself, provoke either: it is only the invidious comparison of *valued* qualities that bites in. But, once this happens, all negative self-feelings tend to run together. Oliver Brachfeld reserves the term 'minus value' for this darker state.

> So long as envy remains in the realm of Having and leaves the roots
> of Being untouched it will be a normal and perfectly justifiable feeling
> of lacking something. But as soon as this lack, this have-not, is
> transmuted into a being-minus, we find ourselves in the realm of
> pathology, of inferiority feelings and all their consequences.[19]

(Footnote continued)
off'.[16] Harold Bloom's *Anxiety of Influence* (1972) sympathetically studies the plight of the poet burdened with the envy of the great predecessor he has made his model.[17]

* 'In most of mankind gratitude is merely a secret hope of further favours' (de la Rochefoucauld).

Scheler paints the darkest picture of this state:

> The most powerless envy is also the most terrible. Therefore *existential envy*, which is directed against the other person's very *nature*, is the strongest source of *ressentiment*. It is as if it whispers continually:
> 'I can forgive you everything, but not that you *are* — that you are *what you are* — that I am not what you are — indeed that I am not you.'[20]

In the deeper layers, feelings of guilt, impotence, insufficiency, insecurity, inferiority and envy all run together in a more or less consciously felt 'lesion in the self-esteeming, self-affirming function' (Brachfeld).

Just as we traced the origins of envy to the child's feelings about its parents, the deepest source of inferiority feelings may be rooted in

> the childhood conflict between the progressive wish to grow up and be like adults on the one hand and the deep regressive force towards the early dependent forms of existence on the other hand. Whenever this regressive wish makes itself felt the ego which identifies itself with the progressive attitude reacts to it with the feeling of inferiority.[21]

Both these essentially narcissistic affects are learnt very early.

Although envious behaviour may thoroughly pervade society — in competition, conspicuous display, denigration and confiscation — we must reconcile ourselves to getting very few glimpses of envy in its raw state. People will almost invariably insist on giving some other name to what they are doing or feeling. We must be prepared, indeed, to infer its presence from the very pressure and strength of the denials that it is at work. But people erect other and more complex defences against its acknowledgement, to which we now turn.

Defences against feeling envy

Knowing the pain of envy, the individual may go to considerable lengths to diminish occasions for it. He may, for example, choose friends or colleagues who are not up to his standard or are clearly worse off in some way, whom he can patronise. Certainly a relationship which continually provokes envy is likely to be felt burdensome, and dropped. Melanie Klein has written of the greedy and ambitious

> type of public figure who, hungry for more and more success, appears never to be content with what he has achieved. One feature in this attitude . . . is the inability to allow others to come sufficiently to the fore. They may be allowed to play a subsidiary part as long as they do not challenge the supremacy of the ambitious person. We also find that such people are unable and unwilling to stimulate and encourage younger people, because some of them might become their successors.[22]

The Australian Prime Minister, Menzies, had, to a notable degree, this Upas-tree effect upon his close following, quickly driving talented ministers from his cabinet, cultivating a personal circle of genial dullards and showing scant regard for the problem of succession. Within six years of his departure, three misfit successors had quite dissipated his party's seemingly invincible lead.

The principal strategies in common use appear to be these:

The envied may be *disparaged* or *devalued*[23] — a spoiled object arouses no envy. As with the fox and the grapes, the message is that what *they* have (that I cannot get at) is not worth having.

The disparity between envied and envier may be *rationalised*, in terms, say, of fate or luck — circumstances having nothing to do with worth. Responsibility for one's relative failure is removed from the self to ineluctable or arbitrary forces.

The envied person or group may be put on a pedestal and *idealised*. Exaggeration of the star's worth strives to keep him or her out of the reach of envy, but it is a precarious strategy, since the closer the star is to the admirer's ideal, the more it *deserves* to be envied: in the long run, envy usually catches up.* I recall a friend of my student days, who held off for two years from joining the Communist party, because he thought Communists must be a wildly superior human type.

Vanity, arrogance and conspicuous display *project* feelings of envy, so that one simply asserts one's own superiority. In this case, the object is 'spoiled' at once by being exposed as, itself, envious.

One may persist in *confusion* and *doubt* about the value of the enviable object. This is a favourite strategy of those confronted by a large, new, seductive idea — one backs off into careful reappraisal, scientific method, and so on.

The simplest defence, *denial* is probably by far the commonest: 'It's nothing to me: there's no comparison being made, and no contrast felt.' If, however, over and above this protestation of indifference, some symbolic reassurance is required that one is not in truth harbouring some envy, one inevitably drops into some logical equivalent of one of the other strategies — as Foster interestingly shows in his review of the forms used in different societies by those who fear they might be suspected of envy: one invokes a blessing, or congratulates in a form that abjures ill-will, or one denigrates the object, or boasts that one does not need it.[24]

Our diarists help us to add some living detail to these categories of envy-defence, although we missed testimony on defence by rationalisation, doubt and denial; relevant items were defined as those anchored in some strongly invidious comparison of qualities or attributes. Disparagement and denigration were the commonest, and took several distinct lines:

Condemnation of others' greed. This included groups making pay claims

---

* As the many celebrity nightclub brawls attest, however, fans have a compulsive need to disparage stars.

(teachers, doctors), or enjoying excessive prosperity ('guzzling' dairy farmers), and a group 'wanting everything' (Women's Liberation). Three foreign celebrities and one local politician were also censured for having or acquiring houses 'ridiculously' large, and one already rich local couple was censured for fighting a 'grasping' family-will case.

Contempt for the pretensions or performance of the powerful, wealthy or over-indulged. This was directed at the élite generally or sections of it: 'those perpetuating the system', 'those who can't see the human issues', 'ivory tower intellectuals', 'everyone's "understanding" while rotten things exist' and the 'disillusioning' parliament (after a visit to it). Contempt was also roused by the absurdity of gentlemen's clubs, of Nixon ('not a big shot'), of a federal minister 'thinking he could run the . . . industry', of a prejudiced judge, of an intelligence chief with a B.A. degree. (All these items contain a tone of strong moral indignation.)

Pleasure (occasionally running as strong as glee) at their discomfiture was felt at the prospect of tax increase on large incomes, at the exploits of a cat burglar specialising in bedside safes, at an art robbery from a decadent heir, and at a 'welcome' rise in the rents of 'pampered' public housing tenants.

Assertion of superiority and projection of envy were also marked:

Attribution of 'pettiness' (including envy) to groups and individuals with whom no sympathy was felt. These included 'our politicians — second-rate compared to those of the U.S.'; student politicians (this was a frequent item); commerce and social-work students and students of Greek descent; home-town bumpkins ('A shock as country bumpkin denigrates me — a real case of envy, with its roots in prejudice and inferiority'); women in general (as too lazy to fight for their rights); and the public at large (exposed as 'reactionary' and 'dull' by an opinion poll, and apt to titter at *Last Tango in Paris*). Four separate small weeklies — of the political left and right, of a country town, and of the Jewish community — struck subjects as 'incredibly rigid', 'doctrinaire', 'myopic'; and so did personal opponents in political arguments — a 'petty, complaining' brother-in-law, for example.

Assertion of patent superiority is a category very similar in kind to that of 'attribution of pettiness', but with the emphasis on 'us' rather than on 'them'. The superiority of one's own suburb was asserted over a poor suburb (as one imagined it to be); of one's own university over an institute of technology ('poor place'); of country over city life-style (there were several of these); and of private over public schooling. This category also included feelings of moral repugnance at the appearance on television of a 'typical, clammy D.L.P. type' — and feelings of triumph over making a success at a Government House reception.

And, finally, there were a good many instances of admiration and ideal-isation. Feelings of this sort were entertained towards individual political leaders, in general terms, or in relation to particular approved policies; and towards striking individuals personally encountered: for example, a leading woman administrator, a couple adopting a Cambodian orphan, and 'tolerant' or 'knowledgeable' elders (carefully described).[25]

Two plain admissions of envy stood out: a Gay Liberation activist envied the 'superior morale and sense of purpose' of Women's Liberation; a conservationist London's 'splendid procedures for preserving historic buildings'.

Individuals differ markedly in their propensity to feel envy, and in their characteristic stratagems for coping with it when they do. At one extreme, the wholly envious man is preoccupied with his treasury of invidious comparisons, insatiable in his greedy ambition for supplies or recognition;[26] at the other, there are those who are apparently oblivious of all rivals, of ill treatment or bad luck, whether through insensitivity, stoicism or schizoid self-enclosure. Oral characters, for example, are said to be peculiarly dependent on others for the maintenance of their self-esteem.[27] The tone may be whining-demanding, accusatory-vindictive, pampered-imperious, or a choked inability to 'impose' or to ask anyone for aid. And a person's envy may pervade his whole life, or it may be tightly confined to certain areas of it — to his professional reputation, say, or to his sexual partner. The harnessing of early greed and envy to ambition, in social life and especially in one's career, seems to be critical. Rivalry with siblings seems particularly to shape the intensity, if not the direction, of this striving.[28]

We expect the envious personality to be attracted to the envious issues in politics, and we expect his approval to go to those political demands or accusations made in a style consonant with the one he has come to depend on in his private dealings with his own immediate circle. Politics, moreover, undoubtedly attracts an undue share of envious personalities to its professional ranks. As Morris Jones has pointed out, it is the quickest status escalator in society,[29] and a large proportion of aspirants turn towards parliament after failure or blockage in a first career. At a deeper level, the politician's demand is for deference, and he pursues status and power 'as a means of compensation against deprivation. *Power is expected to overcome low estimates of the self.* '[30]

An ironical by-product of this selective recruitment is the special attractiveness, especially on the political Left, of demonstrably *unenvious* character-types, both to their colleagues and to the public at large. The relief they afford from the general sour tone of rationalised resentment is enormously welcome: we like 'to hear the Grand Remonstrances of greed, led by the pure' (A. D. Hope). As Ben Chifley's biography shows, however, this stance is sometimes won only by dint of exposure to extravagantly invidious childhood circumstances, and at the cost of severe constriction of affective range.[31]

Envy systems in political use

'Envy,' said Bacon, 'is, together with love, the only passion that fascinates and bewitches.' The phrase catches something of the tendency of envy towards system-building — for the individual bewitched by envy is in its grip over long and obsessive stretches of time. The tendency is remarkable, although in both public and private life, the elaboration of emulatory (or denigratory) schemes proceeds best when it is most rationalised and the raw envy at the root is kept firmly hidden. We lacked till 1912 an extended account of the building of an envy-system. In that year, Max Scheler described the process by which the negative, spoiling aspect of envy hardens into the system of resentment.* Resentment, he wrote, was a 'self-poisoning of the mind which has quite definite causes and consequences'. It was

> a lasting mental attitude, caused by the systematic repression of certain emotions and affects which . . . are normal components of human nature. Their repression leads to the constant tendency to indulge in certain kinds of value delusions and corresponding value judgments. The emotions and affects primarily concerned are revenge, hatred, malice, envy, the impulse to detract, and spite.[32]

He saw it, he tells us, as, in essence, the servant's affect, belonging to those 'dominated at the moment, who fruitlessly resent the sting of authority' — — but powerfully and portentously at work as well among all those 'fated' to inferiority or lodged in society's most keenly invidious niches.

Above all, it was a systematic progression of affects: it begins in a reactive impulse to attack or injure, a desire to hit back, which, however, is stifled because the individual realises that he is too weak and that this is not the time; it gathers strength with hatred, malice, envy; it becomes generalised in the impulse to detract, to disparage and 'smash pedestals', to 'dwell on the negative aspects of excellent men and things'; and it is sharpened in spite, 'always ready to burst forth'. If all this is present and aggression is still checked because of the sense of weakness, and so is hidden and hoarded, *then* there is resentment. To be delivered of it, one must either exercise 'moral self-conquest' and, by a deliberate effort of will, put resentment away from one as unworthy — or act upon it, make one's attack (as criminals do) and thereby relieve it. Short of either of these courses, resentment persists and mounts.

It was the intellectual and moral consequences of the sustained, impotent sense of being inferior that most concerned Scheler. It produced — along lines that combined 'defence by devaluation' with 'defence by projection' — value-delusions of equality or superiority gained by an illusory devaluation of the other's qualities, or a specific blindness to them. The impulse to detract then becomes a fixed attitude, detached from the

---

* Scheler used the French 'ressentiment' throughout, as indicating a permanent state rather than a temporary reaction.

original objects, demanding a falsification of the values themselves, which could bestow excellence on any possible objects of comparison.

> Joy, splendour, power, happiness, fortune, and strength magically attract the man of *ressentiment*. He cannot pass by, he has to look at them, whether he 'wants' to or not. But at the same time he wants to avert his eyes, for he is tormented by the craving to possess them and knows that his desire is vain ... The more the impulse to turn away ... prevails, the more he turns ... to their negative opposites.*[33]

At first, the old values persist, and leave an uncomfortable impression that 'one lives in a *sham world* which one is unable to penetrate', and the well-endowed and powerful are hated in an increasingly abstract and general-ised way. Resentment's final apotheosis, however, lies in a religious 'transvaluation of values' (in Nietzsche's phrase) asserting the primacy of poverty, humility and surrender, whereupon the 'enviable' can be pitied, hatred abandoned, and, at least in the conscious layers of the mind, the resentful man feels 'good, pure and human' at last.

More to the point for politics, however, is the likelihood of fixation at some mid-point in this progression, at which there is some generalisation of the hate-object, some solid hate still, and some vigorous disparagement of the qualities and possessions of the envied —in a word, the denial of superiority 'past one's own level of desire and ability':

> If the awareness of our limitations begins to limit or to dim our *value* consciousness as well — as happens, for instance, in old age with regard to the values of youth — then we have already started the movement of devaluation which will end with the defamation of the world and all its values.[34]

Scheler comes to resentment's political sites only after a leisurely excursion round demographic and occupational situations of 'fated' inequality (echoing Bacon's thought that the most envious are 'deformed persons and eunuchs, old men and bastards — those who *cannot possibly mend their case*'): those in declining life; the aged, especially retired officials; women in general, old maids and mothers-in-law in particular; the priest ('condemned to control his emotions' more than anyone); dwarfs, cripples, the subnormal; all these are particularly subject to resentment. In the structure of society, however, this 'psychological dynamite' lodges where there is the greatest '*discrepancy* between the political, constitutional, or traditional status of a group and its *factual* power'; thus the labour movement, the Jews, the disappearing class of artisans, the petty bourgeoisie and small officials are especially prone to it. Indeed, it is all-pervasive, an ever-mounting pressure, in modern liberal societies with 'wide factual differences in power, property, and education' and a constitutional doctrine of formal equality of rights. He comments pointedly on a form of

* He notes the special appeal of this path to 'apostate' or 'romantic' temperaments.

'resentment criticism' which finds political improvement or reform un-welcome because it undermines oppositionism, permanent and atmos-pheric, and the rhetoric of detraction which is loved for its own sake. The 'spiritual venom' of resentment, the affect *par excellence* of the weak 'common man', is, moreover, extremely contagious.

When it has not been ignored, Scheler's clever essay has been treated with condescension by most later writers.[35] A handful of studies has, however, confirmed its novel and ingenious linkage of a lasting affect-state and the odd cast of political mind it throws forward. Henri de Man, the Belgian political sociologist and socialist deputy, took up in 1920 the question of working-class resentment.[36] Scheler had thought labour leaders a type particularly prone to the rhetoric of negative envy, but he had specifically exempted the industrial proletariat at large from resentment.[37] de Man thought otherwise, and set out, in sensitive interviews with working-class subjects, to establish the centrality of inferiority-feelings in individuals, and the existence of a collective 'social infer-iority complex'. He attributed the latter to the established hierarchy of 'enviable' occupations, to the sense that membership of the working class was a 'fate', a 'life-sentence', and to the actual joylessness and in-security of unskilled manual work. On this ground, 'a social resentment, characterised by feelings of exploitation, oppression, social injustice and working-class solidarity', was certainly taking root; but 'working-class solidarity' was essentially compensatory, and Marxism — though it ap-pealed to the appropriate emotions — ministered hardly at all to real discomforts. (It is a pity that the most recent studies of working-class social outlooks, in the U.S. by Lane[38] and in England by Goldthorpe and Lockwood,[39] have not worked at a depth to engage with these supposi-tions.)

Carl Frankenstein's recent work, however, on the child-rearing prac-tices of poor and ill-educated families in the U.S. and Israel,[40] affirms the basic tie between inferiority reactions and resentful world views, and the two levels that we have called 'political' and 'religious' of Scheler's schema. In *resentment*, Frankenstein argues, society is held responsible for the individual's plight, it has chosen him to be inferior and worthless, and the negative affect 'deprives the "haveable" objects in the environ-ment of their power' to attract or to satisfy. 'Resentment and hatred make direct enjoyment of "having" almost impossible.' At a higher level of self-consciousness, despair supplants inferiority, and 'Regardless of the extent to which . . . material goods are actually available or not, [the individual] experiences them as "unreachable". The world is one in which value is defined as "beyond reach".' Hatred of society and of those not in want drops away and religious belief assures that material conditions and social status are accidental modalities only and not indicators of essential qualities.[41]

Frankenstein's term the 'illusion of knownness' — the refusal to contemplate an external society richer in any detail than the known small world — elegantly complements what Scheler calls the disparaging denial of superiority 'past one's own level of desire and ability'.

Finally, a number of writers have expatiated on the release from resentment and the sense of impotent inferiority afforded by recruitment to aggressive, extremist political groups which assert national, class, ethnic or sexual superiority. Eric Hoffer has described the 'true believer's' flight from a 'spoilt' or 'damaged' self (seen as worthless, guilty, helpless, cowardly or incomplete) and discovery of a new self in the higher, 'historic' identity conferred by membership of a great cause.[42] This is Scheler's delivery from resentment, in political form. The relentless denigration of leaders and would-be leaders in the Women's Movement — 'trashing' — is another most interesting envy-system phenomenon.[43]

Scheler's resentment system is, of course, merely one psychologically comprehensible (and seductive) possibility before those imprisoned in highly invidious settings. He himself mentions a second: the active, bustling emulation of the *arriviste*, who sets out to be highly esteemed for what he shows he has been able to accumulate. His greater constitutional energy, Scheler believes, differentiates him from the resentful man. (We would need a more complex story if we were to interpret in this light, say, the history of modern Japan.) Although it is, of its nature, a self-concerned, and even somewhat anti-political, stance, emulative possessiveness has the power, if it becomes the leading mode in a society, to colour the ends of politics itself: 'development' and the 'spirit of progress', once enthroned, become defined in rather close analogy with practice in the private realm. Some sustained political formations manage to mix both of these envy-systems: rival towns,* for example, achieve a rich combination of mutual denigration and emulation down to the finest detail. Conventionality constitutes a third political envy-system: superiors are accepted as superiors, and admired; the existence of inferiors attests that one is enviable. In extreme cases the upper class is idealised, and the *Woman's Weekly* reader is enabled, by an awed contemplation of the appointments and daily rituals of a royal family, to take the sting out of invidious comparisons with neighbours. (Conventionality is further discussed at the end of chapter 10.)

But, for the most pervasive of all the forms in which envy pours into politics, we must return to our initial quotation from Geoffrey Gorer; perhaps envy is invisible nowadays because it is regarded merely as 'an aspect of a desire for justice'. It is, however, arguable that there was always some sense of fairness embedded in envious feeling, some useful resistance to arbitrary privilege, some inarticulate pressure in the direction of justice —

---

* The very word 'rival' comes from the Latin 'rivalis', meaning 'one who lives on the opposite bank of a stream from another'.

as Leigh Hunt suggested: 'Envy, among other ingredients, has a mixture of the love of justice in it: we are more angry at undeserved than at deserved good fortune.' But which is core and which is coating? Lasswell has taught us that politics is private affects displaced upon public objects, and *rationalised*. The publicly-aired grievance must be couched in the rhetoric of equity.

Of course, the realm of envy is larger than the special populations immured in groups most prone to envy (less homogeneous, perhaps, than most — 'envy makes strange bedfellows') or in sharply-defined envy-processing systems; it includes the whole range of cultural devices designed to preserve citizens from feelings of excessive envy or from excessive fear of the envy of others. These arrangements must be reviewed before we can deal with appropriate and inappropriate envy.

Cultural devices to minimise envy

People in primitive societies, George Foster reminds us, spend a major part of their time contriving to avoid being envied — concealing or denying that they have more valuable belongings or qualities than others, doling out sops or actual shares of their good fortune to those less fortunate.[44] In fact, the poorer the community, the greater the tendency to such preoccupation, since the 'evil eye' and witchcraft generally are proportionately more (and more realistically) feared. Anthropologists talk, indeed, of an 'envy-barrier' standing in the way of even modest material improvement in simple village communities.[45]

The tactic of concealment and denial, Foster argues, is still massively practised in our society.* First, through 'encapsulation', sub-societies are erected in which 'all members ideally have about the same access to what are considered to be the good things in life'.[47] Separated by social, psychological, cultural and often physical boundaries, the enviable in each stands out much less distinctly, and comparisons across the boundaries are discouraged. Secondly, children are firmly taught that envy is shameful and must not be expressed. Notions of fair play, the rules of the game, losing without loss of face, and so on, smooth over a great many potential cases of envy.

Politics begins where efforts are made to reduce the occasions for envy by deliberate strokes of policy.† Systems of wage-fixing, for example,

---

* cf. Edgar Friedenberg: 'Envy, as a social force, in the pre-industrial Arab world — and for that matter, to a lesser degree, even in early nineteenth-century Charleston — led to a characteristic form of urban dwelling for the affluent: a house in a large beautiful garden, totally concealed behind a blank wall that gave no hint of the luxury within to arouse the passions of those excluded from it. In Pacific Palisades or Lake Forest, the luxury is so visible as to be self-deprecating, attesting that the owner is a good old boy who lets it all hang out. The blankness and banality have been internalised; there is no longer anyone to be envied in residence.'[46]

† cf. Politics is 'the manipulation of envy' (Schoeck).[48]

attempt directly to trim income-envy, arbitrators conjuring with ideas of 'comparative wage justice' and attempting to arrange beneficiaries according to their deserts. Or the problem may be tackled with the organisation as the unit, and an effort made to spell out a rationale for every wage-difference.[49] Secondary schemes of redistribution seek next to take from those who have too much and give to those who have too little – in general by taxes and social benefit payments, or by direct provision in particularly invidious fields, such as housing, health or education. The standardising of public services, and, in the broadest sense, of the valued commodities produced in a society, may also be thought to allay envy.

Schoeck points out that this general Welfare State structure has been largely the product of socialist intellectuals who had, individually, a very uncomfortable sense of themselves as enviable, and who accordingly sought a society in which there would be neither envied nor envious. The result, no doubt, is more just, but there is no evidence that envy has been reduced. Indeed, he believes that it is utopian, even wicked, to suggest that any manipulation of the occasions for 'legitimate' envy can ever seriously affect its actual occurrence:

> Envy is ineluctable, implacable and irreconcilable, is irritated by the slightest differences, is independent of the degree of inequality, appears in its worst form in social proximity or among near relatives.[50]

And he judges that the socially equalitarian policies of the last two generations have actually increased the degree of envy that is felt.

For the critic on the Left, the situation is exactly reversed. Such a critic will deplore the success of 'encapsulation' in deflating the sense of 'relative deprivation' in low-paid workers and other groups of the poor in our society, and call for an 'uninhibited reference group choice' in regard to all inequalities. A miner should not compare himself with a fitter, a farm labourer with a boiler-maker. Both men

> have equal reason to compare themselves with clerks or businessmen or Members of Parliament ... [Indeed] the poorest pensioner is entitled to a sense of relative deprivation based on the inequality between himself and the richest man.[51]

We can hardly expect agreement between conservatives and radicals on levels of 'legitimate' envy, but perhaps there is some empirical purchase in the point on which both rely – the special importance of close comparisons in envy-arousal. Although the notion is an ancient one – Hesiod said that 'the potter envies the potter; the carpenter the carpenter; the poor man is jealous of the poor man; the bard of the bard' –the most relevant experience by which to test it is extremely recent, and seems to support Schoeck's view. The lesson of the kibbutz is that the standardisation of childhoods augments envy in adults; and communes, as social experiments designed precisely to deal with this problem, set up conditions which notoriously exacerbate it.

Measurements of envy-levels in larger societies are hardly practicable, although invidious differences in actual life-conditions can be roughly gauged. However, such comparisons *are* possible in anthropology, and do, to a certain degree, already exist. Tribes with similar material culture have evolved strikingly different 'modal personalities' — different not least in their susceptibility to envy and to selected defences against it. In certain of these societies, relatively unenvious character has been encouraged by a combination of chance and intention, on a pattern that does not vary much in individual cases. It is in this realm, if anywhere, that envy is reducible.

Fear, suspicion and paranoia
Feelings of fear

Feelings of fear are unmistakable, if varied; they range from the primitive, animal startle at seeing a snake or spider, the adrenalin surge at a dog's attack, the muscular contraction at an impending blow, to the fear of pain from within one's own body or from one's thoughts as one seeks to avoid in advance even the remotest threat of danger; from the fear of reproof, as we see a brow darken, to the peculiarly human fears of 'invasion by vast and vague forces which are other than [one]self; strangling encirclement by everything that is not safely clarified as allied; and ... loss of face before all-surrounding, mocking audiences' (Erikson).[1] With these various forms of fear come the fear-impulses: the urge to conceal oneself, to shrink away, to run, to cry for help, or to remain silent and immobile; and the contrary urge to defend oneself by aggressive actions.[2] There is also, however, a third possibility — denial that the threat is there at all, or that it is serious. The sensation of fear may be brief and specific — in the special circumstances of, say, driving in heavy traffic, taking exams or making love — but, if serious, it is likely to set up a fear-system to order behaviour some way ahead. We are equipped with many signal patterns constructed to deal with the signs of danger as they accumulate.

What is the difference between fear and anxiety? In common use, anxiety is free-floating and unparticularised. Fear is 'tamed anxiety' in the face of danger (Fenichel),[3] arising once the threat has been defined (although one may fear anxiety itself). In technical writing, however, anxiety is sometimes defined as 'fear of a wholly internalised authority', a property of the ego's relation to the super-ego, successor to the infant's fear of parental disapproval and punishment, while Erikson has suggested that

> Fears are states of apprehension which focus on isolated and recognizable dangers so that they may be judiciously appraised and real-

istically countered. Anxieties are diffuse states of tension (caused by
a loss of mutual regulation and a consequent upset in libidinal and
aggressive controls) which magnify and even cause the illusion of an
outer danger, without pointing to appropriate avenues of defense
or mastery.[4]

Other writers distinguish along the same line between 'true' and 'neurotic'
anxiety.[5] At its highest pitch, in the *Angst* of Kierkegaard and later existen-
tialist writers, we have a 'fear of nothing which is at the same time a fear of
everything', a 'fear of the abyss', in short, a metaphysical distress to which
little short of religious illumination can minister. It is significant that the
Latin root of 'anxiety', and the root of the cognate Greek term, connote
'pressure', 'narrowness', 'the narrow space'.

We are afraid of any number of things — 'meeting gangsters, creditors,
relatives, a former love. . .' (Riezler)[6] but it would be as well to separate at
once serious and general fears (of bereavements, for example, or death)
from what, although serious, is eccentric (fear of cats, of conflict, or of
closed spaces). Polling 20,000 people in 13 countries, Hadley Cantril found
that people's greatest fears, in order of importance, were

> fear of deterioration of present standard of living, fear of ill health,
> accident, death of self, ditto for family, fear about children's welfare
> or opportunities, fear of war, fear of unemployment or inability to
> work, fear of separation from relatives or of not living up to their
> expectations, fear of an unhappy family life, fear of poor or uncon-
> genial work, fear of being dependent on others, fear of not having
> own business or land or not improving it, fear of being unable to
> provide dowry for daughters, fear of not being able to get a house,
> fear of being alone, fear of being emotionally unstable or immature,
> fear of becoming a criminal. . .[7]

The time-span is important: fears of what might happen 'today' (cf.
Riezler's list, above) differ markedly from fears of what might happen
'this year' or 'in the rest of one's life'. Cantril asked for replies in terms of
'worst possible life-future', and concerned himself principally with
national differences. However, it was clear that men and women had
rather different lists (women were more family-centred), and so had the
old, the middle-aged and the young, who were most concerned (respectively) with their health, their children and getting a good job.[8] Cantril
interviewed his subjects on their doorsteps; this approach largely dictates,
of course, the conventional, 'family of man' style of answer; highly
personal or socially unacceptable replies were not to be expected. In a
clinical setting, however, one might find the old talking of loss of status,
the mature of loss of capacity, young people of unloveableness, and
children of disappointing their parents. And personal fears may be deeply
ideologised, as female students currently talk of the fear of confused
identity, of becoming submerged in the roles of wife or mother, or as

kibbutz-dwellers' fears related mainly to the perpetuation and success of the communal enterprise itself.[9] Fears, in this way, are the obverse of hopes.

On the surface, psychoanalysts have been overwhelmingly concerned with particular morbid or neurotic fears — Grinstein's *Index* lists over a hundred papers on individual fear-arousing objects[10] — but, in fact, their strategy for ordering this material has been essentially to relate it back to a common epigenetic model of progress through the psycho-sexual stages of childhood,* and numerous authoritative lists of the basic fears lodged in the various stages of normal growth now exist.[11] It is tempting, indeed, to see childhood as one giant project of mastering anxiety; certainly the earliest infantile fears and anxieties seem the most intense and engulfing — for example, the panic states where the organism is flooded with painful and 'causeless' excitation or where fears of the dark and abandonment hold sway. It is the achievement of the grown child to have substituted for these the conventional array of more or less predictable, manageable 'dangers'.

The analysts' principal lesson is that, while there remain many adult occasions for sharp, realistic apprehension, falling into fear involves, more often than not, the simultaneous reactivation of 'matching' infantile anxieties, which seriously threaten to warp our judgment, and spur us to irrational and disproportionate responses. The study of children's anxiety dreams, which are themselves an important way into the sequential array of prototypical dangers, illustrates that, even with very young children, current fears resonate with those from still earlier developmental periods.[12]

Political fears

While Fromm may be right in suspecting that 'What causes concern and worry (in our time) is the private, separate sector of life, not the social, universal one which connects us with our fellow men',[13] the fact remains that people continue to have political fears, including fears for the future of their community.† Our diarists' apprehensions were, in fact, concentrated on areas of *national* danger (41% of total fear responses). Threats were seen in nuclear technology (French tests, the general nuclear balance, U.S. bases in Australia and nuclear proliferation); in depleted world resources and over-population; in the instability of Russian-Chinese

* Instinctual and traumatic fears, and fears induced by vicissitudes in the *parents'* lives, lie outside this broad central stream.
† cf. Freud's own analysis of national panic or anomie in *Group Psychology* (1921), written soon after the collapse of the Austro-Hungarian empire: 'The loss of the leader in some sense or other, the birth of misgivings about him, brings on the outbreak of panic . . . the mutual ties between the members of the group disappear, as a rule, at the same time as the tie with their leader. The group vanishes in dust.'[14]

or Russian-Czech relations, or in the South-East Asian or Latin American regions generally: in the granting of independence to Papua-New Guinea;* in Japanese rearmament; in the Chinese navy; or in President Nixon's 'megalomania'. In national politics (32% of fears), inflation was the main worry, followed by the new Labour government's political and administrative capacity, especially as evidenced (or tested) in health, security, the arts and aboriginal affairs. City-based fears (17%) included violence, the crime rate, the road toll, pet conservation projects and local Labour party disunity. Personal fears (10%) clustered about the dangerous intensity of student political life, but included the prospect of failure in a civil-service entry bid and of the loss of a tax concession.

When Cantril asked his sample for their fears *for their country*, he found that the replies fell into the following categories:

Political fears (36%) concerned dishonest government, inefficient government, Communist take-over, unrepresentative government, lack or loss of freedom, lack of law and order, disunity, political instability.

Economic fears (30%) concerned instability, unemployment, inadequate or deteriorating standard of living, tax increases, lack of technological advance.

International fears (27%) concerned war, continued armament, no lessening of cold war, becoming isolated from other nations or unable to maintain neutrality.

National status fears (15%) concerned not being a world power, loss of status and importance, failure to exert ideological or moral leadership, lack or loss of independence, threats of foreign aggression.

Social fears (14%) concerned social injustice, continued race or class discrimination, inadequate schools, poor or unfair working conditions, unlimited population growth, no sense of social and political responsibility or awareness; lack of morality, honesty, religion; mechanisation, standardisation, materialism, conformity.[16]

Levels of sensed national insecurity are highly volatile, climbing with crisis, ebbing with détente. Polls, which intermittently ask, '*Do you expect your country to be involved in war within 10 years?*', fix points on this agitated line, as they register at one moment 20% apprehension, at another, 80%.[17] 'Scaring the public half to death and then proposing to save it' (H. L. Mencken) is a familiar conservative tactic, and right-wing parties generally insist on their special competence in defence and national security affairs.[18] Ideas about foreign threats are, of course, peculiarly susceptible to ideological shaping. Indeed, they are doubly ideological, since the foreigners' ideology must first be weighed and analysed, in order

* The Papuans themselves produced the most exotic political fear of 1973: in September rumours swept Port Moresby that the 'snake' around the Queen's neck on the dollar note would jump out and attack people if early independence came.[15] (The 'snake' is a cord holding the Queen's robe in place.)

to determine their intentions; only thus (together with a knowledge of their resources) can the final level of threat be calculated.[19] Though government and/or press leaders can set short-term fear-levels almost at will, they work in a fairly constraining setting, having to justify any marked divergence from the strategic appraisals of allies; and their warnings, to be effective, must run in the familiar 'threat schemas' of the culture (from which they are themselves by no means immune).[20]

How much do those who are personally insecure contribute to the sum of fears for the nation? The only survey so far that has attempted to probe this (in a Norwegian sample)[21] failed to disclose any firm link: it seems that the habit of using politics to exercise anxiety is a necessary bridge, and by no means to be relied on. Nevertheless, in times when no evident or pressing national danger dominates the contemplation of personal futures, influence may well run the other way, and optimism based on personal hopes may become extrapolated to ideas about national security and prosperity as well. Adolescents, particularly, seem prone to conflate aspirations for self and country, using identical phrasing, in a solid exercise in projective identification.[22]

Fear of politics itself is very little studied. (In one month, it threw up 'personal dangers' to 10% of our diarists.) We have a tentative approach to such a study in findings from personality-testing and small-group work about social anxiety and timidity and fear of inter-personal involvement,[23] and, from political socialisation studies, about the onset of indifference to politics.[24] The latter suggest that, by the age of twelve, a good many children, as a result of painful judgment by the peer group and by school authorities, have withdrawn from all attempts to influence group decisions: they 'punish' politics (which they see as the preserve of the prigs) by refusing to attend to it.

Fear systems in politics

Lasswell's *World Politics and Personal Insecurity*, mostly written in 1932,[25] was a pioneering attempt to chart contemporary levels of social insecurity and to forecast what they might portend politically. Politics, he claimed, strove *par excellence* for 'techniques of navigating the tides of insecurity'. It is when people become restless, embittered and afraid, that their allegiance to the symbols and practices of the established order frays, and 'the moment is propitious for the speedy diffusion of opposing myths in whose name power may be seized by a challenging élite'. His lectures assessed the prospects for world Communism in thirty years' time. He predicted containment by parochial and nationalist concerns, a crippling lack of middle-class appeal in the West, a growing inner homogeneity of industrialised societies, and the replacement of the class struggle by the struggle of occupational skills. But the study's continuing interest lies as much in its method of analysis — the deep psychological investigation of the principal fronts on which insecurities impend and the 'unconscious receptivities' available to new 'symbol clusters' — as in the overall results. We may still learn from his descriptions of the situation of the unemployed man, the temporising radical intellectual, the fighter for colonial independence and the anxious defence-planner.* He conceived insecurity-levels in terms of an equilibrium, with phases of insecurity, symbolisation (and propagandising), crisis, and relatively stable readaptation. New symbols were, he thought, apt to assuage superficial rather than deeper insecurities, which, for Western man, he speculated, centre about the fear of self-knowledge and self-analysis, spurring his long historical detour into 'dogmatism, activism, and collectivism' and the externalisation of fantasy. New élites he thought prone to a lazy and self-interested stasis of politics about their own installation as an Establishment.

In a 1951 essay, he added an interesting coda on the control of mass insecurity (and the fear of dissent) in totalitarian régimes and its products, 'the weakened ego and the dependent conscience', and on the lively contemporary threat of the 'garrison state' in the U.S., as fears of foreign assault and internal subversion intensified mutual distrust.[26]

Innumerable studies have shown that mass insecurity presaged Fascism. As Tillich describes it:

> First of all a feeling of *fear* or, more exactly, of indefinite anxiety was prevailing. Not only the economic and political, but also the cultural and religious, security seemed to be lost. There was nothing on which one could build; everything was without foundation. A catastrophic breakdown was expected every moment. Consequently, a longing for security was growing in everybody. A freedom that leads to fear and anxiety has lost its value; better authority with security than freedom with fear![27]

Kurt Riezler stresses that the mood was no mere agglomeration of definite fears (of economic hardship, say, or air raids or arbitrary arrest) but a fundamentally indefinite anxiety, a fear of the unknown, depriving even the reasons for definite fear of a distinctiveness on which to act. Ordinary citizens became paralysed as their whole world of conventional under-standings came under threat, and the social 'universe of discourse split . . . wide apart'. 'Democratic procedure . . . stalled. "Causes" [became] hopelessly entangled; The voice of wavering governments no longer [reached] the average citizen.' Such conditions *create* the totalitarian leader, who

> masters the indefinite fear . . . gives a simple frame of reference, simple causes; whoever joins him gets rid of confusion. . . First things come first — no efficient action without obedience. . . Everybody gets his place in the machine . . . and is told what to do and to think.[28]

---

* The analysis of the anxiety-provoking processes inherent in the operation of an international 'balance' of military power (chapters 3 and 4) is particularly rich and detailed.

Franz Neumann adds that it is the very intensity of the anxiety — regression to full infantile persecutory levels — that makes possible the unreserved 'identification' with the leader-demagogue, who affirms and dramatises the public's special sense of being under persecution. Once in power, the totalitarian leader 'institutionalises' anxiety by propaganda and terror, and, for his special followers, by guilt at the 'crime committed in common'.[29] But we have crossed the border here from fear to paranoia, and must pause to check our map.

Suspicion

Suspicion is an affect falling mid-way between fear and paranoia: fear, its main element, is concentrated in it, moving us along some way towards hatred, but doubt remains, a solid buffer against the terrible certainty of paranoia. Alexander Shand, four years after his *Foundations of Character*, was moved (by the conditions of the time, he hints) to write a separate essay on suspicion, 'this complex and versatile emotion', which becomes prominent in times of war and social crisis.[30] Suspicion concerns itself, however obscurely, with the character and intentions of some person or group thought to have some power for mischief. Doubt remains, however, about whether, or how much, the object is to be feared, and the suspicious person may welcome other people's advice on this, or engage in prudent reality-testing. Doubts *fluctuate*: our wavering thoughts are driven hither and thither by doubt, curiosity and anger.[31] We expect deception, fraud or trickery; one has to get past the appearance of the object in order to reach the real motives, feelings or plans. It is an alert state, attentive to and watchful of its object — but *secretly* watchful. If the emblem of cynicism is the snarl, the emblem of suspicion is the peeping glance:

> It is the stealthiness of its glance and the sudden way in which it is withdrawn, lest it be detected — "peeping" as it were through a lattice — which, joined to the menace in it and to curiosity, seem chiefly to distinguish the expression of Suspicion.

> If fear is one of the roots of Suspicion, anger is another. For the expression of Suspicion on men's faces is always disagreeable, and arouses dislike, because there is a latent hostility in it.[32]

We may, of course, have strong suspicions and yet be little alarmed — if we feel ourselves safely out of the way. ('A citizen of Chile or Argentina may have suspected the German government of aggressive designs before the opening of the Great War, and yet have considered that his country was out of danger.')[33] The biological reason for suspicion, Shand claims, is to accomplish a general preparedness to act, a general deliberate and secret preparation for evil eventualities. There is an element of patience and reflectiveness in it, a wariness, perhaps lifelong.

Helene Deutsch, discussing, in an early essay,[34] four case-histories in which suspicion as a neurotic symptom or a character trait was a feature, stressed the projective element: the menace that these people felt in the environment matched the endopsychic perception of an impulse of danger threatening the ego from the unconscious. She claimed that 'the constitutional strengthening of the anal-sadistic impulses' favours the development of the suspicious character. Deaf people, she noted incidentally, were among those most susceptible, and children disappointed in their first love-objects. Also prone to suspicion, we may suspect, are the 'once-bitten'; and the deceitful themselves; those on the 'losing side'; and those strongly disposed in general to project their feelings. 'When a fear seems out of proportion, it has been bloated by a wish', as Philip Slater warns us in his discussion of parents' suspicions of the 'counter-culture'.[35]

Politically, suspiciousness becomes institutionalised in secret service establishments* and defence-planning generally. Nations suspect each other systematically and comprehensively. In wartime, aliens from enemy countries are set apart and placed under special guard. Suspicion is a major prop of prejudice — along with conventionality, hatred, envy and the special projected badnesses 'appropriate' to each despised ethnic, or other, out-group. The prejudiced personality, though perhaps the best understood formation in political psychology,[36] has proved uncomfortably resistant to liberal therapy.[37]

The Radical Right is permanently suspicious of the Left, but most of all when it appears to be becoming the Establishment, and the Right reacts now with demands for loyalty oaths,[38] and now with para-military drilling to 'forestall' a collapse of order and essential supplies. Lasswell has given us a vivid description of the suspicions foisted on intellectuals, in their turn, when such a season of national mistrust is in full spate: people suddenly

> wonder if the office or home telephone is tapped; or whether a microphone has been installed in the room; or whether the reading of the meter yesterday was done by an agent who was in fact sent to look over the books in the library; or whether the new girl at the office is a police agent; or whether an old friend is now adding to his income by writing reports about what goes on at private dinner parties; or whether one ought to cancel a subscription to a 'liberal' magazine for fear that a hostile neighbor will send in a denunciation; or whether one should stop writing letters to a schoolmate — who may possibly belong to a 'front' organisation. . .; or whether one should express

* It is also institutionalised in a preoccupation with them. Where this becomes group-conventional, as with left-wing suspicion of the security services and the C.I.A., it is often difficult to discover the reality-marker that would separate suspicion from paranoia. When the Australian Labour Senator William Brown suddenly announced in June 1974 that the C.I.A., the Pentagon and the U.S. State Department were planning an anti-Government coup in Australia, his party colleagues called this 'a bit extreme'.

no views whatever about matters of controversial public policy
for fear of adding to a dossier in the police department.[39]

For its part the Labour movement harbours a monumental mistrust of the
'capitalist Press', which is thought to be ceaselessly and cynically misleading its defenceless readers. Yet so close a love-hate relation is it that
the Labour movement does nothing independently to inform its members.
Suspiciousness can finally be 'earthed', Shand reflected, if we can truly
separate ourselves from the troubling object: but most politics goes on
between groups that are indissolubly joined in opposition.

Paranoia

In paranoia the threat-object has become *the enemy*. Doubts have gone;
the paranoiac is not worried by others' disagreement, the thinness of the
evidence, or even by the refusal of intimates to take his delusions seriously.
And the threat has been greatly clarified and magnified: it is now to injure,
disgrace, or kill the self — a case of 'soul-murder' (Schreber). There is now
a conspiracy, a persecution-system, enormous malignity, power, cleverness ranged in opposition, and a terrible urgency.

The fullest account of the paranoid state of mind is David Shapiro's.[40]
He sees the paranoid's rigid, unstable autonomy as his central preoccupation:

> he must always defend that autonomy on two fronts at the same time.
> He must defend it against internal and external threat. The battle on
> the one front results in rigidity; that on the other front in defensive-
> ness... Any weakening of or threat to autonomy that originates
> internally will necessarily intensify the sense of vulnerability to
> external threat as well, and it is likely ... to result in intensification
> not only of rigidity, but also of defensiveness.

The paranoid reaction (built-in and habitual) has two phases: first, a
repudiated impulse or a discomforting affect or idea threatens an already
rigid and defensive sensitivity, and automatically exacerbates both rigidity
and defensive mobilisation; then, in the projective phase, the wound-up
and highly suspicious mind seizes on 'clues' to the external threat, identifies the enemy and constructs the concrete menace. The paranoid's stance
is one of permanent readiness for an emergency, his inner life pervaded
by an 'apprehensive, defensive, and ultimately antagonistic awareness of
external authority and force'. He broods on power, and has an exorbitant
respect for it. The domain subjectively experienced as 'I' shrinks to a tight
and compact administrative centre, all affects constricted and some — the
gentler ones — banned altogether. He searches compulsively and with
intense concentration for tell-tale clues he knows must be there; paranoid
cognition

> resembles a muscle so tense it springs to the touch. This is not
> merely a greater quantity of the normal kind of alertness; and it is not
> merely the alertness of a well-trained soldier or an expert hunter. It

is much closer to the alertness of a soldier or hunter who has begun to tire, experiences increased subjective tension, and, without realizing it, begins to press himself harder. This is the soldier, one imagines, who is likely to shoot at shadows.[41]

He inhabits a world constructed of 'clues', disdaining the obvious, which must be 'seen through'. Despite brilliantly perceptive mistakes, his judgment is radically at fault; he imposes a rigid, autistic interpretative scheme on the world. However, he may accept enough of the ordinary world to achieve some limited adjustment to it, recognising, perhaps, that it is prudent to keep his unusual ideas to himself, and living

> as one might live in a foreign country, with people who, in their ignorance, do not see things clearly and are not even hospitable to those who do but with whom it is nevertheless both necessary and perfectly possible to deal.[42]

Elias Canetti, whose arresting thesis that paranoia is *the* political illness we shall examine presently, also vividly catches the dissimulating and unmasking processes in paranoia: he notes that paranoiacs are so skilful at dissembling the position they imagine they occupy and the importance they arrogate to themselves that many of them are never identified as such. They also have

> a continual urge to unmask enemies. These the paranoiac sees everywhere, in the most peaceful and harmless disguises: he has the gift of seeing through appearances and knows exactly what is behind them. He tears the mask from every face and what he then finds is always essentially the same enemy.[43]

Paranoid projective ideas and preoccupations tend to become incorporated into social attitudes and convictions, and into the images of whole groups or classes of people or social institutions.

> Many paranoid characters ... are to be found among the adherents of fanatical and witch-hunting political or quasipolitical movements, preoccupied with the defense of our country against those who would 'poison its water supply' by fluoridation, pollute its racial purity, [or] undermine its 'will to resist'.[44]

Freud discovered the paranoid projection-mechanism — one of the least contested of his findings — not in a patient, but in a publication, *Memoirs of My Nervous Illness* (1903), by the judge and former parliamentary candidate, D. P. Schreber.* He diagnosed latent homosexuality at the basis of the paranoid delusional system; the original declaration, 'I love him', having to be denied, becomes 'I hate him', which is justified in its turn by, 'He

---

* Niederland, supporting Freud's analysis, stressed the burdensome 'masculine' demands of political work as precipitating factors in Schreber's breakdowns, first in 1884 after he had stood for parliament, then in 1893 when he had just been made chief justice. In each case, 'under the impact of a threatening reality which imperiously demanded of him an active masculine role ... his latent passive feminine tendencies broke into consciousness and he fell ill.'[45]

hates me, and he is out to destroy me.' He traced a libidinal transference from the father to his physician and to God, in the course of the psychosis; and set the fixation-point in libidinal conflict related to repression of the inverted Oedipus situation.[46] One recent revaluation of the *Memoirs* wishes instead to put pre-genital procreation fantasies at the heart of Schreber's system (Schreber was childless); another traces it to his father's sadistic disciplinary methods.[47]

The tendency in later psychoanalytic writing has, however, been to push the date of the lodgement of the paranoid projection-mechanism further and further back from the Oedipal period. An American analyst, remarking that paranoid patients were, in fact, rarely helped by interpretations of homosexuality, asked why the need to love the father was so strong, and why it had to be so vehemently denied. He hypothesised that

> the kind of 'love' involved in Freud's primary proposition 'I love him' is a dangerous, ambivalent love, an intense need to love and be loved to deny the terrific repressed anal-sadistic hate. And the frantic need to deny this love in every way possible is due not to fear of social disapproval of homosexuality as such, but to intense anxiety for the safety of both subject and object because of the destructive anal-sadistic wishes which accompany the attempt to love and obtain passive anal gratification from the object.[48]

Anthony Storr defines it, in a way that is reminiscent of the Gulliver feeling (see below, pp. 375−6), as the condition in which

> the subject regards other people as possessing great, often magical, power for good, or more commonly, ill; and himself as possessing little or no power and being therefore in a weak or helpless position.[49]

He interprets it as the 'persistence into adult life of something which we imagine the baby to feel; the sense that he is at the mercy of [and is the principal concern of] figures who are much more powerful than himself'.

The Kleinian school, however, places the fixation-point of the paranoid stance back in the first three to four months of life, before even the mother is seen as a whole person. Real experience of deprivation and pain are then felt by the baby as threats of annihilation by persecutors, and in his efforts to contain this deep anxiety, he may turn to a variety of restless expedients, all calculated to produce further anxieties in their turn:

> The projection of bad feelings and bad parts of the self outwards produces external persecution [and splitting these into little fragments brings the sense of being persecuted by a multitude of bad objects].
> The reintrojection of persecutors gives rise to hypochondriacal anxiety. The projection of good parts outwards produces the anxiety of being depleted of goodness and of being invaded by persecutors. Projective identification produces a variety of anxieties. The two most important are these: the fear that an attacked object will retaliate equally by

projection; and the anxiety of having parts of oneself imprisoned and controlled by the object into which they have been projected. This last anxiety is particularly strong when good parts of the self have been projected, producing a feeling of having been robbed of these good parts, and of being controlled by other objects.[50]

Paranoid anxieties, then, are universal, but in normal development soon outgrown. It is only where bad experiences predominate drastically over good that the constitution of the ego itself is fatally flawed and paranoid-schizoid* mechanisms are built into it. It is to these desperate early ego-states that psychotics regress.

It has long been suspected that much in politics has a lurking affinity with paranoia. Let us try to clarify the connexions. First, it would seem that paranoiacs are unusually disposed to be active in politics, and, if not too severely disturbed, to look quite attractive as potential leaders — they predominate, for example, on the elected ward-committees of progressive mental hospitals.[51] The paranoid stance, as such, seems to suit political work, which is so much concerned with the identification of threats and dangers, of duplicities, lies, and secret plans in the environment, and with the organising of 'fronts' against them. Paranoiacs make plausible leaders because of their sense of certainty and their readiness for action. Their own belief in themselves, and the secret assurance they draw from their chart of the environment in its stark, military aspects, give them an air of 'natural authority' which the more relaxed and uncertain of us lack. Shapiro saw two distinct paranoid types: the 'furtive, constricted, apprehensively suspicious', and the 'rigidly arrogant, more aggressively suspicious, megalomanic'. It is the second type with which politics has more usually to contend.

Beyond this initial, general aptness and plausibility, paranoiacs have a penchant for crises.† Groups in which deep anxieties have been stirred are ripe for 'caesaristic identification' (Neumann), a regressive form of social huddling based on 'near-total ego-shrinkage'. Ordinary folk, massed and anxious in their plight, are apt to abdicate the res-

---

* The mechanisms are schizoid, too, because early objects, if not persecutory, are dazzlingly idealised.

† The ability to light up one's social plight with lurid paranoid anxiety seems to be a standard accomplishment of adolescent thinking. In seminar discussions, a dozen or more students voiced the opinion that the ecology crisis meant 'we have only fourteen or fifteen years left' or that it was already too late: 'We are doomed — nothing can now be done.' This same conjuring with the idea of a *world spoilt*, and the sense of a whole generation maliciously dealt an unplayable hand, lay behind students' 'certainty' in the 1950s of nuclear holocaust, and behind students' conviction in the 1940s that the war would inevitably destroy their generation to the last man. Yet, together with this panic, goes the idea that if only *this* generation can stay pure and stick together and exert its full will, then the world can be re-made. This is Erikson's 'totalism'; either nothing is possible or everything is.

ponsibility of defining the path ahead, of finding a way out of the situation, to someone who fits the antagonistic stance, and looks as if he is strong and knows what to do.

In large-scale historical situations where crisis leads to dictatorship by a paranoiac, however, we commonly find an additional element — both the leader and the mass of people share a conspiracy theory about their plight. Indeed, the would-be leader is distinguished exactly by the unusually vivid grip which the commonly-seen 'persecutors' have on his imagination. Neumann, in the essay already cited (see above, p. 366), carefully analyses the principal conspiracy theories from the fourteenth-century Roman dictator, Cola di Rienzo, through the French religious wars of the sixteenth century and the Jesuit 'conspiracy' of the seventeenth century, to the American Know-nothings, the Ku Klux Klan and the Populists,[52] the Bolshevik theory of capitalist encirclement[53] and the Nazi theory of Jewish conspiracy. This view of history, he says, is

> never completely false, but always contains a kernel of truth and, indeed, must contain it, if it is to have a convincing effect. The truer it is, one might say, the less regressive the movement; the falser, the more regressive.[54]

The paranoid dictator has the advantage over the ordinary paranoid in that the development of his delusions feeds on, and is validated by, popular support, and he has the opportunity to fulfil his menace with real force.[55]

Once established, the caesaristic movement is compelled to institution-alise persecutory anxiety because it

> can never endure a long wait for power. This is precisely what follows from its affective basis. While the non-affective mass organisation, such as a normal political party, can exist for a long time without disintegrating, the caesarist movement must hurry precisely because of the instability of the cement that holds it together: the libido-charged affectivity. After it has come to power it faces the need of institution-alizing anxiety as a means of preventing the extinction of its affective base by its bureaucratic structure. The techniques are familiar: propaganda and terror.[56]

Once the paranoid stance has become the conventional cultural wisdom, the job is done; the glove has been turned inside out and the paranoia now contains the politics. Every political system, Neumann concludes, is based on anxiety, but 'One may perhaps say that the totally repressive system institutionalizes depressive and persecutory anxiety, the half-way liberal system, true anxiety.'

Elias Canetti makes a fresh look at the Schreber case[57] the pretext for a dark essay on Hitler, Stalin and the political ruler throughout history. Schreber's delusions, he says, lay bare the inner processes of power, no matter that he merely dreamed it, or that repressed homosexuality was at its root. The essence of the *Memoirs* is the structure of the political-delusional world and the way it is peopled. The paranoiac has the sense of an exalted position to defend and make secure,* a position that is greatly threatened, especially by enemy packs. Surrounded by hostility, plotted and conspired against continually, his piercing intellect always unmasks his enemies — he has only to stretch out his hand to drag forth a conspirator. Indeed, he attracts crowds — draws to him, through his illness, the totality of souls. By contact with him, they grow smaller; he consumes them:

> The great man swallows the midgets; they literally go inside him
> and disappear completely. . . Their purpose had actually been hostile;
> originally they were sent to confuse his reason and thus destroy him.
> But it was precisely this threat which gave him the strength to grow;
> and once he knows how to master them, he feels proud of his power
> of attraction.[59]

This is indeed a precise model of political power, the power which feeds on the crowd and derives its substance from it. We note

> The strong and lasting attraction exercised over the individuals who
> are to form a crowd; the ambiguous attitude of these individuals;
> their subjection through being reduced in size; the way they are
> taken into the man who, in his own person, in his *body*, represents
> political power; the fact that his greatness must continually *renew*
> itself in this way; and finally . . . the sense of catastrophe which
> is linked with it, of danger to the world order arising from its sudden
> and rapid increase and unexpected magnetism.[60]

Indeed, he feels himself the last man alive; others about him are '*fleeting, improvised men*'. The ruler sends them to their death. He diverts death on to them — to be spared it himself. His craving for invulnerability and passion for survival merge. He tries on various identities as national champion and saviour of the world, experimenting in thought with crowds he wants to attack or rule (it comes to the same thing).

> The idea that all other human beings had perished dominated him for
> years and this of course meant that he thought of himself as being the
> only one. Gradually, however, this idea was superseded by some-
> thing less extreme: from being the only man alive he became the only
> one who mattered.

> It is difficult to resist the suspicion that behind paranoia, as behind
> all power, lies the same profound urge: the desire to get other men
> out of the way so as to be the only one; or, in the milder, and indeed
> often admitted, form, to get others to help him *become* the only one.[61]

This is, indeed, to see into the 'later champion', who experienced

---

* The paranoid Czech anti-Communist hero of V.I Borin's novel, *The Uprooted Survive* (1961), believes himself 'one of the thirty-six dependable anti-communists in the world'.[58]

Catholics, Jews and Slavs as hostile, swarming crowds, hating them for their very existence and planning the conquest of the world. We need the megalomaniac fantasies spelled out in this way to reassure us that even in nightmare and psychosis there is structure. In routine politics, however, the rulers we have to deal with are likelier to be creatures of daylight.

Powerlessness, disillusion and cynicism

The diarists themselves established this cluster of affects, which had been anticipated loosely as 'political negativism' (working to blacken politics and spur on withdrawal), less by the frequency of their recourse to it (18% of entries) than by the weight of the terms in which they reported it.

Powerlessness

An oppressive sense of powerlessness hung, first of all, over many personal circumstances:

- A trainee teacher has her grant cut; she feels the 'hopelessness' of fighting the 'impenetrable bureaucracy' of the Education Department.
- A social worker feels powerless to alter the 'authoritarian and ineffective procedures' of the psychiatric clinic she is attached to as part of her training.
- A girl doing vacation work as a shop assistant feels her 'utter inability' to get the supervisors to see how her job (and that of her fellow salesgirls) might be made 'more tolerable'.
- A member of the executive of the University Women's Liberation group feels 'totally disillusioned' with her colleagues, and 'totally unable' to see how she could convince them of the reasonableness of her (less radical) views or her good faith.
- A male student becomes very depressed after reflecting 'how utterly dependent' student politics is on the 'ideas of non-students'.
- A radical student leader is refused a South African visa, and a friend of his thinks how 'implacable and unshakeable' the Apartheid regime is.

Somewhat less tied to events, or at least spiralling rapidly up from them into gloomy ideological ruminations:

- Someone sees a film about an attempted Leftist revolt in Argentina which is brutally put down; he feels that the 'struggle against world capitalism is probably doomed to failure'.
- Another (circumstances missing) is led to reflect dolefully on the way 'all organisations confine and restrict', and the 'impossibility of dispensing with them'.
- Another (again, situation not described) finds he has 'rather lost hope for reform, generally'.

– Someone reads Sartre for the first time and gets a full sense of his
  notion of futility.

Further scenarios of gloom are provided by threats to cherished places:
there is no stopping flats or freeways being constructed, or a street being
used as a speedway, or a motel being built in a beauty spot. In the city at
large, people are 'appalled at the way migrants are treated and can see no
real likelihood of improvement'; they are appalled also by the state of
community mental hospitals and the state of the prisons. A girl, for
example, visited the mental hospital and gaol at B——:

> – The only place politics struck in at my personal feelings during the
>   month. I was incredibly affected by the recognition of the
>   inability of the government to really change the situation, and at
>   the loneliness and desperate plight of these poor people... Seeing it
>   made the difference.

In national affairs, people were upset by the powerlessness of the new
Labour government to 'change the general shape of the Budget', or to halt
public-service salary rises, or to stop inflation, 'due basically to selfishness,
materialism and greed', or to check urban sprawl.

> – Someone felt 'frustration and indignation with the whole political
>   system' in a situation where all three right-wing parties announced
>   they would contemplate merging.
> – Another bemoans the 'hopeless state of Australian scientific re-
>   search and the impossibility of improvement'.
> – Someone (provocation missing) has a 'sense of how easily and
>   constantly the powerful manipulate and use ordinary people'.

Internationally, eight diarists bemoaned their powerlessness in face of
the French nuclear tests, one in face of 'the drift of world politics generally',
and two at the trend of affairs in Cambodia.

The quality of melodramatic emphasis – 'utter impossibility', 'total
hopelessness' – is striking, even for diarists. Such extreme terms suggest
immobilisation, paralysis before the task, a touch, indeed, of the 'Gulliver
complex' (Brachfeld)[1] – the sense of being *dwarfed* by problems or opponents. Seeing the situation in these terms frees one from guilt – one cannot
be blamed for not acting when the odds against success are so astrono-
mical. It is odd, perhaps, to see so much of this feeling in young and relatively capable people, yet it may be so marked partly because their original
expectations of achievement are so strong. One sees apathy* rather than
powerlessness in the old and dull. In the very exaggeration of their
language, however, our diarists seem half-conscious of indulging a *mood* –

---

* Leites reminds us that apathy may cloak strong aggression:
   'Affectlessness is ... not only a defense against the various phantasied
   dangers of involvement but also an instrument of aggression against (and contempt for) those persons who expect a fuller response from the [individual].
   The aggression proceeds by spiteful obedience: demands are complied with in
   the letter but not in the spirit.'[2]

such black feelings can surely be expected to pass — and there is a touch of paranoia in the extreme contrast between *'their'* power and *'ours'*.

Powerlessness, disillusion and cynicism are all reactive: they follow some check to an original outward impulse to action and self-affirmation, even if only in fantasy. To be disillusioned, one has first to have illusions. The developmental prototype here is that described by Franz Alexander (see above, p. 350), the regressive pull towards remaining childlike and dependent, as one meets sharp setbacks on the path towards competence and maturity.[3]

We may, perhaps, go a little deeper into this problem with the aid of the Kleinian notion of infantile depressive anxiety. Some time after the fourth month, the infant recognises his mother as whole object, and begins to struggle with the anxieties springing from his ambivalence towards her — above all, the anxiety that his hatred has destroyed her, or will do so in the future.

> At the height of his ambivalence he is exposed to depressive despair.
> He remembers that he has loved, and indeed still loves his mother,
> but feels that he has devoured or destroyed her so that she is no
> longer available in the external world. Furthermore, he has also
> destroyed her as an internal object, which is now felt to be in bits.
> The infant's internal world is felt to be in bits in identification with
> this object and acute feelings of loss are experienced, as well as guilt,
> pining, and hopelessness about regaining it.[4]

This sense of pitifully reduced powers, of paralysis before evil, may be reactivated on many adult occasions, not least in politics. Money-Kyrle has written well of the misreading of political reality through the distorting glass of depression, which erodes the capacity to face up to a long-term danger. The group refuses to take action against the anxiety itself and relies instead on abusing or belittling those who deal with these anxieties in a more aggressive or positive way; rather than have to think about foreign hostility, for example, they will call war-mongers those who insist on re-armament — or else they will magnify the power of an aggressor, and see it as more important to leave him unprovoked than to risk his anger by adopting postures of defence.[5]

Of all who have written on the sense of powerlessness as central to modern politics, the most insistent has been Erich Fromm. His original article, published in 1937, was on the sense of powerlessness in the European bourgeoisie;[6] it dwells, in fact, more on individual psychic distress than does the revised version published in *The Fear of Freedom* (1942).[7] His patients, he says, complained of their powerlessness:

> '. . . I can have no influence on anyone, I can start nothing, I am
> incapable, of my own will, of changing anything either in the external
> world or in myself, I have no strength, I do not exist for others, they
> notice me as little as the air they breathe. . .'[8]

Their complaint is rooted in their childhoods:

> In bourgeois education the child, however affectionately he may
> be treated, is not taken seriously . . . It is a feeling of inferiority in
> the parents which produces this form of education. For . . . the role
> of the adult in bourgeois society, his own impotence in the face of
> forces which he is unable to control or even recognise, deprives him
> of any real autonomy and efficacy.[9]

It is ironic, says Fromm, that the bourgeoisie, at the moment when it has
a greater range of choice (in the matter of life-style and of things to make
and do) than ever before, should cave in in this way, essentially through
a fear of freedom.

He stresses that it is the *unconscious* sense of powerlessness he is talking
about:

> However, this feeling of individual isolation and powerlessness . . . is
> nothing the average normal person is aware of. It is too frightening
> for that. It is covered over by the daily routine of his activities, by the
> assurance and approval he finds in his private or social relations, by
> success in business, by any number of distractions, by 'having fun',
> 'making contacts', 'going places'. But whistling in the dark does not
> bring light. Aloneness, fear, and bewilderment remain; people cannot
> stand it forever.[10]

In short, what people complain of is merely the tip of an iceberg; the rest
they hide from themselves with the illusion that they are coping, being
purposeful or having fun.

Revising the essay for publication in English in 1942, he expanded on
the theme of the inexorable pressure of large-scale technology and organisation; the individual sees himself realistically as in all respects a mere
unit in a manipulated mass — as consumer, producer, audience, and city
resident. It is no accident, he says, that Americans are so taken with
Mickey Mouse, the tiny creature who is in constant flight, and in perpetual danger of being gobbled up. He is truly

> impotent . . . in face of the opaque and highly complicated forces of
> our social structure. Present-day society is rather like a tragi-comical
> performance by millions of dwarfs of a play written for giants.[11]

He forecasts Fascism at the end of every country's road. Individual responsibility will everywhere be abdicated in favour of the strong man,
sado-masochistic hierarchies or automaton conformity.

This prediction has not withstood the test of time. Although technology
and organisation have continued to develop in linear fashion (indeed, we
can now add the multi-national corporation to the array of institutions
we are unable to control), individuals seem not to feel much further down
the road to insignificance. People do seem remarkably able — especially
in small groups, including families — to preserve the human face and the
human scale even through bleak and awesome times.

Disillusionment

The basic mechanism here is very simple: what has been taken as admirable or heroic turns out to be villainous or foolish. Someone or something that claims to be potent, valuable, truthful or innocent is exposed as corrupt, greedy or selfish, or ridiculous, pitiful, of no account. For example:

> — Visited the House of Representatives for the first time. It was very disillusioning: there were eight there, six listening and two asleep! A major forum?
>
> — Bobby Seale runs for mayor — deeply disappointed. The haircut, the whole bit. No more drama in politics. Everyone so 'understanding' while rotten things still exist.
>
> — Struck with the total uselessness of conventional education (Trainee teacher)
>
> — Idealism of the student movement misguided. There are no more Utopias.
>
> — Shocked by the appalling greediness of the children at a picnic our group organised.
>
> — The West Australian election. So prudent, calculating and reactive. Why can't politics sometimes be a matter of right or wrong?
>
> — Visit to the country again — peace and harmony. From here politics seems a matter of little boys playing war — pitiful, conceited little chaps — and I'm for such long stretches taken in by them!

As in the case of powerlessness, we have to deal here with an over-reaction: it is not just disappointment that is being registered, but disillusion. Of course, disillusionment can frequently be justified, and even quite in proportion to the magnitude of the issue — some pieces of politics are, indeed, badly done and, more to the point, grievously belie their promise.

Disillusionment with politics as a whole (as in our last quotation) is of special interest.[12] It often occurs after intense engagement in a single frustrating campaign. But it may be a settled sourness, as with the celebrated reply of the old lady to the canvasser: 'I never vote for them, it only encourages them.'

Cynicism

The cynical reaction follows the same path, but is *forewarned* disillusion: the hero has been 'seen through' in advance, his protestations branded as lies (if he is a villain) or self-delusions (if a fool). Cynicism is an aggressive stance, implicating others in the cynic's negative judgement of events, and bringing them to acknowledge their own mistakes and credulity. It is also, however, self-punishing: and the cynic may, in fact, hurt himself more than he hurts others. As a seventeenth-century don, Henry Aldrich, put it, 'Cynicism is a small brass fieldpiece that eventually breaks and kills the cannoneer.'

We sense that the cynic suffers from some residual excessive idealism that he must keep chastening. Does one get to be cynical only by being at some point massively let down or disappointed, or can one slide into it by stages? Can one, for that matter, be cynical in just one sector – as a trainee teacher, say, might become cynical about the Education Department – or is it by its nature circumambient, and apt to pervade an outlook?*[14] Politics is certainly a large enough target – and an unusually provoking one.

Although most cynicism involves resignation, the withdrawal to a spectator's or a critic's stance (since it is known in advance that action will be unprofitable), there are activist cynics, ambitious men who may achieve political success (they are cynical, it seems, about everything except their own value to the polity). In fact, in some sorts of politics – at court, especially – they may be the main sort of men to be rewarded. Talleyrand's cynicism, for example, superbly capped a system of placeman-politics, where everyone could be bought or disciplined by titles, land or favours.[15] It may be more difficult to get such men past suburban selection committees.[16] Actions cynically planned and carried out may yet, of course, profit the system; this is the large moral, perhaps, of Namier's celebration of the English eighteenth-century Parliament.

Is cynicism an irreversible attitude, or does the possibility always remain of being won back? We sense that cynicism is a shell, an armour (which it should therefore be possible to shed) against the possibility of being found naive or sentimental. One diarist pointed out the importance of fashion:

> – In my first year at college, it was the thing to be cynical about everything. Then in second year, it suddenly dropped right out of fashion.

It may depend on the amount of bitterness that has occasioned the cynical attitude. Some, indeed, have detected at the heart of the cynic stance a secret desire to be proved wrong, and the saying, 'The cynic is one who has remained married to his first love', points us in a promising biographical direction.[17]

There is an interesting association with wit. The several cynical diary-entries had a mildly witty turn:

> – Why all the fuss about Nixon welcoming Whitlam? He'd welcome anyone.
> – Australian politics is so bloody feeble it couldn't even rise to a Watergate.

---

* 'The inner-directed man, when he looks at politics, is likely to be exceedingly cynical about people but not cynical about institutions, constitutions, and ... the value of politics itself. By contrast, the other-directed man, somewhat sentimental about people, is likely to be quite cynical about legal and political institutions, just as he is about the great game of politics itself' (David Riesman).[13]

We recall that Freud saw veiled aggression in jokes; the cynical jibe likewise draws the hearer's latent aggression to the surface. The cynical smile, indeed, has a tab to itself in physiology, as *canicular rictus* – the convulsive contraction of the facial muscles of one side, so that the teeth are shown in the manner of an angry dog (see *O.E.D.*, under 'cynic spasm').

The Greek word denoted both dog and cynic — the man who snarled and barked (and also did not allow himself grandiose dreams). Cynicism attracts intelligence – there are few stupid cynics – and, maybe, especially young intelligence. Bertrand Russell noted that

> Cynicism, such as one finds very frequently among the most highly educated young men and women of the West, results from thé combination of comfort with powerlessness.

It is, at the least, a reliable safeguard against paranoia.

Powerlessness, disillusion and cynicism are all reactive emotions, ways of registering political disappointment and disapproval. Together, they practically exhaust the diarists' negatives; there remain only small clusters of boredom* (best interpreted either as diffuse anger or as feeling 'full of emptiness'),[18] apathy and (accounting for a shamefully small number of admissions) 'confusion/bewilderment'.

> — Disinterested in politics at present. I resent its stagnant parties and its too-far-from-real issues . . .
> — I feel detached. I have to work at my sense of revulsion.

There was little sign of any *tenacious* sense of estrangement from society, as 'alienation' is sometimes defined; one felt more a rhythm of involvement, recoil and re-involvement. But one entry pognantly linked the sense of loneliness with the inability to 'get started' politically:

> — Felt a deep need to join with a super-individual belief or movement, something in which to bury one's efforts and be positive that they don't go in vain. I couldn't think of any such belief or movement — all were tarnished (some more than others) . . . The result was that I felt even more useless and in a state of high, internal conflict.

Bitterness and sourness

These qualities interest us less as affects in their own right than as accents on the negative emotions already discussed. One may feel bitterly or sourly powerless or cynical or disillusioned, and it may sometimes be important to catch the particular tincture. John Alexander's fine paper on this not only suggests a plausible and memorable formula for distinguishing them, but also provides an admirable model for the analysis of the origin of individual affects.[19] Their peculiar quality, he urges, must be

---

* Boredom, however, may rise to epic heights; cf. 'La France s'ennuie' as an explanation of the events of May 1968

sought in specific early sensation-states, universal in their occurrence.[20] He locates bitterness in the infant's taste of regurgitated bile, and sourness in that of regurgitated hydrochloric acid: the 'sour' infant has been left too long between feeds, is neglected and starved; the 'bitter' infant suffers no outright rejection or neglect, but feels he has been given a poisoned breast. Bitterness contains a querulous note;[21] the bitter person is asking the universe *why?*, and hinting at persecution; sourness is less verbal and less rationalised, but just as hostile in an uncompromising way. We feel it as a psychological victory when a defeated person is not embittered. Bitterness is more common in men, sourness in women.

Bitterness may have an independent political significance in circumstances where it leads to demands for the redress of grievances (at a deeper level it is a protest against loss and a goad to desperate efforts towards the reinstatement of the lost object). It may be highly rationalised or only feebly so, and depends for its intensity on a well-developed sense of unfairness or injustice. In extreme cases, this may be used to justify brutal aggression: 'Such persons assert that injustice and treachery have embittered them beyond endurance.'[22] It can have a socially cohesive effect, but usually of a factional character. The overtone of 'Why am *I* singled out for ill-treatment?' links it with paranoia. It tends towards stubborn, 'resuming the struggle' attitudes, projects blame outwards, and girds to an active response; it also keeps deeper depression at bay. The sour person is not concerned with 'justice', but feels more completely rejected than the bitter person. Sourness may be relied on to help turn anger into hatred. The sour disposition predisposes its owner to failures and disappointments, and thus to more sourness.

The elations

Although a mild or moderate admiration of particular leaders or strokes of policy peppered the diaries, only a handful of entries rose to the level of elation:

> — At Conference met M—C— [a senior federal official in the field of Social Welfare] — admired her tremendously — the true, liberated woman. Marvellous to see all the delegates and clients manoeuvre for her ear . . .
>
> — T.V. interview with a young couple who'd just adopted a Cambodian baby. I hope I can do it one day, because I strongly believe it's a constructive way of aiding not only the world situation, but also our own social condition.
>
> — Enormously excited by the Karmel Report [inaugurating grants to all secondary schools]. I want to master it, become its exponent.
>
> — Today great gladness, ideologically-directed: Community Aid Abroad has just come out and declared it will in future support revolutionary activities with its funds.

We need, Bertram Lewin observes, a noun for the 'falsely-struck' emotion, the affect that is felt at a false pitch, where the primary puzzle is the 'discrepancy between the ego's inner emotional perception and the objective situation'.[23] Certainly the hypomania of an ego that is in league with social and cultural ideals is a central political datum.* The manic activity induced, as individuals finally satisfy their conspicuous hunger and thirst for new experiences and new impressions, for new 'food for thought', for new identifications, is often socially efficacious. Neurotic elations, however, cannot do quite as much for the individuals who harbour them. For they are regressive experiences with denial at their heart, denial of negative qualities in the object, and denial of lack and damage in the self.†[26] The elations strive to regain the timelessness, symbiosis, and other gratifications of early infancy. 'Inspiration' is the immediate perception of inexpressible truth, the realness of breast and milk. 'Bliss' (an emotion unlikely to preoccupy the student of politics) replays the experience of satiation. 'Megalomania' recaptures the nipple.[27] 'Elation' repeats 'the oral triad of wishes in symbolic form, the ecstatic portion the later blissful stages of nursing, and the mania proper the postponement of falling asleep and the defensive denials of early dreams'. Elation relives a memory, so external reality is hardly relevant: the manic repudiates the world's teaching and all he has later learnt himself, and dives back to his own original truth.[28] 'Enthusiasm' is the feeding infant on the way to satisfaction, but still recalling previous deprivation and hunger.

We do not have the background to our diarists' elations, although prior doubts seem influential — doubts about feminine adequacy in the first two, about professional adequacy in the first and third (who is possibly a teacher), and a negative-identification with Third World guerillas (in order to upset the father) in the fourth. The onset of political elation is often sudden, prefaced by some disturbing self-doubt or deprivation. Then some idealised object appears, which offers the possibility of satisfaction. A sense of mutuality with the special object lights up the enthusiasm. The enthusiast immediately looks for others to collude in his hopes; he needs them urgently, since his satisfaction is still only partial and prospective, and the memory of the doubting times still haunts. (One fears for the social substantiation — and the longevity — of all four diarists' enthusiasms.)

In short, both depressive and manic moods are defensive, and involve a setting aside of insight and reality-testing. They call on denial as a chief defence. Each is as likely as the other to overshoot the mark and end up in

---

* Where does the extra energy come from that is tapped by enthusiasm? Greenson's answer is that 'The union with an idealized object does away with all tensions between ego and superego; the superego temporarily gives up its functions. Thus, the id is free from pressure and is permitted greater discharge.'[24]

† 'The more pathological the enthusiasm, the more it is created by and used for denial.'[25]

an emotional extreme. No doubt we prefer idealisation; like moral indignation, it seems excusable as likelier to make things happen. But that is itself to show steep cultural bias; there seems to be little to choose between them in terms of mental health. Perhaps our ideal should be the man without illusions.

Sympathy and pity

A review of terms

Standing aside from the central, tough-minded tradition in political criticism, which is epitomised by Hobbes, and given to celebrating the importance of aggression, selfishness and fear in the constitution of political systems, there is a tender-minded school. It is as earnest as the tough-minded tradition, though less ancient, and seems to begin with Hume and Adam Smith and run raggedly down through Herbert Spencer, Kropotkin, Scheler, McDougall and Trigant Burrow,[1] anxious to point to a basic sympathy and altruism in human nature; to our inability to disregard the misfortunes and sufferings of others; and to the steady historical development of social institutions for mutual aid, for the alleviation of suffering and for the elimination of open conflict. Sympathy, this tradition argues, is the primary source and instrument of social cohesion.

What is the difference between sympathy and pity? Used in good part synonymously, they nevertheless strain towards distinctness. First, we feel sympathy with equals, pity for inferiors. Pity is always felt for suffering: it is the affect appropriate to the victim (as moral indignation is appropriate to the criminal). Sympathy is perhaps possible with positive feelings — etymologically, it is just 'feeling with' (as in the allied word 'compassion') — but in ordinary use, our 'sympathy' with another's delight, say, or satisfaction, tends to be guarded, or tinged with some qualification. We reserve 'empathy' for exercises involving conscious and willed efforts to model, or make a replica of, another's feeling.*

Note that offers of pity are often rejected. Perhaps it is healthy that this should be so, since 'pity comes from a suppressed feeling of hostility and superiority and humiliates' because, in essence, it 'signals that one is too damaged to be loved'.[2] Sympathy, too, may be rejected — again, because one refuses the status of victim and accepts responsibility for the misfortune, say, as something self-caused or hazarded or counted on. Yet many actively seek pity — the hypochondriac, for example — in a neurotic variant of the desire to be loved.[3]

---

* Political writings mostly link empathy with leadership — leaders must be able to empathise with the opposing players and with their own followers. We make our own efforts to put ourselves in their places; one diarist, for example, muses, 'Nixon's under such pressure just now, he must be near a heart attack!'

We are inclined to say that sympathy is involuntary: 'When you feel pity, you don't ask others first whether you ought to' (G. C. Lichtenberg). The feelings is not always immediate, however, and there may be a threshold of thought and reflection. We normally recognise grief, for instance, at once; certainly, we are most easily moved when the cause and nature of the suffering is quite patent; but we sometimes notably withhold sympathy where the predicament is not recognised or understood.

Sympathy operates in a way that might be termed a *sympathy slope*. At the minimum, there is the mere recognition that sympathy is in order. One may switch off here, feeling that one can't help, or that sympathy would be unprofitable. At the next level, we allow ourselves to feel sympathy (which is a lightly painful feeling) but only in token quantities, and still as only one's own feeling − 'I know you are in pain, but I feel my sympathy and my pain, not your anguish and your pain'. Again, one may switch off here, as might the diner in an expensive restaurant, who cannot bear to look at the faces of the hungry outside in the dark, because their state is too painful for him to think of. Further down still, one sets oneself to grasp the other's suffering as he feels it by some swift movement of empathy or patient reconstruction of the situation in its details, in order to arrive at a conviction of 'how he *must* feel'. Scheler says, 'Genuine sympathy is an intentional act, a movement, like love . . . In genuine sympathy, the sorrow of the other person is grasped as *his* sorrow and the sympathizer's sorrow is directed toward this fact . . . Genuine sympathy intends . . . not one's own feelings, but the center of awareness of the other person.'[4]

Is there necessarily, at the bottom of the slope, the final step of an impulse to help, an urge to reparative activity? Some have said that pity is essentially 'feminine', a melting and resolving agent that paralyses, quiets, and even prevents active help being given.*[5] It is indeed a feat of identification, of incorporation − we take into ourselves another's heavy feelings and make them our own − and it is over when that has been honestly done. This is linked, of course, with protestations of the uselessness of pity:

> Pity has never helped anyone.   (Old proverb)
> Pity is evil in itself and useless.   (Spinoza)
> If all the people in the world should agree to sympathise with a
> certain man at a certain hour, they would not cure him of his
> headache.   (E. W. Howe)

* Jekels distinguishes this 'passive-identification' pity from 'active-non-identification' pity, the pity of reaction-formation: *he* has it, not *I*; he is damaged/weak, I am whole/strong; which proclaims our difference, immunity, superiority, and distance.[6] (Bergler says that when alms are given, it is 'outdistancing' rather than mere 'conscience' money).[7] His basic contention is that in pity the ego (unconsciously) demonstrates to the super-ego how it would like to be treated, that is, with love and tender concern, this model response being bestowed on some unfortunate in the real world.

and with the cynical use of sympathy as a 'sop':

Tell him all he can have is our heartfelt sympathee.(W. S. Gilbert)

But Scheler, who thought deeply about the matter, insists that 'the act of sympathy is more important than the social consequences of it'. In itself, it is a human and moral feat, and the world is better for it. Most, however, see the giving of help of some sort as the only thing that can dissolve or terminate the pain of sympathy. As with anger or moral indignation, it is essentially a spur to action.

With or without the reparative impulse (but especially *with* it), we have the question of how we gauge the appropriate level of sympathy. Adam Smith thought that we always tend to err on the side of callousness, and that the benevolent person should therefore set himself earnestly to look into the particulars of the victim's situation.* On the other hand, victims are always inclined to ask for too much sympathy, sunk as they are in the very real outrage and misery of their plight. The balance, Smith thought, could be struck if we tried the exercise of imagining an 'impartial spectator' instead of the victim in the victim's plight. (This should answer, too, questions about the appropriate level of *self*-pity.)

The stretching of pity is clearly a humane and creative function. Left to ourselves, we would always produce too little of it; indeed, we can see certain social institutions permanently and centrally involved in this task — the clergy, literature, political leaders and the media.[10]

The objects of sympathy

An American sociologist has propounded a 'law' of declension of sympathy in concentric circles: at the centre are our immediate companions, and children; in the next circle out, other members of our class or nation; next, the human race in general; and, finally, the lower animals.[11] We may certainly predicate at any one time a social 'sympathy schedule' which is a matter of common agreement across a particular community, even though many details — and even some of the underlying principles — may remain obscure. It is obviously worse to be blind than to have a wooden leg, and whole stretches of the law of compensation and pension administration, for example, attempt to spell out such common understandings. Despite (or because of) welfare economics, the 'schedule' is notably under-researched. Kenneth Boulding has only recently drawn our attention to the unsuspectedly large part domestic charity plays in economic life. Only the professionals of public-charity fund-raising have begun

---

* In a notable dissenting judgment, Sophie Bryant defends a 'partial hardening of the heart against the contagion of social feeling [and] sympathetic distraction' under modern conditions. She warns of emotional 'invasion from without' and commends a neutral or cold insight as a more reliable source of help to the suffering.[8] Her essay is striking corroboration of Simmel's famous lecture, *The Metropolis and Mental Life* (1902).[9]

(and that in a frankly manipulative way) to explore the 'drawing power' of particular plights.[12]

Theory, therefore, outruns knowledge, and why we should pity is much more closely discussed than *what*, in fact, we do. Two hypotheses command the field: these are, that we pity what we fear, and that we pity what we have ourselves undergone. Rousseau propounded the latter view: 'We pity in others only those evils we have ourselves experienced.' Personal knowledge of a plight does, indeed, often spur sympathy with fellow-sufferers, and produces the sort of freemasonry that unites, for example, those who have had asthma. One diarist told how the recent shock of her father's death, and the inability of those around her to understand how she felt, had led her to become something of an exponent of grief and to seek out the newly bereaved to share her knowledge with them. The old politician, Webb (see above, pp. 167–72), was able to respond only to those distressing predicaments among his constituents that he himself had experienced as a child. Personal suffering (and self-pity), as encouragements to help, communicate with and, maybe, organise those in the common plight, merge with the close and anxious acquaintance of parents or friends in a particular 'good cause'. It seems unlikely, however, that sympathy alone ever binds a 'plight' group together without coarser cords of anger or fear. Note the additional spur of 'I've come through' as an incentive to helping those who are still in trouble (as is the case with Alcoholics Anonymous). Note, too, the stubborn exceptions: '*I* got through all that without anyone's sympathy, I'm not going to give *them* any.'

Often enough, too, fear is an indispensable element in our sympathy. We especially pity those like us, whose fate could well be ours. Conversely, when we do *not* fear a particular fate, our pity for its victims is the more grudging: we are callous towards the old, because we refuse to believe that we will grow old, too; Australians think that earthquakes, volcanoes and blizzards are somehow faintly unserious — but bush-fires and floods they understand.

Thus, we respond positively to innocence; we sympathise, say, with crippled children more readily than with alcoholics, with those who have cancer of the brain rather than of the lung, with the death of a pedestrian more than with that of a motorist, with the death of a motorist more than with that of a soldier. It is partly that we recognise greater scope in some plights for potential gains and remedial activity (children's, as compared with geriatric, charities). Part, however, is sheer moralism. Moral indignation and sympathy are mutually exclusive. We *can* pity a man whose plight is very largely his own fault, or due to vice or crime, but only in so far as we put out of our minds the culpable elements of the situation. In many cases, we have a frank choice of stressing the pitiable or the blameworthy in a predicament and responding accordingly. Moral indignation *is* a refusal of sympathy, and sympathy an exclusion of moral indignation. The 'shocking history of social reform' has, in fact, been largely a project of enlarging human sympathies, progressively reclassifying 'criminals' as 'victims'. Transpositions can be rapid, indeed: in Australia, for example, in the 1960s, the attitude towards unmarried mothers was perhaps more of moral indignation than of sympathy; now it is the opposite. We are still some way, however, from Samuel Butler's utopian proposal that the criminals be put in hospital and the physically ill gaoled.

It is difficult to feel sympathy with large numbers of people. Although we ought to feel more sympathy as the number of sufferers in a plight increases, we command an uncomfortably low ceiling. A plane crash is worse than a car crash; a riot or natural calamity worse still; but we are unable to lift our response with any adequacy to the victims of Hiroshima — 100,000 or 110,000 — let alone to the six million Jewish victims of Nazism, or the eleven million of both sides killed in 1914–18. The newspapers on this account are full of asymmetrical stories — of the 'Australian dies in Air Crash (and 65 Turks)' variety — or, even more telling, the animal sub-species: of '400 killed in Lima, Peru (page 14), Small dog trapped down well in West Melbourne (page 1)'.

From Chaucer's time, at least, we have been ambivalent about animal lovers. They show an admirable capacity for refined feeling — approaching, indeed, the Buddhist sensibility that can feel for dying flowers, small insects and 'little souls' generally — but we suspect, as we do with the Prioress,[13] some inappropriateness and displacement; dogs are found to be so lovable and worthwhile, so innocent and reliably affectionate, just because humans have turned out to be so disappointing. And we reject the implied reproof. The radical students of Flinders University, unable to get public attention for their anti-Vietnam war campaign, announced that they would next Wednesday napalm a small dog on campus. The animal lovers of Adelaide erupted, and fell into the rather neat trap of demonstrating that the illusory threat to one local dog could arouse more concern in them than the whole carnage of a war.

Sympathy frequently gets entangled with sentimentality, which may be summarily described as the feeling that 'one has been left out'.*[14] One diarist described as her strongest feeling for the month:

> — Inexplicably sad over the burial of that Czech hijacker in Alice Springs. [He had been overpowered and shot by a passenger.] Story seemed to epitomise the agony of the lonely migrant male — he'd only just come from New Zealand, could find no one at all to talk

* cf. the parable of the Good Shepherd and the one lost sheep. The ur-sentimental movie is *The Way of All Flesh*: released from ten years' gaol on Christmas Eve, Wallace Beery peers through the window at his wife and children preparing the Christmas tree . . . realising that they do not miss him, and would get on better without him, he turns and walks away. Snow falls.

to ... Made me wish I could 'adopt' several such people, give them at least a friendly ear.

Drawing, she herself noted (thus modifying the word 'inexplicably'), on the much lighter loneliness of her own arrival as a migrant schoolgirl, she could pierce through — in a way the media made no attempt to — to the youth's emotional state. Sentimental sympathy seems, then, to be a variant of the 'what I've suffered' formula, based on identification with the plight — a variant one might express as 'what I've wanted in childhood and not got (or what I've *not* wanted in childhood and have got all the same)'.

Individual differences

Sympathy, Scheler notes, is a late development in the individual as in mankind; it must be civilised into him. The commentators are agreed that the road from the infant's ruthless egotism and solipsism to the child's respectful care of others' feelings is long and hard. And some learn much more of the lesson than others. One's capacity for sympathetic relations with others seems to depend in large part on the promptness and effectiveness with which one's own affective needs have been met: the well-nurtured can nurture well in their turn. But the steps in the path are not very clear.

We begin, perhaps, around the age of two, with 'mock-mothering' of 'poor baby' (or doll), sick animal or crying mother. Kindergarten children are as busy with sympathetic, as with aggressive, acts.[15] It is not till six or seven, though, that the child can autonomously imagine the plight of the 'poor Indian child (so like, and unlike me)'. Jekels stresses the experience, around five or six, of the beating fantasy, which lays the foundation for 'female' (masochistic) identificatory pity.[16] Reactive, non-identificatory pity, however, he ties to the 'threat', at a similar age, to 'narcissistic masculinity and ... the tenacious defence of this masculinity' (that is, to castration anxiety). Later still, one observes parents singling out a particular child (often the middle one) as the family 'understander', who can be most relied on for the fully sympathetic response, and who then becomes the receptacle for family grievance and pain.[17] Otto Sperling has presented two interesting cases of people working actively for the welfare of the underprivileged, in whom he was able to trace a massive guilt at childhood *over*-privilege, in particular for being the father's favourite, and yet unable to return the great love he showered on them.[18]

Certainly, the larger society at any one time exhibits a striking range of personal differences in the capacity for sympathy* — from President Johnson's 'bleeding hearts' (folk disposed to respond to any and every call on their generous feelings) to the totally callous and ruthless. Among the latter is an interesting political type, the man ignoring this year's deserving cause, who, from his selectively callous perch, berates the

---

* The allied but separate gift of the capacity to communicate sympathy is also most patchily spread.

'windy sentimentalism' of his fellows. Carlyle's denial of sympathy to the anti-slavery movement epitomises the stance.[19]

The notion of a conventional 'sympathy schedule' does not, of course, rule out dramatically idiosyncratic sympathies in individuals — and what a person most pities will show, like the splendid projective device it is, the whole man. People can make creative moral discoveries in this field, stumbling on 'one of those sudden shocks of pity that sometimes decentralise a life' (Edith Wharton). For example, the London *New Society* reported recently the establishment of the Portia Trust; this is the brainchild of a country journalist with no experience of social work who was suddenly and unaccountably shocked at the 'atrocious' gaol sentence given to Pauline Jones in 1971. The trust is designed to befriend and care for women convicted of stealing babies. 'He has been writing to eight convicted baby snatchers, and intends to pursue his sympathetic study of their psychological problems' with backing from the Schizophrenia Association and the National Association of Probation Officers.[20]

Eccentric as this may seem, the story illustrates dependable mechanisms in the politics of pity. An individual suddenly sees a victim where others have seen something quite ordinary or something criminal; he sees that moral indignation and callousness are standing in the way of the fully sympathetic response (cf. the migrant-girl diarist and the hijacker). The crusader[21] is born, however, when, after shock, he is able aggressively to turn back the moral affront against the moralists, in this case, the judges. He is now as indignant with *their* callousness to the sick women, as they have been with the snatchers' callousness to the real mothers. Where we have 'victims', we at once have 'oppressors' — at the least, an oppressive and disabling environment. Still, feeling painfully alone in possession of his moral insight, the crusader reaches out anxiously to all possible supporters and sets his long siege on conventional opinion. A great deal of nineteenth-and twentieth-century politics — from opposition to child labour and negro slavery to the full paraphernalia of the Welfare State and decolonisation — runs in this 'suffering-situation' mould, for 'liberalism is goodwill turned doctrinaire; it is philanthropy organised to be efficient'.[22]

The politics of sympathy

What adjusts and readjusts the 'sympathy schedule'? Deliberate campaigns, both professional and amateur, spring to the eye, but, in looking ahead, one senses that there is a very long way to go in educating our sympathies to a full recognition of 'victimage'. It also seems difficult to promote particular victim-groups too rapidly in public favour without upsetting the 'sympathy status' of others, who are thereby made to feel neglected and under-regarded. For example, opinion polls find that 'Unmarried mothers now have it too easy — a pension, their independence, *and* public sympathy!' Brooding on this, the unhappily married basic-wage earner, who has chosen to abide by the Conventions and quietly to endure his troubles, feels simply disregarded and worse off. Robert Coles's Middle Americans voted Nixon in to get all the 'bums' and ungrateful foreigners off the national payroll.[23] In this way, sympathy is the final coin of politics. Anger and fear may secure short-term victories and dramatically boost the stocks (and takings) of certain groups, but, in the long run, nothing can be sustained without a basis in public sympathy.

That the schedule does, indeed, fluctuate — and not always in response to conscious agitation — a glance at the story of the Australian Returned Servicemen's League will show. At the end of the war, the ex-servicemen were top group, and deserved the best of everything. If not injured, they had at least lost years, and gratitude joined with sympathy to support generous programmes of farm settlement, housing, vocational training and preference in employment and promotion. After ten years, this last was withdrawn: one could not permanently deny promotion to the young; victims or not, the group was coming to have had its 'fair chance'. At the height of the Vietnam War, opposed by Labour and by the young, who resented its assumption of infallible expertise in national security and its demands for hawkish patriotism, the League reached its nadir. There may be a further, Chelsea pensioner, stage ahead, where, publicly housed and dressed in scarlet, ex-servicemen otherwise unoccupied may lend a bright nostalgia to public ceremonial. In any case, the sympathy-curve stands out as basic to the group's fortunes; and it has an organic rhythm, little affected by the conscious strategies of the leadership.

Rather often in our politics, the descrying of a sympathy-plight becomes associated with 'rescue fantasies',[24] which in turn lead to unreal hopes, restless innovation, and bitter disillusionment when programmes fail. The allocation of 'more money' is the obvious opening move, but it soon appears in field after field that skilled help alone will effect real change. Sometimes even this falls short, as in the American Head Start programme. In a similar local case, university student leaders in the mid 1960s founded an Aboriginal Scholarship scheme to keep aboriginal teenagers in secondary school. They stayed — their parents, welcoming the grant, insisted on it — but they slumped at the back of the class, learned nothing and felt miserable. A separate black secondary programme is now advocated. In general, education seems to be at a turning point, where money can buy nothing further that will actually improve the classroom experience; we are back in the hands of an irritable and dishevelled profession.

As the standard of inter-personal emotional and intellectual skills required for the socially acceptable life-performance in our society rises, a higher proportion of people each year fails to reach it and voluntarily seeks, or is declared in need of, help. It is now estimated that, at some point in his life, one person in four will become the client of the welfare professionals — psychiatrists, social workers, probation officers, truant officers, school psychologists, marriage-guidance counsellors (quite apart from requiring the usual services of doctors, teachers and so on). Welfare is therefore very important to politicians. But it is also the most consistently frustrating and disillusioning slice of the public sector. Programmes seem to lag behind requirements, and professional indecision about what should be attempted, and in what way, seems endemic. So we see constant flight to administrative reorganisations which simply rake the existing incompetences into a new pattern. Welfare reform may, indeed, have become professionalised,[25] but the professionals concerned seem singularly unable to come to intellectual grips with their task.

Our earlier question about whether sympathy, if merely token, was worth anything, is made very obvious in the ambivalent status of private charity in our welfare budget. While in Australia we demand that the State meet every detail of schooling-costs, we support hospitals by inventing hundreds of amateur fund-raising expedients. Somehow we feel both that it would be wrong for the Treasurer to be totally charitable on our behalf, and yet chafe under the inefficiencies and snobberies of voluntarism. Could real acts of sympathy in the end be divorced from money?

Loyalty, pride and trust
The feeling of loyalty*

What do we feel when we feel loyal? Is it a throb or spasm of emotion — of pride, perhaps, or love — or is it that 'The participant feels himself to be infused with vital energy from outside himself and elevated by self-transcending purposes'?[1] Or is it barer than this — little more, perhaps, than a sense of connectedness with, or implication in, or oneness with some object? Certainly, it requires some other — a person, a group or a set of ideas with which the ego has become identified, and whose fortunes are now in some sense its own. It is not necessary to *feel* loyal in order to *be* loyal. Indeed, loyalty seems mostly to operate as an implicit system. We set up a loyalty-relationship with an object, we feel directly involved in it — larger for its triumphs and threatened or diminished by any reverse — and, over the years, we behave accordingly, without having to think out each step, hating loyally, fearing loyally,* and acting as a group-member

* We pair 'commitment' with loyalty: loyalty tends to be old, stable and unconscious; commitment tends to be recent, deliberate and energising. Trust and respect are also affects in the loyalty area; they are more sharply focused on the object — leader, institution or régime — than is loyalty, and they are a shade more vivid. Running through the terms in this chapter is an underlying sense of legitimacy, of things being done with piety, in a seemly or proper style.

For a brief discussion of hope as an affect in the loyalty group, see my essay, 'Varieties of hope', in Ross Fitzgerald (ed.), *The Sources of Hope*, Sydney, Pergamon (1979).

† Can one *envy* loyally? Public officials seem especially difficult to envy.

should, fighting, working, co-operating, bragging and lying loyally. The feeling of loyalty can, however, be brought out for inspection, unlike affects such as envy: people may admit to a diminution of loyalty towards a leader who has 'betrayed them', and they may openly proclaim their loyalty on a comparative scale ('The Oblate Fathers are second to none in their adoration of the Virgin').

With or without characteristic sensations (and they *are* somewhat diaphanous), it is significant that the decision to be loyal so often follows criticism of the object. The child, say — and this is likely to be his first experience of the affect — is put on the spot when a playmate or a malicious adult criticises one of his siblings or parents. The criticism may well be familiar, one that he makes himself or recognises as true, but if he rejects it (and he may surprise himself in doing so), he evinces loyalty. Disowning criticism, denying fault, comes near the heart of the loyal response. Not for ever, of course, nor even necessarily for very long (only *blind* loyalty denies the possibility of fault, now or in future), but *for the present*, one decides, the object is going to be stood up for.

Once disloyalty is disowned, the individual has to decide what loyalty requires of him in the particular situation. The nature of the provocation — its degree or novelty — may be uppermost, or it may be wearily familiar: calculation follows choice. The crisis of loyalty may annex a year or a life; one thinks of the Croatian or Lithuanian mother dedicating her son to the liberation army. But it may also precede it, as in qualified loyalty — 'I'll go on supporting the Labour party as long as it spends well on education' — where one specifies some future point at which one may withdraw support. Secondary groups in politics characteristically receive this conditional loyalty, adherents threatening to decamp if and when the group should cross any one of their deeper lines of loyalty.

Loyalty seems peculiarly educable, susceptible to discipline and coaching. Leaders strive to persuade adherents that the group deserves more of their concern, and commitment at still greater strength. They wish to intensify and magnify loyalty. Groups succeed or fail in politics as they pick up or lose cohesion and morale.[2] Politics, Ranyard West claims, *is* the control of loyalty.[3] On the other side, politics appears whenever loyalties conflict.

It is hard to find any trace of the concept of loyalty earlier than the Middle Ages. The word itself (closely connected with the French *loi* and the Latin *lex*) signifies obedience to that which ought to be obeyed — not to the law in the narrow, statute sense,[*] but to the authority whose claim on one's allegiance one freely admits. The first loyalties were to persons, as in the idea of fealty to one's lord. Feudalism built them into a

---

[*] Indeed, 'loyalist' and 'legalist' to this day suggest contrasting types: the latter is to be counted on merely for minimum performance, the former promises high enthusiasm, tireless service and unlimited faithfulness.[4]

polity. They then accreted round the state, as that was redefined in successive constitutions. Attachment, then, to some definite authority, which has a right to be served, is the historic core of the notion: and in the course of history, individuals became progressively freer to choose their attachments. Primitive loyalties were obdurate and inevitable: the accustomed life in the native surroundings was seen as of infinite value, the object, in effect, of religious faith, and worthy of 'devotion through all suffering unto death'.[5] Even today, we still associate feelings of 'special warmth, familiarity and unique existence' with the primary groups of our earliest years.[6]

The loyal company
One early loyalty-formation, more fraternal than filial, continues to haunt the preconscious of contemporary associations — the loyalty-band. In the companies of pre-Christian heroes and of Christian knights, as described in the *Morte d'Arthur* and *The Mabinogion,* comradeship-pacts promised the individual, as long as he was acting in the service of the special vows or of the ideals they had jointly sworn to uphold, total support from all those in the company. Something of the selfless closeness of the chivalric order continues to inform the ego-ideal of present-day sporting clubs, worshipful companies of drapers, and loyal orders of buffaloes (loyal, it should be said, not to the monarch but to the membership) — and, more sympathetically, communes and 'invisible colleges'. Indeed, it does not seem too far-fetched to attribute some of the regular disillusionment that befalls those joining political parties to some vestigial expectation that fellow-members will share an intense dedication to a common set of political ideals and will give each other an unqualified support. The ghost of the loyal company is to be seen as well in the student peer-group: those who, at university, jointly drew up an agenda for political and social renovation, will, long after they have quietly ditched the project, sustain a special regard for (and for the good opinion of) those who knew them in those palmy days when they seemed full of promise.

The loyalty to a vow one has made, inherent in the organisation of the loyal company, can be upheld privately, and this is the basis of the rare but possible usage, 'loyal to oneself', where one understands that an artist, say, takes special care of his daemon, or the ordinary man of his soberest resolutions for himself. The professional man's lifelong performance of work at levels of high quality and difficulty rests on precisely this foundation.

The objects of loyalty
Families do not consciously seek to make children loyal, but there is usually some sense, as we have seen, that the family circle is *special ground.* If this is made very special, vitally different from neighbours, it may later produce extremely vivid 'we-they' conceptions.[7] The unconditional sup-

port, regard and care that family members ideally give each other informs people's hopes in all subsequent groups and associations. But it is often flawed in the original family setting and seems easier to contrive between parents and children than between siblings themselves. Parents often have to work hard to foster inter-sibling loyalty. Parents draw narcissistic satisfaction from the qualities and achievements of their offspring, while children pass through a standard over-estimation of parents, who are only gradually shrunk to more realistic stature. Of course, parents are not always united, and even light competition for a child's regard raises the spectre of disloyalty over confidences. When extreme, it can produce the bitterness of an enduring alliance of the child and one parent in opposition to the other.

If crises of loyalty lie all around the family's perimeter, so, too, do the proximate groups to which the child's loyalties are next attached: the local neighbourhood,* street gang, or church congregation. John Dollard's brilliant reconstruction of the social world of the four- to six-year old illustrates the process by which the child, reflecting on the meaning to 'us' of the principal local social categories, bodies out in these years his social map of loyalties and antipathies.[10] These early face-to-face groups share with the family the power to make their social space encompassing and 'special'. The larger formations they represent — ethnic groups, classes, religious denominations — may function like whole communities, providing so rich and complex an environment that the individual has little cause to venture beyond it. 'Over-estimation' of these native groups (including the nation, the concept of which slowly accretes over the primary school years in the child's mind)[11] is almost universal, especially where they form a closely woven mesh that constitutes a life long integument for the loyalist.

Under the sign of character-building, the *school* deliberately sets out to coach the child in loyalty-behaviour, valuing *a priori* any movement away from pure self-concern. Where it is small, wholly residential and somewhat out of the way, a school may contrive, as a total institution, to generate significant intimacies, that can stir, at least, nostalgia in its alumni. The normal neighbourhood secondary school, however, has to fight to be taken seriously, since pupils tend to see it, realistically enough, as just another filling station along the highway of mass education, and find its 'world' intermittent, and a good deal drabber than the fare provided by the media or the youth culture.[12] Sport is the natural focus for school loyalties (seen at their most etiolated in 'house' competition) and the school status-system — formal and informal — rewards loyal, as well as distin-

---

* City *neighbourhoods* seem to evoke nostalgia[8] more than loyalty — people have their *personal* 'Melbourne', their network joining family, friends, and 'used' sites.[9] But local attachments are still very strong in the countryside. With stationary or declining populations, each family still counts, and the loss of young people to city schools or jobs diminishes the whole.

guished, performance in school affairs. It remains doubtful, however, how far in practice schools can instil capacities for loyalty that are not temperamentally there in the first place. Certainly their efforts are often dysfunctional with a sceptical, intellectual minority, who leave, scarred, as life-long 'anti-groupists'; while the 'professional old boys', whom one can pick out even in their early years at an institution, tend to be neither the happiest nor the most successful pupils. This kind of loyalty among alumni — roughly proportionate, one supposes, to the amount of achieved uniqueness and significant intimacy in the school-experience — is little in evidence in Australian schools, or, for that matter, universities. By and large, all five generations of Australians have felt 'let down' by their education.

Work loyalties: one can be a loyal colleague, a loyal employee, even a loyal customer.* The institutions of economic life, like others, can evoke generous, even zealous, contributions from participants. And they are flanked by a whole set of voluntary, mutual-aid groups — unions, employers' associations, farmers' groups, professional associations —which can call, in their turn, for loyal service and support (enlivened in the union's case with a powerful rhetoric of solidarity, and a demonology of 'scabs', 'blacklegs' and 'enemies of the working class'). It is no longer very clear, however, what 'class loyalties' currently exact. Certainly the desertion of his class by the working-class scholarship boy, beloved of English novelists, is rarely to be found in new countries. There is, perhaps, little more to it now than a readiness at appropriate times to dispense proper sentiments on 'We-They' lines.

American sociologists have found that the staff of large organisations regularly divides into 'locals' and 'cosmopolitans': the former are emotionally attached primarily to the institution, the latter to their profession or skill-group at large.[13] At the time of the loyalty-oath crisis in American universities in the late 1950s, this turned out to be the main predictor of 'loyal' or 'recusant' responses to the Regents' demands.[14] At one stage, too, it appeared that atomic physicists as a profession might have declared it their privilege, and even duty, to put their 'knowledge' at the disposal of mankind, regardless of national loyalties.[15]

Party and ideological loyalties: the residues of innumerable particularistic and incompatible belief-systems, thrown up by the segregated, overvalued and intimacy-restricting primary groups, survive to enliven our politics.[16] A naive sense of the naturalness of each of these sets of group-beliefs, if not a belligerent sense of their certainty, goes hand in hand with a suspicion of the foreignness, hollowness or danger of ideas unconnected with them. Group-beliefs clarify, above all, the circle of 'those with whom it is conceivable to be close' (Gabriele).

In any case, it is these fragments that those leading secondary groups

* South Australian road sign circa 1970 — 'The man you kill may be a customer.'

in politics — and parties are the prime example — must labour to knit into some larger, cogent whole. And party loyalties, no matter how hard the parties try, inevitably tend to be qualified, short-term and calculating.* We know from opinion polls that most people think it makes little difference which party governs, and that even among those who regularly support one party few will wish to call themselves 'strong' supporters. Such tepid partisanship guarantees, of course, that supporters will rarely find themselves at a crisis of loyalty; but it also suggests that, when they do, the tension will tend to be resolved (as with the 1954 Australian Labour party split) in favour of the primary group.

If the rank-and-file is rather lacking in party loyalty, leaders of the second echelon seem almost constantly preoccupied with problems of the precise degree to which they can accept group discipline, this or that leader's formulations, or his tactics. They are also hypersensitive to accusations of disloyalty.[17] A somewhat special framework is perhaps necessary, in any case, to analyse loyalty to *persons*. How does the loyalty-system in friendship, in marriage, or between sponsor and protégé, compare with group-style bonds or constraints? Some degree of identification, of pride, love or respect, of readiness to defend and stand up for the other, is common; but mutuality seems to be more strongly marked in this kind of relation than it is in large groups or systems of ideas.

Loyalists, we have seen, are typically static, unself-assertive, faithful, obedient and little concerned about long-term strategy or the higher conflict of ideas. The *committed*, or 'twice-born', however, deliberately set out to re-make themselves in essentials. They are the men Kenneth Burke was thinking of when he reflected that each man builds his own altar — and it is true only of them. They wish to undo some or all of their core-loyalties, to commit themselves freshly and passionately to some novel project or higher aspiration. The personal exploration and the self-created challenge mark the reformer in politics. From a case-study of abolitionist leaders in the U.S. (none of whom appeared as young men at all likely to espouse this cause or any other),[18] Sylvan Tomkins sketches a step-wise, spiralling pattern of developing commitments, which may be summarised as follows:

> First, a responsiveness to the general idea of the salvation of others; second, risk ventured on behalf of those who need to be saved; third, as a consequence, punishment and suffering; fourth, as a consequence, responsiveness to the original idea of the necessity of salvation deepened, identification with the oppressed increased, and hostility towards the oppressor; fifth, as a result of increased density of affect and ideation, willingness to take even greater risks and more possible punishment and suffering; sixth, increased risk-taking *does* evoke

* 'Bought' loyalty is perhaps characteristic of secondary groups, certainly of those struggling in their claims for service for 'legitimacy'.

more punishment and suffering; seventh, an increased willingness to tolerate the suffering which follows risk-taking together with mounting positive identification with the oppressed and with fellow abolitionists, and mounting negative affect towards the enemy whose apparent power and evil is magnified as the struggle intensifies.

The + − + triad alternates between responsiveness and risk-taking (+), punishment and suffering (−), increased density of positive affect and ideation (+), resulting in increased risk-taking (+), so that the entire triad is endlessly repeated. This cumulatively deepens commitment until it reaches a point of no return − when no other way of life seems possible to the committed reformer. The spiral, composed of + − + triads, is therefore a + − +, + − + set rather than a + − + − + sequence. The increased density of positive affect and ideation at the end of each triad results in an increased positive affect invested in more *risk*, the first + in the next triad.

The pathway from early responsiveness to final commitment is not necessarily without conflict, and some of the suffering comes from within. Each of these men was to doubt greatly at some point whether he should give himself completely to the cause as a way of life.[19]

Lest it be thought that idea-loyalty is all pluck and dynamism, and group-loyalty mere stubbornness and phlegm, we might recall the staunch brigade of 'holders of one position, wrong for years' (Auden), faithful each to some patent political idea which is proclaimed to be ahead of its time, such as esperanto, single tax, Douglas credit, proportional representation, world federation, and so forth, and whose modest boast it is to have kept the spark alive through a damp season.

National loyalties at least introduce one new element: nations alone among contemporary loyalty-objects are apt, at a pinch, to ask for the individual's life in the cause.* But in ordinary times, national loyalties are relatively unstrained, they are, indeed, largely invisible and unconscious. Patiently pursuing his personal ends, the average national runs up against few obstacles placed squarely in his path by his country; indeed, his nation will even seem to him, in those areas that touch him most closely, the 'natural' and inevitable site for his activities.† The fact of his nationality, however, may cling like a burr to the traveller or expatriate

---

* cf. Coser's description: 'The modern world ... continues to spawn organizations and groups which ... make total claims on their members and which attempt to encompass within their circle the whole personality. These might be called *greedy institutions*, insofar as they seek exclusive and undivided loyalty and ... attempt to reduce the claims of competing roles and status positions on those they wish to encompass ... Their demands on the person are omnivorous.'[20]

† 'The belief in a transcendent, spiritually nourishing national life is the product of a repressed longing for the infantile symbiotic relation to the mother in whom all things are found' (Hanly).[21]

(who is uncomfortably often cast as a national 'representative') or the migrant (who must repeatedly ask himself: 'Is this really what I wish to affiliate with?').

Problematic or not, being of a particular nationality is interpreted in a variety of ways by fellow nationals. For the highly political, the master symbols of the nation cluster about its free and seemly institutions of state. These never occur at all to the unsophisticated, who think first of land-scape, the Queen, food and sport.* The precious and precarious 'national culture' that A. devotes himself to, embarrasses B., and passes right over C.'s head. D.'s dire threats to the whole national fabric and future, E. thinks crazy and non-existent. Norwegian students long ago distinguished the 'power-oriented' national from the humanitarian.[23] While the latter takes pride in his country's measure of achievement in certain social ideals, the former needs illusions of national grandeur and superiority to compensate for deep-seated feelings of personal inadequacy and helplessness. Power-types prefer aggressive ways of reacting in situations of international conflict; humanitarians tend to expect other and larger states to forge acceptable compromise solutions. So the weak ego seems to need a strong nation, and the strong ego a modest one. Can the same structure satisfy both?

We have almost everything still to learn about the nature of the con-temporary individual's commitment to his nation, his sensed satisfactions and admitted rights and duties, and his conceptions of position and purpose in the world at large.[24] But it is obvious at once that the nation-alisms of different countries are very different. For example, formal ideology predominates in many countries, and is almost completely absent in others. Ideologies come in different strengths, too — the Chinese practice of brainwashing during the Korean war, for example, showed that it was very much easier to persuade an American out of his national allegiance than a Turk or an Englishman.[25] Some nationalisms seem almost free from hatred; others are compacted with it.† Newer nationalisms often seem

* Some blanket disparagement of 'foreign' life-styles as unpleasing or unpromis-ing is implicit in the standard over-valuation of the national way of life, and may be interpreted partly as a strong and very necessary forward defence against envy. But a handful of debased/degraded alien cultures are usually kept close for use as 'awful examples'. We evidently maintain national pos-tures of idealisation only by 'splitting', and keeping in play a matching 'bad object' set.[22]

† Yeats wrote in 1909: 'The political class in Ireland — the lower-middle class from whom the patriotic associations have drawn their journalists and their leaders for the last ten years — have suffered through the cultivation of hatred as the one energy of their movement, a deprivation which is the intellectual equivalent to the removal of the genitals. Hence the shrillness of their voices... A meditation on sunlight ... affects the nature throughout, producing all that follows from the symbolical nature of the sun. Hate must, in the same way, make sterile, producing many effects which would follow from the

particularly hollow and strident,[28] almost consciously ground out against the models of stronger or older states. In other cases (such as the Eskimos and the Japanese) nationalist feeling is streaked with megalomaniac notions of divine election.

Despite the two world wars in this century[29] — and, for that matter, the Vietnam withdrawal — there appears little sign that people at large are disposed in any decisive way to wind down the claims they feel nations should seek to make on them. The European Economic Community, which drew, after all, on the most sophisticated group of 'post-national' national élites, has despite economic advantages, at the level of affects, merely somewhat exacerbated nationalistic concerns among its members. And while the larger pattern of ideological-bloc rivalry has sustained an uneasy peace, traditional 'national' antagonisms in Belfast, Cyprus, Palestine and Quebec have erupted unappeasably into open violence.

The individual at any one time possesses a *hierarchy* of loyalties, fitting, if he is lucky, into a snug, nesting series,[30] each contributing something to his self-image and offering chances of ego-enhancement with group-success. Politics, however, in its ordinary course, will periodically deal up crises of loyalty in which cross-pressures to readjust priorities of affiliation arise, while crises may force such a drastic reshuffling of emotional investment that identity itself is shaken.

Individual differences in the capacity for loyalty

There are loyalty addicts, who collect badges, insignia, and even the duties of membership in many groups; and loyalty 'sponges', who soak up the full rewards offered in the group for faithfulness in word and deed — and who make full use of the opportunity to become dependent on it. Where loyalty or 'serviceableness' sits high in an ego-ideal, the individual dispenses them in gratifying unit-acts, as others exercise sincerity, promise-keeping or truthfulness. Loyalists in general may have a greater need than normal for security and authority — an external identity. But *converts* as a class show an exaggerated zeal, whether converted to a religion, a political ideology, or, as with migrants, to a nationality. The lukewarmness of the 'native-born' always shocks the converted, whose own over-identification seems partly a matter of defending himself against doubt (they know, after all, what it is like *not* to have had the new ways and beliefs for most of a life) and partly of a conversion experience recent enough to be an emotional success — the new channels that feed self-esteem and displace aggression are still running clear and strong.

(Footnote continued)

meditation on a symbol capable of giving hate.'[26] The national anthem of Nauru (a small phosphate island in the Pacific east of Sydney) opens, 'Death to the foul monsters who disembowelled our fair island . . . ' Ernest Jones has written well on the excessive nationalism of island peoples.[27]

Ranyard West makes a forceful case for the peculiar attraction of patriotism to obsessional personalities,[31] which we may, I think, plausibly extend to their identification with any group they take seriously. The basic problem is, he says, ambivalence — their love and their hate lie too close together. The image of the 'father or mother of earlier times ... whose approval is cherished, whose wrath is feared, and yet upon whom there is a compulsive urge to wreak a vengeance of hate and violence' comes to inhabit whatever group the adult obsessional's loyalty is focused on. He distinguishes himself in the group by his tireless performance of unending duties, often loading himself with those neglected through others' laziness or selfishness. Yet this endless reparative activity (to stifle and deny the hate) carries an undercurrent of subdued aggressiveness, as if, West says, in a memorable formula, they were 'unconsciously seeking legitimate vents for their aggressiveness as close to the objects of their love as they dare go ... The psychological ideal would be for the loved object to sanction and yet survive its own destruction.' Obsessionals have, therefore, an acute craving for intellectual or ideological props to loyalty; they wish to have 'us' painted unambiguously white and 'our' enemies black, and to effect and sustain in this way the separation of love and hate they find so difficult. Once hatred of 'them' is officially sanctioned, the obsessional, now with the 'condonance and encouragement, so he feels, of his conscience-keeper, Society', hates passionately, and with the extra strength of the 'freed hatred to which he dared not expose his friends'. Obsessionals then, tensely loyal, perpetually and unwittingly chivvy their groups into aggressiveness.

Why are some people much *less* loyal than others? If we can follow the testimony of the perceptive André Gorz, who thought his incapacity for loyalty so central a problem that he named his autobiography *The Traitor*,[32] one sufficient condition is a parent so intrusive, so intent on moulding the child to a predetermined shape, that he reads all subsequent overtures to group-affiliation as a deep threat to his precarious autonomy. Such a man would dearly love to belong — above all, to a Great Good Cause — but the moment he approaches, deep fears rise up that his mind would be taken over and unceremoniously managed. To be his own man, he must remain group-shy.

As well as those who are disposed to reject 'given' groups and who are chary about joining new ones, we have others unable to 'stick it out' with the group under duress, when it finds itself in a tight corner — hard-pressed, unpopular and, maybe, at fault. The order in which people left the Communist parties of the West in the 1950s and the 1960s was rooted in temperament as much as ideas, and the personalities of the tiny band persisting into the 1970s would make a fine quarry for the study of loyalist psychology. Ernest Jones, in his piece on the Norwegian wartime collaborator Quisling,[33] points to the type with a 'peculiar inability to face, or even recognise, an enemy', whose lack of capacity to fight springs from an overwhelming unconscious image of an all-powerful (and sadistic) father. Opposition is unthinkable, resistance useless, and ingratiation alone may save the day.

Active disloyalty is rare in modern conditions — 'acts of open disloyalty are not usually relevant to the frustrations and deprivations that individuals commonly face',[34] and, besides, opportunities for treason, sabotage and espionage are hard to come by. Traitors do, however, still emerge (their obliquity is all the greater for their scarcity), and their careers demonstrate a hidden transfer of allegiance, a surreptitious joining of the enemy's camp, the transmitting of damaging secrets given them in trust, and great skill in duplicity and dual role-playing ('a controlled schizophrenia', Fuchs called it). They manage the feat of patriotism in reverse:

> It is plain that . . . there must always have been present some divided attitude towards [their own countrymen] . . . The secret of it lies in some unsatisfactory attitude towards the Mother. Treachery, by allying oneself with the conquering enemy, would seem to be an attempt sadistically to overcome the incest taboo by raping the Mother instead of loving her. Perhaps this is why it is generally regarded as the most outrageous and unnatural of crimes, since it combines disloyalty to both parents.[35]

An American analyst, reviewing those cases of traitors with some known early history,[36] finds them to have in common

> the invasion of emotional relationships by the excessive need for possession and power, growing out of unusually strong and unresolved infantile jealousy; distortion of the sense of identity — sometimes with secondary disturbance in reality-testing; and a fissure-like defect in the super-ego, including the conscience and the formation of ideals.

Future traitors had, when they were children, drastically split loyalties between parents (often enough of different nationalities). Sometimes disappointment with parents led to the concoction of a romantic but hidden ancestry. Vanity, self-love and demands for omnipotence and magic survive infancy to sap the power to shape realistic goals in life or to build stable emotional relationships.

'Sticking it out' is, indeed, the phrase Kim Philby uses for his persistence as a secret member of Russian intelligence 'in the years when some of the worst features of Stalinism became apparent':

> I saw the road leading me into the political position of the querulous outcast, of the Koestler-Crankshaw-Muggeridge variety, railing at the movement that had let *me* down, at the God that had failed *me*. This seemed a ghastly fate, however lucrative it might have been . . . The [alternative] course of action open to me was to stick it out, in the confident faith that the principles of the Revolution would outlive

the aberration of individuals, however enormous ... Graham Greene, in ... *The Confidential Agent*, imagines a scene in which the heroine asks the hero if his leaders are any better than the others. 'No. Of course not,' he replies. 'But I still prefer the people they lead — even if they lead them all wrong.' 'The poor, right or wrong,' she scoffed. 'It's no worse — is it? — than my country, right or wrong. You choose your side once and for all — of course, it may be the wrong side. Only history can tell that.'[37]

Philby's latest biographers, however, suggest that he was by then effectively a prisoner of the Russian, if not also the British, intelligence network.[38] There seems more of the man himself in the concluding sentence of his apologia: 'It is a matter of great pride to me that I was invited, at so early an age, to play my infinitesimal part in building up [Soviet] power [and] ... became a member of the Soviet intelligence service ... When the proposition was made to me, I did not hesitate. One does not look twice at an offer of enrolment in an elite force.'[39]

Pride

Pride has a firm and stable link with loyalty: the steady satisfaction to be drawn from one's affiliations and group membership — directly, and also more largely, as this feeds into one's general reputation and social status. This *social* component of positive self-regard is a good deal less subject to fluctuation than the personal part; it is less occupied with the worth of one's qualities, actions, beliefs or powers — of which one has a closer and less settled view; and people invest in the private and the public self in very individual proportions. The Scots have a useful distinction between 'English' and 'Scottish' pride,* which is almost self-explanatory: the former carries overtones of ostentation, haughtiness, arrogance, contempt† and insolence — the latter connotes self-isolation, dignity and conscious independence. The *Dictionary of Philosophy and Psychology* (1901) observes that

> Pride, unlike vanity, does not involve belief in one's own superiority to others. The most deeply rooted pride may be connected merely with the conception of independence or equality, and may be manifested mainly by a refusal to accept favours or to be under obligation.[40]

This might be described as making a Scottish point.[41]

Pride in a group may be generally stable, but it does have vivid fluctuations. If others should unexpectedly concur with one's own estimation of the group — if they admire or defer to it — one becomes elated; if they should firmly decline to respect it, one feels resentful. Others' scorn or

---

* I am indebted to Neil Whitlock for this point.
† Hume remarked, 'Pride is so strong in "contempt", there is almost nothing else.'

ridicule of the group is pretty unsettling. If the group has a defect exposed, one feels shame — and shame is an instant solvent of pride. But it has to be a defect one acknowledges as such; pride can withstand (and even thrive on) predictable dislike and censure: 'Pride does not feel the cold.' Jacob Arlow has clearly brought out the oral undertones of 'smugness' — 'Say what they like, *I* know I've just been fed, and am chock-full of goodness.'[42] If the group, however, should behave really badly (in a cowardly or sadistic way), one shares the collective guilt. If it succeeds in a difficult or unlikely undertaking, one has the impulse to make sure this is widely known and appreciated.[43]

Pride has, of course, a chequered history.[44] In classical times, it was acceptable enough: all negative force was drawn off in the separate term *hubris*, which denoted insolence rooted in lack of reverence and self-knowledge, and the expression of a self-centred will recognising no power outside itself and no law but its own impulses. The Old Testament condemns pride as self-exaltation in the wicked or foolish, and the prophets inveigh against national pride, as a presumptuous and scornful sense of power. It becomes a sin in the New Testament — diametrically opposed to humility and meekness. And Dante, following St Thomas, puts it first in his list of the Seven Deadly Sins, since it involves non-subjection to God, which is the beginning of all other evils. He groups together on the lowest level of Hell (condemned eternally to recite the Lord's Prayer) the representatives of pride of birth, pride of intellect and pride of dominion. Milton's Satan, of course, follows this pattern. It is, in fact, one of the quiet turning points of the human spirit, when David Hume is able to confide to his readers that pride — as in one's country, one's friends, one's family, or even one's riches — is a *pleasant* feeling, one, indeed, that invigorates the mind.

Yet we remain somewhat torn between the Christian and the humanist interpretations:

> Right now we ought to know all we can about the chemistry of pride. Pride — in a nation, a race, a religion, a party, or a leader — is a substitute for individual self-respect. In other words, pride is a vital necessity when we are in the antechamber of self-respect, and it matters not whether we are in the antechamber on the way in or on the way out. The present fierce craving for pride is indicative of the enormous difficulty experienced by people (particularly educated people) in maintaining their self-respect.[45]

This reflection of Eric Hoffer's is typical in its ambivalence; it places all the strength and badness in the social part of pride and all the goodness and weakness in the personal part. We should probably assent as cheerfully to some rousing affirmation by, say, Philip Slater, of the urgent necessity for contemporaries of learning to transfer the self-satisfaction now vested in individual attainment on to the achieving of richer group-bonds and new, complex dependencies. Or we might assent equally to some bare warning that in no other emotion is the temptation so strong to overdispense.

Trust

Trust, as the reciprocal of suspicion, has already hovered in the wings of earlier discussion, and might even be thought to have been adequately described in terms of its negative. We bring it in here for a single extra point: loyalty creates the space for trust.

The trust that can rise to the occasion, we know from Erikson, has temperamental contours — we emerge from the oral stage either basically trustful or mistrustful.[46] And we know from students of political culture that there are marked differences in the degree of trustfulness shown by different nations.[47] We also know that certain rituals and ceremonies are peculiarly trust-intensifying — a trial,[48] a coronation,[49] a state funeral — and can rapidly restore composure after some wave of mistrust has passed across the polity like a wind over cornfields. De Grazia has written well of our susceptibility to feeling ourselves 'abandoned' by our rulers, and the emotional roots of this susceptibility in separation-anxiety.[50] Boulding alone has seen loyalty and the trust and respect it engenders as a positive 'legitimacy system' in itself, able, in particular, to preserve régimes against great economic shocks, as long as they are thought to be earnest and sincere.[51] The dynamics of this integrative system remain, however, notably obscure, though Kenneth Burke long ago picked piety as, among all the emotions, 'the system-builder'.[52] His account remains of interest.

Piety, he claims, is still deeply at work in contemporary society — though unremarked since we are now 'not religious' — and extends through the whole texture of our lives. Piety is our deepest sense of what properly goes with what, of how the really important and intimate things should be done. It is developed, of course, in our childhood, out of our first patterns of judgement (which we may later wish to revise or amplify but which we find it is possible to do only within limits), and it is sustained and nourished by 'remembrance of things past'. Piety can bring us much pain, requiring of us symbolic expiations for impiety or neglect of observance, sometimes as large and dramatic as martyrdom or intense ambition, especially true when we confront the need to reorganise our outlook to accommodate great social shocks: then we enter the realm of gargoyles, of shattering, fragmentation, rending and tearing, since the new notions we must learn to work with deeply disturb and offend our old understandings.

Burke's account of the system-building propensities of piety runs on perfectly individualist lines. Defined as 'a desire to round things out, to fit experiences together into a unified whole', piety leads to construction in this way:

> If there is an altar, it is pious of a man to perform some ritual act whereby he may approach this altar with clean hands. A kind of symbolic cleanliness goes with altars, a technique of symbolic cleansing goes with cleanliness, a preparation or initiation goes with the technique of cleansing, the need of cleansing was based upon some feeling of taboo — and so on, until pious linkages may have brought all the significant details of the day into coordination, relating them integrally with one another by a complex interpretative network.[53]

The earnest devotee approaches *his own altar* somewhat in this fashion, and dutifully shapes a day, but we need a good deal more work — on perhaps quite different lines — to learn how *causes* construct their calendars.

10   *Compound affects*

Utopianism, fanaticism, tolerance, conventionality and privacy

Depression, it has been argued,[1] is an emotional state that we should not seek to break into its component parts, not merely because this is difficult, but because, where affects are *fused* (as here and, perhaps, in jealousy), we do better to treat them as a whole, a standard and stable compound. Certain political and social 'fused' affects seem to call for the same respectful treatment, and we group them in this chapter, more by this formal property than by any secure understanding of the population they represent. Some are fused by history, others, it seems, by will.

Accidie may most quickly illustrate the type. In the monasteries of the Middle Ages, accidie, the 'noonday sickness', struck with the ringing of the angelus bell. It seemed an age since one had risen, and the day stretched endlessly, pointlessly ahead; one had a sense of vacancy, or of drowning in time.[2] The Fathers of the Church took this disease of the monk who had mistaken his vocation very seriously, analysing in their resourceful Latin its detailed symptoms, so that local authorities might be alert to its onset and prescribe the efficacious extra work or prayer or change of monastery. It was probably the first social emotion to be analysed in the therapeutic mode.* In any case, it is recognisably the progenitor of those nineteenth century emotions of the study, *alienation* and *anomie*, both of which are also alleged to centre about the sense of meaninglessness and purposelessness in work.[3] Yet something of the essence of the original feeling of accidie is lost if we move too far away from the time-experience at its heart. If it is rare in contemporary monastery cloisters, it is certainly not in universities.

Accidie, one feels, should stand at the head† of some illuminating series of historical affects, the consequence of groups of men setting them-

---

* cf. the Silver Latin poets' exploration of the feelings of exile; this exploration, too, was systematic, but the only cure that could be prescribed was an Imperial pardon. cf. also the Odyssean emotion of *nóstos*, homecoming.
† Another early candidate is *contemptus mundi* (and the preoccupation with death associated with it).[4]

selves novel social tasks whose inbuilt strains have uniquely left a mark on their age. We might think first of the slowly emerging professions themselves: if accidie is the monk's negative affect, what are its counterparts in the soldier, the lawyer, the doctor, the engineer and the scientist? Alternatively, we might seek to pin the historical affect to the rising social movement. We do not meet *priggishness*, for example, until the time of the English Puritans.

Only *utopianism* seems so far to have been analysed along these lines. Lewis Mumford first put the question of the origin of the utopian spirit to himself in *The Story of Utopias* in the 1920s. He answered it finally to his satisfaction only in 1965: 'The first utopia was the city itself.'[5] The archetypal ancient city of Egypt or Mesopotamia, built under its mad priest-king by machine-like discipline, with its stunning benefits, ideal pretensions and hallucinations was, indeed, a project of drawing down a piece of heaven to earth. It is precisely this spirit of the first city-builders that, lodged in the collective unconscious, comes back to us when we are seized by utopian dreams.* For Mumford, this hypothesis has the great merit of explaining why savage ideas of regimentation and standardisation invariably accompany the tenderest hopes of ideal commonwealths. For us, his explanation underlines the fact that utopianism, whatever else it may become (ideology or escapade), is at root a *feeling* — the feeling that the world can be remade on awesomely beautiful lines (of which the utopian vision has given only a glimpse) and in a way that promises to ennoble human life. A contemporary psychiatric essay discerns an 'antinomian personality'[7] at the basis of utopian enterprises, a reliable minority of people who believe themselves to be 'exceptions', beyond the rules, and who believe themselves, in fact, to have the *duty* (because of their special qualities) to pioneer and innovate in social arrangements. The instability and impermanence of utopian colonies and communes no doubt owes much to their trying to build with such basically restless, 'free spirit' material.

Although each social movement may enjoy its unique bonding affect, *fanaticism*, which is absent from none, and which is undoubtedly the most portentous emotional input into political history, deserves a longer look.† The contemporary image of the fanatic is quite sharp: he is a man living in fatal relation to an idea. His idea will be unpopular or unknown to most — an ominous state of affairs, since only with this idea may one's actions rise to world-historical significance; without it one may as well not have been born. Service to this master-idea dominates the fanatic's actions; he fights tirelessly to make it known, to secure converts, to

* The 'vision' of the utopia is often literally dreamed. See, for example, Louis Sebastien Mercier's *In the Year 2,500* (1771).[6]
† I summarise here a previously published essay built round the discussion of five recently analysed fanatic 'cases'.[8]

link it with pressing issues, to counter ideas that conflict with or weaken it. He deprecates and minimises his private life (time that might have been spent on his idea) and proudly roots out the more ordinary and comfortable social ties. A sense of imprisonment, even sterility, encloses the image: this life has an inhuman feel, a combination of emotional hysteria and monotony that repels; the very promise seems belied by the desperate way it is put forward. In the grip of his idea, the fanatic seems a man in pain; yet if he breaks free, he is nothing.

Few popular images carry such complex and finely detailed meaning. But then fanaticism has been with us for a very long time, and closely and repeatedly observed. In modern times, indeed, it seems that each generation, as if in some grim societal experiment, has been afforded a fresh chance to confirm the leading elements and vital shape of the composition. In fact, it was even with a sense of *déjà vu* that the term was first introduced into English in the mid seventeenth century as an old humanists' pun to grapple with the provocation of the Puritans. The Romans, too, they recalled, had been alarmed by their *fanatici* — mutilated priests of exotic mother-goddesses, who rushed from the temple, cut themselves with knives, and worked themselves into frenzies in which they prophesied. Roman piety was corporate, external, prudential — a calendar of propitiations; a people having barely brought their gods indoors found it outrageous that a temple (*fanum* — hence our word) could promise personal links with a god, or excite group ecstasies or mortifications. Language, in short, set the root of 'fanatic' in 'possession by a god or demon' (*O.E.D.*). The fanatic is the man who has swallowed his god.

If fanatic ideas were first religious, and then nationalistic, in this century they have been political. To Eric Hoffer, author of *The True Believer*, the great unanswered question was where the support for the ruinous mass movements of Fascism and Communism came from. Why, in our time, have fanatics been so numerous, so full of passionate intensity, so gullible? It is not the ideas themselves, he argues, that matter, it is the desperate need in the followers to find some holy cause, their sense that life without one would be trivial, futile and sinful, that needs to be explained. The fanatic is in flight from himself — from a self he regards as worthless, guilty, helpless, cowardly or incomplete. To lose himself in followership, to strip himself of distinctiveness, of individual will and judgment, is to cast off a spoiled self and assume a higher historic identity.

And, indeed, fanatics from a wide range of causes do exhibit a 'spoilt' life and the flight from a damaged self — and, despite their variety of convictions, they have a common frame of mind. This includes a saving idea desperately championed; aggression, militancy, an 'inhuman' spurning of pleasure; an anathematised present; closed-mindedness; and extravagant yet rigid affects. Exactly how a massive self-dislike is displaced, however, how hatred long battened down suddenly breaks through to an uncensored and conscience-sanctioned outlet in politics, needs fine tracing, which is often very difficult in the individual case. Once securely lodged in its victim, fanaticism is, in any case, very hard to contain, and seems, as if it were a parasitic growth, to seek to fill and dominate the whole personality. Becoming fanatic brings intellectual stultification; categories set, empathy withers and reality-testing falls away. Under enormous pressure to avow and act, the true believer grows impatient, obstinate, arrogant, and tempted to force and fraud. The mind is used, not for discovery, but as a bludgeon in the cause. The general phobic pressure in the fanatic system, however, rises and falls: tight episodes, where the subject lashes out desperately at mis-chosen enemies who are projectively misunderstood, alternate with more relaxed times, when there seems less to be done, and a man can live for a while away from his mission. There is the fanatic flight, as well as the fanatic career.

We turn now to three cooler contemporary compound affects. The first of these is *tolerance*. This, too, is at bottom a feeling (and was reported as such several times in the diaries), as well as a state of mind or a tenet of political belief.* The term was first used to denote a purely physical form of endurance — one tolerated pain, heavy burdens, extremes of heat or cold — but, displaced upwards, it has come to mean the ability to allow the continuance of disturbing advocacy or behaviour, to hold in check a natural and immediate reaction to hate. Notably tolerant individuals seem to have an unusual measure of inner security, enabling them to fend off the anxieties implicit in the provocations (freedom of internal fantasy is the prerequisite for freeing other minds of censure).[9] They are also more at ease, perhaps, with their own aggression; they know they can attack if necessary at a later time, while the intolerant, prone to 'splitting', and unable to bear ambiguity, are ready to explode on contact. The tolerant have firm, but somewhat flexible, opinions, and are more apt in dubious cases to exercise their own judgment than to apply conventional categories. They can laugh at themselves and the groups they belong to, but often treat themselves more harshly than they treat others. Anna N. (see above, pp. 236–43) may be read as a splendid case of this type.

There is, of course, a pathology of tolerance. It can be overdone, or it may merely mask not caring, or it may insult a dissident position by failing to take it seriously enough (Marcuse's 'repressive tolerance'). Some occupations, such as that of tutor, generate a specious open-mindedness, which conceals an incapacity to make up one's own mind, and may even erode the capacity to do so.

In contrasting the intolerant and highly tolerant, we implicitly award the latter more virtue than they deserve. High tolerance may be better seen

---

* In fact, one feels *in*tolerant more often and more vividly, a fact which draws uncomfortable attention to the strict limits to our own open-mindedness.

as a midpoint between intolerance and positive enthusiasm for novelties, dissidence and startling perspectives;[10] this, at least, is how Mill would have us see it.

Conventionality and *conformism* are further compound affects highly relevant to politics. Here, the prompting emotions — of anxiety that one may not feel what one is supposed to feel or act as one is expected to, or of satisfaction that one has actually felt or acted correctly — have been built into a 'system', a need or compulsion to consult group-reactions (even if in fantasy) before deciding on one's own. Both involve an original determination (which may now have become settled habit) to trim and prune one's emotions to standard, allowable dimensions, to suppress tendencies to think and act independently — a 'strain to normality'.

An ingenious study in the early 1950s set out to explore the correlates of this generalised, repetitive need to conform whether the situation called for it or not.[11] A class of psychology students was asked to estimate the distance between two rectangles ($6\frac{1}{2}$ inches, in fact), and then to re-estimate it in the light of the information that the class as a whole judged them to be 12 inches apart. Those who shifted notably towards the class norm were found, indeed, to value conformity generally, to be positively disposed towards authority, and wholeheartedly to endorse conventional morality, and political and religious conservatism. Projective tests disclosed that the conformists had stricter, more dominating parents, whom they idealised and for whom they expressed exaggerated concern, and bore out the hypothesis that

> one origin of compulsive conformity lies in childhood experiences with parents . . . who are punitive, strict, coercive, and dominantly overprotective. The child is punished for expressing and attempting to gratify pleasurable impulses and prevented from exploring the environment at his own pace. . . He is forced to behave in the manner prescribed by his parents though [this may be] alien to his own needs and perhaps beyond his capacities. The child's aggressive responses to such frustrating parental stimuli . . . are punished in such a way as to produce anxiety and feelings of guilt. . . The fact that these frustrating parents also take care of the child and are his main source of support further contribute to the development of guilt. To avoid these . . . guilt feelings the child represses his hostility. . . The reaction formation against hostile impulses toward the parents may involve turning them toward the self and . . . lead to overconcern for the well-being of the parents, overidealization of them . . . and overintrojection of their attitudes and values. . . There exists the basis of a compulsive, guilt-motivated need to conform.[12]

The conformist in many ways — not least in his conventionality — resembles the authoritarian; the critical difference is, however, that he uses projection and displacement far less, and largely internalises guilt and rage. An even more ingenious laboratory routine with volunteer

adults established that conformers were more anxious and more authoritarian; had stronger inferiority feelings and less self-insight; had
disturbed, dejected and distrustful attitudes to others, and exercised rigid
and excessive self-control. While idealising their parents, they carefully
restricted their own children's behaviour.[13] Recent work on obedience to
authority, showing some 65% of subjects prepared to torture victims in a
'scientific' experiment (Australian psychologists found an even higher
percentage), underlines the remarkable force of this need-system.[14]

J. H. Smith, in a neglected article,[15] gives a rather more pointed and
delicate account of the origins of conventionality, which he sees as essentially an anxiety about separateness, and, indeed, about individuality as
such. He places the blame on clumsy mothering just after late infancy, at
the time when the very young child is discovering himself as a separate
individual. Already anxious at the increasing separation from the mother,
the child is made more fearful by the mother's failure to respond sensitively to his own painfully novel feelings, and her insistence on treating
him according to the rules. Conventionality is, above all, despair of ever
being understood on one's own terms, and a desperate, second-best project
of trying to relate to others entirely on theirs. Conventionality is 'anxiety . . .
specifically associated with the person's individuality as such':

> One must postulate . . . that anxiety of the mother is evoked and
> empathically conveyed to the infant in conjunction with the discovery
> of his individuality. Of further importance is the specific way in
> which she deals with that anxiety. The covert operation of the
> mother . . . seems to be one of withdrawing – of denying her anxiety
> about separateness by abruptly engaging in an emotional desertion of
> the infant. Her overt operation is one of overemphasizing the con-
> ventionalities.[16]

Smith quotes a patient's description of a mother who 'spent hours daily
cuddling her infants', but declared, 'I can't stand the childish mind.'
A failure of mutuality and object-relatedness, it prohibits them in its turn.

Pursued as an emotional system – a settled steering of one's affects –
conventionality bites deep, and warps whole lives, lending them an external, 'outside-in' quality, based on the ruthless disparagement of personal
fantasy, as though the individual, playing in a film of his own life, can
applaud only those actions that have the right look. Migrant and other
socially marginal families, who nevertheless feel subtly better than
their environment and are determined to keep up the difference, are
among the most reliable seedbeds of extreme conventionality.

Conformism has, of course, its encyclopaedist in David Riesman, whose
book *The Lonely Crowd* constitutes a kind of gazetteer of the modes of 'other-
direction' – that is, character structure governed throughout life and from
the first by signals from outside – in work, leisure and popular culture in
the United States of the 1950s.[17] He is more concerned, however, with

the consequences of conformity for the individual, rather than with how conformity is produced, or what it feels like to be a conformist. By asking how the person pre-eminently concerned with respectability, for whom 'the act of acting out normalcy becomes a positive value in and of itself', organises himself for the task, Bensman and Vidich take us a little nearer to the subject.[18] Their answer is couched in terms of self-avoidance, 'externalization of the self', automatising of activity and compulsive absorption of work. Note, too, the phenomenon of the 'foreclosed identity' in adolescence, as young people, taking fright at the prospect of unknown and threatening experiences, hastily assume a fixed and simplified life-plan, in an attempt to create an aura of invulnerable, unemotional compet-ence for themselves. 'By imagining the meaning of a class of experiences in advance or apart from living them, a young person . . . insulate[s] him-self in advance from experiences that might portend dislocation and disorder' — and individuality.[19] These mechanisms are fully apparent in our conformist cases, the F types (see above, pp. 163–83).

Conformism, nevertheless, has its satisfactions. There are real re-wards for behaving correctly, such as feelings of justifiable pride; indeed, it becomes at times difficult to separate virtue *from* its rewards. And it does not feel like rigidity from the inside: common standards and under-standings are continually and slowly moving forward. All political groups strive to impose their own conformities; but in politics, conventionality must usually work as a sheet-anchor of conservatism. But conventionality also aids politics by its placing of 'constructive community activity' high among the 'done things'. The rhetoric of public life itself works power-fully to buttress the conventional 'system of illusion' by its endless repetition of high-sounding and sentimental clichés.

If conventionality is trimming one's emotions to conform to others' expectations, the demand in *privacy* is that *others'* emotions be firmly hedged off, especially the intrusive emotions — scorn, envy, moral indigna-tion — which one's own behaviour, if observed, might provoke. Privacy is *sought* aloneness; *undesired* solitude is loneliness.* It has been plausibly argued that current levels of sought privacy are excessive; supported as they are by an 'ideology' of independence and self-reliance of crippling weight,[21] as well as by neurotic demands, the 'autarchy fantasies' (Bergler)[22] of refuting the 'bad' pre-Oedipal mother and the disappoint-ments experienced through her. But the two are interlinked: a compulsive

---

* 'Privacy is neither indifference to others nor a barricading of oneself from the rest of the world, but the capacity and right to be periodically in touch with only oneself, and to have feelings, thoughts, and habits which one need not share with others. Privacy, as a state of being freely at one with one-self, does not make us more distant from others. It is a respectful recognition of that part of ourselves which emerged when we became beings endowed with feelings and ideas' (S. Arieti).[20]

need for privacy is learnt from others who are themselves desocialised or indulging autarchic fantasies. Philip Slater, in *The Pursuit of Loneliness* (1971), has most recently put the case for fuller social participation as critically urgent.[23] We may merely note that as privacy is to the social world, so isolation and detachment in the mental world are strategies for putting distance between oneself and disturbing feelings. The cover can hardly be valuable in itself; it must depend on the use one makes of it.

Lasswell contributed in 1952 an elegant essay on privacy, tracing the conventions enshrining it in law to the conflict between the English nobility and the Crown, and in informal relations to fashions in the 'open ego' and zones of reticence.[24] Privacy is threatened by developments in communications — indeed, communications generally work to restore, in the modern nation, the intensity of contact that can be found in a village. Privacy is threatened, too, by the new technology of surveillance, the new appetites and techniques for the penetration of hitherto inaccessible areas — documentary photography, in-depth reporting, the psychologically rich organisation-dossier, and the security file. Respect for privacy declines as intense concern for the sharing of power within the nation declines, and crusades are mounted against crime, political corruption or subversion. Animosity against privacy, indeed, is one of the major undercurrent drives of our time, drawing strength from the ever-increasing pains of loneliness, disorientation and cold ambition built into metropolitan work-life and social relations.

In the light of these grave psychic costs of individualism, can we continue to justify traditional respect for privacy? The dilemma is that the isolation essential to the creative man drowns the uncreative.

> Our world . . . is confronted with clashing values, as well as con-
> flicting institutional solutions. We need men and women who have
> sought and found a deeply rooted system of belief in human dignity,
> and who have acquired a disciplined sense of responsibility for so
> acting, as to bring into existence the valued modes of human relation-
> ship. Such decisive figures in our turbulent epoch are almost certain
> to acquire much of their firmness on the basis of inner struggle. They
> have sought to put their minds and consciousness in harmony, and
> they have often done this in defiance of many of the prevailing stan-
> dards of the environment in which they were brought up. The capacity
> to endure opprobrium, or worse, with serenity, is often the fruit of
> privacy, not as an end in itself — or as a means of spurning human
> association — but rather as a means of obtaining deeper insight.[25]

Contemporary conventions of privacy also contrive, however, to leave the isolated man to freeze in his own solitude, and to leave the over-burdened man, taking responsibility for himself, to go down to defeat; and the ruthless man is at liberty to spread the poison of cold aloofness and self-concern.

11   *Conclusion*

Far from attempting to tie up loose ends, these final notes tug sharply at several of the more obvious and irritating threads left trailing by earlier pages. We failed to conclude the sections on individual affects at anything approaching a common point, and selected for inspection among the compound emotions merely what was closest to hand, leaving as *terra incognita* even contiguous explorable areas. Satisfied as I am that a formal case has been made for the direct study of each of the emotions detailed, the substance of each review still seems entirely provisional.

Measurement

Clearly, to get any sort of grip on the analysis of political affects, we need agreed measures, and, to close this grip to any degree, we need refined ones. We have talked cheerfully above of anger funds, insecurity levels, sympathy schedules (and could well have added notches of idealisation or disillusionment, envy quotients, fear points, suspicion curves, trust densities and pity ceilings); all of these do not merely presuppose eventual quantification, but seem even peremptorily to demand it.

We get an idea, perhaps, of the sort of thing that is possible from the scales recently devised by Louis Gottschalk to measure anger, fear and suspicion-paranoia (as well as self-hatred and general disorientation) in brief samples of speech or writing.[1] The trick is to attend very carefully to metaphor: repeated or intense play with an affect then shows up in the subject's tally as each unit of consecutive talk (five minutes' worth — say 200–250 words) is scrutinised for its emotional freight. Standard procedure is to ask for an account of 'any interesting or dramatic personal experience', but the scoring categories have proved useful and meaningful with slices of normal psychiatric interview, 'free association', TAT responses, dreams and/or associations to dreams, and there is no reason in principle why they should not be extended to private letters, public speeches or literary works.

Let us look at the anger scale in a little more detail. Gottschalk begins by noting that previous attempts at measuring hostility have managed to draw rather arbitrarily and unevenly on

> four inter-related factors: a) a behavioural act, either physical or verbal,
> called 'aggression', which is interpreted as having a destructive
> function by an outside observer; b) a self-reported attitude of dislike,
> resentment, suspicion toward the world or particular objects, some-
> times called 'hostility'; c) a subjective experience of an affect called
> 'anger' with physiological concomitants; d) a dispositional or poten-
> tial state (rather than an on-going phenomenon) ear-marked by graded
> tendencies to be aroused to 'hostility' or 'aggression'. Furthermore, the
> level of awareness of hostility may range from the perfectly conscious
> to the perfectly unconscious.[2]

Such attempts have, consequently, often disagreed in their testimony.[3]
His solution is to look for a general *anger climate* in which the subject seems
to be moving, and to score up anything that indicates 'hostility in the air',
whether the individual himself makes threats or recalls aggressive deeds,
or whether he contemplates the havoc others may do or are doing or have
done, or whether he even *denies* in the self or in others the presence of
anger, hatred, dislike, cruelty, or an intent to harm. Each glint of anger
or hatred counts; and double and treble marks are awarded to the more
intense manifestations (the use of words such as 'maim', 'smash', or 'kill').
His categories are exhaustive, and leave very little to the judgement of
individual raters.[4]

Having used the anger scale over ten years in a great variety of (mostly
clinical) settings, its inventor is satisfied that the brief-sample score relates
most satisfactorily to material obtained from the same subject over a
period of hours — or even days. Scores on the anger scale correlate closely
with various physiological measures, especially blood pressure; with
aggressive behaviour on the ward; and with subjects' own ratings of their
proneness to anger, admitted either *tout court* or by means of an inventory
of hypotheses ('If someone stepped on my toe, I would...') — although
too close a match here brings into question the adequacy of the methods of
tapping unconscious hostility. Daily anger level, however, varies
somewhat, and to strike a *typical* level for the individual, some half-dozen
tests may be necessary, over a period perhaps as long as a month.

Psychiatrists can, of course, do very much more delicate work than
this. If, to the written-sample text, is added, say, a tape of the subject
actually speaking it, then pitch, volume, tone of voice, accent, rhythm,
cadence and stress can all be ransacked for additional vital clues.[5] If the
subject is video-taped, gestures, facial expression, posture — the whole
extent of the body's complicity in the performance — can clinch points of
uncertainty, and open quite fresh impressions. Pairs of psychiatrists
watching subjects through one-way glass over several days of continuous
subjection to psychological testing have proved perfectly capable of
issuing a stream of agreed scores for anger, anxiety and depression;

in fact, as they warmed to the work, they demanded to be allowed to operate an eighteen-point scale for each, instead of the seven-point one initially agreed on.[6]

Of course, psychiatrists are not ordinarily on hand at the sites of politics — at committee meetings, mass rallies, television debates, bargaining tables, protest marches, and court proceedings. But on the rare occasions when they have been, by fate or design, political observers or participants, they have given us exceptionally fine descriptions — of, for example, decolonisation riots (Mannoni), a Southern lynching (Dollard), wartime collaboration (de Meerloo), concentration camps (Bettelheim, Frankl), brainwashing (Schein, Lifton), integration in Southern schools (Coles), and anti-war agitation (Spock).[7] And it is interesting that the wistful project, first floated in the 1930s, of having psychoanalysts systematically file with some alert centre the politics-relevant reactions of a 'panel' of their patients, as the best (and, perhaps, the only) prospect of getting primary data rich enough to support major conceptual advance, still haunts some of our brightest minds.[8] Sad to say, there is little more definition or sophistication to these psychiatric 'shopping lists' of the 1970s than to those of the late 1930s — indeed, the then contemporary prospectus of the rather eccentric English 'Mass Observers' (pledged to working through entirely untrained volunteer 'anthropologist-detectives') is still, to my taste, the most imaginative of such inventories.[9] Its founders saw the ubiquity of primitive and neurotic elements in our transactions with the secondary environment in darker terms than are warranted by a mere prudent fear of occasional swerves of mass judgment in political crises.

Meanwhile there remains a great need for simple, sturdy, *automatic* instruments, which anyone can read, designed to take the emotional temperature at political sites. We tend, I think, rather to mesmerise ourselves with the spectre of imprecision, and use our undeniable clumsiness as an excuse for inaction.* After all, where social scientists have been shocked out of their professionalism by genuine curiosity and excitement, by the exceptional sense of holding 'History a moment in the hand', they have often produced, using their eyes as much as their tape-recorders (and no laboratory-tested paraphernalia at all), memorable and lastingly useful descriptions of special occasions. The Greenberg-Parker book on the public reaction to the assassination of President Kennedy, for example, did a notable job of mapping something as thoroughly private and unpredictable as grief: who grieved, how deeply, in what way — all the

---

* I recall a story of the first British nuclear test in the Sahara: when all the elaborate and delicate physicists' devices assembled to catch the exact dimensions of the blast were put out of action by its unexpected force, all that enabled some part of the occasion to be reconstructed was the damage done to a ring of old oil-drums that had been filled with sand and propped about the site at the last moment. And that was enough.

information is there, as in a contour map.[10] And later, at their customary observation posts, pollster and psychiatrists proved able to add depth and telling detail, on individuals and special groups, that could be fitted into the original picture produced by 'crisis research.'[11] This, and studies like that of the unemployed man (Bakke), the English 'jitters' of September 1938 (Mass Observation), *The Invasion from Mars* (Cantril), *Wild Cat Strike* (Gouldner), the coronation of Queen Elizabeth II (Shils, Young), the McCarthyite shadow on American universities of the mid 1950s (Lazarsfeld and Riesman),[12] serve in their way as standards against which later occasions of a like kind can be measured. Their value lies, above all, in their having managed, after a fashion, to net the central affect of the occasion — the grief, the anger, the anxiety, the rush of loyalty: words thrown artlessly together can preserve the feeling of the time as dream-records do, which allow the dream experience to be re-lived years later in the re-reading.

One problem attending the measurement of affect in social settings, with special force in politics, is the recourse which is had to silence, secrecy and invisibility; as C. J. Friedrich has said, 'Influence *hides*.' It is more comfortable (sometimes, arguably, it is vital) that not only some part of the reasoning behind a judgment, decision or plan, but also most or all of the emotions that informed it, be kept dark. This is, perhaps, specially true of hostility, suspicion and envy.* For example, E., a difficult fellow, is an applicant for a grant or post. He is not formally inferior to the other nine applicants between A. and J., and they range on to Q. The chairman, however, says, 'I propose that, in a very tight choice, we concentrate our attention on A.—D.' 'What about F.?' says a well-wisher. That is dealt with. 'Can we now take A.—D?' says the chairman. Silence: and E.'s head falls.

How can he — or any third party — establish the committee's lethal hostility? E. may well be able to infer the displeasure or dislike of this or that committee member, but may well have missed some of the most important. He cannot know, however, if these poor impressions have lasted, or if they counted in his being passed over. Committee members may later be indiscreet and speak witheringly of E., or his candidacy, in

---

* A serious instance of this, which has been thoroughly described,[13] is the mystification of the U.S. Embassy in London, throughout the American Civil War, about the sympathies of the British cabinet of the day. Ministers' memoirs twenty years later proved the diplomats to have been quite mistaken — about 'enemies' as much as 'friends'. It is presumably this dependable disclosure of hoarded malice in memoirs that gives the form its discreet charm: we are somehow delighted to learn *at last* of, for example, Shaftesbury's contempt for all his political contemporaries except Palmerston, or Reith's contempt for all his without exception. But a most poignant instance (and a portentous one, since it turned a brilliant young man's ambition from Chief Justice to permanent anti-Chief Justice) is the eighty-year-old Bentham's exquisite analysis of the deathly silence with which the legal establishment greeted his first essay, *A Fragment on Government*.[14]

public; they may even admit that he was simply not discussed. *But they may not:* they may deny dislike if pressed and keep up a front of benevolence for months or even years.

Silence, and a total lack of record, set up an impenetrable screen which we must simply grant. Alternatively, we may have to grapple with testimony that is deliberately bland, impersonal, the fine flower of the official style, burying not only passions but whole persons and their contributions.* Shand has taught us that those in an affect-system do not have each moment to show, or feel, the emotion: and we feel entitled to work back inferentially from the outcome — even a credulous E. is unlikely to apply again to that committee. But political actors in the grip of an emotional system, however carefully they hold themselves in, do not have to say very much at all before their covert feelings begin to show.

The *Edmonton Journal,* for example, in October, 1974, one day before the annual city mayoralty election, in a most carefully worded editorial published on the front page, advised voters to reject one of the six candidates, a former mayor, who had been removed from office some years back for using his position for private gain. (It expressed no preference among the other five.) The editorial was written with painful care to present an *unemotional* case, and, in particular, to avoid any suggestion of personal animus against the ex-mayor. Almost regretfully, it suggested, this paper would have to advise against supporting *anyone* in his position; certain *facts in the record* alone had to be carefully weighed by voters . . .

I had feared that this composition — which was, objectively considered, a notably hostile political act — might, by sheer craft, slip through the net of the Gottschalk anger scale. It did not: the recital of past judicial censures, along with a good deal of editorial tut-tutting, kept the clock busy registering intense covert hostility in each clause. The piece scored almost the maximum possible number of marks. (And next day the rogue was handsomely voted in.)

Numerous special difficulties will no doubt arise in attempts to adjust Gottschalk-type measures to politics — difficulties in enlarging or rewording the scoring categories of existing scales in order to give the optimum range of scores commonly thrown up by political material, as well as difficulties in devising comparable scales for other major political emotions (Gottschalk offers a tentative and rather crude scale for measuring hope). How, for example, do we cope with the intrinsic hollowness and

---

* Dipping even one toe into the cauldron (as A. F. Bentley might *elsewhere* have called it) of committee politics, makes one marvel afresh at Bentley's blind eye for the bureaucratic passions — 'the actual working . . . everyday organisation of our political society . . . goes hammering along . . . undisturbed and uninfluenced, unprodded by specific Spencerian feelings of any kind', he says (see above, p. 294). Is this a prime case of the 'trained incapacity' of the journalist? Money-Kyrle has written well about the 'delusional arrogance' of committees.[15]

'overacting' inherent in declarations of powerlessness? Any prospect of an envy measure was explicitly abandoned on p. 360 above. Particular issues or topics seem to carry an involuntary emotional freight, which protagonists of even widely different temperaments and viewpoints must discharge. For example, it seemed impossible in 1974 for any Canadian speaking on Canadian-American economic relations to avoid the 'mouse and elephant' metaphor (the 'Gulliver' metaphor as discussed at p. 375 above), and this gave an inevitable paranoid texture to his comments — even if he *was* warning against paranoid postures. And possibly a good half of political discourse is pre-empted by attitudes (including emotional attitudes) struck by previous protagonists, and/or traditional opponents. Certain roles, too, impose their leading affect: leaders of the opposition dispense anxiety, doubt and scorn; prime ministers, assurance and hope.

We have also to recognise that, whatever emotional textures politics at a given time presents, individuals and groups are liable to select from them only those elements that they find germane, and can go to extraordinary lengths to screen out of awareness emotional demands they do not wish to meet. Norman Holland has shown, in *Five Readers Reading*, how selectively and characteristically individuals contrive to find only their own message in literary works.[16] The dynamics of political response are hardly less complex.

But for now, the main point to stress is surely that in the prospect of taking the emotional temperature, not only of persons, but of the actual instruments by which they intervene in the political process, we have a new analytic vantage-point of some promise.

The relation to ideology

Despite our earlier grumbles at psychoanalysts for neglecting to study the order in, and processes by, which the individual encounters, confirms and perfects his grip on the principal affects, it happens that one of the most thoughtful schemes so far is Arieti's, which links emotional, with cognitive, epigenesis. This should serve to remind us that in picking over emotional states for so long in isolation from the ideologies — personal and collective — which also help to give political actors their shape and purpose, we have drastically oversimplified.

Arieti distinguishes plausibly between the simple or 'proto'-emotions, characteristic of the first year; the 'second-order' emotions that become available with mental images proper; and the 'higher' emotions that depend on the ability, emerging notably in adolescence, to handle concepts.[17] Thus he lists:

(a) Tension, appetite, fear, rage and satisfaction
    The cognitive component of these feelings consists only of the perception of a definite and circumscribed set of stimuli — for example, direct or impending attack, or threatened immediate

change in homeostasis. These emotions are extinguished in a
few seconds or minutes and are quickly converted into visceral
and motor outlets; in fact, the richness and intensity of endo-
crine, muscular and visceral responses are their leading quality.*

(b) Anxiety, anger, wishing and liking, security (trust), early depression and early love

Second-order emotions are elicited by cognitive processes —
mainly images — which, by making possible an emotional response to what is not present, add a temporal dimension. Anxiety
is imagined fear; anger is rage sustained by images; an image of
what generally evokes appetite arouses (anticipatory) desire.
What belongs to the past and to the future can now be experienced. Emotions last longer, and are less tied to physiology.

Security, as experienced by the year-old child in his contacts
with his mother, is a self-contained emotion, going beyond removal of uncertainty or unpleasant emotions to a positive feeling
of well-being, of pleasant anticipation, of trust in people and
in things to come. It is more fully experienced later in childhood,
when higher cognitive processes permit reflected appraisal and
the building of self-esteem.

Early love and depression centre round images of the absence
or loss of the wished-for (separate) object.

(c) Depression, hate, love and joy

Now joining the 'proto-emotions' and simple emotions, which
continue to be experienced in their original forms, come the
transformations imparted by new forms of cognition, especially
conceptual thinking.

Depression requires a grip on language mature enough to
understand the consequences of loss, and a state of despair premised on a belief that what is lost cannot be retrieved; we overcome depression only by the reorganisation of thinking and
memory on a smaller or larger scale. Hate tends to expand into
a chronic state — 'a stubborn structure of bitter feelings and
accusatory thought' (Allport) — sustained by special thoughts,
especially of enemies, who may be finally coped with by long-
delayed actions. Love, 'felt for anything on which our happiness
is thought to depend', may extend beyond persons to groups,
institutions or ideals, and thoughts of the object — and its value —
sustain the love. Joy, too, has thick cognitive elements, agreeable antecedents, pleasant anticipations of the future.[18]

In short, gratification at the sensorimotor level is bound up with obtaining immediate pleasures or avoiding threats to the body-self; at the 'phan-

---

* When not balanced by other emotions, each 'proto-emotion' may dispose
to a lasting character-type: thus, the fearful person may eventually become
detached (withdrawing from fearful stimuli) or compliant (placating the source
of fear), the rage-filled person aggressive and hostile, the 'appetite-ridden'
hedonistic, the tense hypochondriacal, and the satisfied person smug and
conservative.

tasmic' level with wishing and the fulfilment of wishes; and at the conceptual level with enhancing the acceptability of the self-image and avoiding threats to its stature. In earlier pages, we have nominated paranoia (p. 370) and envy (p. 348 and note 13) as 'proto-emotions' (infants in the Kleinian scheme have an intense and precocious 'image-world'), and we have put powerlessness at least among the earliest and most vivid of the second-order emotions (pp. 376 and 350). Conventionality, as a strategy for ordering affect and behaviour, is readily discernible at three and four years of age (perhaps built upon images of others' judging faces); sympathy, too, is evident in the second-order emotions, although 'true' sympathy may, indeed, require a Piagetian 'reciprocity' (which is perhaps confined to age eight and over). Moral indignation as a second-order affect is at least extensively practised within the long experimentation in 'blaming' and 'being blameworthy',[19] though internalising the moral code is an eminently conceptual task. Tolerance is clearly premised on a sure knowledge of what *is* deviant, dissident or eccentric. Cynical children younger than twelve are rare; and even cynical children who are older than twelve have often been especially badly scarred by bereavement.

In adolescence, concepts emerge as the major part of the self-image, and a prolonged attempt is made to organise them logically. (They remain, however, somewhat resistant to neat organisation, with important affective consequences.) Far, however, from being static and purely intellectual entities, concepts become, if at all important, depositories of affect, and originators of new affect. We recall Scheler's brilliant exploration of the mutual dependence in *resentment* of a 'curdled' emotional state and the 'poisoned', disparaging cast of thought that goes with it.[20]

The construction of the political ego — and ego-ideal — is clearly a major enterprise in the individual life, grappling centrally and simultaneously with affects and concepts. Group-affiliation extends ego-boundaries so that personal and group fortunes are henceforth identified, and the individual's affect-flow is fully harnessed to group occasions. The recruit must also forge a new self-definition in terms of the group ideology, and this is often tinged with manic feelings and illusions of omnipotence. Group concepts may make familiar feelings shameful, or else justify them twice over; they may sharpen blunt affects and point them towards new purposes — for example, new objects of pity, scorn or fear; they may soothe and comfort, taking the sting from envy, and making bitterness less keen; and they may envelop the individual in a warm sense of community, and of sharing a 'just cause'. As with conversion, a late and lurid version of the same endeavour, achievement of the group-aligned self-image dissipates self-hatred; it justifies the use of negative or questionable emotions upon group enemies, since they now serve a purpose, and are being deployed to some good plan; it *energises* — as our discussion of 'harnessing anger' clearly showed (see above, pp. 344–5).

Once achieved, ideology closely regulates the traffic of day-to-day affect in the devotee.* Flickers of approval greet the progress of the admired, anger and indignation thrust at the disliked. Attention narrows to sequences of semi-predictable events – usually in association with some scanning and information-processing device, which rapidly and reliably identifies new provocations and threats, organising a 'para-environment' of confirming instances. The devotee pays, however, for the enduring comfort of his concepts – for the neater, simpler and more purposeful world they bring – by seeing only a small part of what goes on, seeing only the same things over and over again, and seeing them always in the same light; he pays too by increased susceptibility to events, which leaves him both more gullible and more subject to 'bad news'. Ideologies tend to set hard, and themselves become objects of stubborn pride and dependence.

We still need much more detailed work to explicate fully the relationship between ideology and affects. We need to know, for example, the typical steps by which a love for the homeland is evolved within the satisfaction-security-love affect progression, or a cool malice toward its enemies within the rage-anger-hate one. How does pity (not mentioned in Arieti's scheme, but surely incorporable) extend its conceptual bounds? And why, for that matter, are these typically so limited?

We must be equally curious about the *social* contours of political concepts in wide use, since collective belief-systems mobilise emotions on a grand scale. As Kurt Riezler points out, every society

> sets up a system of *pudenda* and *veneranda* – concrete things that must or must *not* be done – on the basis of its interests, conditions and ideas, which it tries to maintain and transmit, and reluctantly modifies as things change.[22]

Intended to be coherent systems, the *pudenda* and *veneranda* are often 'mere aggregates of fragments of diverse traditions, transmitted as habits'. Forever in process of formation and dissolution, they change fastest in the outer layers – 'fundamental principles, mostly intangible and elusive, may be tenaciously clung to in the depths of a culture', while the more visible norms waver, are transmuted, and die. Although each *pudendum* entails a *venerandum*, and vice versa, the *pudenda* may lose their original *veneranda*, and owe their authority to mere habit. In essence,

> each society sets up an image of man, clear or unclear, distinct or blurred, an image formulated in theoretical terms, and represented in remembered or idealised images of exemplary individuals revered as great ... [and counterpointed by] negative images, usually more distinct, of human ways disparaged, detested, abhorred.[23]

* Note that the same public ideological system can and will be used in characteristically different ways – for example, by obsessional, hysteric, paranoid and depressive adherents.[21]

Change in the guiding image of a society is best recognised in movements in hero-worship and the modes of idealisation. Where conditions change rapidly, the official system,

> though still dominating the words, may no longer be the system that secretly guides feelings and actions. Some *pudenda* and *veneranda* in the mouths of parents may already ring hollow to their children; children may even become aware that the *pudenda* and *veneranda* of parental words are no longer those of parental actions; elders may complain about the shamelessness of youth, while youth are already unwittingly setting up new images. Thus the *pudenda* and *veneranda* on the lips of the old may no longer be in their hearts; those in their hearts may no longer be in the hearts of their children; and those in the hearts of their children may not yet have found their words.[24]

Affects and concepts could not be woven more badly together, and, once again, the resetting of the laws and expectations of conduct and decorum has come to seem the critical factor in social change.[25] Riezler stresses the scope always allowed individuals to vary the cultural emphases in working *with shame and awe* to mould their own self-concepts — indeed, it is to these marginal amendments and redefinitions that the whole system owes what flexibility it has. He fears a deficiency in shame and awe less in rebels, who reliably manufacture their own in quantity, than in the power-hungry, in those in want and panic, and in 'the kind of radical enlightenment that denies any secret' (for he sees 'respect for the secret' as what binds shame and awe together into a single emotional system).

> Shame and awe guard the vulnerable. But they themselves are vulnerable, and again and again are trampled to death by violence, cupidity and want. Yet close by the tender plant sprouts anew.[26]

Riezler is surely right to accord these affects their portentous role in the setting and policing of social conventions. Our specialised text has concentrated rather on concepts at the heart of particular affect-systems — the victim in the case of sympathy, the enemy in that of paranoia, the scapegoat for hate, the criminal for moral indignation — around which lengthy passages of politics tend to become organised. The greater the conceptual complexity of the object, of course, the greater the opportunity for refined emotional response; less complexity gives less opportunity.

The tendency in crises for the mass occurrence of emotional and cognitive regression to childish or infantile modes of functioning has been noted several times in these pages — for example, by Lasswell (pp. 305 and 333), by Riezler (p.365), by Neumann (pp.366 and 371), and by the Kleinian school (p. 376). It takes the patrician eye of a great economist, however, to see politics as permanently and in general regressed. 'The typical citizen', Schumpeter complains, drops down to a lower level of mental performance as soon as he enters the political field. He argues and analyses in a way which he would readily recognise as infantile within the sphere of his real interests. He becomes a primitive again. His thinking becomes associative and affective.

We need only compare a lawyer's attitude to his brief and the same lawyer's attitude to the statements of political fact presented in his newspaper in order to see what is the matter. In the one case the lawyer has qualified for appreciating the relevance of his facts by years of purposeful labor done under the definite stimulus of interest in his professional competence; and under a stimulus that is no less powerful he then bends his acquirements, his intellect, his will to the contents of the brief. In the other case, he has not taken the trouble to qualify; he does not care to absorb the information or to apply to it the canons of criticism he knows so well how to handle; and he is impatient of long or complicated argument.

Without the initiative that comes from immediate responsibility, ignorance will persist in the face of masses of information ... People cannot be carried up the ladder.[27]

The core of the trouble is that the individual, finding that in politics he is a 'member of an unworkable committee, the committee of the whole nation', simply gives up the intellectual and emotional task as hopeless. The sense of reality, the responsibility, the will, which mark his behaviour in the private world — and spur on performances of high cognitive maturity — all fall away in the unfamiliar, largely symbolic world of the secondary environment. Keenness of moral discrimination also lapses: the individual will 'occasionally give in to dark urges which the conditions of private life help him to repress', or to the equally injudicious 'burst of generous indignation', as often as not opening himself thereby simply to manipulation. Moreover, policy-makers, who may be men of high principle in private life, do not hesitate to feed audiences with adulterated and selective information, refuse to acknowledge awkward facts, and rule out certain uncomfortable but valid lines of reasoning as undesirable.

Although the picture is a dark one, it does allow shades of maladaptation in thinking and feeling, and this is perhaps the point to fix on. We need to know what triggers ideo-affective regression in general and within each of our principal affect-systems, and what are the stopping-points in these systems — where, for example, a conceptual opponent dissolves into an image of the enemy, which itself dissolves into an internal persecutor — each with its required affect, appropriately nuanced or raw.[28] As we recollect from dreams, regression to an early ego-state not only revives an emotional experience in relation to objects understood at the cognitive level of that age, but also returns us to an earlier body preoccupied with its just-substantiated impulses and skills.

The emotional figure

In the chapters on individual affects, we have, as if inspecting a colour chart, looked quickly in turn at clear, even dense,* samples of selected emotions, with little thought about what they shade off into, or about how rarely, in the 'general mess of imprecision of feeling' (T. S. Eliot), they present themselves unshaded to any degree. Since our leading idea was the affect-system, we have been able cheerfully to ignore tinctures; and, in fact, people seem to have little trouble with mixture-formulae (seven parts anger, two parts fear, one part pride) or 'mixed feelings' generally (the political candidate, we are able to understand, may feel simultaneously excitement as in a game, embarrassment in his self-exposure, a strange openness to insignificant detail, and, underneath all this, stabs of infantile narcissism).† The emotional life of individuals and groups is, indeed, well pictured as a moving current, in which waters from many tributaries mingle in continually changing proportions.

But the 'transformation-potential' of affects (and even affect-systems) sets an altogether more serious problem. To know that our man or group is gripped by fear, say, is something; but is it fear that will shortly be disowned as demeaning, fear that will suddenly, as time runs short, veer into anger, or fear that will grow inexorably into panic, or numbed paralysis? Will this anger-system culminate in a single, large, cathartic aggression, or a dissatisfying one that calls for a whole series of successors, or in no act at all, since hostility is swallowed and kept down? One feels in politics that major affect-systems manage generally to absorb the greater part of the traffic. But many emotions, when they are persisted in, seem inherently disposed to change vector. To guess at the outcome, we need to be able to place them in an *emotional figure*: the unit of analysis thus becomes neither the single intense state, nor the quasi-purposeful affect-system, but the affect-spiral. Let us consider some of the varieties.‡

The time-based spiral

Kurt Riezler extracts an interesting *patience-impatience* figure from the trite case of the missed appointment.[30] The emotions of the person who has been 'stood up' spiral from an initial patience and good-humoured

---

* In Sylvan Tomkins' convenient formula — affect-density = intensity × duration. (Bentham's was a shade more complex, and in verse:
   Intense, long, sure, not distant, fruitful, pure,
   Such marks in pleasures and in pains endure.)[29]

† I am indebted to my friend Arthur Burns for this description.

‡ We wish to reserve the term 'spiral' for extra-system movement, though the reader may recall several figures in the text that might seem otherwise to deserve the name: Tomkins' step-like commitment process (p. 396) within the loyalty-system; the radical students pushed towards totalism (p. 343) within the anger-system; the heaping up of moral indignation against a date and/or an obstinate target, French tests, Nixon (p. 324).

hope before the hour, through a zone of doubt and even anxiety as it recedes, to a final burst of impatience and angry repudiation of concern as he stalks off.

It is a short step to the 'exasperation crises' between nations that Lasswell described in *World Politics and Personal Insecurity*,[31] and his cognate observations on the insecurities exacerbated in military planners' pursuit of balancing strategies, which may be summarised as follows:

> Preoccupation with potential enemy threats and violence reactivates deep early anxieties, especially castration fears. Insecurities, sustained by the necessity of suppressing impulses to vigorous counter-assertion, become heightened when part of the assertiveness is projected on to the other nation, which thereby takes on a more darkly threatening aspect. Changes of alliance, necessary to trim the balance, are read as 'betrayals'. The very caution, restraint and self-control involved in a prolonged balancing strategy itself feeds the pressure for a rash, impulsive outbreak. And, once an enmity crisis is created, negative emotion escalates with hypersensitivity, and a flight into danger becomes a tempting way of ending intolerable insecurities and releasing accumulated aggression.[32]

Such a process occurred in the case of Lord Avon. Condemned to the seemingly endless patience of an emasculating sonship, Eden flared up, when he was finally made premier, into the dangerous and absurd Suez adventure.

The spiral based on external drama

At other times, emotions turn completely round in the wake of public drama: the hero who has long been worked for, hoped in and trusted, turns out a failure, and is 'unmasked' — the moon falls into the sea.[33] At intervals, the trench warfare of party politics ceases for the obligatory scene of reconciliation and mutual regard — at the state funeral, the royal visit or the declaration of the poll.[34] At junctures like this, groups suspend, discard or reverse their emotional systems.

The depth spiral

Common sense, which will easily accept those types of spiral that are controlled by duration and by external circumstance, will have some (perhaps justifiable) difficulty with a spiral that consists of Pleasure, warmth, proffered intimacy — Panic — Hatred and violence (see above, p. 344), or with Mannoni's decolonisation figure: Relaxation of repression — Panic — Violence and riot (p. 344). The missing middle term triggering panic-rage is in the first case, threat of engulfment, of loss of individual boundaries, and in the second, fear of abandonment, suspicion that the sudden 'niceness', indeed, prefigures this. Individual, too, in their vectors were, first, the diarist's 'anti-semitic storm' (see above, p. 336), where anger mounted to a pitch where it frightened, and sparked off guilt and depression; secondly, the Temperance workers' sympathy with the drunkards that swung round to moral indignation, through a middle term like 'But now they dare to *scorn* and *hate* us' (p. 319); and, thirdly, the ideological convert's dramatic, though standard, spiral from passivity, powerlessness and self-hatred to activity, peace, joy and vigorous externalisation of hate (p. 343).

That each figure contains an anger term certainly buttresses that affect's reputation for transformational agility, but the vital term in these spirals is surely the middle one, and, here, fear predominates. We have at present, however, no clear idea of the field of instances of which these examples are a chance handful (with illustrations culled from more perceptive sources we might expect more play with middle-term envy).* In any case, the basic shape — and surprise — of the emotional spiral in politics or elsewhere is simply a corollary of Ernest Jones's layers of affect (see above, p. 300). In moving, or finding ourselves transported, from surface-level

Figure 10.   The transformation of affect.

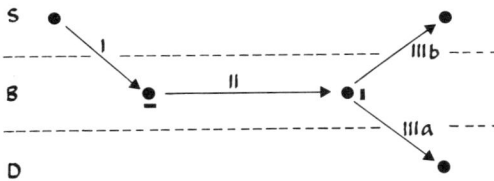

emotion, S, to B, the one beneath (by vector I), we hit an inherently unstable stratum — one that is simply uncomfortable to inhabit. So, after a short spell (vector II), one either drops *with insight* to D, the depth affect (vector IIIa), or throws oneself out into a new S (vector IIIb). Neither D nor the new S is entirely unexpected, but is presaged by the movement from S to B, in much the same fashion as a musical key organises certain possibilities ahead. Note, too, the *defence barriers* operative on level B, first against descent to D, then against persistence in B.

The cultivation of affect

Alexander Shand argued that the larger emotional systems tend to set up their own apparatus within the conscience, developing specialised notions of virtue and vice, defined by what is required for the attainment of each system's object, or its own maintenance.[35] In the first freshness of an affect-system — of sympathy, perhaps, or loyalty — its virtues may develop in a spontaneous way; a little later, however, these

* A figure common in everyday life is this: Interest and delight in another's performance contrive to arouse envy, at once eclipsing interest, and something like boredom is substituted in its place.

qualities may be checked, and effort and reflection be required to overcome 'drudgery', weariness and the competition of other emotions. Then
conscious ideals of, for example, constancy, courage, sincerity or perseverance are apt to be set up, ideals whose pursuit demands constant
concern with how one's accomplishment measures up. Hence *duties* are
established — the duty to be true, constant, loyal, patient, brave and so
forth. As Riezler was to note later of moral behaviour generally, Shand
singled out shame and awe as the emotions specially concerned to police
the maintenance of ideals.*

The moral component within emotional systems did not, Shand
stressed, exhaust the super-ego: 'As [conscience] has no private object,
so has it no private end; its end being to superintend and regulate other
systems, to encourage some, to forbid others, to temper all.'[37] Were it
to disappear, however, he mused, something very like it would reassemble
from the imperatives of, for example, the love-system. As ever, Shand
contemplated here only the primary world of personal relations. We do
not know what modifications he would wish to make in extending the
scheme to an account of the moral impetus of political or social affect-
systems. And this is, indeed, our plight in general: fitfully as the question
of the control or cultivation of the affects has been discussed, it has invariably been in the context of the private life.

Among the philosophers, Spinoza addressed himself most directly to
the strength and control of the affects, in the last three parts of his *Ethics*
(1677). He opposed to the concept of passion the notion of 'action':

> If . . . we can be the adequate cause of any of these affections, I under-
> stand the affect to be an action, otherwise, it is a passion . . . Our
> mind acts at times, and at times suffers: in so far as it has adequate
> ideas, it necessarily acts; and in so far as it has inadequate ideas,
> it necessarily suffers . . . The mind is subject to passions in propor-
> tion to the number of inadequate ideas which it has.[38]

His analysis is set out in two parts: first, a catalogue of the intrinsic merits
and demerits of the individual affects; second, a general strategy for their
control and cultivation. In the first part, he condemns hatred, envy, contempt, pity, humility, repentance, shame and pride as *evil*; his condemnation depends less on original moral insight than on an economical
geometry of interlinked definitions, founded awkwardly on the axiom,
'sorrow . . . is directly evil' (an idea otherwise phrased as 'diminishes
the mind' and passes it 'to a lesser perfection' or 'lesser accomplishment').

* A contrary story in terms of *unpacking* a moral kit has to be told for hate:
  'Hate tends to destroy all restraints and duties that we have formerly acknowledged on behalf of its object, and any others which stand in the way of its
  ends. As soon as we begin to hate anyone the sense of these duties begins
  to decline, until one after another such protections against our enmity are
  abolished, and the man has no longer a right to his own life . . . Hate tends
  to destroy all virtues, ideals, and duties that restrain it from its ends' (Shand).[36]

This part of the analysis has not worn well, but his sketch of a general plan for cultivating the affects altogether escapes this brittleness.

He recommends, in the first place, the study and understanding of the affects themselves as embedded in our living:

> An affect which is a passion is a confused idea ... if, therefore, we form a clear and distinct idea of this affect ... the affect will cease to be a passion. In proportion ... as we know an affect better is it more within our control, and the less does the mind suffer from it ... We have therefore mainly to strive to acquire a clear and distinct knowledge as far as possible of each affect, so that the mind may be led to pass from the affect to think those things which it perceives clearly and distinctly, and with which it is entirely satisfied ... An affect is bad or injurious only in so far as it hinders the mind from thinking.[39]

Since such knowledge is, however, somewhat hard to come by,

> the best thing ... we can do, so long as we lack a perfect knowledge of our affects, is to conceive a right rule of life, or sure maxims ... of life, — to commit these to memory, and constantly to apply them to the particular cases which frequently meet us in life ... For example ... that hatred is to be conquered by love or generosity, and is not to be met with hatred in return.[40]

We can also practise getting rid of fear, for example, if we 'often enumerate and imagine the common dangers of life, and think upon the manner in which they can best be avoided and overcome'. And we should endeavour especially to free ourselves from those affects which bind us to the contemplating of one or a few (obsessional) objects. We suffer less, are less injured, by affects 'related to many and different causes, which the mind contemplates at the same time with the affect itself (since they are more likely to be realistically perceived). We are also fatally prone to under-consider the distant and the long-term, to have weaker affects towards objects not regarded as necessary, possible or contingent.

His second, more radical, strategy is a thoroughgoing detachment from externals: we should

> strive also that the affect may be separated from the thought of an external cause and connected with true thoughts [for we tend to imagine external causes confusedly].
>
> Our sorrows and misfortunes mainly proceed from too much love towards an object which is subject to many changes, and which we can never possess. For no one is troubled or anxious about any object he does not love, neither do wrongs, suspicions, hatreds &c., arise except from love towards objects of which no one can be truly the possessor.[41]

Detachment is abetted by a healthy determinism, by an acknowledgment that 'everything is necessary', by being, indeed, 'philosophical' in the banausic sense: 'For we see that sorrow for the loss of anything good is diminished if the person who has lost it considers that it could not by any possibility have been preserved.'

Thirdly, since fluctuations in objects to which we are attached form the prime threat to equanimity and peace of mind, we should seek out constant objects, which we understand well and 'always truly imagine in the same way'. God is the prime example, and

> clear and distinct knowledge . . . whose foundation is the knowledge . . .
> of God, possesses over the affects . . . the power . . . by which it
> is able, in so far as they are passions, if not actually to destroy them . . .
> at least to make them constitute the smallest part of the mind.[42]

Contemplation of God, moreover, creates love, which 'fills and nourishes the mind'.

It is, I think, quite remarkable that, whenever they focus momentarily on a concrete strategy of affect-cultivation, most of the larger currents in later Western philosophy merely conjure with — without notably modifying — some one or more of the classic axioms of Spinoza. This holds true as much for late Protestant 'Christian Ethics',[43] Nietzschean perspectivism,[44] and theosophical hermeneutics,[45] as for psychoanalysis. Though Philip Rieff finds nothing in his thorough study of Freud as moralist[46] to say on the cultivation of affects, psychoanalysis has established itself as a social institution more than anything else on the basis of Axiom One — the statement that 'merciless dissection of feelings' is the path to self-knowledge and personal freedom.[47] And its main lesson has perhaps been that so many of our deeper feelings are ferociously guarded against consciousness:

> Defences against emotions . . . were studied earlier than defences
> against instinctual drives. As early as 1900, in the *Interpretation of
> Dreams*, Freud mentioned several defences against affects, namely,
> repression, postponement, and displacement. Later he described
> isolation, change of quality, projection and introjection. There are
> special defences against feelings of guilt, for instance, sharing and
> borrowing of guilt, and regression. Against anxiety there are additional defences, e.g. denial, active anticipation, in the turning from
> passivity to activity, in libidinization, etc. Asceticism and intellectualization . . . are . . . defences against the sexual affect.[48]

Thus argued Otto Sperling, in the course of analysing yet another defence — the *spacing* of affects ('out of fear of an excess of emotion, the affect is subdivided and the parts experienced at different times. In the psychological sphere this is similar to certain surgical operations which are performed in two parts, with an interval during which the patient may recover'). Yet his touch falters when he confronts the question of what is *healthy*, if spacing (and its contrary, 'crowding') of emotions is neurotic.

> While philosophers like Aristippus and Epicurus, and religions such
> as the Christian and Mohammedan, present as the most desirable

> form of happiness a continuous state of gentle moderated pleasure,
> our press and entertainment industry seem to have arrived at the
> conclusion that a climactic concentration of pleasure is the most
> desirable ... I would compare the attitude of the ego toward emotions
> with the activities of a sound control man in a radio station. His job
> is not to keep the sound on an equal level — that would make it
> monotonous — but to regulate intensity so as to prevent both extremes
> of loudness as well as faintness.[49]

Younger analysts have, from time to time, rebelled against such tactics
of 'adjustment' and 'adaptation' in psychoanalysis:

> The idealization of self-control, objectivity and detachment springs
> from fear of emotions. It is largely glorified as being scientific, and
> has greatly influenced upbringing, psychiatry, psychoanalytic practice
> and other fields. In my opinion, it does at least as much harm as
> unbridled emotion.[50]

But they misread as 'modern' and 'scientistic' what is really Spinoza's
Axiom Two, and have no clear alternative 'maxims of life' to put in its
place.

It seems, in any case, unlikely that secure maxims for the prudent cultivation of political affect could antedate some substantial resolution of
disputes about control-strategies for emotions in the private realm. If,
for example, hate and envy are to be proscribed *tout court*, it must be in
both fields, and their evil effects on primary relationships must carry
the critical weight. For the secondary environment becomes morally
important only in so far as it puts similar but additional complications
in the way of true feeling. We have, for example, greater difficulty in the
secondary environment in judging how much a reaction is our own, as
opposed to manipulated, mimicked or mocked-up; how much it is 'fresh'
and 'responsive', rather than humdrum, the latest in a long series of
instances (as in Baranger's 'internal organisation of instances');[51] how
much it is 'appropriate' (given the feebleness of our external reality-testing,
and our massive self-ignorance). It is true that 'political culture' can sometimes intervene in almost a voting way to proscribe, in Country A, appeals
made in rage, but in Country B, those in envy or fear; and there is perhaps
in such determinations the hint of an aesthetic resolution. But it seems
most likely that it is in the nature of debates such as those over strategies
for controlling the emotions that they do not get settled. I am content
to have raised questions with which only scholars with refined and forceful capacities for moral analysis can make further headway — journeymen
must be allowed to pose questions with which only masters can cope. The
goal, at least, has been clear as far back as Shakespeare's 'spirits finely
touched to fine issues'.

Notes

Preface

1 Sigmund Freud, *New Introductory Lectures* (1916/17), London, Hogarth Press, 1933, Lecture I.

2 Alexander Grinstein, *The Index of Psychoanalytic Writings*, New York, International Universities Press, vols. I–V (1960), VI–X (1972), XI–XIV (1975).

3 Carl E. Schorske, 'Politics and patricide in Freud's *Interpretation of Dreams*', *American History Review*, 1973, 328–47, and William J. McGrath, 'Freud as Hannibal: the politics of the Brother Band', *Central European History*, 1974, 58–78.

4 Harold D. Lasswell, *Psychopathology and Politics* (1930), University of Chicago Press, 2nd edn, 1960. For an interesting account of his intellectual history, see Bruce Smith's essay and Leo Rosten's delightful personal memoir in Arnold A. Rogow (ed.), *Politics, Personality and Social Science in the Twentieth Century*, Chicago, Chicago University Press, 1969.

5 I think particularly of that remarkable final chapter, 'The politics of prevention'.

6 T. W. Adorno, Else Frenkel-Brunswik, Daniel J. Levinson, and R. Nevitt Sanford, *The Authoritarian Personality*, New York, Harper, 1950.

7 David Riesman, *Faces in the Crowd*, New Haven, Connecticut, Yale University Press, 1951.

8 M. Brewster Smith et al., *Opinions and Personality*, New York, Wiley, 1956; Robert E. Lane, *Political Ideology*, Glencoe, Illinois, Free Press, 1962.

9 I think particularly of Alexander and Juliet George, *Woodrow Wilson and Colonel House*, New York, Day, 1956; Lewis Edinger, *Kurt Schumacher*, Stanford, California, Stanford University Press, 1965; and Arnold A. Rogow, *Victim of Duty — A Study of James Forrestal*, London, Hart-Davis, 1966; and in a brilliant second wave, Arthur Mitzman, *The Iron Cage: An Historical Interpretation of Max Weber*, New York, Knopf, 1970, Lucian Pye, *Mao Tse-tung*, New York, Basic Books, 1976, and John E. Mack, *A Prince of Our Disorder: The Life of T. E. Lawrence*, Boston, Little, Brown, 1976.

10 Fred I. Greenstein, *Personality and Politics*, Chicago, Markham, 1970; Fred I. Greenstein and M. Lerner (eds.), *A Sourcebook for the Study of Personality and Politics*, Chicago, Markham, 1971.

11 Jeanne Knutson (ed.), *Handbook of Political Psychology*, San Francisco, Jossey-Bass, 1974.

12 I think here of James David Barber's *The Presidential Character*, Englewood Cliffs, New Jersey, Prentice Hall, 1972, and especially, perhaps, of his brave chapter on Nixon. Also splendid on Nixon are Eli Chesen, *President Nixon's Psychiatric Profile*, New York, Wyden, 1973, and Edwin Shneidman's classic

piece on the Kennedy-Nixon television debates, 'Personality profile conveyed by the communicator as a function of his logical style', in L. Arons and M. A. May (eds.), *Television and Human Behavior*, New York, Praeger, 1963, pp. 177—99. R. E. Neustadt' *Presidential Power*, New York, New American Library, 1964, and 'Kennedy in the Presidency', *Political Science Quarterly*, 1964, 321 ff, should also be sampled on Presidential style, and his student Doris Kearns has now published a good life of Johnson (best, perhaps, on his Senate years — see above, pp. 73—5). Richard C. Hodgson, Daniel J. Levinson and Abraham Zaleznik, *The Executive Role Constellation*, Boston, Harvard University, Graduate School of Business Administration, Division of Research, 1965, is a superb account of the administrative styles of three men running a large organisation (a psychiatric hospital). Each author reported on one of the executives, and their portraits (which become something of a family set) are far and away the best example of this kind of thing we have.

13 Robert F. Bales, *Personality and Interpersonal Behavior*, New York, Holt, Rinehart and Winston, 1970.
14 Henry A. Murray and Christiana D. Morgan, 'A clinical study of sentiments', *Genetic Psychology Monographs*, 1945, no. 32, pp. 3—311.
15 Nathan Leites, *On the Game of Politics in France*, Stanford, California, Stanford University Press, 1959; *The House without Windows: France Selects a President* (with Constantin Melnik), Evanston, Illinois, Row, Peterson, 1958; *Images of Power in French Politics*, Santa Monica, Rand Corporation, 2 vols, mimeo; *The Rules of the Game in Paris*, Chicago, Illinois, University of Chicago Press, 1966. (And see further work listed below, p. 457, n. 143.) On 'National character/political culture' studies with a special bearing on administration, see below, p. 455, n. 119.
16 Abram Kardiner, *The Individual and his Society*, New York, Columbia University Press, 1939; *The Psychological Frontiers of Society*, New York, Columbia University Press, 1947.
17 Robert F. Bales, *Personality and Interpersonal Behavior*; Philip E. Slater, *Microcosm*, New York, Wiley, 1966; Theodore M. Mills, *Group Transformation*, Englewood Cliffs, New Jersey, Prentice Hall, 1964, *The Sociology of Small Groups*, Englewood Cliffs, Prentice Hall, 1967.
18 Christian Bay, *The Structure of Freedom*, Stanford, California, Stanford University Press, 1965; Erik Erikson, *Insight and Responsibility*, London, Faber, 1966; *Gandhi's Truth*, New York, Norton, 1969.
19 See the invaluable bibliography of this work by the editor of the *History of Childhood Quarterly: A Bibliography of Psychohistory*, ed. Lloyd de Mause, New York, Garland, 1975.
20 Elias Canetti, *Kafka's Other Trial* (1969), London, Calder and Boyars, 1974, p. 79.

Chapter 1. Introduction

1 W. L. Guttsman, in *The British Political Elite*, London, Macgibbon and Kee, 1963, p. 196, offers the estimate that between 2,162 and 2,212 people are actively engaged in British politics. His count includes M.P.s, regularly attending peers, officers of the national party organisations and pressure groups, party agents — local and regional — and 'serious' parliamentary candidates. To neglect senior and middle-range civil servants and journalists is indefensible. Party branch committee members and active campaign workers should also perhaps be included, see D. Marvick (ed.), *Political Decision-makers*, Glencoe, Illinois, Free Press, 1961, pp. 193—217; S. Eldersveld, *Political Parties — A*

Behavioral Analysis, Chicago, Rand McNally, 1964; James Q. Wilson, *The Amateur Democrat*, Chicago, University of Chicago Press, 1962; Colin A. Hughes, 'Political party workers in Brisbane', *Australian—New Zealand Journal of Sociology*, 1969, 32—9. Lord Bryce in 1889 had a count of 3,500.

2   For example, a town clerk or defence official, entitled in his own sphere to the sense of taking a hand in policy, may feel as helpless in the face of the decay of his son's high school or his daughter's university, as the professor or headmaster feels helpless about the endlessly proliferating suburban sprawl or the 'imperatives' of foreign policy or defence.

3   Few kinds of work confer high status faster than politics — hence W. Morris-Jones's definition — 'Who travels where, furthest, fastest?' — in his essay on 'Political recruitment' in Colin Leys (ed.), *Politics and Change in Developing Countries*, London, Cambridge University Press, 1969, p. 113.

4   'I found the younger members of the bureaucracy impressive . . . intelligent, well-educated, socially involved. The raw material with which the [Australian] system of government has to work is basically of good quality. But what is done with it? Discussions with people who had had 20 or so years of experience of the bureaucracy left me with a profound impression of . . . flatness in the quality of their lives, official and unofficial. Years of involvement in routine and ritualistic processes, inability to see the outcome of the work they were doing, and a sense of isolation from those whose affairs they were administering, generally seem to have destroyed the vitality and concern they no doubt [started with].' Dr H. C. Coombs, launching his Report of the Royal Commission on the Public Service, *The Australian*, 12 August 1976, p. 11.

5   Lasswell did not emphasise the term 'work'. He considered that the analysis of political 'practices and tactics' was less promising than the analysis of political 'views'; see *Psychopathology and Politics*, New York, Viking, 1930, 2nd edn 1960, pp. 234—6. Little had then been written analytically on work.

6   Lasswell, *Psychopathology and Politics*, pp. 75—6.

7   A point authoritatively made by ex-President Johnson when speaking of the power to 'stimulate, inspire and unite all the people of the country, which I think is an essential function of the Presidency': 'Now I have never believed that I was the man to do that particular job. Most people won't believe you, because they'll — they'll think you always want power. But the men who really get power are generally people who don't want power; and the fellow that has power is the one that uses it sparingly because you can throw it away very quickly with arrogance and autocracy and without consultation; and you can dissipate it, and most Presidents do . . . I don't think that I can ever explain to you or the American people something that's so deeply embedded in their beliefs as the fact that Lyndon Johnson was an extremely ambitious man who sought power, who enjoyed using it and whose greatest desire was to occupy the top job in American political life . . . I always felt every job that I had was really too big for me.' C.B.S. interview by Walter Cronkite, quoted in *Newsweek*, 5 Jan 1970, pp. 21—2.

8   Perhaps with his group of agitators particularly in mind, he noted: 'The prominence of hate in politics suggests that . . . the most important private motive is a repressed and powerful hatred of [parental] authority.' Lasswell, *Psychopathology and Politics*, p. 75.

9   Lasswell, *Power and Personality*, New York, Norton, 1948; reprinted 1962.

10   *ibid.*, p. 38.

11   The list does not draw at all on his Chicago clinical material collected through the thirties, and suggests, in the confetti of examples from Genghis Khan to the mad King Ludwig, a wet week-end with a biographical dictionary.

12　See the following: Alexander and Juliet George, *Woodrow Wilson and Colonel House*, New York, Day, 1956; Lewis Edinger, *Kurt Schumacher*, Stanford, California, Stanford University Press, 1965 (Edinger acknowledges his debt to the Georges at p. 30, footnote 11); Arnold A. Rogow, *Victim of Duty — A Study of James Forrestal*, London, Hart-Davis, 1966, p. 291; H. D. Lasswell, drawing on L. P. Clark's *Lincoln — A Psycho-biography*, New York, Scribners, 1933, in *Politics: Who Gets What, When, How*, New York, McGraw-Hill, 1936, pp. 417—18. 'We are ... entitled to assume that Winston Churchill was deprived by parental neglect of [an] inner source of self-esteem ... The first and most obvious trait of character which he developed as a response to his deprivation was ambition.' (Anthony Storr in A. J. P. Taylor et al., *Churchill*, London, 1969, Pelican edn, 1973, p. 224.) See also Lucille Iremonger's collective character-isation of English Prime Ministers as 'Phaetons', in *The Fiery Chariot*, London, Secker and Warburg, 1970. The need for power also figures largely in James D. Barber's biographical essay on Nixon in *The Presidential Character*, Englewood Cliffs, New Jersey, Prentice Hall, 1972, pp. 365—74. Its odd relation to alcohol is touched on in David C. McClelland, 'The two faces of power', *Journal of International Affairs*, 1970, 35—6.

13　Alexander L. George, 'Power as a compensatory value for political leaders', *Journal of Social Issues*, 1968, 29—49; Alexander L. George, 'Some uses of dynamic psychology in political biography: case materials on Woodrow Wilson', in Fred I. Greenstein and Michael Lerner (eds.), *A Source Book for the Study of Personality and Politics*, Chicago, Markham, 1971, pp. 78—97. For an entertaining thumbnail sketch of Dominican politician with a notable 'adula-tion' drive, see James L. Payne, 'The Zippo Lighter with the Lark Ad.', in *Incentive Theory and Political Process*, Lexington, Mass., Heath, 1972, pp. 17—27.

14　TAT cards: a projective test designed by Henry A. Murray (see his *Explorations in Personality*, New York, Oxford University Press, 1938) inviting subjects to give free associations to a set of drawings depicting ambiguous but unmistak-ably familial relationships. Using six pictures (an older man talking to a younger one in a rather old-fashioned office; a man sitting at what is ap-parently a drafting-table with a picture of a woman and children in front of him; seven younger men around a table; a man working at a desk in an other-wise dark office, hat and coat piled at the side; a man in city clothes talking to a boy sitting on a farm fence; and a man leaning back in what many people interpret as a seat in an aeroplane with papers or a book on his lap) stories can be simultaneously scored for need for power, need for achieve-ment, and need for affiliation. Points go in the first case, for example, for attempts to control or influence others, or for anticipating or consummating (especially with gusto) such attempts. See David C. McClelland et al., *The Achievement Motive*, New York, Wiley, 1953; idem, *The Achieving Society*, Princeton, New Jersey, Princeton University Press, 1961; and John W. Atkinson (ed.), *Motives in Fantasy, Action and Society*, Princeton, New Jersey, Princeton University Press, 1958.

15　Rufus P. Browning and Herbert Jacob, 'Power motivation and the political personality', *Public Opinion Quarterly*, 1964, 75—90; and Rufus P. Browning, 'The interaction of personality and political system in decisions to run for office: some data and a simulation technique', *Journal of Social Issues*, 1968, 93—110. However, William E. Henry's fine profile of the modal business personality makes no mention of power; see 'The business executive: the psychodyna-mics of a social role', *American Journal of Sociology*, 1949, 286—91.

　　Note also a playful little study measuring need for achievement and need for dominance in twentieth-century Presidential inaugurals: Richard E. Donley and David G. Winter, 'Measuring the motives of public officials at a distance: an exploratory study of American Presidents', *Behavioral Science*, 1970, 227—36.

A recent forthright attempt to net both the psychological traits separating political activists from ordinary people, and leftist activists from centrist and rightist activists (Jeanne N. Knutson, *Psychological Variables in Political Recruitment*, Berkeley, Wright Institute, 1974) brought a disappointing harvest, with little to show in either direction.

16 James D. Barber, *The Lawmakers*, New Haven, Connecticut, Yale University Press, 1965.
17 The same error vitiates the otherwise lucid and resourceful essay by Paul M. Sniderman, *Personality and Democratic Politics*, Berkeley, California, University of California Press, 1975, esp. Ch. 6.
18 Eric Hoffer, *The True Believer*, New York, Harper, 1951.
19 See 'Fanaticism in politics' in Alan Davies, *Essays in Political Sociology*, Melbourne, Cheshire, 1972, pp. 162—83, which discusses biographies by Coles, Lifton and Wolfenstein as well.
20 'Afterthoughts', his thirty-page introduction to the second (1960) edition of *Psychopathology and Politics*, New York, Viking. See also his, 'The selective effect of personality on political participation', in R. Christie and M. Jahoda (eds.), *Studies in the Scope and Method of the Authoritarian Personality*, Glencoe, Illinois, Free Press, 1954, pp. 221 ff.
21 Henry A. Murray, 'An American Icarus', in A. Burton and R. E. Harris (eds.), *Clinical Studies in Personality*, vol. 2, New York, Harper, 1955, pp. 615—41.
22 Iremonger, *The Fiery Chariot*. Maryse Choisy ('Le complexe de Phaeton', *Psyché*, 1950, 715—31) reported that, lacking a father, the orphans lacked a normal super-ego: theirs was both harsher and more severe, and yet inoperative over a large vital area. A compelling conscience (sometimes even inner voices) called on them to exercise restraint, turn their backs on the commonplace pleasures and relaxations of life, to remain 'pure' for some lofty purpose. On the other hand, their demanding consciences were not directed to the realities of life as most people know them, but to their own fantasy world; an infantile omnipotence of thought persisted. Their common fantasy was to perform a feat that would startle the world — to shame it for so drastically and unfairly withholding love from them, to protest their essential superiority and the total miscategorisation of them as inferior, and to exercise their pent up hatred and aggression and draw it to a compelling focus. Inevitably, however, they select a feat beyond their powers, one which is bound to lead them to disaster, since that is what their unconscious all along plans. They are driven — need desperately — to soar, to be seen flying as high as a man may go — to force the unknown father's acknowledgement of them as a 'true son', the world's greatest. Once in the chariot, however, as in the myth, they turn pale from fear, do not know where to head and cannot control the horses.
23 David G. Winter, *The Power Motive*, New York, Free Press, 1973. This model invites immediate comparison with Heinz Kohut's sharply contrasting scenario for the rise of the 'grandiose self' — 'prolonged enmeshment with a narcissistic mother, followed by traumatic rejection and disappointment'. The mother's obvious preference (over the husband) for the thus over-stimulated child is invariably based on a hidden attitude of admiration and reverence towards her own father. 'The son participates in the mother's defensive belittling of his father and elaborates this emotional situation by spinning out grandiose fantasies.' *The Analysis of the Self*, New York, International Universities Press, 1971, pp. 143—4 and 147.)

Lucian Pye follows this model in his magisterial *Mao-tse tung*, New York, Basic Books, 1976, and see also Tilmann Moser, *Years of Apprenticeship on the Couch*, New York, Urizen, 1977, pp. 105–7.

24 Abraham Zaleznik and Manfred F. R. Kets de Vries, *Power and the Corporate Mind*, Boston, Houghton Mifflin, 1975. This curiously invertebrate essay only gets going after fifty pages or so, when Lasswell's theory of the power-centred personality's search for deference as a compensation for early slights is set out — only to be instantly repudiated because of its 'equation of all interests in power with psychopathology'. Lasswell's theory

> minimizes policy issues in politics. It seems reasonable to assume that not all interest in issues is an offshoot of neurotic concerns. There are altruistic and external interests that may draw on emotional commitments but need not draw substantially on infantile reactions. There are many political men who are intent on seeing the world's work placed ahead of private interests and who, as pragmatists, try to find mutuality of interests to draw men together. These men can be distinguished by their anti-ideological positions and by their devotion to . . . the 'art of the possible'. If any question can be raised about their psyches, it may have to do with their being too normal and well adjusted, almost to the point of denying conflict.

In fact, Zaleznik adds, to wade through their TAT protocols is like sitting through a Saturday afternoon at the cowboy films of one's youth — 'There are no neuroses in such characters' — just impacted cliché; they live entirely on the surface, and are pinned firmly into an established vocational tradition. So a different quest is proposed. Not 'Is there a neurotic need for power, and what are its childhood roots?', but 'What in a person's developmental history is likely to lead him, when it falls to his lot as an adult to exercise power, to do so in a neurotic fashion?' For example, while one would not look in Eisenhower for a neurotic power-drive, one could reasonably be curious about why he seemed not to want to use the power of the Presidency when he had it.

The book then settles to a recital of organisational anecdotes illustrative of flaws in the character of principal actors and to a discursive ramble round the sites of childhood, pointing to the places where to get stuck is to become disposed to lifelong habits of misperception and/or misdirected striving. Thus, people with still-active Oedipal conflicts invest authority-relations with melodrama, the orally-fixated strive (like Gandhi) to re-experience 'oceanic feelings' and infantile omnipotence in leadership, and the anally-fixated (like the Krupps) the pleasures of sadism . . . The vicissitudes of narcissism and methods of coping with a 'grandiose' or 'fragmented' self (after Kohut) make a rather more interesting, not to say complex, study, but it should be clear that we are by now well into the territory of *individual styles of work* (characteristic attempts to solve unconscious conflicts by manipulating present objects symbolically). Here, thanks to Lasswell, the general analytic procedures are well-enough understood, and the need (to which Zaleznik, as the author of the 'Dr Suprin' study, has already abundantly contributed) is above all for the well-studied case. There are only case-snippets here, although the book has a sort of cloudy centre in the periodical contrasting sketches of Eisenhower and Nixon.

Some fifty pages on from the repudiation of Lasswell, however, there comes a very striking 'return of the repressed'. Digging away excitedly at one of his 'cases' — it happens to be Portnoy! — Zaleznik drops back into talking naively and with unfeigned awe about the *power-centred personality*. For such men, he exclaims,

The craving for power is an addiction. The erotic sensations that power-hungry people experience during moments when they feel dominant becomes [sic] a compulsion. They need the elation of power; if they do not achieve it, they suffer anger, depression, and the humiliations of dependency.

And he goes on to analyse Jimmy Hoffa and then Nixon in thoroughly Lasswellian terms ('Nixon's mother died, symbolically, when he renounced her as a love object and developed a burning ambition for power'). Real problems have a habit of not yielding to changes in nomenclature, and it seems little advance to replace talk about 'compensation for slights' with talk of the 'Achilles' heel' of 'a secret and grandiose self'.

Just to complete the rout, a little further on, even the boringly obvious, superficial characters, who are only on the political stage to keep things ticking over, become, in the person of the bland, hyper-normal, convictionless 'survivor', Dean Rusk, suddenly themselves, problematical:

Imagine how Rusk must have calculated and manipulated to create this aura of acceptibility [sic]. Indeed, the very genius of Dean Rusk as minimum man was his ability to cloak his ambitions and plans behind the image of Dean Rusk — bland, bumbling, not so smart, nice guy; in all, a person who seemed harmless and probably easy to control.

Rusk now *political man*! Where will it end? Will we have even to look for the Dwight Eisenhower behind the image of Dwight Eisenhower?

25 See the ingenious study of political outlets in a psychiatric hospital by Brent M. Rutherford, 'Psychopathology, decision-making and political involvement', *Journal of Conflict Resolution*, 1966, 387–407. The disproportionate participation of paranoids in ward government is shown to support Lasswell's formulation of political man as a displacer and externaliser.

N. W. Ackerman and Marie Jahoda's somewhat neglected *Anti-Semitism and Emotional Disorder*, New York, Harper, 1950, had already shown that depressives were not anti-semitic; anti-semitism was likely where the individual's typical means of protecting himself from intra-psychic conflict was extrapunitive, that is, where he was prone to projection.

Rutherford notes the apparent contradiction between Lasswell's displacement theory and Lane's participation hypothesis (*Political Life*, Glencoe, Illinois, Free Press, 1959, p. 123).

If an individual suffers from intrapsychic conflict, so much energy will be consumed by the struggle within the person that no surplus will remain to cope with conflict in the political arena. Interpersonal relations and ego strivings will thus suffer to a great extent. Those experiencing intrapsychic conflict, then, would be expected to withdraw from political participation rather than project upon political objects. We would have this proposition: the higher the level of political participation, the greater the psychic energy need, the less the intrapsychic conflict, and, hence, the more rational the participant.

He resolves it neatly — both are right: Lane for 'internalisers', Lasswell for 'externalisers'.

See also David Shapiro's brilliant, *Neurotic Styles*, New York, Basic Books, 1965, for an indirect demonstration of the unsuitability of politics for the purposes of, for example, hysterics; and G. E. Marcus, 'Psychopathology and political recruitment', *Journal of Politics*, 1969, 913–31.

Lasswell's own analysis of Lincoln as a notable 'externaliser' — *Politics: Who Gets What, When, How* (1936), reprinted in *Political Writings of H. D. Lasswell*, Glencoe, Illinois, Free Press, 1951, pp. 413–18 — remains suggestive.

26 'For the authoritarian character activity is rooted in a basic feeling of power-lessness which it tends to overcome'; this hint in Fromm's *Fear of Freedom*, London, Kegan Paul, 1942, p. 148, was not taken up — at least in a developmental sense — by the authors of *The Authoritarian Personality*, New York, Harper, 1950 (T. W. Adorno, E. Frenkel-Brunswik, D. J. Levinson, and R. N. Sanford). Although they made part of their basic definition 'a disposition to view all relations among people in terms of such categories as strong-weak, dominant-submissive, leader-follower, "hammer-anvil"', the disciplinary roots of this disposition were not separately sought.

Despite the urgent case-making of G. J. di Renzo's *Personality, Power, and Politics*, Notre Dame, Indiana, University of Notre Dame, 1957, pp. 98—103, we cannot allow his claim that he derived from administering Rokeach's dogmatism-scale to a sample of Italian politicians any secure understanding of their 'power need', let alone their 'authoritarian orientation toward power'.

27 'The significant question appears to be whether denials of opportunity to play a political role — even a humble one — will destroy the integration of the person. Sometimes the environment performs an 'experiment' for us and imposes such deprivation upon the individual — by forcing him out of office, for instance. As a result the person may attempt an extreme internalisation (suicide) or display somatic conversion symptoms of a severely incapacitating nature, or become mentally disordered. Some of the cases reported in the *Psychopathology* came to the attention of the therapists precisely because of political reversals. They were power-oriented persons in the fullest sense of our definition, since their capacity to continue as integrated members of society depended upon a social situation in which they pursued and exercised power with some success. These personality systems were so rigidly oriented toward the playing of a particular set of rôles that they were unable to maintain their integrity when these opportunities were shut off. 'Lasswell, Afterthoughts', *Psychopathology and Politics*.

28 For a recent careful summary of the psychological and psychoanalytic literature, see W. S. Neff, *Work and Human Behavior*, New York, Atherton, 1968, especially Chs. 6 and 7.

29 Sandor Ferenczi, *Further Contributions to the Theory and Practice of Psychoanalysis*, London, Institute of Psychoanalysis and Hogarth Press, 1926.

30 Elliott Jaques, 'The mental processes in work', Ch. 5. of W. Brown and E. Jaques, *Glacier Project Papers*, London, Heinemann, 1965.

31 Neff, *Work and Human Behavior*, p. 165.

32 Brown and Jaques, *Glacier Project Papers*, p. 75. Indeed Jaques proposes in a later Glacier Paper a rationale for equitable wage-fixing based on this 'time-span of independent work'. If you divide work, he suggests, into its prescribed/discretionary parts, the sense of effort in work is concentrated in the latter, and the weight of responsibility is related to the maximum spans of time during which discretion must be exercised by a person on his own account.

33 Brown and Jaques, *Glacier Project Papers*, p. 84.

34 Abraham H. Maslow: *Eupsychean Management*, Homewood, Illinois, Irwin-Dorsey, 1965, p. 14.

35 Joseph Conrad, *Heart of Darkness* (1902), Harmondsworth, Penguin Books, 1973, p. 41.

36 For a pointed and hard-fought debate about the quality of work of a sample group of 'conflicted' managers, see Abraham Zaleznik et al., *Orientation and Conflict in Career*, Boston, Harvard University, Graduate School of Business Administration, Division of Research, 1970, Ch. 13.

37 Brown and Jaques, *Glacier Project Papers*, p. 78.

38 After nine years' watch, I at last have one nomination — in psychiatry: Noel Bradley's splendidly self-aware piece, 'Theory-making, on scotoma of the nipples, and on the bee as nipple', *International Journal of Psychoanalysis*, 1973, 301—13. If only this mode would catch on in analytic communications . . .

39 See especially A. Zaleznik, R. C. Hodgson and D. J. Levinson, *The Executive Role Constellation*, Boston, Harvard University, Graduate School of Business Administration, Division of Research, 1965, Ch. 7.

40 Elliott Jaques, 'Death and the mid-life crisis', *International Journal of Psychoanalysis*, 1965, 502—13.

41 Lasswell, *Psychopathology and Politics* (2nd edn), pp. 234—8.

42 Lasswell, *Power and Personality*, especially pp. 62—5.

43 Shapiro, *Neurotic Styles*, p. 38.

44 The Wolf-man's 'repression of his overpowerful homosexuality . . . reserved that important impulse for the unconscious, kept it directed towards its original aim, and withdrew it from all the sublimations to which it is susceptible in other circumstances. For this reason the [Wolf-man] was without all those social interests which give a content to life . . . [or] attachment to the great common concerns of mankind.' Sigmund Freud, 'From the history of an infantile neurosis', reprinted in Muriel Gardiner, *The Wolf-man and Sigmund Freud*, London, Hogarth Press, 1972, p. 214.

45 This addition seems to draw on I. de Sola Pool's ingenious experiment with apprentice journalists — having them write stories with, or across, the grain of their temperamental preference for dispensing good or bad news. Ithiel de Sola Pool and Irwin Schulman, 'Newsmen's fantasies, audiences and newswriting', *Public Opinion Quarterly*, 1959, 145—58.

46 Lasswell, *Psychopathology and Politics*, 1960 edn, p. 151.

47 Lasswell, *Power and Personality*, pp. 89—91.

48 *ibid.*, pp. 92—3.

49 H. D. Lasswell, 'Agitation', *Encyclopedia of the Social Sciences*, New York, Macmillan, 1930, vol I, pp. 487—8.

50 Hoffer, *True Believer*, pp. 130—51.

51 Lucian Pye, 'Administrators, agitators and brokers', *Public Opinion Quarterly*, 1958, 342—8.

52 It is unclear, for example, what status his propositions about narcissism and latent homosexuality in agitators have. Both are prominent in his cases, but are they 'type-necessary' elements? Neither is required, or seems to fit neatly into the broader Object-relations frame. And one thinks readily of agitators who are notably non-narcissistic: for example, Ralph Nader.

A second example of strain between type-description and case comes in the distinction between orator and publicist. From the general frame set up, the publicist might be expected to be less a 'personaliser' (in fact, Lasswell *says* he is less a 'personaliser') than the orator, who moves more freely towards people. Lasswell's text tells us that agitators will be either 'model children' (imposters) consciously attached to, but unconsciously hostile to, their parents, and therefore choosing remoter objects and building more elaborate political thought-systems, or children consciously aggrieved by their parents, and therefore free to choose particular persons and groups as targets. And this seems to match the orator seeking a live audience to stir, while the publicist sets his audience firmly at one remove. It happens, however, that Lasswell's orator, Mr A., is the imposter, and his publicist, Mr B., the exponent of the journalistic exposé of persons.

The matter of preference for a certain distance from contemporaries is in any case eminently researchable. People have reports to make on it: for example,

'I want to be the sort of person only my friends know about' (young philosopher); 'I'm afraid I don't make proper use of other people. I hate parties,
for example — don't think I've been to one for eight years . . . I'm forced
dangerously back on my own, pretty static pool of ideas' (feature journalist,
in flight from frightening, over-close nuclear-family relations); 'During the
campaign . . . the candidate . . . becomes utterly surfeited with people, including his close friends on whom he nevertheless depends.' The politician has
no device, as the physician or lawyer has, for keeping people at a proper
distance (David Riesman, Introduction to Stimson Bullitt's *To be a Politician*,
New York, Anchor, 1961, pp. xi and xvi); the professional politician has 'an
inordinate capacity for multiplying human relationships without ever becoming deeply involved emotionally. Despite his appearance of friendliness and
warmth, the professional may in fact carry a cool detachment that many
citizens would find it impossibly wearisome to sustain.' It is easy to confuse
this posture with cynicism, for it so frequently is cynicism. (R. A. Dahl,
Who Governs? New Haven, Connecticut, Yale University Press, 1961, p. 298.)

53 Fred Greenstein grapples with Lasswell's saddening re-statement of the
quest, the logic of political personality typologies in Ch. 11 of Greenstein and
Lerner, *A Source Book for the Study of Personality and Politics*.

54 Fenichel gives a useful account of the concept of fixation:
'In mental development the progress to a higher level never takes place
completely; instead characteristics of the earlier level persist alongside of or
behind the new level to some extent. Disturbances of development may occur
not only in the form of a total arresting of development but also in the form
of retaining more characteristics of earlier stages than is normal. When a new
development meets with difficulties, there may be backward movements in
which the development recedes to earlier stages that were more successfully
experienced. Fixation and regression are complementary to each other. Freud
used the simile of an advancing army in enemy territory leaving occupation
troops at all important points. The stronger the occupation troops left behind,
the weaker is the army that marches on. If the latter meets a too powerful
enemy force, it may retreat to those points where it had previously left the
strongest occupation troops. The stronger a fixation, the more easily will a
regression take place if difficulties arise.

What are the factors responsible for evoking fixations? Unquestionably there
are hereditary tendencies that account for the various erogenous zones being
charged with different amounts of cathexis or different degrees of ability for
discharge. Little is known about such constitutional factors. Psychoanalysis did
succeed, however, in studying the kinds of experience that favor the development of fixations.

1. The consequence of experiencing excessive satisfactions at a given level
is that this level is renounced only with reluctance; if, later, misfortunes occur,
there is always a yearning for the satisfaction formerly enjoyed.

2. A similar effect is wrought by excessive *frustrations* at a given level. One
gets the impression that at developmental levels that do not afford enough
satisfaction, the organism refuses to go further, demanding the withheld satisfaction. If the frustration has led to repression, the drives in question are thus
cut off from the rest of the personality; they do not participate in further
maturation and send up their disturbing derivatives from the unconscious
into the conscious. The result is that these drives remain in the unconscious
unchanged, constantly demanding the same sort of satisfaction; thus they also
constantly provoke the same defensive attitudes on the part of the defending
ego. This is one source of neurotic 'repetitions'.

3. One frequently finds that excessive satisfactions as well as excessive frustrations underlie a given fixation; previous overindulgence had made the person unable to bear later frustrations; little frustrations, which a less spoiled individual could tolerate, then have the same effect that a severe frustration ordinarily has.

4. It is understandable, therefore, that abrupt changes from excessive satisfactions to excessive frustrations have an especially fixating effect.

5. Most frequently, however, fixations are rooted in experiences of instinctual satisfaction which simultaneously gave reassurance in the face of some anxiety or aided in repressing some other feared impulse. Such simultaneous satisfaction of drive and of security is the most common cause of fixations.' O. Fenichel, *The Psychoanalytic Theory of Neurosis*, London, Routledge and Kegan Paul, 1946, pp. 65—6.

55 See, for example, Fenichel, *Psychoanalytic Theory of Neurosis*, pp. 62—80; Erik Erikson, *Childhood and Society*, New York, Norton, 1950, Ch. 2.

56 G. E. Swanson, 'Agitation through the Press: a study of the personalities of publicists', *Public Opinion Quarterly*, 1956, 441—56, and 'Agitation in face-to-face contacts: a study of the personalities of agitators', *Public Opinion Quarterly*, 1957, 288—94.

57 Leo C. Rosten, *The Washington Correspondents*, New York, Harcourt, Brace, 1937, pp. 243—4. A study of some 127 'active political correspondents' writing news-dispatches or columns of national political content for daily U.S. newspapers or press associations of a large general circulation. Rosten had been a student of Lasswell's at Chicago.

58 Swanson, 'Agitation through the Press', p. 442.

59 cf. Martin Birnbach, *Neo-Freudian Social Philosophy*, Stanford, California, Stanford University Press, 1961, p. 161.

60 Swanson, 'Agitation through the Press', p. 444.

61 Erich Fromm summarises various clinical manifestations of oral passivity in his 'receptive orientation'; see Fromm, *Man for Himself*, New York, Holt, Rinehart, 1947, pp. 62—3.

62 The Krout scale had an immaturity cluster (dealing with preferences for 'working with subordinates or in a dependent role as over against having contacts with one's equals') and a maturity and generativity cluster (dealing with the 'ability to face unpleasant realities without being overwhelmed ... tolerance ... willingness to be ruthless if "reality" demands it. [All in all] a flexibility in the face of widely diverse and trying circumstances — the ability to face and do variously unpleasant things from dominating to submitting to suffering embarrassment to drudgery to putting up with petty annoyance to exploitation to being impartial under duress'.). (See Swanson, 'Agitation through the Press', pp. 441 ff.)

Incidentally, it is not clear why oral sadism was not predicted of at least a proportion of journalists, those working with cutting, biting speech, and an incisive style.

63 Otto Sperling, 'Psychoanalytic aspects of bureaucracy', *Psychoanalytic Quarterly*, 1950, 88—100.

64 Freud, 'Character and anal eroticism' (1908) in *Collected Papers*, London, Hogarth Press, 1924, vol. 2, p. 45.

65 H. Orlansky, 'Infant care and personality', *Psychological Bulletin*, 46, 1—48.

66 Sperling, 'Psychoanalytic aspects of bureaucracy', p. 98.

67 S. Kakar, *Frederick Taylor*, Boston, Mass., M.I.T. Press, 1970.

68 M. L. Farber, 'The anal character and political aggression', *Journal of Abnormal and Social Psychology*, 1955, 486—9.

Chapter 2.   *Agitating*

1   James D. Barber, *The Presidential Character: Predicting Performance in the White House*, Englewood Cliffs, New Jersey, Prentice-Hall, 1972.
2   For these terms, see H. D. Lasswell and A. Kaplan, *Power and Society*, New Haven, Connecticut, Yale University Press, 1950.
3   Mr A., in Lasswell, *Psychopathology and Politics*, Ch. 7.
4   Sigmund Freud and William C. Bullitt, *Thomas Woodrow Wilson — A Psychological Study*, London, Weidenfeld and Nicolson, 1967.
5   See Erik Erikson, review of Freud and Bullitt in *International Journal of Psychoanalysis*, 1967, 462—8.
6   Freud and Bullitt, *Woodrow Wilson*, pp. 63—4.
7   *ibid.*, p. 26. As the Georges show, Wilson was poor at negotiation and face-to-face persuasion, and, in the earlier stages of his Presidency, simply delegated this to House. It went deeper than this, however. He was prone in all one-to-one relationships to sense a challenge to his authority (always internally precarious), and, in whatever position of authority, he invariably ended up in conflict with one principal 'enemy' in a style showing more than a trace of paranoia. See Alexander L. George and Juliette L. George, *Woodrow Wilson and Colonel House*, New York, Dover, 1956, p. 26.
8   Freud and Bullitt, *Woodrow Wilson*, p. 6.
9   *ibid.*, p. 148.
10   *ibid.*, p. 168.
11   George and George, *Woodrow Wilson*, p. 320.
12   Freud and Bullitt, *Woodrow Wilson*, p. 88.
13   *ibid.*, p. 89.
14   William Bayard Hale, *The Story of a Style — A Psychoanalytic Study of Woodrow Wilson*, New York, W. B. Huebsch, 1920. See also Ernest Jones's review, *International Journal of Psychoanalysis*, 1921, 385.
15   Lasswell, *Psychopathology and Politics*, p. 97. This accusation was movingly levelled against himself by the Italian Communist leader, Antonio Gramsci, aged 30, in a letter to his future wife:
>How many times have I wondered if it is really possible to forge links with a mass of people when one has never had strong feelings for anyone, not even for one's own parents; if it is possible to love a collectivity when one has not been deeply loved oneself, by individual human creatures? Hasn't this had some effect on my life as a militant, has it not tended to make me sterile and reduce my quality as a revolutionary by making everything a matter of pure intellect, of mere mathematical calculation? (Quoted in Giuseppe Fiori, *Antonio Gramsci: Life of a Revolutionary* (1965), London, NLB, 1970, p. 157.)
16   Freud and Bullitt, *Woodrow Wilson*, pp. 3—4.
17   *ibid.*, p. 57.
18   *ibid.*, pp. 15—16.
19   *ibid.*, p. 97.
20   *ibid.*, p. 70.
21   *ibid.*, p. 94.
22   See E. M. House, *Phillip Dru — Administrator*, New York, Huebsch, 1908, For an informative discussion of Wilson's brief espousal of imperialism, and his eventual settling on 'leadership in the bureaucratic state' (involving, incidentally, the invention of the academic specialism of public administration) as the path of heroism — against a close comparison of Max Weber's parallel struggle

against a similarly oppressive paternalism and sense of historical stasis — see Michael Rogin, 'Max Weber and Woodrow Wilson: the Iron Cage in Germany and the U.S.', *Polity*, 1971, 557—75.

23 See note 14 above.

24 Ernest Jones, review of W. B. Hale in *International Journal of Psychoanalysis*, 1921, 385. Hale's book was known to Freud. 'Reading an American journalist's criticism of President Woodrow Wilson which applied the Freudian doctrine of unconscious processes to Wilson's mode of expressing himself, Freud exclaimed to Theodore Reik, "What do you say to the fact that psychoanalysis is here put in the service of polemics? People will never understand that our method cannot be used for aggression. It can only be applied to excuse human actions."' A. B. Feldman, *The Unconscious in History*, New York, Philosophical Library, 1959, p. 118.

Erikson notes in his review of Freud and Bullitt, *Woodrow Wilson*, that Freud was always interested in Wilson because they were born in the same year. See *International Journal of Psychoanalysis*, 1967, 462—8.

25 See, for example, Senator Carter Glass's speech on the abandonment of the Gold Standard, in Kenneth Burke, *A Grammar of Motives*, New York, Prentice Hall, 1945, pp. 432 ff.

26 See Richard E. Donley and David G. Winter, 'Measuring the motives of public officials at a distance: an exploratory study of American Presidents', *Behavioral Science*, 1970, 227—36.

27 Personality profile conveyed by the communicator as a function of his logical style, in L. Arons and M. A. May (eds.), *Television and Human Behavior*, New York, Praeger, 1963, pp. 177—99.

28 Lewis Edinger, *Kurt Schumacher*, Stanford, California, Stanford University Press, 1965, final chapter. On Nixon's use of rhetoric as a way to release aggression, see Barber, *Presidential Character*.

29 Robert Michels, *Political Parties*, Glencoe, Illinois, Free Press, 1949, p. 75.

30 J. A. La Nauze, *Alfred Deakin*, Melbourne, Melbourne University Press, 1965.

31 Alfred Deakin, *New Pilgrim's Progress*, Melbourne, privately printed, 1877, p. 64.

32 L. Pierce Clark, *Lincoln — A Psychobiography*, New York, Scribners, 1933, p. 302; Leo Abse, *Private Member*, London, Macdonald, 1973, p. 57.

33 La Nauze, *Alfred Deakin*, pp. 250 and 246.

34 William Empson, *Seven Types of Ambiguity* (1930), New York, New Directions, 1947, p. 17.

35 Deakin's first memory is of being on his mother's knee, 'white-gowned and glowing from his hot bath, out of which his sister had just tenderly lifted him', gazing at his father, reading by an oil-lamp. His shy, ambitious, *talkative*, 'emotional, affectionate, expressive, versatile, impressionable and reckless' father was a prodigious reader aloud, 'enunciating clearly in "a flexible and tuneful voice"' by the hour. The books he read were the Victorian classics: he named his son Alfred Tennyson. See La Nauze, *Alfred Deakin*, pp. 12—15.

36 Gustav Bychowski, *Dictators and Disciples*, New York, International Universities Press, 1948, pp. 202—3.

37 La Nauze, *Alfred Deakin*, p. 643.

38 J. D. Barber, 'Classifying and predicting presidential styles: two weak presidents', in F. I. Greenstein (ed.), 'Personality and politics', *Journal of Social Issues*, 1968:4, 51—80; L. F. Crisp, *Ben Chifley*, Melbourne, Longmans, 1960; Alex Gottfried, *Boss Cermak of Chicago*, Seattle, University of Washington Press, 1962; J. D. Barber, 'Adult identity and presidential style: the rhetorical emphasis', *Daedalus*, 1968:3, 938—68.

39 'Prudence condemned me to acquiesce in the humble station of a mute. I was not armed by Nature or education with the intrepid energy of mind or voice ... timidity was fortified by pride; and even the success of my pen [with the publication of the first volumes of his *History*] discouraged the tryal of my voice.' *Memoirs of My Life* (1796), (ed. Georges A. Bonnard), London, Nelson, 1966, p. 156. For the familial background, see David P. Jordan, 'Edward Gibbon', *Daedalus*, 1976:3, 1—12.

40 André Gorz, *The Traitor* (1954), English translation, London, Calder, 1960; see also 'The case of André Gorz' in Alan Davies, *Essays in Political Sociology*, Melbourne, Cheshire, 1972.

41 Mr Justice Crisp, reported in the *Melbourne Herald*, 18 March 1969.

42 Arnold L. Green, 'The ideology of anti-fluoridation leaders', *Journal of Social Issues*, 1961:4, 13—25.

43 Green, 'Anti-fluoridation leaders', 16—17.

44 See Alan Davies, 'The child's discovery of nationality', *Australian—New Zealand Journal of Sociology*, 1968, 107—125, and Henry A. Murray and Christiana D. Morgan, 'A clinical study of sentiments', *Genetic Psychology Monographs*, 1945, no. 32, pp. 3—311.

45 Rousseau's mother also died giving birth to him. He left us a philosophical system based on the repudiation of Original Sin and the celebration of natural man. For the family background of American women's liberationists, see C. Cherniss, 'Personality and ideology', *Psychiatry*, 1972, 109—24. The observations about Women's Liberation and Abortion Law Reform groups were given me by friends.

46 *Politics: Who Gets What, When, How* (1936), reprinted in *Political Writings of H. D. Lasswell*, Glencoe, Illinois, Free Press, 1951, pp. 414—15.

47 At the same time, the proportion of political manoeuvring contributed by the fixed adherents of the large encompassing ideologies of individualism and socialism dwindles. See Frank Parkin, *Middle Class Radicalism: The Social Bases of the British Campaign for Nuclear Disarmament*, Manchester, Manchester University Press, 1968.

48 Lasswell, *Politics: Who Gets What, When, How*, p. 383.

49 R. E. Lane and D. Sears, *Public Opinion*, New York, Prentice-Hall, 1968, pp. 75—6.

50 H. D. Lasswell and Dorothy Blumenstock, *World Revolutionary Propaganda — A Chicago Study*, New York, Knopf, 1939, pp. 283—300. This is still one of the very few psychological studies of a group of radical political actors. (Of late, only student radicals have fallen under review: see K. Keniston, *Young Radicals*, New York, Harcourt, Brace, 1968, and Robert Liebert, *Radical and Militant Youth*, New York, Praeger, 1971.) Lasswell's thoughts on 'externalised rage' are supplemented by his case study of 'Some of the problems in the synthesis of motive and skill in politics — the mature years of Abraham Lincoln' (*Politics — Who Gets What, When, How*, Ch. 8). Lincoln is seen as a 'partially inhibited-rage type', as well as an agitator *par excellence*.

51 Don Aitken, *The Colonel: A Political Biography of Sir Michael Bruxner*, Canberra, Australian National University Press, 1969, p. 277.

52 See, for example, Judd Marmor, 'The psychodynamics of political extremism', *American Journal of Ortho-psychiatry*, 1968, 561—8; Gilbert Abcarian, 'Radical Right and New Left' in W. J. Crotty (ed.), *Public Opinion and Politics*, New York, Holt, Rinehart and Winston, 1970, pp. 168—89; I. L. Horowitz, *The Struggle is the Message*, Berkeley, Glendessary Press, 1970, especially Ch. 8.

53 Leo Lowenthal and Norbert Guterman, *Prophets of Deceit: A Study of the Techniques of the American Agitator*, New York, Harper, 1949, p. 9. Note too the shrewd comments on the rightist's 'insider stance' and 'kite-flying improvisations'.

54 Lowenthal and Guterman, *Prophets of Deceit*, p. 17. It might be a useful exercise to score Herbert Marcuse on these 'reactionary' themes; and see Horowitz, *Struggle*, Ch. 8.

55 Lowenthal and Guterman, *Prophets of Deceit*, p. 141.

56 John Halverson, 'The psychopathology of style: the case of right-wing rhetoric', *Antioch Review*, 1971, 97—108.

57 For an impressive recent study showing that the cancer metaphor is central to Hitler's thinking, see Richard A. Koenigsberg, *Hitler's Ideology*, New York, Library of Social Science, 1975; and for discussions of its persuasiveness, see Bychowski, *Dictators and Disciples*, especially pp. 202—6, and Ernest Kris, 'The "danger" of propaganda, *American Imago*, 1941, 3—42, which discusses 'suggestibility' at length, linking it with anxiety and disappointment: 'it is a regular stage in childhood'. Note also the comment by the columnist 'R' in *Encounter*: his oratory 'was of the kind that speaks neither to the mind nor to the heart of his audience, but plays upon its nerves until they are strung to such a pitch of intensity that they shriek for release in action'. (*Encounter*, November 1975, p. 44.) For further discussion of this matter, see Walter Langer's magisterial *The Mind of Adolf Hitler*, New York, Basic Books, 1972, pp. 47—9, 65—6, 129—30 and 203—6.

58 R. Money-Kyrle has interpreted such moments of manic elevation as at bottom the fantasy of regaining the nipple. See 'Megalomania', *American Imago*, 1966, 142—54. He also presents in *Psychoanalysis and Politics* a neat case of a young man's 'sense of a vitally important mission' constructed upon an 'omnipotent phantasy of reparation' following a father's early death (London, Duckworth, 1951, pp. 173—6).

For an illuminating discussion of the prevalence of a sense of inner superiority and 'specialness' in schizoid/theorist types generally, based on 'a secret over-valuation of personal contents, mental as well as physical; and . . . identification with . . . internalised libidinal objects (e.g. the maternal breast and the paternal penis)', see William Ronald Fairbairn, *Psychoanalytic Studies of the Personality*, London, Routledge, 1952, pp. 22—3.

59 Freud and Bullitt, *Woodrow Wilson*, p. xi.

60 Alfred Deakin, *Quentin Massys*, Melbourne, privately printed, 1879, p. 17.

61 Heinz Kohut, 'Creativeness, charisma and group psychology', *Psychological Issues*, 1976, 379—425.

62 E. V. Wolfenstein, 'Some psychological aspects of crises leadership' in L. J. Edinger (ed.), *Political Leadership in Industrialized Societies*, New York, Wiley, 1967, pp. 155—81 (Churchill, Hitler, Lenin and Gandhi); Stanley Hoffman, 'Heroic leadership: the case of modern France', *ibid.*, pp. 108—54 (Petain, de Gaulle, Mendès-France).

63 Personal communication from Claire Rosemberg.

64 For an eloquent statement of this general predicament, see Lawrence Kubie, 'Some unsolved problems of the scientific career', p. 245, in Maurice Stein, Arthur J. Vidich and David Manning White (eds.), *Identity and Anxiety*, New York, Free Press, 1960.

65 David Riesman, Introduction to Stimson Bullitt, *To be a Politician*, New York, Anchor, 1961, p. xix.

66 William H. Whyte, 'The dissemination of viewpoints', S. M. Farber (ed.), *Conflict and Creativity*, New York, McGraw Hill, 1963, pp. 329—34.

67 Karl Deutsch, *The Nerves of Government*, New York, Free Press, 1963, p. 174.

68 See, for example, Peter Heydon, *Quiet Decision: A Study of George Foster Pearce*, Melbourne, Melbourne University Press, 1965, p. 31.

69   But note J. S. Gusfield, *Symbolic Crusade*, Urbana, Illinois, University of Illinois Press, 1963, on the U.S. Temperance movement, a case study that proceeds at an admirable depth; and Phyllis Keller, 'G. S. Viereck — a psycho-biography', *Journal of Interdisciplinary History*, 1971—2, especially pp. 79—84; E. Victor Wolfenstein, *Personality and Politics*, California, Dickenson, 1969, Ch. 3 (Malcolm X.); Michael Abdul Malik's splendid autobiography, *From Michael de Freitas to Michael X*, London, Deutsch, 1968; W. L. Warner's clowning mayor, 'Biggy Muldoon', in part v of *The Living and the Dead*, New Haven, Connecticut, Yale University Press, 1959; Leo Abse's sharp portrait of Sidney Silverman in Ch. 6 of *Private Member*, London, Macdonald, 1973; and now Angus McIntyre, *Political Styles and Political Change in the Communist Party of Australia*, University of Melbourne Ph. D. thesis, 1975, which contains five case-studies of party leaders.

70   Summarised from Herbert Blumer, *New Outlines of the Principles of Sociology*, ed. A. M. Lee, New York, Barnes and Noble, 1951, pp. 199—220.

71   *ibid.*, pp. 203—5.

72   David Truman, *The Governmental Process*, New York, Knopf, 1951, Chs. 6—7.

73   See Mark Benney, *What Great Beast?*, London, Peter Davies, 1936.

74   See Bill Hornedge, *Chidley's Answer to the Sex Problem*, Sydney, Review Publications, 1971.

75   James D. Barber, *The Lawmakers*, New Haven, Connecticut, Yale University Press, 1965.

76   *ibid.*, p. 214.

77   That this reality sense is the prime gift of the successful politician is the message of Oliver's spirited introduction to his life of Walpole (F. S. Oliver, *The Endless Adventure*, London, Macmillan, 1930, vol. 1, part 1). It is also emphasised in Edinger's *Schumacher*, which contains some quite careful discussion about the measurement problems that must be considered when writing the biography of a paranoid. There is some evidence that selection committees, the press, and party and cabinet colleagues are increasingly able to recognise and reward it.

78   A Congressman, according to Lewis A. Dexter, very largely gets back what he puts out. He associates more with some kinds of people than with others, listens to some kinds of messages more than others. He controls what he hears, both by his attention and his attitudes. He *makes* the world to which he thinks he is responding. 'One Congressman with an eye on issues will listen with concern to arguments put forward by constituents, whereas another Congressman with an eye on local social groups will feel no pressure from pompous statements about issues as he tries to keep track of births, marriages, and deaths. The Representative who is known to have arranged for the non-quota entrance of relatives of members of a given ethnic group will receive similar requests from other such persons. The Congressman who establishes his home office in a working-class section, where his secretary gives advice on social-security cases, will get such cases, which perhaps take more time than any other service. The Congressman who has interested himself in taxes will hear about taxes.' His activities determine which of his constituents know him, and their past experience tells them what their Congressman will respond to. If he has come to church suppers before, he will be invited again. If he has given speeches on foreign policy, that is what he will be invited to do. The job is largely what the Congressman makes it. See Lewis A. Dexter, 'The job of the Congressman' in R. E. Wolfinger (ed.), *Readings in American Political Behavior*, New York, Prentice Hall, 1966, 2nd edn 1970, pp. 5—25.

Chapter 3.   Administering

1   See Paul Ferris, *The House of Northcliffe*, London, Weidenfield, 1971.
2   See Lord Reith's autobiography, *Into the Wind*, London, Hodder and Stoughton, 1949. The Viceroy fantasy was aired in a television interview with Malcolm Muggeridge on Reith's eightieth birthday. Andrew Boyle gives an alternative account of Reith's 'autonomous' style, basing it on neurosis, if not paranoia, in *Only The Wind Will Listen: Reith on the B.B.C.*, London, Hutchinson, 1972.
    The psychological literature, clinical or theoretical, on failure and disappointment in career is scant. See, however, Abraham Zaleznik, 'The management of disappointment', *Harvard Business Review*, 1967; G. Rochlin, 'The psychology of failure' in his *Griefs and Discontents*, London, Churchill, 1965; and S. Kakar, *Frederick Taylor*, Boston, Mass., M.I.T. Press, 1970, Ch. 8.
3   Arnold A. Rogow, *Victim of Duty — A Study of James Forrestal*, London, Hart-Davis, 1966.
4   Lasswell, *Psychopathology and Politics*, pp. 135—9.
5   For example, R. G. S. Brown's 'shallows' and 'deeps', in his 'Organisational Theory and Civil Service Reform', *Public Administration* (London), 1965, 313—30; R. Presthus's 'upward mobiles' and 'ambivalents' in his *The Organizational Society*, New York, Vintage Books, 1965; the more routine public administration dichotomy of 'generalists' and 'specialists' or 'professionals', as in A. J. A. Gardner, 'Specialists and the Administrative Career', *Public Administration* (Sydney), 1963, 30—46; and the distinction already made in this book between 'single cause' and 'general purpose' agitators (see above, pp. 36—9). The specialist in one administrative *technique* which may be applied impartially in a number of fields stands rather outside our purview.
6   Dag Hammarskjöld's biographer, Henry P. Van Dusen, writes:
    Between the despairing plaints [in *Markings*] of late 1952 and the positive and profoundly religious affirmations of early 1953, something had occurred in his interior self . . . It has been generally assumed that the event which effected such a radical alteration in outlook was Hammarskjöld's elevation to the United Nations Secretary-Generalship. Unquestionably, this was an important factor in consolidating the change.' He wrote to an old friend, 'In this international work I have lost the sense of inner cleavage that I felt at home in Sweden.' (*Dag Hammarskjöld: A Biographical Interpretation of 'Markings'*, London, Faber, 1967, p. 99.)
    Sweden was his *father's* country — he was Prime Minister during much of Dag's childhood ('A box on the ear taught the boy / That father's name / Was odious to them'), and Hammarskjöld noted: 'I . . . stand in the centre of a perpetual conflict with a dominating father (in many things deeply unlike me) whose pressure I hated and whose weaknesses I always saw very clearly.' (Van Dusen, *Dag Hammarskjöld*, p. 15.) His father's death at this time gave him the freedom to be himself, 'to answer *Yes* to Someone — or Something' (*ibid.*, p. 100).
7   cf. J. A. La Nauze, *Alfred Deakin*, Melbourne, Melbourne University Press, 1965, pp. 84—6. For the link between inventors' and engineers' preoccupations with irrigation and childhood struggles with bed-wetting, see K. Eissler, *Leonardo*, New York, International Universities Press, 1961, p. 167, and Kakar, *Frederick Taylor*, p. 81.
8   See Parrin Stryker, *The Character of the Executive*, New York, Harper, 1961, for a case study of management succession and changes in corporate strategy in Sears Roebuck.
9   W. Lloyd Warner, Paul P. Van Riper, Norman H. Martin and Orvis F. Collins,

The American Federal Executive, New Haven, Connecticut, Yale University Press, 1963, pp. 194 ff.

10 *ibid.*, p. 219.

11 *ibid.*, pp. 225—36.

12 Meyer A. Zeligs, *Friendship and Fratricide: An Analysis of Whittaker Chambers and Alger Hiss*, New York, Viking Press, 1967. See also the careful review of this book in John E. Mack's survey of psycho-biography, *Journal of the American Psychoanalytical Association*, 1971, 163—6.

13 One may conjecture that it was hostility to the mother that broke through in his spying. Chambers notes: 'The outstanding fact about Alger Hiss was an unvarying mildness . . . Only very rarely did a streak of wholly incongruous cruelty crop out. From the first, my wife and I had been charmed by Baltimore and sometimes said so. "Baltimore," Alger once answered, "is the only city in the country so backward that it still lights its streets by gas. It's a city of dying old men and women." He was so unnecessarily savage that, by way of easing matters, I said: "They seem to be pleasant and harmless old people." "Yes," he said, "the horrible old women of Baltimore!" . . . The same strange savagery cropped out in a conversation about Franklin Roosevelt. Hiss's contempt for Franklin Roosevelt as a dabbler in revolution who understood neither revolution nor history was profound . . . He startled me, and deeply shocked my wife, by the obvious pleasure he took in the most simple and brutal references to the President's physical condition as a symbol of the middle-class breakdown.' (Whittaker Chambers, *Witness*, New York, Random House, 1952, quoted in Zeligs, *Friendship and Fratricide*, pp. 209—10.) Mother, Baltimore matriarchy, the posturing, sedentary President — all epitomise feeble, illegitimate authority that ought to die or disappear but refuses to do so. Russia — under the cover of Marxist—Leninist ideology — stands for Aunt Lila, 'the quick, intelligent, ethical little woman' who showed him simple warmth and understanding.

    For a recent study that strongly supports the Hiss-as-spy thesis, see Allen Weinstein, *Perjury: the Hiss-Chambers Case*, New York, Knopf, 1978, and Garry Wills's review, *New York Review of Books*, 20 April 1978, pp. 29—30.

14 Zeligs, *Friendship and Fratricide*, pp. 150—1.

15 *ibid.*, p. 155.

16 Chambers, *Witness*, p. 258.

17 Lasswell, *Psychopathology and Politics*, p. 151.

18 *ibid.*, p. 135.

19 See Elliott Jaques, 'Social systems as defence against persecutory and depressive anxiety', in Melanie Klein (ed.), *New Directions in Psychoanalysis*, London, Hogarth Press, 1953.

20 William E. Henry, 'The business executive: the psychodynamics of a social role', *American Journal of Sociology*, 1949, 286—91. The hundred or so executives interviewed were mostly 'from distributive (rather than manufacturing) businesses of moderately loose organisational structure'. The interviews ('short, undirected'), were accompanied by a Thematic Apperception Test, and a projective analysis of a number of traditional personality tests.

    For a later study of the successful executive's traits through the analysis of projective materials, see Z. A. Piotrowski, *The Perceptanalytic Executive Scale*, New York, Grune, Stratton, 1963, which singles out: the drive for power; foresight and the anticipation of challenge; self-confidence and mental and physical health; the capacity for friendly co-operation and competition; integration and spontaneity; mental productivity; and controlled aggressiveness and obsessiveness. In the Rorschach Test, such men are distinguished by the number and quality of their responses to human movement, colour and wholeness. They have few depressive moods, play roles with inner conviction, and have a genuine capacity for growth.

21 Henry, 'Business executive', p. 290.

22 Melville Dalton, *Men Who Manage*, New York, Wiley, 1959, pp. 6—7 and 246—8.

23 Abraham H. Maslow, *Eupsychean Management*, Homewood, Illinois, Irwin-Dorsey, 1965, pp. 141—2.

24 *ibid.*, pp. 130—1.

25 Lasswell, *Psychopathology and Politics*, pp. 139—42.

26 Maslow, *Eupsychean Management*, pp. 193—4.

27 Henry, 'Business executive', p. 290.

28 See also Presthus, *Organizational Society*, Ch. 8, 'The Ambivalents'.

29 Rogow, *Victim of Duty*, pp. 288—91.

30 *ibid.*, pp. 291—3. I also drew gratefully for several details on the deft presentation of this case in Joseph H. di Rivera, *The Psychological Dimension of Foreign Policy*, Columbus, Ohio, Bobbs Merrill, 1968, pp. 200—6.

31 Martin H. Stein, 'A psychoanalytical view of mental health: Samuel Pepys and his Diary', *Psychoanalytic Quarterly*, 1977, 82—115. There is unfortunately no childhood detail.

32 I draw this paragraph directly from the discussion of Henry's study by Robert Endelman in his *Personality and Social Life*, New York, Random House, 1966, pp. 361—4. Compare Erikson's 1946 report on the preoccupation in the dreams of a run of veteran patients, struggling 'to regain access to the non-reversible escalator of free enterprise'; 'their traumatised ego fights and flees an evil identity which includes elements of the crying baby, the bleeding woman, the submissive nigger, the sexual sissy, the economic sucker, the mental moron — all prototypes the mere allusion to which can bring these men close to homicidal or suicidal rage'. ('Ego development and historical change', *The Psychoanalytic Study of the Child*, New York, International Universities Press, 1946, p. 387.)

33 See on this the perceptive comments by Zaleznik in Abraham Zaleznik and Manfred F. R. Kets de Vries, *Power and the Corporate Mind*, Boston, Houghton Mifflin, 1975, pp. 85—7.

34 Orvis Collins and David G. Moore, *The Organisation Makers: A Behavioral Study of Independent Entrepreneurs*, New York, Appleton-Century-Crofts, 1970, especially pp. 34—8. Autobiographies and TATs are most resourcefully used, and the analysis extends to the details of institutional development.

    For a sardonic side-glance at the type of entrepreneurial success based on the repudiation of group ties and the hypostasis of personal technique and will, see Mary Douglas, *Natural Symbols*, London, Cresset, 1970, Ch. 9. She moves magisterially from the Melanesian 'Big Man' and his cosmology of success to Lord Thomson of Fleet (ex-Toronto) for whom 'the feasts, the balance sheets, the dynamism' serve identical ends.

35 Collins and Moore, *Organisation Makers*, pp. 34—5.

36 Australian cases that spring to mind are those of Atlee Hunt, who built the Federal Prime Minister's department and whose father died when Hunt was twelve (see Helen Davies, *The Administrative Career of Atlee Hunt, 1901—1910*, M.A. thesis, University of Melbourne, 1968), and J. T. Lang, who had to leave primary school and work to help support the family when his father lost his business, and whose attitude to the Labour party was 'I'll join, if I lead' (see Miriam Dixson, *'Greater than Lenin'*, Melbourne Politics Monographs, Melbourne University Press, 1976).

37 Sir Henry Taylor, *The Statesman*, New York, Mentor, 1958, p. 44.

38 M. B. and R. A. Cohen, 'Personality as a factor in administrative decisions', *Psychiatry*, 1951, 47—53.

39 Kenneth Burke, *A Grammar of Motives*, New York, Prentice-Hall, 1945, p. 391.

40 See, for example, N. H. Martin and J. H. Sims, 'Power Tactics', *Harvard Business Review*, 1956, 25—9.

41 Richard Christie, 'Some consequences of taking Machiavelli seriously', in Edgar F. Borgatta and William W. Lambert (eds.), *Handbook of Personality Theory and Research*, Chicago, Rand McNally, 1968, pp. 959—73; Richard Christie and Florence L. Geis, *Studies in Machiavellianism*, New York, Academic Press, 1970.

42 Christie and Geis, *Studies*, p. 3.

43 *ibid.*, p. 353.

44 Christie, 'Some consequences', p. 960.

45 See Christie and Geis, *Studies*, pp. 352—3.

46 Stanley S. Guterman, *The Machiavellians: A Social Psychological Study of Moral Character and Organisation Milieu*, Lincoln, Nebraska, University of Nebraska Press, 1970. Bursten disagrees with Guterman that Machiavellians must be incapable of empathy: 'the expert deceiver must also be able to intuit the other's character, his interests, his prohibitions, his propensity for guilt, his anxieties, loyalties, etc ... the deceiver uses empathy to fashion the other person. One person will be influenced by an appeal to his vanity, another by an appeal to his ambition or loyalty to the values of some group. One person will change his goal if made to feel guilty; another ... if the manipulator gives him false but convincing information.' See Ben Bursten, *The Manipulator — A Psychoanalytic View*, New Haven, Connecticut, Yale University Press, 1973, p. 78. And see also Speer on Hitler, summarised in a footnote to p. 69 above.

47 Bursten, *The Manipulator*, especially pp. 156—61.

48 Alan C. Elms, *Personality and Politics*, New York, Harcourt Brace, 1976, pp. 140—7.

49 Lewis J. Edinger, 'Political science and political biography (ii)', *Journal of Politics*, 1964, 665. That the ability to 'see things as they really are' is also the leading trait of successful entrepreneurs is persuasively argued in Harry Schrage, 'The R. & D. entrepreneur: profile of success', *Harvard Business Review*, 1965, 56—69. 'High ... awareness of self, the market, and his employees' joined high achievement motivation and low power motivation to predict success.

50 Nelson N. Foote and Leonard S. Cottrell, *Identity and Interpersonal Competence*, University of Chicago Press, 1955, pp. 84—90.

51 *ibid.*, p. 90.

52 See, for example, S. Ferenczi, 'Stages in the development of the sense of reality' (1913), Ch. 8 of his *Contributions to Psychoanalysis*, New York, Dover, 1956; E. Bergler, 'Thirty years after Ferenczi's "Stages"', *Psychoanalytic Review*, 1945, 125—45; R. Money-Kyrle, *Man's Picture of his World*, London, Duckworth, 1961, Ch. 3.

53 But see S. de Grazia, 'The universality of political and religious belief systems', part i of his *The Political Community*, University of Chicago Press, 1948.

54 See, for example, F. Wittels, 'A neglected boundary of psychoanalysis', *Psychoanalytic Quarterly*, 1949, 44—53; Avery D. Weisman, 'Reality sense and reality testing', *Behavioral Science*, 1958, 228—61, especially pp. 246—52; and Money-Kyrle, *Man's Picture of his World*, Ch. 4.

55 E. Weiss, 'The sense of reality', in his *The Principles of Psychodynamics*, New York, Grune, Stratton, 1950, pp. 45 ff.

56 Sigmund Freud, 'On Negation' (1925), in his *Collected Papers*, London, Hogarth Press, 1950, vol. 5, p. 183.

57   Money-Kyrle, *Man's Picture of his World*, p. 79.

58   There have been several attempts to describe the special 'sense of reality' peculiar to each of the psycho-sexual stages: for example, R. Laforgue, 'The ego and the conception of reality', *International Journal of Psychoanalysis*, 1939, 403–12, and B. Lewin, 'Elation and the sense of reality', in his *The Psycho-analysis of Elation*, New York, Norton, 1950.

59   Money-Kyrle, 'On the avoidable sources of conflict', in his *Man's Picture of his World*, Ch. 10.

60   *ibid.*, p. 157.

61   It is hard to improve on George Eliot's comprehensive formulation of this accomplishment and its possible distortions: '... a security of distinction between what we have professed and what we have done; what we have aimed at and what we have achieved; what we have invented and what we have witnessed or had evidenced to us; what we think and feel in the present and what we thought and felt in the past'. See George Eliot, *Impressions of Theophrastus Such*, Edinburgh, Blackwood, 1879, p. 125.

62   Ernest G. Schachtel, *Metamorphosis — On the Development of Affect, Perception, Attention and Memory*, New York, Basic Books, 1959, Ch. 11.

63   Weisman, 'Reality sense and reality testing', p. 259.

64   This summary was made by the columnist 'R' in *Encounter*, November 1975, pp. 42–4.

65   Robert E. Dahl and Charles E. Lindblom, *Politics, Economics and Welfare*, New York, Harper, 1953, p. 333.

66   John Power argues that the demands of urban planning have created a new political function, that of 'reticulist'; reticulists are men specialising in the gathering, production and reticulation of information and knowledge relevant to public policy-making, and concerned with the relations between knowledge and power. See John K. Friend, J. M. Power and C. J. L. Yewlett, *Public Planning: The Intercorporate Dimension*, London, Tavistock, 1974, especially pp. 44 and 364–72.

67   James G. March and Herbert A. Simon, *Organizations*, New York, Wiley, 1958, pp. 129–31. See also Paul A. Diesing's useful gloss in *Reason in Society*, Urbana, Illinois, University of Illinois Press, 1962, pp. 174–6 and 196–8. From this convention it follows that 'A bargaining process ... is held together primarily by power distribution, by a few shared rules of procedure, and often by some form of mediator.' Some mistrust and disapproval of the other groups must be assumed. There are also structural constraints: 'Bargaining structures are most effective when they are differentiated into a few, ideally two, clearly defined groups. Bargaining takes place between two opposed groups, so the more subgroups there are in a structure the more difficult it is to work out a series of agreements satisfactory to all. Moreover, if agreements are to be kept the bargaining groups must have enough continuity of purpose and of responsible leadership to carry out an agreement over a period of time.' (Diesing, *Reason in Society*, p. 196.)

68   Collins and Moore, *The Organisation Makers*, p. 90.

69   Dahl and Lindblom, *Politics, Economics and Welfare*, p. 333.

70   Stanley Hoffman, 'Heroic leadership: the case of modern France', in L. J. Edinger (ed.), *Political Leadership in Industrialized Societies*, New York, Wiley, 1967, pp. 119–20.

71   Hesketh Pearson, *G.B.S.*, New York, Harper, 1942, p. 156 (quoted by Dahl and Lindblom in *Politics, Economics and Welfare*, p. 334).

72   F. S. Oliver, *The Endless Adventure*, London, Macmillan, 1930, pp. 1–111.

73   Review in *The Times Literary Supplement*, 30 June 1972, p. 747, of A. J. P. Taylor, *Beaverbrook*, London, Macmillan, 1972.

74 Doris Kearns, *Lyndon Johnson and the American Dream*, New York, Harper, 1976, pp. 110—11.

75 *ibid.*, pp. 117—24.

76 *ibid.*, p. 129.

77 On bargaining as Benjamin Franklin's central talent, see Richard L. Bushman, 'Conflict and conciliation in Benjamin Franklin', *History and Theory*, 1966, 225—40. It can also, perhaps, be regarded as the key skill in the party manager's role; for an early sketch, see Harold F. Gosnell, 'Thos. C. Platt — political manager', *Political Science Quarterly*, 1923, 443—69.

78 Taylor, *The Statesman*, p. 31.

79 *ibid.*, p. 96.

80 Thomas Collins, 'Secretary McNamara', *Newsday*, 6 June 1970.

81 Herbert Simon, 'Administrative theory', *International Encyclopedia of the Social Sciences*, New York, Macmillan-Free Press, 1968, vol. 1, p. 76.

82 Chester Barnard, *The Functions of the Executive*, Cambridge, Mass., Harvard University Press, 1956, p. 186.

83 Simon, 'Administrative theory', p. 77.

84 *ibid.*, p. 77.

85 See Richard M. Cyert and James G. March, *A Behavioral Theory of the Firm*, Englewood Cliffs, New Jersey, Prentice Hall, 1963.

86 Joseph de Rivera, *The Psychological Dimension of Foreign Policy*, Columbus, Ohio, Bobbs Merrill, 1968, and Irving L. Janis, *Victims of Groupthink*, Boston, Houghton Mifflin, 1972. See also the analysis of J. Foster Dulles as a decision-maker in Ole R. Holsti, 'The belief system and national images — a case study', *Journal of Conflict Resolution*, 1962, 244—52.

87 W. R. Dill, 'The Varieties of Administrative Decision', in H. J. Leavitt and L. R. Pondy (eds.), *Readings in Managerial Psychology*, Chicago, University of Chicago Press, 1964, pp. 447—56.

88 See J. D. Thompson and A. Tuden, 'Strategies, structures and processes of organisational decision', in Leavitt and Pondy, *Readings in Managerial Psychology*, pp. 496—515.

89 March and Simon, *Organizations*, p. 185.

90 Charles Lindblom, 'The science of "muddling through"', *Public Administration Review*, 1959, 78—88. See also P. Selznick, *Leadership in Administration*, Evanston, Illinois, Row, Peterson, 1957, Ch. 2, and H. A. Kissinger, 'The policy maker and intellectual', *The Reporter*, 1959, 30—5. Brian Chapman, *The Profession of Government*, London, Allen and Unwin, 1959, pp. 317—20 finds that a 'schizophrenic attitude of progressive conservatism' is the leading characteristic of European senior civil servants. Erikson related the bargaining temper of American politics to the democracy of U.S. family decision-making (*Childhood and Society*, New York, Norton, 1950, pp. 275—7). Perhaps 'majority concurrence' in the nuclear family may be posited for notable 'bargainers' in any society?

91 Irving Janis, 'Decisional conflicts: a theoretical analysis', *Journal of Conflict Resolution*, 1959, 6—27.

92 Irving Janis, 'Motivational factors in the resolution of decisional conflicts', *Nebraska Symposium on Motivation*, 1959, pp. 198—231.

93 Janis, 'Decisional conflicts', p. 17.

94 Janis's ideas include better briefing on home government and public opinion, more pre-testing of policy moves (by trial balloons, for example, or international relations gaming), privileged access to potential home critics (to give persuasion more purchase), and a status closer to that of a judge for international representatives. de Rivera's *The Psychological Dimension of Foreign Policy* traverses this ground thoroughly, and adds a proposal that a 'devil's advocate'

should be included in each foreign policy making team. And now see Irving L. Janis and Leon Mann, *Decision Making*, New York, Free Press, 1977, especially pp. 395—400, and A. L. George, 'Adaptations to stress in political decision making', in G. V. Coelho et al. (eds.), *Coping and Adaptation*, New York, Basic Books, 1974.

95   Edward C. Banfield, 'The training of the executive', *Public Policy*, 1960, 27.
96   *ibid.*, p. 35.
97   Abraham Zaleznik and D. Moment, *Role Development and Interpersonal Competence*, Boston, Harvard University, Graduate School of Business Administration, Division of Research, 1963, Ch. 8.
98   Managers' actual performance in problem-solving sessions, yielding groupings which held firm under detailed psychological investigation, was used by Zaleznik and Moment in *Role Development and Interpersonal Competence*, Ch. 1.
99   Zaleznik and Moment, *Role Development and Interpersonal Competence*, and Zaleznik et al., *Orientation and Conflict in Career*, Boston, Harvard University, Graduate School of Business Administration, Division of Research, 1970, Ch. 12.
100 The leading executives of a famous private psychiatric hospital were the subjects of organisational study and a team biography: see A. Zaleznik, R. C. Hodgson and D. J. Levinson, *The Executive Role Constellation*, Boston, Harvard University, Graduate School of Business Administration, Division of Research, 1965.
101 Zaleznik et al., *Orientation and Conflict*, passim.
102 Zaleznik, Hodgson and Levinson, *Executive Role Constellation*, p. 231. In politics, too, we recognise that certain leadership positions offer scope for special talents and unusual combinations of preferences. R. A. Butler, for example, reflecting on what three times just prevented his being made Prime Minister, seized on a missing talent: 'I was reading *Great Contemporaries* by Winston Churchill, and he describes, in the chapter on Asquith, how Asquith was talking about a Prime Minister being a butcher; and I think the Prime Minister has to be a butcher, and know the joints. That is perhaps where I have not been quite competent in knowing all the ways that you cut up a carcase.' (*The Listener*, 28 July 1966.)

Aitken's biography of Sir Michael Bruxner notes that he relished the leader-subordinate amalgam, the 'position of honourable junior partner', required of the minority party leader in coalition governments:

'He played [both roles] superbly ... because both ... came very naturally to him: they represented the working out in his adult life of dispositions he had acquired in childhood. Their origins lay in the coincidence of a long illness and a kindly elder brother. Harry was not a rival for his mother's affections: Michael's long sickness and her enfolding care ensured that. Instead, he became the boyhood hero who did everything well, and who did not tarnish this image by neglecting his frail and helpless brother. As an infant Michael adored Harry; as he grew older and stronger he longed to emulate him, to be strong and admired himself. Yet the years of dependence left their mark. The warmth and emotional richness of the security given him by his brother's love, the praise for his halting efforts in play, the ready support when support was needed, became rewards he sought and worked for in his relationship with others. Emulation and dependence were the intertwined roots of his personality.' (Don Aitken, *The Colonel: A Political Biography of Sir Michael Bruxner*, Canberra, Australian National University Press, 1969, p. 274.)

103 Carl N. Edwards, 'Interactive styles and social adaptation', *Genetic Psychology Monographs*, 1973:2, 123—74.

104 R. R. Sears, E. E. Maccoby and H. Levin, *Patterns of Child Rearing*, New York, Harper, 1957.
105 For a third scheme, designed primarily with political performances in mind, see David Brereton, 'Leadership: a conceptual framework', *Melbourne Journal of Politics*, 1975—6, 38—43. This scheme distinguishes among interactive styles which emphasise the work, the mass communication, and the inter-personal aspects of tasks, and suggests developmental paths to each of them. Brereton's term 'inter-personal' is roughly equivalent to Edwards's 'co-operational', and Brereton's 'work' to Edwards's 'instrumental', but the skills of public performance are stressed (rather than analysis) because they are more commonly met with.
106 Graham Little, *Faces on the Campus*, Melbourne, Melbourne University Press, 1976. His discussion of Edwards's typology may be found at pp. 230—3.
107 Edwards, 'Interactive styles', p. 132.
108 Summarised from M. Brewster Smith, J. S. Bruner and Robert W. White, *Opinions and Personality*, New York, Wiley, 1956, pp. 133—6.
109 Daniel R. Miller and Guy E. Swanson, *The Changing American Parent: A Study in the Detroit Area*, New York, Wiley, 1958, especially Chs. 2 and 8.
110 Leonard V. Gordon, 'Measurement of bureaucratic orientation', *Personnel Psychology*, 1970, 1—11.
111 Leonard V. Gordon, 'Weber in the classroom', *Journal of Educational Psychology*, 1971, 60—6.
112 Kenneth Keniston, *The Uncommitted: Alienated Youth in American Society*, New York, Dell, 1965, p. 360.
113 *ibid.*, p. 367.
114 *ibid.*, p. 368
115 *ibid.*, p. 370
116 Philip Slater, *The Pursuit of Loneliness*, Boston, Beacon, 1970.
117 Jules Henry, *Pathways to Madness*, London, Cape, 1972, pp. 345—55.
118 Michel Crozier, *The Bureaucratic Phenomenon*, London, Tavistock, 1964, especially pp. 194ff, on 'the bureaucratic vicious circle'. Crozier has remarkably little about the French family. Stanley Hoffman carries his analysis enthusiastically forward in 'Heroic leadership: the case of modern France' in L. J. Edinger (ed.), *Political Leadership in Industrialized Societies*, New York, Wiley, 1967, pp. 108—54, and in 'The French psychodrama: De Gaulle's anti-Communist group', *The New Republic*, 31 August 1968, 15—21. See also Fred I. Greentein and Sidney G. Tarrow, 'The study of French political socialisation', *World Politics*, 1969, 95—138.
119 Lucian Pye, *Politics, personality and nation-building: Burma's search for identity*, New Haven, Connecticut, Yale University Press, 1962, especially Chs. 15—16. British administrators prefer the comfort of protective arrangements to competition; see Eleanor Wintour, 'Bringing up children, the U.S. and British way'. *Harpers Magazine*, August 1964, 58—63; S. White, 'The underdeveloped British businessman', *Atlantic*, January 1966, 75—8; and H. R. Wolf, 'British fathers and sons, 1773—1913 — from filial submissiveness to creativity?', *Psychoanalytic Review*, 1965, 53—70. On Turkey, where employees are evaluated in terms of loyalty to the manager rather than by objective job performance, see N. Bradburn, 'Interpersonal relations within formal organisations', *Journal of Social Issues*, 1963, 61—7. On Japan, see John Fischer, 'Japan's intellectuals', *Harpers Magazine*, September 1964, 14—15.
120 Frank Crowley, *Forrest*, St Lucia, Queensland, University of Queensland Press, 1971, p. 269.
121 Sir Henry Taylor, *The Statesman* (1836), New York, Mentor, 1958, Ch. 32.

122 Barber, *The Presidential Character*, Chs. 2 and 3.
123 Joseph Bensman and Arthur J. Vidich, *The New American Society*, Chicago, Quadrangle, 1971, p. 256.
124 Henry Kissinger, interview with Oriana Fallaci, *New Republic*, 16 December 1972, 21.
125 David E. Lilienthal, *The Journals*, H. S. Commager, (ed.), New York, Harper, 1964 — in progress. L. F. Crisp tells me that the National Library in Canberra has recently acquired an equivalent MS — in reserve for 20 years — by Peter Heydon, the late Secretary of the Department of Immigration. For an admirable account of Heydon's personality and career, see L. F. Crisp, *Peter Heydon — A Memoir*, Canberra, privately printed, 1972.
126 See, for example, Howard Becker, *Boys in White*, Chicago, University of Chicago Press, 1961.
127 Taylor, *The Statesman*, Ch. 6, especially this: 'The leading rule is to be content to be commonplace ... avoid express metaphors ... and use only such as lie hid in common language, and will not attract specific notice. [However] the exclusion of metaphorical invention does not negative such an exercise of imagination as shall detect the latent metaphors of language, and so deal with them as to give to the style a congruity and aptitude otherwise unattainable.'
128 L. F. Crisp, 'Public administration as a profession', *Public Administration* (Sydney), 1969, 122—140.
129 See Herbert E. Krugman, 'Organisation structure and the organisation man', in J. G. Peatman and E. L. Hartley (eds.), *Festschrift for Gardner Murphy*, New York, Harper, 1960, pp. 241—8.
130 Ithiel de Sola Pool, 'The head of the company — conceptions of role and identity', *Behavioral Science*, 1964, 147—56.
131 See Edwin E. Ghisetti and Douglas A. Johnson, 'Need satisfaction, managerial success and organisational structure', *Personnel Psychology*, 1970, 569—76.
132 For a pleasantly full review of psycho-biographies of American figures, see John E. Mack, 'Psychoanalysis and historical biography', *Journal of the American Psychoanalytical Association*, 1971, 143—79. See also Alan Davies, 'The tasks of biography', Ch. 8 of *Essays in Political Sociology*, Melbourne, Cheshire, 1972.
133 Richard Neustadt, *Presidential Power*, New York, Mentor, 1960. There is also a kiddies' version, Erwin C. Hargrove, *Presidential Leadership and Personality and Political Style*, New York, Macmillan, 1966.
134 Neustadt, *Presidential Power*, p. 147.
135 Richard Neustadt, 'Kennedy in the Presidency', *Political Science Quarterly*, 1964, 321—37. On Kennedy's style, see also E. S. Shneidman, 'Personality profile conveyed by the communicator as a function of his logical style', in L. Arons and M. A. May, (eds.), *Television and Human Behavior*, New York, Praeger, 1963, pp. 177—99; J. McG. Burns, 'What sort of man? What sort of President?'. in James D. Barber (ed.), *Political Leadership in American Government*, Boston, Little, Brown, 1964, pp. 15—34; J. K. Galbraith, *Ambassador's Diary*, Boston, Houghton Mifflin, 1965, appendix A, 'J.F.K.'s Style of Work'; R. G. Tugwell, 'The President and his helpers: a review article', *Political Science Quarterly*, 1967, 253—65; James D. Barber, *The Presidential Character*, Englewood Cliffs, New Jersey, Prentice-Hall, 1972, Ch. 9; Nancy Clinch, *The Kennedy Neurosis*, New York, Grosset and Dunlap, 1972.
136 Ulrich Ellis, 'Sir Earle Page — a study in leadership', in his *A History of the Australian Country Party*, Melbourne, Melbourne University Press, 1963, pp. 320—9, See also Earle Page, *Truant Surgeon: The Inside Story of Forty Years of Australian Political Life*, Sydney, Angus and Robertson, 1963.
137 Peter Heydon, *Quiet Decision — A Study of George Foster Pearce*, Melbourne,

Melbourne University Press, 1965, especially Ch. 11. See also George Pearce, *Carpenter to Cabinet*, Sydney, Hutchinson, 1951.

138   Barber, *Presidential Character*. See also his vigorous and persuasive defence of his methodology, 'Strategies for understanding politicians', *World Politics*, 1974, 443—67.

139   Barber, *Presidential Character*, p. 10.

140   *ibid.*, p. 418.

141   *ibid.*, pp. 368ff. See also the somewhat tasteless M. Rogin and J. Lottier, 'The inner history of Richard M. Nixon', *Transaction*, November/December, 1971. And for a highly sophisticated and psychological analysis of the texts of the Kennedy-Nixon Debates of 1960 and their predictive potential, see Edwin Shneidman's 'Personality profile' in Arons and May, *Television and Human Behavior*.

142   Eli S. Chesen, *President Nixon's Psychiatric Profile*, New York, Wyden, 1973. Work-style is rather skimped in Mazlish's full-length psycho-biography: Bruce Mazlish, *In Search of Nixon: A Psycho-historical Enquiry*, New York, Basic Books, 1972. And now see David Abrahamsen, *Nixon vs. Nixon*, New York, Farrar, 1977. James D. Barber's second edition of *The Presidential Character* (1977) contains his predictions about President Carter.

143   Nathan Leites's studies are as follows: *The Operational Code of the Politburo*, New York, McGraw-Hill, 1951; *A Study of Bolshevism*, Glencoe, Illinois, Free Press, 1953; *On the Game of Politics in France*, Stanford, California, Stanford University Press, 1959; *The House without Windows: France Selects a President* (with Constantin Melnik), Evanston, Illinois, Row, Peterson, 1958; *Images of Power in French Politics*, 2 vols, mimeo., Rand Corporation, Santa Monica, 1962; *The Rules of the Game in Paris*, Chicago, University of Chicago Press, 1966.
      Alexander George, 'The "Operational Code": a neglected approach to the study of political leaders and decision-making', *International Studies Quarterly*, 1969, 190—222, has helped the transfer of this approach to individual actors.

144   Robert D. Putnam, 'Studying elite political cultures: the case of "Ideology"', *American Political Science Review*, 1971, 651—81. And see Anthony A. D'Amato, 'Psychological constructs in foreign policy prediction', *Journal of Conflict Resolution*, 1967, 294—310.

145   David S. McLellan, 'The "Operational Code" approach to the study of political leaders: Dean Acheson's philosophical and instrumental beliefs', *Canadian Journal of Political Science*, 1971, 52—75, and a set of papers, read at the 1973 American Political Science Association Conference, but still apparently unpublished, on the operational codes of Senators Vandenberg, Fulbright and Frank Church, and Dean Rusk, by Joel Anderson, Kurt Tweraserer, L. Johnson and G. Gutierrez. See also Lloyd Etheridge, 'Personality and foreign policy', *Psychology Today*, 1975, 37—42.

146   Shneidman, 'Personality profile'.

Chapter 4.   Theorising

1   cf. Lewis Feuer: 'In the beginning was the emotion; then came the idea and last the deed. The emotional need for an ideology is the primary theme in the history of intellectuals; it is their longing for a generational myth of a mission, and of the validation of their claim to rule ... Every so-called generation in politics, literature, or art will have its corresponding ideology.' (*Ideology and the Ideologists*, New York, Harper and Row, 1975, p. 79.) We might, however, distinguish between 'independent' and 'cause-serving' intellectuals; this distinction was made by Lasswell ('Political constitution and character', *Psy-*

choanalysis and the Psychoanalytic Review, 1959, 15) and roughly parallels the distinction made above, pp. 63—4, between 'entrepreneurs' and 'executives/functionaries'; the key thing psychologically is the need to feel attached to, or independent of, an established structure of ideas bestowing comfort and guaranteeing authoritativeness.

2   See also, Richard Wollheim, *A Family Romance*, London, Cape, 1969, 177—88 and 246—7 for as startling a discovery of speech as what-gives-one-away, with the intrusive parent, the father.

3   Konrad Kellen, Introduction to Jacques Ellul, *Propaganda*, New York, Knopf, 1971, p. vi.

4   Compare Theodore Reik's charming tale of transfixing, as a child, his grandfather's Talmudic circle's discussion of the creation of Eve, with the cry, 'Tomer verkehrt' ('the opposite more likely'), which he had noticed was a frequent resource of the group. See Reik, *The Creation of Woman*, New York, Braziller, 1966, p. 17.

And a recent critic of one of our early modern minds notes: 'One has sometimes the feeling that whenever Machiavelli read the statement of another writer or heard about a generally accepted view, his first reaction was to doubt these notions and to try to discover what would happen if the opposite was maintained'. (Felix Gilbert, *Machiavelli and Guicciardini*, Princeton, New Jersey, Princeton University Press, 1965, pp. 164—5.)

5   John Dollard acutely notes of 'intellectuals' pleasure in the "power of ideas" — it is an echo of their childhood pleasure in turning seemingly categorical absolutes against their parents in order to coerce them.' (*Fear in Battle*, New Haven, Connecticut, Yale University Press, 1943, p. 356.)

6   H. Lasswell, *Power and Personality*, New York, Norton, 1948, pp. 92—4. The Reichian Elsworth F. Baker also sees 'protestation of concern' as the liberal intellectual's defining mark — the 'substitution of intellectual for direct emotional response. He feels, rightly, an element of unreality or insincerity in voicing this concern for others, and to the extent that he is not deceived himself by the image he presents, he feels he is deceiving others. He is therefore driven to prove his sincerity by showing even more concern. Thus begins an endless self-perpetuating process, which can be halted only if he will stop trying to escape from his own problems to those of others.' *Man in the Trap*, New York, Avon, 1974, pp. 198—9.

And, more darkly, see the Kanner 1943 paper on autism, quoted by Martin James in *International Journal of Psychoanalysis*, 1975, 107, which reports on 400 cases of autistic children up to 5 years of age, the 'great majority' of whom 'came from homes where both parents were intellectuals' and showed, in convincing and 'alarmingly homely' examples, a signal failure to understand what babies need.

7   A 'high incidence of childhood physical illness [precipitated] ... a shift from action to thought, fantasy and words arising out of inactivity and introspection'. Philip M. Spielman, reviewing Arthur Burton (ed.), *Twelve Therapists*, San Francisco, Jossey-Bass, 1972, in *International Journal of Psychoanalysis*, 1975, 119—20.

8   *The Education of Henry Adams* (1905), Boston, Houghton Mifflin, 1918.

9   *ibid.*, p. 4.

10   *ibid.*, p. 6.

11   *ibid.*, p 7.

12   *ibid.*, p. 26.

13   *ibid.*, p. 253.

14   *ibid.*, pp. 164—5.

15 Ronald Fairbairn, 'Schizoid factors in the personality' (1940), reprinted in his
    Psychoanalytic Studies of the Personality, London, Routledge, 1952, pp. 3—27.

16 J. S. Mill, *Autobiography* (1873), London, World's Classics edn, p. 113. See also
    A. W. Levi, 'The writing of Mill's Autobiography', *Ethics*, 1950—1, 291—2.

17 Mill, *Autobiography*, p. 119. I draw here on the acute analysis of A. W. Levi,
    'The "mental crisis" of John Stuart Mill', *Psychoanalytic Review*, 1945, 86—101.
    This is retold to be 'better understood by students of Mill and politics' in R. V.
    Sampson, *Equality and Power*, London, Heinemann, 1965, pp. 69—92; it is made
    the centre of Bruce Mazlish's analysis in Ch. 10 of his *James and John Stuart
    Mill*, London, Hutchinson, 1975. Mazlish also stresses the importance of his
    year in France in assisting his detachment from his father.

18 John Durham, 'The influence of John Stuart Mill's mental crisis on his
    thought', *American Imago*, 1963, 376.

19 See 'Symposium on the obsessional character', *International Journal of Psy-
    choanalysis*, 1966, 116—217.

20 E. G. Howe, 'Compulsive thinking as a castration equivalent', *British Journal
    of Medical Psychology*, 1929, 159—77. For a discussion (including a short case
    history) of theorising primarily as a defence against depression, see R. E.
    Money-Kyrle, *Psychoanalysis and Politics*, London, Duckworth, 1951, pp. 173—6,
    and his later *Man's Picture of his World*, London, Duckworth, 1961, pp. 151—2.

21 Anna Freud, *The Ego and the Mechanisms of Defence*, London, Hogarth Press,
    1939, Chs. 10—11.

22 E. Bergler, 'The psychoanalysis of writers', *Psychoanalysis and the Social
    Sciences*, 1947, 247—96, reprinted in his *Selected Papers*, New York, Grune and
    Stratton, 1969.

23 J. T. MacCurdy, 'Mental constitution of compulsive thinking', *British Journal
    of Medical Psychology*, 1926, 159—78.

24 J.-P. Sartre, *Words*, London, Hamish Hamilton, 1964, p. 113. For a sharp note
    on Sartre's childhood as a nightmare of social categorylessness, see Mary
    Douglas, *Natural Symbols*, London, Cresset, 1970, pp. 31—2.

25 Ann Rowe, 'A psychological study of eminent psychologists and anthropolo-
    gists, and a comparison with biological and physical scientists', *Psychological
    Monographs*, 1953, no. 352, 1—55. See also her *The Making of a Scientist*, New
    York, Dodd, Mead, 1952, especially Chs. 7—10.

26 Liam Hudson, *Contrary Imaginations: A Psychological Study of the English School-
    boy*, London, Methuen, 1966; *Frames of Mind*, Harmondsworth, Penguin Books,
    1968; and *The Cult of the Fact*, London, Cape, 1972. See also the excellent
    account of the science mind by David C. McClelland, 'The psychodynamics of
    creative physical scientists', in McClelland, *The Roots of Consciousness*, Princeton,
    New Jersey, Van Nostrand, 1964, Ch. 7.

27 Hudson, *Contrary Imaginations*, p. 134.

28 Hudson, *Cult of the Fact*, pp. 68—9.

29 Liam Hudson, 'Fertility in the arts and sciences', *Science Studies*, 1973, 305—10.

30 *ibid.*, p. 307.

31 For a complex model for the analysis of an organisation's changing leadership
    requirements over time, see E. Spencer Wellhofer, 'Dimensions of party
    development: a study in organisational dynamics', *Journal of Politics*, 1972,
    153—82. See also W. Roche, 'The bureaucrat and the enthusiast', in B.
    McLaughlin (ed.), *Studies in Social Movements*, New York, Free Press, 1969.

32 Edward Shils, 'Ideology', *International Encyclopedia of the Social Sciences* (ed.
    David L. Sills), New York, Macmillan-Free Press, 1968, vol. 7, pp. 66—75.

33 Clifford Geertz, 'Ideology as a cultural system', in D. Apter (ed.), *Ideology and
    Discontent*, New York, Free Press, 1964, pp. 56—7.

34 Shils, 'Ideology', p. 75.

35 Erik Erikson, *Young Man Luther*, London, Faber, 1958, p. 39.

36 *ibid.*

37 'Rousseau and the politics of sensibility', in Alan Davies, *Essays in Political
    Sociology*, Melbourne, Cheshire, 1972.

38 See above, p. 445, note 45.

39 Nathan Leites, *A Study of Bolshevism*, Glencoe, Illinois, Free Press, 1953.

40 This demand is not made only by victim-groups. In fact, the best ideology-
    analysis we have is F. X. Sutton, *The American Business Creed*, Cambridge,
    Mass., Harvard University Press, 1956. See also David Apter, 'How ideologies
    are formed', in D. Apter (ed.), *The Politics of Modernisation*, Chicago, University
    of Chicago Press, 1965, pp. 319–23.

41 Aitken, *The Colonel*.

42 *Miriam Dixson, 'Greater than Lenin'*, Melbourne Politics Monographs,
    Melbourne University Press, 1976, p. 27.

43 See R. N. Rosecrance, 'Australia', in Louis Hartz (ed.), *The Foundation in New
    Societies*, New York, Harcourt, Brace, World, 1964, for an argument that all
    Australian politics is locked inside a single culture-chip — that of the free
    immigrant's upper-working-class chartism.

44 cf. Peter Loveday's dogged elucidation of the *implicit* political ideas of the
    ordinary working federal parliamentarian. The most recent of his several
    pieces is 'Liberals and the idea of "development"', *Australian Journal of History
    and Politics*, 1977, 219–26.

45 E. H. Erikson, 'The problem of ego identity', in 'Identity and the life cycle',
    Psychological Issues, 1959, 102–110; *Young Man Luther*, London, Faber, 1958,
    Ch. 4; 'Youth: fidelity and diversity' in Erikson (ed.), *Youth: Change and Chal-
    lenge*, New York, Basic Books, 1963; *Gandhi's Truth*, London, Faber, 1970. The
    Shaw piece is in the first article listed; Hitler is treated in *Childhood and Society*,
    New York, Norton, 1950, Ch. 9, and *Young Man Luther*, pp. 100–6. An excel-
    lent introduction to Erikson's work is Lucian W. Pye, 'Personal identity and
    political ideology', in Dwaine Marvick (ed.), *Political Decision-Makers*, New
    York, Free Press, 1962.

46 H. A. Murray and Christiana D. Morgan, 'A clinical study of sentiments',
    Genetic Psychology Monographs, 1945, No. 32, 3–311; Kenneth Keniston, *The
    Uncommitted*, New York, Harcourt, Brace, 1965; Robert Lane, *Political Thinking
    and Political Consciousness*, Chicago, Markham, 1969; Philip M. Helfaer, *The
    Psychology of Religious Doubt*, Boston, Beacon, 1972; Graham Little, *Politics and
    Personal Style*, Melbourne, Nelson, 1973.

47 Willy Baranger, 'The ego and the funtion of ideology', *International Journal
    of Psychoanalysis*, 1958, 191–201.

48 See, for example, Jerome D. Frank and Earl H. Nash, 'Commitment to peace
    work: a preliminary study of determinants and sustainers of behavior change',
    American Journal of Orthopsychiatry, 1965, 106–19.

49 David Larg, *John Ruskin*, London, Peter Davies, 1932, p. 75.

50 Leon Salzman, 'The psychology of religious and ideological conversion',
    Psychiatry, 1953, 177–87, argues that 'progressive or maturational' conversions
    are healthy, 'sudden or regressive' conversions psychopathological. See also
    Benjamin Weininger, 'The interpersonal factor in the religious experience',
    Psychoanalysis, 1954–5, 27–44; Eric Hoffer, *The True Believer*, New York,
    Harper, 1951, pp. 39–125; Robert J. Lifton, *Thought Reform and the Psychology
    of Totalism*, London, Gollancz, 1961, Ch. 22. The master-text on ideological
    conversion remains Kenneth Burke, *Permanence and Change*, Los Altos,
    California, Hermes, 1935/1954, part II, 'Perspective by incongruity'.

51 E. Victor Wolfenstein, *Personality and Politics*, Belmont, California, Dickenson, 1969, pp. 40—68; M. Parenti, 'Collective psychodynamics of Black Muslims', in R. Endelman, *Personality and Social Life*, New York, Random House, 1967, pp. 510—24.

52 From *Farrago* (University of Melbourne students' weekly paper), 8 May 1972, p. 7.

53 Whittaker Chambers, *Cold Friday*, New York, Livewright, 1964, pp. 207—8. See also Gilbert Abcarian, 'Psychodynamics and political defection', a paper given at the International Political Science Association Conference, 1970.

54 See Hugh Stretton, *The Political Sciences*, London, Routledge, 1969, for a powerful plea that social science 'must be persuaded to stop indoctrinating its recruits with the peculiarly stupid ideals of generality, objectivity and cumulation' (p. 262); and also Amitai Etzioni, *American Behavioral Scientist*, 1968, 25 — 'Sociology should be the institutionalised desire to help'.

55 See Christian Bay's celebrated essay complaining of empty work in political science and attacking a 'supposedly neutral literature ... generally conservative and in a special sense anti-political': 'Politics and pseudopolitics', *American Political Science Review*, 1965. Bay pleads for more normative and *psychological* research, and for a theory of real needs. 'If advice-giving social scientists don't feel called on to invest their best intellectual energies in studying the ultimate ends of our national policies, it is unlikely that anyone else of influence will.'

56 cf. Stretton, *Political Sciences*, pp. 146 ff.

57 'Sociology as vocation', in John Seeley, *The Americanisation of the Unconscious*, New York, Science Books, 1967.

58 Burford H. Junker, *Field Work*, Chicago, University of Chicago Press, 1960.

59 L. A. Coser, 'Georg Simmel's style of work', *American Journal of Sociology*, 1958, 635—40.

60 Arthur Mitzman, *The Iron Cage: An Historical Interpretation of Max Weber*, New York, Knopf, 1970. Ironically, this perfectly orthodox psychoanalytic study is far and away the best example we have so far of the supposedly new 'ego psychological (Eriksonian)' biographical mode, aggressively championed by, for example, Cushing Strout ('Ego psychology and the historian', *History and Theory*, 1968, 281—97). This mode is said to do three perfectly novel, highly sophisticated and only recently accomplishable things. It directs us, first of all, Strout says, to the class of deeply conflicted, articulate and creative men, whose lives commonsense can make least of — and who have the knack of bringing the issues of their times to a more vivid, intense and clarifying focus. Secondly, it directs us to a relatively short but vital stage of their lives, their identity crisis of late adolescence and early manhood, during which their leading ideas are forged in the course of facing the identity-defining choices of vocation and mate — and this is the stage that abounds in self-conscious and mature literary evidence of the subjects' thinking to pore over. Thirdly, it fixes no labels, but requires the biographer to think his way into the subject's concrete situation in an effort 'to see how in detail his thoughts, feelings, and actions can be understood as a process over time of an unconscious effort — *in conjunction with conscious aims* — to assimilate and reject in a new configuration aspects of identity which the significant others in his family (or their surrogates) represent for him'. This requires psychological skill, but also a 'sensitivity to the *intersections* of the development of family-centered difficulties with social and cultural history, for they interact and resonate with each other'.

Strout himself has contributed several interesting essays along this pattern on William James, without so far engaging with intellectual style. One essay which does, however, is E. Victor Wolfenstein, *Personality and Politics*, Belmont, California, Dickenson, 1969, Ch. 5, which considers the psychological meaning of fragmentation and integration as attributes of Nietzsche's style. It should be said that much good intellectual history seems just on the point of taking up this challenge; see, for example, Richard Ashcraft, 'Hobbes's Natural Man: a study in ideology formation', *Journal of Politics*, 1971, 1076—117.

    For an example of Weber's powerful influence as a role-model for younger social scientists, see the closing pages of John M. Cuddihy, *The Ordeal of Civility*, New York, Delta, 1974, which expatiates on his '"secret", inner-worldly discipline' of breaking the whole person into 'necessary' role requirements, but then staking his whole being in each and every separate role.

61   See H. H. Gerth and C. Wright Mills, *From Max Weber*, London, Kegan Paul, 1948, p. 126.

62   Mitzman, *Iron Cage*, p. 218.

63   H. L. Wilensky, 'The professionalization of everyone?', *American Journal of Sociology*, 1964, 158.

64   D. P. Moynihan, 'The professionalization of reform', *The Public Interest*, 1965, 6—16.

65   See also J. Salwyn Schapiro, 'Lamartine: a study of the poetic temperament in politics', *Political Science Quarterly*, 1919 (34), 639—42; Jose Vasconcelos, *A Mexican Ulysses*, Westport, Connecticut, Greenwood, 1972; and George Seferis, *Days of 1945—51: A Poet's Journal*, Cambridge, Mass., Harvard University Press, 1974, especially the striking dreams on the pressure of people (pp. 13 and 466).

66   André Malraux, *Antimémoirs* (1967), English trans., London, Hamish Hamilton, 1968, p. 136.

67   Quoted in Moynihan, 'Professionalization', 12.

68   I transpose here from art to politics some arresting formulations in Walter Abell's *The Collective Dream in Art* (1957), New York, Schocken Books, 1966, Ch. 18.

Chapter 5.   The classification of world views

1   Robert F. Bales, *Personality and Interpersonal Behaviour*, New York, Holt, Rinehart and Winston, 1970.

2   A generation-and-a-half ago, Dollard and Lasswell in Chicago declared for 'scientific' biography, but failed to write it. (See 'The tasks of biography' in Alan Davies, *Essays in Political Sociology*, Melbourne, Cheshire, 1972, pp. 109—17.) Contemporary 'psycho-biographers' have revived the aspiration, but again without the assurance that they will actually write the stuff. (See, for example, Betty Glad, 'Contributions to psycho-biography', Ch. 10 of Jeanne Knutson (ed.), *Handbook of Political Psychology*, San Francisco, Jossey-Bass, 1973, and Cushing Strout, 'Ego psychology and the historian', *History and Theory*, 1968, 281—97.)

3   Bales, *Personality*, p. 169.

4   These axes are, fascinatingly enough, the 'attitudes' that Lasswell had chosen in 1930 to use for the basis of his (and the world's) first political psychology case, 'Mr A.' (see above, pp, 189—93).

5   This convention is a very cramping one, and it is not made much more useful by the occasional abrupt expansions into two-by-two tables, as proposed by, for example, A. L. Lowell, *Public Opinion*, London, Macmillan, 1910 (whose categories were 'change good', 'change bad', 'change fast' and 'change slow'), H. J. Eysenck, *The Psychology of Politics*, London, Cassell, 1958 (whose catego-

ries were 'tough-minded', 'tender minded', 'left' and 'right') or, most recently, Martin Selinger, *Ideology and Politics*, Allen and Unwin, 1976, especially Ch. 7.

6 Henry A. Murray and Christiana Morgan, 'A clinical study of the sentiments', *Genetic Psychology Monographs*, 1945, pp. 13–311. The interviews were carried out in 1941.

7 *ibid.*, p. 126.

8 *ibid.*, p. 125.

9 *ibid.*, pp. 171 and 174.

10 *ibid.*, pp. 172–3.

11 *ibid.*, p. 253.

12 *ibid.*, p. 255.

13 Bales, *Personality*, p. 374.

14 *ibid.*, p. 263.

15 *ibid.*, p. 321.

16 *ibid.*, p. 263.

17 See, for example, Helmut Schoeck, *Envy*, London, Secker and Warburg, 1969, Ch. 7.

18 Murray and Morgan, 'Clinical study', p. 76.

19 *ibid.*, pp. 175–6.

20 *ibid.*, p. 176.

21 *ibid.*, p. 177.

22 *ibid.*, p. 212.

23 *ibid.*, pp. 209–10 and 178.

24 *ibid.*, pp. 210–11.

25 It seems discourteous of Bales not to refer here to Murray's celebrated description of 'n. REJ' (the need for rejection) in *Explorations in Personality*, New York, Oxford University Press, 1938, pp. 177–8.

26 Bales, *Personality*, p. 294.

27 Murray and Morgan, 'Clinical study', p. 116.

28 *ibid.*, pp. 244–5.

29 *ibid.*, p. 245.

30 Bales, *Personality*, p. 280.

31 See *ibid.*, pp. 273–4.

32 *ibid.*, p. 279.

33 *ibid.*, p. 336.

34 *ibid.*, p. 363.

35 *ibid.*, p. 363.

36 *ibid.*, p. 374.

37 *ibid.*, p. 366.

38 See Ernest Jones, 'The God complex' (1913), reprinted in *Psycho-myth, Psycho-history*, New York, Hillstone, 1974, vol. II, Ch. 13.

39 Bales, *Personality*, p. 332.

40 *ibid.*, p. 280.

41 *ibid.*, p. 338.

42 *ibid.*, p. 338.

43 *ibid.*, p. 335.

44 *ibid.*, p. 239.

45 *ibid.*, p. 243.

46 *ibid.*, p. 270.

47 *ibid.*, p. 269.

48 *ibid.*, p. 327.

49 Ernest Jones, 'The psychology of Quislingism', *International Journal of Psychoanalysis*, 1941, 1–6.

50 Bales, *Personality*, p. 328.

51   *ibid.*, p. 279.

52   G. D. Wilson and J. R. Paterson, 'A new measure of conservatism', *British Journal of Social and Clinical Psychology*, 1968, 264—9; R. Boshier, 'To rotate or not to rotate: the question of the Conservatism scale', *British Journal of Social and Clinical Psychology*, 1972, 313—23.

53   Herbert McClosky, 'Conservatism and personality', *American Political Science Review*, 1958, 27—45. This conservatism scale was built, oddly, without reference to Robert A. Nisbet's magisterial essay on the ten basic propositions of nineteenth-century conservatism, 'Conservatism and sociology', *American Journal of Sociology*, 1952—3, 167—75.

54   L. Berkowitz and K. G. Lutterman, 'The traditional socially responsible personality', *Public Opinion Quarterly*, 1968, 169—85.

55   Giuseppe di Palma and Herbert McClosky. 'Personality and conformity', *American Political Science Review*, 1970, 1054—73.

56   For this case, see M. Brewster Smith, Jerome S. Bruner and Robert W. White, *Opinions and Personality*, New York, Wiley, 1956, pp. 113—53.

57   See J. C. Wahlke et al., *The Legislative System*, New York, Wiley, 1962, Ch. 12.

58   James D. Barber, *The Lawmakers*, New Haven, Connecticut, Yale University Press, 1965, pp. 23—63.

59   *ibid.*, pp. 116—62.

60   Webb was first interviewed in 1960. See Alan Davies, *Private Politics*, Melbourne, Melbourne University Press, 1966, pp. 92—148.

61   *ibid.*, p. 101.

62   See Keith Dunstan, *Wowsers*, Melbourne, Cassell, 1968, for a good-humoured introduction to wowserism, and Elsworth F. Baker, *Man in the Trap*, New York, Avon, 1967, pp. 189—95 (the emotional plague character), for an implacably hostile, Reichian account.

63   For this case, see Graham Little, *Politics and Personal Style*, Melbourne, Nelson, 1973, pp. 33—52.

64   See, for example, John Edwards, *Life Wasn't Meant To Be Easy — A Political Profile of Malcolm Fraser*, Sydney, Mayhem, 1977.

65   Plato, *The Republic*, London, Everyman edn, 1935, pp. 244—5.

66   Lawrence F. Schiff, 'The obedient rebels', *Journal of Social Issues*, 1964:4, 74—95, 86.

67   For this case, see James A. Walter, 'The Perception of Conflict: Profiles from Student Politics', M.A. thesis, Politics Department, La Trobe University, 1974, pp. 232—70.

68   L. F. Schiff, 'The Conservative Movement on American College Campuses', unpublished doctoral dissertation, Harvard University, 1964. It is summarised in the article cited in note 66, above.

69   Harold D. Lasswell, *Psychopathology and Politics*, 1930, Viking edn, New York, 1960, pp. 153—7.

70   I take this sketch, in fact, from the profile of a research chemist's work-style; see Morris I. Stein et al., 'A case study of a scientist', in Arthur Burton and Robert E. Harris (eds.), *Clinical Studies in Personality*, New York, Harper, 1955, vol. II, pp. 726—67. There are, indeed, many other grounds for classifying 'Dr Baker' as an F representative but, since his social outlook was not explored, I have not sought to present his case in fuller summary.

Gregory Bateson adds an interesting reflection on the relation of conventionality of mind and schooling: 'Learning to "find a trick and use it" or to accept a rule on authority and use it without hoping to understand are ... wide-reaching lessons ... taught repeatedly in our schools ... Such lessons can pervade life as general premises to be applied in all situations. When they fail, the person whose approach to life has been patterned in this way has only to say that he tried the wrong trick or failed to accept authority with sufficient conviction. Understood so, the failure strengthens the generalization instead of calling it in question. Thus, such premises have the special quality of being self-validating.' See Mary C. Bateson (ed.), *Our Own Metaphor*, New York, Knopf, 1972, p. 114.

71 See Jerome S. Bruner, 'Hilary Sullivan', in Smith, Bruner and White, *Opinions and Personality*, pp. 154—88.

72 Bales, *Personality*, pp. 306—7.

73 For this case, see Lasswell, *Psychopathology and Politics*, Ch. 7.

74 For this case, see Graham Little, *Politics and Personal Style*, pp. 15—32.

75 For a detailed comparison of Compton and Lasswell's Mr A. as agitators (giving Compton his maximum activist potential), see Little, *Politics and Personal Style*, pp. 77—80 and 91—2.

76 Bales, *Personality*, p. 311.

77 East was interviewed in 1960. See Alan Davies, *Private Politics*, Ch. 3.

78 For this case, see Kenneth Keniston, 'Inburn: an American Ishmael', in Robert W. White (ed.), *The Study of Lives*, New York, Atherton, 1963, pp. 40—70; reprinted as Ch. 2 of Keniston's *The Uncommitted: Alienated Youth in American Society*, New York, Harcourt, Brace, 1965.

79 From *The Study of Lives*, p. 67.

80 Keniston, *The Uncommitted*, pp. 164—72.

81 Bales, *Personality*, p. 355.

82 Keniston, *The Uncommitted*, Chs. 3—6.

83 *ibid.*, pp. 482—3.

84 Kenneth Keniston, *Young Radicals*, New York, Harcourt, Brace, 1968, especially pp. 349—58.

85 For this case, see Diane Wienecke, 'The Schizoid Basis of Idealism', M.A. thesis, Politics School, University of Melbourne, 1975, pp. 27—55, and 'Transcripts of Interviews', pp. 138—259.

86 Philip M. Helfaer, *The Psychology of Religious Doubt*, Boston, Beacon, 1972, pp. 220—1.

87 For discussions of the dynamics of the 'ideal self' in suicide, see S. Lorand, 'Adolescent depression', *International Journal of Psychoanalysis*, 1967, 53—60, and Norman L. Farberow and Edwin S. Shneidman (eds.), *The Cry for Help*, New York, McGraw-Hill, 1961, especially pp. 239—42 and 250—3.

88 Henry Hart, 'Masochism, passivity and radicalism', *Psychoanalytic Review*, 1952, 309—210.

89 Bales, *Personality*, p. 351.

90 Hart does not, perhaps, give enough attention to his patients' styles *as party members*. But for a spirited and ruthless essay describing a participation-style which is basically dependent, anxious, alienated, stereotyped and lacking deep personal commitment, see Philip Selznick, 'Stalinoid Liberals' (1952), reprinted in his *Organizational Weapon — A Study in Bolshevik Strategy and Tactics*, New York, Free Press, 1960, pp. 297—308.

91 Herbert Krugman, 'The role of hostility in the appeal of Communism in the U.S.', *Psychiatry*, 1953, 253—61.

92 For this case, see Robert Lindner, *The Jet-Propelled Couch*, London, Secker, 1955, pp. 75—113.

93 André Gorz, *The Traitor* (1955), English translation, London, Calder, 1960 (with an introduction by J.-P. Sartre). I abstract from my previously published essay, 'The case of André Gorz', in *Essays in Political Sociology*, pp. 148—61.

94 Gorz, *Traitor*, p. 72.

95   *ibid.*, p. 71.
96   See *ibid.*, pp. 207 and 219—20.
97   *ibid.*, p. 44.
98   *ibid.*, p. 128.
99   *ibid.*, p. 274.
100 *ibid.*, p. 140.
101 *ibid.*, p. 279.
102 *ibid.*, p. 290.
103 However, for an account of a strikingly similar childhood which prompted,
     not a career of radical passivity, but one of aggressive (or, at least, highly con-
     fident) psychiatry, see Arthur Burton, 'The therapist has a small pain' in
     Arthur Burton (ed.), *Twelve Therapists*, San Francisco, Jossey-Bass, 1972,
     pp. 192—4. In his case, he feels that his 'commanding' mother managed to
     make sexuality 'the riddle', as well as loading upon her eldest son the
     responsibility for the family's happiness or unhappiness.
104 Shirley MacLaine, *You Can Get There From Here*, New York, Bantam, 1975,
     p. 189 (a reflection prompted by a visit to Yunan).
105 Arnold Rogow, *The Dying of the Light*, New York, Putnams, 1975, p. 307.
106 T. W. Adorno, Else Frenkel-Brunswik, Daniel J. Levinson, and R. Nevitt
     Sanford, *The Authoritarian Personality*, New York, Harper, 1950, p. 971.
107 In *The Authoritarian Personality*, Ch. 19 ('Syndromes found among low
     scorers', pp. 771—86), Adorno distinguished among the following categories:
     rigid (clenched-teeth brotherly love), *protesting* (compulsive disobeyers),
     impulsive (undiscriminating) and *easy-going* (a category that is hard for the
     reader to pin down; at one time, it is 'those who know no fear of women',
     at another, it is people who have a neurotic 'fear of hurting'). This charac-
     teristically unsatisfying Adorno chapter concludes that 'low scorers are as a
     whole less "typed" [i.e. homogeneous?] than the high scorers'. The 'genuine
     liberal' case offered (pp. 785—6) is derisory.
108 Lawrence A. Dombrose and Daniel J. Levinson, 'Ideological "militancy" and
     "pacifism" in democratic individuals', *Journal of Social Psychology*, 1950,
     101—13.
109 Harold D. Lasswell, 'Democratic character', in *Political Writings of Harold D.
     Lasswell*, Glencoe, Illinois, Free Press, 1951, pp. 465—525, especially pp. 495—
     514. I have been greatly helped in my reading of this, at times, elusive essay
     by Fred I. Greenstein's deft popularisation of it, 'Harold D. Lasswell's concept
     of democratic character', *Journal of Politics*, 1968, 696—709.
110 Alex Inkeles, 'Towards the delineation of the democratic character', in F.L.K.
     Hsu (ed.), *Psychological Anthropology*, Homeward, Illinois, Dorsey, 1961,
     pp. 193—9.
111 Robert E. Lane, *Political Ideology*, Glencoe, Illinois, Free Press, 1962, especially
     'Notes on a theory of democratic personality', pp. 400—12; and James G.
     Martin, *The Tolerant Personality*, Detroit, Wayne State University Press, 1964,
     especially pp. 119—23.
112 Daniel J. Levinson, 'Idea systems in the individual and society', in G. K.
     Zollschan and W. Hirsch (eds.), *Explorations in Social Change*, Boston, Houghton
     Mifflin, 1964, p. 305.
113 Helfaer, *The Psychology of Religious Doubt*, pp. 227—61. Another case derived
     from clinical work, which opposes to the bland, once-born model democrat of
     the theorists an ideological composition built upon deep unconscious conflict,
     is described in R. E. Money-Kyrle, *Psychoanalysis and Politics*, London, Duck-
     worth, 1951, pp. 173—7. This young 'theorist of equality' has an ideology
     based on reaction to the early death of his father.

114 Bales, *Personality*, p. 204.
115 R. J. Lifton, *Death in Life*, Harmondsworth, Penguin Books, 1971, pp. 250—6. Charles Berg's 'Case xiv' gives us a brief but vivid *female* DPF case; see his *War in the Mind*, London, Macaulay, 2nd edn, 1944, pp. 122—9.
116 Mark Considine, 'Case Study and Transcript of Interview with "Anna (Natoli) Williams"', unpublished MS, Politics School, University of Melbourne, 1975.
117 Ernest Jones, 'The psychology of Quislingism', *International Journal of Psychoanalysis*, 1941, 1—6.
118 R. N. Sanford and H. S. Conrad, 'Some personality characteristics of morale', *Journal of Abnormal and Social Psychology*, 1943 3—20. It is whimsical to note that the future author of *The Authoritarian Personality* also concluded from this survey that it was easier, using personality and family-background data, to spot democratic characters than anti-democratic ones.
119 R. N. Sanford and H. S. Conrad, 'High and low morale as exemplified in two cases', *Character and Personality*, 1944, pp. 207—27. We skip for the moment the companion portrait in the same article — matched for age, course, class, ethnic background and religion — of a high scorer. This article, written before the collaboration on *The Authoritarian Personality* study had begun, is remarkable not only for describing substantively the first 'local "potential fascist"', but also for its general advocacy of grounding the study of ideology in personality, and the study of that, in turn, in family pattern. Its closing passages go on to adumbrate a double strategy of inquiry — a strategy with the scope of a survey, yet using instruments which draw on clinical insights and which function with a maximum of opacity and indirection. These passages so closely presage the eventual strategy of *The Authoritarian Personality* that one is led to question what, besides some hysterical politics (Ch. 17, for example), the Frankfurt School researchers brought to the project. For a well-informed but unremittingly charitable account of this interesting matter, see Martin Jay, *The Dialectical Imagination*, London, Heinemann, 1973, especially, Ch. 7. Sanford's own account appears in his essay, 'The approach of *The Authoritarian Personality*' (1956), reprinted in Fred I. Greenstein and Michael Lerner (eds.), *A Source Book for the Study of Personality and Politics*, Chicago, Markham, 1971, pp. 319—29.
120 R. Nevitt Sanford, 'Identification with the enemy: a case study of an American Quisling', *Journal of Personality*, 1946—7, 53—8.
121 Adorno et al., *The Authoritarian Personality*, especially pp. 32—56 and 787—802. Intermediate passages deal with Mack's test scores and his performance on TAT and projective questions. The initial contact (questionnaire) was made in 1945 (*The Authoritarian Personality*, p. 21).
122 Edward Shils, 'Authoritarianism "Right" and "Left"', in R. Christie and M. Jahoda (eds.), *Studies in the Scope and Method of the Authoritarian Personality*, Glencoe, Illinois, Free Press, 1954, pp. 24—49, especially Shils's footnote 4.
123 Sanford, 'The approach of *The Authoritarian Personality*', p. 321.
124 See Bales, *Personality*, pp. 223—8.
125 Else Frenkel-Brunswik, 'Patterns of social and cognitive outlook in children and parents', *American Journal of Orthopsychiatry*, 1951, 543—58.
126 For this case, see Robert Coles, *Children of Crisis*, Boston, Little Brown, 1967, pp. 238—52. My summary was previously published in Davies, *Essays in Political Sociology*, Melbourne, Cheshire, 1972, pp. 167—9.
127 Ephraim Rosen, 'John X — self portrait of a fascist', *Journal of Abnormal and Social Psychology*, 1949, 528—50.
128 Robert Lane, *Political Ideology*, Glencoe, Illinois, Free Press, 1961 (especially

pp. 98—112), and *Political Thinking and Consciousness*, Chicago, Markham, 1970.

129 Robert Lane, *Political Man*, New York, Free Press, 1972, pp. 128—39.

130 Rupert Wilkinson, 'Roger Stanton', *The Broken Rebel*, London, Croom-Helm, 1972, pp. 295—309.

131 Norman F. Dixon, *On the Psychology of Military Incompetence*, London, Cape, 1976, Ch. 22. This chapter also contains what is probably the best current two-paragraph description of the authoritarian personality as it currently haunts the psychology departments (pp. 258—63). Rosen's 'John X', incidentally, waxes lyrical, from his NCO point of view, on the Army s 'bringing out the best' in him.

132 The left-wing authoritarian theme was first propounded by Edward Shils in 'Authoritarianism "Right" and "Left"'.

133 For example, Roger Brown, *Social Psychology*, New York, Free Press, 1965, pp. 526ff, especially pp. 542—3.

134 Adam Curle, *Mystics and Militants*, London, Tavistock, 1972, pp. 40—1.

135 For this case, see R. N. Sanford, 'The freeing and acting out of impulses in adolescence', in R. W. White (ed.), *The Study of Lives*, New York, Atherton, 1963, pp. 9—24.

136 The best theoretical statement of the authoritarian personality remains Daniel Levinson, 'Idea systems in the individual and society', in G. K. Zollschan and W. Hirsch (eds.), *Explorations in Social Change*, Boston, Houghton Mifflin, 1964, pp. 305ff.

137 Leo Lowenthal, 'Knut Hamsun', *Zeitschrift fur Sozialforschung*, 1937, 295—345, reprinted in Lowenthal, *Literature and the Image of Man*, Boston, Beacon, 1957, pp. 190—220.

138 Bales's scheme also works retrospectively to validate earlier one-off comparisons that may have seemed at the time merely eccentric — for example, Milton M. Miller's yoking together of Proust's Marcel and Thomas French's celebrated railwayman patient, 'John', as archetypal asthmatics (*Nostalgia*, Boston, Houghton Mifflin, 1956). Both come up plainly as Bales DBs.

139 Robert Bales, *Personality and Interpersonal Behavior*, New York, Holt, Rinehart and Winston, 1970, pp. 46—7.

140 David Riesman, 'Horace Weinstein', in *Faces in the Crowd*, New Haven, Connecticut, Yale University Press, 1951, pp. 485—517.

Chapter 6.   Attending to an outlook

1   I use this term in place of 'world view' merely to signalise the adoption of the new 'inside-out' perspective; there is little enough substantive difference. It is not a technical term. Amusingly, neither 'outlook' nor 'world view' appears in Robert Lane's careful list of 43 near-synonymous terms used over the last generation by American social scientists to denote 'a bundle of political beliefs'; see Jeanne Knutson (ed.), *Handbook of Political Psychology*, San Francisco, Jossey-Bass, 1973, pp. 83—4.

The word 'outlook' made, in fact, a brief appearance in the closing pages of *The Authoritarian Personality*:

The most crucial result of the present study . . . is the demonstration of close correspondence in the type of approach and outlook a subject is likely to have in a great variety of areas, ranging from the most intimate features of family and sex adjustment through relationships to other people in general, to religion and to social and political philosophy. (p. 971)

The authors claimed to have delineated two opposite types of outlook — the democratic and the authoritarian. But when Levinson turned, a decade or so later, to his careful methodological essay on these compositions, outlooks

had become 'idea-systems' — see 'Idea-systems in the individual and society',
Ch. 12 of G. K. Zollschan and W. Hirsch (eds.), *Explorations in Social Change*,
Boston, Houghton Mifflin, 1964. Lane himself also finally settles for 'belief-
system', after much use of 'personal' or 'latent' 'ideology' — although he, too,
drops into 'social outlook' from time to time for stylistic relief. In any case,
some inclusive term, with suitably vague boundaries, is required as our unit
of study, to lift us above the aridity of having to consider component ideas,
opinions, beliefs, attitudes, values, principles or ideals. Our object of study,
however it be named, is (as the novel was once defined) *the world through a
temperament*.

Those demanding a formal definition may, however, consider this: 'The
world view of any individual is a set of very wide-range vectors [a private
term roughly equivalent to 'very broad propensities to bias'] in that individual's belief space (a) that he learned early in life and that are not readily
changed and (b) that have a determinate influence on much of his observable
behavior, both verbal and nonverbal, but (c) that he seldom or never verbal-
izes in the referential mode, though (d) they are constantly conveyed by him
in the expressive mode and as latent meanings.' (W. T. Jones, 'World views:
their nature and function', *Current Anthropology*, 1972, 83.) A very similar
treatment of 'core beliefs' is given in A. B. Gabriele, 'The principle of
irrational loyalty', *Psychoanalytic Review*, 1966, 69—84.

2 For example, David Barber can, for his purpose of predicting work-style,
conclude of President Carter that 'the drive for excellence . . . comprises . . .
about a third of the Carter world-view and illustrates an important outgrowth
of his character . . . Perhaps as important, he had been, and felt, lucky.' (*The
Presidential Character*, Englewood Cliffs, New Jersey, Prentice Hall, 1977, pp.
509—10.) The President himself is unlikely to allot two-thirds of his subjective
space in this way.

3 Robert Redfield, *The Little Community*, Chicago, Illinois, University of Chicago
Press, 1955, p. 91.

4 Peter L. Berger, *Invitation to Sociology* (1963), Harmondsworth, Penguin Books,
1966, pp. 70—5.

5 Robert E. Lane, *Political Thinking and Political Consciousness*, Chicago, Markham,
1969, p. 313.

6 A. F. Davies, *Private Politics*, Melbourne, Melbourne University Press, 1966,
pp. 243—4.

7 I take this phrase — and the whole subsequent skeleton of the divergent
approaches to outlooks — from W. T. Jones's magisterial essay, 'World views:
their nature and function', *Current Anthropology*, 1972, 86—90, where they
are deployed in the form of a report on the behaviour of anthropologists and
others at a conference on the subject.

8 As reported by Daryl J. Bem, *Beliefs, Attitudes and Human Affairs*, Belmont,
California, Brooks/Cole, 1970, pp. 38—9. See also Philip E. Converse's disillusioned essay, 'The nature of belief systems in mass publics', in D. E. Apter
(ed.), *Ideology and Discontent*, New York, Free Press, 1964.

9 For an explicit argument to this effect, see Daniel J. Levinson, 'The importance
of personality for political participation', *Public Opinion Quarterly*, 1958, 3—10,
and, more generally, the much anthologised piece by Dennis Wrong, 'The
over-socialised conception of man in modern sociology', *American Sociology
Review*, 1961, 173—83. Kenneth Burke put it most concisely: 'The relations of
any one individual to the public medium can be understood only by examining
the "clusters" or "equations" in his particular "psychic economy".' (*A
Grammar of Motives*, New York, Prentice Hall, 1945, p. 114.)

10 This phrasing sharpens only slightly a sentence in R. Money Kyrle, 'Political ethics', *International Journal of Psychoanalysis*, 1944, 166—71.

11 cf. R. G. Collingwood's distinction between the 'static and dynamic aspects of thought':

> The business of St Thomas ... is not to expound Thomism, but to arrive at it ... Ever since Pythagoras (or so we are told) invented the word philosophy, in order to express the notion of the philosopher not as one who possesses wisdom but as one who aspires to it, students of philosophy have recognized that the essence of their business lies not in holding this view or that, but in aiming at some view not yet achieved: in the labour and adventure of thinking, not in the results of it. What a genuine philosopher (as distinct from a teacher of philosophy for purposes of examination) tries to express when he writes is the experience he enjoys in the course of this adventure, where theories and systems are only incidents in the journey. For the poet, there is, perhaps, none of this dynamism of thinking. He finds himself equipped, as it were, with certain ideas, and expresses the way in which it feels to possess them.
>
> (*The Principles of Art*, London, Oxford University Press, 1936, p. 297)

The poet, in this view, is a pure R type.

12 See Henri de Man, *The Re-making of a Mind*, New York, Scribner, 1919; Arthur Koestler, *Arrow in the Blue*, New York, Macmillan, 1952, especially part v, which re-works more fully the story originally told in R.H.S. Crossman (ed.), *The God that Failed*, New York, Harper, 1949; Whittaker Chambers, *Witness*, New York, Random House, 1952, and *Cold Friday*, New York, Random House, 1964; André Gorz, *The Traitor* (1955), English translation, London, Calder, 1960; and Michael Harrington, *Fragments of the Century*, New York, Saturday Review Press, 1973, especially Ch. 7. I wish I could be surer that the two last named are genuine apologies for this trope, and not merely sad exhibits of it.

13 As Daryl J. Bem observes, 'A recently published book called *Theories of Cognitive Consistency: a Sourcebook* (known affectionately by the in-group as TOCCAS) contains 84 chapters, 830 pages of text, 41 pages of references (about 1000 references), and more about cognitive consistency than almost anyone would care to know ... Inconsistency, they seem to be trying to tell us, motivates belief and attitude change.' (See *Beliefs, Attitudes and Human Affairs*, p. 34.)

Let us try quickly to characterise this enterprise. First, it amends the intellectual quest from, 'What gives opinions their strength?' (to which one plausible and *psychological* answer might be, 'Strong primitive beliefs hidden inside or beneath them'), to the much more drab, 'What strengthens or weakens an opinion?' So it becomes interesting to experiment with manipulating small changes in belief by, for example, hypnotism, false information, slanted information, propaganda, emotional appeals, exposure to shocks, debate, group pressure, or personal confrontations with opponents — that is, it becomes interesting to concentrate on behaviour when chivvying a man's reasoning has a *commonsense* outcome. Secondly, it shifts the focus from beliefs *in* (that is, our earliest, surest, and most private 'knowledge') to beliefs *that* (the world of information, that is, of factual inference, and 'proof'). Thirdly, it implicitly adopts the model of a close-reasoning mind, operating in circumstances pressing strongly for consistency.

The cognitive-dissonance approach does not deny that opinions may be, and usually are, clung to for emotional reasons (it simply does not try to analyse that, as if emotions were out of bounds); and it does not assume an impossible rationality (it allows an ample measure of irrationality to be caught in the denials and rationalisations summoned to defend cherished opinions against telling contrary evidence). But it does narrow the whole problem down to one of faulty intellection. Of course, along the way, things of interest crop up — for example, personal styles of denying or rationalising away awkwardness (where A. will seek out other supporting beliefs in order to swamp the inconsistency, B. will split the belief-object into one part where the trouble-some new bit is true, and another part where it is not, while C. will 'trans-cend' the problem, seeing two disparate beliefs as part of a larger unity). Abelson's computer mock-up of a right-wing Senator, using a minimum of some 200 unit-beliefs, is a salutary exercise in contemplating what goes to make up a brutally simple political mind. (See Robert P. Abelson and J. D. Carroll, 'Computer simulation of individual belief systems', *American Behavioral Scientist*, 1965, 24—30.)

14 Note particularly the parrot cry, 'The source of a belief is logically irrelevant to its validity . . . the truth of a proposition is to be assessed quite indepen-dently of how it happened to be arrived at.' Behind this priggish utterance there lies a massive, indeed tribal, defence against insight. Logical validity is one thing, empirical validity another, but — in politics especially — the *existential* validity of opinions, their 'truth-to-this-person', will often matter still more. The 'validity' of the stand a person takes before an issue will depend, from his point of view, not only on its congruence with those of his beliefs which indicate that the situation has certain features (which new inform-ation may change), but equally on how it fits in with his beliefs *in* various objects (beliefs which he may be permanently saddled with). Anyone wishing to re-think an attitude may thus value new light on the 'prototypes' of his beliefs, the archaic fires still burning in them, as much as on the reality-features of a current issue. Identifying the 'psychotic factor of interest' (Kenneth Burke) in one's own opinions may damage them as much as ex-ternal attacks — indeed, the latter will perhaps only strike home through the former. (For a fuller exposition of this point, see Davies, *Private Politics*, pp. 258—61.) Critics and readers must learn to press philosophers more insistently with the question, 'But why are *you* telling us all this?'

15 Joan Evans, *Taste and Temperament*, London, Cape, 1939.

16 See, for example, Henry Murray's specification of fourteen basic 'needs' (the frame upon which rests much of the concision and acuity of his case-studies) in *Explorations in Personality*, New York, Oxford University Press, 1948; or the classifications of character-types in Erich Fromm, *Man for Himself*, London, Routledge, 1948, especially part III; or the classification of 'neurotic types' in Karen Horney, *Neurosis and Human Growth*, London, Routledge, 1951, or of 'neurotic styles' in David Shapiro, *Neurotic Styles*, New York, Basic Books, 1965. There is also a considerable experimental psychological literature on 'cognitive styles', unfortunately mostly in terms of discrete paired alternatives (sharpener/ leveller, field-dependent/field-independent, and so on). For an early essay in this mode, see G. S. Klein, 'The personal world through perception', in R. R. Blake (ed.), *Perception*, New York, Ronald, 1951. For an up-to-date review of the field, see Klein's *Perception, Motives and Personality*, New York, Knopf, 1970.

17 These are the three 'vectors' which, he demonstrates, account for the main enduring disagreements among philosophers (see W. T. Jones, 'Philosophical disagreements and world views', *American Philosophical Association Proceedings*, 1969—70, 24—42). For wider purposes (anthropological, for example), he adds 'simple/complex', 'sharp-focus/soft-focus' and 'spontaneous/constrained' (Jones, 'World views', especially pp. 85—6). His original statement, *The Romantic*

Syndrome, The Hague, Nijhoff, 1961, made play also with 'order/disorder', 'inner/outer' and 'this world/other world', but see now his current ordering in the appendix to the second edition, 1974.

18 This is a relatively open system of content-analysis applicable to small samples of writing. The manual is Ralph K. White, *Value Analysis*, Ann Arbor, Michigan, Society for the Psychological Study of Social Issues, 1951; and there are applications by White himself: 'Black boy: a value analysis', *Journal of Abnormal and Social Psychology*, 1947, 440—61, and 'Hitler, Roosevelt and the nature of war propaganda', *Journal of Abnormal and Social Psychology*, 1949, 157—74; by William Eckhardt: 'War propaganda, welfare values and political ideologies', *Journal of Conflict Resolution*, 1965, 345—59; 'Can this be the conscience of a conservative?', *Journal of Human Relations*, 1967, 443—56; and 'Communist values', *Journal of Human Relations*, 1970, 778—88; and by Howard W. Cummins: *Mao, Hsiao, Churchill and Montgomery: Personal Values in Decision Making*, Beverley Hills, Sage, 1973. White's scheme was evolved over a decade or more of work on propaganda analysis for the U.S. Government in a programme launched at the outbreak of the Second World War by Lasswell himself. Leites's 'operational code' procedures are very similar and of similar derivation.

19 Milton Rokeach, *The Nature of Human Values*, New York, Free Press, 1973, especially parts 1, 3 and 5. This is a rough scheme; the key term 'value' drifts about from 'concern' to 'ideal' — and how conscious a value is assumed to be, is not a problem that is faced. This is, in a sense, a child's version of the Lasswell and Kaplan scheme in *Power and Society*, New Haven, Yale University Press, 1969, pp. 55—8, and especially the table on p. 87, 'Forms of influence and power — Base values × Scope values'.

20 E. S. Shneidman: 'Psycho-logic: a personality approach to patterns of thinking', in J. Kagan and G. S. Lesser (eds.), *Contemporary Issues in Thematic Apperception Methods*, Springfield, Illinois, Thomas, 1961, pp. 153—90; 'The case of Jay', *Journal of Projective Techniques*, 1952, especially pp. 44—7; 'The logic of El.: a psycho-logic approach', *Journal of Projective Techniques*, 1961, 390—403; and 'Personality profile conveyed by the communicator as a function of his logical style', in L. Arons and A. May (eds.), *Television and Human Behavior*, New York, Appleton Century, 1963, pp. 177—9.

21 Norman N. Holland briefly analyses J. S. Mill, Carlyle, Matthew Arnold and Cardinal Newman in 'Prose and minds: a psycho-analytic approach to non-fiction', in George Levine and W. Maddern, *The Art of Victorian Prose*, New York, Oxford University Press, 1968, pp. 314—37. His *Five Readers Reading*, New Haven, Yale University Press, 1975, exposes the full scheme.

22 Quoted in Robert J. Lifton, *Death in Life* (1967), Harmondsworth, Penguin Books, 1971, p. 92.

23 Quoted in Jerome D. Frank and Earl H. Nash, 'Commitment to peace work', *American Journal of Orthopsychiatry*, 1965, 106—119.

24 See the brilliant discussion of 'Transference as fear of death', in Ernest Becker, *The Denial of Death*, New York, Free Press, 1973, pp. 148—50.

25 See 'L'Année Horrible' (1935) in Sybille Bedford, *Aldous Huxley*, London, Constable, 1973, vol. 1, pp. 298—314.

26 See Silvano Arieti, 'The microgeny of thought and perception', *Archives of General Psychiatry*, VI, 454 ff; and his *The Intrapsychic Self*, New York, Basic Books, 1967, pp. 5—8.

27 There has been much polling in search of 'stratum ideology', but the most interesting reading is still Alfred Lee's theoretical scheme (*Multivalent Man*, New York, Braziller, 1966, part III) sketching the 'probable outlooks' of four

status-grades within four vocational styles inside the typical large modern organisation — or profession.

28   See John Dollard, *Class and Caste in a Southern Town*, New Haven, Connecticut, Yale University Institute of Human Relations, 1957, pp. 364—89.

29   Paul Schilder, 'The analysis of ideologies as a psychotherapeutic method, especially in group treatment', *American Journal of Psychiatry*, 1936—7, 601—17.

30   For a study of a body of factory workers of roughly similar views, half of whom were promoted to foreman and half shunted sideways into unionism, and who, three years later had largely re-worked their views accordingly, see Seymour Lieberman, 'The effects of changes in roles on attitudes of role occupants', *Journal of Human Relations*, 1956, 385 —402. And for opinion changes in a very mobile man (moving in twelve years from union representative to middle management) see Davies, *Essays in Political Sociology*, pp. 147—8 and Ch. 7, which also discusses earlier 'group theory' writing on 'cross-pressured' individuals.

   Mary Douglas adds an interesting comment on world views (she calls them cosmologies) as rooted in, and shifting with, changes in social conditions: 'Anyone who finds himself living in a new social condition must . . . find that the cosmology he used in his old habitat no longer works. We should try to think of cosmology as a set of categories that are in use. It is like lenses which bring into focus and make bearable the manifold challenge of experience. It is not a hard carapace which the tortoise has to carry forever, but something very flexible and easily disjointed. Spare parts can be fitted and adjustments made without much trouble. Occasionally a major overhaul is necessary to bring the obsolete set of views into focus with new times and new company. This is conversion. But most of the time adjustments are made so smoothly that one is hardly aware of the shifts of angle until they have developed an obvious disharmony between past and present. Then a gradual conversion that has been slowly taking place has to be recognised . . . and . . . old, irrelevant rituals . . . laid aside. They no longer have meaning because the social action in which they inhered no longer exists' (*Natural Symbols*, London, Cresset, 1970, p. 144). Those recalling our description of 'resigned' and 'phallic' attitudes might wish to test their sense of it on this passage: is it R or P? (For my taste, it is both too 'outside in' and too expectant of smooth flexibility.)

31   See John Strachey, *The Strangled Cry*, London, Bodley Head, 1962, pp. 12—13; the passage is also quoted by Lewis S. Feuer, *Ideology and the Ideologists*, Oxford, Blackwell, 1975, p. 108.

32   Kenneth Burke, *The Rhetoric of Religion*, University of California Press 1970, which underlines the movement of surrender as well as of resolve in the critical moment, and the 'partialness' of the conversion — less the exchange of one faith for another than the change to a more exacting stance towards the faith already accepted, 'as with persons who suddenly feel "called" to study for the ministry in a religion to which they already subscribed' (p. 104); see also Burke's *Permanence and Change* (1935), Los Altos, California, Hermes, 1954, for the brilliant part II, 'Perspective by incongruity'.

33   Leon Salzman, 'The psychology of religious and ideological conversion', *Psychiatry*, 1953, 177—87. See also Eric Hoffer, *The True Believer*, New York, Harper, 1951, especially pp. 39—125 — 'The social contexts of conversion — the potential converts and characteristic beliefs and affects'; B. Weininger, 'The interpersonal factor in the religious experience', *Psychoanalysis*, 1954—5, 27—44; E. H. Schein, 'The Chinese indoctrination programme for prisoners of war', *Psychiatry*, 1956, 149—72; R. J. Lifton, *Thought Reform and the*

Psychology of Totalism, London, Gollancz, 1961, Ch. 5, and conclusion; C. W. Christiansen, 'Religious conversion', *Archives of General Psychiatry*, 1963, 207—81, and Gilbert Abcarian, 'Romantics and renegades — political defection and the radical Left', *Journal of Social Issues*, 1971, 123—39. On particular conversions, see W. N. Evans, 'The conversion of John Bunyan', *International Journal of Psychoanalysis*, 1943, 76—85; Charles Kligerman, 'A psychoanalytic study of the Confessions of St. Augustine', *Journal of the American Psychoanalytic Association*, 1957, 469—84; E. Victor Wolfenstein, *Personality and Politics*, Belmont, California, Dickenson, 1964, Ch. 3 (Malcom X), and, on the same subject Michael J. Parenti, 'Black nationalism and the reconstruction of identity', in Robert Endelman (ed.), *Personality and Social Life*, New York, Random House, 1967, pp. 514—23.

34 Bertrand Russell, *Autobiography*, London, George Allen and Unwin, 1967, vol. I, p. 146.

35 I follow here Bennett and Nancy Simon, 'The pacifist turn: an episode of mystic illumination in the *Autobiography* of Bertrand Russell', *Journal of the American Psychoanalytic Association*, 1972, 109—21.

36 See Willy Baranger, 'The ego and the function of ideology', *International Journal of Psychoanalysis*, 1958, 191—5.

37 They are, of course, P types to a man. Mary McCarthy has gently satirised the self-dramatising portentousness with which ideologues retrospectively clothe their larger shifts of view. In 'My Confession' (1953) in her *On the Contrary*, London, Heinemann, 1962, she represents her own moves into and out of Communism as almost wholly subliminal drift — for example, the Moscow trials constituted 'a break or rupture, not very noticeable at first, that gradually widened and widened, without any conscious effort on my part, sometimes to my regret. This estrangement was not marked by any definite stages; it was a matter of tiny choices. Shortly after the Moscow trials, for instance, I changed from the *Herald Tribune* to the *Times*; soon I had stopped doing crossword puzzles, playing bridge, reading detective stories and popular novels. I did not 'give up' these things; they departed from me, as it were, on tiptoe, seeing that my thoughts were elsewhere.' 'During that year, I simply realized, with a certain wistfulness, that it was too late for me to become any kind of Marxist.'

38 See Fred I. Greenstein, *Children and Politics*, New Haven, Yale University Press, 1965; David Easton and Jack Dennis, *Children in the Political System*, New York, McGraw-Hill, 1969; R. D. Hess and Judith Torney, *The Development of Political Attitudes in Children*, Chicago, Aldine, 1967; R. W. Connell, *The Child's Construction of Politics*, Melbourne, Melbourne University Press, 1971; and Davies, 'Political Socialisation', in F. J. Hunt (ed.), *Socialisation in Australia*, Melbourne, Australia International Press, 1978, pp. 301—14.

39 It is only fair to say that this has hardly been a major aim of the 'political socialisation' workers, but also that their work has been in consequence unusually directionless.

40 The best short account of this is Jane Loevinger, 'The meaning and measurement of ego development', *American Psychologist*, 1966, 195—206. For the earliest sampling of conventional social values — in four-year-olds — see Mary Goodman, 'Emergent citizenship' in *Childhood Education*, 1958—9, 248—51.

41 Of course, only a small proportion of young adults win through to a fully-rounded and mature outlook. cf. Robert E. Lane, *Political Thinking and Political Consciousness*, Chicago, Markham, 1969, and Richard M. Merelman, 'The development of policy thinking in adolescence', *American Political Science Review*, 1971, 1033—47, who both put adolescent samples through schemes of

levels of sophistication in political thinking incorporating Kohlberg's stages of moral development. Lane points up the possibility on this basis of rating adult political discourse (Is this leader selling this issue morally short? Is he nuancing it too finely for popular acceptance?) and the sense in which one perhaps only wins a political argument by raising a point to a higher level, showing something morally lacking in the less inclusive, empathetic view of it. Merelman raises the idea that maturity in the moral mode is only one of several styles of fully-developed outlook — others possibly emphasise 'causal', 'socio-centric', or 'imaginative' maturity (Merelman, 'Development', p. 1047). For further testimony on how rare a worked-up outlook is in sixteen-year-olds, see Connell, *The Child's Construction of Politics*, ('Fred'), and Joseph Adelson, 'The political imagination of the young adolescent', *Daedalus*, 1971:4, 1013—50, who each report one case only — a young Communist and a Utopian scientist — from large secondary-school samples.

42 See Fred I. Greenstein and S. Tarrow, *Political Orientations of Children*, New York, Sage, 1971; and Jeanne Knutson, 'Pre-political ideologies', in R. Niemi (ed.), *The Politics of Future Citizens*, San Francisco, Jossey-Bass 1974, pp. 7—40.

43 For a general discussion of reproach in children's ideals, see M. N. Searl, 'Infantile Ideals', *International Journal of Psychoanalysis*, 1936, especially pp. 35—6.

44 Harold G. McCurdy (ed.), *Barbara: the Unconscious Autobiography of a Child Genius*, University of North Carolina Press, 1966, especially Ch. 3.

45 Anna Freud, *The Ego and the Mechanisms of Defence*, London, Hogarth Press, 1937, Ch. 12, especially pp. 167—72. For an account of the institutionalising of the twelve-year-old 'call' in the career-path of the conservative clergyman, see Helfaer, *The Psychology of Religious Doubt*, Boston, Beacon, 1972, part II.

46 Mary McCarthy, *Memoirs of a Catholic Girlhood*, Harmondsworth, Penguin Books, 1958.

47 James Agee, *The Morning Watch*, London, Peter Owen, 1950.

48 James Baldwin, *Go tell it on the Mountain*, London, Michael Joseph, 1953.

49 cf. Michael Oakeshott:

> Politics is an activity unsuited to the young, not on account of their vices but on account of what I at least consider to be their virtues ... Everybody's young days are a dream, a delightful insanity, a sweet solipsism. Nothing in them has a fixed shape ... everything is what can be made of it. The world is a mirror in which we seek the reflection of our own desires ... Since life is a dream, we argue (with plausible but erroneous logic) that politics must be an encounter of dreams, in which we hope to impose our own ... [But for] most there is what Conrad called the 'shadow line' which, when we pass it, discloses a solid world of things, each with its fixed shape, each with its own point of balance, each with its price; a world of fact, not poetic image, in which what we have spent on one thing we cannot spend on another; a world inhabited by others besides ourselves who cannot be reduced to mere reflections of our own emotions. And coming to be at home in this commonplace world qualifies us (as no knowledge of 'political science' can ever qualify us), if we are so inclined and have nothing better to think about, to engage in what the man of conservative disposition understands to be political activity.
>
> To rein in one's own beliefs and desires, to acknowledge the current shape of things, to feel the balance of things in one's hands ... these are difficult achievements; and they are achievements not to be looked for in the young. (From 'On being Conservative', in Oakeshott, *Rationalism in Politics*, London, Methuen, 1962, p. 195).

50 Erik H. Erikson, 'Autobiographical notes on the identity crisis', *Daedalus*,
    1970:1, 730—59.
51 Anna Freud, *The Ego and the Mechanisms of Defence*, p. 180.
52 Silvano Arieti, 'The role of cognition in the development of inner reality',
    J. Hellmuth (ed.), *Cognitive Studies*, New York, Brunner-Mazel, 1970, p. 103.
53 Erikson's most severe critic is Nathan Leites, who claims (*The New Ego*, New
    York, Aronson, 1973, part II) that the very notion of 'identity' promotes
    imprecision and ambiguity, and is so popular exactly because it allows people
    to talk about, *and not understand*, central personal concerns. Joseph Barnett
    objects that ideology-adoption, far from being generally a positive (or even
    necessary) step in the attainment of identity and maturity, is often a psycholo-
    gically conservative and dependent move, especially in those who will remain
    'ideologues' (see 'On ideology and the psycho-dynamics of ideologues', *Journal
    of the American Academy of Psychoanalysis*, 1973, 381—95).
        A very useful extension of Eriksonian thinking to diagnostic university
    counselling is J. A. Marcia, 'The development and validation of ego-identity
    status', *Journal of Personality and Social Psychology*, 1965, 551—8, which shows
    how, by the use of interviews on occupational choice, religious beliefs and
    political ideology, students may be classified as identity-*achieved* (this describes
    those who have been through a crisis and are now 'committed'), in *morato-
    rium* (those who are in crisis, with their commitments still vague), *foreclosed*
    (those who have experienced no crisis, but are committed to parents', or
    others', earlier goals and values), and *diffused* (those with no commitment,
    regardless of crisis). This makes clear, as does Lawrence Kohlberg, 'The
    adolescent as philosopher', *Daedalus*, 1971:4, 1051—86, that Erikson's picture
    of an adolescent stage of identity-crisis and resolution, since it presupposes
    the attainment of considerable intellectual skill and moral sophistication, fits
    the experience only of a small, developmentally élite group in any body of
    young people. See also Anne Constantinople, 'An Eriksonian measure of per-
    sonality development in college students', *Journal of Developmental Psychology*,
    1969, 357—72, and James M. Donovan, 'Identity status and interpersonal
    style', *Journal of Youth and Adolescence*, 1975, 37—55.
        For a polemical defence of 'no jargon' in analysing the identity crisis, see
    Cushing Strout, 'Ego psychology and the historian', *History and Theory*, 1968,
    281—97.
54 Carl C. Jung, 'The stages of life', *Collected Works*, New York, Bollingen, 1960,
    vol. 6, part 6; Elliott Jaques, 'Death and the mid-life crisis', *International
    Journal of Psychoanalysis*, 1965, 502—14; Erik Erikson, 'Dr Borg's life-cycle',
    in Erikson (ed.), *Adulthood*, New York, Norton, 1978, pp. 1—32.
55 'John Chatwell' (see M. Brewster Smith, Jerome S. Bruner and Robert W.
    White, *Opinions and Personality*, New York, Wiley, 1956, Ch. 6), who was 'cased'
    as an undergraduate and then again seven years later, looks at first like an
    ideal test, but it seems that he did not see the results of the first assessment.
56 Ernest Jones, 'The concept of a normal mind', in *Papers on Psychoanalysis*,
    London, Baillière, Tindall and Cox, 5th edn, 1958, pp. 207—8.
57 The title of Paul Schilder's piece, 'The analysis of ideologies as a psycho-
    therapeutic method', *American Journal of Psychiatry*, 1936—7, 601—17, promises
    at first sight to be a notable exception, but the 'ideologies' that Schilder
    concerned himself with turn out to be ideas about '(1) Body and beauty; (2)
    health, strength, efficiency, superiority and inferiority in a physical sense;
    (3) aggressiveness and submission; (4) masculinity and femininity; (5) the
    relation of sex and love; (6) the expectation for the future; (7) the meaning of
    death'. His purpose was to bring out, in a *group*-treatment setting, the inherent

logical flaws in many of his patients' private concepts in these realms and to get them to consider how they had allowed such notions to get such a leverage over their actions.

58 cf. Carl Rogers and S. Dymond, *Psychotherapy and Personality Change*, Chicago, University of Chicago Press, 1954, Ch. 11.

59 Another example is Baranger's Case B, a philosophy student with delusions of superiority and a 'philosophy of quality'; 'I am sure', the author says, 'that the analysis of B would have been quite impossible without an examination of his theory of "quality" and the processes at its basis. B had remained practically unproductive up to the moment of the analysis of those processes; this allowed him, in a way, to regain contact with the split-up aspects of his objects and his ego.' (See Willy Baranger, 'The ego and the function of ideology', *International Journal of Psychoanalysis*, 1958, 194—5.) cf. R. E. Money-Kyrle's comment on 'an experience which is fairly common in analysis':

'The experience is the almost accidental discovery of the clinical importance of certain beliefs, usually of a religious or philosophical nature, which a patient has hitherto belittled rather than concealed. He has always been aware of them, but they have seemed to him to be quite irrelevant to his analysis and he has hardly mentioned them. If, however, he is asked about them, another reason for his previous avoidance of the subject may come to light. He may, for example, find to his surprise that he cannot describe them clearly to his analyst even when he tries; and this at once suggests that they must be important after all, and that he unconsciously wants to conceal them because he is very much afraid of their being undermined. He may then admit that he does feel them in some obscure way to be the mainspring of his life which would be meaningless without them. This may be all that can be elicited at first. But it is enough to make the analyst suspect that, whether true or false in themselves, they are being used to deny some truth which is felt to be intolerable' (*Psychoanalysis and Politics*, London, Duckworth, 1951, p. 173).

60 Ranyard West, *Conscience and Society*, London, Methuen, 1942, pp. 135—52.

61 This was confirmed in West's 'An analysis in retrospect', *Acta Psychotherapeutica*, 1964, 299—317, which provides further details of the original analysis. West also pursues the similarities between Freud's and Mr C.'s social views in 'The social significance of the uncompleted psychoanalysis of Sigmund Freud', pp. 131—40 of West's *International Law and Psychology*, New York, Oceana, 1974.

62 This story is told slightly more fully in Davies, *Private Politics*, pp. 256—8.

63 Sigmund Freud, *The Interpretation of Dreams*, London, Hogarth Press, 1954, p. 553.

64 Determining in private one's opinion on a political question is not a bit like debating. Kenneth Burke noted the difference between privately following one's own thoughts and ordering them to present to others: 'Consider all the logical modulations which one adds in the attempt to socialise his point of view: how spontaneously he puts forward, as his grounds for belief, many points and progressions of thought which had never even occurred to him until he sat down to the business of motivating his argument for his public. The very considerations which are almost wholly elided during the inception of one's thesis often constitute the main burden of his efforts, once he sets about it to recommend his beliefs to others. In externalising or impersonalising his thesis, he seeks to translate it into a system of motivations which will be cogent to his readers'. (See Burke, *Permanence and Change*, 2nd edn, pp. 24—5.) cf. Paul Valéry: 'When we think we lose the thread.'

65 A. F. Davies, *Images of Class*, Sydney, Sydney University Press, 1965.

66 Sebastian de Grazia, *The Political Community*, Chicago, University of Chicago Press, 1948, pp. 11—18.

67 A. B. Gabriele, 'The principle of irrational loyalty', *Psychoanalytic Review*, 1966, p. 71.
68 This is Helfaer's suggestion in *The Psychology of Religious Doubt*, Ch. 3, section 2.
69 See the case of Forrestal, above, pp. 61—3.
70 G. Handel (ed.), *The Psychosocial Interior of the Family*, New York, Basic Books, 1967, Conclusion.
71 See the works by Jones and Shneidman cited above at notes 17 and 20.
72 cf. M. N. Searl, 'Infantile ideals', *International Journal of Psychoanalysis*, 1936, especially pp. 33—6.
73 John Dollard, 'The life history in community studies', *American Sociological Review*, 1938, 103—17.

Chapter 7.   The neglect of affects

1 Lewis Namier, 'Human nature in politics', in *Personalities and Powers*, New York, Harper, 1965, p. 5.
2 Graham Wallas, *Human Nature in Politics*, London, Constable, 1908, Ch. 1.
3 Arthur F. Bentley, *The Process of Government*, Evanston, Illinois, Principia Press, 1908, part I.
4 Bentley, *Process of Government*, p. 55.
5 David L. Sills (ed.), *New International Encyclopedia of the Social Sciences*, New York, Macmillan-Free Press, 1968, 17 vols.
6 William James, *Textbook of Psychology*, London, Macmillan, 1892, pp. 374—6.
7 D. Krech and R. S. Crutchfield, *Elements of Psychology*, New York, Knopf, 2nd edn, 1969, pp. 519—64.
8 S. S. Tomkins, *Affect, Imagery and Consciousness*, vols. II, New York, Springer, 1962.
9 *ibid.*, especially vol. 1, Ch. 3.
10 A. F. Shand, 'Feeling and thought', *Mind*, 1898, 477—505, is excellent on this.
11 See G. Piers and M. B. Singer, *Shame and Guilt*, New York, Norton, 1971, p. 18.
12 E. C. Banfield, *The Moral Basis of a Backward Society*, Glencoe, Illinois, Free Press, 1958, pp. 111—12.
13 Peter Mark Roget, *Thesaurus of English Words and Phrases*, London, Longman, 3rd edn, 1955, pp. 231—88.
14 Joel R. Davitz, *The Language of Emotion*, New York, Academic Press, 1969.
15 Davitz, *Language of Emotion*, pp. 144—5. However, he nominates as 'neutral' apathy and boredom — I have always found the latter painful.
16 Or, alternatively, 'inner-directed, outer-directed and bi-polar'; see Robert C. Solomon, *The Passions*, New York, Anchor, 1976, pp. 256—8.
17 On signal affects, see D. Rapaport, 'On the psychoanalytic theory of affects', *International Journal of Psychoanalysis*, 1953, 177—87. Engel speaks of 'signals of signals'. See George L. Engel, 'Towards a classification of affects', in P. Knapp (ed.), *Expression of the Emotions in Man*, New York, International Universities Press, 1963, pp. 266—94.
18 Paul Federn, *Ego Psychology and the Psychoses*, New York, Basic Books, 1954, p. 87.
19 See O. Fenichel, 'The ego and the affects', Ch. 15 of his *Collected Papers* (second series), London, Routledge, 1955.
20 Edith Jacobson, 'The affects and their pleasure-unpleasure qualities in relation to psychic discharge processes', in R. M. Loewenstein (ed.), *Drives, Affects and Behavior*, New York, International Universities Press, 1953, pp. 38—66.
21 See S. Novey, 'A clinical view of affect theory in psychoanalysis', *International Journal of Psychoanalysis*, 1959, 94—101.

22 Franz Alexander, 'The logic of the emotions', *International Journal of Psychoanalysis*, 1935, 399–413; and see Alexander and Wilson, 'Quantitative dream studies', *Psychoanalytic Quarterly*, 1935, 371–93 – 'an attempt to obtain a picture of the economic distribution of the fundamental dynamic tendencies in a personality'.

23 cf. Stuart Hampshire, *Spinoza*, Harmondsworth, Penguin Books, 1951, p. 135.

24 William McDougall, *Social Psychology*, London, Methuen, 1908. This line of thought has recently been extended in R. Plutchik, *The Emotions: Facts, Theories and a New Model*, New York, Random House, 1962, which distinguishes eight basic patterns of 'adaptive' behaviour – destruction, reproduction, incorporation, orientation, protection, deprivation, rejection and exploration – to which, it claims, most affects may be annexed.

25 Alexander Shand, *The Foundations of Character*, London, Macmillan, 1912, Ch. 1.

26 Erik Erikson, *Childhood and Society*, New York, Norton, 1950, Ch. 7.

27 See, for example, Hanna Segal, *Introduction to the Work of Melanie Klein*, London, Heinemann, 1964; R. Money-Kyrle, *Man's Picture of his World*, London, Duckworth, 1961, Chs. 2 and 3.

28 Edward Glover, 'The psychoanalysis of affects', *International Journal of Psychoanalysis*, 1939, 299–307.

29 cf. Hanna Segal, *Introduction to the Work of Melanie Klein*, Ch. 3.

30 Glover, 'The psychoanalysis of affects', p. 301.

31 Here, I follow Roy Schafer, 'The clinical analysis of the affects', *Journal of the American Psychoanalytic Association*, 1964, 275–99.

32 Ernest Jones, 'Fear, guilt and hate', *International Journal of Psychoanalysis*, 1929, 383–97.

33 For a striking case in which the problem is massive 'inauthenticity of affect', see Paul H. Seton, 'Uses of affect observed in a histrionic patient', *International Journal of Psychoanalysis*, 1965, 226–36.

34 Thomas M. French, *The Integration of Behavior*, Chicago, University of Chicago Press, 1952, vol. 1, p. 144.

35 Engel, 'Towards a classification of affects', p. 267: putting feelings into words involves 'oversimplification and impoverishment' and is 'fundamentally inconsistent' with the nature of affects. His remarks on empathy are also on p. 267.

36 A point emphatically made by R. G. Collingwood, *Principles of Art*, London, Oxford University Press, 1938, Ch. 7. I owe the reference to A. L. Burns. Ernest Becker has carried it further still with the proposition that anxiety is due to lack of words – rather than inner impulses or reservoirs of feeling. Insight depends on words: we direct our feelings rather than purge them. See Becker, *Revolution in Psychiatry*, New York, Free Press, 1964, p. 178.

37 Fenichel, *Collected Papers*, vol. ii, p. 221.

38 I am aware of, indeed sympathetic to, a reforming current that would 'purify' psychoanalytic and psychological terminology with a dose of linguistic analysis: see, for example, Roy Schafer, 'A psychoanalytic view of emotion', *Philosophical Studies*, 22, 156–67, and 'Psychoanalysis without psychodynamics', *International Journal of Psychoanalysis*, 1975, 41–55; M. Edelson, 'Language and Dreams', *Psychoanalytic Study of the Child*, 1972, 208–83; and, more broadly, Anatol W. Holt's declaration of war on nouns, as reported in Mary Catherine Bateson (ed.), *Our Own Metaphor*, New York, 1972, pp. 176–84. This line of thought leads to a resolute replacement of *substantives* (here, 'affect', 'affect-system' and the individual affects themselves) by an 'action' (that is, verb-and-adverb) convention. On a later occasion I may, indeed, attempt this exercise. For the present, however, the propositions I wish to advance seem sufficiently

modest and artless (and the new 'language' so far still conspicuously graceless). I hope I will be forgiven my persistence in low-grade metapsychology.

39 Max Scheler, *Ressentiment* (1912), New York, Free Press, 1961, and *The Nature of Sympathy* (1913), London, Routledge, 1954.

40 However, Shand discussed them with some zest in his earlier, 'Character and the emotions', *Mind*, 1896, 203—26, especially 208—12.

41 Fenichel, 'The ego and the affects', p. 217.

42 See the fine descriptions of the 'styles' in David Shapiro's *Neurotic Styles*, New York, Basic Books, 1965.

43 David Riesman, *Faces in the Crowd*, New Haven, Connecticut, Yale University Press, 1950, p. 68.

Chapter 8.   Affects in politics

1 W. B. Yeats, *Memoirs* (ed. D. Donoghue), London, Macmillan, 1972, p. 283.

2 Lasswell, *Psychopathology and Politics*, p. 76. The Adams quotation is from *The Education of Henry Adams* (1905), Boston, Houghton Mifflin, 1918, p. 7. For a useful discussion of guilt in politics, see R. E. Money-Kyrle, *Psychoanalysis and Politics*, London, Duckworth, 1951, pp. 163—72.

3 See Norman H. Holland, *The Dynamics of Literary Response*, Oxford University Press, 1968, Ch. 11, for an account of how literature 'involves a structuring process which we introject', and can evoke both 'neater' and 'less messy' but also 'stronger, more profound' emotions than everyday life.

4 Lasswell, *Psychopathology and Politics*, Ch. 10.

5 Gregory Zilboorg, 'Affects, personal and social', *Psychoanalytic Quarterly*, 1945, 28—45.

6 Lasswell, *Psychopathology and Politics*, pp. 74—5.

7 Quoted in K. S. Eissler, *Talent and Genius*, New York, Quadrangle, 1971, p. 200.

8 See Lasswell, *Psychopathology and Politics*, pp. 183—6, 189 and 193—4.

9 *ibid.*, p. 184.

10 *ibid.*, pp. 185—6 and 265.

11 Zilboorg, 'Affects, personal and social', p. 42.

12 Lasswell, *Psychopathology and Politics*, p. 184.

13 Zilboorg, 'Affects, personal and social', pp. 41—3.

14 *ibid.*, p. 44.

15 Gregory Zilboorg, 'The emotional problem and the therapeutic role of insight', *Yearbook of Psychoanalysis*, 1953, pp. 202—3.

16 David Riesman, *Faces in the Crowd*, New Haven, Yale University Press, 1952, p. 64.

17 David Riesman, 'Criteria for political apathy', in Alvin W. Gouldner (ed.), *Studies in Leadership*, New York, Harper 1950, especially pp. 547—56.

18 Paul Federn, *Ego Psychology and the Psychoses*, New York, Basic Books, 1954, p. 87.

19 Riesman, *Faces in the Crowd*, p. 68.

20 Willy Baranger, 'The ego and the function of ideology', *International Journal of Psychoanalysis*, 1958, 191—5, 195.

21 Lord Moran, *Winston Churchill: the battle for survival, 1940—65*, London, Constable, 1966, p. 285.

22 Albert Camus, *Selected Essays and Notebooks*, Harmondsworth, Penguin Books, 1972, p. 192.

23 Calvin Hall, *The Meaning of Dreams*, New York, McGraw-Hill, 1953, 2nd edn, 1966, p. 40.

24 As Herbert Hyman remarks in 'Surveys in the study of political psychology',

in Jeanne Knutson (ed.), *Handbook of Political Psychology*, San Francisco, Jossey-Bass, 1973, p. 345, it is astonishing that, of the hundreds of thousands of opinion polls, only one should seem to bear directly on political affects — and that happens to relate to feelings about elections. The following table shows the distribution of those who sometimes felt pleasure, anger or contempt — and those who regularly felt only apathy. The survey was made in 1959.

	U.S.	U.K.	Germany	Italy
Pleasure	66%	52%	28%	18%
Anger	57%	41%	46%	20%
Contempt	58%	37%	46%	15%
Apathy	12%	26%	35%	54%

(*Source*: G. A. Almond and S. Verba, *The Civic Culture*, Princeton, New Jersey, Princeton University Press, 1963, table 13.)

25 James C. Davies, *Human Nature in Politics*, New York, Wiley, 1963, Ch. 1.
26 Robert Coles, 'Social struggle and weariness', *Psychiatry*, 1964, 305—15.
27 John P. Roche and Stephen Sachs, 'The bureaucrat and the enthusiast', *Western Political Quarterly*, 1965, 248—61.
28 Lasswell, *Psychopathology and Politics*, p. 197.

Chapter 9.   The principal affects

Moral indignation
1 Svend Ranulf, *The Jealousy of the Gods and the Criminal Law at Athens —A Contribution to the Sociology of Moral Indignation*, two vols., London, Williams and Norgate, 1933, p. 7.
2 Emile Durkheim, *The Division of Labour in Society* (1893), translated by George Simpson, New York, Free Press, 1964, p. 108.
3 G. H. Mead, 'The psychology of punitive justice', *American Journal of Sociology*, 1918, 577—602.
4 Franz Alexander, 'The social psychology of punishment' (1926), pp. 221—35 of *The Criminal, the Judge and the Public*, New York, Collier, 1962. See also Gregory Zilboorg, *The Psychology of the Criminal Act and Punishment*, London, Hogarth Press, 1955.
5 Svend Ranulf, *Moral Indignation and Middle Class Psychology*, New York, Schocken, 1964.
6 J. R. Gusfield, *Symbolic Crusade*, University of Illinois Press, 1963, p. 180.
7 For this term, and for a fuller discussion of the outlook it involves, see above, pp. 162—72 and p. 464 n. 62.
8 Alan Davies, *Private Politics*, Melbourne, Melbourne University Press, 1957, Ch. 2.
9 David Riesman, *The Lonely Crowd*, New Haven, Yale University Press, 1950, pp. 228—30.
10 Gusfield, *Symbolic Crusade*, p. 116.
11 P. F. Strawson, *Freedom and Resentment*, London, Methuen, 1974, p. 14.
12 *ibid.*, pp. 16—17.
13 Dennis Altman, *Homosexual*, New York, Outerbridge and Dienstfrey, 1971, last Ch.
14 Leo Abse, *Private Member*, London, Macdonald, 1973.
15 Quoted in Altman, *Homosexual*, p. 100.
16 Wilhelm Reich, *Character Analysis*, New York, Orgone Press, 1945, p. 169.

17 Riesman, *Faces in the Crowd*, p. 312, Riesman follows Aristotle here: 'There
    are some things at which we ought to feel angry', *Nicomachean Ethics*, Bk. III,
    Ch. 1. This is quoted in Gabriele Taylor, 'Justifying the emotions', *Mind*, 1975,
    390—402, who is most interesting on *not* feeling as a failing; she notes that
    when we should feel angry, sorry, jealous, or grieving, but do not, it is usually
    through conceit, humility or inability to take threatened values seriously
    enough.
18 T. W. Adorno et al., *The Authoritarian Personality*, New York, Harper, 1950,
    pp. 406 ff.
19 For a general discussion of anal metaphors in politics, see L. Lowenthal and
    N. Guterman, *Prophets of Deceit: A Study of the Techniques of the American Agi-
    tator*, New York, Harper, 1949, theme 1.
20 See, for example, the unfashionable demurrers in S. M. Lipset and Earl Rabb,
    Commentary, Sept. 1973, pp. 7—13.
21 G. H. J. Pearson, *Adolescence and the Conflict of Generations*, New York, Norton
    1958.
22 Robert Coles, *The Middle Americans*, Boston, Little, Brown, 1971.
23 Frank Parkin, *Middle Class Radicalism: The Social Bases of the British Campaign
    for Nuclear Disarmament*, Manchester, Manchester University Press, 1968,
    defines them as school teachers, clergymen, scientists, architects, university
    and college lecturers, social workers, journalists, artists, novelists, M.P.s and
    librarians (p. 180).
24 Lenski noted 'relatively strong support for liberal political programs from
    such diverse groups as College professors, Jewish businessmen, Hollywood
    actors, and the Protestant clergy'. These groups shared, he thought, strongly
    incongruent statuses — ethnic, occupational, economic and educational. See
    Gerhard E. Lenski, 'Status crystallisation: a non-vertical dimension of social
    status', *American Sociological Review*, 1954, 405—13. Parkin felt in the C.N.D.
    it was the other way about: C.N.D. types simply chose predominantly service
    occupations because they believed in the work (*Middle Class Radicalism*, pp.
    184—6).
25 Lasswell, 'Introduction' to S. Ranulf, *Moral Indignation*, p. xiii.
26 *ibid.*
27 Parkin, *Middle Class Radicalism*, pp. 16, 36, 39 and 85.
28 Riesman, *The Lonely Crowd*, p. 198.
29 See too Lasswell's splendid essay, 'Political constitution and political character',
    Psychoanalysis and the Psychoanalytic Review, 1959, 3—18, and further references
    cited at p. 506, note 25.
30 See Kenneth Keniston, *The Uncommitted*, New York, Harcourt, Brace, 1965,
    and Bruno Bettelheim, *The Children of the Dream*, New York, Macmillan, 1969.
31 Robert Lane, *Political Thinking and Political Consciousness*, Chicago, Markham,
    1969, p. 212. See also Herbert Fingarette, *The Self in Transformation*, Glencoe,
    Illinois, Free Press, 1957, Ch. 4, for an account of the evolution of the capacity
    to blame and bear blame.
32 Lasswell reproves Ranulf for neglecting this. See Else Frenkel-Brunswik, 'A
    study of prejudice in children', *Human Relations*, 1949, 295—306, and her Ch.
    10 of *The Authoritarian Personality*, New York, Norton, 1950.
33 See K. R. Eissler, 'Crusaders', *Psychoanalytic Study of Society*, 1964, 329—55.
34 I take this to be a permissible translation of Lasswell's term 'partial rage
    inhibited' type, used in his study with Dorothy Blumenstock of the Chicago
    black community, *World Revolutionary Propaganda: a Chicago Study*, New York,
    Knopf, 1939, and in this passage:
        The inner turbulence occasioned by incompatible standards, and especially
        by different degrees of severity in sanctioning policy, favors the formation

of egocentric and partially inhibited rage types of character. Egocentricity is fed by the alienation engendered in multiple exposure to contradictory requirements. The rage which is provoked by erratic acts of deprivation in family, school and neighborhood is only partly inhibited. There are therefore strong dispositions to escape from internal tension by 'acting out' instead of relying on neurotic symptoms. Among the more extreme types are persons who seek to avenge themselves against fate by committing individual acts of violence. A lone wolf assassin — like Oswald — is more often an indignant, desperate and alienated moralist than a cautious calculator.

From Lasswell, 'Introduction' to Ranulf, *Moral Indignation*

35 Arthur Koestler, *Arrow in the Blue*, New York, Macmillan, 1962, pp. 272—3.
36 Consider the possible action of unconscious fear: (a) where the fear (perhaps not altogether unreasonable) of being blamed oneself for a part of the 'outrage', drives one out ahead of the pack to censure others, 'those *really* to blame' (onlookers have then to conclude that a person of such virtue and proper feeling could not possibly have been the culprit); (b) where a fear resonates in the memory of what one might be led to do (as one did in the past), if carried away again in a fit of righteous anger.

Anger and hatred

1 Alexander Shand, *The Foundations of Character*, London, Macmillan, 2nd edn, 1920, part II, Chs. 3 and 4. Compare the list of instigations in Leonard Berkowitz, *Aggression*, New York, McGraw-Hill, 1962, p. 45; Berkowitz argues that, although frustration can lead to other things, and aggression can be inhibited, the general rule is that aggression presupposes frustration, and that frustrations always lead to some form of aggression. Favouring strong arousal are: strong instigation to the frustrated response, strong interference with it, a large number of frustrations, arbitrary and unreasonable frustrations, frustrations blocking a goal, and small danger of punishment. Robert Solomon, however, contests the whole stimulus-response convention: 'One does not become angry because the comment *is* offensive: the comment is offensive by virtue of its being an object for anger.' (Solomon, *The Passions*, New York, Anchor, 1976, p. 196.) A listing of the whole range of angers and aggressions, across a moral spectrum from 'life-enhancing' to 'necrophiliac', is given in Ernest Becker, *The Birth and Death of Meaning*, New York, Free Press, 2nd edn, pp. 167—74.
2 Quoted in Shand, *Foundations of Character*, p. 264.
3 *ibid.*, p. 251. Luther can be cited to similar effect: 'I have no better work than anger and jealousy, for when I am angry ... I can pray and preach; then my whole disposition is quickened, my understanding sharpened, and all unpleasant cogitations and vexations do depart.' (Luther, *Table Talk*, quoted in N. Kemp Smith, *The Philosophy of David Hume*, London, Macmillan, 1941, p. 158.)
4 Shand, *Foundations of Character*, p. 251.
5 *ibid.*, p. 252.
6 James Alexander, 'The psychology of bitterness', *International Journal of Psychoanalysis*, 1960, 514—20.
7 G. W. Allport, *The Nature of Prejudice*, Cambridge, Mass., Addison-Wesley, 1954, p. 363.
8 Phyllis Greenacre, *Swift and Carroll*, New York, International Universities Press 1955, p. 275.
9 Howard E. Gruber, *A Psychological Study of Scientific Creativity*, New York, 1974, pp. 128—9.
10 Solomon, *The Passions*, p. 219.

11 D. Horton and R. R. Wohl, 'Mass communication and para-social interaction', *Psychiatry*, 1956, 215—30.

12 See Betty E. Fried, 'Ego-strengthening aspects of hostility', *American Journal of Orthopsychiatry*, 1956, 179—87.

13 O. Holsti, 'The image of the enemy' in D. J. Finlay et al., *Enemies in Politics*, Chicago, Rand McNally, 1967, p. 26. Finlay's Introduction to the three case studies of this book is also a useful piece.

14 John Dollard, 'Hostility and fear in social life', *Social Forces*, 1938, 19.

15 Harold D. Lasswell, *Propaganda Technique in World War I* (1927), 2nd edn, Boston, Mass., M.I.T. Press, 1971, p. 77.

16 Adolf Hitler, *Mein Kampf*, Boston, Houghton Mifflin, 1943, p. 118.

17 Theodor Herzl, *A Jewish State*, London, Nutt, 1896. See also Franz Alexander, *Social Forces*, 1938, 27—9. Lucian Pye (*The Spirit of Chinese Politics*, Boston, Mass., M.I.T. Press, 1968, especially Ch. 5) characterises Chinese politics during the 1960s as a 'search for enemies' and a deliberate incitement to hate.

18 T. Shibutani, 'On the personification of adversaries', in Shibutani (ed.), *Human Nature and Collective Behavior*, Englewood Cliffs, New Jersey, Prentice Hall, 1970, pp. 223—33. See also Orrin E. Klapp, 'Notes toward the study of vilification as a social process', *Pacific Sociological Review*, 1959, 71—6; H. C. Kelman (ed.), *International Behavior*, New York, Holt, Rinehart and Winston, 1966, part i; and Ralph K. White, 'Misconceptions and the Vietnam war', *Journal of Social Issues*, 1966, 1—164.

19 See Urie Bronfenbrenner, 'The mirror image in Soviet-American relations,' *Journal of Social Issues*, 1961, 45—56, and also the sharply witty 'inversion-substitution' exercise in which Ranyard West rewrites George Kennan's 1957 Reith lectures as a Russian would have given them, simply substituting U.S. for U.S.S.R., Truman for Stalin, Eisenhower for Krushev, etc., *International Law and Psychology*, New York, Oceana, 1974, pp. 121—30.

20 See Anna Freud, *The Ego and its Mechanisms of Defence*, London, Hogarth Press, 1931, Ch. 9.

21 For a darker illustration still, see Bruno Bettelheim, *The Informed Heart*, Glencoe, Illinois, Free Press, 1960, pp. 217—31.

22 I largely follow here Berkowitz, *Aggression*, Ch. 6.

23 See section 'Hajj' in article 'Arabs', in *Encyclopedia of Religion and Ethics*, Edinburgh, T. and T. Clark, 1908—26, 16 vols.

24 Sir James Frazer, *The Golden Bough*, abridged edn, London, Macmillan, Chs. 45—8; and for medieval practices see, for example, Lynn White, 'Death and the Devil' in R. S. Kinsman (ed.), *The Darker Vision of the Renaissance*, Berkeley, California, University of California Press, 1974, pp. 43 ff.

25 R. Money-Kyrle, *The Meaning of Sacrifice*, London, Hogarth Press, 1930, p. 254.

26 See, for example, H. Loeblowitz-Leonard, 'The Jew as symbol', *Psychiatric Quarterly*, 1947, 33—8; Martin Wangh, 'National Socialism and genocide of the Jews', *International Journal of Psychoanalysis*, 1964, 386—95; and Bela Grunberger, 'The Anti-Semite and the Oedipal conflict', *International Journal of Psychoanalysis*, 1964, 380—5.

27 Originally in Burke's essay, 'On human behavior considered "dramatistically"', especially parts v-vii, in *Permanence and Change*, Los Altos, California, Hermes, 1930. For later additions, see the useful précis in H. D. Duncan, *Communication and the Social Order*, London, Oxford University Press, 1968, under 'scapegoat' in index.

28 Quoted G. W. Allport, *The Nature of Prejudice*, p. 243.

29 For a well-studied case, see Nathan Leites, *Ritual of Liquidation*, Santa Monica, California, Rand Corporation, 1954. And see Augusta Bonnard, 'The meta-

psychology of the Russian trials confessions', *International Journal of Psychoanalysis*, 1954—5, 208—12.

30 Burke, *Permanence and Change*, p. 287.

31 Allport, *Nature of Prejudice*, pp. 257—9, which also quotes Aristotle.

32 See Neal E. Miller, 'Theory and experiment relating psychoanalytic displacement to stimulus-response generalisation', *Journal of Abnormal and Social Psychology*, 1948, 155—78.

33 For more on the Government as anger-target, see Robert Lane, *Political Thinking and Political Consciousness*, Chicago, Markham 1971, pp. 156—9.

34 Adapted from Allport, *Nature of Prejudice*, pp. 247—8.

35 Heinz Kohut, 'Narcissism and narcissistic rage', *Psychoanalytic Study of the Child*, 1972, 360—400. This paper follows his path-breaking book on narcissism, *The Analysis of the Self*, New York, International Universities Press, 1971, and takes up the challenge of exploring the interrelations of narcissism and aggression.

36 Kohut, speaking at a 1976 seminar at the Chicago Institute of Psychoanalysis.

37 cf. William L. Davidson's definition: 'When revenge pursues its object spitefully with unremitting persistence, and finds zest in every pretty infliction of evil on him, it is *vindictiveness*' Article 'Anger', *Encyclopedia of Religion and Ethics*, Edinburth, T. and T. Clark, 1908—26); and Elias Canetti's account of vengeance and 'the sting' in *Crowds and Power*, London, Gollancz, 1962, pp. 110—19.

38 He finds in *Michael Kohlhaas* (1808) 'a gripping description of the insatiable search for revenge after a narcissistic injury'. Kohlhaas has also been discussed as a prime case of querulance, by Melitta Shmideberg, 'On querulance', *Psychoanalytic Quarterly*, 1946, 478—81, and as a prime case of fanaticism, by Lambert Boltrauer, 'The psychology of fanaticism', *International Journal of Psychoanalysis*, 1952, 263, and the present author, *Essays in Political Sociology*, Melbourne, Cheshire, 1972, pp. 176—83. Kleist's novel is cleverly modernised in E. L. Doctorow's *Ragtime* (London, Pan Books, 1976) in the character 'Coalhouse' Walker. See also the case of Wolf Tone, and the 'insulting neglect', the 'lack of a letter' that had been the excuse for Tone's conversion to separatism. 'Tone had written to William Pitt the younger, offering to found a British colony on one of the islands which Captain Cook had discovered in the Pacific; his idea was that it would provide a base against the Spaniards. When Pitt did not bother to reply, Tone had registered a vow to make him sorry — and, but for the persistent easterly gale which prevented the French expeditionary force from landing in Ireland in 1796, he might well have redeemed that pledge.' Brian Inglis, *Roger Casement*, New York, Harcourt, Brace, Jovanovich, 1973, p. 142.

39 Emil Ludwig, biographer of Wilhelm II (1926) explained his subject's 'readiness to take offense and to turn toward war as reactions to the sense of a specific organ inferiority. The Emperor had been born with a withered arm.' Freud, however, pointed out in his *New Introductory Lectures* (1933) that 'It was not the birth injury in itself which resulted in the Emperor William's sensitivity to narcissistic slights, but the rejection by his proud mother who could not tolerate an imperfect child' (Kohut, 'Narcissism and narcissistic rage').

40 Kohut, 1976 seminar.

41 Talcott Parsons, 'Certain primary sources and patterns of aggression in the social structure of the Western world', *Psychiatry*, 1947, 167—81.

42 Clyde Kluckhohn, *Navaho Witchcraft* (1944), Boston, Beacon Press, 1967. See also Kluckhohn's 'Group tensions: analysis of a case history', in L. Bryson et al., (eds.), *Approaches to National Unity*, New York, Harper, 1945.

43 Parsons, 'Primary sources', p. 177 fn. 10.

44 Arnold Rogow, *The Dying of the Light*, New York, Putnams, 1975, p. 280.

45 However, see Rex Nettleford, 'Aggression, violence and force: containment and eruption in the Jamaican history of protest, in P. P. Wiener and J. Fisher (eds.), *Violence and Aggression in the History of Ideas*, New Brunswick, N.J., Rutgers University Press, 1974, pp. 133—57 for an extraordinarily interesting essay on Jamaican politics as on a permanent knife-edge of violence — in a state of *dread*: 'One still expects from the *status quo* uncorrupt politicians, compassionate judges, less brutal policemen, and a juster society. But one also expects decision-makers with insights and *creative daring*. It is the absence of this, which could activate the violence potential in *dread*' (p. 155).

46 Abram Kardiner, *The Psychological Frontiers of Society*, Columbia University Press, 1945, p. 372.

47 See D. C. McClelland, *Personality*, New York, Holt, Rinehart, 1951, pp. 512—19; Allport, *Nature of Prejudice*, Ch. 22; and Berkowitz, *Aggression*, Ch. 8.

48 Lasswell, *Power and Personality*, p. 45.

49 Erich Fromm, *Man for Himself* (1949), London, Routledge paperback edn, 1971, p. 215.

50 For a good deal more of the same, see H. Guntrip, *Some Aspects of Psychoanalytic Therapy*, New York, International Universities Press, 1952, pp. 102ff. For political case studies centring round inability to show hostility, see Robert Lane, *Political Thinking and Political Consciousness*, Chicago, Markham, 1969, Ch. 9, and Leon Saul, *The Hostile Mind*, New York, Random House, 1965, Ch. 6, Cases C and G.

51 Maurice L. Farber, 'The anal character and political aggression', *Journal of Abnormal and Social Psychology*, 1955, 486—9. (But note William Rabinowitz, 'Anality, aggression and acquiescence,' *Journal of Abnormal and Social Psychology*, 1957, 140—2, which argues that the relationship is an artefact of acquiescence response-set.) The point is also made by Joseph Barnett, 'On ideology and the psychodynamics of the ideologue', *Journal of the American Academy of Psychoanalysis*, 1973, 391: 'The obsessional's style of aggression and hostility is covert and inhibited. Anger is contained, denied and imploded; and hostility is expressed more often through acts of omission than commission.'

52 T. W. Adorno et al., *The Authoritarian Personality*, New York, Harper, 1950, p. 557.

53 See Abraham Maslow, 'The authoritarian character structure', *Journal of Social Psychology*, 1943, 401—11.

54 See for example Karen Horney, 'The value of vindictiveness', *American Journal of Psychoanalysis*, 1948, 3—12; and Harold F. Searles, 'The psychodynamics of vengefulness', *Psychiatry*, 1956, 31—9.

55 Edrita Fried, 'Ego-strengthening aspects of hostility', *American Journal of Orthopsychiatry*, 1956, 179—87.

56 R. T. Green and G. Santori:, 'A cross-cultural study of hostility and aggression', *Journal of Peace Research*, 1969, 13—22.

57 Berkowitz, *Aggression*, p. 100. Paranoiacs, similarly, inhibit their paranoia; see Henry A. Alker, 'A quasi-paranoid feature of students' extreme attitudes against colonialism', *Behavioral Science*, 1971, 218—27.

58 Pye, *Spirit of Chinese Politics*, especially Ch. 5.

59 Leon Salzman, 'Religious and ideological conversion', *Psychiatry*, 177—87.

60 James A. Walter, *The Perception of Conflict: Profiles from Student Politics*, M. A. thesis, Politics Department, La Trobe University, Melbourne, 1974, pp. 28—37.

61 David Finlay et al., *Enemies in Politics*, Chicago, Rand McNally, 1967, pp. 169ff. And see E. D. Hoedemaker, 'Distrust and aggression: an interpersonal inter-

national analogy', *Journal of Conflict Resolution*, 1968, 69—81, for three case studies where healthier nations have ameliorated 'unrealistic distrust and aggressive postures' (which 'may represent an unconscious, unverbalized expression of a need for support and help') in developing countries.

62 Fried, 'Ego-strengthening aspects of hostility', pp. 181—3.

63 O. Mannoni, *Prospero and Caliban: The Psychology of Colonisation* (1950), New York, Praeger 1964, part III, Ch. 2.

64 This has been worked out in some detail for a small sample of New York recruits to Communism in the late 1930s and early 1940s, who were subsequently patients in analysis. See Herbert E. Krugman, 'The role of hostility in the appeal of Communism', *Psychiatry*, 1953, 253—61.

65 Salzman, 'Religious and ideological conversion', p. 186, and Malcolm X., *Autobiography*, New York, Grove Press, 1966.

66 Abram Kardiner, *The Mark of Oppression*, New York, World Publishing Company, Meridian paperback edn, 1962. And see Edward Glover, *On the Early Development of Mind*, London, Hogarth Press, 1950, Ch. 13, for a discussion of the 'mastering of rage' through psychosis, addictions and sexual perversions.

67 Kardiner, *Mark of Oppression*, p. 304.

68 *ibid.*, pp. 332—3.

69 Robert Coles, *Children of Crisis*, Boston, Little, Brown, 1967.

70 Destiny Deacon, 'Being black in another world', *Farrago*, (Melbourne University students' weekly paper), 10 May 1974, p. 18.

Envy, inferiority and resentment

1 cf. Churton Collins's saying to the same effect: 'Envy and fear are the only passions to which no pleasure is attached. Every other sin hath some pleasure annexed to it or will admit of some excuse, envy alone wants both.'

Illustrative quotations here and throughout this chapter have been drawn from a wide variety of dictionaries of quotations: these include the *Oxford Dictionary of Quotations*, London, Oxford University Press, 1953; the *Penguin Dictionary of Quotations*, Harmondsworth, Penguin Books, 1960; *Bartlett's Familiar Quotations*, Macmillan, 1968; *Stevenson's Book of Proverbs, Maxims and Familiar Phrases*, London, Routledge, 1949; J. B. Simpson, *Contemporary Quotations*, New York, 1964; R. Flesch, *The Book of Unusual Quotations*, London, Cassell, 1959; Bergen Evans, *Dictionary of Quotations*, New York, Delacorte, 1968; H. L. Mencken, *A New Dictionary of Quotations*, New York, Knopf, 1942; *Bartlett's Unfamiliar Quotations*, London, Allen and Unwin, 1971; and a number of others.

2 George M. Foster, 'The anatomy of envy', *Current Anthropology*, 1972, 166.

3 Geoffrey Gorer, *Exploring English Character*, London, Cresset, 1955, pp. 284—5.

4 Helmut Schoeck, *Envy*, London, Secker and Warburg, 1969.

5 'From envy, hatred, malice, and all uncharitableness, Good Lord deliver us.' The Litany, *Book of Common Prayer*.

6 See Peter Wertheim's sensitive analysis in his 'Morality and advantage', *Australian Journal of Philosophy*, 1964, 375—87. Max Scheler emphasises at this point a sense of one's own impotence (*Ressentiment* (1912), New York, Free Press, 1961, Ch. 2.)

7 Harry Stack Sullivan, *Clinical Studies in Psychiatry*, New York, Norton, 1956, p. 129.

8 Isca Salzberger-Wittenberg, *Psychoanalytic Insight and Relationships*, London, Routledge, 1970, Part II, Ch. 4. She expounds formulations originally to be found in Melanie Klein, *Envy and Gratitude*, London, Tavistock, 1957, and Hanna Segal, *Introduction to the Work of Melanie Klein*, London, Hogarth Press, 2nd edn, 1973, Ch. 3.

9   See for example, William Davidson, 'Envy', *Encyclopedia of Religion and Ethics*, 1925; Salzberger-Wittenberg, *Psychoanalytic Insight and Relationships*, pp. 113—14.

10 Foster, 'The anatomy of envy', p. 168.

11 Hamed Ammar, *Growing up in an Egyptian Village*, London, Routledge, 1954, pp. 108—9, quoted Foster, 'The anatomy of envy', p. 174.

12 Segal, *Introduction to the Work of Melanie Klein*, p. 28; and see Wertheim, 'Morality and advantage', pp. 377—80 for an argument that envy, once established as a trait of character, has a 'vortex quality', and tends to erode autonomy, inhibit or cripple the intelligence, destroy the conditions necessary for cooperation or friendship with others, and by its compulsiveness and excessive self-concern generate malice and hatred.

13 Hanna Segal paraphrases Melanie Klein's view as follows:

> Envy stirs as soon as the infant becomes aware of the breast as a source of life and good experience; the real gratification which he experiences at the breast, reinforced by idealization, so powerful in early infancy, makes him feel that the breast is the source of all comforts, physical and mental, an inexhaustible reservoir of food and warmth, love, understanding and wisdom. The blissful experience of satisfaction which this wonderful object can give will increase his love and his desire to possess, preserve and protect it, but the same experience stirs in him also the wish to be himself the source of such perfection; he experiences painful feelings of envy which carry with them the desire to spoil the qualities of the object which can give him such painful feelings.
>
> Greed aims at the possession of all the goodness that can be extracted from the object, regardless of consequences; this may result in the destruction of the object and the spoiling of its goodness, but the destruction is incidental to the ruthless acquirement. Envy aims at being as good as the object, but when this is felt as impossible, it aims at spoiling the goodness of the object, to remove the source of envious feelings. It is this spoiling aspect of envy that is so destructive to development, since the very source of goodness that the infant depends on is turned bad, and good introjections, therefore, cannot be achieved.
>
> (Segal, *Introduction to the Work of Melanie Klein*, pp. 28 and 27)

14 Ralph Greenson, 'On enthusiasm', *Journal of the American Psychoanalytic Association*, 1962, 4.

15 Foster, 'The anatomy of envy', p. 169—70.

16 Roger Money-Kyrle has noted that 'Some analysts believe that envy, which seems to be inherited in unequal measure, imposes, in those who have it strongly, an insuperable barrier to insight.' Money-Kyrle, *Man's Picture of his World*, London, Duckworth, 1961, p. 185.

17 Harold Bloom, *Anxiety of Influence*, New York, Oxford University Press, 1973.

18 It was one of Franz Alexander's 'emotional syllogisms' that the sense of inferiority naturally stimulated aggression and competitive striving — as opposed to the sense of guilt, which typically immobilised. See Alexander, 'The relation of inferiority feelings to guilt feelings', *International Journal of Psychoanalysis*, 1938, 41—9. cf. Max Scheler, *Ressentiment*, p. 52: 'Envy does not strengthen the acquisitive urge, it weakens it.' We have already quoted Luther, (see above p. 483, note 3) to the effect that envy (clearly this is what we can take his 'jealousy' to mean) as well as anger, 'sharpens his wits and quickens his whole disposition'.

19 Oliver Brachfeld, *Inferiority Feelings in the Individual and the Group*, London, Routledge, 1951, p. 110.

20 Scheler, *Ressentiment*, p. 52.

21 Alexander, 'Relation of inferiority feelings', p. 47.

22 Melanie Klein, *Our Adult World and its Roots in Infancy*, London, Tavistock, 1960, pp. 13—14.

23 I draw in these next paragraphs on Salzberger-Wittenberg, Segal and Foster, works cited above, notes 2 and 8.

24 Foster, 'The anatomy of envy', pp. 182—4.

25 These included personal encounters with 'a tolerant old blacksmith, aged 89, who'd fought in Russia 1919 ... made me feel humble', and 'a really knowledgeable old man who knew all about the U.S. in the thirties — made me determined to study it up'. Three cases of extreme idealisation are discussed on pp. 381—3 below.

26 Such a man, Melanie Klein notes, 'in spite of all his successes, always remains dissatisfied, in the same way as a greedy baby is never satisfied'. Such men cannot be content with what they have achieved, partly because 'their interest is not so much devoted to the field in which they are working as to their personal prestige'. See Klein, *Our Adult World*, pp. 13—14. For Maryse Choisy's view of this as a characteristic of 'Phaetons', see above, p. 436 n. 22.

27 Otto Fenichel, *The Psychoanalytic Theory of Neurosis*, New York, Norton, 1945, pp. 488—92. Note also Erich Fromm's popularising of oral passive and oral sadistic character under the labels: the 'receptive type', who believes good things only come as gifts from others, and the 'exploitative type', who believes that everything worthwhile must be taken from someone else.

28 For a striking case of envy 'split off' in childhood remaining as a 'governor' to moderate adult ambition, see Hanna Segal, *Introduction to the Work of Melanie Klein*, Ch. 3. •

29 See Morris Jones's essay, 'Political recruitment', in Colin Leys (ed.), *Politics and Change in Developing Countries*, London, Cambridge University Press, 1969, p. 113.

30 Lasswell, *Power and Personality* (1948), New York, Viking, 1962, p. 39; and see above, pp. 5—7.

31 See L. F. Crisp, *Ben Chifley*, Melbourne, Longmans, 1960. With the birth of a younger brother, Chifley was sent at the age of four to live indefinitely with a grandfather; he was not taken back into the home till eight years later.

32 Scheler, *Ressentiment*, pp. 45—6.

33 *ibid.*, p. 74—5.

34 *ibid.*, p. 59.

35 It was assailed with special venom by Svend Ranulf, (*Moral Indignation and Middle Class Psychology*, New York, Schocken Books, 1964, Appendix) who, as he admits, might have been uniquely expected to welcome it, for its convergence on his own envy thesis. Plausible guesses, he complained, cannot do the work of science — and, besides, Scheler was philosophical rather than empirical, and did no content-analysis.
     Writers who have made something of his work include: Albert Camus, *The Rebel*, London, Hamish Hamilton, 1953, pp. 23—5; Robert K. Merton, *Social Theory and Social Structure*, New York, Free Press, 1962, p. 145; Donald W. Ball, 'Covert political rebellion as ressentiment', *Social Forces*, 1964—5, 93—101 (an empirical demonstration that a sizeable group of college students in the early 1960s were turning their backs on politics as part of a rebellion against their fathers); and Herbert H. Hyman, 'Mass communication and socialization', in W.P. Davison and F.T.C. Yu (eds.), *Mass Communications Research*, New York, Praeger, 1974.
     Its most enthusiastic proponent, however, has been Edgar Z. Friedenberg —

in the somewhat incongruous context of an essay on R. D. Laing (*Laing,* London, Fontana, 1973, pp. 97—108). He sees the Resentful Common Man as horribly on top in contemporary America: such men are intrusive ('Having an inadequate sense of their own selfhood, the alienated cannot be sensitive to the selfhood of others; they cannot really tell, and do not much care, where their lives leave off and those of the others with whom they are involved, but who seem no more real than themselves, begin') and censorious in personal taste, sexual morality and the arts. 'They have little capacity for empathy, which is one of the feelings that frighten them. And they have very little *sense of process,* in Rebecca West's phrase' (they are, that is, no judge of any sort of skill, since complacently without any themselves). 'In the United States, today', Friedenberg says, and in other societies like it, envy

> has become a prime motivating force, and one whose primacy is taken for granted as a matter of ordinary political sense. The country is continually obsessed with the possibility that someone may be getting something for nothing. As a rough check on the importance of envy as a political force in any society, consider the proportion of expenditure for amenities, social services, or welfare which is actually used for administrative safeguards against 'abuses' rather than to further the ends presumably sought ... We now assume that the state must ... behave in a suspicious and mean-spirited manner.

When envy, 'perhaps the most divisive of emotions', becomes institutionalised in the egalitarian, industrial society as a major social force, its consequences include (though the somewhat choking incoherence which takes over at this point makes summary difficult) a school system so ruthlessly standardised that it quenches imagination, malevolent brooding on the favouritism of authorities, the weak ganging up to eliminate a stronger competitor and, in general, trained incapacity and suppression of individual talent.

Women, and housewives in particular, have also recently been nominated as group lodged in a notably resentment-producing position. Rose Laub Coser, in 'The housewife and her "greedy family"' (in Lewis A. Coser, *Greedy Institutions,* New York, Free Press, 1974, p. 99) writes: 'Modern American society ... values equality of opportunity for its members, yet women can hardly avail themselves of opportunities as long as they accept the cultural mandate that their major loyalty should be to their family. What is offered them formally is withdrawn normatively. Such contradictory patterns are likely to be highly anxiety-producing for many women and to evoke ambivalence and *ressentiment.*'

36 Henri de Man, *Au delà du Marxisme,* Paris, Alcan, 1925. Trade union leaders remain a most dependable source of resentment rhetoric. Here, for example, a postal workers' union leader rebuts a suggestion by an academic publisher that mail and telephone installation services are peculiarly inefficient:

> Sir, Mr R.'s letter on the postal workers brings to mind Mark Twain's famous words on the virtues of hard work — 'I can watch it all day', he said.
>
> It may be a little uncharitable to visualise Mr R. rising at noon (by which time thousands of PMG linesmen have done half a day's work in murky manholes) to spend a productive afternoon peering out the window of his Parkville town house study and making notes on the progress of his telephone installation.
>
> Mr R. pours scorn on the idea of postal workers being liable to heart disease as a result of the rigours of their jobs. Apart from any conclusions he may have drawn from reading scholarly journals of management studies, he is almost certain to have had many years' personal experience of the

restful, if not positively luxurious, nature of pick-and-shovel jobs.

What perturbs me most is that Mr R. — whose contribution to the community's productivity so dramatically overshadows that of millions who work with their hands — must surely himself be in grave peril of collapsing with coronary or some other disease.

Mr R., our sympathies go out to you as you perch intensely on the edge of your armchair, the veins standing out on your brow, while that mighty brain strives to attain new heights of sarcasm for your latest diatribe against postal workers. The next time you take a few seconds' pause from your valiant labours to restore your flagging metabolism with a sip of sherry, you might reflect on the fact that you are not alone in your ceaseless struggle against those great parasites of history — the working class.

(*The Age*, Melbourne, 11 July 1973)

Mr R.'s letter was certainly provocative and demanded a spirited reply — suggesting, for example, that postal inefficiency was management's fault, or a fraction of that in Mr R.'s bookshop — but it got a peculiarly *envious* and *resentful* one: manual workers had to be defended by totally denigrating brain workers. The envy is particularly patent in the loving catalogue of Mr R.'s privileges — rising at noon, study, armchair, sherry . . . Perhaps one can always suspect envy underneath 'heavy humour'?

37 Scheler, *Ressentiment*, pp. 51—2 and 66.

38 Robert E. Lane, *Political Ideology*, Glencoe, Illinois, Free Press, 1962. See, however, pp. 242—6 and 411—12, where work is judged mainly as bolstering self-esteem, and the politics of the minority of 'disparagers' is related to self-disparagement. Lane's chapter giving the views of 'disparagers' on equality is also a valuable source for the study of defences against feelings of low status. Richard Sennett and J. Cobb, *The Hidden Injuries of Class*, New York, Knopf, 1972; now takes us more deeply into working-class emotional discomfort but, unfortunately, altogether eschews the concept of envy. There are frequent references, however, to such burdens as 'the feeling of not getting anywhere despite one's efforts, the feeling of vulnerability in contrasting oneself to others at a higher social level, the buried sense of inadequacy that one resents oneself for feeling' (p. 58).

39 John H. Goldthorpe, David Lockwood et al., *The Affluent Workers in the Class Structure*, Cambridge University Press, 1969. Sebastian de Grazia makes the case that working-class envy of the arrogant extravagance of the U.S. upper class in the 1880s and 1890s was behind the violence and bitter class consciousness of the time. (*The Political Community*, University of Chicago Press 1948, pp. 115—22.)

40 Carl Frankenstein, *The Roots of the Ego*, Baltimore, Williams and Wilkins, 1966, and *Psychodynamics of Externalisation*, Baltimore, Williams and Wilkins, 1968.

41 Frankenstein, *Roots of the Ego*, pp. 205—6.

42 Eric Hoffer, *The True Believer*, New York, Harper, 1951, p. 8. Oliver Brachfeld has neatly caught the appeal of such movements' ambience of violence and aggression:

Totalitarian regimes owe their success to the use of violence as their chief weapon of publicity. Acts of violence — often unpunished — impress upon the minds, or rather the unconscious minds, of the public the superiority of the aggressors. Especially if these aggressors dress themselves up in uniforms, hoist military insignia of all sorts, and use every device to convince themselves and the public that they are strong, terrible and immune from punishment. A characteristic example of this was the fashion indulged in by the early Fascists of wearing long hair and long beards. We

have it from Aldous Huxley that when questioned as to the reason for
this growth on their faces they replied 'per essere piu terribili!' In
this way do men overcome their own feelings of inferiority, and then
produce in the amorphous neutral mass that constitutes the raw material of
all political movements, the feeling that only by belonging to the faction of
violence can they overcome their own feeling of littleness: only so can
one acquire a 'superiority complex'.

(Brachfeld, *Inferiority Feelings*, pp. 9—10)

43   See Kate Millett, *Flying*, New York, Ballantine, 1975, *passim*, and 'Joreen' (pseud.), 'Trashing', *Ms*, April 1976, pp. 49ff.
44   Foster, 'The anatomy of envy', pp. 175—82.
45   Schoeck, *Envy*, p. 197 and Ch. 7.
46   Friedenberg, *Laing*, p. 108.
47   Schoeck, *Envy*, pp. 249—51.
48   *ibid.*, p. 198.
49   Elliott Jaques, *Equitable Payment*, London, Tavistock, 1967.
50   Schoeck, *Envy*, p. 247.
51   W. G. Runciman, quoted by Schoeck, *ibid.*, p. 209.

Fear, suspicion and paranoia
1   Erik H. Erikson, *Childhood and Society*, New York, Norton, 1950, p. 362.
2   Alexander Shand, *The Foundations of Character*, London, Macmillan, 2nd edn, 1920, pp. 199—206.
3   Otto Fenichel, The *Psychoanalytic Theory of Neurosis*, London, Kegan Paul, p. 133.
4   Erikson, *Childhood and Society*, pp. 362—3. See also Lasswell's distinction between 'real' and 'neurotic' fear, *World Politics and Personal Insecurity*, New York, Free Press, 1965, p. 188.
5   Franz Neumann, 'Anxiety and politics' (1954), Ch. 11 of *The Democratic and Authoritarian State*, Glencoe, Illinois, Free Press, 1957.
6   Kurt Riezler, 'The social psychology of fear,' *American Journal of Sociology*, 1944, 489—98.
7   Hadley Cantril, *The Pattern of Human Concerns*, New Brunswick, New Jersey, Rutgers University Press, 1965, pp. 276—7.
8   *ibid.*, pp. 311 and 407.
9   *ibid.*, pp. 107—10.
10   Alexander Grinstein, *The Index of Psychoanalytic Writings*, New York, International Universities Press, 1960, vol. v, pp. 2385—6, vol. ix, pp. 4492—3.
11   See, for example, Erikson, *Childhood and Society*, pp. 364—7; H. Segal, *Introduction to the Work of Melanie Klein*, London, Heinemann, 1964, Chs. 2 and 3; and especially Carl Frankenstein, 'Structural factors in the anxiety of the child', *Acta Psychologica*, 1956—7, 301—25.
12   John E. Mack, 'Nightmares, conflicts and ego development in childhood', *International Journal of Psychoanalysis*, 1965, 403—28.
13   Erich Fromm, *Escape from Freedom*, New York, Rinehart, 1941, p. 140, quoted Bjorn Christiansen, *Attitudes towards Foreign Affairs as a Function of Personality*, Oslo, Oslo University Press, 1959, p. 60.
14   S. Freud, *Group Psychology and the Analysis of the Ego* (Standard Edition, vol. 18, London, Hogarth Press, 1955, p. 97.
15   *The Age*, Melbourne, 5 September 1973, p.l.
16   Adapted from Cantril, *Pattern*, pp. 171—3.
17   See Otto Klineberg, *Tensions Affecting International Understanding*, New York, Social Science Research Council, 1950, quoted Christiansen, *Attitudes towards Foreign Affairs*, p. 59. For example, the percentage of Australians expecting a

new war rose from 42% in 1944 to 67% in 1948 — in which year 28% of Finns, 35% of Englishmen and 57% of Americans were similarly apprehensive — and had declined to 34% in 1966. See also Alan Hughes, *Psychology and the Political Experience*, Cambridge University Press, 1974, Index, 'war, threat of'.

18 And see L. F. Crisp, 'Australian Conservatisme sans doctrines' (Unpublished MS., 1973), p. 7. He adds that in Australia 'such anti-Communist, anti-trade union boss' campaigns seem to delude the 'conscript third of a-political voters' drawn in by compulsory voting. Service 'threat-experts' also develop a professional alarmism — for example:

> Brigadier J. G. Hooten, former director of Army Intelligence, who is one of the many top-level officers who have now resigned from the services, says that Australia is now in the most dangerous defence position since the height of the Japanese campaign in New Guinea.
>
> 'I have a great deal of respect for the public service,' he told the Constitutional Association of Australia, 'but the government is now getting advice from a bunch of utterly inept armchair strategists.'
>
> (*Herald*, Melbourne, 6 July 1974)

19 Australian polls, for example, from 1967 to the end of 1970, on China as a threat to Australia's security, found no significant differences between apprehensive and other respondents sorted by sex, age, education, occupational level, urban/rural region or religion — *only* by vote intention: the D.L.P. audience was 'threat-oriented', and the L.C.P. audience 'loyalty-oriented'. Arthur Huck, 'The idea of "China" in Australian politics', *Australian Outlook*, 1970, 309—19.

20 On the existence of 'the threat from the North' schema in kindergarten children in Australia, see R. Connell, *The Child's Construction of Politics*, Melbourne, Melbourne University Press, 1972.

21 Christiansen, *Attitudes towards Foreign Affairs*, Ch. 9. For an essay on Jewish anxiety, see Aaron Antonovsky, 'Identity, anxiety and the Jew', in Maurice R. Stein (ed.), *Identity and Anxiety*, Glencoe, Illinois, Free Press, 1960, pp. 428—34.

22 See A. A. Staley, 'Student activists', *Politics* (Sydney), 157—60 for illustrations of self-images 'flooding' national images.

23 Joseph Sandler et al., 'Patterns of anxiety: the correlates of social anxiety', *British Journal of Medical Psychology*, 1957—58, 24—31, which reduces a 'general factor' of social timidity to more pointed fears of revealing inferiority, of loss of control (especially of bodily control), and of exhibitionism. The authors argue for a general typology of the anxious, noting the *focus* of fears: inner psychic self; body-self; intimates; acquaintances and strangers. On the many varieties of timid group-style, see R. F. Bales, *Personality and Interpersonal Behavior*, New York, Holt, Rinehart, Winston, 1970.

24 See Alan Davies, 'Political socialisation', in F. J. Hunt (ed.), *Socialisation in Australia*, Sydney, Angus and Robertson, 1972, pp. 228—9.

25 Cited at note 4, above.

26 H. Lasswell, 'Propaganda and mass insecurity', in A. H. Stanton (ed.), *Personality and Political Crisis*, Glencoe, Illinois, Free Press, 1951, pp. 29—30.

27 Paul Tillich, *The Protestant Era*, Chicago, 1947, p. 245, quoted Rollo May, 'The centrality of the problem of anxiety in our day', in M. R. Stein et al. (eds), *Identity and Anxiety*, New York, Free Press, 1960 p. 125.

28 Riezler, 'The social psychology of fear'.

29 Neumann, 'Anxiety and politics'.

30 A. Shand, 'On Suspicion', *British Journal of Psychology*, 1922—3, 195—214.

31 *ibid.*

32 *ibid.*, p. 199.

33 *ibid.*
34 Helene Deutsch, 'On the psychology of suspicion', abstract in *International Journal of Psychoanalysis*, 1920, 343—5.
35 Philip Slater, *The Pursuit of Loneliness*, Boston, Little, Brown, 1970.
36 As well as *The Authoritarian Personality* and its offshoots, there are two excellent monographs: B. Bettelheim and M. Janowitz, *Dynamics of Prejudice*, New York, Harper, 1950, and Gordon W. Allport, *The Nature of Prejudice*, New York, Addison-Wesley, 1954. See also Robert A. LeVine and Donald T. Campbell, *Ethnocentrism*, New York, Wiley, 1972, especially Ch. 9.
37 Note, however, the interesting finding in R. M. Jones, *An Application of Psychoanalysis to Education*, Springfield, Illinois, Thomas, 1960, that the 'loosening' of fantasy in free-discussion classes relaxed suspicions of out-groups in a secondary school.
38 Edward Shils, *The Torment of Secrecy*, London, Heinemann, 1956, especially Ch. 5; Nevitt Sanford, 'Individual and social change in a community under pressure: the Oath controversy', *Journal of Social Issues*, 1953—4, 25—42.
39 Lasswell, 'Propaganda and mass insecurity', pp. 29—30.
40 David Shapiro, 'Paranoid style', in his *Neurotic Styles*, New York, Basic Books, 1965, pp. 54—107.
41 *ibid.*
42 *ibid.*
43 Elias Canetti, *Crowds and Power* (1960), New York, Viking, 1963, pp. 378—9.
44 Shapiro, 'Paranoid style'.
45 W. G. Niederland, 'Three notes on the Schreber case', *Psychoanalytic Quarterly*, 1951, 579—89.
46 S. Freud, 'Psychoanalytic notes on an autobiographical account of a case of paranoia', *Collected Papers*, London, Hogarth Press, 1925, vol. III, pp. 390ff.
47 Ida Macalpine and R. A. Hunter (eds.), *Schreber: Memoirs of My Nervous Illness*, London, Dawson, 1955, Discussion' pp. 372—412; and Morton Schatzman, 'Paranoia or persecution: the case of Schreber', *History of Childhood Quarterly*, 1974, 62—88.
48 Robert P. Knight, 'The relationship of latent homosexuality to the mechanism of paranoid delusions', *Bulletin of the Menninger Clinic*, 1940, 149—59.
49 Anthony Storr, *Human Destructiveness*, London, Chatto and Heinemann, 1972, pp. 80—1.
50 See Hanna Segal, *Introduction to the Work of Melanie Klein*, London, Heinemann, 1964, p. xii and Ch. 2, especially pp. 17 and 21.
51 Brent M. Rutherford, 'Psychopathology, decision-making and political involvement', *Journal of Conflict Resolution*, 1966, 387—407.
52 See also Richard Hofstadter, *The Paranoid Style in American Politics*, New York, Knopf, 1963.
53 See also on this, Nathan Leites, 'Panic and defences against panic in the Bolshevik view of politics', *Psychoanalysis and the Social Sciences*, 1955, 135—43.
54 Neumann, 'Anxiety and politics'.
55 Gustav Bychowski, 'Dictatorship and paranoia', *Psychoanalysis and the Social Sciences*, 1955, 127—33, which analyses Robespierre's paranoia. See also his *Dictators and Disciples*, New York, International Universities Press, 1948.
56 Neumann, 'Anxiety and politics'.
57 Canetti, 'The case of Schreber', in *Crowds and Power*, pp. 434—62.
58 V. I. Borin, *The Uprooted Survive*, Sydney, Comet, 1961.
59 Canetti, 'The case of Schreber'.
60 *ibid.*
61 *ibid.*

Powerlessness, disillusion and cynicism

1 Brachfeld reminds us that Swift had been reading Berkeley's *New Theory of Vision* and brooding on the statement 'that there is no absolute magnitude and that all measurement is relative'. In his first two voyages, he sees men through a telescope, with the big lens Lilliput, the small lens Brobdingnag, minimising and maximising the self. (See *Inferiority Feelings in the Individual and the Group*, London, Routledge, 1951, p. 11.)

   Phyllis Greenacre gets a little nearer the emotional heart of the Gulliver experience:

   > In the First Voyage, Gulliver is an enormous figure of overwhelming importance, cast up out of the sea, and endangering those around him by his very existence. This may very well express the primary narcissistic omnipotence of the infant who did threaten the welfare of those who cared for him. In the Second Voyage, he is reduced to a small size among giants, expressive of the helplessness of the child and the awareness of his small size which must become apparent to an infant between a year and eighteen months.

   (*Swift and Carroll*, New York, International Universities Press, 1955, p. 96)

2 Nathan Leites, 'Trends in affectlessness', *American Imago*, 1947, 97. He is here commenting principally on the hero of Camus's *The Stranger*. He diagnoses his withdrawal of conscious affect as a reaction to 'the guilty rage induced by the severe deprivations imposed by an absent father, an indifferent mother, and a withholding wider environment'. 'Conscious indifference and intense unconscious destructiveness are not only a possible but even a typical combination' (*ibid.*, p. 102).

3 Sandor Ferenczi, indeed, locates the origin of the Gulliver feeling in the child's comparison of the size of his own and the adult genital, 'Gulliver fantasies', *International Journal of Psychoanalysis*, 1928, 283—301.

4 Segal, *Introduction to the Work of Melanie Klein*, p. 57.

5 R. Money-Kyrle, *Man's Picture of his World*, London, Duckworth, 1961, pp. 148—51.

6 Erich Fromm, 'The feeling of powerlessness' [in German], *Zeitschrift für Sozialforschung*, 1937, 95—119. Brachfeld, *Inferiority Feelings*, gives a useful summary, especially pp. 27—30.

7 The revision evidently appears at pp. 102—16 of *The Fear of Freedom*, London, Kegan Paul, 1942.

8 Fromm, 'The feeling of powerlessness', as quoted in Brachfeld, *Inferiority Feelings*, p. 27.

9 *ibid.*, p. 28.

10 Fromm, *The Fear of Freedom*, pp. 115—16.

11 Brachfeld discussing Fromm in *Inferiority Feelings*, p. 30.

12 For a wonderfully strong example of such disillusion, see Henry Adams's description of his feelings about President Grant, in whose administration he had been hoping to play a part, in *The Education of Henry Adams*, Boston, Houghton Mifflin, 1918, pp. 260—5; and see above, p. 104.

13 David Riesman, *The Lonely Crowd*, New Haven, Yale University Press, paperback edn, 1970, p. 196.

14 For an attempt to compare, using the semantic differential, cynicism about persons (parents, self) with cynicism about politics, see John Fraser, 'Personal and political meaning: correlates of political cynicism', *Midwest Journal of Political Science*, 1971, 347—64. Other studies 'mapping' negative affects in the general public include R. E. Agger et al., 'Political cynicism — measurement and meaning', *Journal of Politics*, 1961, 477—506; J. E. Horton and W. Thompson, 'Powerlessness and political negativism', *American Journal of Socio-*

logy, 1962, 485—93; Edgar Litt, 'Political cynicism and political futility', *Journal of Politics*, 1963, 312—23; F. A. Pinner, 'Parental overprotection and political distrust', *Annals*, 1965 (361), 58—70; M. Rosenberg, 'Misanthropy and political ideology', *American Sociological Review*, 1956, 690—5; T. J. Agnello, 'Aging and political powerlessness', *Public Opinion Quarterly*, 1973, 251—9; and Herbert McClosky, 'Cynicism in British politics', *British Journal of Political Science*, 1975, 1—21.

15 See Edmund Bergler, *Talleyrand-Napoleon-Stendahl-Grabbe* [in German], Vienna, Internationale Psychoanalytische Verlag, 1935. Bergler's ambitious early essay on cynicism remains untranslated. The gist of it, however, appears in 'On the psychology of the cynic', in his *Collected Papers*, New York, Grune, Stratton, 1969, pp. 846—9.

16 However, John Gorton, Australian Prime Minister 1968—71, who combined joviality and cynicism in equal parts, managed briefly to attract the support of a majority of his parliamentary colleagues. It was said of Asquith, 'It is possible, indeed, that he cared nothing in his whole life for a single person or institution.'

17 Sanford's Mack, who is more famous as an authoritarian than as a cynic, nevertheless presented this as a leading trait — 'projecting his contemptibleness', in Sanford's words. His mother died when he was six. (T. W. Adorno et al., *The Authoritarian Personality*, New York, Harper, 1950, especially pp. 32—56, 274—5 and 787—802, summarised above, pp. 248—52. There may be a small but well-marked path to cynicism through bereavement in childhood.

18 For the first interpretation, see Edmund Bergler, 'On boredom and its psychopathology', *Psychiatric Quarterly*, 1945, 38—57, reprinted as Ch. 54 in his *Collected Papers*. For the second, see Ralph R. Greenson, 'On boredom', *Journal of the American Psychoanalytical Association*, 1953, 7—21.

19 John Alexander, 'The psychology of bitterness', *International Journal of Psychoanalysis*, 1960, 514—20.

20 For earlier clear advocacy of this strategy — and an excellent illustration of it — see Bertram Lewin, *The Psychoanalysis of Elation*, London, Hogarth Press, 1951, especially pp. 168ff. 'If we wish to use Freud's ideas on anxiety as a model for the analysis of other emotional conditions, we should posit a primal, "idealess", physiologically determined basic state, then establish its purpose, and finally determine what ideas become attached to the repetitions of the basic response during development.' One can only wish for concerted effort along this *'anlage'* front. Writers speak altogether too casually of 'early' or 'late' emotions (for example, of moral indignation or guilt being 'late' because they involve the ego-ideal), rarely specifying their origin or reinforcing visitations. Wonder, for example, might plausibly be traced back to the infant's first looking into mother's eyes *as mother's eyes* — that is, recognising the whole person, not merely the familiar parts and ministering environment. This 'recognition' involves a massive intellectual/cognitive leap — clearing up a large part of the environment. But it is a step wholly informed by the affect of wonder accompanying and, indeed, carrying it. The infant now has the capacity to draw on wonder on all apt future occasions.

21 And see Melitta Schmideberg, 'On querulance', *Psychoanalytic Quarterly*, 1946, 472—501. She notes, 'Several of my querulant patients had half-conscious fantasies of saving the world, or future generations. These dictated patients' choices of professions as economist or psychotherapist, and in another case the decision to become a communist. The querulant phase usually started either as a reaction to injured narcissism, being rudely disturbed in some preconscious fantasy of grandeur, or to everyday frustrations which were felt as a kind of lèse majesté.'

22 Alexander, 'Psychology of bitterness'.

23 Lewin, *Psychoanalysis of Elation*, Ch. 7.

24 Ralph R. Greenson, 'On enthusiasm', *Journal of the American Psychoanalytical Association*, 1962, 3—21.

25 *ibid.*, p. 11.

26 *ibid.*, p. 10.

27 R. E. Money-Kyrle, 'On megalomania', *American Imago*, 1966, 142—54.

28 Lewin, *Psychoanalysis of Elation*, p. 169.

Sympathy and pity

1 See N. Kemp Smith, *The Philosophy of David Hume*, London, Macmillan, 1941, pp. 169—77, which stresses a debt to Butler's *Sermons* (1726). Also see L. G. Wispé 'Sympathy and empathy', in David L. Sills (ed.), *International Encyclopedia of the Social Sciences*, New York, Macmillan-Free Press, 1968, vol. 15, pp. 441—7. Evidently only Empedocles among the ancient philosophers suggests himself as a forerunner. Hobbes's low view of pity, indeed, directly provoked Bishop Butler's Sermon v, 'Upon compassion' (see W. A. Spooner, article 'Pity', *Encyclopedia of Religion and Ethics*, Edinburgh, Chapman, 1925).

2 T. Benedeck, *Insight and Personality Adjustment*, New York, Ronald Press, 1946.

3 Marc H. Hollender, 'The seeking of sympathy or pity', *Journal of Nervous and Mental Diseases*, 1958, 579—84. Hypochondriacs are, he suggests, the reverse type to the seekers of admiration (for achievement), and both strategies are neurotic distortions of the desire to be loved.

4 Max Scheler, *On Sympathy*, quoted Wispé, 'Sympathy and empathy', p. 443.

5 See Ludwig Jekels, 'The psychology of pity' (1930) in his *Selected Papers*, London, Imago, 1952, pp. 88—96.

6 *ibid.*

7 E. Bergler, 'Pity as an unconscious disguise of terror-like fear', *Quarterly Review of Psychology and Neurology*, 1951, 241—5.

8 Sophie Bryant, article 'Sympathy', *Encyclopaedia of Religion and Ethics*. She also analyses personal antipathy as 'a peculiar sense of revulsion, as towards something put into us against our will'.

9 Reprinted in Kurt H. Wolff (ed.), *The Sociology of Georg Simmel*, Glencoe, Illinois, Free Press, 1950.

10 For a fine reflective essay on the contribution of the media to the widening of sympathy, see Herbert H. Hyman, 'Mass communication and socialization', *Public Opinion Quarterly*, 1973—4, 524—40.

11 Lester Ward, quoted Wispé, 'Sympathy and empathy', p. 442.

12 Intrafamily 'transfers' come to almost a third of the G.N.P. Grants, Boulding notes, come either from the 'threat system' (from fear), or from the 'integrative system — that aspect of society that deals with status, identity, community, legitimacy, loyalty, and benevolence' (from love). See Kenneth Boulding, *The Economy of Love and Fear*, Belmont, California, Wadsworth, 1973, p. 70.

13 Chaucer's prioress:
   She was so charitable and so piteous,
   She would weep if that she saw a mouse
   Caught in a trap, if it were dead or bled.
   Of smallë houndës had she, that she fed
   With roasted flesh, and milk, and wastel bread.
   But sore she wept if one of them were dead,
   Or if men smote it with a yardë smart:
   And all was conscience and tender heart.
                    ('General Prologue', *The Canterbury Tales*, lines 143—50.)

14 A very similar account may be found in Theodore Branfman, 'The psychology

of sentimentality', *Psychiatric Quarterly*, 1954, 624—34. Branfman defines sentimentality as a 'mood of teary-eyed wistful sadness, not consciously painful'. He stresses the quality of passive observation, the 'silent' crying, and the frequent alliance with the sense that 'time is passing' (nostalgia). 'The individual wistfully observes what he has wanted in childhood and not got (or not wanted and got) . . . he is, however, not aggressive, just watching.' See also A. Winterstein and E. Bergler, 'The psychology of pathos', *International Journal of Psychoanalysis*, 1935, 414—24.

15 Lois Murphy, *Social Behavior and Child Personality: an Exploratory Study of the Roots of Sympathy*, New York, Columbia University Press, 1937, quoted in Hyman, 'Mass communication and socialization'.

16 S. Freud, 'A child is being beaten' (1919), *Collected Papers*, vol. II, pp. 172—201.

17 For a case, see Davies, *Private Politics*, Ch. 4; and for an off-shoot in ideology, Davies, *Images of Class*, p. 69 ('middle-mix').

18 Otto E. Sperling, 'A psychoanalytic study of social-mindedness', *Psychoanalytic Quarterly*, 1955, 256—69. Beating and beating fantasies abound in this case material.

19 For example, 'Shooting Niagara: and after' (1867) in Thomas Carlyle, *Critical and Miscellaneous Essays*, London, Chapman and Hall, 1869, vol. VI, pp. 343—6: 'To me individually the Nigger's case was not the most pressing in the world, but among the least so.' He had written his 'Occasional Discourse on the Nigger Question', *ibid.*, pp. 171—210, fourteen years earlier as 'pretty much in a "minority of one" in the present era of the world'.

20 'Relief for snatchers', *New Society*, 26 July 1973.

21 For a somewhat mordant sketch of the Crusader type, see Orrin E. Klapp, *Collective Search for Identity*, New York, Holt, 1969, Ch. 8. His dark comment, 'The crusade classifies as a type of vilifying movement', builds on his, 'Vilification as a social process', *Pacific Sociological Review*, 1959, 71—6.

22 K. R. Minogue, *The Liberal Mind*, London, Methuen, 1967, especially pp. 7—13.

23 Robert Coles, *The Middle Americans*, Boston, Little, Brown, 1971.

24 See Freud's 'A special type of object-choice made by men' (1910), *Collected Papers*, London, Hogarth Press, 1950, vol. V, Ch. XI.

25 See Daniel P. Moynihan, 'The professionalisation of reform', *The Public Interest*, 1965, 6—16.

Loyalty, pride and trust

1 Charles Hanly, 'A psychoanalysis of nationalist sentiment', in Peter Russell (ed.), *Nationalism in Canada*, Toronto, McGraw-Hill, 1966, p. 305.

2 David Truman, *The Governmental Process*, New York, Knopf, 1951, Chs. 6—7.

3 Ranyard West, *Conscience and Society: A Study in the Psychological Prerequisites of Law and Order*, London, Methuen, 1942, p. 226.

4 I follow here Sophie Bryant, article 'Loyalty', *Encyclopedia of Religion and Ethics*, Edinburgh, T. and T. Clark, 1908—26, vol. 8, pp. 183—8, as also on the 'loyal company' in the paragraphs that follow.

5 Bryant, 'Loyalty', p. 187.

6 Anthony B. Gabriele, 'The principle of irrational loyalty', *Psychoanalytic Review*, 1966, 68—84.

7 See, for example, K. Deutsch and N. Wiener, 'The lonely nationalism of Rudyard Kipling', *Yale Review*, 1963, 499—517; and Kim Philby, *My Silent War*, London, McGibbon and Kee, 1968.

8 See Nandor Fodor, 'Varieties of nostalgia', *Psychoanalytic Review*, 1950, 25—38.

9 See Graham McInnes, *The Road to Gundagai*, London, Hamish Hamilton, 1965, for an account of Hawthorn, a Melbourne suburb, as remembered thirty years later in Ottawa.

10 John Dollard, 'The life history in community studies', *American Sociological Review*, 1938, 724–37.

11 See Alan Davies, 'The child's discovery of nationality', *Australian-New Zealand Journal of Sociology*, 1968, 107–26.

12 See Edgar Z. Friedenberg, *The Vanishing Adolescent*, New York, Dell, 1962; and Jules Henry, *Culture Against Man*, New York, Vintage, 1963.

13 Alvin W. Gouldner, 'Cosmopolitans and locals', *Administrative Science Quarterly*, 1957, 281–306, and 1958, 444–80.

14 Paul F. Lazarsfeld et al., *The Academic Mind: Social Scientists in Time of Crisis*, Glencoe, Illinois, Free Press, 1958, pp. 263ff.

15 Rebecca West, *The Meaning of Treason*, New York, Viking, 1964. And see Phyllis Greenacre, 'Treason and the traitor', *American Imago*, 1969, especially pp. 217–25, for the case of Klaus Fuchs.

16 I follow here Anthony Gabriele's formulation in 'The principle of irrational loyalty', p. 69, but his verb is 'plague'.

17 'It is lack of loyalty or nothing,' said the judge of the New South Wales Supreme Court, hearing the case of the weekly, *Nation Review*, sued by veteran Labour politician, Arthur Calwell, for libel in an article of 25 April 1971, which carried the imputation that he was lacking in loyalty, presumably to the then leader of the A.L.P., Whitlam, and/or to the party itself. He awarded Calwell $18,000 damages. At the paper's appeal, their counsel argued that it was not defamatory to say a person 'lacked loyalty' without relating the lack to someone or something; that changing loyalties and realignment of loyalties are the very stuff of politics, and that therefore 'lacking loyalty' in a political sense is not defamatory of a politician (the judge remarked here: 'This introduces the concept of the right to criticise the public conduct of public men too early'). They said thirdly that the article dealt prominently with his loyalty to those he considered the political giants of his hey-day and asserted that these loyalties were at the root of his lack of expressed loyalty to the present party leaders; and, finally, that the article attributed no base motives to him, and dealt with matters on which the public ought to be informed. The appeal was successful, and Calwell got no damages.

18 Sylvan S. Tomkins, 'The psychology of commitment', Ch. 6 of Tomkins (ed.), *Affect, Cognition and Personality*, New York, Springer, 1965. It is efficiently condensed in 'Some varieties of psychological organisation', Ch. 16 of Marianne L. Simmel (ed.), *The Reach of Mind: Essays in Memory of Kurt Goldstein*, New York, Springer, 1968.

19 Tomkins, 'Some varieties of psychological organisation', pp. 229–30.

20 Lewis A. Coser, *Greedy Institutions: Patterns of Undivided Commitment*, New York, Free Press, 1974, p. 4. The text discusses Jesuits, Communists and Utopian sects (by definition, those 'who have cut themselves off from the main body of society').

21 Hanly, 'A psychoanalysis of nationalist sentiment', p. 306.

22 See *ibid.*, p. 308, for answers to the question, Why does nationalist sentiment require a hate-object?

23 Christian Bay et al., *Nationalism — a Study of Identification with People and Power*, Oslo, Institute for Social Research, 1950, 2 vols. And see Bjorn Christiansen et al., *Attitudes towards Foreign Affairs as a Function of Personality*, Oslo University Press, 1959.

24 See Herbert C. Kelman (ed.), *International Behavior — a Social-psychological Approach*, New York, Holt, Rinehart, Winston, 1966, pp. 12ff; and A. Inkeles, 'Participant citizenship in six developing countries', *American Political Science Review*, 1969, 1120–41. E. H. Erikson writes valuably on the special adolescent

appetite for loyalty in 'Youth: fidelity and diversity', in Erikson (ed.), *The Challenge of Youth*, New York, Norton, 1961.

25 E. H. Schein, 'The Chinese indoctrination program for prisoners of war', *Psychiatry*, 1956, 149—72; R. J. Lifton, '"Thought reform" in Western civilians in Chinese Communist prisons', *Psychiatry*, 1956, 173—95.

26 W. B. Yeats, *Memoirs* (ed. D. Donoghue), London, Macmillan, 1972, p. 177.

27 Ernest Jones, 'The island of Ireland: a psychoanalytic contribution to political psychology' (1922), Ch. 8 of Jones, *Psycho-myth, Psycho-history*, New York, Stonehill, 1974.

28 See Paul A. Linebarger, 'Mimesis in Asian nationalism, *Psychiatry*, 1959, 79—86.

29 See Edmund Stillman and William Pfaff, *The Politics of Hysteria*, New York, Harper, 1964, for an impressive attempt to ground contemporary political disorders in the international history of this century.

30 See A. McC. Lee, *Multivalent Man*, New York, Braziller, 1966, Chs. 9—10, for an extended discussion of concentric and overlapping group memberships.

31 West, *Conscience and Society*, pp. 218—26.

32 André Gorz, *The Traitor*, English trans., London, Calder, 1960. Gorz's case is epitomised above, pp. 221—5, and see also 'The case of André Gorz', Ch. 11 of Alan Davies, *Essays in Political Sociology*, Melbourne, Cheshire, 1972.

33 Ernest Jones, 'Psychology of Quislingism', *International Journal of Psychoanalysis*, 1941, 1—6. A. M. Meerloo has an interesting essay on wartime collaborators in Holland, *Aftermath of Peace*, New York, International Universities Press, 1946, pp. 11—30.

34 Morton Grodzins, *The Loyal and the Disloyal*, University of Chicago Press, 1956, especially pp. 29—35 and Ch. 8. Carl J. Friedrich dissents both from this scarcity thesis and from the general assumption of the psychological approach that *principled* treason, pure and simple, is non-existent. See Friedrich, *The Pathology of Politics*, New York, Harper, 1972, part II. For a useful case-study of an American traitor at the time of the First World War, see Phyllis Keller, 'G. S. Viereck', *Journal of Interdisciplinary History*, 1971—2, especially pp. 79—84.

35 Jones, 'Psychology of Quislingism', p. 6.

36 Greenacre, 'Treason and the traitor'.

37 Philby, *My Silent War*, pp. xvii—xviii.

38 Patrick Seale and Maureen McConville, *Philby*, London, Hamish Hamilton, 1973.

39 Philby, *My Silent War*, p. xviii.

40 J. M. Baldwin (ed.), *Dictionary of Philosophy and Psychology*, New York, Macmillan, 4 vols, 1901—5.

41 We skirt quickly here — since our focus is 'pride *in the group*' — a portentous dichotomy on which much earnest ink has been expended, and to which A.O. Lovejoy's *Pride in Eighteenth Century Thought*, New York, Braziller, 1955, is a splendid introduction, notable for its grasp of post-Freudian psychology. 'Modern' discussions of the portentous pair include: McDougall, *An Introduction to Social Psychology*, London, Methuen, 1908, who speaks of 'self respect' and its contrasting type, an exaggerated form of self-regard which admits of no personal failing or limit; Paul Federn (1936), who contrasts 'healthy' with 'pathological narcissism' (*Ego Psychology and the Psychoses*, New York, International Universities Press, 1952, pp. 334—42); Henry A. Murray (1955), who speaks of 'Icarian' as against 'Solar' bids for fame ('An American Icarus', in A. Burton and R. E. Harris (eds.), *Clinical Studies in Personality*, vol. II, New York, Harper, 1955, pp. 615—41) and who extended this into an analysis of

'malevolent pride' in the figure of Captain Ahab, in G. Lindzey and C. S. Hall, *Theories of Personality: Primary Sources and Research*, New York, Wiley, 1966, pp. 153—61; Peter Wertheim (1964), who contrasts 'acceptable' pride with 'corrupt' pride ('Morality and advantage', *Australian Journal of Philosophy*, 1964, 375—87); J. Diggory (1966), who has 'gratuitous' as against 'realistic' pride (*Self-Evaluation*, New York, Wiley, 1966, pp. 110—14); and Abraham Zaleznik (1975), who contrasts ambition with hubris — 'the failure of an individual to modify or relinquish a grandiose self-image' (*Power and the Corporate Mind*, Boston, Houghton Mifflin, 1975, pp. 6—7 and 102—8).

In assessing the character and analysing the behaviour of political actors, this effort to disentangle health from pathology in narcissistic absorption, ambition and assertion will often seem absolutely critical.

42 Jacob Arlow, 'On smugness', *International Journal of Psychoanalysis*, 1957, 1—8.

43 And see Harry Levin and Alfred L. Baldwin, 'Pride and shame in children', *Nebraska Symposium on Motivation*, 1959, especially pp. 141—6.

44 I draw gratefully here on R. Martin Pope, article 'Pride', *Encyclopedia of Religion and Ethics*, vol. 10, pp. 5—8.

45 Eric Hoffer, *Working and Thinking on the Waterfront*, New York, Perennial, 1969, pp. 139—40.

46 Erik Erikson, *Childhood and Society*, New York, Norton, 1950, pp. 72—80 and 247—51. S. Arieti, *The Will to be Human*, New York, Quadrangle, 1972, pp. 72—4 and 76—9, usefully extends Erikson's discussion.

47 See, for example, Lucian Pye, *Politics, Personality and Nation-building: Burma's Search for Identity*, New Haven, Yale University Press, 1962; Morris Carstairs, *The Twice-Born*, London, Hogarth Press, 1957; and Donald F. Miller, 'Australian and Indian Politicians — a cultural comparison', *Melbourne Journal of Politics*, 1972, 12—29. For a useful summary of Almond and Verba's several attempts through surveys to compare German and U.S. levels of trust, see Herbert H. Hyman, 'Surveys in the study of political psychology', in Jeanne Knutson (ed.), *Handbook of Political Psychology*, San Francisco, Jossey Bass, 1973, pp. 346—7.

48 Thurman W. Arnold, *The Symbols of Government*, New Haven, Yale University Press, 1935, Ch. 6.

49 Edward Shils and Michael Young, 'The meaning of the coronation', *Sociological Review*, 1953—4, 63—81. Other auspicious occasions include royal visits, state openings of Parliament, Royal Commissions of inquiry, Question Time, public fireworks and, of course, the ballot.

50 Sebastian de Grazia, *The Political Community*, Chicago, Illinois, University of Chicago Press, 1946.

51 Kenneth Boulding, *Collected Essays*, vol. II, pp. 356ff and vol. III, pp. 209—15.

52 Kenneth Burke, *Permanence and Change*, Belmont, California, Allcorn, part II.

53 *ibid.*

Chapter 10. Compound affects

1 Edward Glover, 'The psychoanalysis of affects', *International Journal of Psychoanalysis*, 1939, 299—307.

2 C. Taylor, *Encyclopedia of Religion and Ethics* (Edinburgh, 1925), gives a brief, workmanlike description, and recommends, as the major account, F. Paget, *The Spirit of Discipline* (1891). See now, however, P. Alphandéry, 'De quelques documents médiévaux relatifs à des états psychasthèniques', *Journal de Psycho-*

logie, 1929, 763—87. What affects are fused in accidie? Painful affectlessness, disillusion, powerlessness, boredom (that is, suppressed rage), despair — in all, a sense of drowning and vacancy?

3   For recent discussions see J . Israel, *Alienation: from Marx to Modern Sociology*, Boston, Allyn and Bacon, 1971; R. Schacht, *Alienation*, London, Allen and Unwin, 1971; and A. Hughes, *Psychology and the Political Experience*, London, Cambridge University Press, 1974, pp. 75—89 and 117—42. Sound as a bell, but maybe premature, was Alfred McC. Lee, 'An obituary for alienation', *Social Problems*, 1972, 121—7.

4   See Lynn White, 'Death and the Devil', in R. S. Kinsman (ed.), *The Darker Vision of the Renaissance*, University of California Press, 1974, for an exciting prospectus of work relating 'velocity of cultural change' to creativity, destructive ritual (the scapegoat, for example) and forms of private neurosis.

Mention should also be made of the stimulating (if mainly methodological) essay, 'History and emotional climates' (Ch. 3 of Zevedei Barbu's *Problems of Historical Psychology*, New York, Grove Press, 1960), which not only discusses a variety of episodes in which anxiety and rage have been critical, but also, while disowning psychoanalytic influences, traces their manifestation in displaced, compensatory or regressive guises.

'Atimia' is the most recent nomination as a compound social affect. Gustavo Lagos sees it as the painful affect experienced by underdeveloped countries and especially by their leaders as they join an already stratified international community. It is a self-disesteem; a loss of status and honour relative to other nations as Germany and Japan once experienced it. See Lagos, *International Stratification and Underdeveloped Countries*, Chapel Hill, University of North Carolina Press, 1963, Ch. 1.

5   Lewis Mumford, 'Utopia, the city and the machine', in F. Manuel (ed.), 'Utopias and utopian thought', *Daedalus*, Spring 1965, 3—24.

6   This has been reprinted in F. E. and F. P. Manuel (eds.), *French Utopias*, New York, Schocken Books, 1971, pp. 131—41. See also F. Manuel, 'Towards a psychological history of utopias', in B. McLaughlin (ed.), *Studies in Social Movements*, New York, Free Press, 1969.

7   N. Adler, 'The antinomian personality', *Psychiatry*, 1968, 325—38.

8   A. F. Davies, *Essays in Political Sociology*, Melbourne, Cheshire, 1972, Ch. 9. See also J. Rudin, *Fanaticism — a Psychological Analysis*, Notre Dame, Indiana, University of Notre Dame Press, 1965, and 'The Roots of Fanaticism', *Et Cetera*, 1977:1 (a whole issue devoted to this topic).

9   I draw here on J. C. Flugel, 'The psychology of toleration', *The Listener*, 16 September 1954, pp. 441—2, which is itself an efficient condensation of his own 'Tolerance', in George B. Wilbor and Warner Muensterberger (eds.), *Psychoanalysis and Culture*, New York, International Universities Press, 1951, pp. 196—217. James G. Martin, *The Tolerant Personality*, Wayne State University Press, 1964, especially pp. 119—23, corroborates these points, and adds that the tolerant are also more empathetic and self-insightful. His tolerant subjects mostly had 'permissive' parents.

cf. 'Regardless of whether the specific topic was ambivalence or aggression or passivity, the outstanding finding was that the extremely unprejudiced individual tends to manifest a greater readiness to become aware of unacceptable tendencies and impulses in himself. The prejudiced individual, on the other hand, is more apt *not* to face these tendencies openly, and thus to fail in integrating them satisfactorily with the conscious image he has of himself.' (Else Frenkel-Brunswik, quoted in Richard M. Jones, *An Application of Psychoanalysis to Education*, Springfield, Illinois, Thomas, 1960, p. 47 — itself a source on the teaching of tolerance.) And see P. J. Leach, 'Teaching tolerance', *International Review of Education*, 1964, 190—204. For the idea that tolerance in children, which is *rare*, is linked with self-esteem and divergent-thinking, see, G. L. Zellman and D. O. Sears, 'Childhood origins of tolerance for dissent', *Journal of Social Issues*, 1971, 109—36.

10 cf. this celebration of the 'power to deal courteously with eccentricity': 'Courtesy signals intellectual as well as emotional strength; it requires seeing how aberrant behavior is not merely compulsive but the expression of variant conventionality ... it supposes that we try to see the meaning of unfamiliar patterns of word and gesture, and credit the intelligence behind them, even where we do not find the effect congenial. In this sense the business of criticism is high courtesy.' (Alvin C. Kibel, 'Logic and satire in *Alice in Wonderland*, *American Scholar*, 1973—4, 605—29.)

11 Martin C. Hoffman, 'Some psychodynamic factors in compulsive conformity', *Journal of Abnormal and Social Psychology*, 1953, 383—94. His later study, 'Conformity as a defence mechanism and a form of resistance to genuine group influence', *Journal of Personality*, 1957, 412—24, unfortunately fails to carry things much further. (He attributes the idea for the study to Fromm's phrase, 'automaton conformity', in *The Fear of Freedom*.) See also Marie Jahoda, 'Conformity and independence', *Human Relations*, 1959, 8—24; Louis Breger and Charlotte Ruiz, 'The role of ego-defense in conformity', *Journal of Social Psychology*, 1966, 73—85; and Chas. A. and Sara B. Kiesler, *Conformity*, Don Mills, Ontario, Addison-Wesley, 1969.

12 Hoffman, 'Some psychodynamic factors', p. 383.

13 R. C. Crutchfield, 'Conformity and character', *American Psychologist*, 1955, 191—8. On the origins of conformity, see also N. Sanford, *Self and Society*, New York, Atherton, 1966, pp. 207—10, and Robert F. Bales, *Personality and Interpersonal Behavior*, Englewood Cliffs, New Jersey, Prentice Hall, 1970, especially pp. 336—8 (on conditional-love upbringing), excerpted above at pp. 145—6.

Compare the rare but significant by-product of a writer's extremely conventional upbringing in the case of Christopher Isherwood: his mother's stuffy and rigid orthodoxy was an immense challenge to her novelist son. 'One of the aims of his writing, he confesses, "was to seduce her into liking it in spite of herself" ... It was so often the efforts to make her see something which forced him to write really well.' (Ronald Blythe, reviewing Isherwood's *Kathleen and Frank* in the *New York Times Book Review*, 23 Jan. 1972.)

14 Stanley Milgram, *Obedience to Authority*, New York, Harper and Row, 1974.

15 J. H. Smith, 'The metaphor of the manic-depressive', *Psychiatry* 1960, 375—84.

16 *ibid.*, p. 382.

17 David Riesman, *The Lonely Crowd*, New Haven, Connecticut, Yale University Press, 1950.

18 Arthur J. Vidich and Joseph Bensman, *Small Town in Mass Society: Class, Power and Religion in a Rural Community* (1958), New York, Anchor edn, 1960, pp. 297—320. This essay was originally published as 'The future of community life — a case study and some reflections', in B. Nelson (ed.), *Psychoanalysis and the Future*, New York, National Psychological Association for Psychoanalysis, 1958. Some quite valuable concluding strictures (pp. 181ff) on the pathology of the 'normal' personality were dropped in transit. Taking us even closer to the psychoanalysis of the conformist, there is J. McDougall, 'L'antianalysant en analyse', *Revue Française Psychanalyse*, 1972, 167—84.

19 Richard Sennett, *The Uses of Disorder: Personal Identity and City Life* 1970), Harmondsworth, Penguin Books, 1973, Ch. 1.

20 S. Arieti, *The Will to be Human*, New York, Quadrangle, 1972, pp. 250—1.

21 Paul Halmos, 'The ideology of privacy and reserve', Ch. 6 of his *Solitude and Privacy*, London, Routledge, 1952.
22 Edmund Bergler, 'Psychoanalysis of writers and of literary productivity', *Psychoanalysis and the Social Sciences*, 1947, 247–96.
23 Philip Slater, *The Pursuit of Loneliness*.
24 H. Lasswell, 'The threat to privacy', in R. M. McIver (ed.), *Conflict of Loyalties*, New York, Institute for Religious and Social Studies, 1952, pp. 121–40.
25 *ibid.*, p. 136.

Chapter 11. Conclusion

1 Louis A. Gottschalk and Goldine E. Gleser, *The Measurement of Psychological States through the Content Analysis of Verbal Material*, Los Angeles, University of California Press, 1969; Louis A. Gottschalk et al., *Manual of Instructions for using the Gottschalk-Gleser Content Analysis Scales: Anxiety, Hostility, and Social Alienation-Personal Disorganisation*, University of California Press, 1969.
2 Louis A. Gottschalk et al., 'Three hostility scales applicable to verbal samples', *Archives of General Psychiatry*, 1963, 254–79.
3 Not only have inter-correlations between different measures been low, but 'projective measures have been plagued with different results', with different tests and scores 'not predictive of behaviour or responses in contexts other than the test situation. Self-report and inventory techniques encounter varying levels of awareness and unwillingness to admit culturally frowned on feelings. Purely physiological measures fail to differentiate anger from, for example, sadness or fear. Even presumptive hostility-arousing experimental situations may provoke anxiety instead, or some conglomeration of affects.' (Gottschalk, 'Three hostility scales', p. 255.) It is especially interesting that TAT and Rorschach give rather different readings – for a full analysis, see A. J. Hafner and O. J. Kaplan, 'Measurement of hostility in Rorschach and TATs', *Journal of Projective Techniques*, 1960, 137–43. The prize for the most ingeniously indirect measure of aggression through projective methods goes to Bjorn Christiansen, who inferred it from the presence and magnitude of unresolved impulse patterns and psycho-dynamic conflicts disclosed in responses to the Blacky pictures; see *Attitudes towards Foreign Affairs as a Function of Personality*, Oslo University Press, 1959. Unfortunately, after all that, no strong links with political opinions showed up.
4 This differentiates his approach from the one it most closely resembles, John Dollard and F. Auld, *Scoring Human Motives*, New Haven, Yale University Press, 1959, which requires skilled-scorer judgment. Leon Saul's 'The quantification of hostility in dreams with reference to essential hyper-tension', *Science*, 1954, 382–3, gave preliminary scoring categories.
5 For example, D. T. Dittman and L. C. Wynne, 'Linguistic techniques and the analysis of emotionality in interviews', *Journal of Abnormal and Social Psychology*, 1961, 201–4, and Robert E. Pittenger et al., *The First Five Minutes*, New York, Martineau 1960, who conjure with 'breathiness, clicking, clipping, drawling, exhalation, fracture, gasp, glissando, glottal closure, nasalisation, over-fast, over-high, over-loud, pouting, quaver, sigh, slur, squeeze, swallow, throat-clear and whisper'!
6 See David A. Hamburg et al., 'Classification and rating of emotional experiences', *Archives of Neurology and Psychiatry*, 1958, 415–26.
7 O. Mannoni, *Prospero and Caliban: The Psychology of Colonisation* (1950), New York, Praeger, 1964; N. E. Miller and John Dollard, *Social Learning and Imitation*, New Haven, Connecticut, Yale University Press, 1941, Chs. 14–15; Jost

de Meerloo, *Aftermath of Peace*, New York, International Universities Press, 1946; Bruno Bettelheim, *The Informed Heart*, Glencoe, Illinois, Free Press, 1960; Vicktor E. Frankl, *From Death-camp to Existentialism*, Boston, Beacon Press, 1959; E. H. Schein, 'The Chinese indoctrination program for prisoners of war, *Psychiatry*, 1956, 149—72; R. J. Lifton, *Thought Reform and the Psychology of Totalism*, New York, Norton, 1961; Robert Coles, *Children of Crisis*, Boston, Little, Brown, 1967; Benjamin Spock, 'The professional man's muzzle', *American Journal of Orthopsychiatry*, 1965, 37—40, and *Decent and Indecent*, Greenwich, Connecticut, Fawcett, 1969, Chs. 3—4.

8   I compare here specifically Fred I. Greenstein, 'Private disorder and the public order: a proposal for collaboration between psychoanalysts and political scientists', *Psychoanalytic Quarterly*, 1968, 261—81, and Robert Dorn and Arnold A. Rogow, 'Psychoanalysts, patients, and crisis situations: the impact of events on private lives' (Unpublished MS, 1968), with Harold D. Lasswell, 'What psychiatrists and political scientists can learn from each other', *Psychiatry*, 1938, 33—9, and Edward Glover, 'Psychological effects of war conditions', *International Journal of Psychoanalysis*, 1941, 132—46 and 1942, 17—37. (This paper includes the reports of twenty analysts on the reactions of a hundred cases to the Munich crisis, the declaration of war, and, more patchily, the 'blitz' of 1940—1: Glover was then research secretary of the British Psychoanalytic Association.) The critical paragraph of the Rogow-Dorn memorandum might be summarised as follows:

How did the patient first experience the crisis — did he hear of it from radio, T.V., newspapers, cab drivers, friends? What was his immediate reaction (thinking behaviour, actions, physical or emotional response)? How did the crisis subsequently affect appetite, digestion, elimination; sex life; sleep; dreams; consumption of alcohol, tobacco, tranquillisers, drugs or medicines; physical health in general; interpersonal relations — marriage, relations with children, friends, employer or employees; job performance; attitudes towards life — money, the future, happiness; tension and/or anxiety levels, guilt feelings; acting out and acting in? What was the duration of these effects in hours, days, weeks? (Analysts may want to be on the alert for evidence that the patient somehow feels responsible for the crisis; relief that it happened, or, alternatively, profound anguish; welcomes it; is reminded of earlier personal crises; or feels nothing between the manifest and latent contents of crisis, or very little difference.)

(Dorn and Rogow, 'Psychoanalysts, patients and crisis situations', pp. 4—5)

9   Charles Madge and Tom Harrisson, *Mass-Observation*, London, Muller, 1937. Their strategy envisaged panel reports on typical days as well as days of crisis or predictable mass emotion; and their list of topics that they might shortly investigate included what is on the mantelpiece, behaviour at war memorials, low flying aeroplanes, contents of shop windows and the cultural significance of the indoor plant.

10   B. S. Greenberg and E. B. Parker, *The Kennedy Assassination and the American Public*, Stanford University Press, 1965.

11   Martha Wolfenstein (ed.), *Children and the Death of a President*, New York, Doubleday, 1965. cf., for example, P. Lacombe, 'Unconscious reactions to the international conflict of the Suez Canal', *Revue Française Psychanalyse*, 1948, 827—37.

12   E. W. Bakke, *The Unemployed Man*, London, Nisbet, 1934; Hadley Cantril, *The Invasion from Mars*, Princeton University Press, 1940; Alvin Gouldner, *Wild Cat Strike*, Yellow Springs, Ohio, Antioch Press, 1954; Mass Observation, *Britain, 1940*, Harmondsworth, Penguin Books, 1940; Edward Shils and

Michael Young, 'The meaning of the Coronation', *Sociological Review*, 1953—4, 63—81; P. F. Lazarsfeld et al., *The Academic Mind*, Glencoe, Illinois, Free Press, 1958.

13   Henry Adams, *The Education of Henry Adams*, Boston, Houghton, Mifflin, 1918, Chs. 8—10.

14   J. Bentham, 'Historical Preface to the Second Edition of *A Fragment on Government* (1828)', *Collected Works* (John Bowring, ed.), Edinburgh, Tait, 1838, vol. 2.

15   R. Money-Kyrle, 'On megalomania', *American Imago*, 1966, 152—3.

16   Norman Holland, *Five Readers Reading*, New Haven, Connecticut, Yale University Press, 1975.

17   Silvano Arieti, *The Intrapsychic Self: Feeling, Cognition and Creativity in Health and Mental Illness*, New York, Basic Books, 1967, especially pp. 38—42, 70—78 and 115—20. The author efficiently summarises this discussion in his later essay, 'The role of cognition in the development of inner reality', in J. Hellmuth (ed.), *Cognitive Studies*, New York, Bruner-Mazel, 1970, pp. 91—110.

18   Summarised from Arieti, *The Intrapsychic Self*.

19   See Herbert Fingarette, *The Self in Transformation*, Glencoe, Illinois, Free Press, 1957, Ch. 4.

20   See Max Scheler, *Ressentiment* (1912), New York, Free Press, 1961, and our earlier discussion at pp. 354—6.

21   See Joseph Barnett, 'On ideology and the psychodynamics of the ideologue', *Journal of the American Academy of Psychoanalysis*, 1973, 381—95.

22   Kurt Riezler, 'Shame and awe', Ch. 8 of his *Man, Mutable and Immutable*, Chicago, Regnery 1950. See also his, 'The social psychology of shame', *American Journal of Sociology*, 1943, 4—20. See also Hildred Geertz's admirable article, 'The vocabulary of emotion — Javanese socialisation processes', *Psychiatry*, 1959, 225—37, which deals with the child's learning not merely of what behaviour is expected, but how to feel about his actions.

23   Riezler, 'Shame and awe'.

24   *ibid.*

25   For other discussions of generational agenda-setting, see R. E. Money-Kyrle, *Psychoanalysis and Politics*, London, Duckworth, 1951, pp. 106—22; H. D. Lasswell, 'Political constitution and political character', *Psychoanalysis and the Psychoanalytic Review*, 1959, 3—18; Everett E. Hagan, *On the Theory of Social Change*, Homewood, Illinois, Dorsey, 1962, pp. 210ff; Arthur Mitzman, *The Iron Cage*, New York, Knopf, 1970 (and the review of it by Michael Rogin in the *Journal of Interdisciplinary History*, 1971, 557—75); and L. S. Feuer, *Ideology and the Ideologists*, Oxford, Blackwell, 1975, Ch. 3.

26   Riezler, 'Shame and awe'.

27   Joseph A. Schumpeter, 'Human nature in politics', in his *Capitalism, Socialism and Democracy*, New York, Harper, 1945, 3rd edn, 1950, pp. 256—64. The echo of Graham Wallas's title is deliberate; indeed, Schumpeter pays him fulsome tribute.

28   For a graceful admission of this cognitive-affective parallelism, see Jean Piaget, 'The affective unconscious and the cognitive unconscious', *Journal of the American Psychoanalytical Association*, 1973, 249—61.

29   Quoted in Mary P. Mack, *Jeremy Bentham*, London, Heinemann, 1962, p. 139.

30   Riezler, 'Shame and awe', pp. 115—16.

31   Lasswell, *World Politics and Personal Insecurity* (1933), New York, Free Press, 1965, especially Ch. 3.

32   Summarised from *ibid.*, pp. 50—1. See also Maurice L. Farber, 'The Armageddon Complex: dynamics of opinion', *Public Opinion Quarterly*, 1951—2, 217—24.

33   Charles Rycroft, 'On idealisation, illusion and catastrophic disillusion', in his

Imagination and Reality, London, Hogarth Press, 1968, pp. 29—34. The image of the moon falling into the sea was reported by Rycroft's patient from a dream.

34 See Richard Merelman, 'The dramaturgy of politics', *Sociological Quarerly*, 1969, 224.

35 Shand, *Foundations of Character*, Book 1, Ch. 11, 'Of the relative ethics of the sentiments'. This chapter was picked out for special praise by Carveth Read in his review of the second edition in the *British Journal of Psychology*, 1920—1, 271—3. The first edition was unaccountably not noticed by that journal.

36 Shand, *Foundations of Character*, Book 1, Ch. 11.

37 *ibid.*

38 Spinoza, 'Ethic', in John Wild (ed.), *Spinoza Selections*, New York, Scribner, 1958, pp. 207—8.

39 *ibid.*, pp. 369, 370 and 373.

40 *ibid.*, p. 375.

41 *ibid.*, pp. 370 and 382.

42 *ibid.*, p. 382.

43 John Macmurray, *Reason and Emotion*, London, Faber, 1935. See also the articles on the individual affects in the *Encyclopaedia of Religion and Ethics*, Edinburgh, T. and T. Clark, 1908—1925, 16 vols. — a work that could bear the sub-title, What every young Presbyterian minister should know.

44 cf. Nietzsche's 1897 aphorism, 'Conquest of passions':

> The man who has conquered his passions has entered into possession of the most fertile soil ... To sow on the soil of conquered passions the seed of good works of the mind then becomes the pressing next task. The conquest itself is only a *means*, not a goal; if it is not so regarded, there soon grow, on the rich soil that has been left empty, all sorts of weeds and devilish nonsense.

> (Quoted in K. R. Eissler, *Talent and Genius*, New York, Quadrangle, 1971, p. 241)

Nietzsche was also Spinozian in demanding freedom from externally imposed values. However, unlike Spinoza — or Freud — he called for *unreflective* (that is, anti-Axiom One) regeneration. For a neat contrast of Nietzschean and Freudian 'therapies', see Mitchell Ginsberg, 'Nietzschean psychiatry', in Robert Solomon (ed.), *Niezsche — A Collection of Critical Essays*, New York, Anchor, 1973, pp. 293—316. For an extended and exemplary analysis, see John Carroll, *Break Out from the Crystal Palace*, London, Routledge, 1974, Ch. 2. Robert C. Solomon's welcome full-length book *The Passions*, New York, Anchor, 1976, is strongest in its philosophical polemics, which advocate a Shandian assumption of responsibility for one's affects; it is weakest where it is faintly Nietzschean, in its concluding part, 'Towards an ethics of emotion'.

45 See, for example, P. D. Ouspensky, *The Psychology of Man's Possible Evolution*, New York, Knopf, 2nd edn, 1974, and R. Nichol's *Commentaries* [on Ouspensky and Gurdyieff], London, n.d., vol. I, especially 'Work on negative feelings'.

46 Philip Rieff, *Freud — The Mind of the Moralist*, New York, Viking, 1959. See, however, Stuart Hampshire, *Spinoza*, Harmondsworth, Penguin Books, 1951, pp. 141—4, for a comparison of Freud's ethics with Spinoza's.

47 'When ... Freud reaches the end of his life, he will have made "dissection of feelings" [an echo of a phrase in a letter he wrote to a friend at age 17 — "I do not mean to suggest that if you find yourself in a doubtful situation, you should mercilessly dissect your feelings, but if you do, you will see how little about yourself you are sure of. The magnificence of the world rests after all on this wealth of possibilities, except that it is unfortunately not a firm basis for self-knowledge."] the only firm basis for self-knowledge.'

(Eissler, *Talent and Genius*, p. 276.)

48 Otto Sperling, 'On the mechanisms of spacing and crowding emotions',
    International Journal of Psychoanalysis, 1948, 232—5.
49 *ibid.*, p. 235.
50 Melitta Schmideberg, 'Hypocrisy, detachment and adaptation', *Psychoanalytic
    Review*, 1957, 409.
51 Willy Baranger, 'The ego and the function of ideology', *International Journal of
    Psychoanalysis*, 1958, 191—5; and see our earlier discussion at pp. 309—10
    above.

Author index

Subject index

A., Mr (case), 15, 24–5, 189–93, 196–7, 264, 440
accidie, 316, 406
achievement drive, 53, 58, 62, 88, 153
Adams, Henry, The Education of, 102–4, 304
Adenauer, Konrad, 67
administrators, 14–16, 51–99, 201
adolescence, 28–9, 42–5, 67, 281–2, 371n, 421
adolescent moratorium; 113, 281n; *see also* age, generational agenda
affect spiral, 342, 425–7
affects: defined, 295–6; appropriate, 308–10; in committees, 417–18; cultivation of, 427–31; developmental plan of, 419–21; fused with issue, 34, 40, 419; as homeostatic, 301; individual hierarchies of, 302–3; and insight, 308n, 427; layers of, 300; neglect of, by psychologists, 294–5, 301; neglect of, by students of politics, 293–4; obstacles to study of, 295–301; paralysis of, 105; poverty of, 17, 65, 101, 154, 225; preconscious, 309n; problems of measurement of, 414–19; of student sample, 310–14; as systems, 301–2; transformation of, 342, 426–7; unconscious, 299–300; in work, 9
age: and outlook, 355; and political performance, 46, 53–4, 75, 111n; *see also* adolescence, political socialisation
agitators, 14–15, 17–18, 24–50, 189–91, 397
alienated personality: case of East, 197–201; case of André Gorz, 221–5; case of Inburn, 202–7; case of Katie, 207–15; case of Mac, 220–1; case of Yawl, 156–8; composite case of, 214–20; discussed, 325–6; *see also* beat personality
altruistic personality: case of Finch, 158–9; case of Nack, 158; discussed, 243
ambition, x, 6–7, 58, 131; parents', 55, 152–4, 181; *see also* sense of mission

ambivalence, 7n, 11, 179, 225, 299n, 307, 400
anal character, 22–3, 67, 341
anal metaphors in politics, 326
anarchists/anarchism, 49, 157–8, 202–14, 264
anger, 329–46, 414–15
Anna N. (case), 236–43, 270
antinomian personality (Bales UNB), 407
anti-Semitism, 247–8, 250–1, 255, 258, 261, 335, 438n. 25; *see also* ethnocentrism
appeasement, 244–5; *see also* Quislingism
architecture and envy, 358n
Asquith, Herbert, 73, 496
atimia, 502n. 4; *see also* inferiority sense
attitude psychology, 273, 470n. 13
Augustine, St, 278, 473–4
authoritarian personality, xi, 125, 159; case of Mack, 248–52; case of Mr Q., 247–8; case of Vito, 245–7; E. Jones's cases, 243–5; discussed, 252–5, 259–62, 325n, 328, 341, 349n. 26
Authoritarian Personality, The (Adorno et al.), 252–5, 261
awe, 304, 432, 428
axes of value, 124–7, 286–9

B., Mr (case), 15, 34, 440
Baldwin, James, 280
Baldwin, Stanley, 25
Bales, Robert F.: his axes of value, 124–7; classification of personality types, 128–9 (table); climates of childhood axes, 160n; typology of world views, 123–30, 262–6
Barbara (case), 280
bargaining, 70–5
Baruch, B., 71
beat personality: case of Inburn, 202–7; case of Katie, 207–14; compared to democrats, 228–9
Beaverbrook, Lord, 71, 73
Bentham, Jeremy, 293, 417n, 425n, 506n. 14

517

LIBRARY OF DAVIDSON COLLEGE

Books on regular loan may be checked out for **two weeks**. Books must be presented at the Circulation Desk in order to be renewed.

A fine is charged after date due.

Special books are subject to special regulations at the discretion of the library staff.